# Prepare with The Power of Classroom Practice

## Register for **MyEducationLab**
today at www.myeducationlab.com

## What is MyEducationLab?

MyEducationLab is easy to use and integrate into this book. Wherever you see the MyEducationLab logo in the margins or elsewhere in the text, follow the simple instructions to access the videos, strategies, cases, and artifacts associated with these assignments, activities, and learning units on MyEducationLab. MyEducationLab is organized topically to enhance the coverage of the core concepts discussed in the chapters of your book. For each topic on the course you will find most or all of the following resources:

### Students:

- Take **Practice Tests** for each chapter of your text.
  - Completion of each practice test generates a **study plan** that is unique to you.
  - The study plan links to text excerpts, activities with feedback, and videos and other media that can help you master concepts covered in your text.

- Complete **Assignments and Activities** to apply text content to real classroom situations.

- Explore the **Building Teaching Skills and Dispositions** exercises to practice and strengthen the skills that are essential to teaching.

### MyEducationLab offers:

- Authentic **classroom video** shows real teachers and students interacting, and helps prepare you for the classroom.

- **Case studies** offer real-life perspectives on common issues and challenges faced in the classroom.

- Authentic student and teacher **classroom artifacts** provide you with the actual types of materials encountered every day by teachers.

**CONNECTION TO NATIONAL STANDARDS:** Now it is easier than ever to see how coursework is connected to national standards. Each topic on MyEducationLab lists intended learning outcomes connected to the appropriate national standards. And all of the Assignments and Activities and all of the Building Teaching Skills and Dispositions in MyEducationLab are mapped to the appropriate national standards and learning outcomes.

**ASSIGNMENTS AND ACTIVITIES:** Designed to save instructors preparation time and enhance student understanding, these assignable exercises show concepts in action (through video, cases, and/or student and teacher artifacts). They help students synthesize and apply concepts and strategies they read about in the book.

Children: "Oo"
Teacher: Good job.

## BUILDING TEACHING SKILLS AND DISPOSITIONS

These learning units help students practice and strengthen skills that are essential to quality teaching. Students are presented with the core skill or concept and then given an opportunity to practice their understanding of this concept multiple times by watching video footage (or interacting with other media) and then critically analyzing the strategy or skill presented.

## STUDY PLAN

A MyEducationLab Study Plan is a multiple choice assessment tied to chapter objectives and supported by study material. A well-designed Study Plan offers multiple opportunities to fully master required course content as identified by the objectives in each chapter:

- **Chapter Objectives** identify the learning outcomes for the chapter and give students targets to shoot for as they read and study.
- **Multiple Choice Assessments** assess mastery of the content. These assessments are mapped to chapter objectives, and students can take the multiple choice quiz as many times as they want. Not only do these quizzes provide overall scores for each objective, but they also explain why responses to particular items are correct or incorrect.
- **Study Material: Review, Practice and Enrichment** give students a deeper understanding of what they do and do not know related to chapter content. This material includes text excerpts, activities that include hints and feedback, and interactive multi-media exercises built around videos, simulations, cases, or classroom artifacts.
- **Flashcards** help students study the definitions of the key terms within each chapter.

## GENERAL RESOURCES ON YOUR MYEDUCATIONLAB COURSE

The Resources section on MyEducationLab is designed to help students pass their licensure exams, put together effective portfolios and lesson plans, prepare for and navigate the first year of their teaching careers, and understand key educational standards, policies, and laws. This section includes:

- **Licensure Exams:** Contains guidelines for passing the Praxis exam. **The Practice Test Exam** includes practice multiple-choice questions, case study questions, and video case studies with sample questions.
- **Lesson Plan Builder:** Helps students create and share lesson plans.
- **Licensure and Standards:** Provides links to state licensure standards and national standards.
- **Beginning Your Career:** Educate Offers tips, advice, and valuable information on:

  o Resume Writing and Interviewing: Expert advice on how to write impressive resumes and prepare for job interviews.
  o Your First Year of Teaching: Practical tips on setting up a classroom, managing student behavior, and planning for instruction and assessment.
  o Law and Public Policies: Includes specific directives and requirements educators need to understand under the No Child Left Behind Act and the Individuals with Disabilities Education Improvement Act of 2004.

## What if I need help?

We've got you covered 24/7.
There is a wealth of helpful information on the site, under "Tours and Training "and" Support."
Technical support is available 24 hours a day, seven days a week, at http://247pearsoned.custhelp.com.

Visit **www.myeducationlab.com** for a demonstration of this exciting new online teaching resource.

**SECOND** EDITION

# Special Education for Today's Teachers

## AN INTRODUCTION

Michael S. Rosenberg
Johns Hopkins University

David L. Westling
Western Carolina University

James McLeskey
University of Florida

**PEARSON**

Boston   Columbus   Indianapolis   New York   San Francisco   Upper Saddle River
Amsterdam   Cape Town   Dubai   London   Madrid   Milan   Munich   Paris   Montreal   Toronto
Delhi   Mexico City   Sao Paulo   Sydney   Hong Kong   Seoul   Singapore   Taipei   Tokyo

Vice President and Editor in Chief: Jeffery W. Johnston
Executive Editor: Ann Castel Davis
Editorial Assistant: Penny Burleson
Development Editor: Heather Doyle Fraser
Vice President, Director of Marketing: Quinn Perkson
Marketing Manager: Erica DeLuca
Senior Managing Editor: Pamela D. Bennett
Production Editor: Sheryl Glicker Langner
Senior Operations Supervisor: Matthew Ottenweller
Operations Specialist: Laura Messerly

Senior Art Director: Diane C. Lorenzo
Text and Cover Designer: Candace Rowley
Photo Coordinator: Sandy Schaefer
Cover Image: Fotosearch
Media Producer: Autumn Benson
Media Project Manager: Rebecca Norsic
Composition: S4Carlisle Publishing Services
Printer/Binder: Worldcolor/Dubuque
Cover Printer: Lehigh/Phoenix
Text Font: Garamond

Credits and acknowledgments borrowed from other sources and reproduced, with permission, in this textbook appear on appropriate page within text.

Every effort has been made to provide accurate and current Internet information in this book. However, the Internet and information posted on it are constantly changing, so it is inevitable that some of the Internet addresses listed in this textbook will change.

Photo Credits: See page xxiv.

**Library of Congress Cataloging-in-Publication Data**
Rosenberg, Michael S.
    Special education for today's teachers: an introduction / Michael S. Rosenberg, David L. Westling, James McLeskey.
— 2nd ed.
        p. cm.
Includes bibliographical references and index.
ISBN-13: 978-0-13-703397-3 (pbk.)
ISBN-10: 0-13-703397-4 (pbk.)
1.   Children with disabilities—Education—United States.  2.   Special education—Study and teaching—United States.
3.   Special education teachers—United States I. Westling, David L. II. McLeskey, James, 1949- III. Title.

LC4031.R678 2011
371.90973—dc22
                                                                                            2009036930

10 9 8 7 6 5 4 3 2 1

www.pearsonhighered.com

ISBN 10:     0-13-703397-4
ISBN 13: 978-0-13-703397-3

To Irene and Daniel—So Much! Again and Always.
MSR

To Wendy, Jen, Jess, & Mere—Thanks for your love and support.
DLW

To Nancy, Gaby, and Robby, your support was priceless!
JLM

# Preface

Landmark legislation (No Child Left Behind and the Individuals with Disabilities Education Improvement Act of 2004) requires that all teachers be highly qualified, a designation that for the first time is actually specified by federal statute. As a result, the ways in which our teacher workforce is being prepared are changing significantly. In this changing environment, we have tried to create a text that addresses the needs of all people interested in the profession of teaching, whether they are traditional special education students, traditional general education students, or alternative certification students.

During the writing of this text, one question has remained in the forefront of our minds: "Regardless of who you are, are you prepared to serve and teach all students?" With this question guiding our writing, we have crafted a succinct and approachable text in which the information and research-based, practical strategies are presented in a realistic manner. We provide the most valuable information regarding each disability area so that all who read this book can acquire a working knowledge of the characteristics and learning needs of students who have exceptionalities. This book serves as a foundations of special education text and a recruitment text that will:

- Provide basic foundational knowledge of special education (Chapters 1–5),
- Provide a broad view of effective practices in the classroom while also examining the defining characteristics of disabilities (Chapters 6–15), and
- Provide an understanding of and a commitment to professionalism and the issues that underlie the field of special education (Chapters 1 and 16).

## NEW TO THIS EDITION

- MyEducationLab is integrated throughout the text with margin notes that direct readers to Assignments and Activities and Building Teaching Skills and Dispositions learning units on the course. Additionally, readers are directed to take advantage of Study Plans on the site that allow students to check their understanding of chapter content and then enhance their understanding with review, practice, and enrichment activities.
- Chapter 1 has been significantly revised to better focus the reader on the three themes carried throughout the text: professionalism, effective instructional practice, and reflection.
- A NEW feature entitled "The Real World: Challenges and Solutions" appears in Chapters 2–15 and focuses on the daily problem solving and reflection typical of teachers of students with special needs.
- A greater emphasis is now made on the response to intervention (RTI) framework as it guides many aspects of special education practice. (Substantial changes in Chapters 4, 5, and 6 with regard to RTI.)
- Chapter 4 has been significantly revised to emphasize a process approach with regard to RTI and individualized education programs (IEPs).
- Chapter 5 (Effective Instruction in a Well-Managed Classroom) has been significantly revised to include coverage of RTI and to focus on the connection between effective classroom management and effective classroom instruction.

- Chapters 2–15 now conclude with a provocative section that addresses at least two "Prevailing Issues, Controversies, and Implications for the Teacher."
- Chapter 8 has been significantly revised to include the full continuum of intellectual disabilities (from mild to severe) in one chapter.
- Traumatic brain injury (TBI) is now presented with severe and multiple disabilities in a revised Chapter 12.

Additionally, as you look at the table of contents and examine not only the chapter content but also the pedagogical features that support the narrative, you will notice the strong focus on professionalism, instructional application, and reflection. These three themes drive this new edition and our thinking on key issues related to education in general, and special education in particular.

# A FOCUS ON **PROFESSIONALISM**

## MY PROFESSION, MY STORY

Each chapter begins with a story of a teacher. Some have found their way to education through traditional routes and others have come by way of different life experiences, but all are engaged in teaching students in today's diverse classrooms. These stories focus on the backgrounds of the teachers, how they came to the profession, their dispositions and characteristics, and how all of this relates to their teaching and classroom experiences. Periodically throughout the chapters, these teachers are brought back into the discussion to further elaborate on chapter content. Additionally, many of these teachers are featured on video within the Assignments and Activities and Building Teaching Skills and Dispositions learning units on MyEducationLab.

## THE REAL WORLD: CHALLENGES AND SOLUTIONS

Throughout the book (Chapters 2–15), we highlight teachers and situations that show the daily problem solving and reflection typical of teachers of students with special needs.

## CHAPTER 16—Continuing a Successful Career: Professionalism, Effective Instruction, and Reflection

All special education teachers—regardless of the manner in which they are prepared—require certain general skills to succeed in their work. Although it lies beyond the scope of this text—or a course in which it is used—to develop those skills, novice teachers and teacher education students must be made aware early in their programs of the importance of communication, collaboration, and commitment to ongoing professional development. The text concludes with a discussion of how readers can continue their own professional development and personal growth as they progress through their training, and later in their careers, in special education.

## ADDRESSING THE PROFESSIONAL STANDARDS AND PRAXIS CORRELATION MATRIX

Following the summary of each chapter, we have included the CEC Core Knowledge Standards that best reflect the content covered in the chapter. Additionally, three appendices in the text connect to the standards. Appendix A shows the correlation of the Coverage of Content Areas for PRAXIS II® Test to the core content in the text, chapter by chapter. Appendix B is a complete listing of the CEC Knowledge and Skill Standards Common Core highlighted at the ends of chapters. Appendix C is the CEC Code of Ethics and Standards for Professional Practice referred to in Chapter 16. Readers can use these guides to make sure they are aware of the standards set for the profession and can also use them when they are studying for their licensure and PRAXIS™ exams.

# ⬛ A FOCUS ON **INSTRUCTIONAL APPLICATION**

Go to the Assignments and Activities section of Topic 13: Autism in the MyEducationLab for your course and complete the activity entitled *Communication and Social Skills of Students with Autism Spectrum Disorders.*

## HIGHLY EFFECTIVE INSTRUCTIONAL PRACTICE

MyEducationLab is woven into the text with marginal notes and at the end of every chapter. These notes point to Assignments and Activities, Building Teaching Skills and Dispositions learning units, and other activities and resources that highlight evidence-based practices discussed in the text. In addition, students can use the Study Plans on MyEducationLab to check comprehension on the core content covered in each chapter.

## CAN YOU HELP ME WITH THIS STUDENT?

This feature (Chapters 2–15) depicts an e-mail exchange between a new teacher and a mentor) teacher (or a related area specialist) in which the new teacher is facing a difficult or challenging situation with a student. A step-by-step list of supports suggested by the mentor teacher follows the new teacher's dilemma as well as resources for the new teacher (suggested readings). Finally, "Extend and Apply" activities encourage readers to think beyond the stated situation and put themselves in the place of the new teacher.

## TECHNOLOGY FOR ACCESS

Technology is a huge part of today's teaching. This feature gives snapshots throughout the text of different technologies that enable students with exceptionalities to better access the general education curriculum.

## CHAPTER 5—EFFECTIVE INSTRUCTION IN A WELL-MANAGED CLASSROOM

Teaching, learning and behavior management are inherently linked in every lesson or unit that the teacher plans. In order to provide readers with the best understanding possible of these underlying principles, we have devoted an entire chapter to this subject. Here we include coverage of Response to Intervention (RTI) and focus on the connection between effective classroom management and effective classroom instruction.

# ◼ A FOCUS ON **REFLECTION**

## CHAPTER 1—TEACHING STUDENTS WITH SPECIAL EDUCATIONAL NEEDS: PROFESSIONAL ROLES AND RESPONSIBILITIES

Chapter 1 encapsulates what it means to be a teacher in today's classroom and discusses what your role will be—whatever path you choose in education. It requires you to really think about and reflect upon the choices you will be making regarding your career and if you have the dispositions and attitudes necessary to become a successful teacher in general, or a special education teacher in particular.

## REFLECT UPON FOCUS QUESTIONS

These focus questions at the beginning of each chapter orient the reader to chapter content and serve not only as an advance organizer but also as items for reflection. Additionally, each question aligns with a major section of the chapter and connects to the chapter summary.

> **REFLECT UPON**
> - How are learning disabilities defined?
> - What are the characteristics of students with learning disabilities?
> - How many students are identified with learning disabilities, and what are the major causes?
> - How are students with learning disabilities identified?
> - What principles guide effective instruction for students with learning disabilities?
> - What are the prevailing controversial issues related to learning disabilities?

## REFLECTIVE EXERCISE MARGIN NOTES

These margin notes (all chapters) engage readers in thought-provoking reflective exercises that extend the content of the narrative and allow readers to really examine their beliefs about and perceptions of special education.

> **REFLECTIVE EXERCISE**
>
> #10  Based on what you have read in this chapter, what role can you play, and what activities can you engage in as a teacher to increase the value of persons with intellectual disabilities in your classroom? In your school? In the community?

# MYEDUCATIONLAB

## THE POWER OF CLASSROOM PRACTICE

"Teacher educators who are developing pedagogies for the analysis of teaching and learning contend that analyzing teaching artifacts has three advantages: it enables new teachers time for reflection while still using the real materials of practice; it provides new teachers with experience thinking about and approaching the complexity of the classroom; and in some cases, it can help new teachers and teacher educators develop a shared understanding and common language about teaching. . . ."[1]

As Linda Darling-Hammond and her colleagues point out, grounding teacher education in real classrooms—among real teachers and students and among actual examples of students' and teachers' work—is an important and perhaps even an essential, part of training teachers for the complexities of teaching in today's classrooms. For this reason, we have created a valuable, time-saving Website—MyEducationLab—that provides you with the context of real classrooms and artifacts that research on teacher education tells us is so important. The authentic in-class video footage, interactive skill-building exercises, and other resources available on MyEducationLab offer you a uniquely valuable teacher education tool.

MyEducationLab is easy to use and integrate into both your assignments and your courses. Wherever you see the MyEducationLab logo in the margins or elsewhere in the text, follow the simple instructions to access the videos, strategies, cases, and artifacts associated with these assignments, activities, and learning units on MyEducationLab. MyEducationLab is organized topically to enhance the coverage of the core concepts discussed in the chapters of your book. For each topic covered in the course, you will find most or all of the following resources:

## CONNECTION TO NATIONAL STANDARDS

Now it is easier than ever to see how your coursework is connected to national standards. In each topic of MyEducationLab, you will find intended learning outcomes connected to the appropriate national standards for your course. All of the Assignments and Activities and all of the Building Teaching Skills and Dispositions in MyEducationLab are mapped to the appropriate national standards and learning outcomes as well.

## ASSIGNMENTS AND ACTIVITIES

Designed to save instructors preparation time, these assignable exercises show concepts in action (through video, cases, or student and teacher artifacts) and then offer thought-provoking questions that probe your understanding of these concepts or strategies. (Feedback for these assignments is available to the instructor.)

## BUILDING TEACHING SKILLS AND DISPOSITIONS

These learning units help you practice and strengthen skills that are essential to quality teaching. You are presented with the core skill or concept and then given an opportunity to practice your understanding of this concept multiple times by watching video footage (or interacting with other media) and then critically analyzing the strategy or skill presented.

[1] Darling-Hammond, l., & Bransford, J., Eds.(2005). *Preparing Teachers for a Changing World*. San Francisco: John Wiley & Sons

## IRIS CENTER RESOURCES

The IRIS Center at Vanderbilt University (http://iris.peabody.vanderbilt.edu)—funded by the U.S. Department of Education's Office of Special Education Programs (OSEP) develops training enhancement materials for pre-service and in-service teachers. IRIS Center works with experts from across the country to create challenge-based interactive modules, case study units, and podcasts that provide research-validated information about working with students in inclusive settings. In your MyEducationLab course we have integrated this content where appropriate to enhance the content coverage in your book.

## TEACHER TALK

This feature links to videos of teachers of the year across the country discussing their personal stories of why they teach. This National Teacher of the Year Program is sponsored by the Council of Chief State School Officers (CCSSO) and focuses public attention on teaching excellence.

## GENERAL RESOURCES IN YOUR MYEDUCATIONLAB COURSE

The Resources section in your MyEducationLab course is designed to help you pass your licensure exam, put together an effective portfolio and lesson plan, prepare for and navigate the first year of your teaching career, and understand key educational standards, policies, and laws. This section includes:

Licensure Exams: Access guidelines for passing the Praxis exam. The *Practice Test Exam* includes practice questions, Case Histories, and *Video Case Studies*.

Portfolio Builder and Lesson Plan Builder: Create, update, and share portfolios and lesson plans.

Preparing a Portfolio: Access guidelines for creating a high-quality teaching portfolio that will allow you to practice effective lesson planning.

Licensure and Standards: Link to state licensure standards and national standards.

Beginning Your Career: Educate yourself—access tips, advice, and valuable information on:

- Resume Writing and Interviewing: Expert advice on how to write impressive resumes and prepare for job interviews.
- Your First Year of Teaching: Practical tips to set up your classroom, manage student behavior, and learn to more easily organize for instruction and assessment.
- Law and Public Policies: Specific directives and requirements you need to understand under the No Child Left Behind Act and the Individuals with Disabilities Education Improvement Act of 2004.

## BOOK-SPECIFIC RESOURCES

### Study Plan

A MyEducationLab Study Plan is a multiple-choice assessment tied to chapter objectives, supported by study material. A well-designed Study Plan offers multiple opportunities to fully master required course content as identified by the objectives in each chapter:

- Chapter Objectives identify the learning outcomes for the chapter and give you targets to shoot for as you read and study.

- Multiple-Choice Assessments assess mastery of the content (tied to each chapter objective) by taking the multiple-choice quiz as many times as needed. These quizzes not only provide overall scores for each objective, but also explain why responses to particular items are correct or incorrect.
- Study Material: Review, Practice and Enrichment gives you a deeper understanding of what you do and do not know related to chapter content. This can be accessed through the Multiple-Choice Assessment (after you take a quiz you receive information regarding the chapter content on which you still need practice and review) or through a self-directed method of study. This material includes text excerpts, activities that include hints and feedback, and media assets (video, simulations, cases, etc.).

***Visit www.myeducationlab.com for a demonstration of this exciting new online teaching resource.***

# ■■ INSTRUCTOR **SUPPLEMENTS**

We have created an instructor and student support package that is both comprehensive and easy to use. Our package includes access to the Introduction to Special Education MyEducationLab course (discussed above), an Online Instructor's Manual with Test items, Pearson MyTest assessment software, and a PowerPoint Lecture Presentation.

## ONLINE INSTRUCTOR'S MANUAL WITH TEST ITEMS

The Online Instructor's Manual (available online at the Instructor's Resource Center, described below, at www.pearsonhighered.com) includes numerous recommendations for presenting and extending text content. It is organized by chapter and contains chapter objectives, chapter summaries, presentation outlines, discussion questions, application activities, MyEducationLab homework assignments, and test items. The test item bank contains over 600 questions. These multiple-choice, short-answer, and essay questions can be used to assess students' recognition, recall, and synthesis of factual content and conceptual issues from each chapter.

## PEARSON MYTEST

Pearson MyTest is a powerful assessment generation program that helps instructors easily create and print quizzes and exams. Questions and tests are authored online, allowing ultimate flexibility and the ability to efficiently create and print assessments anytime, anywhere! Instructors can access Pearson MyTest and their test bank files by going to www.pearsonmytest.com to log in, register, or request access. Features of Pearson MyTest include:

**Premium assessment content**

- Draw from a rich library of assessments that complement your Pearson textbook and your course's learning objectives.
- Edit questions or tests to fit your specific teaching needs.

**Instructor-friendly resources**

- Easily create and store your own questions, including images, diagrams, and charts using simple drag-and-drop and Word-like controls.
- Use additional information provided by Pearson, such as the question's difficulty level or learning objective, to help you quickly build your test.

**Time-saving enhancements**

- Add headers or footers and easily scramble questions and answer choices—all from one simple toolbar.
- Quickly create multiple versions of your test or answer key, and when ready, simply save to MS-Word or PDF format and print!
- Export your exams for import to Blackboard 6.0, CE (WebCT), or Vista (WebCT)!

## POWERPOINT LECTURE PRESENTATION

The lecture presentation—available in PowerPoint slide format at the Instructor Resource Center, described below, at *www.pearsonhighered.com*—highlights key concepts and summarizes content from the text.

# INSTRUCTOR RESOURCE CENTER

The Instructor Resource Center at *www.pearsonhighered.com* has a variety of print and media resources available in downloadable, digital format—all in one location. As a registered faculty member, you can access and download pass-code protected resource files, course management content, and other premium online content directly to your computer.

Digital resources available for *Special Education for Today's Teachers: An Introduction* include text-specific PowerPoint Lectures and an online version of the Instructor's Manual with Test Items.

To access these items online, go to *www.pearsonhighered.com,* click on the Instructor Support button, and then go to the Download Supplements section. Here you will be able to log in or complete a one-time registration for a user name and password. If you have any questions regarding this process or the materials available online, please contact your local Pearson Education sales representative.

# ACKNOWLEDGMENTS

Throughout the second edition of this text, we stress the importance of professionalism, reflection, and application. In particular, we emphasize repeatedly the value of collaboration and teamwork when educating students with disabilities and learning differences. We have seen first-hand how teams of committed and creative educators have positive and long-lasting effects on the lives of children and adolescents. Developing a comprehensive textbook to reach a variety of readers interested in teaching students with disabilities successfully is no different. At every stage of this project we were awed by the creativity, knowledge, and accessibility displayed by friends and colleagues, old and new, and we consider ourselves extremely fortunate to have had their enthusiastic support and cooperation.

First, we wish to recognize the Herculean efforts of the professionals at Pearson. Along with Editor in Chief Jeff Johnston, Ann Davis provided much needed initial momentum for our entry into this project. With her keen eye for what works in the real world of textbook development, Ann made sure that we stayed *on message* with minimal tilting at windmills. Our many inquiries to the offices in Columbus were addressed cheerfully and expediently by Penny Burleson. Sandy Schaefer in the photo editing department ensured that we had excellent images to supplement our text. Luanne Dreyer-Elliott copyedited our manuscript with skill, grace, and speed. We are also appreciative of efforts of Tammy Feil, Nancy Hunt, and Blanche Glimps, who developed the extensive student and instructor ancillaries that complement the text. Finally, we are grateful for the creative coordination of Sheryl Langner, Senior Production Editor, who made sure that all the pieces of this project fit together in an attractive and logical fashion.

Special thanks to our lifeline at Pearson, Senior Development Editor Heather Doyle Fraser. Heather's unparalleled editorial and organizational skills are exceeded only by her grace, charm, and diplomacy. There were times when we dreaded the additional work associated with one of her calls. However, Heather's gifts of task analysis, keeping mercurial authors on task, and providing constructive feedback with encouragement made the iterative process of rewriting both energizing and productive.

We wish to recognize Dorene Ross, Margaret Kamman, and Maria Coady of the University of Florida, who co-wrote Chapter 3; Sunil Misra of Johns Hopkins University who contributed to Chapter 10; and also Eric Jones of Bowling Green State University and W. Thomas Southern of Miami University of Ohio who co-wrote Chapter 15. Thank you for your time, effort, and expertise in carefully writing and revising these chapters to meet our needs and those of our reviewers.

We owe a great debt to the many teachers and students who agreed to be featured in the text and ancilllaries. Our cadre of featured master teachers gave of their time liberally and shared with candor their views of what it takes to succeed in today's schools. Specifically, we are indebted to Carol Sprague, Amanda Adimoolah, Bobby Biddle, Andrea Craine, Kathy Blossfield, Meridith Taylor-Strout, Kim Thomas, Kathleen Lance Morgan, Margaret Otwell, Ryan Hess, Shannon Hunt, Julie Lenner, Steve Kennedy, Steve Williams, and Monique Green. Graduate students at Johns Hopkins University also shared their views as to why they are pursuing careers in special education. For their time and expert opinions, we thank Melissa Geraci, Jacqueline LeVine, Shana Alter, Annaleese Boyd, Tonette Campbell, Jacqueline Cantara, Howard Caplan, Joyce Chapman, Sharie DeGross, Michael Ensslen, Catherine Kalafut, Dawn McCrea, Nina McQueen, and John Sancandi.

The staff at all three of our universities assisted with tasks large and small. At Johns Hopkins we are appreciative of the efforts of Shanise Winters and Sharon Lampkin. Sunil Misra graciously assisted in the development of the original glossary as well as serving as an extraordinary research associate. We also thank Chad Kramer for providing his dissertation results as one of our features.

At Western Carolina University, we appreciate the advice and comments of our colleagues who provided feedback on various concepts, ideas, and chapter drafts. Most notably we appreciate the help of Karena Cooper-Duffy, Bill Ogletree, and David Shapiro for their strong input on chapter content, as well as the help of numerous undergraduate and graduate students for various forms of support that contributed both directly and indirectly to this work. At the University of Florida, we'd like to thank Shaira Rivas-Otero, Linda Parsons, Vicki Tucker, Michell York, and Penny Cox for their support in a range of activities, big and small, as well as for picking up the slack when deadlines approached.

Numerous drafts of chapters were sent out for review and we are indebted to the many teacher educators who took the time to provide extensive and highly constructive feedback. Specifically we thank Martha J. Meyer, Butler University; Melissa A. Miller, University of North Carolina at Chapel Hill; Linda Seybert, Park University; and Scott Zimmerman, University of Wisconsin, Madison.

Finally, each of us is blessed with the love and support of our families—wives Irene, Wendy, and Nancy; children Daniel, Jennifer, Jessica, Meredith, Matthew, Zeke, Gaby, and Robby; and grandchildren Hayden, Riley, Dylan, and Ethan.

MSR
DLW
JLM

# Brief Contents

# Contents

## 5 Effective Instruction in a Well-Managed Classroom   106

## 7 Emotional and Behavioral Disabilities   168

# Photo Credits

iStockphoto.com, pp. 1, 51 (top), 169 (top), 258, 319 (bottom), 370, 371 (top), 399 (top), 419; Krista Greco/Merrill, pp. 2, 153, 435; Creatas Images/Jupiter Unlimited, p. 3 (top); Comstock Images/Jupiter Unlimited, pp. 3 (bottom), 23 (bottom), 79 (bottom), 233 (bottom), 259 (bottom), 399 (bottom); ©Royalty-Free/Corbis, p. 4; ColorBlind Images/Getty Images–Photodisc/Royalty Free, p. 5; Anthony Magnacca/Merrill, pp. 9, 14, 53, 129, 187, 193, 220, 232, 324, 426; Chris Schmidt/iStockphoto.com, p. 13; Kathy Kirtland/Merrill, p. 19; EyeWire Collection/Getty Images–Photodisc/Royalty Free, pp. 20, 328, 366; Stockdisc, pp. 22, 50, 398; Stockxpert/Jupiter Unlimited, pp. 23 (top), 137, 139 (top), 168, 169 (bottom), 305, 319 (top), 338, 383; Lyrl Ahern, p. 27; AP Wide World Photos, p. 29; Reprinted with permission from Blatt, B., & Kaplan, F. (1974). *Christmas in Purgatory: A Photographic Essay on Mental Retardation*. Syracuse, NY: Human Policy Press, p. 30; Jacksonville–Courier/Clayton Statler/The Image Works, p. 31; Scott Cunningham/Merrill, pp. 38, 58, 216, 291; Liz Moore/Merrill, p. 41; Creatas/Dynamic Graphics, Inc., p. 49; AbleStock.com/Jupiter Unlimited, pp. 51 (bottom), 201 (top); Creatas Images/Punchstock, p. 57; David Young-Wolff/PhotoEdit Inc., pp. 62, 263, 413; Bob Daemmrich/Bob Daemmrich Photography, Inc., pp. 64, 92; Creatas/SuperStock, p. 78; Comstock Royalty Free Division, pp. 79 (top), 80, 201 (bottom), 259 (top); Laura Bolesta/Merrill, pp. 86, 190, 273; Tony Freeman/PhotoEdit Inc., p. 89; Mark E. Gibson/Creative Eye/MIRA.com, p. 98; Juice Images/Fotosearch.com, p. 106; Rafa Irusta/Shutterstock, p. 107 (top); Patrick White/Merrill, pp. 107 (bottom), 139 (bottom), 144, 162, 207, 245; Pearson Learning Photo Studio, pp. 109, 200; Robin Sachs/PhotoEdit Inc., p. 114; Tom Watson/Merrill, pp. 119, 152, 400; Katelyn Metzger/Merrill, p. 120; Getty Images, Inc.–Stone Allstock, p. 122; Thinkstock Images/Jupiter Unlimited, p. 138; Leah-Anne Thompson/iStockphoto.com, p. 141; David Buffington/Getty Images, Inc.–PhotoDisc, p. 145; Richard Hutchings/PhotoEdit Inc., pp. 147, 174; Michael Newman/PhotoEdit Inc., pp. 177, 348, 359; Myrleen Ferguson Cate/PhotoEdit Inc., pp. 178, 322; © Ellen B. Senisi/Ellen Senisi, p. 210; Todd Yarrington/Merrill, p. 212; Kati Molin/iStockphoto.com, p. 214; Lori Whitley/Merrill, p. 224; © Dorling Kindersley, pp. 233 (top), 241; Robin Nelson/PhotoEdit Inc., p. 234; Stockbroker/Getty Images/Digital Vision, p. 242; Maria B. Vonada/Merrill, p. 243; George Dodson/PH College, pp. 249, 289 (bottom), 318, 414; Valerie Schultz/Merrill, pp. 271, 277, 421, 425, 429; Mary Kate Denny/PhotoEdit Inc., p. 274; Bruce Ayres/Getty Images Inc.–Stone Allstock, p. 275; PhotoObjects.net/Jupiter Unlimited, p. 288; iofoto/Shutterstock, p. 289 (top); EMG Education Management Group, p. 294; Laima Druskis/PH College, p. 300; Michal Heron/PH College, p. 321; Bob Daemmrich/The Image Works, p. 334; © BananaStock Ltd., p. 344; Lushpix Royalty Free Photography, p. 345 (top); Scott T. Baxter/Getty Images, Inc. –PhotoDisc, p. 345 (bottom); Getty Images–Stockbyte, Royalty Free, p. 346; Pete Souza/The White House Photo Office, p. 350; Ellen B. Senisi/The Image Works, p. 355; Bold Stock Royalty Free Photography, p. 371 (bottom); Frank Siteman/PhotoEdit Inc., p. 372; Jonathan Nourok/PhotoEdit Inc., p. 375; Marc Anderson/PH College, p. 378; Roy Ramsey/PH College, p. 385; Getty Images–Photodisc/Royalty Free, p. 393; Linda Kauffman/Merrill, p. 402 (top); Richard T. Nowitz/Corbis–NY, p. 402 (bottom); BananaStock/Jupiter Unlimited, p. 405; Dynamic Graphics/Jupiter Images–FoodPix–Creatas, p. 420; Michaeljung/Shutterstock, p. 423.

# Becoming a Professional
## What Are the Foundations of Special Education?

part one

# chapter 1

# Teaching Students with Special Educational Needs

## Professional Roles and Responsibilities

### REFLECT UPON

- What is "special" about special education, and what are the professional roles and responsibilities of special education teachers?
- What are the rewards and challenges of being a special education teacher?
- How do general educators work professionally and effectively with students with special needs?
- Who are the other personnel who provide services to students with special needs?
- What are the keys for being a good teacher for *all* students?

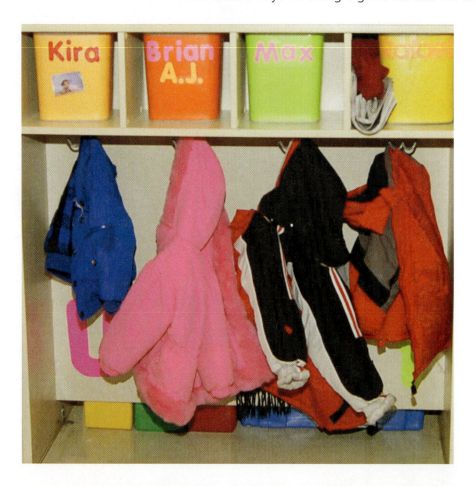

"Before entering the field, special education struck me as merely teaching basic skills in small segregated classrooms, giving kids as much time as they needed to complete tasks, and speaking slowly with a louder voice. In college, I learned that effective special education is much more. I observed firsthand how specialized supports, creative accommodations, and caring professionals contribute to important academic and behavioral student outcomes. I was taken by the thought that, with the right training, I could impact the lives of others."

Michael S. Rosenberg

"When I went to college, I really had no idea what I was going to do. At some point I decided to be a high school English teacher, but that didn't work out. Then I found my way into special education. Honestly, I never would have thought about it as a career, but I have to tell you, it's been great in so many ways."

David Westling

"I never planned to become a teacher. However, I couldn't find a job in my chosen profession and stumbled into a teaching position with students who were labeled with mild and moderate intellectual disabilities. My classroom was in a Quonset hut on a dusty, remote corner of the campus of a modern vocational high school. On the first day of class, I had no idea what to expect. I arrived early and was greeted by one of my students, Henry. I was struck by how 'normal' Henry was—much more like me than he was different. From that day on, special education has been a challenge as I've learned new things almost every day. It's also been the most enjoyable and rewarding career I could imagine."

James McLeskey

What role will you play as an educational professional working with students with special needs?

**REFLECTIVE EXERCISE**

**#1** *Special education* means different things to different people. What words, phrases, characterizations, thoughts, and emotions come to mind when you hear the term? Would you characterize your responses as positive, neutral, or negative?

**PEARSON**
**myeducationlab**

To check your comprehension on the content covered in Chapter 1, go to the Book-Specific Resources in the MyEducationLab for your course, select your text, and complete the Study Plan. Here you will be able to take a chapter quiz, receive feedback on your answers, and then access Review, Practice, and Enrichment activities to enhance your understanding of chapter content.

It is often interesting to learn about how people arrived at their current jobs or stations in life and the paths they traveled to get there. One of the oldest icebreakers goes something like, "So why did you decide to become a nurse?" or "When did you first think about being a firefighter?" Because you are reading this text, we assume that you may be on the road to your future, a future that could include teaching or working with students with disabilities or special needs.

Are you planning to become a special education teacher? Or will you be a general education teacher, an administrator, or a related service professional who will work with students with special needs? If you are choosing any of these professions, your roles and responsibilities will be similar in some ways and different in others. The similarities for all educators and other professionals working with students with special needs should include having a commitment to *professionalism*, providing *effective* instruction to *all* students, and *reflecting* on the quality of their practice. These personal attributes should inform all your unique roles and responsibilities with students with special needs.

We will stress these themes—professionalism, effective instruction, and reflection—throughout this text because we believe these characteristics will lead to positive outcomes for all students. We provide you with examples of professionalism when we introduce you to successful teachers at the beginning of chapters and then again when we invite you to consider "The Real World: Challenges and Solutions," included in Chapters 2 through 15. You will also practice becoming an effective professional when you meet students with special needs and are asked, "Can You Help Me with This Student?" Finally, you may engage in meaningful reflection throughout the text when we present you with reflective exercises. Our goal in the rest of this chapter is to provide you with useful information about those who work with students with special needs. Let's begin by considering the fundamental question, What is "special" about special education?

## WHAT IS "SPECIAL" ABOUT SPECIAL EDUCATION?

*Special education* is a term that often evokes emotion and passion. The nature and content of reactions vary, however, depending on who is responding. For the parent-advocate who has a teenager with a severe disability, special education represents a hard-fought civil rights victory for a free and appropriate education. For the school board member, special education usually involves concern about finances and expenses associated with delivering services required by federal law. To the 10th-grade science teacher, special education is the "inclusion section" of biology in which several students with disabilities need content enhancements to participate in required activities. And for the third-grade student with a hearing impairment, special education is the service through which she can acquire the phonic ear that helps her participate in class activities with her classmates.

If you ask a group of special education teachers what "special education" means, you will probably get as many different answers as the number of teachers you ask. But one that we feel is universally acceptable is that *special education means providing individualized instruction and supports that lead to better life outcomes for students with special needs.*

Traditionally, special education has been defined primarily in terms of the nature of instruction provided directly to students with special needs. For example, according to IDEA, "the term 'special education' means specially designed instruction, at no cost to parents, to meet the unique needs of a child with a disability" (Individuals with Disabilities Education Act [IDEA] Sec. 602 (29); 20 U.S.C. 1401). From this perspective, instructional methods used in special education are intended to be more precise, intense, structured, and systematic than most general education methods. Special education can also mean that the content of instruction, or what we teach students with special needs, may differ from what other students are taught. While students with special needs must receive instruction in the same general curriculum as all other students, they may also need to learn supplementary or complementary skills. For example, some students in special education may need to learn how to interact in socially acceptable ways, others may need to use a motorized wheelchair, and some may need additional instruction in reading or other basic skills. To help students achieve their learning needs, special educators will often use (or recommend) different instructional strategies and tactics, and sometimes different materials, equipment, and devices, that will facilitate students' learning and behavioral success (Kauffman & Hallahan, 2005).

While this concept of special education remains valid, it is no longer enough. As society has moved more toward accepting and including individuals with special needs, instructional provisions for these school-age students are no longer considered the responsibility of only special educators. Nor is special education defined by separate settings. Today, special education should be thought of as a service that requires collaboration and consultation among professional educators. It must include co-planning and co-teaching and must involve both special educators and general educators. While "specially designed instruction" remains necessary for students with special needs, the delivery of this instruction must be done in a way that maximizes the student's participation in the general curriculum and in the general education classroom and minimizes the student's separation and stigmatization as much as possible. Couched within the key themes we introduced earlier, we suggest that "what makes special education special" are the essential components listed in Table 1.1.

## REFLECTIVE EXERCISE

#2 Have you been closely acquainted with a special education teacher? How did this individual enter the field? In a typical fashion or by a more nontraditional route? Did this person influence your interest in teaching?

## Are Special Educators Special?

According to the U.S. Department of Education (2009), around 440,000 special education teachers provide instruction to over 6.7 million eligible students between the ages of 3 and 21 years. What has drawn so many people to this profession? Is it because they themselves are special?

Through our work in public schools and as teacher educators, we have come to know many special education teachers. And one thing we have noticed is that they became special educators for many different reasons. Some had siblings or family members with disabilities, some were tutors or "best buddies" in high school, and some came into the field simply because someone who knew them well suggested it.

We don't know if special education professionals are truly "special," but if you talk to veteran special educators, chances are you won't find them or their lives trivial or routine. Throughout your professional development, you will meet special education teachers and other professionals supporting students with special needs; and, as you will see, many have very interesting stories about how they got to where they are.

Today special education requires collaboration among many different professionals.

What's your story? Maybe you are currently attempting to determine the correct career choice for yourself. If you are, we have a short questionnaire that will allow you to reflect on the reasons why you might want to be a special education teacher.

## TABLE 1.1 • WHAT MAKES SPECIAL EDUCATION SPECIAL?

***Professionalism*** **occurs in special education when . . .**

- Teachers show respect for individual students and maintain healthy dispositions about their potential as participants within learning communities.
- Special educators and general educators collaborate to provide instruction in the most inclusive setting possible.
- Teachers stay abreast of current knowledge about students with special needs and how to teach them.
- Teachers accept additional tasks necessary for improving quality-of-life conditions for their students such as helping a student become a member of a school club or learning about a new assistive technology device that could help a student learn to read or communicate.

***Effective instruction*** **for students with special needs means . . .**

- Teachers use evidence-based instructional procedure in the least restrictive environment possible.
- Teachers deliver instruction with adequate structure, intensity, and frequency necessary for learning to occur.
- Teachers focus instruction based on the general curriculum but also address students' unique learning needs.
- Teachers use a positive approach both to improve academic skills and to foster appropriate personal and social behavior.
- Teachers monitor student progress in order to change instructional approaches and behavioral improvement methods when necessary.

**Teachers of students with special needs are *reflective* when . . .**

- They give adequate consideration to the progress of individual students.
- They realize their relationship with students can affect student progress.
- They create learning environments sensitive to the needs of all of their students.

"Becoming a special education teacher was not something that I planned early in my life or even early in my career. My academic career was uneventful, but my teaching career quickly took a new direction as I practiced my craft. I quickly realized that, within any given classroom, students had a wide range of skills and abilities both academically and behaviorally, and I didn't have the knowledge to meet their needs and work with struggling readers. Thankfully, I met a teacher who became my mentor and encouraged me to become a special education teacher."

Carol Sprague, an elementary special education teacher in Thomas County, Georgia

In Figure 1.1 you will see the future special educator's motivation scale. If you wish, you can complete this survey to gain personal insight about what may draw you to the field of special education. You can also compare your responses with your classmates'. As with most surveys, there are no right or wrong answers, just an opportunity to think about some factors that might be important to you as a future professional.

## Who Do Special Education Teachers Teach? Where Do They Teach?

In Chapters 6 through 15 of this textbook, we will introduce you to students with special needs and describe many of the services they receive. Federal law requires that these students be placed into different disability categories. As a point of reference for our present discussion, Table 1.2 presents the federal disability categories. Students who have the disabilities that are defined in the table, as well as students who are gifted or talented, are typically those who receive special education and related services. Most will be taught by special education teachers and

FIGURE 1.1 • **THE FUTURE SPECIAL EDUCATOR'S MOTIVATION SCALE**

Rate each of these reasons for why you believe you may want to become a special education teacher. Use the following rating scale:

1 = Strongly disagree
2 = Disagree
3 = Somewhat disagree
4 = Agree and disagree
5 = Somewhat agree
6 = Agree
7 = Strongly agree

| | |
|---|---|
| 1. I am drawn by the opportunity to have smaller class sizes. | 1 2 3 4 5 6 7 |
| 2. I look forward to the challenge of teaching difficult students. | 1 2 3 4 5 6 7 |
| 3. I like the idea of the possibility of extra pay. | 1 2 3 4 5 6 7 |
| 4. I have an interest in specific disabilities (e.g., autism, Down syndrome). | 1 2 3 4 5 6 7 |
| 5. I know that special education has good job availability and offers various opportunities. | 1 2 3 4 5 6 7 |
| 6. I am excited by the opportunity to witness student improvement in knowledge, skills, or behavior. | 1 2 3 4 5 6 7 |
| 7. I have a high level of regard for people with disabilities. | 1 2 3 4 5 6 7 |
| 8. My personal characteristics fit well with the special educator's job (e.g., I am very patient or not easily stressed). | 1 2 3 4 5 6 7 |
| 9. I have a friend or family member with a disability. | 1 2 3 4 5 6 7 |
| 10. I have worked or volunteered with students with disabilities before and found it to be extremely rewarding. | 1 2 3 4 5 6 7 |

TABLE 1.2 • PUBLIC SCHOOL DISABILITY CATEGORIES

| Disability | Definition |
|---|---|
| Autism | *Autism* is a developmental disability significantly affecting verbal and nonverbal communication and social interaction, generally evident before age 3, that adversely affects a child's educational performance. Other characteristics often associated with autism are engagement in repetitive activities and stereotyped movements, resistance to environmental change or change in daily routines, and unusual responses to sensory experiences. The term does not apply if a child's educational performance is adversely affected primarily because the child has an emotional disturbance. A child who manifests the characteristics of autism after age 3 could be diagnosed as having autism if the criteria in this paragraph are satisfied. |
| Deaf-blindness | *Deaf-blindness* means concomitant hearing and visual impairments, the combination of which causes such severe communication and other developmental and educational needs that they cannot be accommodated in special education programs solely for children with deafness or children with blindness. |
| Deafness | *Deafness* is a hearing impairment so severe that the child is impaired in processing linguistic information through hearing, with or without amplification, and that adversely affects a child's educational performance. |

*(continued)*

**TABLE 1.2** • PUBLIC SCHOOL DISABILITY CATEGORIES    (continued)

| Disability | Definition |
| --- | --- |
| Emotional disturbance | *Emotional disturbance* is a condition exhibiting one or more of the following characteristics over a long period of time and to a marked degree that adversely affects a child's educational performance:<br>1. An inability to learn that cannot be explained by intellectual, sensory, or health factors<br>2. An inability to build or maintain satisfactory interpersonal relationships with peers and teachers<br>3. Inappropriate types of behavior or feelings under normal circumstances<br>4. A general pervasive mood of unhappiness or depression<br>5. A tendency to develop physical symptoms or fears associated with personal or school problems<br>The term includes schizophrenia. The term does not apply to children who are socially maladjusted, unless it is determined that they have an emotional disturbance. |
| Hearing impairment | *Hearing impairment,* whether permanent or fluctuating, adversely affects a child's educational performance but is not included under the definition of deafness. |
| Mental retardation | *Mental retardation* means significantly subaverage general intellectual functioning, existing concurrently with deficits in adaptive behavior and manifested during the developmental period, that adversely affects a child's educational performance. |
| Multiple disabilities | *Multiple disabilities* are concomitant impairments (e.g., mental retardation–blindness, mental retardation–orthopedic impairment), the combination of which causes such severe educational needs that they cannot be accommodated in special education programs solely for one of the impairments. The term does not include deaf-blindness. |
| Orthopedic impairment | *Orthopedic impairment* means a severe structural impairment that adversely affects a child's educational performance. The term includes impairments caused by congenital anomaly (e.g., clubfoot, absence of some member), impairments caused by disease (e.g., poliomyelitis, bone tuberculosis), and impairments from other causes (e.g., cerebral palsy, amputations, and fractures or burns that cause contractures). |
| Other health impairment | *Other health impairment* means having limited strength, vitality, or alertness, including a heightened alertness to environmental stimuli, that results in limited alertness with respect to the educational environment, that<br>1. Is due to chronic or acute health problems such as asthma, attention deficit disorder or attention deficit hyperactivity disorder, diabetes, epilepsy, a heart condition, hemophilia, lead poisoning, leukemia, nephritis, rheumatic fever, and sickle cell anemia; and<br>2. Adversely affects a child's educational performance. |
| Specific learning disability | *Specific learning disability,* in general, means a disorder in one or more of the basic psychological processes involved in understanding or using language, spoken or written, which may manifest itself in the imperfect ability to listen, think, speak, read, write, spell, or do mathematical calculations. The term includes such conditions as perceptual disabilities, brain injury, minimal brain dysfunction, dyslexia, and developmental aphasia. It does not include a learning problem that is primarily the result of visual, hearing, or motor disabilities; of mental retardation; of emotional disturbance; or of environmental, cultural, or economic disadvantage. |
| Speech or language impairment | *Speech or language impairment* means a communication disorder, such as stuttering, impaired articulation, a language impairment, or a voice impairment that adversely affects a child's educational performance. |
| Traumatic brain injury | *Traumatic brain injury* means an acquired injury to the brain caused by an external physical force, resulting in total or partial functional disability or psychosocial impairment, or both, that adversely affects a child's educational performance. The term applies to open or closed head injuries resulting in impairments in one or more areas, such as cognition; language; memory; attention; reasoning; abstract thinking; judgment; problem solving; sensory, perceptual, and motor abilities; psychosocial behavior; physical functions; information processing; and speech. The term does not apply to brain injuries that are congenital or degenerative or to brain injuries induced by birth trauma. |
| Visual impairment including blindness | *Visual impairment including blindness* means an impairment in vision that, even with correction, adversely affects a child's educational performance. The term includes both partial sight and blindness. |

Source: Adapted from regulations to IDEA 2004.

also general educators. Additionally, a sizable number will receive related services such as speech therapy, physical therapy, or occupational therapy.

Public schools often provide special education and related services in various settings, and the special educators working in these settings have different roles. Figure 1.2 shows the full range of settings in which special educators are employed, often referred to as the "continuum of services." Even though you will find special educators working in all of these settings, usually they will teach in one of three types of settings: as co-teachers with general education teachers in general education classrooms, in resource rooms, or in self-contained special classrooms (in either general education or special schools). As you read about these settings and what teachers do in them, you should reflect on how each appeals to you.

### Co-Teaching in the General Education Classroom

Many students with special needs spend a significant amount of time in the general education classroom, as the diagram in Figure 1.3 shows. To serve these students, special education teachers work as co-teachers in these classrooms with their general education colleagues.

When working in these classrooms, special educators typically provide instruction and support for students of various backgrounds and with different needs. Most of these students participate in the general curriculum with students without disabilities. Although most students with disabilities in the general education classroom are likely to have high-incidence disabilities including **learning disabilities, emotional disturbance/behavior disorders,** or **mild intellectual disabilities;** others may have more severe or low-incidence disabilities such as **autism spectrum disorders; moderate, severe, or profound intellectual disabilities;** or perhaps **multiple disabilities** (see Figure 1.3).

As a co-teacher, the special educator will plan with the general education teacher to make sure that students with special needs can participate meaningfully in the general curriculum. The special educator will also help students work toward achieving any other **individualized education program (IEP)** goals. In classrooms where the special educator and the general education

The special education teacher and the general education teacher must plan together so that students with special needs can participate meaningfully.

---

FIGURE 1.2 • **THE CONTINUUM OF SERVICES IN SPECIAL EDUCATION**

- The general education classroom, with supplementary aids and services (such as special education teacher or paraeducator support)
- A part-time special class or a resource room for part of the day, with the student spending the remainder of the day in the general education classroom or in activities with students who do not have disabilities
- A full-time, self-contained special class within the regular school, with no or only a few opportunities to be integrated into other classes or settings
- A full-time, self-contained special class in a separate special school that serves only students with disabilities
- A residential placement in a state-operated or private residential school
- Instructional services in the student's home or a hospital

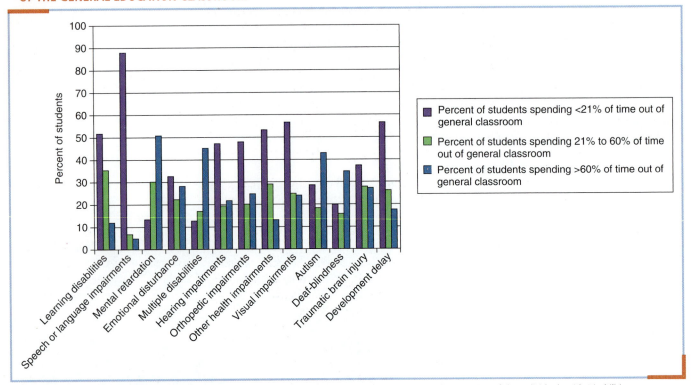

Source: Data from U.S. Department of Education. (2009). *28th Annual Report to Congress on the Implementation of the Individuals with Disabilities Education Act,* 2006, vol. 2, Washington, DC.

teacher both work for the entire day, their roles are often indistinguishable because both usually teach all of the students.

Sometimes the special education co-teacher will not be in the general education classroom full-time. Instead, he or she may co-teach for shorter periods and serve as a consultant to the classroom teacher so that students with disabilities may continue to receive services when the special educator is not there. Under this arrangement, the special educator will consult with the general education teacher and the **paraeducator** to support students when they are in the general education classroom. He or she also may serve students directly in a resource room.

### Teaching in a Resource Room

Resource rooms are separate, part-time, special classrooms where students with disabilities go to improve their academic skills or receive supports to assist them in achieving the knowledge and skills required by the general curriculum. Although they may spend most of their time in the general education classroom, some students with disabilities report to the resource room for intensive, small-group instruction on subjects they find especially difficult. They might also work to improve other areas such as their study skills, organizational and test-taking skills, problem-solving skills, or other strategies that will help them succeed in the general education classroom. The resource room teacher usually works with students one-on-one or in small groups.

"Visiting one of the schools that I once attended, I was flabbergasted at how badly things had deteriorated. There was little authority and order, and students with learning needs were being ignored. After seeing this, I decided to apply to the District of Columbia Teaching Fellows Program to become a special education teacher."

Monique Green, on why she decided to become a special education teacher for students with learning disabilities

It is quite common for special education teachers to spend at least a part of their school day in a resource room because most students with disabilities attend resource rooms for at least part of the day. Like other special educators, this teacher will provide direct instruction but will also meet with parents and other professionals, assess students' academic skills, work on IEPs, and plan instruction.

### Teaching in a Self-Contained Special Classroom

Some special educators teach in self-contained classrooms in elementary, middle, or high schools or in separate **special schools.** Usually, students with more severe intellectual, behavioral, physical, or sensory disabilities attend special classes, although it isn't uncommon for some of them to attend general education classrooms as well. On the other hand, you will find some students with milder disabilities served solely in self-contained special classes.

Important distinctions exist between teaching in a self-contained special class and working as a co-teacher or a resource room teacher. The special class teacher has more direct contact with the students and more responsibility for instruction in all curricular areas, and he or she works with the same students for the entire day. Also, self-contained special classes generally have fewer students, typically between 7 and 12. Often one or more paraeducators assists the teacher in self-contained settings, depending on the nature of the students' needs. This can be an important factor because it means the teacher must know how to work effectively with the paraeducators just as he or she works effectively with the students.

## THE REWARDS AND CHALLENGES OF BEING A SPECIAL EDUCATION TEACHER

Many experienced teachers will tell you that teaching students with special needs can be very rewarding. In reference to the question we raised earlier about whether special educators are special, we have noted that many "ordinary" people become special education teachers, but most do it for reasons that are not so ordinary. Next we discuss some reasons why many of these teachers value their work.

### Recognizing Potential and Seeing Progress

Many teachers receive positive reinforcement for their work when they see their students' progress. They say things like, "It's wonderful to see them grow," and, "It is rewarding to know that you are having a positive effect."

For some people, having a role in the improvement of others is extremely rewarding: helping them learn something, showing them how to perform a new skill, finding a way for them to overcome some boundary. Certainly, with the great diversity of students with special needs, significant student outcomes can mean achievement in a number of different areas. From improved behavior or better academic skills, to something as simple as learning to feed yourself or put on your pants: these are the essential sources of reinforcement for many special educators.

### Achieving Respect, Admiration, and Gratitude

Many people achieve respect by holding influential positions in industry or government. Others do so by giving large amounts of money to important causes. Still other people achieve respect by the nature of the work they do. Special educators fall into this category. Like nurses, paramedics, firefighters, and police officers, special education teachers realize that most of society values and respects the work they do. And knowing they are doing good work is enough to keep them doing it.

**REFLECTIVE EXERCISE**

#3 If you plan to be a special educator, have you thought about the type of position you would like to have? Is it one of those we have just discussed? If so, why does this position appeal to you?

"I loved it. It just felt really good and right."

Kathy Blossfield, preschool special education teacher from Asheville, North Carolina, on how she felt when she first worked with children with disabilities at a summer camp

## Taking on Challenges

Being a special education teacher can sometimes present challenging work-related conditions. For many teachers, their day-to-day challenges stimulate their efforts. They wish to do more, to do better, to improve their understanding of their students, to find more successful ways to teach. They wish for their students to learn despite their shortcomings and to help their students find happy, successful lives despite the odds. Students with special needs form a very heterogeneous group. Even within a particular disability category, such as autism spectrum disorders, you won't find two individuals who are the same. Many teachers of students with special needs love these differences and know that they will constantly be challenged to find a way to work effectively with their students.

While the challenges you face might motivate you to be more effective, they can also feel a bit daunting—especially in the first years on the job—and it is important for you to be prepared for them. As a new special educator, you may have students who have weak academic skills and some who exhibit inappropriate behavior. In some cases you may feel that your class size or case load is too large; that you do not have sufficient materials; that you have too much paperwork, too many meetings, and too little time to do all that you need to do. Finally, as you encounter these problems, you may sometimes feel that you do not have enough support from your administrator, your supervisor, or your colleagues. Certainly, these types of conditions can be very trying (Billingsley & Tomchin, 1992; Busch, Pederson, Espin, & Weissenburger, 2001; Kilgore & Griffin, 1998; Kilgore, Griffin, Otis-Wilborn, & Winn, 2003; Mastropieri, 2001).

In a very interesting study, Kilgore and her associates (2003) interviewed and observed 36 new special educators over a 2-year period to learn about their problems and what helped them deal with those issues. They found that teachers reported many of the problems just listed, such as having several content areas to teach to students at different ability levels and sometimes not having enough time or resources. According to Kilgore et al., "in many respects, these novice teachers had curricular responsibilities exceeding their general education peers, yet they struggled to find curricular resources to assist them in developing appropriate materials for their students" (p. 46). The new teachers also reported having insufficient opportunities for planning. One teacher pointed out that, unlike the students of general educators, none of her students went to "specials" (music, PE) at the same time. This meant that she was never completely without students and thus never had sufficient time to plan.

## Avoiding and Reducing the Challenges

Fortunately, along with the challenges noted by Kilgore and her colleagues (2003), they also reported several sources of support for many new teachers. Very often the new special educators said that other, more experienced colleagues, including both special and general educators, provided them with needed information, materials, and guidance. Veteran teachers were often good models for planning and teaching and gave valuable advice about the operations of the school and curriculum development. Many others were also helpful. When principals supported the teachers, the teachers really liked it. One teacher said, "As a first year teacher, it's been really nice to know that I could walk into my principal's office and talk with her like a tenured teacher" (p. 45).

There is probably no way a new special education teacher can avoid all of the difficult working conditions that may arise. But there are ways to lessen the stress that many teachers face, and many of these are related to a school's working conditions. As you consider schools where you may wish to teach, keep the following in mind:

- Support from principals, other teachers, and central office administrators will be important to your success. Try to gauge how much support will be available to you in your position as a special educator.
- A healthy school climate is also important. Look at how well teachers work together, how well student behavior is generally managed, the degree of mutual

respect between teachers and students, and the relationships between school personnel and parents and other members of the community.

- Relevant professional development opportunities will allow you to learn more as you seek to improve your teaching skills. Find out about the quality and quantity of learning opportunities.
- Have a clear understanding of your responsibilities and duties, and try to avoid conflicting directives, as these can be a source of confusion and stress. Know who you can turn to for help in prioritizing and solving problems.
- Determine if the school culture encourages teachers to engage in meaningful and substantive conversations and provides them with opportunities to do so. This will allow you to feel much more a part of a learning community and thus you will be better able to benefit from your colleagues' knowledge and experience.
- Focus on improving your classroom and behavior management skills. Many teachers become distressed at relatively minor but irksome student behavior problems. Develop positive strategies that you can use to reduce these behaviors and increase student productivity.
- Take care of your mental and physical health. Have a life outside your work, stay physically active, have a sense of humor. Realize that you cannot solve all your students' problems, and if you are not of sound body and mind, you will likely not help any of them (Botwinik, 2007; Clunies-Ross, Little, & Keinhuis, 2008; Gersten, Keating, Yovanoff, & Harniss, 2001; Grayson & Alvarez, 2008).

Good collegial relationships, a sense of humor, and having a life outside your work can help maintain mental health.

## A CRITICAL PLAYER: THE GENERAL EDUCATION TEACHER'S CONTRIBUTION TO STUDENTS WITH SPECIAL NEEDS

If you are planning to become an early childhood, elementary, or high school general education teacher, you will be the primary teacher for many students with special needs. In this section, we discuss the importance of your role in their education.

### The Responsibilities of the General Education Teacher

As you saw in Figure 1.3, many students with special needs, in fact over 95%, spend at least some, if not most, of their time in general education classrooms (U.S. Department of Education, 2009). Clearly, their success in these classrooms depends a great deal on how well general and special educators can collaborate to deliver an appropriate educational program.

As you probably know, general education teachers have the primary responsibility for teaching subject matter from the **standard course of study (SCOS)** to students from the time they are in kindergarten until they complete high school. Most general educators are well prepared to teach students who have "typical" learning abilities, and many are able to offer differentiated instruction for students based on their individual characteristics. Most often their students can acquire information efficiently through verbal and written instruction or through other kinds of meaningful learning activities. Among their varied responsibilities, general education teachers must plan lessons, prepare materials, organize instructional activities, and use instructional media and materials to teach specific content. Like special educators and other school personnel, their responsibilities keep their plates very full.

> "I strongly believe that every child can learn, and . . . I think kids want to belong and be with their peers. . . . I think it's important for kids to be around all kinds of kids."
>
> Shannon Hunt, second-grade teacher in Asheville, North Carolina, on why she likes to have children with special needs in her general education classroom

## The General Education Teacher and the Inclusive Classroom

Many students with special needs require alternative forms of instruction or have learning goals that fall outside those of other students, and so general education teachers may require support to find ways to instruct them and include them in the general classroom and as learning participants in the general curriculum. As you will learn in Chapter 2, federal law requires that, to the maximum extent possible, all students have an opportunity to be in, and learn in, normalized school environments.

The practice of including students with disabilities in general education classrooms and encouraging their participation in the general curriculum, which is always the preferred option under IDEA, places the general education teacher in a critical role. For this reason, a general education teacher often serves on IEP teams and works closely with the special education teacher to accommodate students with special needs. Although we can't expect that general education teachers will have the preparation or the breadth or depth of knowledge about students with disabilities that a special educator should have, it is fair to expect that the general education teacher can *share* in the responsibility for providing instruction to students with disabilities in general education classrooms.

## Creating a Positive Inclusive Classroom

**REFLECTIVE EXERCISE**

**#4** If you plan to be a general education teacher, what types of support do you think you would need to successfully include students with disabilities?

Formal preparation, an open mind, and a willingness to collaborate are required for a classroom teacher to succeed in teaching students with disabilities in the general education classroom. The teacher not only needs to help students with disabilities feel that they belong with their peers without disabilities but also needs to be a catalyst for acceptance. Most important, special education teachers and general education teachers must learn to plan, teach, and problem solve collaboratively. Working closely on addressing issues related to inclusion will allow teachers to work more effectively than working separately (Hobbs & Westling, 2000).

The teacher should be a catalyst for acceptance.

# MEET THE REST OF THE TEAM: OTHERS WHO WORK WITH STUDENTS WITH SPECIAL NEEDS

Besides special education teachers and general education teachers, many other professionals provide direct or indirect services to students with special needs, and we need to recognize their significance.

## Related-Services Professionals

Federal law requires that schools must provide "related services" to students in special education to the extent that these services are necessary to help them benefit from other school services. For example, if a student needs physical therapy to participate in learning activities, then the school must provide physical therapy. The result of this legal requirement is that public schools employ many professionals besides teachers to serve students with special needs.

According to data from the U.S. Department of Education (2009), U.S. public schools employ approximately 18,300 **social workers,** about 44,000 **speech/language pathologists (SLPs),** more than 7,300 **physical therapists,** and nearly 15,200 **occupational therapists** to work with students with disabilities. Additionally, educational administrators, counselors, rehabilitation specialists, and school psychologists play significant roles in the education of students with special needs (U.S. Department of Education, 2009). Table 1.3 lists and briefly describes the roles of some who commonly work with students with special needs.

"At first I wanted to pursue being a pediatrician; I knew I wanted to work with children . . . and then my dad said, 'Well, why don't you think about being a speech pathologist?' And I decided that indeed was what I wanted to pursue, to work with children, to make a difference."

Kathleen Lance Morgan, on why she became a speech/language pathologist

**REFLECTIVE EXERCISE**

#5 What has been your experience with different professionals who have worked with students with disabilities? What did they do? Did they like their jobs? What aspects of these jobs do you think you would like or dislike?

**TABLE 1.3 • OTHER PROFESSIONALS WHO WORK WITH STUDENTS WITH DISABILITIES**

| Professional | Role |
|---|---|
| School psychologists | The primary role of the school psychologist is to conduct assessments to determine the present level of cognitive, academic, social-emotional, and adaptive behavioral functioning of students with disabilities. |
| Physical and occupational therapists (PTs and OTs) | The PT evaluates, plans, and develops interventions to improve posture and balance; to prevent bodily misformations; and to improve walking ability and other gross-motor skills. The PT works primarily with students who have severe disabilities. The OT has knowledge and skills similar to the PT's but has an orientation toward purposeful activities or tasks such as the use of fine-motor skills related to daily living activities. |
| Speech/language pathologists (SLPs) | The SLP evaluates a student's speech and language abilities and develops appropriate goals in this area if necessary. SLPs also may work with students with more severe disabilities to develop alternate or augmentative communication systems. |
| Social workers | Social workers address many issues that occur outside the school. They may deal with family matters and will often make home visits to help resolve conflicts or improve parent–child interactions. They also can arrange for other service agency support. |
| School guidance counselors | Guidance counselors can help provide direction for academic or behavioral improvements. They will work one-on-one with students or with groups. |
| Art, music, and recreational therapists | Professionals in these areas use their particular specialties to help improve students' functioning in different ways, such as improving their communication or social skills. |

FIGURE 1.4 • **DUTIES APPROPRIATE FOR PARAEDUCATORS**

- Supervise individuals and small groups
- Provide individual assistance to students when necessary
- Help prepare materials and arrange the classroom
- Be responsible for keeping the classroom neat and orderly
- Assist in preparing materials, bulletin boards, adaptive equipment, classroom furniture, etc.
- Collect student performance data
- Help implement positive behavioral support plans
- Intervene in medical emergencies and contact an appropriate individual for emergency medical services
- Engage in clerical tasks that free teachers to spend more instructional time with students

Source: Adapted from Giangreco, Broer, & Edelman, 1999; Giangreco & Doyle, 2002; Westling & Fox, 2009.

## Paraeducators

As a special educator, a general education teacher, or another professional who works with students who have special needs, you are likely to find that paraeducators (also referred to as paraprofessionals, teacher assistants, or teacher aides) also play a major role in the education of these students. Although paraeducators often work closely with teachers in self-contained special classes, more of them are now working with students with disabilities in general education classrooms (Giangreco & Doyle, 2002; Giangreco, Edelman, Broer, & Doyle, 2001; McKenzie & Lewis, 2008). The U.S. Department of Education (2009) reports that approximately 367,000 individuals are employed as paraeducators for students with disabilities.

Paraeducators may perform many duties similar to those carried out by teachers, including instructional and noninstructional activities. The primary differences between teachers and their assistants are (1) teachers must hold at least a 4-year degree from a college or university, whereas paraeducators need 2 years of college or the equivalent; (2) teachers are the primary planners and decision makers responsible for developing instructional programs, whereas paraeducators may play a role in the delivery of instruction; and (3) teachers are held accountable for students' learning, whereas paraeducators may be held accountable for assisting teachers. In Figure 1.4 we list some duties that are appropriate for paraeducators. Such duties must always be carried out under the direction and supervision of a certified teacher.

## PROFESSIONALISM, EFFECTIVE PRACTICES, AND REFLECTION: THE KEYS TO BEING A GOOD TEACHER OF *ALL* STUDENTS

As you have seen, special education teachers can work in different types of settings, each with different sets of responsibilities. Furthermore, you know that general education teachers and other professionals also play important roles in the education of students with special needs. But whether you are a special educator, a general educator, or a related service professional, you should ask yourself, What does it take to be really good at my job? What knowledge, skills, qualities, and attributes are important for me to have a positive impact on all of my students? Returning to the key themes we introduced earlier, we propose that for you to be your best in your chosen career, it is vital that you become a *committed professional*, who uses the most *effective practices* known, and that you *continuously reflect* on the quality of your performance.

## Being a Committed Professional

### Developing and Maintaining Appropriate Dispositions

Working as a professional who provides instruction or support for students requires that you have a *disposition* that values the nature of human differences and recognizes the importance of being equally committed to all students. We believe that dispositions are just as important as having appropriate content knowledge and pedagogical skills. Many public school students have challenges that test the skills of the best teachers. But if you intend to be a *professional*, you must accept that you have a responsibility to work with all students regardless of their different challenges or special needs.

Organizations concerned with the preparation and continued success of teachers recognize the importance of appropriate teacher dispositions. The National Council for the Accreditation of Teacher Education (NCATE, 2008) states that future teachers should "demonstrate classroom behaviors that create caring and supportive learning environments" and "should recognize when their professional dispositions may need to be adjusted" (p. 20). NCATE further writes, "candidates [future teachers] must develop knowledge of diversity in the United States and the world, [and] professional dispositions that respect and value differences, and skills for working with diverse populations" (p. 31).

The Interstate New Teacher Assessment and Support Consortium (1992), a program of the Council of Chief State School Officers, has voiced a similar position:

> The teacher believes that all children can learn at high levels and persists in helping all children achieve success. The teacher appreciates and values human diversity, shows respect for students' varied talents and perspectives, and is committed to the pursuit of "individually configured excellence." The teacher respects students as individuals with differing personal and family backgrounds and various skills, talents, and interests. The teacher is sensitive to community and cultural norms. The teacher makes students feel valued for their potential as people, and helps them learn to value each other. (pp. 18–19)

As you can see, having an appropriate disposition to be a teacher means having an outlook that maintains that all students are important and should be valued as members of the learning community. Without a disposition of this nature, the quality of a teacher is likely to be diminished. This is especially true if you want to teach students with special needs.

### Displaying Positive Attitudes

The dispositions that you maintain as a teacher will be reflected in your attitudes toward different students, and, as you might surmise, teachers' attitudes can be a critical factor in the success of their students. Teachers of students with disabilities in inclusive settings often have mixed attitudes about these students. Research shows that teachers of these students are sometimes more likely to be indifferent toward them, have more of an inclination to reject them, and may be less attached to them than they are to students without disabilities. At the same time, teachers may have greater concern for these students and therefore make extra efforts to provide for their instructional needs (Cook, Cameron, & Tankersley, 2007).

### Caring, Fairness, and Respect

Caring, fairness, and respect are not just good qualities for teachers to have; they are essential. A teacher who cares about his or her students is more likely to have a positive impact. Bell (2003) suggests that, for schools to succeed with all students, teachers must be instructionally effective and show caring and patience for their students: "You can be the reason some kid gets up and comes to school when his life is tough. You can be the reason some student 'keeps on keeping on' even though her parents are telling her she can't succeed. You can inspire your at-risk students" (p. 34). In an

**PEARSON myeducationlab**

To enhance your understanding of what it means to teach students with special needs, go to the IRIS Center Resources section of Topic 8: Intellectual Disabilities in the MyEducationLab for your course and complete the Module entitled *What Do You See? Perceptions of Disability.*

**REFLECTIVE EXERCISE**

#6 Before you read ahead, what do you think are necessary attitudes for being an effective teacher?

**REFLECTIVE EXERCISE**

#7 From a student perspective, how have you been affected by the care, fairness, and respect of a teacher? Describe some positive and negative experiences.

interesting study, Langer (2000) compared students in demographically similar schools who were considered to be at risk for failure. She wanted to know why some teachers' students were succeeding while others were not. Although Langer found several important differences, one of the most important was that the teachers of the more successful students showed signs that they cared more about their students and about their success.

Fairness and respect are also important attitudes for teachers. *Fairness* means that teachers provide the instruction and support that individual students need without bias. *Respect* means that a teacher interacts with students in ways that acknowledge their humanity and strengths. Teachers who are fair and who show respect will monitor their own behavior to make sure that their interactions do not fluctuate as a function of a person's background or personal characteristics. Stronge (2002) reports that students feel most strongly about the following:

- They expect teachers to treat them as people.
- They view effective teachers as those who do not ridicule students or allow them to be embarrassed in front of their peers.
- They believe effective teachers are fair with regard to gender, race, and ethnicity.
- They see teachers who are consistent and allow students to have input into the classroom as fair and respectful.
- They believe effective teachers offer all students opportunities to participate and to succeed.

### Enthusiasm, Motivation, and Dedication to Teaching

Experience suggests that students' interest is affected by the teacher's interest. Teachers who are excited about what they are doing tend to increase the excitement and interest of their students (Brophy, 1998; Stronge, 2002). For example, in one study researchers found that when teachers exhibited more enthusiasm during instruction of students with learning disabilities, the students learned more and exhibited fewer behavior problems (Brigham, Scruggs, & Mastropieri, 1992). Teachers can show enthusiasm in different ways. Look at some characteristics of enthusiastic teachers in Figure 1.5, and see if you can suggest others.

**REFLECTIVE EXERCISE**

#8 How important are a teacher's enthusiasm, motivation, and dedication? How would you rate your own? Is it possible to be an effective teacher without these characteristics?

If you are a person who is not only dedicated to teaching but also motivated to be an effective teacher, you will have interest in both your students' learning and your own. You will always be searching for better ways to teach and more effective ways to get your students to learn. You will take courses, participate actively in professional development sessions, and attend professional conferences. You will also collaborate with other professionals, share and receive ideas, and often volunteer to contribute to needs in the school or community.

## Maximizing Your Effectiveness

### Teacher Expectations and Personal Teaching Efficacy

Teachers who are most effective, regardless of their teaching assignment, strongly believe that they can have a positive impact on their students, *regardless of the nature or degree of the students' needs.*

**REFLECTIVE EXERCISE**

#9 Although you are planning to be a teacher, how much confidence do you have in yourself about teaching students in a classroom? Have you had any successful experience in teaching someone to do something? How did this make you feel?

FIGURE 1.5 • SIGNS OF A TEACHER'S ENTHUSIASM

- Uses humor and appears to enjoy the subject
- Relates personal experiences to students about the topic
- Shows excitement when discussing the topic
- Is animated when presenting the lesson
- Maintains an active pace when covering the topic

Your view of your potential for success as a teacher is known as your "personal teaching efficacy." Teachers with high levels of personal teaching efficacy believe that they can positively influence student achievement and motivation (Bandura, 1977; Rotter, 1966; Tschannen-Moran, Woolfolk Hoy, & Hoy, 1998). Research has shown that teacher efficacy correlates positively with student achievement, teachers' willingness to implement innovations, less teacher stress, less negative affect in teaching, and teachers' willingness to stay in the field (Carlson, Lee, & Schroll, 2004; Ross, 1994; Soto & Goetz, 1998; Tschannen-Moran et al., 1998).

Effective teachers will use different avenues to pursue lifelong learning.

### Using Evidenced-Based Teaching Approaches

While we cannot underestimate the importance of appropriate dispositions and attitudes for teachers, we also need to state quite frankly that these are not enough. Successful teaching requires using the most effective teaching practices. This is especially true when the student has learning difficulties or special needs.

Teachers often cite a number of reasons for teaching the way they do or for using a particular instructional method. But all methods are not equal. To be most effective, teachers must seek and use **evidenced-based** instructional approaches whenever possible. Evidenced-based methods are those that are supported by scientific research and have been shown to demonstrate a relatively high degree of success in terms of student learning outcomes.

Although evidenced-based practices have been promoted for many years in other professions (e.g., medicine), they are a new concept in much of education, including special education. In our field, we have only recently begun to think about what we mean by scientifically based evidence and what is suitable to drive what schools and teachers do (Odom et al., 2005).

PEARSON
**my**education**lab**

Go to the Assignments and Activities section of Topic 1: Law, LRE, & IEPs in the MyEducationLab for your course and complete the activity entitled *Research-based Interventions*.

## Maintaining Quality Through Continuous Reflection

We hope that at this point you have started to develop a picture of the professional lives of teachers and other professionals regarding their work with students with special needs. We hope that as you have learned about those who teach students with special needs, you have reflected on your own potential as a professional and how you might be as effective as possible. If you have, then we feel you are moving in a very positive direction.

Before you continue with this textbook and your course, reflect on your part. Do you believe that providing an important service to others will lead to personal satisfaction? If so, then teaching may well be the right choice for you. Do you think that there is value in helping to form the lives of young people, improving the quality of our society, or experiencing a lifetime of self-growth? If so, then you probably have identified a good reason to be a teacher (Kauchak, Eggen, & Carter, 2002).

What about being a *special education* teacher? Is this what you think you should do? Let's return to the future special educator's motivation scale that we presented in Figure 1.1, and consider your responses. We developed this self-assessment to help you evaluate your reasons for becoming a special educator. Using the rating system provided, you could rate the importance of each item as it relates to your becoming a special education teacher. Look at your responses now, and consider the meaning of your answers.

**REFLECTIVE EXERCISE**

#10 How did you answer on the future special educator's motivation scale, in Figure 1.1? Do you still think you should be a special education teacher?

Society values special education teachers.

If you had relatively high ratings on items 1, 3, 5, and 8, a choice of special education as a career *might* be related to personal comfort and convenience. On the other hand, if your ratings on items 4, 7, and 9 were high, you probably have a particularly high regard for the idea of providing support to individuals with disabilities. Finally, if you marked items 2, 6, and 10 high, then you are probably a person who will enjoy the challenges and benefits often associated with the work of a special education teacher. While any of these factors might lead you to want to become a special education teacher, which do you think are more likely to predict your happiness in the field of special education?

# 1 SUMMARY

Many special education teachers enter the field for different reasons, and many people have different perspectives about what special education means. But special education teachers, general education teachers, and many other professionals make significant contributions to the lives of students with special needs.

## Why Special Education Is "Special," and the Roles and Responsibilities of Special Education Teachers

- Special education is often seen as providing instruction that is more precise, intense, structured, and controlled than instruction provided through general education. Teachers must often use different strategies and tactics to promote learning in students with special needs.
- Most special education teachers will work as co-teachers in general education classrooms, resource rooms, or part-time special classes, or separate self-contained classes for students with special needs.

## Rewards and Challenges of Teaching Students with Special Needs

- Some of the rewards of teaching students with special needs include the opportunity to see progress; accepting challenges that others would not; and achieving the respect, admiration, and gratitude of many members of society.
- Some challenges include teaching students who have weak academic skills, dealing with inappropri-

ate behavior, having class sizes or case loads that are too large, having too much paperwork and too many meetings.
- To reduce challenges, you should seek support from more experienced colleagues and administrators, work in healthy school climates where there is a high degree of mutual respect, take advantage of professional development activities, have a clear understanding of your responsibilities, be effective at managing student behavior, and take care of your own mental and physical health.

## The Role of the General Education Teacher for Students with Special Needs

- Most students with special needs are taught in regular education classrooms for at least a part of the instructional day. The general education teacher thus plays an important role in their education.
- The general education teacher's willingness to collaborate with special education teachers will be one of the most important factors leading to a student's success in the general education classroom.

## Other Professionals Who Provide Services to Students with Special Needs and Their Roles

- Related-services professionals in public schools commonly include speech/language pathologists (SLPs) and physical and occupational therapists.
- Additional key professionals include school psychologists, administrators, social workers, and various other therapists.

- Paraeducators also play an important role in educating students with special needs.

### Keys for Being a Good Teacher for All Students

- Enhance your professionalism by developing appropriate dispositions and attitudes such as acceptance, caring, fairness, and respect for all students. Teachers should also be enthusiastic and motivated and maintain a high level of dedication.

- Maintain a positive attitude about your teaching abilities. To be more effective, teachers should believe in their ability to succeed—that is, they should have a high level of personal teaching efficacy. In addition, teachers must use evidenced-based teaching methods.

- Reflect on your practice in order to be able to offer your students the instruction and support they need.

 **Council for Exceptional Children**

## ADDRESSING THE PROFESSIONAL STANDARDS

Council for Exceptional Children (CEC) Knowledge Standards addressed in the chapter:

ICC1K1, ICC1K3, ICC1K5, ICC1K9, GC1K1, GC1K4, GC1K5, ICC1S1, ICC5K4, ICC6K2, ICC7K5, ICC9K1-ICC9K4, ICC10K4

Appendix B: CEC Knowledge and Skill Standards Common Core has a full listing of the standards referenced here.

**PEARSON myeducationlab**

Now go to Topic 1: Law, LRE, & IEPs in the MyEducationLab for your course, where you can:

- Find learning outcomes for the broad concepts covered in this chapter along with the national standards that connect to these outcomes.
- Complete Assignments and Activities that can help you more deeply understand the chapter content.
- Examine challenging situations presented in the IRIS Center Resources.
- Apply and practice your understanding of the core concepts and skills identified in the chapter with the Building Teaching Skills and Dispositions learning unit.

- Check your comprehension on the content covered in the chapter by going to the Study Plan in the Book-Specific Resources section for your text. Here you will be able to take a chapter quiz, receive feedback on your answers, and then access Review, Practice, and Enrichment activities to enhance your understanding of chapter content.
- Access video clips of CCSSO National Teachers of the Year award winners responding to the question, "Why Do I Teach?" in the Teacher Talk section.

# chapter
# 2

# Special Education Today
## An Unfinished History

**REFLECT UPON**

- What are the shared characteristics and accomplishments among the notable historical figures involved in the social history of special education and disability?

- What are the major components of the Individuals with Disabilities Education Improvement Act (IDEA, 2004)? How has historic legislation and precedent-setting litigation influenced the development of the act?

- What are the five characteristics of the No Child Left Behind Act (NCLB)? How do they represent a major expansion of the federal role in the education of all students?

- How do Section 504 of the Rehabilitation Act and the Americans with Disabilities Act (ADA) influence service delivery to students with disabilities?

- What are two prevailing and controversial issues associated with special education service delivery and accountability?

Monique Green has experienced the rewards and frustrations associated with providing a free appropriate public education to students with disabilities. As a beginning teacher in an inner-city urban school district, Monique was disappointed to find that students with special needs were treated as if they could not learn and were not considered part of the neighborhood school community. For the most part, the strong educational and due process requirements of the Individuals with Disabilities Education Act (IDEA), as well as Monique's advocacy, ensured that students received books, supplies, and services. However, the laws, rules, and regulations that provide due process rights to students with disabilities can also provide challenges and frustrations. Currently, Monique is facing a difficult case in which parents and advocates believe that a student with a history of frequent violent outbursts is best served by being included in the general school environment. Monique and her team believe that the student would be better served in a setting that can provide more intensive therapeutic support. Monique, her team, parents, and advocates have attended long meetings, often characterized by adversarial and frustrating deliberations.

Monique Green did not set out to be a special educator. She completed her degree in communications from American University and was following news reports of her local urban school district's inability to bridge the achievement gap, retain qualified teachers, or be in compliance with the requirements of federal special education laws. However, what most impacted Monique was a visit to her former middle school. She was flabbergasted and appalled at how things had deteriorated; there was little discipline and little instruction being provided for students, and those with special needs were contained rather than educated. This was a pivotal moment: After this visit, Monique applied to the District of Columbia Teaching Fellows (DCTF) program, a preparation program sponsored by the school district and George Washington University. The students deserved more than they were receiving.

Although her first year of teaching was quite difficult, Monique survived. DCTF provided a solid foundation of instruction in the characteristics of students with disabilities and the importance of legal protections afforded to those with learning and behavioral disabilities. A mentor also helped by providing feedback on Monique's instruction and behavior management techniques. The reality of working with challenging students became apparent on her first day in the classroom. When one of her students could not find his pencil, he decided to toss a chair

across the room! Monique considered this a welcome to the real world of teaching students with extreme behaviors—a crash course in what is not provided in the textbooks.

For Monique, the greatest rewards of teaching are exposing students to new things (she took her students to the opera) and seeing her students light up when they realize that they could succeed in the classroom ("Wow, Ms. Green, I'm really not stupid!"). Still, there are frustrations. Although she is organized, she does not seem to have enough time to document all of the information required by the school district. Moreover, many transfer students come from other schools with little information, requiring intensive assessments for instruction. Monique believes that her organizational skills, creativity, and persistence allow her to develop systems that track student progress. Most important, Monique loves her students and sees herself as a change agent.

For those thinking of becoming a teacher, Monique emphasizes the need to understand that, regardless of observed deficits and disabilities, parents are sending us their beloved children. In addition to being an educator, we become therapist, friend, advocate, mediator, and sometimes magician for the family. To meet these multiple roles, teachers must be aware of current practices and stay organized, flexible, and caring.

## FAQ Sheet
### UNFINISHED HISTORY

| | |
|---|---|
| Why should we be aware of the social history of special education? | Knowledge of our history sheds perspective on current issues, helps us understand the changing cultural contexts of schools, and decreases the possibility of holding on to policies and procedures that don't work. |
| What will tomorrow's historians identify as today's key issues? | Prevailing issues occupying center stage in special education include service delivery alternatives, ensuring that every student with a disability receives an appropriate education, and the overrepresentation in special education of students from certain racial and ethnic groups. |
| What are the major components of NCLB? | Five principles form the core of the NCLB legislation:<br>• Strong accountability for results<br>• Increased flexibility and local control of schools<br>• Teaching methods based on scientific research<br>• Expanded options for parents<br>• Highly qualified teachers |
| What are the major components of IDEA 2004? | The major requirements of IDEA include<br>• Nondiscriminatory identification, assessment, and evaluation<br>• Least restrictive environment<br>• Individualized educational programs<br>• Procedural safeguards |
| What other relevant legislation influences the education of students with disabilities? | Section 504 of the Rehabilitation Act of 1973 provides protections for those with disabilities who do not fit the definitions under IDEA.<br><br>The Americans with Disabilities Act (ADA) is civil rights legislation that prohibits discrimination and requires accessibility to buildings and their physical facilities. |

Special education is a profession shaped by a rich social history, landmark legislation, past and current political events, as well as the courageous actions of parents, teachers, and advocates. As you prepare to teach students with disabilities, you will undoubtedly formulate your own view, or **conceptual framework,** of special education. Such thinking will allow you to develop a well-articulated and coherent vision of what you hope to accomplish with the students in your classroom. You will be able to expand your focus beyond the immediacy of daily professional activities and reflect on why certain practices—due process and least restrictive environment, for example—are essential to student success. Developing your own conceptual framework is neither quick nor easy; a personal view of special education requires knowledge, experience, and opportunities for reflection. Specifically, why do we prepare individual educational programs and use specialized methods for students with disabilities? How did schools and society treat students with disabilities and their families before civil rights advocates fought for due process of law? What social and civil actions prompted the right to education, **deinstitutionalization,** and inclusion movements? We believe that you will find that having an awareness of the social history of our field is essential in the development of professional competence and, more important, one's personal commitment to the field.

## SPECIAL EDUCATION STORIES: THE SOCIAL HISTORIES OF OUR FIELD

Consider the value of knowing the social history of special education. First, knowledge of our history provides new or different perspectives on current issues and challenges (D. J. Smith, 1998). Being aware of how individuals with disabilities were warehoused into isolated, overcrowded facilities provides insight about the motivation of those who advocate for full inclusion. Second, the history of special education parallels the histories of public education, psychology, medicine, law, and politics (J. M. Kauffman, 1981). By examining the development of our field, we can understand the changing cultural context of our schools and society. Third, knowledge of history increases the application of effective classroom interventions and professional practices. In contrast, educators who are unaware of successful practices in special education have a tendency to jump quickly on bandwagons, adopt reconstituted fads, and cling to empirically baseless interventions (J. M. Kauffman, 1981; Mostert & Crockett, 2000; Yell & Drasgow, 2005). Finally, a historical view of special education allows for a more complete understanding of the people and social circumstances associated with precedent-setting events. Much of this history inspires and provides direction; unfortunately, some of this history is frightening and signals the need for caution and reexamination of our present-day ethics and values (see Figure 2.1).

**my**education**lab**

To check your comprehension on the content covered in Chapter 2, go to the Book-Specific Resources in the MyEducationLab for your course, select your text, and complete the Study Plan. Here you will be able to take a chapter quiz, receive feedback on your answers, and then access Review, Practice, and Enrichment activities to enhance your understanding of chapter content.

## Beyond Cruelty and Neglect: Times of Recognition, Charity, and Education (1500–1900)

Before 1500, individuals with disabilities, if they were fortunate enough to survive infancy and early childhood, had lives filled with a mixture of brutality, hardship, derision, and neglect (Safford & Safford, 1996). Most physical and mental exceptionalities were viewed as divine or satanic messages: Those with disabilities and/or their families were being punished for secret sins, and their afflictions could not be altered through human or "earthbound" intervention. With the exception of individuals who were blind—who many believed were compensated with special powers—those with physical or mental differences were feared and treated as inferior beings. What would it take to change misunderstandings and ill treatment of those with disabilities? We examine three stories of people who advanced the quality of life for individuals with disabilities.

### Pedro Ponce de Leon: Teaching Deaf Adolescents

One of the earliest known efforts to truly educate persons with disabilities took place in Spain toward the end of the 16th century (Winzer, 1998). Pedro Ponce de Leon, a Benedictine monk, instructed wealthy boys who were deaf. Financial concerns motivated de Leon's efforts: The sons of the wealthy nobility needed to read in order to qualify for their inheritance and property ownership. However, such activities were revolutionary in that they challenged Plato's and Aristotle's prevailing views that, without speech and hearing, people could not learn. Even more courageous, de Leon broke with the prevailing church view that people who were born deaf could not have faith because they could not hear the word of God (Deaf Culture Information, 2005).

### Itard and the Wild Boy of Aveyon

A wild "man-animal" found in the forests of France in 1799 was a curiosity to the citizens of Europe. Considered an "incurable idiot," he was a dirty, inarticulate young boy of approximately 11 years of age who trotted and grunted like the beasts of the field. Incapable of attending to or perceiving heat and cold, he spent much of his time rocking back and forth like an animal in the wild and took great pleasure in only the basic biological functions of eating, sleeping, and sheltering himself from the unwanted attentions of others.

Jean-Marc-Gaspard Itard claimed that the boy's aberrant behavior was the result of a severe lack of social contact with other human beings. Consequently, Itard believed the boy's behaviors could be changed. Similar to the current-day educators

# FIGURE 2.1 • HISTORICAL OVERVIEW OF SPECIAL EDUCATION

## Beyond Cruelty and Neglect (up to 1900)

1590    Pedro Ponce de Leon teaches deaf young men, linking hand configurations to letters of the alphabet.

1799    Jean-Marc-Gaspard Itard works with Victor, the Wild Boy of Aveyon.

1817    Thomas Gallaudet opens the American Asylum for the Education of the Deaf and the Dumb.

1832    Samuel Howe opens the New England Asylum for the Blind.

1841    Dorothea Dix begins her work on behalf of people with disabilities incarcerated in jails and poorhouses.

1848    The first residential institution for people with mental retardation is founded by Samuel Gridley Howe at the Perkins Institution in Boston.

1860    Simon Pollak demonstrates the use of braille at the Missouri School for the Blind.

1869    The first wheelchair patent is registered with the U.S. Patent Office.
         Edouard Sequin founds the Association of Medical Officers of American Institutions for Idiots and Feebleminded Persons. It is later renamed the American Association on Mental Retardation.

## Steps Forward and Back (Early 20th Century)

1903    Helen Keller, the first deaf-blind person to enroll in college, publishes her autobiography, *The Story of My Life.*

1906    Elizabeth Farrell institutes a program of ungraded classes as an alternative to institutionalization.

1912    Building on Galton's view of eugenics, Henry H. Goddard publishes *The Kallikak Family,* a book linking disability with immorality and alleging that both are tied to genetics.

1922    The Council for Exceptional Children (CEC) is founded.

1924    The Commonwealth of Virginia legalizes sterilization of the feebleminded, insane, depressed, and mentally handicapped.

1927    Franklin Roosevelt co-founds the Warm Springs Foundation at Warms Springs, Georgia. The facility for polio survivors becomes a model rehabilitation and peer-counseling program.

1943    Congress passes the Vocational Rehabilitation Amendments, known as the LaFollette-Barden Act, adding physical rehabilitation to the goals of federally funded vocational rehabilitation programs.

1949    The United Cerebral Palsy Organization is founded.

## Civil Rights and Access (1950–1990)

1950    The Association for Retarded Children, now called the ARC, is founded.

1954    The *Brown v. Board of Education* court ruling ends the separate but equal philosophy.

1961    President Kennedy appoints a special President's Panel on Mental Retardation to investigate the status of people with mental retardation and develop programs and reforms for its improvement.

1963    The Association for Children with Learning Disabilities is founded.
         President Kennedy, in an address to Congress, calls for a reduction "over a number of years and by hundreds of thousands, [in the number] of persons confined" to residential institutions.

1964    The Civil Rights Act, a model for subsequent disability rights legislation, is passed.

1966    *Christmas in Purgatory,* by Burton Blatt and Fred Kaplan, is published, documenting the appalling conditions at state institutions for people with developmental disabilities.

1969    Swedish educator Bengt Nirge coins the term *normalization.*

1972    Wolf Wolfensberger popularizes the term *normalization* in the United States.
         *PARC* and *Mills* rulings guarantee the right to education of all children with disabilities.

1973    Section 504 of the Rehabilitation Act is passed. It prevents discrimination based on disability.

1975    The Education for All Handicapped Children Act, later renamed the Individuals with Disabilities Education Act (IDEA), is passed.

1984    *Rowley v. Hendrick Hudson School District* ruling declares that schools must provide services that students require to benefit from education.

1986    The reauthorization of IDEA mandates services for preschoolers with disabilities and requires that individualized family service plans (IFSPs) be developed for each student receiving services.

1990    The Americans with Disabilities Act (ADA) is passed. The reauthorization of IDEA mandates that transition be addressed for adolescents in special education.

1997    Reauthorization of IDEA requires that students with disabilities be included in state- and district-wide assessments and that IEPs address access to the general education curricula.

2002    The No Child Left Behind Act (NCLB) is passed. It mandates accountability for results, methods based on scientific research, expanded parent options, and highly qualified teachers in every classroom.

2004    The most recent reauthorization of IDEA is passed, emphasizing the need to reduce burdensome paperwork and improve methods used to identify students with learning disabilities.

Source: Adapted from Cimera, 2003; Rehabilitation Research and Training Center, 2002.

## FIGURE 2.2 • ITARD'S "IEP" GOALS FOR VICTOR

**Goal 1**  To interest him in social life by rendering it more pleasant to him than the one he was then leading, and above all more like the life which he had just left.

**Goal 2**  To awaken his nervous sensibility by the most energetic stimulation, and occasionally by intense emotion.

**Goal 3**  To extend the range of his ideas by giving him new needs and by increasing his social contacts.

**Goal 4**  To lead him to the use of speech by inducing the exercise of imitation through the imperious law of necessity.

**Goal 5**  To make him exercise the simplest mental operations upon the objects of his physical needs over a period of time, afterward inducing the application of these mental processes to the objects of instruction.

Source: Adapted from Itard, 1962.

who develop individualized education programs (IEPs), Itard generated five goals related to the mental and moral education of the young boy (see Figure 2.2). Victor (the boy's given name) benefited significantly from Itard's efforts. Although not completely "cured," he developed into an affectionate young man who, despite his inability to develop speech, could appreciate relationships with those who cared for him and understand what was said to him. Beyond the positive changes in Victor, Itard's efforts are significant because the methods used to educate the boy signaled to the world that a specific set of procedures to improve the behaviors of those believed to be untreatable actually existed (Humphrey, 1962).

### Laura Bridgeman and Samuel Gridley Howe

Consider the observations of Charles Dickens upon meeting 13-year-old Laura Bridgeman during a tour of the United States in 1842:

> I sat down . . . before a girl, blind, deaf, and dumb; destitute of smell; and nearly so of taste: before a fair young creature with every human faculty and hope, and power of goodness and affection inclosed [sic] within her frame, and but one sense—the sense of touch. . . . Her face was radiant with intelligence and pleasure. Her hair, braided by her own hands, was bound about a head, whose intellectual capacity and development were beautifully expressed in its graceful outline, and its broad open brow.

At age 2, Laura Bridgeman was stricken with scarlet fever that left her deaf and blind. At 7 years of age, Laura attended the Perkins Institution for the Blind in Boston, where she had the rare good fortune to be taught by the founder, Samuel Gridley Howe. A teacher of the blind, Howe believed that special instructional techniques could allow students with visual impairments to learn as much as those with sight. For Laura, Howe developed a system that used raised letters that spelled out words that corresponded to common objects. Building on her ability to distinguish among shapes, Howe taught Laura the relationship between words and objects, and ultimately Laura acquired a manual alphabet that allowed her to communicate with others. Laura's desire to learn was legendary, and Howe's methodology was widely disseminated and applied to children with

Jean-Marc-Gaspard Itard believed that the behaviors of Victor, the Wild Boy of Aveyon, could be changed.

multiple disabilities. Interestingly, his work had a dramatic effect on Anne Sullivan, the well-known teacher and "miracle worker," who employed many of Howe's techniques in her work with Helen Keller.

## Steps Back, Steps Forward: Early 20th Century

The optimism exemplified by the efforts of de Leon, Itard, and Howe did not extend to all individuals with disabilities, nor were they maintained over time. Although professional organizations were founded to address the needs of individuals with sensory and orthopedic disabilities, those with intellectual deficits received little or poor attention. Two stories reflect the events of this period.

### Goddard and Eugenics

**REFLECTIVE EXERCISE**

#1 How do current issues involving bioethics (e.g., stem-cell therapy, genetic mapping) remind some people of the dark days of eugenics? Can you think of similarities and differences between these situations?

**Eugenics,** or the science of human improvement by better breeding (Davenport, 1910), dominated much of the social thinking in the early 20th century. For those with cognitive disabilities, this meant subjecting them to segregation and sterilization to keep them from reproducing and polluting the "good genetic stock" (Kauffman, 1981). Such thinking is not new: In ancient Greece, Plato advocated selective reproduction. In the mid-19th century, Sir Francis Galton, using the theories of his cousin, Charles Darwin, asserted that society could not be saved from mediocrity unless the less intelligent stopped outreproducing those with greater intelligence. However, Henry Goddard's case study, "The Kallikak Family: A Study in the Heredity of Feeble-Mindedness," claimed it was *scientific fact* that mental disabilities and criminality were based on heredity. Consistent with this "science," Goddard and other eugenicists advocated reproduction restrictions among criminals, prostitutes, and those with undesirable social behaviors and said that a mental age of 12 should be the minimum level for people who were permitted to have children. Responding to such calls, nearly every state segregated people with cognitive disabilities in institutions, and 32 states enacted compulsory sterilization laws. Approximately 60,000 people in the United States were sterilized (Larson, 2002).

### Elizabeth Farrell and Ungraded Classes

During the popular eugenics movement, many reform-minded educators provided needed services to students who differed from the mainstream population. Recall that the beginning of the 20th century was a time of great immigration to our nation, and cities were home to many poor families who had not acquired the language or culture of their new surroundings. Not surprisingly, the new science of intelligence testing identified a disproportionate share of children from immigrant families, along with other "idiots" and "cripples," as defective. In 1899, Elizabeth Farrell got her start as a teacher of these "misfits" on New York's Lower East Side, an area of high immigrant concentration. Based on her success with these challenging students, Farrell was appointed in 1906 as head of the city's newly formed Department of Ungraded Classes.

Farrell's goals for these classes differed from those held by many of the leading educators of the times. Rather than viewing her classrooms as mere holding centers, Farrell believed that attendance in the classes could awaken the constructive, acquisitive, and initiative instincts in the child (Hendrick & Macmillan, 1989; Safford & Safford, 1996). With activity being the major theme, Farrell's curriculum emphasized motor skills and allowed for increased emphases on socialization and self-expression. Farrell collected follow-up data on many of her "defective" students. Rather than being institutionalized in wholesale fashion, 54.8% were employed, and 8.8% were not working but were considered able. The most compelling outcome: Only 4% of Farrell's former students were in institutions (Safford & Safford, 1996).

# Civil Rights and Access (1950–1990)

The **civil rights movement** of the mid-20th century had a monumental effect on the lives of many members of disenfranchised groups, including individuals with disabilities. As was the case with young African American schoolchildren, advocates for those with disabilities used the schools as a prominent battleground in efforts to achieve equal rights and due process of law. In fact, many of the original decisions rectifying the exclusion and segregation of students based on race were expanded to include students with disabilities (Murdick, Gartin, & Crabtree, 2002). Characterized as "a quiet revolution," in this movement, parents and civil rights advocates took on state governments and large school districts to ensure that students with disabilities had access to resources necessary to meet their individualized needs (Weintraub & Abeson, 1976). Next we focus on a few individuals who brought the plight of students with disabilities to the forefront of our national consciousness.

## Blatt and Rivera: Dignity and Disability Rights

Burton Blatt was a prolific writer and distinguished educator at Syracuse University who founded the Center on Human Policy in 1967; Geraldo Rivera was a young reporter beginning his broadcasting career at WABC television in New York City in 1972. Both men, from very different walks of life, share the distinction of having brought the horrors of institutional life for those with disabilities to the general public. Through photographic essays, textbooks, and a novel (e.g., *Christmas in Purgatory* [Blatt & Kaplan, 1966], *Exodus from Pandemonium* [Blatt, 1970], *Revolt of the Idiots* [Blatt, 1976]), Blatt exposed the inhumane conditions, pain, and drudgery inflicted on those in institutions. Using a hidden camera, Blatt and his collaborator, Fred Kaplan, took photos that made the American public aware of the cruelty and neglect that was hidden from view. Blatt's work contributed to a growing call for the deinstitutionalization of those with disabilities and the development

The civil rights movement of the mid-20th century was a time of advocacy for all disenfranchised groups, including those with disabilities.

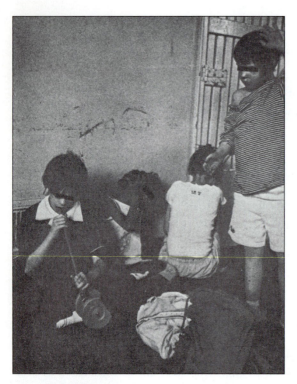

Burton Blatt's photographic essays exposed the inhumane conditions inflicted on those in institutions.

of community-centered residential facilities to actually habilitate those disabilities (Herr, 1995).

It took the power of television to bring the horrors of institutional life fully into America's homes. In early 1972, Geraldo Rivera, along with a cameraman, was able to sneak into the Willowbrook State School, an institution located on New York City's Staten Island. The facility housed 6,000 residents of varying disabilities and levels of intelligence. Rivera shared the following with his viewers:

> The ward residents, who were children, slept on wooden benches and straight back chairs in the dark cold ward. Some had no clothes. One was drinking water like a dog from an open toilet. The odors were foul beyond description. (Rivera, 2004)

The initial reports of the Willowbrook tragedy resulted in an explosion of public outrage. A number of organizations filed suit against the state for violation of the civil rights of the children, and Willowbrook was eventually shut down (Goode, 1998). One of the more compelling images was that of Bernard Carabello, an 18-year resident of the facility who had cerebral palsy but not mental retardation, as he was finally being moved out of the institution. This and the many horrific images presented by Blatt and Rivera spurred a generation of family members and advocates to use the courts (and the court of public opinion) to fight for appropriate, inclusive, and community-based educational and rehabilitative services.

## REFLECTIVE EXERCISE

#2 Investigative journalism played a key role in the attainment of civil rights and educational services for individuals with disabilities. Today, our ever-present media have focused on a number of controversial special education issues. Can you identify these issues and comment on the impact of the media on them?

### Sam Kirk: Recognizing Learning Disabilities

In 1963, Sam Kirk recognized an entirely new group of students with special needs whose characteristics had previously been misunderstood and misdiagnosed: students with learning disabilities (Chalfant, 1998; Gallagher, 1998). A prolific academic, Kirk established the Institute for Research at the University of Illinois in 1951 and wrote extensively on numerous topics in special education. Kirk was also extremely active in the formulation of some of the first federal public policies involving students with exceptionalities. For example, after Kirk served on the Presidential Committee on Mental Retardation in the early 1960s, President Kennedy named him the first director of the Division of Handicapped Children and Youth in the U.S. Office of Education. He was involved in strengthening professional organizations such as the Council for Exceptional Children (CEC) and instrumental in assisting in the formation of parent organizations advocating for the education of children with mental retardation and learning disabilities.

Kirk created formal mechanisms for identifying and assessing learning disabilities and developed the diagnostic-prescriptive approach to teaching, a process that links diagnosis and remediation of learning difficulties. His conceptualization of **intraindividual differences,** the variability of strengths and weaknesses within a student, is generally regarded as the hallmark of learning disabilities and serves as the basis for discerning learning disabilities from other types of cognitive and psychological difficulties and disabilities (Minskoff, 1998).

### Tomorrow's History: Inclusion, Accountability, and Overrepresentation

What will the historians of tomorrow identify as the key issues that face special education today? We believe that three of the field's current issues reflect our era:

(1) service delivery, (2) assurances that an appropriate education is being provided to every student with a disability, and (3) the overrepresentation of students from certain racial and ethnic groups in special education. For example, in their history of the inclusion movement, Fuchs and Fuchs (1994) assert that vocal "inclusionists" advocate dismantling the continuum of placements and refashioning general education classes to accommodate all children. Although it will take years to fully assess the impact of such policies on student outcomes, it is clear that inclusive philosophies are driving a number of historic special education reforms.

Similarly, while there is little argument about the need for accountability in the delivery of instruction to students with special education needs, we are only in the initial stages of developing valid and reliable methods for making appropriate test accommodations. As you will see in later sections of this chapter, federal legislation (e.g., No Child Left Behind) requires all students to pass state tests or alternate assessments (Thurlow, Elliott, & Ysseldyke, 2003). Finally, future historians of special education will note how this generation of leaders addressed issues associated with the overrepresentation of certain minority groups in special education. As we fully describe in later chapters, it is likely that two interacting areas will continue to be investigated: (1) the role of demographic, social, and economic factors and (2) school processes (e.g., referral and assessment systems) that are insensitive to cultural and linguistic differences (Coutinho & Oswald, 2000).

**REFLECTIVE EXERCISE**

#3 We have identified three current issues surrounding the delivery of special education. Which issues do you believe will be the focus of historians 30 years in the future?

# FEDERAL LEGISLATION

Two major legislative acts, the **Individuals with Disabilities Education Improvement Act of 2004 (IDEA 2004)** and the **No Child Left Behind Act (NCLB)** of 2001, shape how teachers do their jobs. In our discussions of each, we consider the historical developments that led to their passage, describe the major components of the legislation, and conclude with a discussion of how these laws impact the professional lives of teachers.

## Individuals with Disabilities Education Improvement Act

IDEA 2004, the most recent iteration of the landmark Education of All Handicapped Children Act (EAHCA) of 1975, is arguably the most significant piece of legislation supporting the education and treatment of children and youth with disabilities. Figure 2.3 provides a quick introduction to IDEA 2004.

### Legal Basis for IDEA 2004

Approximately 40 years ago, there was no guarantee that a child with a disability could get a free appropriate public education. In 1970, approximately 1 million children between the ages of 7 and 17 were not enrolled in school. Their absence from school was not a family choice. Instead, school officials decided, often arbitrarily, that such children were beyond their responsibility (Abeson, Bolick, & Hass, 1976). Also, highly restrictive

The due process rights afforded to students with disabilities and their families are, in large part, the result of grassroot parent activism and advocacy.

institutions that provided little more than food, clothing, and shelter were homes for approximately 200,000 individuals with significant disabilities. Schools in our nation educated only one in five children with disabilities, and many states had laws that explicitly excluded students with certain types of disabilities.

FIGURE 2.3 • SELECTED QUICK FACTS: IDEA 2004

**Free Appropriate Public Education (FAPE)**
All children regardless of severity of disability can learn and are entitled to a free appropriate public education.
Special education and related services are provided at public expense in conformity with an IEP.

**Nondiscriminatory Assessment**
All testing and evaluation used to identify and assess students with disabilities are not to be racially or culturally discriminatory.
Evaluations requiring tests are to be in the child's native language or appropriate mode of communication and must be validated and administered by trained personnel.

**Least Restrictive Environment (LRE)**
The preferred placement for students with disabilities is the general education classroom.
When success in the general education classroom cannot be achieved even with significant alterations, alternatives on the continuum of placements are to be considered.

**Individualized Education Program (IEP)**
An IEP must be developed for each student with a disability and include (1) current levels of performance; (2) annual goals; (3) extent of participation in general education programs; (4) beginning dates and anticipated duration of service; and (5) evaluation methods.
Participants in IEP planning must include at least one special and general educator, a representative of the local education agency, an evaluation specialist, related-service specialists, and parents.

**Parent Participation**
Written permission is needed for all testing, evaluation, and changes in services.
Parents actively participate in IEP development and annual reviews.

**Procedural Safeguards**
Adequate notice is provided for meetings.
Disagreements can be settled through mediation and due process hearings.

Obviously, many changes in educational policy have occurred, changes that now guarantee students with disabilities a free and appropriate public education. Significant **legislation** (laws and their accompanying interpretive regulations) have resulted in explicit rights for students with disabilities and their families as well as a range of responsibilities for professionals who work in schools and treatment centers. IDEA 2004 updates and amends earlier landmark legislation that served as the legal basis for the education of those with disabilities (EAHCA of 1975; the 1983 and 1986 EAHCA amendments; and the IDEA of 1990, 1992, and 1997). Keep in mind that legislation is temporary, fluid, and subject to the influence of political pressure. For example, much of the legislation involving students with disabilities in schools has resulted from the tireless efforts of parents and disability-rights advocates who lobbied Congress for equal rights, due process, and educational equality for all learners. Figure 2.4 lists and describes earlier legislation that has had an impact on our current IDEA.

In addition to evolving legislation, **litigation** (legal cases in which a judge or a jury interprets the law in situational disputes) influenced the initial passage and prompted improvements in the provisions of IDEA 2004. Following are the legal principles that have had the most influence in the development of special education law. After reading them, review the cases in Table 2.1, and try to identify the principles that the courts used in making their decisions.

- **Due process.** The due process clauses of both the 5th and 14th Amendments of the Constitution require that laws be applied to all with sufficient safeguards. For students with disabilities, this means fair and specific procedures related to

## FIGURE 2.4 • EVOLUTION OF IDEA 2004 LEGISLATION

- **PL 83-531, Cooperative Research Act (1954),** involved cooperative research in education, including students with mental retardation.
- **PL 88-164, Mental Retardation Facilities and Community Mental Health Center's Construction Act (1963),** brought together into one unit expanded teacher-training programs and a new research program for the education of students with disabilities.
- **PL 88-164, Research and Demonstration Projects in Education of Handicapped Students Act (1964),** made grants to state and local agencies to educate students with handicaps and provided funds for construction, equipment, and operation of facilities for research and training of research personnel.
- **PL 89-313, Elementary and Secondary Education Act Amendments (1965),** encouraged programs to educate students with disabilities who were residing in institutions and similar state-operated or -supported residential facilities.
- **PL 89-750, Title VI, Education for Handicapped Students (1966),** allowed grants to states through the Elementary and Secondary Education Act (ESEA) for special-needs students.
- **PL 90-538, Handicapped Students' Early Education Assistance Act (1968),** was developed exclusively for students with disabilities to establish experimental preschool and early education programs for special-needs students.
- **PL 92-424, Economic Opportunity Amendments (1972),** mandated that a minimum of 10% of the enrollment slots in Head Start programs be made available to students with disabilities.
- **PL 93-112, 504, 29 U.S.C. 794, Rehabilitation Act (1973),** specified that no handicapped individual in the United States shall, solely by reason of his or her handicap, be excluded from the participation in, be denied the benefits of, or be subjected to discrimination under any program or activity receiving federal financial assistance.
- **PL 93-380, Education Amendments (1974),** increased monies available to public agencies for the education of students with special needs and protected the confidentiality of school records, provided procedures to challenge questionable information contained in the records (Buckley Amendment), and required states to locate and serve all students with disabilities.
- **PL 94-142, Education for All Handicapped Children Act (1975),** the precursor to IDEA 2004, often referred to as the Bill of Rights for students with disabilities, guaranteed the availability of a "free appropriate public education," "due process," and "individualized educational plans" to all students with disabilities.
- **PL 98-199, Parent Training and Information Centers (1983),** entailed the training and provision of information to parents and volunteers.
- **PL 99-457, Education for All Handicapped Students Act Amendments (1986),** extended the mandate from PL 94-142 to include special education and related services beginning at age 3 and created a discretionary early intervention program to serve students from birth through age 2.
- **PL 101-476, Individuals with Disabilities Education Act (1990),** further amended the provisions of PL 94-142 and PL 99-487, renamed the act IDEA, and mandated that the IEP include a statement of transition services.
- **PL 101-336, Americans with Disabilities Act (1990),** prohibited discrimination based on disabilities in the areas of employment, public services, transportation, public accommodations, and telecommunications.
- **PL 101-392, Carl D. Perkins Vocational and Technology Education Act (1990),** provided resources for improving educational skills needed in a technologically advanced society, guaranteeing full vocational educational opportunities for all special populations.
- **PL 103-239, School to Work Opportunities Act (1994),** encouraged partnership models between school- and employment-based sites at the local level by encouraging schools and employment-site personnel to plan, implement, and evaluate integrated school- and work-based learning. It encouraged interagency agreements; technical assistance; and services to employers, educators, case managers, and others.
- **PL 102-476, Individuals with Disabilities Education Act: IDEA (1990), amended in 1997 as PL 105-17,** established a number of new provisions designed to improve outcomes for students with disabilities. Provisions inherent in the reauthorized law (IDEA 1997) include requirements that students with disabilities be included in state- and district-wide assessments, that students' IEPs address the issue of access to general education curricula, and that states establish performance goals and indicators for students with disabilities.

Source: Adapted from Rosenberg, Michael S.; O'Shea, Lawrence J.; O'Shea, Dorothy J., *Student Teacher to Master Teacher: A Practical Guide for Educating Students with Special Needs,* 4th edition, © 2006. Electronically reproduced by permission of Pearson Education, Inc., Upper Saddle River, New Jersey.

assessment, identification, and placement of children in special education (Turnbull, Stowe, & Huerta, 2007).

- **Equal protection.** The equal protection clause of the 14th Amendment forbids states from denying anyone equal protection of the laws without justification. Therefore, states must provide the same rights and benefits (e.g., opportunities to have qualified teachers, go on field trips, and participate in extracurricular activities) to students with disabilities as to those without disabilities.

**TABLE 2.1 • COURT CASES INFLUENCING THE DEVELOPMENT OF IDEA 2004**

| Case/Date | Context and Findings |
|---|---|
| *Brown v. Board of Education of Topeka, Kansas* (1954) | The U.S. Supreme Court ruled that African American students who were required to attend segregated schools were not receiving an equal education. The "separate but equal" doctrine was struck down. |
| *Hobson v. Hansen* (1967) | The system used to place a disproportionate number of African American students into the lower tracks of the Washington, DC, school system was invalidated. Special classes were allowed as long as testing and retesting procedures were frequent and rigorous. |
| *Diane v. State Board of Education* (1970) | California was ordered to correct biases in assessment procedures used with culturally and linguistically diverse students. |
| *Mills v. Board of Education* (1972) | Students with disabilities are to have access to a free appropriate public education and due process regardless of the school district's financial status. |
| *PARC v. the Commonwealth of Pennsylvania* (1972) | In a consent degree agreement, the Commonwealth of Pennsylvania assured the court that a free appropriate public education would be provided to all students and that there would be no exclusion of students with mental retardation. |
| *Wyatt v. Stickney* (1972) | Institutionalized students with mental retardation had a constitutional right to treatment. |
| *Armstrong v. Kline* (1979) | The 180-day school year violates some children's rights to a free appropriate public education, and the state must supply instruction to meet individualized needs without limitation. |
| *Larry P. v. Riles* (1972, 1984) | Use of IQ tests as a measure for placing African American students in special education was determined to be discriminatory. |
| *Board of Education v. Rowley* (1982) | The requirement to provide an appropriate education does not mean that a school must provide the "best" education or one to maximize student potential. |
| *Jose P. v. Ambach* (1984) | To increase delivery of services in a timely fashion, no more than 30 days should elapse between referral and evaluation. |
| *Daniel R. R. v. State Board of Education* (1989) | Although a program need not be modified beyond recognition, the general education curriculum must be modified for a student who requires accommodations and supports. The student with disabilities need not be expected to learn at the same rate as other students in the class, and schools are to consider broader educational benefits. |
| *Schaffer v. Weist, Montgomery County Schools* (2005) | Parents who demand better special education programs for their children have the burden of proof in their challenges with the school districts. |

- **Zero reject.** No child with a disability can be excluded from school, and all school agencies are to follow a policy of zero reject.
- **Free and appropriate public education (FAPE).** Individual students must be provided with a full range of appropriate direct and related educational services at no cost to students or their families.
- **Least restrictive environment (LRE).** Schools must deliver services in settings that best meet the needs of the student and are closest to the typical general education setting.
- **Nondiscriminatory assessment.** Biased evaluation instruments and/or procedures constitute a denial of equal access to education. Students can be harmed by assessments that wrongly label them and mistakenly place them in environments that deprive them of opportunities for advancement.

## From Law to Classroom: Major Components of IDEA 2004

Undoubtedly, IDEA 2004 and its preceding litigation and legislation guide how we view, approach, educate, and evaluate students with disabilities. In many respects, the components of IDEA 2004 form a core of competencies reflecting what all teachers should know and be able to do when teaching students with disabilities in their classrooms (Rosenberg et al., 2006).

**Nondiscriminatory Identification, Assessment, and Evaluation.** A major component of the original IDEA legislation was literally to locate the large number of children with disabilities who were unserved when the law passed in 1975. IDEA 2004 continues these child-find activities and mandates school systems to identify children who could benefit from early intervention. The law requires that schools and community agencies evaluate students to determine if a disability is present and, if so, to identify the full spectrum of educational services needed for the student to succeed in school or preschool settings. When conducting such evaluations, the law requires that educators

1. Employ testing materials and procedures in the student's primary language or mode of communication.
2. Use more than one test or procedure to determine disability or placement status.
3. Provide a full-scale evaluation in all areas of functioning related to the suspected disability.
4. Have only qualified personnel administer validated tests that assess how students function in classroom situations.
5. Ensure that tests and procedures are not racially, culturally, or ideologically biased or discriminatory.
6. Secure written consent and input from parents and guardians for both initial evaluation and reevaluations; summarize data into a format that is readily accessed and understood.

Keep in mind that IDEA 2004 requires that a multidisciplinary team determine disability status, eligibility for special education services, as well as the extent of participation in general education settings and activities.

**Least Restrictive Environment.** Is there a best setting or level of intensity in which to deliver special education services? Is it better to "mainstream," "include," "segregate," or "integrate"? Many people are surprised to learn that the federal law does not include any of these frequently used terms. The language used by IDEA 2004 requires that the education of students with disabilities occur in the least restrictive environment (LRE), meaning that

- Education placement is determined at least annually and is based on an individual student's educational needs.
- To the greatest degree possible, students with disabilities receive services close to their home, be educated with nondisabled peers, and have access to the general education curriculum and extracurricular activities.
- Removal from the general education environment occurs only when the nature and the severity of the disability precludes the satisfactory delivery of educational services with appropriate supplemental aids and services (Murdick et al., 2002).

To ensure that services are provided in the LRE, IDEA 2004 regulations require that school districts develop and implement a continuum of alternative placements, historically referred to as a cascade or hierarchy of educational placements. Having a continuum means that a variety of options is available to meet the specific educational needs of students. Such services typically range from indirect consultative arrangements that help general education teachers modify instruction to direct instruction in

Go to the Assignments and Activities section of Topic 1: Law, LRE, & IEPs in the MyEducationLab for your course and complete the activity entitled *LRE and the Continuum of Services*.

## CAN YOU HELP ME WITH THIS STUDENT?

| To... | Jean Sutherland, District Special Education Supervisor |
|---|---|
| From... | Shanise Saunders, Elementary Special Education Teacher |
| Subject: | Addressing the needs of a third-grade student with Down syndrome |

Dear Jean,

For more than 2 months I have been trying to get Junior B., a 9-year-old student with Down syndrome, to acquire basic math, reading, and social skills. A little background: At the insistence of his parents, Junior has been included in a general education third-grade class. This is the second year that he has been fully included, with my limited support, in a classroom comprised of 24 students without disabilities. As one of the special educators in our school, I work directly with Junior for 1 hour a day. (I have a caseload of 15 students in the building.) I also provide regular consultative support to Ms. Grenier, the third-grade teacher. I am an advocate for my students and believe that they should be included in the general education classroom with the necessary supports whenever appropriate. However, I am beginning to sense that this is not the most appropriate learning environment for Junior. In both academic and social domains, his needs are quite intensive, and Ms. Grenier has done her best to engage Junior. Several parents of other children have complained that Junior requires so much attention that Ms. Grenier cannot fully attend to other students who have difficulties. I worry about Junior and believe that we are not providing the most appropriate education for his needs. In spite of his parents' objections, I would like to see him placed in a setting where he can get more intensive academic and social instruction. My principal agrees that a change of placement is best for Junior but is afraid that the advocacy for inclusion in our district (advocacy, I should add, that we support) may hamper our efforts. What can we do? Any and all advice is welcome.

Thanks in advance,
Shanise

---

From:     Jean Sutherland, District Special Education Supervisor
To:         Shanise Saunders, Elementary Special Education Teacher
Subject:  RE: Addressing the needs of a third-grade student with Down syndrome

Dear Shanise,
Thanks for contacting me. I agree that the majority of students with disabilities, given appropriate accommodations and supports, can receive much or all of their education in the general education classroom. However, in spite of the most Herculean of collaborative efforts among special and general educators, a few students will need intensive and structured programming that requires removal from the general education classroom. As you consider any change in placement for Junior, consider the four factors cited in the *Daniel R. R.* (1989) precedent used to evaluate the appropriateness of a placement:

- Can teachers provide an appropriate education for the student, including supplemental aids and supports, in the general education placement?

- Have teachers made all available accommodations that could allow the student to succeed in the classroom?

- What are the benefits of placement in the general education classroom?

- What are the effects of the placement on the other students in the classroom?

Using these criteria, you may be able to make a strong case to Junior's parents that you and the principal are justified in advocating for a change in placement. Junior's consistent lack of performance in the general education enviroment, despite the best efforts of the team, overrides parental preference for full inclusion. I have listed some resources that may help in your discussions with the parents.

Douvanis, G., & Hulsey, D. (2002). *The least restrictive environment mandate: How has it been defined by the courts?* Retrieved on April 11, 2006, from http://ericec.org/digests/e629.html

Thomas, S. B., & Rapport, M. J. (1998). Least restrictive environment: Understanding the direction of the courts. *Journal of Special Education, 32*(2), 66–79.

Yell, M. (1995) *Clyde K. and Sheila K. v. Puyallup School District:* The courts, inclusion, and students with behavioral disorders. *Behavioral Disorders, 20*(3), 179–189.

Do know that we in the central office are available to help. Let me know if you would like for me to join you when you meet with Junior's parents.

Jean

---

**EXTEND AND APPLY**

- Junior's teachers clearly believe that he is not succeeding in the inclusion setting. How can they apply the court findings of the *Daniel R. R.* (1989) case (see Table 2.1) to this situation?

- Junior's parents continue to push for his placement in the general education classroom. How might Junior's teachers approach the parents to resolve this delicate placement issue? What type of information would you recommend the teachers share during this meeting?

---

specialized facilities for students who require intensive levels of support and supervision. Placement at one point of the continuum is not permanent, and service providers work to move students to a less restrictive, less segregated level of service. When the needs of a student require more intensive levels of service, movement to more restrictive settings is both necessary and appropriate.

**Individualized Education Programs.** IDEA 2004 requires that each student identified as having a disability receive an **individualized education program (IEP)**, a document that informs and guides the delivery of instruction and related services. Requirements for the development of an IEP are quite specific in terms of information included and the individuals who develop the plan. Six categories of information are required:

1. The student's current levels of academic and functional performance, with particular emphasis on how the student's disability affects participation and progress in the general education curriculum
2. Measurable annual goals related to meeting the student's needs resulting from the disability and enabling progress in the general education curriculum or, when necessary, short-term objectives for those students who participate in alternative assessments
3. A description of how the student's progress toward meeting annual goals is measured, how often progress is reported, and to whom it is reported (e.g., periodic reports to parents)
4. A statement of special education and related services and supplementary aids and services, based on research to the extent practicable, provided for or on behalf of the student

**PEARSON myeducationlab**

Go to the Assignments and Activities section of Topic 1: Law, LRE, & IEPs in the MyEducationLab for your course and complete the activity entitled *Individualized Education Programs*.

PEARSON
**myeducationlab**

Go to the Building Teaching Skills and Dispositions section of Topic 1: Law, LRE, & IEPs in the MyEducationLab for your course and complete the activity entitled *Conducting or Participating in an IEP Meeting.*

**REFLECTIVE EXERCISE**

**#4** In spite of all of the effort involved in developing IEPs, their use during classroom instruction is limited. Can you think of ways to make IEPs user friendly?

5. The extent, if any, to which the student will not participate with nondisabled students in the general education environment
6. The projected date for the beginning of services and the anticipated frequency, location, and duration of those services and modifications

The IEP team will also address postsecondary transition issues for students turning 16 (or younger, if deemed necessary by the team). Consequently, the IEP must include measurable goals and corresponding services based on appropriate transition assessments. Finally, as the student approaches the state's legal age, the IEP must include a statement that the student has been informed of his or her rights in regard to IDEA 2004.

Because the IEP is the focal point for planning, coordinating, and evaluating education services, successful development and implementation requires input from a number of informed stakeholders. IDEA 2004 requires that the IEP team include

- At least one general education teacher of the student (if he or she is, or is planning to, participate in general education activities)
- At least one special educator of the student
- A school district representative who is knowledgeable about available service-delivery options and programs as well as the general education curriculum and related-service availability
- An evaluation specialist who can interpret the instructional implications of assessments
- Other specialists who can provide important information, such as related-service providers, transportation specialists, physicians, lawyers, and advocates
- Parents, guardians, surrogate parents, and, when appropriate, the student

To reduce some of the logistical burdens on IEP meeting participants, IDEA 2004 excuses a team member from attending if that member's area is not being discussed or if there is agreement that written input is acceptable.

**Procedural Safeguards.** IDEA 2004 requires that schools ensure that parents (or guardians or surrogates) have the opportunity to participate in every decision related to the identification, assessment, and placement of their child. In addition to providing adequate notice for meetings and scheduling them at a mutually agreed-on time and place, school district personnel must notify parents when considering changes in educational programming or related services.

What happens if parents believe that their rights have been violated or if there is disagreement regarding the development of their child's IEP? An initial step is *mediation,* a voluntary process in which a qualified, impartial facilitator works with the parties to come to resolution. If mediation does not satisfy the parties, IDEA 2004 mandates the convening of a due process hearing. These hearings allow injured or dissenting parties to question decisions and actions. Parties also have the right to appeal due process hearing decisions in federal court if they remain unsatisfied. IDEA 2004 urges states to strengthen

Mediation is a voluntary first step designed to resolve IEP disagreements between parents and school districts.

their mediation procedures in the belief that structured opportunities for purposeful discussion between parties can reduce the need for protracted and costly legal activities associated with due process hearings and appeals.

**Suspensions and Expulsions.** For suspending, changing the placement, or expelling a student for violations of school rules, IDEA 2004 protections are prominent and somewhat controversial. Most people agree that schools must deliver legally correct and educationally relevant consequences fairly, regardless of the student's disability status (Rosenberg et al., 2006). For those inappropriate behaviors deemed not a manifestation (i.e., caused by or related substantially to the disability or a failure to implement IEP procedures) of the student's special needs, schools can apply disciplinary actions in the same manner as they do for students without disabilities (as long as special education services continue). However, schools cannot remove a student with a disability from his or her current placement for more than 10 days if educators determine that the problem behaviors are a function of the disability. After a number of debates during the reauthorization process (i.e., on the difficulty of determining whether specific behaviors are a result of a disability; the safety of other students in school), IDEA 2004 provided schools with the authority to consider unique circumstances on a case-by-case basis to change a student's placement for violations such as (1) bringing a dangerous weapon to school, (2) selling or possessing illegal drugs, and (3) inflicting serious bodily injury on another person while at school or at a school function. In such cases, the school district may unilaterally place a student in an interim alternative placement for up to 45 school days.

**Confidentiality and Access to Information.** Student information, including the results of all assessments and reports, is confidential. In fact, IDEA 2004 requires that one official in each school district assume responsibility for ensuring confidentiality of school records and ensuring that those who have contact with student records are trained in records-management procedures. Parents by law have the right to inspect and review all information on their child, and it is not unusual for them to request an explanation regarding the information in the records.

**Services to Infants, Toddlers, and Preschoolers.** Historically, many states did not provide services to infants, toddlers, and preschoolers with disabilities. It was not until 1986, and an early reauthorization of IDEA, that federal law mandated preschool special education services for children ages 3 to 5 and provided incentives to states encouraging the development of programs for infants, toddlers, and their families. Preschoolers are afforded the same services and protections available to school-age children. Because infants and toddlers with disabilities often require medical, psychological, and human service interventions, as do members of the entire family, the federal government has encouraged the development of state-wide, multidisciplinary, interagency programs by offering increased grant support.

**Response to Intervention.** No longer is a local education agency required to use the controversial aptitude–achievement discrepancy method for identifying learning disabilities. Instead, the district can use a process that considers the child's response to scientific, research-based methods, an identification method known as **response to intervention (RTI).** As we highlight in later chapters, IDEA also encourages the use of RTI as a method of prereferral early intervention (EI) activities. Teachers provide academic and behavioral support in the general education classroom as one way of preventing special education identification (Hollenback, 2007; Zirkel & Krohn, 2008).

### IDEA Outcomes and Improvements

Recall that, before 1975, large numbers of students with disabilities received minimal services, often in highly restrictive, segregated settings. As a result of IDEA, most of today's children and youth with disabilities are educated in their neighborhood schools in general education classrooms with their nondisabled peers. Moreover, postschool employment rates for people with disabilities, although not where they should be, are twice those of older adults with similar profiles who did not have the rights and protections of the law. Even more heartening are the numbers of students with disabilities who attend college; compared to 1978, the number of first-year college students

**REFLECTIVE EXERCISE**

#5 Consider the issues of equity involved in having different standards for suspension and expulsion. Is manifestation of a disability justification for having differing disciplinary consequences? How should we address the breaking of school rules by students with disabilities?

To enhance your understanding of response to intervention, go to the IRIS Center Resources section of Topic 1: Law, LRE, & IEPs in the MyEducationLab for your course and complete the Module entitled *RTI (Part 1): An Overview.*

with disabilities has more than tripled (U.S. Department of Education, n.d.). IDEA also supports the development of quality model programs in the areas of early childhood special education, culturally relevant instructional methods, parent training, and teacher development as well as improved protocols for promoting transition to the world of work and strategies for assisting students to acquire content-rich curricula.

Even with these considerable accomplishments, advocates continue to identify aspects of the law that require improvement. Influenced by a presidential commission report, changes in the most recent reauthorization of IDEA were particularly significant. A key theme that emerged from the report centered on the burdensome paperwork and administrative duties required to comply with the legal requirements of IDEA. In trying to reduce these burdens, IDEA 2004

## REFLECTIVE EXERCISE

**#6** Consider the major accomplishments of IDEA since its original enactment in 1975. Has the law fulfilled its mission of providing a free appropriate public education to all students? What can improve the act?

- No longer requires short-term objectives on students' IEPs except for those who take alternate assessments in place of the state's standardized assessment program
- Authorizes pilot projects in up to 15 states to develop multiyear IEPS, not to exceed 3 years
- Creates a 15-state paperwork demonstration program that allows states to test methods of reducing administrative reporting requirements without affecting applicable civil rights requirements

## No Child Left Behind

NCLB of 2001 is a comprehensive federal initiative designed to improve the educational performance of *all* students. Although it is a reauthorization of earlier Elementary and Secondary Education Acts (ESEA), NCLB represents a major expansion of the federal government's role in public education. Rather than merely providing financial assistance to states in their efforts to set standards and improve student achievement, the act explicitly mandates compliance to high standards and sanctions states and schools that fail to meet set criteria (Hardman & Muldur, 2004; Yell & Drasgow, 2005). Figure 2.5 offers a quick introduction to NCLB.

## REFLECTIVE EXERCISE

**#7** Federal government involvement in education is a hot political issue. Do you believe that federal agencies and national policy makers should influence the policies of neighborhood schools? If so, under what circumstances do you believe that states and local governments should object to such influence?

With governance of schools the purview of individual states, the federal government cannot enact laws that mandate uniform policies and procedures. Nonetheless, it influences schools powerfully by invoking other provisions of the U.S. Constitution. Just imagine for a moment how different our schools would be if the Constitution did not protect our rights as citizens. In ***Brown v. Board of Education (1954)***, the landmark case that struck down racial segregation in public schools, the

FIGURE 2.5 • **SELECTED QUICK FACTS: THE NO CHILD LEFT BEHIND (NCLB) ACT OF 2001**

**Accountability for Results**
- Creation of state assessments to measure what children know and learn
- Annual report cards on school performance allowing parents to know about the quality of the children's schools, the qualifications of teachers, and progress in key subjects
- Statewide performance reports disaggregated according to race, gender, and other relevant criteria to assess closing of achievement gap

**Expanding Options for Parents**
- Parents with children in failing schools allowed to transfer child to a better-performing public or charter school
- Title I funds available for supplemental educational programs (e.g., tutoring, after-school services, summer school) for children in failing schools
- Expanded federal support for charter schools

**Strengthening Teacher Quality**
- A highly qualified teacher in every public school classroom by 2005

Supreme Court used the 14th Amendment to rule that separation between groups prevented equal educational opportunities. Without such federal intervention, states would have had the option of continuing the practice of "separate but equal." In enacting NCLB, Congress was asserting that states were not doing enough to ensure that all students were performing adequately in school. Many students, once again, were being denied equal opportunities for success.

## Major Components of NCLB

NCLB legislation is based on five core principles: (1) strong accountability for results; (2) expanded flexibility and local control of schools; (3) an emphasis on teaching methods based on scientific research; (4) expanded options for parents, particularly those whose children attend low-performing schools; and (5) highly qualified teachers.

**Strong Accountability for Results.** Among educators, the letters of the alphabet that most closely follow NCLB are AYP. AYP refers to **adequate yearly progress,** the minimum standard, or benchmark, expected of every student and school. NCLB makes it very clear that states must develop clearly defined goals, or proficiency standards, and then assess if individual students and schools meet these targets. Comparing student performance data to the standards enables parents to know how their child is doing at school. In turn, policy makers and school leaders can assess how individual schools and school districts are performing in relation to state standards. In addition to measures of performance for all students across schools and districts, states are required to parse out, or disaggregate, data for specific groups of students, including those who are economically disadvantaged, members of varying culturally and linguistically diverse groups, and students with disabilities. Schools that meet their AYP goals receive positive public acknowledgment of effort. Those that do not meet their goals for 2 years running are deemed in need of improvement.

What about students with disabilities? Historically, students with disabilities were excluded, both formally and informally, from school and district assessments, perpetuating low expectations throughout their educational careers. Although many have welcomed inclusion, questions remain regarding the appropriateness of including students with severe cognitive disabilities in overall determinations of school effectiveness. To address this concern, NCLB allows school districts and states to exempt 1% of all students from the usual assessments. This 1% represents about 9% of those with disabilities and includes those with the most severe disabilities. Responding to concerns voiced by state and local officials, the U.S. Department of Education allows additional flexibility: an additional 2%, those identified as being in need of modified standards and assessments, can be assessed through alternative measures rather than the usual tests.

**Expanded Flexibility and Local Control.** NCLB recognizes that local officials have greater sensitivity to the needs of neighborhood schools than do federal administrators in Washington, DC. Consequently, NCLB provides the freedom for school districts to transfer up to 50% of federal funds among a number of programs without the need to obtain prior government approval. The act also allows school districts to consolidate funds from several programs and to enter into flexible state-local partnerships.

**REFLECTIVE EXERCISE**

**#8** Critics of NCLB have asserted that the rhetoric of the act is admirable but in some cases unreasonable. For example, is it realistic to expect that *all* students will be able to meet state-mandated proficiency levels?

**REFLECTIVE EXERCISE**

**#9** The transferring and consolidation of funds between and among programs can be controversial. What are the potential advantages and disadvantages associated with this flexibility? Why might advocates for students with disabilities be concerned by this practice?

NCLB requires that schools have clearly defined proficiency standards and methods to assess if individual students meet these targets.

**Teaching Methods Based on Scientific Research.** Monique Green, our featured teacher, was concerned that few students with disabilities in her neighborhood school received specialized accommodations and supports. Policy makers are also concerned that educational research has limited influence on school and classroom practices. Far too often, educators adopt programs and teaching methods based on fads, bandwagons, anecdote, and personal whim, usually with dismal results (Kauffman, 1981; Yell & Drasgow, 2005). With NCLB, federal support is targeted to only those programs that have a proven track record, demonstrating effectiveness through rigorous scientific research.

**Expanded Options for Parents.** Imagine for a moment that you are a parent of a second-grade student who attends a low-performing school that has had more than its share of discipline issues. You fear for your child's well-being and long-term academic prospects. Under NCLB you have options. First, if the school has not met state goals for two consecutive years, you can choose to have your child transferred to a better-performing school in the district, with transportation provided. Second, if the school fails to meet goals for three consecutive years, your child is eligible for a range of supplemental activities, including free tutoring and after-school instruction.

**Highly Qualified Teachers.** NCLB requires that all teachers be highly qualified. This has special meaning in NCLB: **Highly qualified teachers** are defined as being appropriately licensed and having the requisite qualifications in core academic subject areas. For content-area teachers, this requirement is fairly straightforward. To continue teaching, one must (1) have a college degree; (2) have full state certification or licensure; and (3) demonstrate competency in the areas he or she teaches by passing subject-specific, state-administered tests. The situation is not so clear-cut for special educators; for many, these requirements are confusing, controversial, and potentially burdensome. In addition to developing their special education skills, those who teach at the elementary level must pass a test of subject knowledge and teaching skill in the standard elementary curriculum (e.g., reading, writing, mathematics). Special education teachers at the middle and high school levels must be highly qualified in each of the core subject areas they teach. Because secondary special education teachers often teach multiple subjects to their students, they must demonstrate content knowledge tests in each of those subject areas.

## NCLB Outcomes

Go to the Assignments and Activities section of Topic 1: Law, LRE, & IEPs in the MyEducationLab for your course and complete the activity entitled *No Child Left Behind*.

Have the initial outcomes of NCLB justified all of the effort, reform, confusion, and expense? Although evaluation of the highly qualified teacher provisions will need to wait for the collection of reliable data, we do know that the AYP system has succeeded in identifying schools that need improvement (Hall, Wiener, & Carey, 2003). In fact, in many areas of the country, the general public is keenly aware of the magnitude of achievement gaps across their state and in their neighborhood schools. The AYP system has recognized improvements in low-performing schools, demonstrating that schools can and do move off the needs-improvement list. However, some in the disability community are concerned that the individualized, non-normative nature of special education is inconsistent with the use of predetermined, standardized measures of quality, a core element of NCLB. Many students with disabilities do not respond to the general education curriculum on the same schedule as their typically achieving peers or receive the supports and accommodations necessary for success at grade level. Consequently, students with disabilities could become the scapegoats for their schools' failures or blamed unfairly for requiring disproportionately more resources to meet standards (Allbritten, Mainzer, & Ziegler, 2004; Hardman & Nagle, 2004).

# Other Relevant Legislation

Two pieces of significant legislation, **Section 504 of the Rehabilitation Act** and the **Americans with Disabilities Act (ADA)**, have elements that influence how we deliver educational services to students with disabilities.

## Section 504

Section 504 is a component of the Rehabilitation Act of 1973 (PL 93-112) that authorizes federal support for the rehabilitation and training of individuals with physical and mental disabilities. It is significant for students with special needs because it provides protections for those whose disabilities do not match the definitions under the IDEA statute. In addition to using a categorical approach to disability, Section 504 protects students with (1) communicable diseases; (2) temporary disabilities arising from accidents; and (3) allergies, asthma, or environmental illnesses. Students who do not qualify for services under IDEA may qualify under Section 504. In essence, it considers that a child has a disability if he or she functions as though disabled (Murdick et al., 2002), and it provides these students with equal opportunities to obtain the same results, benefits, and levels of achievement as those without disabilities. Section 504 also extends protections against discrimination beyond school settings to employment and social and health services. If violations of 504 are found, agencies risk losing federal financial assistance.

How are the protections of Section 504 different from those provided by IDEA? According to Rosenfeld (2005), Section 504 levels the playing field by eliminating barriers that exclude those with disabilities from full participation in activities. These barriers can be physical (e.g., architectural impediments that stop a person with a physical or sensory disability from accessing a building), or they can be programmatic (e.g., not giving a student with attention-deficit/hyperactivity disorder supports and accommodations so that he or she can benefit from instruction). IDEA is remedial and typically requires the provision of intensive services and programs in addition to those made available to people without disabilities. Similar to IDEA, Section 504 has specific requirements for identification, evaluation, placement, and procedural safeguards. (In Chapter 4, we discuss Section 504 plans.) Unfortunately, because Section 504 is an unfunded mandate, the protections have been minimal, and many parents and teachers still remain unaware of its potential benefits (Richards, 2003; Rosenfeld, 2005; Shaw & Madaus, 2008).

Eligibility for Section 504 services is based on a team's determination of the presence of a substantial limitation to major life activities resulting from physical and learning-related impairments (Zirkel, 2009). Once a determination is made, teachers develop an individual accommodation plan. The accommodation plan is not as extensive as an IEP but should include clear information on how school personnel can implement accommodations to meet individual student needs.

## Americans with Disabilities Act

Passed in 1990, the Americans with Disabilities Act (ADA) (PL 101-336) requires, among other nondiscriminatory protections (i.e., equal opportunity to participate fully in community life and have equal opportunity to live independently), that all buildings and their physical facilities be accessible to those individuals with disabilities. Similar to Section 504, the ADA is civil rights legislation for those with disabilities. However, beyond receipt of federal funds, the ADA applies to all segments of society—employment, education, and recreation services—with the exception of private schools and religious organizations. Considered the Emancipation Proclamation for individuals with disabilities, it prohibits discrimination in employment, governmental entities, and public accommodations (T. E. C. Smith, 2001). Consider the frustration experienced by a student in a wheelchair unable to eat with peers because of an architectural barrier precluding entry to the cafeteria. The ADA requires removal of existing physical barriers or the provision of alternative means of service implementation. Students with contagious diseases, such as HIV/AIDS, are also protected from discrimination as long as they do not threaten the health and safety of others (Murdick et al., 2002). Finally, the ADA also requires that students have access to supplementary aids and devices that enable success in the LRE.

# PREVAILING ISSUES, CONTROVERSIES, AND IMPLICATIONS FOR THE TEACHER

## Accountability in a Time of Standards

Meeting the many requirements of IDEA 2004, NCLB, and the other laws governing the education of students with disabilities can be challenging. A combination of factors—including the intensive needs of the students, the shortage of qualified special educators, and the lack of adequate fiscal resources—has meant that some school systems have been cited for not delivering legally mandated appropriate education services to students in their districts. Several districts continue to be under the supervision of federal judges and special masters who monitor district activities and help achieve compliance.

What can teachers do? First, keep in mind that all teachers have both a legal and professional responsibility to have a basic working knowledge of legislation and litigation that affect students. Every effort should be made to ensure that the legal requirements of federal laws are being met. The following are recommended for demonstrating and enhancing your compliance to legal requirements (Billingsley, 2005; Rosenberg et al., 2006):

- Keep a readily accessible prompt sheet of the legal and professional guidelines that ensure fairness in the planning, delivery, and evaluation of educational services.
- Be a reliable teammate: Keep up with your share of the paperwork, participate in the development of IEPs, and attend all IEP conferences.
- Be aware of the goals and requirements of your state's and local district's testing programs, and provide the necessary accommodations as indicated on students' IEPs.
- Reduce your stress, and adopt an attitude of flexibility and adaptability: Educational requirements change continually in response to laws, regulations, and political pressures.
- Keep up with current events, participate in conferences and workshops, and subscribe to professional journals.
- Join local, state, and national advocacy groups to increase political awareness and influence public policy. Many positive changes in the past happened because individuals had the courage to question the inadequate and discriminatory practices they encountered.
- Interact regularly with members of the school and local community, advise families of their rights, and serve as a resource to your colleagues.

## Evolving Roles in Changing Education Systems

Changing legal requirements and rising standards will require changes in the way we do our jobs. For example, in this chapter, we introduced RTI, a process used in both the identification of students with learning disabilities and the delivery of early intervention services. As we fully describe in later chapters, many educators consider RTI a comprehensive conceptual framework for responding to the needs of *all*

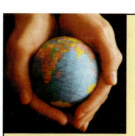

# THE REAL WORLD Challenges and Solutions

## Do the words we use to describe students matter?

*Sylvia Juarez, a special education teacher at San Jacinto High School for 10 years, is gratified that her collaborative work with general education colleagues has resulted in students with special needs receiving inclusive high-quality, supported subject-area instruction. Ms. Juarez consults and co-teaches with content-area specialists, and she has helped develop a peer-support network that pairs students with disabilities with high-achieving peers. San Jacinto has many indicators of success: Attendance rates are up, report card grades are improving, and standardized test scores are heading in the right direction. Still, Ms. Juarez is troubled by the way several of her colleagues refer to the students with disabilities. When speaking of a specific student, some on the faculty refer to the disability first, failing to recognize that the person is much more than just an educational or psychological diagnosis. For example, Ben, a student with intellectual disabilities, is often referred to as the retarded kid. Austin, who has autism, is typically talked about in negative terms, suggesting that he is a helpless student afflicted with a hopeless disease. Even Suzie, the cheerleader who has mild learning disabilities, is referred to as "that LD girl on the squad." Ms. Juarez is tempted to correct her colleagues but wonders if it is worth upsetting good working relationships with an issue that many believe is an exercise in political correctness.*

Do the words we use to describe students affect them and influence how they are perceived and treated by others? Or, are protestations to employ more sensitive language in our descriptions of people with differences and disabilities merely a "touchy-feely" fad or an exercise in political correctness? According to Snow (2009), the words we use to describe people are powerful, and the inappropriate use of old, inaccurate, and medically based descriptors remains the largest obstacle facing individuals with disabilities. In fact, when we use descriptors based on medical or educational diagnoses, we marginalize individuals and fail to recognize that they are much more than their disabilities.

The American Psychological Association (APA, 2003) suggests avoiding language that (1) implies the person as a whole is disabled, (2) equates persons with their disability, (3) implies negative overtones, and (4) is regarded as a slur. Such language implies that individuals with disabilities do not have the capacity or right to express themselves as resourceful and contributing members of society. Ms. Juarez should suggest that her colleagues consider the following guidelines (APA, 2003; Russell, 2008) when referring to students with disabilities.

**Put People First:** Avoid the implication that the person as a whole is disabled.
  **No:** learning disabled student
  **Yes:** student with learning disability

**Use Emotionally Neutral Descriptors:** Avoid expressions that suggest helplessness and negativity.
  **No:** birth defect
  **Yes:** youngster who has a congenital disability

**Emphasize Abilities Instead of Limitations:** Employ positive statements that reflect functioning.
  **No:** confined to homebound instruction
  **Yes:** student taught at home

**Focus on Capacity to Express Control:** Use language that reflects the person's ability to express goals and self-determine services and supports.
  **No:** placement decisions
  **Yes:** discussions of appropriate service delivery

**Reflect Person as a Resource Rather than Burden or Problem:** Language should reflect that service delivery involves inclusion and supports rather than solving a problem.
  **No:** problem of autism
  **Yes:** challenges faced by students with autism

### Valuable Resources for the Teacher

American Psychological Association. (2003). Guidelines for non-handicapping language in APA journals. Retrieved March 3, 2009, from www.apastyle.org/disabilities.html

Russell, C. L. (2008). How are your person first skills? A self-assessment. *Teaching Exceptional Children, 40*(5), 40–43.

Snow, K. (2009). *People first language.* Retrieved March 3, 2009, from http://www.disabilityisnatural.com/peoplefirstlanguage.htm

### Final Thoughts

Treating persons with disabilities with dignity involves recognizing that they are, first and foremost, people. Like most of us, they assume a number of varied and overlapping roles—parents, sons, daughters, friends, colleagues, co-workers, entertainers, researchers, and, yes, sometimes even irritating store clerks. Consequently the guiding principle when referring to individuals with disabilities is to recognize individuals as whole human beings.

students who experience academic, social, or behavioral difficulties in school. The central element of RTI is a tiered continuum of services. The first tier is a high-quality, universal, evidence-based general education program; Tier-2 instruction supplements Tier-1 instruction with focused, targeted interventions for those students who do not meet expected patterns of growth and achievement. Tier-3 instruction is highly intensive intervention—often provided by special education teachers—designed for students who do not respond to Tier-2 efforts (CEC, 2007; Hoover & Patton, 2008; Martinez, Nellis, & Prendergast, 2006).

Consider how a multitiered RTI framework would require a change in teachers' roles and responsibilities. For example, it is likely that general educators will be responsible for delivering research-based Tier-1 instruction to all students. Although special educators would likely support students at risk and with disabilities in all three tiers, all teachers would need to remain current on what constitutes effective practices for learners in a variety of skill and subject areas (Mastropieri & Scruggs, 2005). Teachers would also engage in data-driven decision making, provide differentiated instruction and behavioral supports, and participate in collaborative planning and practice (Hoover & Patton, 2008). Are most general and special education teachers fully prepared to fulfill these new roles? A major challenge may be to ensure that school districts address gaps in training as tiered instructional delivery becomes more prominent in schools.

## 2 SUMMARY

Special education has been influenced by historical events, significant litigation, landmark legislation, and the courageous actions of advocates, teachers, and parents.

### Social History: Individuals and Events Shaping Current Practices

- Although 1500 to 1900 is a period that can be characterized as "beyond cruelty and neglect," the stories of Pedro Ponce de Leon, Jean-Marc-Gaspard Itard, Laura Bridgeman, and Samuel Gridley Howe illustrate how the typical maltreatment of some with disabilities was beginning to change.
- During the early 20th century, the work of Henry Goddard and other eugenicists represented fear and contempt for people with disabilities. At the same time, advocates such as Elizabeth Farrell developed curricula that helped students with disabilities obtain employment.
- Between 1950 and 1990, a period characterized by the fight for civil rights, advocates, legislators, and parents made significant efforts to ensure that students with disabilities had access to appropriate educational services and treatment.

### IDEA 2004

- IDEA 2004, the most recent iteration of the landmark EAHCA of 1975, is the most significant legislative effort supporting the education of students with disabilities.

- IDEA, a confluence of significant legal decisions and principles, ensures that all students, regardless of their disability, receive a free appropriate public education in the least restrictive environment.
- Because of IDEA, the majority of children with disabilities are educated in their neighborhood schools and, to a large extent, in general education classrooms.

### No Child Left Behind

- NCLB is a comprehensive federal initiative designed to improve the educational performance of *all* students.
- NCLB mandates compliance to high standards, and it sanctions states and schools that fail to meet set criteria.
- The major components of NCLB—strong accountability for results, expanded flexibility, scientifically based teaching methods, expanded options for parents, and highly qualified teacher requirements—are having a substantial impact on how all students are being educated.
- Students and their families have procedural due process protections and are assured of receiving a nondiscriminatory assessment of strengths and weaknesses.
- An individualized education program containing current levels of functioning, annual goals, special education and related services, projected dates, and the extent of participation in the general education environment guides instructional efforts.

## Section 504 and the ADA

- Section 504 and the ADA are significant pieces of legislation that provide protections for people with disabilities who do not match the definitions provided under the IDEA statutes.
- Section 504 considers a child to have a disability if he or she functions as disabled.
- ADA expands protections to prohibit discrimination in employment and public accommodations.

## Prevailing Issues, Controversies, and Implications for the Teacher

- Although challenging, teachers have both a legal and professional responsibility to have a basic working knowledge of legislation and litigation that affect students.
- Many general and special education teachers are not fully prepared to fulfill the new roles associated with an RTI educational delivery system, and a major challenge may be how best to address gaps in training.

 ## ADDRESSING THE PROFESSIONAL STANDARDS

Council for Exceptional Children (CEC) knowledge standards addressed in the chapter:

ICC1K1, ICC1K2, ICC1K6, ICC1K8, GC1K3, GC1K4, GC1K5, ICC9S8,

Appendix B: CEC Knowledge and Skill Standards Common Core has a full listing of the standards listed here.

## myeducationlab

Now go to Topic 1: Law, LRE, & IEPs in the MyEducationLab for your course, where you can:

- Find learning outcomes for the broad concepts covered in this chapter along with the national standards that connect to these outcomes.
- Complete Assignments and Activities that can help you more deeply understand the chapter content.
- Examine challenging situations presented in the IRIS Center Resources.
- Apply and practice your understanding of the core concepts and skills identified in the chapter with the Building Teaching Skills and Dispositions learning unit.

- Check your comprehension on the content covered in the chapter by going to the Study Plan in the Book-Specific Resources section for your text. Here you will be able to take a chapter quiz, receive feedback on your answers, and then access Review, Practice, and Enrichment activities to enhance your understanding of chapter content.
- Access video clips of CCSSO National Teachers of the Year award winners responding to the question. "Why Do I Teach?" in the Teacher Talk section.

# Teaching Effectively in the Classroom

## What Can You Expect?

part two

# chapter
# 3

# Accepting Responsibility for the Learning of All Students

## What Does It Mean?

**by Dorene Ross, Margaret Kamman, and Maria Coady,**
*University of Florida*

**REFLECT UPON**

- How are the demographics of public school students changing?
- How is the increasing diversity of the student population reflected in special education?
- What is the demographic divide, and why is it important?
- How are the significant discrepancies in educational outcomes for students who vary by ethnicity, culture, socioeconomic status, language, and learning differences explained?
- What do successful teachers believe and do to enhance the educational futures of all students?
- What are the prevailing issues related to students from diverse backgrounds?

# MY PROFESSION, MY STORY: AMANDA ADIMOOLAH

Amanda Adimoolah is a third-year teacher in a fourth-grade inclusion class at the P. K. Yonge Developmental Research School at the University of Florida. Amanda can't remember a time when she didn't want to be a teacher. For her, school was always a positive place, and helping others learn even when she was still a student was something that brought her great satisfaction.

Amanda is highly qualified as a teacher. She has a bachelor's degree in elementary education and a master's in special education from the University of Florida. She is dually certified in these two fields and also holds an endorsement for teaching second-language learners. She believes her teacher preparation gives her a solid foundation of practical and theoretical knowledge that she draws on regularly as she makes decisions about practice. At the same time, it is abundantly clear that Amanda's life experiences in general and her mother in particular have had a powerful influence on who she is as a teacher, and how she defines her role.

Amanda was one of two children born to Caribbean parents who grew up poor. Her mother had no indoor plumbing until early adulthood and raised Amanda and her brother as a single parent for most of Amanda's formative years. Her mother's experiences in the army meant that Amanda moved regularly through her teens, and she feels this broadened her perspective and made her open to other people and experiences, making her well suited to address the needs of a diverse student population. She described her single, black mother as a stereotype breaker. Her mother was a loving, stable, disciplined, highly involved parent who somehow made sure that her children had everything they needed and grew up believing they could achieve their dreams. Amanda developed her vision of a strong teacher from her mother, and she strives to give her children the values her mother gave to her. Yet she also talks regularly about her partnerships with parents, about respecting what parents give to their children, and about the significance of the people who have the "night shift" with her students.

Amanda sets high expectations for her students, establishes clear routines and procedures that enable them to succeed, and reteaches any content that challenges a child until mastery. Although these are important to the success of her students, she believes the real secrets to successful teaching are relationships and partnerships. She sees it as her job to build a strong relationship with every child and every family. She also works to help children build strong relationships with one another. Amanda believes the development of these relationships is particularly important for the children in her class who lack economic resources, who lack social skills and self-discipline, or who struggle academically, whether officially identified with a disability or not. Although she feels pressure to ensure academic success for her students, Amanda's real passion is making sure that they have the social skills and self-discipline necessary to get along with one another and to persevere in learning. She believes that as a teacher of color she serves as an especially important role model in this regard for all the children, but especially for children of color. This is her passion, for she believes that equipping students with these skills establishes habits of learning that can carry them through their educational career.

Amanda Adimoolah also is adamant that parents and teachers must be partners and that the major barrier to involving parents is that many teachers lack the perseverance to reach out as many times as it takes to engage the parents. Once she meets parents, she believes the key to developing a partnership is to be a great listener, to get to know the parents as individuals, and to find out what they care about and what their dreams are for their children. Then her job is to work with the child and family to help them achieve their dreams.

As an observer in special education classrooms, you may note that a disproportionate number of students with disabilities are from diverse **cultures** and **ethnic** backgrounds (i.e., non–European American backgrounds, where **standard English** is often not spoken in the home). In addition, many of these students are from families with low socioeconomic status. To better meet the needs of students with disabilities from diverse backgrounds, researchers have recommended strategies similar to those used by Amanda Adimoolah. They recommend that all teachers

- Better understand students' cultural and language backgrounds
- Learn how they can adapt their teaching based on this information to ensure successful student outcomes

In this chapter we provide information that addresses the cultural, language, racial, and economic backgrounds of students and how these factors affect student learning. This information is useful for students from diverse backgrounds, regardless of whether they have a disability, and is intended to complement the instructional approaches that we discuss in each of the categorical chapters in this text.

Before you read any further, take a moment to answer a few questions about your own background to create a framework for understanding the information in this chapter (see Figure 3.1).

## THE CHANGING SCHOOL POPULATION

Are today's students really so different from the students who entered school 15 to 20 years ago? Let's examine how the ethnicity, language, poverty, and disability rates of students have changed and continue to change.

### Ethnicity

Throughout our history, European Americans have been in the majority. According to the U.S. Census Bureau (2008), in 2008 they made up 66% of the population. However, the percentage of persons from other, diverse backgrounds continues to rise. It is projected that by 2015 European Americans will only make up 58% of the population. Hispanics are one of the fastest-growing populations and are expected to increase as a proportion of the total population from 22% in 2008 to 39% in 2050. In fact, the "minority" population is expanding so rapidly that, by the year 2023, it is likely that half of all students will be non–European American. Moreover, several

FIGURE 3.1 • **PERSONAL DEMOGRAPHIC QUESTIONNAIRE**

**IMPORTANT: DO NOT SKIP THIS QUESTIONNAIRE!!**
We know that most students don't really take the questionnaires they find in textbooks. Make an exception and do this one. It will help you think about who you are. Teachers who take the time to think about their own background are more likely to be effective with students whose backgrounds are different from their own.

1. Before you read any of the other questions (and don't cheat!), list as many words as you can think of to describe yourself.
2. What is your race?
3. Unless you are American Indian or an Alaska Native, note how your ancestors came to this country and where they came from.
4. What is your family's socioeconomic status?
5. Do you or members of your family speak another language fluently?
6. What are some of your culture's traditions and expectations?
7. What ethnicity were the majority of your teachers?
8. What was the typical demographic makeup of your K–12 classrooms?

Classrooms are becoming increasingly diverse in all areas of the United States.

states (e.g., California, Hawaii, New Mexico, Texas) do not have any group that represents a majority of the state's population (U.S. Census Bureau, 2008).

## Language

Confounding this rapid change in ethnic demographics are factors of language. Currently, one in five U.S. students comes from a home in which a language other than English is spoken (U.S. Census Bureau, 2007). Census 2000 figures predict that, by 2030, 40% of 5- to 17-year-olds will not have English as their first language (National Center for Education Statistics, 2006). Almost 10% of the **culturally or linguistically diverse (CLD)** student population are classified as **English-language learners (ELL)** and are entitled to general education services to address their limited English proficiency.

The number of students who are English-language learners demonstrates stark differences by region. For example, a rural district in Arkansas (total student population, 15,543) reported 2,247 (14%) English-language learners who spoke 16 different languages. In contrast, Houston Independent School District, the nation's seventh-largest public school system (total student population, 208,945), served 58,000 (28%) English-language learners, representing more than 80 languages (National Center for Education Statistics, 2005). Any school district where you will work likely will have a large number of students who are English-language learners.

## Poverty

Economic segregation is perhaps the most significant trend in the United States. The poverty rates in the United States may surprise you: 13.2 million children were living in families below the poverty level in 2008 (Fass & Cauthen, 2008). Of even more concern is the number of children living in poverty as compared to the total population (see Figure 3.2). These statistics present us with the reality of increasing poverty and the challenges facing teachers for the foreseeable future.

## Abuse and Neglect

Abuse and neglect cross the lines of ethnicity and social class. Substantiated child abuse cases in 2007 included 794,000 victims of child maltreatment, including neglect (59%), physical abuse (10.8%), sexual abuse (7.6%), and psychological abuse (4.2%) (U.S. Department of Health and Human Services, 2009). Victims of child abuse may experience psychological, behavioral, social, educational, and neurological development problems (Child Welfare Information Gateway, 2008).

PEARSON
**myeducationlab**

Go to the Assignments and Activities section of Topic 4: Cultural/Linguistic Diversity in the MyEducationLab for your course and complete the activity entitled *Culture and Diversity*.

FIGURE 3.2 • **CHILDREN VS. ALL PEOPLE IN POVERTY**

Children vs. All People in Poverty

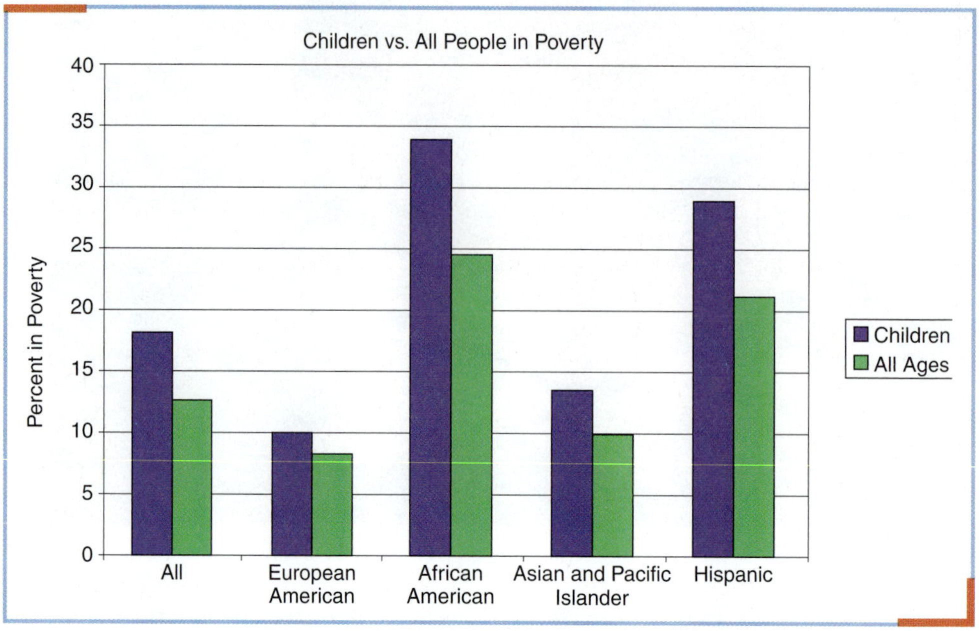

Source: Data from Fass, S., & Cauthen, N. (2008). *Who are America's poor children: The official story.* Retrieved May 15, 2009, from http://www.nccp.org/publications/pub-843.html

**REFLECTIVE EXERCISE**

**#1** Have you experienced the changing demographics of schools during your experience as a student? How well prepared do you feel to address the diverse needs of students? What strengths do you have to build on (e.g., knowledge of students from a particular cultural background) as a teacher?

According to the U.S. Department of Health and Human Services (2006), more children suffer from neglect in the United States than from any other type of abuse. *Neglect* is defined as an act of omission or the absence of an action. Neglecting children's needs can be as damaging as physically harming them. Consequences include problems with attachment, low self-esteem, increased dependency and anger, impaired cognitive development, and delayed academic achievement.

## DIVERSITY IN SPECIAL EDUCATION

Now that you have a better picture of the student population in general, we review how this diversity intersects with the population of students with disabilities. In 2007, almost 5.9 million students with disabilities aged 6 to 21 were served under IDEA (U.S. Department of Education, 2009). Obviously, disabilities are found in students of all ethnicities and language backgrounds. For the 2007–2008 school year, European American students made up 57% of students with disabilities; 20% were African American; 18% were Hispanic; 2% were Asian/Pacific Islander; and 2% were American Indian/Alaska Native (U.S. Department of Education, 2009). Additionally, approximately 6.4% of students with disabilities were identified as second-language learners in 2007 (U.S. Department of Education, 2009).

A critical issue related to the diversity of the special education population is the overrepresentation of certain groups of students. **Overrepresentation** means that, for certain demographic groups, the proportion of students identified for special education services is higher than the proportion of that group in the general population. Overrepresentation of non–European American students in special education has been discussed extensively and continues to be very controversial (Coutinho & Oswald, 2000; Hosp & Reschly, 2004). Specifically, African American and American Indian/Alaska Native students are significantly overrepresented in the intellectual disability, learning disability, and emotional and behaviorial disability categories (U.S. Department of Education, 2009). How could disproportionate representation be addressed by school professionals? See "The Real World" for more information on this topic.

## What can teachers do to address disproportionate representation?

*At Evans Elementary School, the teachers are assembled for a faculty meeting. The district Director of Special Education, Mr. Norton, is there to address them. He begins by assuring them of his faith in them as capable teachers. However, he says, "Like many of the other schools in this district, you have a disproportionate number of African American students identified with intellectual disabilities. Proportionately, you identify twice as many African American students as you should. As I said, this is not just an issue in your school—in fact, this is an issue across the nation—but it is an issue we need to address because it cannot continue. I am confident you will find solutions to this problem. I wish I could stay to talk with you further about this, but I've been called to a meeting at the district office. I'll be happy to return at a future meeting if you want to talk further." As the district supervisor leaves, teachers begin to murmur— "What are we supposed to do?" "Many of these students are so far behind and no one at home helps them." "How can I be expected to catch students up when they begin school so far behind?" The principal quiets the teachers and prepares to initiate a conversation. Her strategy will be to ask teachers to study the problem, do some reading, generate possible solution strategies, and study their impact. What information might help these teachers?*

As the district administrator noted, a disproportionate number of African American students are identified with intellectual disabilities in many school districts across the United States. Specifically, more than twice as many African American students are identified with intellectual disabilities as would be expected based on the number of African Americans in the school-age population. Why is this viewed as a significant problem?

First, the *intellectual disability* label is viewed as more stigmatizing than some other special education labels (e.g., learning disability). Second, students who are identified with intellectual disabilities are most often provided with services in a highly segregated setting and grouped with students who have similar disabilities (Skiba, Poloni-Staudinger, Gallini, Simmons, & Feggins-Azziz, 2006; Williamson, McLeskey, Hoppey, & Rentz, 2006). Third, many view the segregated settings in which these students are educated as ineffective and inappropriate for meeting students' needs (Freeman & Alkin, 2000; Williamson et al., 2006). Finally, in some schools or districts, disproportionate representation results in racial segregation in separate special education classes (Skiba et al., 2006; Zhang & Katsiyannis, 2002).

Two primary reasons are cited for the disproportionate representation of African American students in the intellectual disability category. First, African American students are more likely to come from very poor or low-income homes (Zhang & Katsiyannis, 2002). Students from these economic backgrounds often enter school less well prepared academically and socially and have lower achievement levels than their more affluent peers. Cultural difference is also often cited as a factor. For example, some have suggested that there is an African American behavioral style that may create a conflict between teachers' expectations for student behavior and those of their African American students (Hosp & Reschly, 2004). We'll address this topic in more detail later in this chapter.

### Valuable Resources for the Teacher

The best thing a teacher can do to address overrepresentation well is to make sure that cultural differences are accounted for, as all students are taught well. We provide more information regarding how to provide culturally responsive instruction and behavior management later in this chapter. Resources that may be helpful include the following:

Banks, J., & McGee Banks, C. (2006). *Multicultural education: Issues and perspectives* (6th ed.). Hoboken, NJ: Wiley.

Ladson-Billings, G. (2009). *The dreamkeepers: Successful teachers of African American children* (2nd ed.). Hoboken, NJ: Jossey-Bass.

### Final Thoughts

To some degree, overrepresentation of African American students with intellectual disabilities has been addressed by identifying fewer students with this disability (Beirne-Smith et al., 2006). Instead, increasing numbers of African American students have been identified using the less stigmatizing learning disability label. However, in spite of this practice, the overrepresentation of African American students in the intellectual disabilities category persists. To address this concern, several actions are needed, including the following:

- Prevent disabilities by providing improved health care and high-quality early education programs.
- Provide early intervention in school settings to address the needs of students who are at risk for developing academic problems (which may be addressed, to some degree, by the response-to-intervention [RTI] approach to student identification).
- Improve initial preparation and ongoing professional development for teachers related to addressing the needs of students from diverse backgrounds.

## FAQ Sheet
### DIVERSITY AND DISABILITY

| | |
|---|---|
| What is the prevalence of disability by ethnicity? | • European American—8.5%<br>• African American—12.2%<br>• Hispanic—8.5%<br>• Asian/Pacific Islander—4.8%<br>• American Indian/Alaska Native—14.4% |
| Are there differences in ethnicity by disability category? | • Significantly more African American and American Indian/Alaska Native students are identified with disabilities than are students from other groups.<br>• African American and American Indian/Alaska Native students are overrepresented in the intellectual disability, learning disability, and emotional and behaviorial disability categories. |
| How do graduation rates compare? | • Only 48% of Hispanic and American Indian/Alaska Native and 39% of African American students with disabilities graduate with a standard diploma, compared to 61% of European American students. |
| Where are students educated? | • African American students with disabilities are the least likely of any racial group to be educated in a general education classroom. Of these students, 41% are educated in general education settings for most of the school day, compared to 57% of European American students.<br>• While 13.3% of European American students with disabilities are educated in separate special education classes or schools for most of the school day, 26% of Hispanic and 27% of African American students with disabilities are educated in these settings. |
| Who is living in poverty? | • Students with disabilities are more likely to be poor than are students in the general population.<br>• About one fourth of elementary and secondary students with disabilities live in poverty, compared with 20% of the general population. |

Sources: U.S. Department of Education, 2007, 2009.

**REFLECTIVE EXERCISE**

#2 Think back to how you responded to the questionnaire at the beginning of this chapter. How does your background fit with the changing population of students? How will these differences influence how well prepared you are to teach students from diverse backgrounds?

In addition to overrepresentation, the FAQ sheet above shows that, while all students with disabilities have low graduation rates with a standard diploma, rates for Hispanic, American Indian/Alaska Native, and African American students are substantially lower than for European American students. Finally, African American and Hispanic students with disabilities are substantially more likely to be educated for most of the school day in separate special education classrooms or schools than are European American students.

Without question, the demographic changes in the United States will necessitate changes in how we educate children. Increasing identification rates for students with disabilities, coupled with high rates of child poverty, increasing numbers of English-language learners, and a demographic shift in which minorities are becoming the majority in many schools means that educators must adapt their classroom practices to meet the needs of diverse students.

## STUDENT DIVERSITY AND ACADEMIC ACHIEVEMENT

Students from diverse backgrounds often struggle to meet academic expectations in school. This has resulted in an achievement gap between these students and European American students. In the sections that follow, we describe this achievement gap and address resource inequities that contribute to it.

## Academic Proficiency

The achievement gap is usually discussed as the difference between European American students' achievement scores and those of other groups such as African American and Hispanic students. To illustrate, research examining the achievement gap revealed the following levels of proficiency among fourth-grade students in reading: European American, 40%; African American, 10%; Hispanic, 11%. A similar achievement gap exists in math. Research shows that these achievement gaps arise in the early grades and widen by the end of high school (Education Trust, 2009).

Poverty accounts for much of the difference in achievement, as poor students score substantially lower than their middle- and upper-income peers at all three tested grades (4th, 8th, and 12th) and in all subjects (National Center for Education Statistics, 2008). Additionally, in science, math, and history, three to four times as many middle- and upper-income students received proficient scores when compared with poor students. This and other research consistently confirms that the higher the levels of poverty, the lower the levels of student achievement (Books, 2007).

To enhance your understanding of why students from diverse backgrounds might struggle to meet academic expectations in school, go to the IRIS Center Resources section of Topic 4: Cultural/Linguistic Diversity in the MyEducationLab for your course and complete the Module entitled *Cultural and Linguistic Differences: What Teachers Should Know*.

## High School Graduation Rates

*The 28th Annual Report to Congress* (U.S Department of Education, 2007) reported that only 55.5% of all students with disabilities graduate with a standard diploma and 31.1% drop out. Culturally and linguistically diverse (CLD) students with disabilities are at the highest risk of dropping out. Only 47% of Hispanic, 48% of American Indian/Alaskan Native, and 39% of African American students with disabilities obtain a standard diploma. In general, students from CLD backgrounds are "three times more likely to be low achievers than high achievers, two times more likely to be at least one grade level behind in schools, and four times more likely to drop out than their native-English-speaking peers" (American Association of Colleges for Teacher Education, 2002).

## Access to Resources

Both direct and indirect effects of poverty contribute to the achievement gap. Consider the resources available to support a student's education. For decades, the Education Trust (Arroyo, 2008) has analyzed state data documenting the disparities in resources for high-poverty schools that enroll a high percentage of students from non–European American backgrounds. Their most recent report indicates improvements in some states, while inequality persists in others. Currently, 16 states have a funding gap, with a nationwide discrepancy between high- and low-poverty districts of $1,532 per student. Many high-poverty schools struggle with deteriorating facilities. They also are less likely to employ experienced, qualified, knowledgeable, effective teachers (Arroyo, 2008). Students in high-poverty schools are almost twice as likely as other students (34% vs. 24%) to have novice teachers (Peske & Haycock, 2006). This lack of highly qualified teachers is likely to be even more extreme for special education teachers in high-poverty schools (Tyler, Yzquierdo, Lopez-Reyna, & Flippin, 2004).

Not all classrooms have access to the necessary resources to meet student needs.

All too often, the diversity of the teaching force does not match the diversity of students.

## The Demographic Divide Between Teachers and Students

Another factor that contributes to the achievement gap is the lack of teachers from culturally and linguistically diverse backgrounds. The nation's teaching force is predominantly European American (84.6%), female (more than 75%), and middle aged (average age of 42). African American (8.4%) and Hispanic teachers (5.5%) make up only a small proportion of the total teaching force (National Center for Education Statistics, 2008).

The increasing diversity of the school population, coupled with the homogeneity of the teaching workforce, creates a demographic divide in many schools. According to a 2003 National Commission on Teaching and America's Future report, individuals of African American, Hispanic and Latino, Asian, and American Indian/Alaska Native descent make up 14% of K–12 teachers, while 36% of the students are from these backgrounds. In the nation's largest urban schools, students from diverse backgrounds make up 69% of the population, while only 35% of their teachers are from similar backgrounds (National Education Association, 2003).

We do not mean to suggest that teachers from the majority culture cannot successfully teach students from diverse backgrounds. However, it is important that the teacher workforce include a reasonable proportion of teachers who share the cultural and language experiences of their students. These teachers can serve as a rich resource for other teachers and ensure that the diverse backgrounds of students are used to enrich the lives of everyone in the school (Tyler et al., 2004). In the next section, we discuss how all teachers can bridge the demographic divide.

## REFLECTIVE EXERCISE

#3 Have you experienced or observed the demographic divide in a school? How important do you think this divide is for students from diverse backgrounds? Why?

## THE ROLE OF CULTURE IN EXPLAINING DIFFERENTIAL OUTCOMES

Clearly, significant differences occur in educational outcomes for students who vary by class, ethnicity, and home language. Factors such as access to resources, access to high-quality teachers, the nature of family support, and the demographic divide between teachers and students all help to explain these discrepancies. However, these factors do not predetermine educational outcomes. For example, Gruwell (2007) documents the success of all 150 students she worked with in a poverty high school in Los Angeles. With their teachers' help, these students all graduated, and many went on to college despite overwhelming odds (i.e., poverty, second-language background, gang culture, teenage pregnancy, homelessness).

Additionally, it is important to emphasize that students are not defined by any one factor. Each student has a complex history that encompasses varied factors such as social class, ethnicity, language, family structure, medical history, school history, ability, and disability. For example, the school experience and probable educational outcomes for a middle-class European American student with a moderate learning disability will not be the same as those of a student with a similar disability who is from a poor migrant family and is an English-language learner. Yet great variability occurs in the educational outcomes within groups as well. The connections (or lack of connections) between students and their teachers often facilitate or impede academic success.

One might think that the more points of difference between the students and the teacher, the more difficult it is for students to succeed. However, more significant than the number of differences is how teachers perceive difference. While human variation falls along a continuum (Salend, 2008), the human tendency is to perceive difference as dividing people and behavior into two groups, "normal" and "abnormal." We tend to perceive those most like us as "normal" and those who differ from us in significant ways as "abnormal." For most of us, these perceptions are implicit feelings. Try a little experiment to help you think about your perceptions of "normal" and how hard it is to alter one's perceptions.

Cross your arms across your chest in the way that you habitually cross them (called the akimbo position), and notice which hand is on top. Now cross your arms so that the *other* hand is on top. Many of our students find this so "abnormal" that it takes several tries to cross their arms in the nonhabitual way, but there is nothing inherently "normal" about having one's left (or right) hand on top. Yet even when you *know* that there is nothing abnormal about the new position, it feels weird; and without deliberate intention, you will habitually return your arms to their accustomed position.

In school, teachers often define "normal" students as those who come prepared to behave in particular ways and to handle a specific type of academic structure. For example, "normal" students might be those who

- Sit and listen for extended periods of time.
- Take turns speaking in class; use standard grammar.
- Are deferential to adults.
- Look teachers in the eye when reprimanded.
- Use a logical sequential communication style.

If you are a White, European American, middle-class female who has spoken English from birth, these characteristics probably seem "normal." Yet each of those characteristics is outside the norm for one or more cultural groups. This can mean that the teacher perceives actions that fall within the norms for students' cultures as "abnormal."

Although few teachers talk about students or their families as abnormal, teachers' lack of familiarity and/or comfort with the norms of other cultures and backgrounds can lead to the following kinds of perceptions about students or families:

- He just has no idea of appropriate behavior. He is out of his seat *all* the time and talks constantly when he should be listening.
- Those parents just don't care. They never return my phone calls, never come to parent conferences, and don't even sign the student's planner.

When a teacher's implicit evaluation of a student leads to the conclusion that the child's academic or social behavior is outside the norm of appropriate behavior, the teacher may make well-intended decisions that are unlikely to enhance the child's educational success.

One example of the influence of culture concerns the decision to refer a child for possible identification with a disability. This is an inferential decision. That is, the teacher makes a decision to refer the student because he or she *believes* that the student's academic or social behavior is so far outside the expectations for "normal" behavior that special services are warranted.

Notice the word *believes*, because teachers' beliefs are influenced by their cultural expectations. A review of studies on ethnicity and special education placement revealed that school districts with predominantly European American populations enrolled a higher percentage of students from diverse backgrounds in special education than did districts with higher percentages of students from non–European American backgrounds (Fletcher & Navarrete, 2003). These findings suggest that students who fall outside the norms of behavior expected by European American, middle-class teachers are at greater risk for being referred to special education.

# What Is Culture, and Why Is It So Important?

Culture is a concept that helps teachers understand the implicit evaluations they make and the reasons behind some of the behaviors of students that "seem" atypical. Nieto and Bode (2007) define culture as "the values; traditions; social and political relationships; and worldview created, shared, and transformed by a group of people bound together by a common history, geographic location, language, social class and/or religion" (p. 436). As this definition suggests, culture is dynamic and socially constructed by participants, and it involves an invisible web of shared meanings (Geertz, 1973). Because culture is invisible, it can be very difficult to perceive the defining characteristics of one's own culture (Greenfield, Raeff, & Quiroz, 1996). In addition, the invisible rules (or norms) of culture, including behaviors, values, and beliefs that guide human interaction, may be confusing to people when they attempt to participate in a different culture.

## Cultural Norms and School: An Example

Some societies are considered *individualist* in their culture and communication style, while others are *collectivist*. **Individualist cultures** emphasize individual achievement, initiative, and competition (Tileson & Darling, 2008). Students are motivated by individual recognition. For example, the teacher might publicly display achievement by hanging individual student work on the wall with stars and stickers for accomplished work. Or a teacher might praise individual students for good behavior and refer to an individual as a "model" student. The United States is an example of an individualist culture.

The emphasis in **collectivist cultures** is on the collective and not the individual. Working for the common good is more highly valued than individual achievement. Students from collectivist cultures may prefer to work in groups, and each member's contribution is "successful" to the degree that it enhances the whole group. Individuals from collectivist cultures may not be motivated by individual praise and displays of accomplishment; instead, they may be motivated by group productivity and accomplishment (Trumbull, Rothstein-Fisch, & Greenfield, 2000). Examples of collectivist cultures include Native American, Native Hawaiian, Latin American, African, and Asian (Tileson & Darling, 2008). Although cultural groups have tendencies toward individualism or collectivism, these qualities fall along a continuum, and all cultures have both individual and collective traits. Thus, much variation exists among individuals within cultures with regard to these qualities.

## The Impact of Culture on Education

Cultural tendencies impact the way students participate in education. Table 3.1 describes different expectations about "normal" school behavior for students from individualist and collectivist cultures. As you review this information, take a moment to think about how teachers who lack knowledge about culture might interpret the behavior of a child from a collectivist culture. These differences may cause educators to inaccurately judge students from some cultures as poorly behaved or disrespectful. In addition, because cultural differences are hard to perceive, students may find themselves reprimanded by teachers but fail to understand what they did that caused concern.

Another cultural contrast involves the role of parents in education. Although parents from all cultures value education and want to be involved with their child's education, parents from some cultural backgrounds (e.g., Hispanic) are more likely to expect initial contact and an invitation to participate to come from the teacher (Wong & Hughes, 2006). In contrast, European American parents are more likely to initiate contact with teachers and request opportunities to volunteer and assist teachers. These cultural differences may cause educators to make inaccurate judgments

**TABLE 3.1** • INDIVIDUALIST AND COLLECTIVIST CULTURAL PERSPECTIVES ON EDUCATION

| Individualist Perspective | Collectivist Perspective |
|---|---|
| Students work independently; helping others may be cheating. | Students work with peers and provide assistance when needed. |
| Students engage in discussion and argument to learn to think critically. | Students are quiet and respectful in class in order to learn more efficiently. |
| Property belongs to individuals, and others must ask to borrow it. | Property is communal. |
| Teacher manages the school environment indirectly and encourages student self-control. | Teacher is the primary authority, but peers guide each other's behavior. |
| Parents are integral to child's academic progress and participate actively. | Parents yield to teacher's expertise to provide academic instruction and guidance. |

Source: Adapted from The Education Alliance. (2002). Individualist and collectivist perspectives on education. In *The Diversity Kit*. Providence, RI: Author.

regarding the value that non–European American families place on education. While it is important to keep in mind that different cultural groups *tend* to follow particular language and interaction styles, tremendous variability occurs within cultural groups. Thus, educators need to understand individual histories and ideologies regarding education and learning as well as the cultural patterns and beliefs of groups. Next, we provide a couple of cases, so you can examine in more detail how culture impacts educational interactions.

## Understanding Culture Through the Lens of Ethnicity, Class, and Student Behavior

To illustrate the significance of culture, consider the case of a fourth-grade African American male student identified with an emotional and behavior disability, Deshawn, who has been retained twice, is 2 years older and appreciably larger than most of his classmates. His academic work is significantly below grade level, and he has difficulty controlling his anger in school. Marks (2005) describes an incident involving this child with Ms. Payton (pseudonyms are used for this teacher and student), an African American teacher.

> At the end of the day students were given 20 minutes of free time to read or catch up on writing and [Deshawn] who was having a difficult day wanted to leave school early. He was hovering around the classroom door holding his backpack and looked like a caged tiger walking back and forth. This was a management problem waiting to explode. (Marks, 2005, p. 85)

Although Deshawn was not a model student for Ms. Payton, his anger seldom erupted in her class, even though he was a constant problem for other teachers and had many referrals from them. Here's how she handled the situation:

> "Come over here baby. Come and talk to your mama." The student walked over to Ms Payton, kicking his backpack. Ms Payton asked in a quiet voice, "What are you doing?" He responded that he wanted to go home. "Baby we got 20 more minutes of school. You can't stand there for 20 minutes.

REFLECTIVE EXERCISE

#4 What would be a professional response to this situation? What would you say to Deshawn? What would you do? And how would you want the teacher to respond if Deshawn were *your* child?

Go find something to do. Hang in there, then you can go and do whatever you want. Just hang in there with me." (Marks, 2005, p. 85)

At this point, Deshawn joined Ms. Payton and a small group of students in an activity at her desk. Ms. Payton used her relationship with the student to support and guide him to resolve his problem. Teachers' responses to any student's behavior are grounded in their culturally derived judgments. If the behavior is judged as inappropriate, the teacher then makes a determination about how severe the infraction is. Where others might judge Deshawn as defiant, Ms. Payton recognizes that many African American children and youth, particularly males, behave more defiantly with adults whom they regard as untrustworthy (Gregory & Weinstein, 2008). She interprets his resistance as an expression of discontent or disconnection and recognizes that, as an overage, low-achieving fourth grader, Deshawn's strongest desire is to escape. Rather than asserting her authority, she grounds her response in her relationship with him, drawing on their shared culture as a way to connect. Then, drawing on her knowledge of culturally responsive classroom management, she provides both structure and choice, insisting on appropriate behavior but avoiding a power struggle and preserving Deshawn's autonomy and self-respect in the process (Brown, 2004; Gregory & Weinstein, 2008). It is important to note, however, that the ability to attend to cultural differences does not require that the teacher share the same culture as the student (Bondy, Ross, Gallingane, & Hambacher, 2007).

## Understanding Culture Through the Lens of Language and Disability

Let's explore another set of cultural factors as we consider the experiences of Carlos, a 7-year-old, second-grade boy who has been living in the United States for 10 months. His family speaks only Spanish in the home, and both parents are literate in Spanish. Upon his arrival in the United States, Carlos was enrolled in the local elementary school and participated in a general education classroom with English-language learner (ELL) support provided in a separate classroom setting. Berta, his mother, has been increasingly concerned about Carlos's performance in school. She receives notes from the teacher about her son's work, but she cannot respond due to the language barrier. Berta wants the teacher to know that her son was receiving speech services in Mexico because he had been identified as having special needs as a result of limited oxygen at birth. Neither the general education teacher nor the ELL teacher has noticed Carlos's special needs, and Berta is concerned that he is disengaged in school and seems to be making little progress academically. Moreover, she is not sure how to initiate communication around this issue with his teacher, due to the language difference.

In the United States, some view **bilingualism** as a deficit (Klingner, Hoover, & Baca, 2008). This can lead educators to misidentify students who are acquiring English as having a learning disability or a communication disorder (Connor & Boskin, 2001; Escamilla & Coady, 2001). Just as problematic, however, is the possibility that teachers fail to perceive a language disability (Escamilla & Coady, 2001; Klingner et al., 2008) because they believe that a student's low performance is a result of second-language acquisition rather than a disability (Klingner et al., 2008). The complexity of these issues is illustrated by Ms. Finn's request for help in "Can You Help Me with This Student?"

Students bring many language backgrounds to the classroom.

| To... | Gabriela Ramirez, District ELL Supervisor |
| From... | Adele Finn, First-Grade Teacher |
| Subject: | Subject: Concerns regarding an ELL student, Josue |

Gaby, I need your assistance with a boy in my class, Josue. You may remember him, as I brought him up briefly when we last met for our mentoring meeting. He is 7 years old and moved here from Mexico in August. Josue received no formal education in Mexico, he can't read or write in Spanish or English. He is in my class for math, science, and social studies and is bused to the district's English-as-a-second-language program each day, where he receives ELL support in reading and language arts. I'm concerned about Josue's limited progress over these first 3 months of the school year. He has a short attention span, and some simple tasks, such as counting money, seem difficult for him. In addition, for much of the school day, he is silent or uses one-word responses. I have heard that his parents are migrant workers. I'm not sure how to respond to Josue's needs. Should I contact the family? Do the family's migrant lifestyle and culture influence Josue's education? I'm also concerned that he may have a learning disability. I would like to talk with you next week during our mentoring meeting about Josue, but in the meantime, any assistance or advice you have time to provide would be most appreciated.

Thanks,
Adele

---

To:      Adele Finn
From:    Gabriela Rodriguez
Subject: RE: Concerns regarding an ELL student, Josue

Adele, I would be most pleased to talk with you about Josue when we meet next week. I've had many students with backgrounds similar to his, and I have some suggestions that you may find useful. In the meantime, I've provided some ideas below for you to consider.

As you work with Josue, keep in mind that second-language learners frequently experience a period of time when their oral production is limited. This period, known as the silent or nonverbal period, may continue for 4, 5, or 6 months (Krashen, 2006). Josue's ability to use one-word responses is promising and demonstrates his understanding of ways to communicate his needs. Although it is possible that Josue has a learning disability, his newcomer status suggests it may be too soon to initiate assessment. In assessing his language competence, here are some things to consider (Baca & Cervantes, 2004):

- Look for other indications of communicative competence (e.g., communicating through gestures, pictures, drawings).

- Observe receptive language skill, and determine if he is developing an understanding of spoken English.

- Observe his first-language skills informally when he is interacting with peers from the same language group.

- Make a referral for assessment only if you observe problems in receptive and expressive communication in both languages.

You might also consider contacting the ELL teacher, Ester Thompson, to discuss Josue's progress. Ester can work with you to determine which instructional techniques might facilitate his learning and to identify books and materials related to Josue's background that should stimulate his interest in the curriculum. To establish stronger communication with Josue's family, you might consider arranging with the parents to make a home visit during a time when they will be home from work. The district's migrant education advocate, Maria Otero, may be available to assist you and can serve as a valuable resource as you work with Josue and his parents. Finally, classroom-related documents (newsletters, homework) should be translated into Spanish whenever possible.

If you'd like more information about the process of acculturation, teacher strategies that support English-language learners, and information on children of migrant farm workers, the following resources should be helpful:

Diaz-Rico, L. T. (2008). *A course for teaching English learners.* Boston: Allyn & Bacon Publishers.

Verplaetse, S., & Migliacci, N. (Eds.). (2007). *Inclusive pedagogy for English language learners: A handbook of research-informed practices.* New York: Erlbaum.

Vocke, K. S. (2007). *Where do we go from here?: Meeting the unique educational needs of migrant students.* Thousand Oaks, CA: Corwin Press.

I hope you find this information useful, and I look forward to meeting with you next week to further discuss Josue.

Gaby

**EXTEND AND APPLY**

- Imagine that Ms. Finn has several Spanish-speaking students in her classroom. How might Josue benefit from grouping strategies that combine students who speak Spanish?
- What additional information might Ms. Finn want to know about Josue's background that can inform her instruction and work with him?

Not all parents feel free to interact with and ask questions of their child's teacher.

## How Culture Mediates School Experience

Looking at school achievement through different cultural lenses demonstrates the ways in which teacher and student behaviors are mediated by culturally derived values, experiences, and beliefs (Wilder, Taylor Dyches, Obiakor, & Algozzine, 2004). The challenge for teachers is that students vary in so many ways. The examples we provided describe just a few of the many variations and suggest the complex interaction of factors.

In addition to describing the many ways in which students vary—by ethnicity, ability, disability, birth language—we mentioned that students vary simultaneously across many factors. Given that students vary in many ways both within and across cultures and that the problems of poverty are pervasive and beyond teachers' control, you may be feeling overwhelmed and somewhat discouraged about your capacity to make a difference. We want to be clear that schools and teachers play a critical role and can make a significant difference in the lives of students from CLD backgrounds. In fact, research demonstrates that teachers who accept the responsibility to make a difference with *every* child have a powerful impact on achievement. This difference is magnified when teachers and administrators in entire schools accept this mission (Corbett, Wilson, & Williams, 2002; Irvine, 2002; Ladson-Billings, 2009).

# WHAT CAN TEACHERS DO? GUIDELINES FOR CULTURALLY RESPONSIVE TEACHING

The remainder of this chapter draws on the literature about **culturally responsive teaching and management** to suggest guiding principles for teachers of students with disabilities from diverse backgrounds. This information is intended to complement and extend the information regarding specific pedagogy for students with disabilities that is provided in other chapters in this text. Used in combination, these guidelines will better equip you to address the needs of all of your students, regardless of their background.

## What Is the Goal?

Although improving students' achievement-test scores is important, raising scores is too limited a goal. The real goal is to help students develop their capacity to be resilient. **Resilience** has been defined as the ability to succeed despite adverse circumstances and challenges (Downey, 2008). Resilience is not the result of innate abilities, but is a capacity available to all students that is bolstered by supportive factors (Bempechat, 1998; Benard, 2004). The goal, then, is to assess students' strengths and build on them by tailoring instruction toward their strengths while building capacity in weaker areas. In this way teachers help students believe in themselves, their futures, and their capacity to succeed.

Teachers and the school environment are critical protective factors for fostering resilience. Imagine how a teacher who believes each student has cultural and learning strengths that must be enhanced and accommodated might approach instruction differently from a teacher who perceives that students have cultural and learning deficiencies that must be remediated. How we think about disabilities and cultural differences becomes very important. Consider the example in Figure 3.3 regarding different ways in which we think about disabilities.

## Know Yourself and the Role That Culture Plays in Perception

Culturally responsive teachers are simultaneously curious about culture and introspective. They strive to learn more about who they are, what they believe, and how their beliefs and experiences influence their perceptions of and interactions with students and their families.

### Become a Student of Culture and Difference

No teacher will possess comprehensive knowledge about all of the possible cultures, languages, disabilities, and economic influences on learning. While knowledge is important, a teacher's underlying curiosity about culture and difference is more important (Banks et al., 2005). A teacher who is culturally curious recognizes that all people are influenced by their background, culture, and experience.

While we are all inevitably influenced by our culture, the pervasiveness of the dominant (European American, heterosexual, middle-class) culture can make it invisible to those who have grown up inside that culture. Think back to how you answered the first question on the demographic questionnaire at the beginning of the chapter. If you are white, middle-class, monolingual, and of European descent, and you omitted these characteristics, your answers suggest that parts of your culture are invisible to you.

The culturally responsive teacher actively strives to see alternative perspectives. One strategy is to critically examine the impact of your differences from others. In this chapter you have learned about some of the ways that people from various

## REFLECTIVE EXERCISE

#5 Research has revealed that students' beliefs in their capacity to succeed were stronger predictors of success in school than IQ or achievement test scores (Bempechat, 1998). How would a teacher ensure that students believe in their capacity to succeed?

## REFLECTIVE EXERCISE

#6 How do you think about disabilities? Which of the two models in Figure 3.3 (medical and interactional) better characterizes your perspective? Discuss with another member of class your perspective on these models. Is your perspective about disabilities important?

## FIGURE 3.3 • HOW WE THINK ABOUT DISABILITIES: DOES IT MAKE A DIFFERENCE?

Historically, disabilities have been defined much like diseases, from a medical perspective. The words that were used (and continue to be used by some) reflected this perspective. Individuals were "diagnosed" with disabilities (much like diseases), and "treatments" were sought to fix or cure the diagnosed deficiency. The assumption was made that the disability resided within the person (again, like a disease), and external factors had little influence on the disability. This view of disability is commonly referred to as the *medical model* (Hahn, 1985; Kavale & Forness, 1995; Sleeter, 1995).

In reaction to the medical model, leaders in the field of disability studies have advocated for an interactional model (Hahn, 1985; Sleeter, 1995). They argue that disability originates from the interaction between the individual and society and that the remedy for disability-related problems is a change in these interactions (Hahn, 1985). This may seem to be a relatively trivial change, but consider the following differences in how people think about disabilities using these models.

| Medical Model | Interactional Model |
|---|---|
| Disability is a deficiency. | Disability is a difference. |
| A disability is negative. | A disability is neutral. |
| A disability resides within a person. | A disability results from the relationship (or the interaction) between a person and society. |
| The professional is the expert. | An expert can be the person with the disability, an advocate, or anyone who changes the social relationship. |

Obviously, the medical model views disability from a negative perspective and places the responsibility (and, in some cases, blame) for the disability on the person with the "deficiency." In contrast, the interactional model views disability not as a deficiency to be fixed but as a difference that creates challenges to be addressed. The interactional model does not ignore the disability or the challenges that a person with a disability will face. Rather, the disability is no longer perceived in a negative light but is viewed from a neutral or positive perspective, and the influence that society has on a disability, for good or bad, is recognized.

To illustrate, for most of the 20th century, most persons with disabilities that limited their mobility lacked access to many buildings because most buildings were not designed to be accessible (a societal decision). This lack of access was produced by a lack of convenient parking, the use of steps rather than ramps for entering buildings, heavy doors that required much arm strength to open rather than automatic doors, restrooms that were not accessible, and lack of elevators to access different floors of a building, among other things.

During the last 25 years of the 20th century, society made a decision (with the passage of Section 504 of the Rehabilitation Act and the Americans with Disabilities Act) that persons with disabilities that reduced their mobility should have access to buildings. Thus, newly constructed buildings were required to be accessible (e.g., with designated parking spaces, ramps, automatic doors, elevators, accessible restrooms), greatly enhancing the independent access to these settings.

PEARSON
**myeducationlab**

Go to the Assignments and Activities section of Topic 4: Cultural/Linguistic Diversity in the MyEducationLab for your course and complete the activity entitled *Cultural Diversity and Special Education*.

cultures view parenting, teachers, authority, social interaction, and disability. Our hope is that this has made you curious about other perspectives.

## Develop a Vision of Students Who Succeed

Culturally responsive teachers recognize the impact of poverty but accept no excuses when students fail to learn. Although teachers probably do not want to believe they have low expectations, in fact, teachers who excuse students' failures because they are poor, are second-language learners, lack motivation, or have a disability have low expectations. As noted, these students do, in fact, have challenges that impact their success. It would be unrealistic to suggest that all students, despite the challenges they face, will achieve to the same level within schools as currently constituted. Nevertheless, culturally responsive teachers *must* believe they can reach every child and work to accomplish this goal. To give up ensures that certain groups of students will continue to fail.

One strategy for developing this vision is to seek out examples of students whose background and experience differ from the norm but who succeed in school. You can read about teachers who succeed in reaching all students (Clark, 2004; Esquith, 2007; Gruwell, 2007). Additionally, visiting the classrooms of outstanding teachers in your district will help you see what successful teaching looks like. If others can do it, so can you. Effective teaching for *all* students is not magic, and it is not a bag of pedagogical skills (though you certainly need many skills!). Effective teaching for *all* students is the constant pursuit of the mission to help all students succeed. The first step is to develop the belief that success is possible and a picture of what success looks like.

### Learn Not to Judge

Remember that the way we have grown up and experienced life defines "normal" for each of us. Working effectively with students from diverse backgrounds requires us to constantly question our reactions to students and their families and to check the human tendency to judge different as "abnormal." Learning not to judge requires that you analyze your affective reactions. For example, we all tend to judge parents based on our experiences and background, which at times can result in misperceptions when parents' actions contradict our assumptions about how "good" parents interact with their children and with the school. Consider the example in Figure 3.4, which addresses a parent's reaction to her son's disability.

## Communicate Care to All Students and Families

As Amanda Adimoolah stressed, teachers who care about children communicate in varied ways that they believe in them and expect them to succeed (Benard, 2004). The concept of care means more than loving children. Teachers who care treat students with respect, require them to treat others with respect, perceive them as capable, and accept them unconditionally, even as they help them change undesirable behavior (Benard, 2004).

Go to the Assignments and Activities section of Topic 4: Cultural/Linguistic Diversity in the MyEducationLab for your course and complete the activity entitled *Working with Families of Culturally Diverse Students*.

FIGURE 3.4 • **UNDERSTANDING THE PERSPECTIVES OF PARENTS**

In *Learning Outside the Lines* (Mooney & Cole, 2000), Jonathan, a young man who has coped with a reading disability throughout his academic life, tells the story of his second-grade year, when he struggled in spelling and reading. His mother often kept him out of school on Friday, which was spelling-test day. Can you think of two ways to explain this mother's decision?

One explanation is that the mother did not care about her son's academic future and did not understand how important school attendance is. A child with a disability needs school even more than others and cannot afford to miss even one day. This mother kept her son out often. Her behavior was irresponsible and unjustifiable.

The explanation that Jonathan provides is that school and particularly spelling-test day were so challenging for him during that year that his mother was struggling to preserve his sense of himself as a valuable, capable person. By taking him out of school on a high-stress day, a day when failure was inevitable, she believed she was saving him and making future success more likely because she knew that, if he saw himself as a failure, he would eventually stop trying.

### Learn About Students, Their Backgrounds, and Their Experiences

Culturally responsive teachers must really *know* their students in order to teach them. Here is a story from one of this chapter's authors:

> Alton and Barry challenged me daily. They were quick to get angry and fight and demonstrated little interest in any academic activities. I remember an evening conversation with my mother. I began railing against the behavior of these two "troublemakers." I wondered how I was to teach when they wouldn't cooperate and when no punishment I devised seemed to affect them. My mother's response helped shape the teacher I became. "Honey," she said, "those boys are not out to get you. Whatever they say and do is, to them, the most appropriate response to the situation as they perceive it. Your job is to see things as they see things. Then you'll know what to do."

Long before educators began to address cultural issues, this mother was teaching her daughter the foundational principle of culturally responsive teaching. To teach students, we must know them, know how they perceive the world, know their language, know their family traditions and customs, know their interests, know their dreams, know their learning strategies, and know what they care about (Banks et al., 2005).

There are no magic strategies for learning about students and their families. The process is as simple, and as complicated, as spending time with them and, as Amanda Adimoolah stressed, listening to them. Culturally responsive teachers spend time in students' communities, visit homes, interact with families, and attend relevant cultural and family-oriented activities. Parents know them and see them in the community, and the teachers know families well enough to know the cultural and experiential resources in students' homes. This has been called knowing the "funds of knowledge" within students' homes (Gonzalez, Moll, & Amanti, 2005; Moll et al., 1992).

It is also important to develop specific knowledge about students through questionnaires, informal conversations with students and parents, observation, and analysis of students' work. Moreover, it is important to become a student of children's culture. What are their favorite television shows? Movies? Music? Video games? Where do they go, and what do they do after school? What significant events have happened in the community? As Ms. Adimoolah stressed, the more you know about the children, the greater your capacity to link schoolwork to their culture and experience. The importance of this type of information is illustrated in the "Can You Help Me with This Student" feature that addresses Zaquan's behavior.

### Establish an Ethos of Care in the Classroom

Research on classrooms that support students' motivation to achieve (Patrick, Turner, Meyer, & Midgley, 2003; Weinstein, 2002), on classrooms that scaffold student resilience (Benard, 2004; Tileson & Darling, 2008), and on culturally responsive classroom management (Brown, 2004; Bondy et al., 2007) suggests guidelines for establishing an ethos of care in the classroom.

**Create a Sense of Community in the Classroom.** Culturally responsive teachers bring themselves into the classroom and enable students to do the same. The teachers share their families, their interests, and their lives and use structures like class meetings to enable students to know one another. They communicate that respect for others is highly valued by respecting and listening to students and teaching students to respect and listen to one another.

**Teach Classroom Rules, Routines, and Procedures Explicitly.** Culturally responsive teachers explicitly teach the behaviors and routines they expect students to demonstrate (Emmer & Evertson, 2008). Teachers who neglect this important step may believe that stating the rule is enough, but the result is that the teachers

| To... | Ms. Lakesha Bowman, Middle School Assistant Principal |
|---|---|
| From... | Lionel Shaker, Middle School Social Studies Teacher |
| Subject: | Assistance in addressing a student behavior problem |

Lakesha, as you know from our previous conversations during mentoring sessions, I have an eighth-grade African American student, Zaquan, in my social studies class who has caused me some problems. He always seems to be challenging my authority (four times this week!). Today he came up to my desk before class and asked (in a very loud voice) why we have to do current events, and said nobody liked this topic. I tried to be patient (at least at first), and reminded Zaquan that he had asked this question earlier in the week. I told him then that current events are an important part of the curriculum, and I can't just skip it. I went on to tell him that I get that he doesn't like current events, but he needs to stop arguing with me about this. Then I told him to sit down, but he didn't give up. He said that I never listen to him, and that class is dumb, nobody likes it. I then insisted that he sit down, as all the other students were in class and the tardy bell had rung. Zaquan still stood in front of the class and glared at me. I then got very firm with him (and a bit irritated, I must admit), and told Zaquan to sit down, now! Zaquan then shouted an obscenity at me and shoved a desk that tipped over and hit another student. I wrote Zaquan up for this offense, and as district rules require, he was suspended. I was surprised when Ms. Tobias, the assistant principal, came to my room after school and questioned me about Zaquan's behavior (this is my third referral for him in the last month) and about my interactions with other African American students. I agreed with her that most of my referrals this year have been for African American males, but I only make a referral when their behavior violates a school rule. Anyway, I'm very frustrated about all of this. I won't tolerate inappropriate behavior, but I want to figure out how to better address behavior problems in my class. Maybe part of the problem relates to cultural differences that I just don't understand? Can you give me some quick ideas about strategies I might use or things to think about?

Many thanks for your help!!
Lionel

---

To:     Lionel Shaker
From:   Lakesha Bowman
Subject:    RE: Assistance in addressing a student behavior problem

Lionel, thanks for sharing with me the details of your interactions with Zaquan. As you know, African American youth (especially boys) receive a disproportionate number of school sanctions such as referrals and suspensions (Wald & Losen, 2007). For example, in one study of a high school, the majority of referrals were for student defiance of adult authority (Gregory, 2007). In this school, 80% of the African American students who received referrals had at least one for defiance, as compared to fewer than 50% of the European American students who received referrals. One finding in this study that intrigued me was that while African American high school students received more defiance-related referrals, students were not uniformly defiant. That is, a student who was defiant with one teacher might be cooperative with another. This suggests that the acceptance of teacher authority is often grounded in students' perceptions that teachers care about them, genuinely believe in their academic potential, and are acting in their best interest (Gay, 2000).

Given these research findings, it becomes important that teachers look at their own and their students' behavior in new ways. This helps in gaining a better understanding regarding the possible cultural sources of student resistance or defiance. From our previous conversations, I know that most of your management challenges come from African American boys who resist and become confrontational when reprimanded and that many of these issues arise during current events. I suggest that you begin by talking with some of your students regarding why they don't like current events. It may be that they lack access to newspapers or other material at home and therefore find it difficult to complete some assignments. Or perhaps, as was the case with one student you talked with me about previously, their relatives are occasionally mentioned in articles that are less than complimentary, and reviewing them in class creates negative interactions with peers.

Let's talk about this further when we next get together for a mentoring meeting later this week. In the meantime, you might find the following references useful, as they provide information regarding how students view teachers and school and provide strategies for building positive connections with students.

Cushman, K. (2003). *Fires in the bathroom: Advice for teachers from high school students*. New York: The New Press.

Cushman, K., & Rogers, L. (2008). *Fires in the middle school bathroom: Advice for teachers from middle schoolers*. New York: The New Press.

Wilson, B. L., & Corbett, H. D. (2001). *Listening to urban kids: School reform and the teachers they want*. Albany: State University of New York Press.

---

**EXTEND AND APPLY**

- Imagine how a teacher might benefit from talking even once a week with one or two resistant learners about how a particular lesson helped or didn't help them and what might have made the lesson more beneficial.
- How would you make a current events class more meaningful and motivating to Zaquan?
- Can you think of other ways teachers can make their high school classes more culturally responsive? Reading about students' cultural backgrounds? Visiting students' communities? Talking with parents? Talking with other teachers?

---

## REFLECTIVE EXERCISE

**#7** How can it be so difficult for a student to remember a simple rule like raising one's hand to speak? What if, in a child's family, multiple people often speak simultaneously? Can you think of other classroom rules that might differ from a student's cultural experiences?

implement an escalating sequence of consequences and punishments and develop a negative classroom environment where many fail to thrive.

The following principle may help you: Assume that students will behave appropriately if they know and remember what the teacher expects. Culturally responsive elementary classroom teachers state their expectations, provide models and demonstrations, require student restatement of expectations, provide opportunities for practice with feedback, repeat instruction as necessary, and remind students of and reinforce appropriate behavior (Bondy et al., 2007).

**Protect the Classroom Community Through Teacher Insistence.** All teachers want their students to abide by classroom rules. Some, in trying to be fair, give students "chances" that send inconsistent messages. Others do not know how to insist respectfully and become punitive and threatening. Both kinds of teachers undermine the classroom community—the former by allowing disrespectful behavior, and the latter by treating students disrespectfully. Effective teachers strategically and respectfully insist that students abide by rules and procedures and that they respect one another and the teacher (Patrick et al., 2003). Yet in their "insistence," they always preserve the respectful and caring connection to each student.

## Have High Expectations for Student Achievement

**Never Give Up on a Child.**  Culturally responsive teachers take to heart the adage "If at first you don't succeed, try, try again!" These teachers view student learning as a puzzle that they are constantly striving to solve (Banks et al., 2005; Corbett et al., 2002). They accept responsibility for student learning and look for other ways to accomplish the goal. These are teachers who simply refuse to believe there is any child who cannot be reached, and they actively communicate this belief to students.

**Provide Explicit Instruction Linked to Meaningful Activity.**  Culturally responsive teachers provide a challenging curriculum that stresses critical thinking, develops curiosity, and equips students with the skills and knowledge to succeed. These teachers provide explicit instruction and opportunities for meaningful use of skills and knowledge (Banks et al., 2005; Tileson & Darling, 2008). Explicit instruction is sometimes misunderstood as drill of low–cognitive-level skills. While explicit instruction includes this kind of drill, it involves a great deal more. In determining whether they are providing clear, explicit instruction that is meaningful to students, teachers must ask themselves whether they have provided authentic opportunities for students to use newly acquired skills and competencies.

This question is critically important. Imagine joining a soccer team where you practice drills every day but never play a game. Not only would you lose interest in practice, but also your mastery of the skills would be shallow, because you would not understand the context of their use. This is the case in classrooms where students practice skills and concepts, are tested on them, and then move on to the next set of skills and concepts. The result is that they lose interest in participating in practice, and their learning is shallow.

**Insist on Completion and Quality.**  Culturally responsive teachers do not allow students to do less than their best (Conchas, 2006; Corbett et al., 2002). They insist that students complete and revise their work until it meets the standard. Important learning inevitably involves struggle, and effective teachers not only convey that the struggle is important, but insist that students persist through barriers and support them until they succeed. Teachers who provide this support encourage students to try, refuse to allow students to get by with incomplete or sloppy work, give them opportunities to make up work, provide after-school tutoring, make work relevant to students' lives, and reteach using varied strategies until everyone understands (Conchas, 2006; Wilson & Corbett, 2001).

## Use Culturally Relevant Curriculum

Obviously, culturally relevant curriculum must be culturally specific. In this section we provide examples drawn primarily from literature on culturally relevant practice for low-income African American children and youth.

### Tailor Curriculum Materials to the Students and the Context

The school curriculum is not culturally neutral. The curriculum as represented in texts, in national and state standards, and in the lived experience of most teachers is a reflection of the dominant culture (Hollins, 1996). For example, texts will mention the names of a small, often-repeated group of African American men and women who fought for freedom, voting rights, and economic equity in the United States (e.g., Rosa Parks; Martin Luther King, Jr.; Harriet Tubman), but the detail devoted to this struggle for freedom receives far less attention in our history than the struggle of our revolutionary period. Few of us learn about men like James Armistead, a slave who was freed for his surveillance efforts during the struggles of that time (Selig, 2005).

Culturally responsive teachers know that students need to see themselves in the curriculum. If the faces in the textbook are predominantly European American, students learn that history and scientific achievement are the work of European

### REFLECTIVE EXERCISE

#8 Do you think that a teacher who gives a student an *F* when he or she fails to complete an assignment or performs poorly rates low in professionalism because the teacher has low expectations? Why or why not?

### REFLECTIVE EXERCISE

#9 Take a minute to list as many famous European Americans as you can; then list as many famous African Americans as you can (no sports or entertainment figures). Assume that the difference in your lists is *not* because African Americans never did anything of historical significance. What does this mean?

Americans. To be effective, teachers need "wide ranging knowledge of subject matter content, so that they can construct a curriculum that includes multiple representations addressing the prior experiences of different groups of students" (Banks et al., 2005, p. 251; Conchas, 2006). One important way to connect culturally and linguistically diverse students to the school context is to use children's literature that reflects their cultural background and life experiences. When students see themselves in their books, they enjoy reading and make a connection to literature. Students build vocabulary and language skills that assist them academically.

### Connect Pedagogy to Students

Previously, we explained that culturally responsive teachers develop knowledge about children's culture, traditions, and interests. This knowledge is critical in linking the curriculum to what students know and the ways that they learn.

**Link Students' Interests, Experiences, Families, and Home Culture.**  Many students find school knowledge irrelevant to their out-of-school lives and perceive no reason to learn it. When teachers link school knowledge to students' real-world interests and experiences, students are more likely to be engaged and to retain what they learn. The most effective teachers find ways to link concepts to everyday experiences. For example, a local math teacher links place value to students' knowledge of families by introducing them to the 100s family, the 1,000s family, the 10,000s family, and so on. Esquith (2007) makes economics and money relevant to students by developing a classroom economy that requires they work to pay for things such as their desk, the location of their desk, and essential classroom supplies.

Links to students' background and experiences are important for the same reasons. For example, African American culture has a strong oral tradition reflected in both poetry and rap music. Study of the use of language and rhythm in rap music can provide a strong background for an introduction to poetry. The point is *not* that we should teach rap music. The point is that we link schoolwork to students' culturally derived knowledge to help them access and understand concepts and skills that would otherwise seem to be isolated pieces of "school" knowledge with little relevance to their interests.

Additionally, effective teachers find ways to link to students' families and family traditions. Previously, we noted that parents from some cultures maintain a respectful distance from the school unless invited to engage by teachers. Educators who expand their definitions of "involvement" find ways to incorporate family traditions into the school. For example, Kyle, McIntyre, Miller, and Moore (2006) describe a family traditions event where parents work with their children informally, helping children record family stories to create a family history. Drawing on their knowledge of families, culturally responsive teachers tap the funds of knowledge (Gonzalez et al., 2005) within families to enable parents to share their expertise and enhance the education of children.

**Empower Students to Seek Equity and Social Justice.**  Even preschoolers have a strong sense of fairness and equity. Empowering students to act on these perceptions is a way to strengthen the curriculum, engage students, and pursue an equity agenda.

What might an equity agenda look like? At times, it may be as simple as encouraging a child to speak out when he or she perceives inequity. Pelo and Davidson (2000) describe a preschool child who became upset when she saw classmates laughing at two men who were hugging. She knew the men, friends of her two mothers, and was angry that her classmates had laughed. Her teacher encouraged her to share her feelings, empowering her to work toward a change she believed should happen and that increased the knowledge and sensitivity of her classmates.

For older students, teachers can integrate lessons related to social justice and equity into the curriculum. For example, students can compare the report of historical events in their textbook to the account of the same events in *Lies My Teacher Told Me* (Loewen, 2007). Or they can use the Internet to search for alternative

PEARSON
**myeducationlab**

To hear an expert discuss more on the topic of tapping into students' real-world interests and experiences and how this can shape teaching practice, go to the IRIS Center Resources section of Topic 4: Cultural/Linguistic Diversity in the MyEducationLab for your course and listen to the Podcast entitled *Episode 2: Diane Torres-Velasquez on diverse learners.*

accounts of historical events and scientific discoveries and write essays about the discrepancies and the possible reasons for those discrepancies.

Similarly, they can draw on local and national current events to raise questions related to equity. Consider, for example, the various issues raised by news coverage of the 2008 presidential primary race between Barak Obama and Hillary Clinton. Students could talk about the differences in news coverage for a woman candidate versus a man, and for a white candidate versus a multiracial candidate. They could talk about the role ethnicity played in the election by considering issues such as the controversy over Obama's pastor, Reverend Jeremiah Wright. They could debate the advantages and disadvantages of being the first African American or first woman candidate for president.

Other issues, such as Hurricane Katrina in the fall of 2005, present important opportunities for dialogue about issues related to the differential impact of national disasters on low-income families and the role of government versus individuals in responding to citizens' needs. Students can also engage in social action projects, for example, taking food to a homeless shelter or writing to local officials about changes they believe would improve their communities. In this way the academic curriculum empowers students to believe they can impact their world and again helps them to see school as connected to life.

**Ensure That Students Understand What Equity Means.**  According to *The New Oxford American Dictionary* (Jewell & Abate, 2001), *equal* refers to "being the same in quantity, size, degree, or value" (p. 573). In contrast, *equitable* refers to being "fair and impartial" (p. 574). *Equity* is sometimes a difficult concept for students to grasp. Many come into a classroom with the perspective that *fair* means treating everyone the same (e.g., providing the same, or *equal,* instruction for everyone). As we have emphasized throughout this chapter, treating everyone equally is not always equitable and does not result in effective instructional practices or desired educational outcomes. This is especially the case for students from diverse backgrounds and students with disabilities but is true for other students as well.

In this chapter we provided many examples of the need to adapt classroom practices based on student characteristics and needs. We will provide similar suggestions in Chapters 6 to 15, which address specific disabilities. These suggestions are built on the assumption that equitable treatment of students is giving what they need, not treating all students the same. It is important that teachers discuss this distinction with their students and help them understand why some students need different types of support and instruction to succeed.

**REFLECTIVE EXERCISE**

**#10** You have a student with a physical disability included in a general education classroom. The student uses a voice-activated computer for writing activities. A student has complained that this student receives preferential treatment and that all students should be treated equally. Discuss how you would respond with a peer in your class.

PEARSON
**myeducationlab**

Now that you have some background about the guiding principles of culturally responsive teaching and managemnet, go to the Building Teaching Skills and Dispositions section of Topic 4: Cultural/Linguistic Diversity in the MyEducationLab for your course and complete the activity entitled *Providing Culturally Reponsive Instruction.*

# PREVAILING ISSUES, CONTROVERSIES, AND IMPLICATIONS FOR THE TEACHER

Teachers can do many things to impact the educational outcomes for students who come from diverse backgrounds. Two prevailing issues that we mentioned previously in this chapter play significant roles in teacher impact and therefore warrant further examination here.

## The Issue of Culture, Parent Expectations, and Disability

Cultural values and beliefs influence how people view disability (Wilder, Taylor Dyches, Obiakor, & Algozzine, 2004). Some Hispanic mothers, for example, may view caring for a child with a severe disability as a form of devotion, while others may view this as a curse or a result of a *mal ojo,* or evil eye, based on their spiritual practices. Linguistic differences also affect a cultural group's understanding of disability. For example, some Asian languages have no word for autism (Wilder et al., 2004). The lack of vocabulary to describe a disability may indicate a different cultural idea related to the disability itself.

Correa and Tulbert (1993) outline several cultural tendencies that may provide a better understanding of how to work effectively with Hispanic families. First, many Hispanic families are large, extended units. The broad social network of families provides a sizable source of information for educators. This network may include the godparents of Hispanic children as well as grandparents, aunts, and uncles.

Second, many Hispanic parents place high value on respect for individuals and the family as well as affection for children. As such, family members, including extended family members, may provide emotional and economic support for each other. This corresponds to collectivist notions of culture. As a result, Hispanic children tend to work well in cooperative groups, and educators who appear impartial or objective in working with children may be perceived as uncaring (Correa & Tulbert, 1993).

Third, for many, Hispanic notions of being well educated often include a balance of academic achievement and appropriate behaviors such as respect toward adults (Escamilla & Coady, 2001). As a result, parental expectations of children may not align with educators' emphasis on the importance of attaining high test scores and grades.

As you think about culture, it is also important to remember that tremendous variation in beliefs occurs within cultural groups (i.e., not all Hispanic families have the same beliefs regarding disability). Obviously, it is very important for teachers to know their students and understand an individual family's cultural perspectives about medicine and disability. This information is crucial in guiding interactions with parents. However, acquiring this information is a significant challenge. Teachers may not speak the family's home language, and accessing information about cultural definitions of disability from the literature, while useful, may misrepresent the actual perspectives of a particular family about their particular child (Correa & Tulbert, 1993). To acquire this information, finding an interpreter and having conversations with parents often best serve teachers. These conversations are not easy, and it may take time for family members to trust a teacher from outside their culture enough to say what they really think.

## The Issue of Poverty

As teachers, we accept the challenge to help all the students who come to our classrooms thrive and succeed. Yet, the challenges children and families living in poverty face are formidable, and it is idealistic to suggest that good teaching is enough to meet these challenges. The lack of economic resources limits the ability of parents and children to access medical care, prenatal care, high-quality preschool, therapy, tutors, after-school and summer enrichment programs, stable housing, and healthy food. And as we've noted previously, living in poverty often limits access to good schools and certified teachers. In these and other ways too numerous to mention, poverty diminishes the opportunities for success. Consider just a few of the specific ways in which poverty undermines achievement.

The rate of asthma is significantly higher for children from lower-class backgrounds than for those from the middle or upper classes (Rothstein, 2008). Children from high-poverty backgrounds are less likely to receive treatment for asthma, which impacts sleep patterns, ability to be attentive in school, and school attendance. Each of these factors in turn influences achievement. In addition, children from non–European American and low-income backgrounds experience high levels of untreated problems with vision, hearing, and oral health. Research suggests that attention to these problems might impact school achievement more substantially than changes in teaching practice (Rothstein, 2004).

Students from diverse and high-poverty backgrounds who have disabilities often struggle to meet the academic expectations that state and local education agencies place on schools. These expectations have increased in most states over the past few years as a result of state and federal legislation (e.g., the No Child Left Behind Act). Figure 3.5 provides an example of the special challenge that high-stakes testing and changing expectations present for these students.

## REFLECTIVE EXERCISE

#11 High-stakes testing requires that states balance the need for high standards with equitable treatment of all students. What issues do states face in achieving this balance?

## FIGURE 3.5 • THE SPECIAL CHALLENGE OF HIGH-STAKES TESTING

With the passage of the No Child Left Behind Act in 2001, many states began to implement high school exit exams. By 2006, 25 states had or were phasing in mandatory exit exams (Center on Education Policy, 2006). These exams are intended to make the high school diploma "mean something," ensuring that the recipient has a certain level of knowledge and skills that are needed to succeed in a job and other aspects of daily life (Bhanpuri & Sexton, 2006). Thus, students face high stakes when they take the exam, as graduation from high school with a regular diploma is contingent on achieving a certain score.

Most professionals recognize that high-stakes tests in general, and high school exit exams in particular, can be a very good thing for students who historically have not achieved at a high level (including students with disabilities, English-language learners, and students from non–European American backgrounds who live in poverty) (Johnson & Thurlow, 2003; O'Neil, 2001; Ysseldyke, Dennison, & Nelson, 2004). For example, these tests are intended to

- Ensure high expectations for all students
- Hold schools accountable for the achievement of all students (e.g., before NCLB, most states did not hold local schools accountable for the achievement of students with disabilities)
- Ensure that all students participate in the general education curriculum
- Reduce differences among groups of students (e.g., students with disabilities and those who do not have disabilities)
- Improve instruction to better meet the needs of students who do not do well on high-stakes exams
- Serve as a catalyst for school improvement in settings where students do not achieve at appropriate levels

In spite of these positive intended outcomes, controversy has emerged regarding the use of high-stakes tests. Critics fear that they will increase the dropout rate, reduce the number of students who receive a regular diploma, and lower student self-esteem due to repeated failure on exit exams (Johnson & Thurlow, 2003). Some also contend that a single test should not be the basis for making a high-stakes educational decision and that alternative assessments should be available (O'Neil, 2001). Perhaps the greatest concern raised by critics is that schools will not have the resources to provide remedial support for students who do not make adequate progress toward achievement goals (Center on Education Policy, 2004).

Alternatives for exit exams are beginning to emerge in some states, in part as a result of high failure rates for certain groups of students, including students with disabilities, English-language learners, and students from non–European American backgrounds (Bhanpuri & Sexton, 2006). These alternatives include waivers or exemptions (e.g., for students with disabilities based on IEP goals), substitute tests, and alternate diplomas (Center on Education Policy, 2004). Critics fear that these alternatives will result in lowered expectations for students. Moreover, individual accountability is crucial if students are to be held to high standards (O'Neil, 2001). If students are "issued diplomas regardless of performance, their degrees may be tainted with a stigma and their achievements discounted" (pp. 187–188).

Data from other sources reveal that the life circumstances of children living in poverty mean they begin school behind, and most never catch up (Books, 2007). These findings are not intended to dismiss the significant role that schools play in creating opportunities for these students. Powerful education can alter the life circumstances for students living in poverty (e.g., Gruwell, 2007). We all know teachers who use their personal resources to provide school materials and food for students, and who volunteer their time to help students prepare for testing, to collect clothing and food to help families, and to raise funds for trips that build background knowledge.

However, decreasing the achievement gap cannot rest in the hands of teachers as superheroes or missionaries. Solving the achievement gap requires social policy that directly tackles the challenges of poverty rather than suggesting that schools alone can solve the problem. Although teachers cannot solve these problems alone, they can partner with families to try to address them. Often this is a political battle requiring that teachers fight for additional resources. This requires meeting with legislators, addressing school board members, and helping families learn to advocate for their children. These activities take many teachers out of their comfort zone, and each teacher must wrestle with what kinds of actions he or she can and will take to address the achievement gap.

# 3 SUMMARY

As teachers enter classrooms each year, they are faced with an increasingly diverse range of students. All too often the backgrounds of these students differ significantly from the background of the teacher, creating a demographic divide. In this chapter, we addressed this demographic divide and described strategies that may be used to meet the needs of students from diverse backgrounds.

## How Are the Demographics of Public School Students Changing?

- The demographics of public school students are rapidly changing in terms of ethnicity, language, poverty, and disability as classrooms across the United States become more diverse.
- By 2023, more than one half of all students will be non–European American, and 40% will not have English as their first language.

## What Is the Demographic Divide, and Why Does It Matter?

- The demographic divide describes the disparity between the demographics of teachers and students. Students from diverse backgrounds make up 36% of the school population, while 14% of teachers are from similar backgrounds.
- This demographic divide contributes to an achievement gap that exists for many students from diverse backgrounds, demonstrating that schools are not consistently successful in teaching non–European American students, children in poverty, English-language learners, and students with disabilities.

## How Can the Significant Discrepancies in Educational Outcomes for Students Who Vary by Ethnicity, Culture, Socioeconomic Status, Language, and Learning Differences Be Explained?

- The demographic divide is at least partially responsible for this discrepancy.
- The lowest-performing schools typically have lower per-pupil expenditures, fewer highly qualified teachers, and lower-quality curriculum and materials.
- The demographic divide and fewer resources do not destine a student to failure. Many students within and across these groups are achieving substantial success. By exploring these cases, we can better learn how to help students with complex histories succeed in the classroom and cross the border of language, culture, and disability.

## What Do Successful Teachers Believe and Do to Enhance the Educational Futures of All Students?

- Culturally responsive teaching is designed to foster resilience in students, improve student outcomes, and enhance the educational futures of students.
- Culturally responsive teachers are those who
  - Reflect on the role that culture plays in their perceptions.
  - Adopt an attitude of inquiry about culture and difference.
  - Create a vision of non–European American, non–middle-class English-language learners and students with disabilities who succeed.
  - Communicate care to all students and families.
  - Commit to learning about students, their backgrounds, and their experiences.
  - Create a classroom centered on care.
  - Teach classroom rules, routines, and procedures explicitly.
  - Have high expectations for student achievement.
  - Incorporate culturally relevant curriculum.

## ADDRESSING THE PROFESSIONAL STANDARDS

Council for Exceptional Children (CEC) Knowledge Standards addressed in the chapter

ICC1K7, ICC1K8, ICC1K9, ICC1K10, ICC2K3, ICC2K4, ICC3K3, ICC3K4, ICC3K5, ICC5K7, ICC5K8, ICC5K9, ICC5K10, ICC6K1, ICC6K2, ICC6K3, ICC9K1, ICC10K4

Appendix B: CEC Knowledge and Skill Standards Common Core has a full listing of the standards referenced here.

**PEARSON myeducationlab**

Now go to Topic 4: Cultural/Linguistic Diversity in the MyEducationLab for your course, where you can

- Find learning outcomes for the broad concepts covered in this chapter along with the national standards that connect to these outcomes.
- Complete Assignments and Activities that can help you more deeply understand the chapter content.
- Examine challenging situations presented in the IRIS Center Resources.
- Apply and practice your understanding of the core concepts and skills identified in the chapter with the Building Teaching Skills and Dispositions learning unit.

- Check your comprehension on the content covered in the chapter by going to the Study Plan in the Book-Specific Resources for your text. Here you will be able to take a chapter quiz, receive feedback on your answers, and then access Review, Practice, and Enrichment activities to enhance your understanding of chapter content.
- Access video clips of CCSSO National Teachers of the Year award winners responding to the question, "Why Do I Teach?" in the Teacher Talk section.

chapter

4

# Identification and Planning for Students with Special Needs

**REFLECT UPON**

- How do teachers make decisions to refer students for possible special education services?
- What procedures do teachers use to identify students with special needs?
- How do teachers identify infants, toddlers, and preschool-age children with special needs for special services?
- What is an IEP, and how do teachers use it to plan for students with special needs? What other approaches do teachers use to plan for students with special needs?
- How do teachers plan for infants, toddlers, and preschoolers with special needs?
- What are the prevailing issues related to identification and planning for students with special needs?

Different paths might lead one to become a special education teacher, and the one Kathy Blossfield took was different from many and not particularly easy. But Kathy, who works for the Asheville, North Carolina, City School System, has reached a point of real satisfaction. Within the past few years, she finished her master's degree, received her national board certificate in special education, and found her "dream job" in an inclusive preschool program. What reinforces her love for the work she does? "I love seeing the children make progress. I love seeing them be able to connect with their peers or be able to communicate in some way, or be able to learn some skills, to have some tools, that will help them in school. It's just so gratifying to see them make progress in so many different ways." But it wasn't always easy for Kathy.

Kathy had no idea what she wanted to do when she left high school; but being a little rebellious, she knew she didn't want to follow in the footsteps of her parents and become a teacher. So she spent time outdoors, traveled some, and became a whitewater rafting guide in western North Carolina. Seeking jobs in the outdoors led Kathy to become a counselor for children with special needs at a camp in Michigan. After that summer, she thought that working with children with special needs was what she wanted to do, but she wasn't sure about the particulars. Still, she knew she was ready to settle down, so she bought some land to build on, found a nice small college in North Carolina, and plugged away to complete a bachelor's degree in psychology. When she finished, Kathy started working at odd jobs, including substitute teaching, and finally decided that she needed to get her teaching certificate and become a legitimate special educator. Because she had to work during this time, it took 7 years before she was eligible to teach students with special needs. "I was entirely on my own and had to work three jobs to pay my bills, so there was no other way to do it," she said. Yet she persisted.

When Kathy finally finished her certificate requirements, she wondered if she had not made the worst mistake of her life. The teaching job she found didn't match what she had been prepared to do. Instead of working with small groups of students in a resource room on reading and math skills, she found herself in a self-contained special class with children who had serious emotional and behavioral problems. She was at a loss and was rapidly becoming emotionally drained. "The classroom was totally, totally different. I was very frustrated. I cried every day on the way home. I really questioned whether or not I had made the right choice."

How was Kathy able to hang on to become a great special educator? Three keys led to her success. First, she

couldn't quit. There was no noble reason for this. She owed money, had adopted a child with special needs, and needed a job. Although she wasn't getting rich, being a teacher paid fairly well, and she knew what it was like to scrape by on low-paying jobs. Second, her fellow teachers provided her with support. They helped her develop lessons and gave her ideas for working with her students. Third, she found support through a special project called the Teacher Support Program at Western Carolina University. A faculty member involved in this program came to her school, helped her reorganize her classroom, and provided her with reading material and instructions on how to implement positive behavior support practices. Because of this contact, Kathy returned to graduate school part-time and, after another several years of schooling, finished her master's degree.

Kathy can't imagine doing anything else now. After 13 years as a teacher, she knows the tough side of special education, but she also knows that this work can be great. She feels bad for other teachers whose working conditions aren't as good as hers; but she couldn't ask for a situation that suits her better.

Many students are identified with disabilities after experiencing academic or social problems in school.

We hope you take two important lessons from Kathy Blossfield's story: one about you and another about the students you may teach. First, finding your best niche may not come easily or quickly, but by persisting you can find that niche and become a very successful teacher. Second, wide variation exists among the students we identify with disabilities. Some of these students may be a better fit for your skills and abilities than others. In this chapter we help you understand the procedures that teachers use to identify students with special needs and how teachers plan special education services. We hope this will provide you with information regarding the different types of students with special needs and will help you make a good decision about the teaching position that is right for you.

We're sure you've noticed that many students struggle at times to meet academic or social expectations in school. Most anyone reading this chapter could identify times when they have struggled in school with academics or social interactions. Or think of a friend who struggled to learn geometry, creative writing, or music. Others might have had difficulty getting along with a teacher or experienced conflict with one or more of their peers. Most of these problems are short term and will be forgotten in a matter of weeks or months. A disability has more persistent, long-term effects.

We think of special education as support services that teachers provide to students who struggle to meet expectations in school. Identifying these students would be a simple matter if special education services were provided to everyone who struggled in school, but that is not the intended use of these services. The limited resources available in special education must be used to support students who need assistance the most. This makes it very important that we have methods in place to identify the students who are *most* in need of assistance from special education. These are students whose struggles are the most persistent and long term. Furthermore, after we identify these students, we need a process for planning student supports that will lead to success in school and beyond. We summarize many of the important features of planning in the "FAQ Sheet."

## REFLECTIVE EXERCISE

# 1 How would you expect parents to react if they suspected their child had a disability? What would your reaction be if you were a parent?

# IDENTIFYING STUDENTS WITH SPECIAL NEEDS

## The Current Status of Student Identification

The very nature of how we identify students with special needs is currently in a state of flux. Many professionals have criticized the traditional approach that educators have used for many years to identify students with special needs. This has resulted in the

# FAQ Sheet

## IDENTIFICATION AND PLANNING

| | |
|---|---|
| What are early intervening services? | • Teachers use early intervening services to provide support and interventions for addressing difficulties students face in general education classrooms.<br>• Teachers design these interventions to prevent minor learning or behavior problems from becoming more serious, as well as to reduce the number of referrals of students who have minor problems and won't be found eligible for special education services. |
| What is response to intervention (RTI)? | • Teachers design RTI models to provide high-quality, effective instruction or behavior support in the general education classroom to any student who struggles to learn basic academic skills or has behavior problems.<br>• Ultimately, teachers may use the information collected as part of an RTI model to identify a student with a disability. |
| What is an individualized education program (IEP)? | • An IEP is a document that lists the educational goals for a student with special needs, the special education and related services the student is to receive, the placement of the student, and other important information.<br>• The IEP team develops and approves the IEP. The team includes professionals and the student's parents. |
| What is a 504 Plan? | • A 504 Plan is developed for students who under Section 504 of the Rehabilitation Act are considered to be people with a disability but who under IDEA 2004 do not qualify for special education services.<br>• Students who qualify under Section 504 have the right to plans that specify any accommodations or adaptations that they need to participate in school activities. |
| What is a behavior intervention plan (BIP)? | • A BIP is a plan to address challenging student behavior that threatens to lead to placing the student in a more restrictive setting.<br>• Many schools develop BIPs for any student who regularly engages in inappropriate behavior.<br>• A school psychologist or behavior specialist typically works with the teacher to develop and implement the BIP. |
| What is a statement of transition services? | • When a student with special needs turns 16, the IEP must include a statement about transition from school to adult life.<br>• The transition services statement includes the preparation that will occur in high school to meet various needs in adulthood such as postsecondary education, employment, or residential living. |
| What are Part C services, and for whom are they provided? | • States may offer Part C services for children with special needs under age 3 and their families.<br>• States may apply for federal funds to offer these services. The services are named after the part of the law (Individuals with Disabilities Education Act [IDEA] 2004) that describes them. |
| What is an individualized family service plan (IFSP)? | • An IFSP is the document used to plan the services for infants and toddlers served by Part C services.<br>• The plan can include services for the child and the family. |
| At what age does a child become eligible for special education services? | • When a child is 3 years old, he or she has the right to a free appropriate public education (FAPE) under IDEA if eligibility requirements are met. This right continues until the child turns 21. |

inclusion of a new approach to student identification, **response to intervention (RTI),** which was approved by Congress as part of IDEA 2004. Many states are rapidly moving toward using an RTI approach to identify many students with special needs. In the sections that follow, we describe both a traditional approach to student identification and the RTI approach.

It is important to note that RTI does not fit neatly into our traditional conceptions of student identification. Traditionally, identification has been a process that is mostly removed from planning and providing instruction for students with special needs. RTI is an attempt to address many of the shortcomings of the traditional model of student identification, and does this by closely integrating student instruction and identification and requiring that general and special educators collaborate in this process. In short, RTI models are designed to both provide high-quality instruction for students who struggle in learning academic content, and to provide data and information for student identification and program planning. In the sections that follow, we describe how teachers use RTI to provide high-quality instruction and to identify students.

## Overview of Student Identification

Most students who are identified with learning disabilities, mild intellectual disabilities, or other "mild disabilities" are identified during elementary school after they experience problems with their academic work or social behavior. Before entering school, these children might lag behind others in a developmental area (e.g., motor, language, social skills), but these differences are minor and seem more typical than atypical to both parents and professionals. However, once these students enter school and struggle meeting grade-level expectations for academic work or social behavior, these difficulties come to the attention of teachers and other school personnel, and often result in the initiation of a process for determining if the student has a disability.

In contrast, students with more severe disabilities (e.g., severe intellectual disabilities, multiple disabilities, autism) are usually recognized as having special needs earlier in life, even when they are infants or toddlers. These children generally exhibit serious medical needs or have very uncommon developmental characteristics that lead their parents to seek professional services. You saw that Kathy Blossfield was teaching in a preschool program. The children she supports in their fully inclusive classrooms were identified earlier rather than later because it was apparent from an early age that their development was atypical.

Once a student is in elementary school, the identification process proceeds in two distinct phases: (1) early intervening services and referral to special education and (2) student identification. As we present information about these procedures, keep in mind that while federal laws apply to all school districts and schools in the United States, state and local laws may also be applied, and they may vary. Therefore, as a new teacher, whether in special education or general education, you should familiarize yourself with local policies that address referral, identification, and planning procedures for students with special needs.

While teachers make most referrals of students for possible special education services, others may also make referrals (e.g., parent, administrator). As you think about the referral process, keep in mind that many students have difficulty progressing at some time during their years in school. This often makes it difficult for a teacher or other professional to make a decision regarding which children have problems that will disappear over time and which have problems that are so persistent and extreme that they merit referral for possible special education services. This is especially true for students with less obvious, mild disabilities. This difficulty has led to the development of what have been called **prereferral interventions** or, more recently, **early intervening services** that teachers use before referring a student for special education services.

## Early Intervening Services

Federal law does not mandate that teachers must use early intervening services or prereferral interventions before referring a student for possible special education services. However, to ensure that students who might need special education services are appropriately referred, many states either mandate these interventions or strongly recommend their use (Buck, Polloway, Smith-Thomas, & Cook, 2003). Teachers use these interventions to provide support for addressing difficulties students face in general education classrooms and to reduce the number of referrals of students who have minor problems and won't be found eligible for special education services.

While prereferral interventions have been used for at least the last 30 years (Chalfant, Pysh, & Moultrie, 1979; Chalfant & Pysh, 1989; Sindelar, Griffin, Smith, & Watanabe, 1992), an increase in the use of these interventions has occurred since the passage of IDEA 2004. This law now allows school districts to use a portion of their federal special education funds (up to 15%) to "develop and implement coordinated, early intervening services . . . for students in kindergarten through grade 12 (with a particular emphasis on students in kindergarten through grade three) who have *not* been identified as needing special education or related services but who *need* additional academic and behavioral support to succeed in a general education environment" (U.S. Department of Education, 2005b, italics added). This suggests a strong preference in federal law that schools successfully serve students in general education classrooms rather than identifying them as having a disability and providing special education services.

Early intervening services may take many forms. Two of the most widely used forms of these interventions are student-support teams (also called instructional support teams, intervention assistance teams, students success teams, and teacher assistance teams in different parts of the country) (Buck et al., 2003), and the use of RTI models (Gersten, Compton, Dimino, Santoro, Linan-Thompson, & Tilly, 2009). Student support teams are often specifically designed to provide services to teachers when they have students experiencing difficulty in their classroom. In contrast, RTI is a more general approach that not only results in the provision of early intervening services but also entails planning the delivery of systematic instruction and providing data for student identification. Both of these approaches are subsequently described.

## Student Support Teams

Student support teams (SSTs) serve a range of purposes, but here we focus on the use of these teams to provide early intervening services or prereferral interventions for students with possible disabilities, or to provide teachers with support in addressing any student problems that may arise (Buck et al., 2003; Chalfant & Pysh, 1989; Lane, Pierson, Robertson, & Little, 2004). Approximately 3 of every 4 states require or recommend the use of this type of building-based support team in local schools (Buck et al., 2003).

Student support teams are typically composed of professionals such as teachers and specialists (e.g., a school psychologist or a special educator) who collaborate to come up with tactics that will help a teacher increase the student's success. Teams meet with a referring teacher and use a structured, collaborative, problem-solving approach to develop intervention strategies (Bangert & Cooch, 2001). The intervention is usually tried for a specific amount of time and then evaluated. These interventions can include modifications in different areas such as changes in the curriculum, instructional procedures, classroom management, or the classroom environment (Mastropieri & Scruggs, 2010).

Most student problems that are referred to the SST relate to work habits, classroom behavior, interpersonal behavior, attentional problems, and reading difficulties. Referring teachers often report success with the recommended interventions (Lane et al., 2004). Some students for whom recommendations are not successful may be referred to special education (if they are not already identified with a disability), to determine if they need more intensive interventions. The SST process often significantly reduces the number of referrals to special education. Furthermore,

PEARSON
**myeducationlab**

To enhance your understanding of early intervening services, go to the IRIS Center Resources section of Topic 1: Law, LRE, & IEPs in the MyEducationLab for your course and complete the Module entitled *The Prereferral Process: Procedures for Supporting Students with Academic and Behavioral Interventions.*

when students are referred to special education after being referred to the SST, they are most often identified with a disability.

## Response to Intervention

**PEARSON myeducationlab**

To enhance your understanding of the assessment aspect of response to intervention, go to the IRIS Center Resources section of Topic 1: Law, LRE, & IEPs in the MyEducationLab for your course and complete the Module entitled *RTI (Part 2): Assessment.*

Schools have increasingly begun to use a more comprehensive approach to early intervening services that is built upon RTI. Teachers and other professionals design RTI models to provide high-quality, effective instruction in the general education classroom to any student who struggles to learn basic academic skills. This involves the reorganization of instructional services to provide seamless tiers of instruction to better meet the needs of all students. Ultimately, teachers may use information collected as part of an RTI model to identify a student with a learning or other disability (Gersten et al., 2009). However, the aspects that we address here relate to the use of RTI to provide early intervening services in the general education classroom before referral.

The components of RTI that general education teachers use before referral to special education include the provision of high-quality, effective core instruction in the general education classroom (Tier-1 instruction), and supplementary instruction in the general education classroom for students who struggle learning basic skills (Tier-2 instruction). This supplementary instruction may include peer tutoring or small-group (three to six students) instruction in particular skills areas. When teachers use an RTI model, they closely monitor a student's progress using quick and frequent assessments that are directly tied to the curriculum being taught. Teachers then use this continuous progress monitoring to determine if the student is making sufficient progress in an academic area. An alternative for students who do not make sufficient progress after receiving a Tier-2 intervention is referral for possible special education services and the development of more intensive, Tier-3, interventions to address their needs.

Many approaches have been used to implement RTI. One such approach includes the following steps (L. Fuchs & Fuchs, 2007; Gersten et al., 2009; Vaughn & Roberts, 2007):

1. General education teachers provide high-quality, core instruction in the general education classroom (or Tier-1 instruction). For example, in reading, this instruction is typically built on a curriculum that includes the basic components of early reading instruction (i.e., phonemic awareness, phonics, reading fluency, and comprehension). Instruction then entails the use of evidence-based practices to ensure that students learn these basic skills.

2. As they provide high-quality, Tier-1 instruction, teachers use universal screening measures to determine which students are struggling to learn the content. For students who are identified, teachers then monitor progress more systematically over time using a **curriculum-based measure (CBM)** to determine if the students are having a significant problem. Students who have a significant problem then receive Tier-2 intervention (L. Fuchs & Fuchs, 2007).

3. Tier 2 is more intensive, systematic instruction than is typically provided in the general education classroom. This instruction is delivered in small groups (approximately three to six students) for 15 to 30 minutes each day, and it may last up to 20 weeks. General education teachers provide these interventions in addition to Tier-1 instruction. Teachers coordinate Tier-2 interventions with the curriculum of the general education classroom and target them to specific student skill deficits (L. Fuchs & Fuchs, 2007; Vaughn & Roberts, 2007).

4. As teachers deliver Tier-2 instruction, they closely monitor student progress using a CBM weekly or biweekly. Teachers use these measures to indicate if a student has progressed sufficiently to ensure success in the general education classroom. For those who have not progressed sufficiently, a multidisciplinary team meets to discuss the student's eligibility for special education and, as appropriate, to develop a Tier-3 intervention (Gersten et al., 2009).

5. A Tier-3 intervention is closely coordinated with general education instruction; it is more intensive and focused on specific skills than Tier-2 instruction; it is provided in addition to general education content area instruction; and it entails frequent progress monitoring to ensure that the intervention is working (L. Fuchs & Fuchs, 2007; Vaughn & Roberts, 2007). Tier-3 instruction should be delivered in groups of two to three students, and it should last longer than Tier-2 instruction (for 50 minutes or more) (Vaughn & Roberts, 2007).

Thus, RTI is an approach that teachers may use to provide early intervening services in general education classrooms for students who struggle learning to read or have difficulty in other academic areas (e.g., mathematics [D. Fuchs, Fuchs, Compton, et al., 2007]). The use of RTI in mathematics would be similar to the steps used with reading intervention. It is important to note that teachers may also use this approach to provide support for students with behavior problems (Fairbanks, Sugai, Guarding, & Lathrop, 2007; Gresham, 2005), using a somewhat different approach.

To address student behavior problems, Tier-1 intervention should consist of a school-wide approach to "identify and explicitly teach school-wide expectations; implement a system to acknowledge expectation-compliant behavior; define and consistently apply consequences for inappropriate behavior; and regularly review progress towards school-wide goals. Such a universal system reflects the features of positive behavior support" (Fairbanks et al., 2007, p. 289). General education teachers provide Tier-2 interventions to support the development of specific social behavior/skills for small groups of students; while Tier-3 interventions would provide intensive, individual support for more extreme student behavior problems that persist over time.

Whether addressing academic or behavioral struggles of students, RTI models provide high-quality instruction or behavior management and continuous progress monitoring. Many students will overcome minor difficulties using these strategies. However, students who continue to struggle may be referred to special education for possible identification with a disability and for more intensive special education services. RTI models are designed to improve services in the general education classroom, provide students with interventions that may prevent the development of more severe problems, and provide the teacher with a more systematic approach to determine who should be referred for possible special education services.

## Referral for Special Education Services

Many students who might be considered for special education can be successfully supported in general education classrooms using these effective interventions (L. Fuchs et al., 2003; Gersten et al., 2009). However, if the student's difficulties are too challenging, if the general education intervention is not effective, or if no early intervening services are available, educators will refer the student to be evaluated for possible special education services. When this occurs, school professionals follow procedural guidelines that are included in IDEA 2004.

The formal path for a school-age student into special education typically begins when the classroom teacher or another school professional submits a written referral for evaluation. This form describes concerns regarding the student's academic or behavioral performance in school. Through this action, the teacher asks that the child be evaluated to determine eligibility for special education. Parents or other interested persons may also submit such a request to the school.

The referral is typically sent to a designated individual in the school such as the school counselor or an assistant principal, and this person then forwards the referral to the central district administrative office. A placement specialist at the administrative office then arranges a schedule for conducting the necessary evaluations. If parents have not yet been involved in a prereferral or early intervening process or have not yet been notified that their child is having difficulty, federal law

PEARSON
**myeducationlab**

To enhance your overall understanding of response to intervention, go to the IRIS Center Resources section of Topic 1: Law, LRE, & IEPs in the MyEducationLab for your course and complete the Module entitled *RTI (Part 4): Putting It All Together.*

**REFLECTIVE EXERCISE**

#3 Prereferral interventions and early intervening services seem to make a lot of sense, and many school districts use these approaches. What do you perceive to be the pros and cons of these practices?

Schools must provide a full and individual initial evaluation to determine eligibility for special education services.

requires that they be notified when a referral is submitted, *except* under the following circumstances (U.S. Department of Education, 2005b):

- Despite reasonable efforts to do so, the agency cannot discover the whereabouts of the parent of the child.
- The rights of the parents have been terminated in accordance with state law.
- The rights of the parent to make educational decisions have been subrogated by a judge in accordance with state law, and consent for an initial evaluation has been given by an individual appointed by the judge to represent the child.

School district personnel often meet with parents at this point to make sure that they understand their child's status and the procedures involved in evaluating the child. Although rare, some parents may disagree with the school's desire to evaluate their child for special education placement and not provide the required permission. When this happens, schools have the option to pursue the evaluation through due process or mediation procedures or not to proceed with the evaluation.

## Student Identification

When teachers submit a referral, IDEA 2004 requires that for the initial evaluation and any subsequent evaluation:

- the individualized education program (IEP) team and other qualified professionals, as appropriate, shall review existing evaluation data on the child,
- and, on the basis of that review, and input from the child's parents, identify what additional data, if any, are needed to determine,
    - Whether the child has a disability,
    - The educational needs of the child, or, in the case of a reevaluation of a child, whether the child continues to have such a disability and such educational needs, and
    - The present levels of academic achievement and related developmental needs of the child (IDEA 2004, Sec. 614[c][1][b]).

After the school receives parental consent, educators then schedule and conduct any necessary additional evaluations. You should note that if the school district conducts an evaluation and the parents disagree with the results, the parents have the right to have an independent evaluation conducted. Or if a parent feels that an evaluation should be conducted but the school disagrees, the parent may initiate an evaluation, and the results must be considered by the school district.

Assuming parents and the school district agree that the child should be evaluated and considered for special education, then the school district has 60 days to conduct a "full and individual initial evaluation" to determine eligibility for special education services. Most school districts employ school psychologists to administer tests, conduct observations, and conduct interviews with key individuals such as the student's teacher and parents to gather necessary evaluative information.

Educators use many different types of tests to identify students with special needs. The particular tests vary based on the nature of the student's difficulties; tests may include measures of intelligence, achievement, behavior, social skills, and adaptive behavior. We discuss many of these tests and evaluation procedures in later chapters as we address particular disabilities. For more information on this topic and resources that may prove useful to help you become informed regarding these tests, see the "Real World" feature at the end of this chapter.

After the placement specialist has collected all relevant test results and other data, school district personnel call a meeting of the IEP team to consider the information and make a decision about whether the child has a disability. If the child is found to be eligible for special education, the team develops an IEP, which is then implemented. The IEP team is made up of the parent, guardian, or surrogate; a general education teacher; a special education teacher; a school district representative who is knowledgeable about available service-delivery options; an evaluation specialist (usually a school psychologist) who can interpret test results; other professionals as needed; and the student, as appropriate. At this initial meeting, a written copy of the evaluation report is given to the parents, and parents (and their supporters) may present information they believe is relevant. To determine the student's eligibility for special education, the school district personnel must consider information coming from multiple sources, including the results of early intervening services, tests, parent input, and teacher recommendations.

Ultimately, the committee must decide if the child meets the criteria for a specific disability and, if so, which one. Three factors would make the child *ineligible* to receive special education services. (1) The child's inadequate performance in school is due to poor instruction in an academic content area. (2) The learning problems are related to inadequate English proficiency. (3) The child clearly does not meet any of the requirements for having a disability.

### The Use of Response to Intervention for Student Identification

Earlier in this chapter we discussed the use of an RTI model for providing early intervening services. Educators also use RTI in many states as an alternative for identifying students with disabilities, especially students with learning disabilities and emotional and behavioral disabilities (Fairbanks et al., 2007; Gersten et al., 2009). RTI was initially included as an alternative for identifying students with disabilities as part of IDEA 2004 (Reschly, 2005).

The use of this approach for student identification is based on the assumption that students should only be identified with a disability after they have been provided high-quality instruction or behavior interventions and continue to struggle. This places emphasis on making sure that the suspected disability is not the result of poor instruction. As we noted earlier in this chapter, this high-quality instruction includes Tier-1 instruction (high-quality instruction or behavior support in the general education classroom); Tier-2 instruction (instruction or behavior intervention in small groups in addition to general education instruction); and Tier-3 instruction (intensive, individualized instruction or behavior support focusing on specific student needs [Fairbanks et al., 2007; L. Fuchs & Fuchs, 2007; Gersten et al., 2009], which is typically provided by special education).

Student progress is closely monitored during the delivery of these tiers of instruction, to determine if the interventions are effective, and whether the student needs more intensive instruction or behavior support. For students who do not respond to increasingly intensive, highly effective interventions, this information is used, at least in part, in making a decision about whether the student should be identified with a disability.

The use of an RTI model can be effective in preventing learning and behavior problems. Research has shown that, for many students who are at risk or who struggle in early elementary school, the use of tiers of instruction has been effective in increasing the number of students whose reading skills improve and enabling them to succeed with grade-level material (Torgeson et al., 2001; Vellutino, Scanlon, Small, & Fanuele, 2006). For example, after providing kindergarten and first-grade interventions consisting of small-group and individualized tutoring for students who were at risk for reading problems, Vellutino and colleagues found that well over one half of these students were no longer at risk, and the students continued to achieve at this level through third grade. This suggests that a tiered approach to delivering

**REFLECTIVE EXERCISE**

**#4** When it originated, IDEA was considered to be a strong "parents' rights" law. How important do you think it is for parents to consent to have their child evaluated for special education services? How much effort do you believe school districts should make to get parental consent?

REFLECTIVE EXERCISE

#5 The use of RTI to identify students with disabilities is a major shift in thinking for both general and special educators. It might portend important changes in future populations of students classified as having special needs. What is your opinion of this change? Will it be helpful? Who will support it, and who will oppose it?

high-quality instruction may prevent many reading problems and reduce the number of students who are identified with disabilities. Research on tiered behavior interventions for students with behavior problems has resulted in similar findings (Fairbanks et al., 2007).

## IDENTIFYING CHILDREN WITH DISABILITIES BEFORE THEY ENTER SCHOOL

IDEA 2004 requires that states identify children with special needs who are between the ages of 3 and 21 and, if they meet the eligibility requirements, provide them with a free appropriate public education. Some children will show evidence of special needs very early in life, many before they are 3 years old. These infants or toddlers and their families may receive special services, and states can apply to the federal government for grants to assist them in providing these services.

### Identifying Infants and Toddlers with Special Needs

According to federal legislation, an "infant or toddler with a disability" is a child under 3 years of age who needs early intervention services because he or she "is experiencing developmental delays" in one or more areas, including "cognitive development, physical development, communication development, social or emotional development, and adaptive development," or has a "physical or mental condition that has a high probability of resulting in developmental delay." If individual states decide, this term can also include "at-risk infants and toddlers" (IDEA 2004, Part C, Sec. 632).

To help identify and serve children with special needs, states must use a **child-find system**. Under IDEA 2004, Congress required that states' child-find systems focus especially on identifying infants and toddlers who may have special needs who reside in foster care, those living with homeless families, those who are wards of the state, and those who have been exposed to domestic violence and abuse (U.S. Department of Education, 2005b).

The child-find system operates as a public awareness program that distributes information about early intervention and preschool programs through the media, doctors' offices, health service agencies, and other public agencies. Also, many states have birth-defect surveillance programs that identify newborns with characteristics such as **chromosomal anomalies** (e.g., **Down syndrome**) or **musculoskeletal disorders** (e.g., limb abnormalities), so early intervention programs can begin as soon as possible (Farel, Meyer, Hicken, & Edmonds, 2003). Under IDEA 2004, the early intervention lead service agency must target parents of children who are born prematurely or with other "physical risk factors associated with learning or developmental complications" and provide them with information about early intervention services (U.S. Department of Education, 2005b).

States vary significantly in the number and characteristics of infants and toddlers who are actually identified (Shackelford, 2006; Wolery & Bailey, 2002). This occurs because individual states (not the federal government) must decide which children under the age of 3 are eligible for **Part C services** (so-called because of the section of the law in which the services are located).

Parents and professionals are most likely to identify infants or toddlers who either have clear characteristics of specific syndromes or show significant evidence of delay in key developmental areas. Once children are identified, after an initial referral, agencies can begin to provide services if assessments by skilled clinicians show that a child is experiencing a substantial delay. The clinicians will conduct their evaluations using **developmental assessments** to determine how much of a delay is occurring in different areas. States use different criteria in determining a significant delay, but typically they include a substantial delay in one area (e.g., a 50% delay from the norm) or a significant, but less serious, delay in more than one area (e.g., a 25% delay in two or more areas) (M. McLean, 2004).

## Identifying Preschoolers with Special Needs

Beginning when a child with an eligible disability is 3 years old and until he or she reaches age 21, the child has the legal right to special education and any necessary related services. As we have described, agencies *may have been* providing services to children from the time they were infants. When the children turn 3, however, this is no longer an option; public schools *must* provide services. If the child has been in a Part C program, IDEA requires a smooth transition between the early intervention program and the preschool program.

In general, professionals often find it difficult to accurately determine if a young child has a disability unless the child shows clear physical characteristics or indicators that suggest a disability. These characteristics are usually associated with conditions such as cerebral palsy, visual disabilities, hearing impairments, severe intellectual disabilities, or multiple disabilities. Aside from such indicators, professionals must rely on developmental lags and behavioral characteristics that might suggest that the child has a disability such as autism or an intellectual disability. The younger the child and the less pronounced the developmental lag, the more challenging it is to make a definitive determination regarding a disability. This is primarily because the child might outgrow the delay. However, educators don't know if this will occur, and research shows that the earlier the intervention when a child has a disability, the better. The accuracy of early identification therefore is always a critical issue. For an example of this dilemma, review the information that we provide about Jeremy, a child who may have a disability, in "Can You Help Me with This Student?" Once you've examined this information, consider the following questions. Does this child have a disability? How would you have reacted if you were the child's preschool teacher?

Part C services for infants and toddlers might not include children such as Jeremy, simply because when such a child is younger, professionals cannot always reliably determine that he has special needs. As the child grows a little older, however, the needs become more apparent, and he is likely to be served in a preschool program. Children who are good candidates for preschool programs show risks primarily in two areas: communication delays and challenging behaviors. Certain sociocultural factors also suggest a child may be at risk for later delays, and we discuss all of these risk factors next.

### Communication Delays

Lagging communication is the most prevalent symptom of developmental delays. However, if no other disability is readily observable, these children often will not be recognized until they are 2 to 3 years old (Wetherby, Goldstein, Cleary, Allen, & Kublin, 2003). Some **prelinguistic communication** characteristics have been shown to be associated with later language abilities. For example, before children can use words, they typically regulate communication by using eye gaze, affect, gestures, and vocalizations. A lack of these prelinguistic characteristics may predict later language delays, and such language delays are characteristic of children with **autism spectrum disorders**, which includes **autism** and related disorders such as **Asperger's syndrome** (Wetherby et al., 2003). Indicators such as the conditions listed in Figure 4.1,

PEARSON
**myeducationlab**

Go to the Assignments and Activities section of Topic 18: Early Intervention in the MyEducationLab for your course and complete the activity entitled *Programs for Infants and Toddlers and Their Families.*

Professionals must involve parents in developing an individualized family service plan.

| To... | Denise Phillips, Early Childhood Intervention Specialist |
|---|---|
| From... | Melissa Shaw, Preschool Teacher |
| Subject: | Subject: Your insight regarding Jeremy |

Denise, I need your help with a student in my nursery school class. His name is Jeremy, and he's 18 months old. After his first birthday, his mom started to worry about him. What concerned her was that Jeremy was becoming less and less interested in her and the other members of the family and spent longer amounts of time engaged with the same toy, a stuffed beagle puppy. He was also using his few words less and less often and not in ways you might expect. Sometimes when she began to change his diaper, he would arch his back and contort his face and scream, "Cook, cook!" Jeremy's pediatrician said it was too early to worry about anything and that Jeremy was probably going through a phase that he would outgrow. Now that Jeremy is 18 months old, nothing has improved. In my class, while the other toddlers follow each other around from one interesting activity to another, Jeremy often crouches against the wall, holding and smelling his stuffed beagle. I've never had a child like Jeremy. I don't want to overreact, but I'm beginning to agree with Jeremy's mom that something might be wrong in spite of the fact that Jeremy is physically one of the most attractive and able children in the toddler room. Please let me know what you think I should do!

---

To:       Melissa Shaw
From:     Denise Phillips
Subject:  RE: Your insight regarding Jeremy

Melissa, I'm glad you checked with me about Jeremy. This is definitely something that we should check into further. I recommend that we meet with his mother to discuss possible responses to Jeremy's lack of progress and social behavior. During this meeting, we should explain our concerns to her and assure her that in your class you encourage Jeremy to become actively involved in class, and that you often invite the other children to play with him and talk to him. We also need to explain that further evaluation is needed to help us better understand Jeremy's difficulties. With this in mind, we should recommend the following:

- At home, we should encourage Jeremy's mother to try different ways to get him to respond and interact with her and other family members. She and other family members should also spend as much time with him each day as possible, prompting him to make eye contact, look at different items, and repeat names of items.

- The family's pediatrician should refer Jeremy to a pediatric neurologist for an examination. Someone with experience with developmental delays is preferable.

- Contact the state developmental disabilities office, and ask for a developmental assessment by a speech/language specialist who can evaluate language skills.

Based on the description you've provided, I fear that Jeremy may have autism, but we should wait until professionals make that determination before discussing this with his mother. In the meantime, you should consult the following resources for further information:

Prizant, B. M., Wetherby, A. M., Rubin, E., & Laurent, A. C. (2003). The SCERTS Model: A transactional, family-centered approach to enhancing communication and socioemotional abilities of children with autism spectrum disorder. *Infants and Young Children, 16,* 296–316.

Wetherby, A. M., Woods, J., Allen, L., Clearly, J., Dickinson, H., & Lord, C. (2004). Early indicators of autism spectrum disorders in the second year of life. *Journal of Autism and Developmental Disorders, 34,* 473–493.

**EXTEND AND APPLY**

- Do you believe Melissa and Denise have developed a good plan of action? Would you have done something else?

- What are some natural ways you might try to get Jeremy more engaged with his peers?

- Are there some things you might say to Jeremy's peers to encourage them to play with and talk to Jeremy?

FIGURE 4.1 • **INDICATORS OF COMMUNICATION PROBLEMS**

- No babbling by 12 months, no single words by 16 months, or no two-word spontaneous utterances by 24 months
- Failure to respond when name is called by familiar person
- No engagement in joint attention
- Limited gestures by 12 months
- No imitation of another's facial or body movements
- Apparent lack of emotional concern for others, such as when another person is accidentally hurt
- Limited interest in toys, playing, and pretending; focusing more on specific items and actions (e.g., twirling a string)
- Loss of language or social skills at any age

Source: Adapted from Kasari & Wong, 2002; Woods & Wetherby, 2003.

which can be seen very early, even during the infant and toddler years, could suggest a problem in the development of communication skills. At the least, such conditions would call for a formal assessment by a skilled psychologist or speech/language pathologist.

## Challenging Behavior

In addition to early language delays, inappropriate and uncommon behavior in young children, such as acts of aggression or ongoing disruptive behavior, may signal long-term behavioral problems (Drotar, 2002). **Self-injurious behaviors (SIBs)** such as head banging, self-scratching, or self-biting are also very troubling. Sometimes such behaviors appear as a part of normal development and then disappear. When they do not, however, concern about severe developmental delays may be warranted. SIBs are often associated with specific developmental disability syndromes, including **Cornelia de Lange**, **Fragile X**, **Lesch-Nyhan**, **Smith-Magenis**, and **5p (or cri-du-chat)** (MacLean & Symons, 2002).

## Sociocultural Factors

Certain sociocultural factors can place children at risk for later cognitive, academic, and behavioral difficulties in school. These factors can even affect children whose physical and behavioral development appear to be typical. The impact of sociocultural factors has been identified in studies since the mid-20th century or earlier (Uzgiris, 1970), and children exposed to these conditions may be identified in the first 15 months of life based on some of these factors. For example, La Paro, Olsen, and Pianta (2002) found that children younger than 16 months who were from poor homes in which parents provided little stimulation, whose mothers lacked sensitivity, and who exhibited behavior problems early in life were well below average in

**REFLECTIVE EXERCISE**

**#6** Do the indicators of communication problems in Figure 4.1 suggest to you that Jeremy, the child described in "Can You Help Me with This Student?" may have a disability? What do you think would be the best way to communicate with a parent if you suspect a child has a special need?

language development and intellectual development at 36 months of age. The authors noted that, when such children are young, they often are not identified or are not eligible for special services, even though it is likely that they will later end up in special education. During their early years, they may have speech and language problems or difficulty in learning basic concepts (e.g., numbers, alphabet, days of the week, colors, shapes), and they may be restless and easily distracted. Sometimes these children have trouble interacting with their peers or could have difficulty in following directions or routines, and their fine-motor skills may be slow to develop (Schwab Foundation for Learning, 1999).

## PLANNING FOR STUDENTS WITH SPECIAL NEEDS

Since 1977, the IEP has been the central document devoted to specifying the nature of special education services for students with special needs. Additionally, other key documents specify the nature of services that a school district can provide to a student. We examine the IEP and other approaches that teachers use to plan for students with special needs in the following sections.

### Individualized Education Program

In Chapter 2, we addressed the makeup of the IEP team, the components of the IEP, and procedural safeguards regarding the IEP. Here we address the IEP as a planning document for addressing the needs of students with disabilities. The content of an IEP is very clearly spelled out in the law. Although different school districts may use different forms and formats when creating an IEP, the minimum content cannot vary. The initial IEP and all subsequent IEPs must include the following parts:

1. **A statement of the child's present level of educational achievement and functional performance.** What are the student's educational skills, and how do these skills affect the child's participation and performance in the general education curriculum? For preschool children, this information must tell how the disability affects the child's ability to participate in age-appropriate activities.

The IEP team considers information from various sources.

2. **A statement of measurable annual goals and, for students evaluated through alternate assessments, benchmarks, or short-term objectives.** These goals relate to meeting the child's needs that result from the disability and enabling the student to participate in the general education curriculum or for a preschool child to participate in appropriate activities. The goals must also address each of the child's other educational needs that result from the disability. IDEA 2004 eliminated the need for short-term objectives for most students with special needs, requiring them only for students who must be evaluated through alternate assessments (primarily students with more severe special needs).

3. **A statement of the special education and related services and supplementary aids and services to be provided to the child.** This section of the IEP contains a statement of the program modifications or supports that will be provided so that the student can advance appropriately toward attaining annual goals, can participate and progress in the general education curriculum, and can participate in extracurricular and other nonacademic activities with children with and without special needs. To ensure effectiveness, the services provided must be based on "peer-reviewed research to the extent practicable" (IDEA 2004, Sec. 614[d][1][a]).

4. **An explanation of the extent, if any, to which the child will not participate with children who do not have disabilities in the general education classroom and in other school activities.** The assumption is that a child with a disability *will* be included in the general education classroom, will participate in the general curriculum, and in other ways will be involved in school activities. To the extent that this does not occur, the IEP must include an explanation.

5. **A statement about the child's participation in state- or district-wide assessments of student achievement.** This statement includes any individual modifications in the administration of state- or district-wide assessments that are needed for the child to participate in the assessment. If the IEP team determines that the child will not participate in a particular state- or district-wide assessment, the IEP must state why that assessment is not appropriate for the child and how the child will be assessed.

6. **The projected dates for beginning services and modifications.** These dates refer to services described in item 3 and their anticipated frequency, location, and duration.

7. **A statement of how the child's progress toward the annual goals will be measured and how the child's parents will be regularly informed.** Parents of children with special needs must be informed of their children's progress at least as often as other parents are informed of their children's progress. The progress reports must tell parents about a child's progress toward his or her annual goals and the extent to which that progress is sufficient to enable the child to achieve the goals by the end of the year.

As these components suggest, the purpose of the IEP is to ensure that students with special needs receive the high-quality services they need to address their disability. As part of these services, the student must be provided access to the general education curriculum. This access has been explicitly required since 1997 (IDEA, 1997), and it was strengthened in 2004 by mandating that students with disabilities have this access "in the regular classroom" [P.L. 108-446, 601(c)(5)(A)]. Thus, the curriculum used to educate students with disabilities has become the general education curriculum, and accountability measures are aligned with this curriculum.

The general education curriculum is typically tied to standards that are used in a particular state. For example, in Florida, the general education curriculum and accountability measures are tied to the Next Generation Sunshine State Standards (SSS)

Go to the Building Teaching Skills and Dispositions section of Topic 1: Law, LRE, & IEPs in the MyEducationLab for your course and complete the activity entitled *Conducting or Participating in an IEP Meeting.*

(for more information, see http://www.fldoe.org/bii/curriculum/sss/), which include content standards in reading/language arts, mathematics, science, social studies, and other areas.

It is noteworthy that the Florida Next Generation standards are designed to meet the needs of all students in the state. For example, these standards include expectations for students with significant intellectual disabilities to access the general education curriculum, called *access points*. These access points are embedded in the state standards, and they reflect the content of a particular standard but with a reduced level of complexity. Three levels of complexity are provided, which are described as *participatory* (least complex), *supported*, and *independent* (most complex). Florida has developed an alternate assessment that educators use to measure student achievement related to the access points in reading, mathematics, science, and writing.

The development of state standards has resulted in the use of standards-based IEPs in many states (Ahearn, 2006). These IEPs are based on state standards, rather than focusing on student skill deficits, as has often been the case in the past. This ensures that the IEP is aligned with the general education curriculum and tied to accountability measures that are used in a given state. For example, to address the IEP requirement related to current levels of performance, discussion should begin with a review of the state standards the student has achieved, and how this knowledge will allow the student to work toward grade-level standards. Furthermore, information from testing and other sources should be used to "identify the skills and knowledge the individual student needs to achieve the academic standards for the current or subsequent grade level" (Ahearn, 2006, p. 5). Thus, the standards-based IEP is used to bridge the gap between the student's current level of knowledge and where the student needs to be with regard to state standards.

Using state standards to plan a student's IEP (Ahearn, 2006) has many advantages:

- It eliminates a separate, often fragmented curriculum for special education.
- Special education teachers teach toward a coherent, well-defined set of curriculum standards.
- General education teachers see a correlation between what they teach and what is needed for students with disabilities. They then assume greater ownership for the academic achievement of these students.
- When students with disabilities are taught using state standards, the curriculum is aligned with accountability measures.
- Students with disabilities who are taught using state standards achieve at higher levels than previously anticipated.
- More students with disabilities pass state high school exit exams when they are taught using state standards.

Finally, IDEA 2004 mandates that students be invited to IEP planning meetings, beginning at the age of 14. This mandate was included in the law, at least in part, to ensure that students have some ownership for planning for their school experience. In addition, participation in planning the IEP has been viewed as an opportunity to provide students with knowledge regarding their disability, as well as to gain skills in self-advocacy. Unfortunately, research has shown that most students are passive and talk infrequently during IEP meetings (Martin et al., 2006).

## Reevaluations and Updating the IEP

Neither the student's placement in special education nor his special education goals are permanent. After a student begins to receive special education services and supports, subsequent reevaluations for eligibility and meetings for updating the IEP are necessary and required to continue planning for the student's success.

According to IDEA 2004, school districts should conduct reevaluations if the student's academic or functional progress seems to have been sufficient to warrant a reevaluation or if the parents or a teacher request a reevaluation. However, schools are not required to conduct reevaluations more than once a year, unless the school district and the parent both agree that it is necessary. On the other hand, schools must conduct reevaluations at least every 3 years unless the district and the parents agree that it is not necessary to do so to establish the eligibility of the student.

At least once a year, or more often if the parents or school personnel feel it is necessary, an IEP meeting must be held so that the student's progress toward his annual goals and participation in the general curriculum can be reviewed. If necessary, the IEP may be revised at this meeting to change the goals; include any recent evaluation results or any relevant information provided by the parents; change the services, supports, or placement; or make any other relevant changes.

## Family Participation in Planning

As we have discussed previously, parents have the right to approve the initial evaluation of their child and attend the meeting where eligibility will be determined and an initial IEP developed. They also have a right to active involvement in decisions regarding the placement of their child and all other components of the IEP. Schools are required to do all that is possible to facilitate parents' attendance and participation in meetings, including having meetings at a place and time when the parents can attend and providing an interpreter if a parent speaks a language other than English or is deaf. If parents' physical attendance is not possible, the law allows telephone or video conferences. IDEA 2004 allows for IEP team members to *not* attend IEP meetings under two circumstances: (1) if the parents and school district agree that a team member need not attend because her area of expertise will not be discussed or (2) if the parents and the school district agree that input from a particular team member may be made in writing.

After the IEP has been written and signed by members of the IEP team, school officials must give the parents a copy. Because they are members of the IEP team, ideally, parents will have full knowledge of the contents of the IEP, will have agreed to it, and will also have agreed to the placement decision that is required as part of the IEP. However, suppose that parents *do not agree* to have special education services provided for their child. What then? Under IDEA 2004, the school district may not provide these services and may not appeal through due process procedures to require the child to participate in special education. The law clearly states, "If the parent of a child for whom an agency is seeking consent to provide special education and related services refuses to consent to services . . . the LEA [local education agency] shall not provide special education and related services to the child by utilizing the [due process] procedures" (614[a][1][D][i][II], [ii][II]). Further, the law states, "If the parent of such child refuses to consent to the receipt of special education and related services, or if the parent fails to respond to a request to provide such consent":

- The LEA shall not be considered to be in violation of the requirement to make available a free appropriate public education (FAPE) to the child for the failure to provide such child with the special education and related services for which the LEA requests such consent; and
- The LEA shall not be required to convene an individualized education program (IEP) meeting or develop an IEP under this section for the child for the special education and related services for which the LEA requests such consent. (IDEA 2004, Sec. 614[a][1][d])

REFLECTIVE EXERCISE

#8 Reevaluations and meetings to update IEPs are time-consuming and costly. Do you believe they are worth the time and effort? Do you think they should occur more or less often?

PEARSON
myeducationlab

Go to the Assignments and Activities section of Topic 3: Parents & Families in the MyEducationLab for your course and complete the activity entitled *Parent Participation in Special Education.*

Notwithstanding this condition of the law, it is important for teachers and other school personnel to know that parental agreement to the initial evaluation and their acceptance of the results of the evaluation *does not* mean that the parents have agreed to a specific special education placement for their child (e.g., a special classroom or special school). This requires a separate consent. As you saw in Chapter 1, the law requires a continuum of placements in special education, and parents have the right to express their opinion about the placement they desire for their child and to argue their case through the due process procedures outlined in the law.

## 504 Plans

Two criteria are required for determining eligibility for special education services under IDEA, because the student must be (1) identified with a disability and (2) determined to need special education services. Any student who meets both of these criteria will have an IEP. A student who is identified with a disability but who is not determined to need special education services may be eligible for a 504 Plan. Just over 1% of the school-age population have 504 Plans (Zirkel, 2009).

Section 504 of the Rehabilitation Act of 1973 is not an education law but is a civil rights act like the Americans with Disabilities Act (ADA). This act prohibits discrimination on the basis of a disability in any program or activity that receives federal funding, and it ensures that individuals with special needs are provided all activities and services that are available to others in public schools. Section 504 is not funded, and carrying out this act is the responsibility of general education, not special education. More specifically, a 504 Plan may specify any accommodation or adaptation that is needed to allow the student to participate in school activities.

Because public schools receive federal funds, they must comply with Section 504. However, because a disability is more broadly defined under the Rehabilitation Act than under IDEA legislation, students in public schools who are not in special education may still be considered to have a disability that "substantially limits a major life activity." For example, a student who has asthma may not need special education services because her school performance may be adequate. However, he or she may still qualify for supports and services under Section 504. Similarly, a student with attention-deficit hyperactivity disorder may have adequate school performance and not need special education services, but the student's disability may affect performance on tests and result in the need for an accommodation on a high-stakes test (e.g., additional time to complete the test).

A collaborative team is used to develop a Section 504 Plan, once a student has been determined to have a disability and is eligible for these services. This team is most often headed by a general education administrator (i.e., principal or assistant principal). It includes the parent and may include other school personnel such as the school counselor, school psychologist, social worker, general education teacher, and special education teacher (Madaus & Shaw, 2008). Members of the Section 504 team should include individuals who have knowledge about the child, possible accommodations that may be used to meet the child's needs, and evaluation data that are used for student identification and program planning (Zirkel, 2009).

Congress passed amendments to the ADA in 2008 (effective January 1, 2009), which unobtrusively connected this law to Section 504 and revised the definition of disability in Section 504 (Zirkel, 2009). This revision results in an even broader definition of disability under Section 504 and will likely result in increasing numbers of students with 504 Plans in the coming years.

## Behavior Intervention Plans

Some students exhibit such challenging behavior that school personnel must develop a formal plan to improve the student's behavior. This plan, called a **behavior intervention plan (BIP)**, is required by law for students with disabilities if the challenging behavior threatens to lead to a more restrictive placement. For example, if a student in a general education classroom were exhibiting behavior that might require the student to be placed in a separate classroom or school, a BIP would be written. Most schools also develop BIPs for any student who regularly engages in inappropriate behavior.

A school psychologist or behavior specialist who has training in **applied behavior analysis (ABA)** and **positive behavior supports (PBSs)** is usually the lead person who develops the BIP. This person will complete a **functional behavior assessment (FBA)** by interviewing the teacher and directly observing the student. The FBA will provide information regarding the nature of the problem behavior and how the behavior might be successfully addressed. Based on this assessment, the behavior specialist develops a BIP and reviews it with the teacher to determine if the teacher understands the intervention and feels that she can implement it in the classroom.

Successful BIPs are often characterized by three factors. First, the goal of these plans is often to replace negative, disruptive behaviors with more appropriate behaviors. Second, BIPs may address behaviors of students who misbehave because they lack the skills to act productively in the classroom and school. For these students, teachers use direct instruction related to social skills to improve social competence and reduce problem behaviors. Finally, teaching of self-management provides students with the skills to assume a significant role in their behavior change efforts. This allows students to control their own behavior independently (Polsgrove & Smith, 2004).

While BIPs for some students are relatively straightforward and are not difficult for the teacher to implement, other plans are more complex. For example, a plan that requires social skills training using a particular curriculum or the development of self-management skills can become quite complicated. When educators develop these more complex plans, school psychologists or behavior specialists are typically available to provide support to the teacher as the plan is implemented and evaluated. These professionals work collaboratively with the teacher to determine the effectiveness of the program and to make changes as necessary to better meet the student's needs.

## Transition Services

For students who are adolescents and approaching adulthood, IDEA 2004 requires that the IEP include a statement of **transition services**. According to IDEA 2004, *transition services* means a "coordinated set of activities" that

- Is "results-oriented" in that it focuses on "improving the academic and functional achievement" of a student and facilitates "movement from school to postschool activities"
- May include postsecondary education, vocational education, integrated employment (including supported employment), continuing and adult education, adult services, independent living, or community participation
- Is based on individual needs that consider the student's strengths, preferences, and interests
- Includes instruction, related services, community experiences, the development of employment and other postschool adult living objectives, and, when appropriate, acquisition of daily living skills and functional vocational evaluation (IDEA 2004, Sec. 602[34])

Transition services for each student with a disability must begin at age 16. These services are indicated in the IEP by a statement of measurable postsecondary goals. The goals are based on assessments that report the student's skills in areas of training, education, employment, and, when appropriate, independent living skills. To help the student reach these goals, the IEP must have a statement of transition

Go to the Assignments and Activities section of Topic 19: Transitions in the MyEducationLab for your course and complete the activity entitled *Describing Transition Services.*

Transition services must begin by age 16.

services, including courses of study (e. g., participation in advanced-placement courses or a vocational education program), and a statement of the interagency responsibilities or any links needed to coordinate supports.

Much of transition planning addresses either preparation for employment or for postsecondary education (Brooke, Revell, & Wehman, 2009; Gil, 2007; D. Johnson, Mellard, & Lancaster, 2007). One of the major areas addressed in transition planning is self-determination, or the student's belief in himself, ability to make decisions and self-advocate, and willingness to initiate actions to reach goals (Gil, 2007). Another critical aspect of transition planning often addressed is social skills, which is closely related to self-determination (Pierson, Carter, Lane, & Glaeser, 2008). Others have recognized the need for specific skills that are necessary to successfully transitioning to a work setting. For example, the "Road to Success" curriculum has been developed to provide students with specific skills needed as they plan and prepare for employment (D. Johnson et al., 2007). This program includes curriculum and instruction related to learning skills and behaviors that help in getting and maintaining employment, and it helps prepare individual students as they are "making connections with local employment options and support services" (D. Johnson et al., 2007, p. 28).

For an adolescent, transition planning is often one of the most important parts of the IEP. When the student is 21 years old, he is no longer entitled to a free appropriate special education and does not receive extensive support from special educators to ensure success. As you might anticipate, much more independence and skill in decision making are required to succeed in postsecondary education or employment settings. Thus, preparation for adult life is a critical issue. Take a look at Jeffrey, in "Can You Help Me with This Student?" Can you make any recommendations for his transition plan?

## CAN YOU HELP ME WITH THIS STUDENT?

| To... | Jean Rafferty, District Special Education Supervisor |
|---|---|
| From... | Alice Staley, High School Special Education Teacher |
| Subject: | Transition planning for Jeffrey |

Jean, I need your expertise regarding a transition planning issue for a student in my class. Jeffrey is 15 years old and a really nice guy. For the most part, he has done well in school, notwithstanding the fact he has a learning disability and reads on about a sixth-grade level. Jeffrey's measured intelligence is in the average range, he is quite capable of taking care of himself, and he makes average grades in most of his subjects, with support from his special education teacher. He has not thought about college (his mom and dad did not attend college) and has assumed (until now) that he will get a job after high school in the nearby furniture factory or maybe drive a truck. After talking to his dad, though, Jeffrey doesn't know if this is going to be possible. I'm sure you saw the recent announcement in the local newspaper that the furniture factory is closing next year. Furthermore, his dad told Jeffrey that the price of fuel is making trucking less and less profitable. So Jeffrey has been thinking more about the community college. He doesn't know what he will study, and he's not sure how he'll do, but he can't think of many other options. We have a transition planning meeting coming up in a couple of weeks. Do you have recommendations regarding what we should do in planning for this meeting? Thanks for any help you can provide!

—Alice

From:     Jean Rafferty

To:       Alice Staley

Subject:   RE: Transition planning for Jeffrey

Alice, I'm glad you contacted me regarding transition planning for Jeffrey. As you know, Jeffrey has many options after he graduates from high school. Unfortunately, most high school students only consider a limited number of options. Of course, that's where transition planning becomes so important! Here's what I'd recommend that you and Jeffrey do before your meeting:

- Have Jeffrey take a vocational interest inventory such as the Strong Interest Inventory Revised Edition (Donnay, Morris, Schaubhut, & Thompson, 2004) to help him think about an initial career direction.

- Brainstorm about possible options, including the community college, but also other ideas for possible jobs that would be a good fit for Jeffrey. There may be jobs besides factory work and truck driving that are appealing to Jeffrey.

- Talk to the coordinator of disability services at the community college, and find out about the supports the school offers and some possible areas of study that might be interesting and beneficial for Jeffrey.

- Think about what additional courses in high school might be helpful for whatever direction is decided.

I hope these suggestions help. I'd be glad to talk further with you about this as you and Jeremy move through the transition planning process. You might also consult the following resources for additional information about transition planning and postsecondary planning for students with learning disabilities.

Hitchings, W. E., Luzzo, D. A., Ristow, R., Horvath, M., Retish, P., & Tanners, A. (2001). The career development needs of college students with learning disabilities: In their own words. *Learning Disabilities Research & Practice, 16,* 8–17.

Kochhar-Bryant, C., & Greene, G. (2008). *Pathways to successful transition for youth with disabilities: A developmental process* (2nd ed.). Upper Saddle River, NJ: Merrill/Pearson Education.

Trainor, A. A. (2005). Self-determination perceptions and behaviors of diverse students with LD during the transition planning process. *Journal of Learning Disabilities, 38,* 233–249.

**EXTEND AND APPLY**

- Do you believe Ms. Staley is being helpful to Jeffrey? What else would you have done?

- You might find it helpful and interesting to look at support services offered in nearby colleges and universities for students with learning disabilities (and other disabilities, for that matter). More and more students with disabilities are participating in postsecondary education.

## Planning for Infants and Toddlers with Special Needs and Their Families

Federal law provides financial support for states that choose to offer special services to infants or toddlers with special needs. If a state offers the service, it must designate a lead agency (usually the health and human services agency) to operate the program. To provide appropriate services, agencies must develop a written **individualized family service plan (IFSP)**. The IFSP includes the types of services provided to the infant or toddler and the child's family. Because of the young age of the child, services for the child should not be separated from the needs of the parents and family members. Thus, the IFSP addresses not only the child's needs but also how to

**REFLECTIVE EXERCISE**

#9 Many educators and parents have found the development of effective transition services to be very difficult. Why do you think this is the case? What transition services do you think are most important to ensure that students with disabilities are successful in employment settings? Postsecondary settings?

support the family to help meet these needs. Services for an infant or toddler are often provided in the family's home, but the child may also be served in a special center. A change in the most recent version of the law (IDEA 2004) requires that services be "based on scientifically based research" and include "preliteracy and language skills, as developmentally appropriate for the child" (U.S. Department of Education, 2005b).

When professionals prepare an IFSP, they must involve the parents and other family members. Friends or advocates of the child and family can participate in the process as well, if the parents so desire. A service coordinator who is identified by the public agency providing the services oversees the design and implementation of the IFSP. Other professionals will also help write the IFSP if they have conducted evaluations of the child and/or will provide services to the child or the family. The IFSP itself is a rather extensive document that must include several key components (see Figure 4.2).

## Planning for Preschoolers with Special Needs

Under IDEA 2004, if a child has been in a Part C program, states may develop a plan that allows parents to keep their child in this program, if they wish, until he or she reaches kindergarten age. Parents can choose this option instead of transferring the child into a preschool program, which would be the typical placement for children who are 3 to 4 years old (U.S. Department of Education, 2005). If parents choose this option, the IFSP continues as the planning document for the child until he or she reaches kindergarten age. Even if a child receiving Part C services transfers to a preschool program at age 3, the IFSP developed when he was enrolled in a Part C program may still serve as the child's IEP until the next IEP is developed.

When children like Jeremy (see "Can You Help Me with This Student?"), who most likely were not served in a Part C program, begin preschool, public school officials will create an individualized education program for them. The IEP will specify the services for the child, just as it does for school-age students.

Public schools may use early childhood or early childhood special education settings to serve preschool-age children with identified disabilities and may offer either full- or part-time services. The schools will often use the designation "child with a disability" when referring to a preschooler with special needs instead of placing the child in a specific disability category. They may use this classification until the child is 9 years old.

FIGURE 4.2 • **REQUIRED COMPONENTS OF THE INDIVIDUALIZED FAMILY SERVICE PLAN**

1. Information about the child's status, including physical health, cognitive development, communication development, social-emotional development, and adaptive development
2. Family information (if the family agrees to provide it) about family needs, resources, and priorities related to the development of the child
3. The type of early intervention services to be provided "based on peer-reviewed research to the extent possible," the natural environments in which they will be provided, how often they will be provided, and who will provide them (IDEA 2004, Sec. 636 [d] [4])
4. A statement of measurable results or outcomes, including preliteracy and language skills, as developmentally appropriate for the child
5. Other services that will be provided, such as medical services
6. The dates on which services will be provided and the duration of services
7. The name of the service coordinator who will be responsible for implementing the IFSP and coordinating all of the services to be provided
8. A description of appropriate transition services to help the child and the family when it is time for the child to move from the early interventions program into a preschool program

Early childhood settings that serve students without disabilities are used to serve more than a third of the preschool-age children with special needs (U.S. Department of Education, 2003). This allows them the opportunity to interact with their typical peers, who will model appropriate communication and social skills.

Research has shown that preschool programs for children with special needs can be very effective. These programs "(1) ameliorate, and in some cases, prevent developmental problems; (2) result in fewer children being retained in later grades; (3) reduce educational costs to school programs; and (4) improve the quality of parent, child, and family relationships" (Salisbury & Smith, 1993, p. 1). The most effective preschool programs include the following characteristics (Salisbury & Smith, 1993):

- Encourage the involvement of parents to reinforce critical skills in natural contexts
- Occur early in the child's life
- Operate from a more structured and systematic instructional base
- Prescriptively address each child's assessed needs
- Include normally developing children as models

**REFLECTIVE EXERCISE**

#10 Do you think more preschool programs for children with special needs should be inclusive? What are the advantages of having children with and without special needs together at a young age?

# PREVAILING ISSUES, CONTROVERSIES, AND IMPLICATIONS FOR THE TEACHER

Since Congress passed IDEA in 1975, great progress has been made related to the identification and program planning for students with special needs. However, in spite of this progress, challenges and controversial issues remain. Two critical issues at present relate to providing highly qualified teachers for students with special needs and ensuring that these students meet accountability standards while being educated in the least restrictive setting. In addition, we address the need to provide parents with information regarding tests that are used as accountability measures with their children in the "Real World" feature.

## Highly Qualified Teachers for All Students

Can we provide highly qualified teachers for all students with special needs? Researchers have consistently recognized that the most important factor in high levels of student achievement is a highly effective teacher (McLeskey & Billingsley, 2008; Rivkin, Hanushek, & Kain, 2002). This research has demonstrated that teacher quality contributes more to student achievement than any other factor, including class composition, class size, or student background (Sanders & Horn, 1998). Two key factors in determining whether a teacher is highly qualified are certification status and knowledge of the content being taught (Darling-Hammond, 2001; McLeskey & Ross, 2004; Walsh, 2001).

District administrators have reported great difficulty in hiring sufficient numbers of highly qualified special education teachers (Westat Corp., 2002). This difficulty results in large part because of a severe, chronic shortage of certified special education teachers across the United States (Boe & Cook, 2006; McLeskey, Tyler, & Flippin, 2004). Data from 2006 reveal that over 11% (approximately 45,000) of special education teachers were not certified (U.S. Department of Education, 2009). These teachers served approximately 765,000 students with special needs.

A second issue related to highly qualified teachers is the extent to which a teacher has a deep knowledge of the content being taught. Research has consistently revealed that most secondary-level special education teachers do not have certification or the necessary content expertise in the subject areas they teach, including English, math, science, or social studies (Billingsley, Fall, & Williams, 2006; McLeskey & Billingsley, 2008).

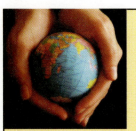

*Ms. Yon is a third-year special education teacher in an elementary school. She has attended several meetings in which students have been identified with a disability, as well as meetings in which IEPs have been developed or changed. On several occasions, parents have asked her about standardized, norm-referenced tests that were used to make decisions about their children. Ms. Yon initially sought assistance in responding to these questions from the school psychologist who works in her school. One of her primary concerns related to just what a "norm-referenced" test is. The psychologist was most helpful in providing Ms. Yon with information and also suggested resources for obtaining additional information about tests that are often used to identify students with special needs or to make instructional decisions.*

The school psychologist who works in Ms. Yon's school was very helpful in helping her understand the basics regarding tests that are used to identify or plan programs for students with special needs. She explained that tests can be either norm referenced or criterion referenced. She also explained that a norm-referenced test compares a student's score to a large peer group of students who have taken the test under the same, or standardized, conditions. For example, if you give a student a norm-referenced reading test, you can determine how well she did by comparing her score to an average score for her age or grade group. A percentile score is often provided to make this comparison. For example, a student may score better than 50% of all students who took the test, or at the 50th percentile rank. A low-scoring student might score at the 15th percentile, or better than 15% of students who took the test. Intelligence tests, behavior rating scales, many achievement tests, and developmental assessments are norm referenced.

In contrast to norm-referenced tests, criterion-referenced tests are not designed to compare a student's performance to a selected normative group. Instead, educators use criterion-referenced tests to determine if a student can perform a skill to a predetermined criterion level. For example, if the criterion of interest is to read 80% of the words on a sight-word reading list, then you could give a criterion-referenced test to determine if the criterion has been met. While all nationally norm-referenced tests are commercially produced, criterion-referenced tests may be commercially produced or created by a teacher, a school, or a school district.

### Valuable Resources for the Teacher

For more information on tests that are frequently used to identify or plan instruction for students with special needs, you may want to consult the following resources:

Overton, T. (2009). *Assessing learners with special needs: An applied approach* (6th ed.). Upper Saddle River, NJ: Merrill/Pearson Education.

Salvia, J., Ysseldyke, J., & Bolt, S. (2010). *Assessment in special and inclusive education* (11th ed.). Belmont, CA: Wadsworth.

### Final Thoughts

You should be well informed about tests that are used to identify or plan programs for students with special needs. This information can help you better interpret and use test information in working with a student with a disability. In addition, you can provide information for other teachers so that they can better understand and use test information. Perhaps most importantly, many parents may feel frustrated by the jargon that educators often use as they describe tests that are used to make critical decisions about their children. Your ability to explain the nature of tests and test results in "plain English" will be extremely important for many parents, because this will allow them to understand how and why tests are used, and how decisions are made about their children.

The No Child Left Behind Act addresses the need for a highly qualified teacher for every student. As part of this act, support has been provided for developing alternative routes to certification to increase the number of teachers entering the profession. Many state education agencies and local school districts have developed alternative routes to certification to attract persons with bachelor's degrees from the local population into teaching (Rosenberg & Sindelar, 2007). These alternative routes to certification have contributed to a decrease in the number of uncertified teachers over the last 5 years (U.S. Department of Education, 2009).

Some local education agencies have addressed the shortage of secondary special education teachers with content area expertise by altering the delivery of services to students with special needs. These districts have begun to increasingly use co-teachers in secondary classrooms that include a general education teacher with expertise in the content area, and a special education teacher with expertise in meeting diverse student needs. While these actions have had some effect on reducing the shortage of special education teachers, it is anticipated that this shortage will continue into the foreseeable future.

## Meeting Accountability Standards

Can we ensure that all students with special needs meet accountability standards while providing access to the general education curriculum in the least restrictive environment? An uncompromising promise was made in NCLB and IDEA 2004 that all students will meet high achievement standards. This legislation boldly states that all students will be on grade level by 2013, if schools use a rigorous curriculum and teachers use evidence-based practices in classrooms (Hardman & Dawson, 2008). While some have begun to question whether all students can meet these high standards, all continue to agree that if current knowledge regarding effective instructional practices is consistently used in schools, the academic achievement levels of students with disabilities can be significantly improved (McLeskey & Billingsley, 2008). To achieve these high levels of achievement, students with disabilities must participate in the general education curriculum, be taught to the same standards as other students, and be provided intensive instruction to meet their individual needs (Ahearn, 2006; Hardman & Dawson, 2008).

These mandates suggest that programs that are provided for students with disabilities must be both effective and inclusive. Although some evidence suggests that schools can be inclusive and highly effective (Salend & Garrick Duhaney, 2007; Waldron & McLeskey, 1998), some inclusive programs have not significantly improved student achievement (Baines, Baines, & Masterson, 1994; Fox & Ysseldyke, 1997). These results suggest that there are many challenges ahead in developing effective, inclusive programs that result in significantly improved student outcomes. Challenges include (Hardman & Dawson, 2008; McLeskey & Waldron, 2006; Waldron & McLeskey, 2009):

- Creating content standards that are broad enough to meet the needs of all students, including those with special needs
- Developing an assessment system that includes students with special needs who need accommodations to demonstrate knowledge and skills
- Using assessment to improve instructional practices and student outcomes
- Developing inclusive programs that include effective core instruction in the general education classroom, as well as opportunities for more intensive instruction based on individual student needs
- Creating schools where teachers work collaboratively to meet the needs of all students.

# 4 SUMMARY

Effective special education practices begin with identification and planning. Sometimes this will begin when children are very young and sometimes not until they reach the early school years.

## Initial Referral of School-Age Students for Possible Special Education Services

- Initial recognition of students with special needs during the school years usually occurs because of academic or behavioral challenges.

- Screening tests or teacher or parent concerns can lead to an initial referral for possible special education services.
- Most of the time, early intervening services are used in the general education classroom before referral for possible special education services.
- If a student does not succeed after early intervening services, school personnel make a referral for evaluation to determine if the student is eligible for special education services.

## Identification of School-Age Students with Special Needs

- Most students with disabilities are identified in elementary school. This includes most students with mild disabilities (e.g., learning disabilities, mild intellectual disabilities).
- Once a student is referred, a multidisciplinary team of professionals collect information (e.g., test data, classroom observations) and meet with the parent to determine if the student has a disability and needs special education services.
- The student must be reevaluated for eligibility no more than once a year and at least every 3 years unless the school district and the parents agree that there is no need for an evaluation to maintain eligibility.

## Identification of Infants, Toddlers, and Preschool-Age Children with Special Needs

- Some children show signs of special needs very early in life, even as infants or toddlers. Most of these children have recognizable physical or sensory disabilities and experience cognitive, physical, communicative, and/or adaptive delays.
- Professionals document these delays using developmental assessments. Sometimes states also serve infants or toddlers who are considered at risk for delays, even if the delays have not yet occurred.
- Preschool personnel recognize children with special needs because of delays in language or because they exhibit uncommon challenging behavior.
- When a preschool-age child is suspected of having a special need, a school psychologist will conduct assessments to determine if the child is eligible for special education services.

## Planning for Students with Special Needs Using an IEP and Other Special Plans

- If the results of the evaluation indicate the student has a disability and needs special education services, an individualized education program (IEP) is developed by the IEP team.
- The IEP includes the special education goals for the student, the placement setting, how the student will participate in the general curriculum, and other critical information. When a student with special needs reaches age 16, the IEP must include a statement of transition needs.
- Schools must have an IEP when a student begins special education, and an IEP must exist as long as the student continues to receive special education services.
- The IEP team will generally update the IEP at least once a year.
- The IEP team includes professionals, the student's parents, and, when appropriate, the student.
- Students who have a disability but are not eligible for special education services may be provided accommodations using a 504 Plan.
- Behavior intervention plans (BIPs) are used to plan for the needs of students with challenging behavior.

## Planning for Infants, Toddlers, Preschool-Age Children, and Their Families

- Individualized family service plans (IFSPs) are used to plan for the needs of infants and toddlers with special needs and their families. Parents participate in constructing these plans, and a planning coordinator oversees their implementation.
- Preschoolers who receive special education services may have these services directed by the IFSP if one was developed for them as participants in a Part C program or by an IEP.

## Prevailing Issues

- A severe, chronic shortage of highly qualified teachers to address the needs of students with special needs continues to be a problem. Many states have begun to address the need for highly qualified teachers by developing alternative certification programs.
- Students with special needs must meet the same accountability standards as all other students. While some educators have expressed concern regarding whether these standards can be met, all agree that student achievement levels can be significantly increased if current knowledge regarding effective instruction is consistently used in schools.

 **Council for Exceptional Children**

# ADDRESSING THE PROFESSIONAL STANDARDS

Council for Exceptional Children (CEC) Knowledge Standards addressed in the chapter:

ICC1K5, ICC1K6, ICC1K7, IGC1K1, IGC1K5, IGC2K3, ICC8K1-5, GC8K1-4

Appendix B: CEC Knowledge and Skill Standards Common Core has a full listing of the standards referenced here.

**PEARSON** **myeducationlab**

Now go to the MyEducationLab for your course, where you can:

- Find learning outcomes for the broad concepts covered in this chapter along with the national standards that connect to these outcomes.
- Complete Assignments and Activities that can help you more deeply understand the chapter content.
- Examine challenging situations presented in the IRIS Center Resources.
- Apply and practice your understanding of the core concepts and skills identified in the chapter with the Building Teaching Skills and Dispositions learning units.

- Check your comprehension on the content covered in the chapter by going to the Study Plan in the Book-Specific Resources section for your text. Here you will be able to take a chapter quiz, receive feedback on your answers, and then access Review, Practice, and Enrichment activities to enhance your understanding of chapter content.
- Access video clips of CCSSO National Teachers of the Year award winners responding to the question, "Why Do I Teach?" in the Teacher Talk section.

# Effective Instruction in a Well-Managed Classroom

**REFLECT UPON**

- What practices allow for communicating instruction and behavior management in a positive and professional manner?
- What is the general education curriculum? What tools are used to adapt instruction for students who have special education needs?
- What are the major approaches to instruction that teachers use to guide their systematic teaching?
- How can teachers develop systematic, proactive, and positive behavior management systems in their schools and classrooms?
- What are two prevailing and controversial issues associated with effective teaching in well-managed classrooms?

If any one teacher has experienced it all, Bobby Biddle is that person. Currently teaching environmental science to seventh graders in Fairfax County, Virginia, Bobby has certification and degrees in biology and special education. Since she graduated from Duke University with a degree in zoology in 1969, Bobby has taught adolescents in public and private schools, adults in the military in need of basic-skills remediation, and teachers in need of professional staff development. Not surprisingly, Bobby is an award-winning teacher who has been recognized several times as an educator of the year.

Bobby is a "natural" teacher. Although she lacked significant training in teaching methods during her first years in the classroom, Bobby felt immediately comfortable in her instructional role and was able to motivate most of her students. Still, she quickly recognized the need for additional training in instructional methods. After taking several education courses at the local community college, Bobby was recruited into a funded special education master's program, an opportunity that provided her with a diversified repertoire of instructional and behavior-management strategies. This combined training and comfort in both science and special education made Bobby a teacher who has great success making content-rich lessons accessible to a diverse range of learners.

Success in her own classroom teaching is not enough. In her current assignment at Herndon Middle School, Bobby is an active participant in all aspects of school improvement and collaborative governance. She finds interacting with students and adults in the building rewarding and craves opportunities for teachers to work together in productive projects. Bobby is an active member of her school's PAR committee (a positive behavior support effort), which was instrumental in developing supports for Herndon's schoolwide behavior-management program. Bobby also recognizes the importance of communicating with her students and enjoys chatting informally whenever possible. Opportunities to talk with students informally allow her to build relationships with the middle schoolers, an important precondition for respect, motivation, and appropriate school behavior.

On occasion, Bobby feels frustrated that things do not flow smoothly. For example, she is irritated by the few teachers and staff members who are resistant to schoolwide initiatives (e.g., Herndon's behavior program) and the lack of consistency among adults when doling out consequences for students who misbehave. A major challenge is trying to inspire those few students she cannot reach. Not that she lacks desire or motivation; Bobby feels that there is just not enough time to do all that a teacher needs to do. There are so many lab reports to grade, and many students with special needs require supports, accommodations, and remediation. Still, Bobby's greatest gifts—remaining positive and flexible—allow her to meet all challenges. She enjoys the variety that each day brings as well as the promise of improving the lives of her students, one child at a time.

As we have highlighted in previous chapters, teachers of students with special needs assume diverse and important roles. However, a teacher's major responsibility—and, arguably, toughest challenge—is to deliver effective and efficient instruction in a safe and orderly environment. We recognize that you will receive considerable experience in the overlapping areas of teaching and discipline as you continue to pursue your teaching career. Our goal in this chapter is to highlight four essential elements that must be in place if teaching is to have maximum impact. First, instruction and behavior management are best communicated with authenticity, civility, and respect. Second, teachers must know what to teach (i.e., the curriculum) and how to develop appropriate academic goals for the variety of learners in their classrooms. Third teachers should deliver the curriculum using evidence-based instructional delivery techniques—activities and environmental conditions shown repeatedly to help students achieve. Finally, student behavior should be managed in a tiered, proactive, and positive fashion. Do not underestimate the importance of these four interrelated areas: Research has demonstrated that teacher quality contributes more to student outcomes than any other factor, including class size, class composition, or student background (Goe, 2007; Rivkin, Hanushek, & Kain, 2001; Sanders & Horn, 1998).

Teachers like Bobby Biddle recognize the dynamic relationships between teaching and behavior management, as well as the importance of communicating them effectively. Although these issues are often talked about separately, she recognizes that they are highly interrelated. Specifically, Bobby recognizes that her creative efforts to ensure that all students in her classroom learn critical academic skills is one of the most important things she can do to prevent the occurrence of problem behaviors. Correspondingly, she knows that, without the application of systematic and positive behavior management techniques, even the most interesting and supportive of her lessons runs the risk of failing to reach students.

## COMMUNICATING INSTRUCTION AND BEHAVIOR MANAGEMENT

**PEARSON**
**myeducationlab**

To check your comprehension on the content covered in Chapter 5, go to the Book-Specific Resources in the MyEducationLab for your course, select your text, and complete the Study Plan. Here you will be able to take a chapter quiz, receive feedback on your answers, and then access Review, Practice, and Enrichment activities to enhance your understanding of chapter content.

Arguably, the most important consideration in teaching and managing student behavior is the manner in which teachers view their role and interact with students and colleagues. As we're sure you noticed, it is not just what teachers say, but the manner in which they approach their tasks and how they communicate with others. Effective teachers convey to their students that they truly care about them and approach challenging academic and behavioral situations as problem-solving opportunities.

### Developing Authentic Relationships

Mr. Andrew Del Priori, known as Mr. Del to both students and adults at the local middle school, teaches one of the most difficult math classes, Introduction to Algebra, to students with a wide range of abilities. He has the reputation of having high expectations for all students and for being a strict but fair evaluator. His students report that he runs a tight, structured classroom in which instructional time is valued with ferocity. Mr. Del is one of the most popular teachers in the school. Students congregate in his room before and after school, and many talk with him when facing confusing situations in their academic and personal lives. What is it about Mr. Del that makes him so popular with students? Why do they confide in him when faced with problems? Students who know Mr. Del trust him and believe he cares about them as both developing young people and advanced math students. Mr. Del projects openness and concern and appears to really enjoy interacting with students (even the ones considered challenging).

How does a teacher develop authentic relationships with students? First, realize that relationship building is more evolution than revolution. Relationships with students take time to develop and are influenced by the many brief contacts and interactions that you have with students every day. Small investments of teacher energy such as greeting students at the start of the day, expressing appreciation for their efforts, recognizing special

# FAQ Sheet

## EFFECTIVE INSTRUCTION IN A WELL-MANAGED CLASSROOM

| | |
|---|---|
| What strategies help in communicating instruction and behavior management? | Strategies that contribute to effective communication include<br>• Development of authentic relationships<br>• Civility and respect<br>• Conveying appropriate expectations<br>• Cultural sensitivity<br>• Maintaining credibility and dependability<br>• Keeping things in perspective when problems occur<br>• Being a response to intervention (RTI) problem solver |
| What is curriculum, and how is it adapted for students with special education needs? | • Curriculum is the content taught in local schools. Tools employed to adapt curriculum include taxonomies, universal design for learning, planning pyramids, and instructional accommodations. |
| What evidence-based practices enhance the delivery of instruction? | Effective teachers make use of evidence-based practices in the areas of<br>• Instructional grouping<br>• Presenting content<br>• Providing opportunities for practice<br>• Monitoring student progress<br>• Using technology to support instruction |
| How do effective teachers approach the management of student behavior? | • Behavior management is best viewed in a culturally responsive framework in which rules and procedures exist alongside community and family standards.<br>• The utility of speculating on the etiology of misbehavior is questionable; it is more useful to understand the functions associated with a student's actions. |
| What are the major components of an effective behavior-management plan? | Effective management plans consist of five key elements:<br>• A mission statement<br>• Rules, procedures, and supports<br>• Consequences for appropriate and inappropriate behavior<br>• Crisis procedures<br>• Document presenting the management plan |

talents, as well as taking an interest in aspects of their activities and personal lives will enhance the development of productive relationships (Koenig, 2000). As exchanges accumulate, students assess teacher credibility, seeing if what they do corresponds with what is said. Second, authentic relationships are based on listening to students rather than just reacting to them. As observed by Postman and Weingartner (1969) in their classic text, *Teaching as a Subversive Activity,* listening is the only way to learn what students view as relevant and the one true way to validate if what they say deserves attention, even if it is not always on target. Finally, developing children and adolescents often choose to express themselves through a variety of creative ways, including dress, speech, demeanor, and belief systems. Relationships grow when teachers accept students for who they are, encourage them to maintain their individuality, and make continued attempts to understand the world from their point of view.

Brief contacts and interactions often lead to the development of positive relationships with students.

## Civility and Respect

*Civility* means being cognizant that all our actions have consequences for others and anticipating what those consequences may be (Forni, 2002). *Respect* refers to one's basic human right to be acknowledged and treated with dignity. Teachers model civility and respect by engaging in many of the behaviors that maximize effective interpersonal communication, including (1) a vocal tone that conveys patience and understanding and uses a minimum of judgmental language; (2) focused active listening with accompanying eye contact; and (3) regular private interactions that convey a desire to know students and their individual opinions and concerns (Kauffman Mostert, Trent, & Hallahan, 2002; Rosenberg et al., 2006).

It is important to treat students with respect even when you are frustrated by their academic performance or disappointed by their behaviors. Although this is often difficult, you should emphasize that their problematic behaviors are the focus of disapproval, not the students themselves. Keep in mind that up to 90% of what we communicate is transmitted in ways other than the actual words we use. Nonverbal communication, facial gestures and body language, and the rate, pitch, and volume of speech often reflect values and acceptance of students. Although unintended, actions as simple as diverting one's eyes, stepping back, looking at one's watch, or speaking quickly send negative signals to students seeking our approval.

## Credibility, Dependability, and Assertiveness

Credibility with students develops when (1) what teachers say coincides consistently with what they actually do and (2) students perceive that their teachers are prepared and doing all they can to help them succeed in the classroom (Rosenberg et al., 2006). Credibility will not develop if teachers break their own rules and standards (e.g., socializing with other teachers during "sacred" reading instruction time), choose not to follow inconvenient school-wide procedures, or are inconsistent in enforcement of a behavior-management plan. Finally, it is important that we realize that conveying authority need not involve threat, intimidation, or intrusiveness. Strong leaders convey their authority with tact, subtlety, diplomacy, and even humor. Consider these interpersonal communication guidelines (Curwin & Mendler, 1999; Westling & Koorland, 1988):

- Use positive, calm, controlled, and defined statements when requesting student attention and compliance.
- Be confident, self-assured, and consistent; speak without hostility when delivering consequences.
- Be firm, use a soft voice, and avoid arguing with students.
- Let students know that their concerns will be addressed in a timely, caring, and constructive manner.
- Treat students respectfully (e.g., don't embarrass a student in front of peers).

## Being Professional: Keep Things in Perspective

Even with the best of plans and communication strategies, events are going to happen that are frustrating, unfair, and sometimes infuriating. Things will not always go as planned; and like all aspects of life, there will be individuals, both students and colleagues, who appear disillusioned and manipulative. Some of the more challenging situations associated with teaching and behavior management involve people and events peripheral to the classroom. For example, teachers may have heated disagreements with colleagues regarding the correct way to meet the academic needs of a student, administrators may fail to support disciplinary actions adequately, and parents may fight well-intentioned efforts to improve a student's academic performance or turn a pattern of inappropriate behavior around.

What can you do to respond in a professional manner? First, be patient, keep things in perspective, and be aware of the big picture. Schools are microcosms of

### REFLECTIVE EXERCISE

#1 Think of a situation when another person's nonverbal communication appeared in sharp contrast to the words being expressed. How did this situation make you feel? What were your thoughts regarding the honesty and integrity of that individual?

PEARSON
**myeducationlab**

Go to the Assignments and Activities section of Topic 6: Classroom/Behavior Management in the MyEducationLab for your course and complete the activity entitled *Classroom Climate and Respect*. After completing this assignment, go to the Building Teaching Skills and Dispositions section and complete the learning unit entitled *Creating an Inclusive Classroom Climate* to deepen your understanding of this concept.

society, and events do not always go as planned or desired. Don't take it personally. Second, remain diplomatic and consider the perspective of the individual causing the disagreement or even the *function* of that person's actions. For example, think about the frustrations experienced by the parent of a student who is repeatedly in trouble at school or the pressures on an administrator who must sort through multiple sources of information related to a disciplinary infraction.

Third, remain poised and try to settle conflicts in ways that are in the best interests of the student. Keep in mind that how you comport yourself during difficult and stressful circumstances is a public display of your competence. Furthermore, your successful navigation through delicate circumstances is a model of behavior for students. Finally, reflect on your own role in the situation. Consider what actions you are taking that may be contributing to the conflict. As Kottler (2002) has aptly observed, we are the primary authors of our own life stories, and we must determine what we are doing to either produce or maintain our disagreements with others.

### Being an RTI Problem Solver

In earlier chapters we discussed response to intervention (RTI), a model of instruction that provides high-quality, effective instruction to any student who has academic and/or behavioral difficulties. RTI is based on the premise that educational services are best provided as seamless tiers of instruction that vary in terms of intensity and support. Tier-1 instruction involves the provision of high-quality core instruction in the general education classroom. Students who have problems learning the required content receive a Tier-2 intervention, characterized by more focused and intensive instruction. Typically, this instruction supplements Tier-1 efforts, and teachers deliver Tier-2 instruction in small groups within the general education classroom. Students who continue to fall short of expectations will require Tier-3 interventions, necessitating enhanced assessment and specialized educational plans.

RTI provides teachers with a systematic means for allocating instructional time and resources to students who struggle academically and behaviorally. Tiered instruction requires an expansion of traditional roles and responsibilities. Consider several of the roles required of RTI problems solvers (Hoover & Patton, 2008; Little, 2009):

To enhance your understanding of response to intervention, go to the IRIS Center Resources section of Topic 1: Law, LRE, & IEPs in the MyEducationLab for your course and complete the Module entitled *RTI (Part 4): Putting It All Together.*

- Conduct data-based decision making: Analyze a variety of student performance data sources to identify strengths and weaknesses; use data to make informed instructional decisions and evaluate selected interventions.
- Identify evidence-based interventions: Be knowledgeable of practices that result in increased student performance and of ways to support implementation of such practices.
- Differentiate instruction: Convey a range of supports and accommodations that can be applied to assist struggling learners in diverse educational settings.
- Provide positive behavioral supports: Conduct functional behavioral assessments to determine how best to address behavioral challenges.
- Collaborate with colleagues, students, and parents: Work and communicate with the variety of stakeholders involved in developing and sustaining education programs.

## WHAT TO TEACH: CURRICULUM AND STUDENTS WITH SPECIAL NEEDS

One of the most important decisions that educators and parents make involves what students learn in school, or the curriculum. Defined broadly, *curriculum* is the content taught in a school, school district, or state. As recently as 15 years ago, decisions regarding curriculum were largely the responsibility of local school districts and, to a lesser degree, local schools. Today, state governments are much more involved in

| To... | Sylvia Cossetti, District Academic Coach |
| --- | --- |
| From... | Steve Payton, Principal, Southwood Elementary |
| Subject: | Why does one third-grade class outperform another? |

Sylvia,

I hope you can help me with this inconsistency in our third-grade student performance data. Here is what started this: I have long been curious about why students in Ms. Rivera's class seem to routinely win third-grade spelling contests. Using our school-wide data, I found that the standardized test scores of Rivera's students were significantly higher than the scores of students in other third-grade classes in spelling, vocabulary development, and reading. Why is Ms. Rivera so successful in teaching language arts to her students, and why is one of the other third-grade teachers, Ms. Chamblee, for example, less successful? Can you conduct some observations and let me know what is going on? As you can imagine, I would like to help the students by providing the teachers with some instructional feedback.

Thanks in advance,

Steve

---

From:     Sylvia Cossetti
To:        Steve Payton
Subject:  RE: Why does one third-grade class outperform another?

Dear Steve,

As you can probably guess, your star teacher Ms. Rivera regularly applies many of the basic principles of curriculum planning and effective instruction, which include:

- Use instruction in other content areas to support spelling.
- Have different expectations for students: She expects some to learn the entire spelling list and others to learn a reduced number of spelling words.
- Meet with the parents of each student who is struggling to learn spelling words and provide them with information on how to improve spelling, reading, and vocabulary development.

(I can go on, Steve, but I believe you get the point.)

In contrast, Ms. Chamblee doesn't set aside a specific amount of time for spelling. Instructional time allocated to spelling does not seem well planned, varies each week, and consists almost entirely of drill and practice. Ms. Chamblee does little to make adaptations in curriculum for individual student needs, provides little structure for students as they learn the spelling words, and includes little variation in the type of activities students engage in as they prepare for their weekly spelling test. In essence, it is a "one-size-fits-all" approach. Although some of her students learn their spelling words using this approach, students who struggle do not do well. I suggest that we get a coach or mentor assigned to her (and perhaps some of your other teachers) ASAP. In the meantime, I suggest you provide Ms. Chamblee the following user-friendly resources on effective ways to allocate instructional time and plan on how best to use it.

deBettencourt, L. U., & Howard, L. (2007). *The effective special education teacher: A practical guide for success.* Upper Saddle River, NJ: Pearson.

Rosenberg, M. S., O'Shea, L., & O'Shea. D. J. (2006). *Student teacher to master teacher: A practical guide for educating students with special needs.* Upper Saddle River, NJ: Pearson.

Let's talk soon,

Sylvia

deciding the curriculum and evidence-based practices for local schools (i.e., when each subject and specific skills will be taught and how schools will be held accountable for ensuring that students have mastered the curriculum). All 50 states and the District of Columbia have developed standards in core content areas that constitute the curriculum for local schools state-wide (American Federation of Teachers, 2008; Skinner & Staresina, 2004). If you are thinking that teachers now have much less say about the curriculum, you are correct. However, keep in mind that teachers are still involved in making decisions regarding materials and resources (e.g., DVDs, books) that will be used to enrich the curriculum. Furthermore, teachers still make many decisions regarding adaptations and accommodations to the curriculum to address the needs of all students.

Wherever you teach, a state-wide curriculum and related accountability system will be in place, and most students with disabilities will be expected to participate and make progress in this general education curriculum. Effective teachers recognize that students differ in their ability to learn, retain, and apply information and that not all students will learn everything in the curriculum. Clearly, some aspects of any content area are critical for *all* students to learn to proficiency, and these aspects of content are often defined by a given state's curriculum or content standards. However, other aspects of the curriculum will be acquired by only a smaller proportion of students.

How do effective teachers adapt curriculum? While certain content areas, such as spelling (see the preceding example in "Can You Help Me with This Student?"), are relatively straightforward, other areas of the curriculum present greater challenges. Indeed, you will find that effectively delivering instruction to a diverse range of students is a task that requires specific skills. Many teachers find four tools to be particularly useful when adapting instruction: taxonomies for teaching, learning, and assessing; universal design for learning; planning pyramids for designing units and lessons; and techniques for adapting curriculum and instruction.

## Taxonomies

A *taxonomy* is a framework used to organize information. Taxonomies help teachers organize instruction into well-defined units, provide a meaningful sequence of instructional activities, and signal when supplemental materials and activities are used to reteach information. When planning instruction, teachers use taxonomies to (1) clarify their instructional goals; (2) determine the knowledge and cognitive levels of the material being taught; and (3) ensure consistency among goals, learning activities, practice, seatwork, homework, and assessment. The most commonly applied taxonomy, **Bloom's taxonomy** (see Figure 5.1), is useful in planning instruction for diverse learners (Anderson & Kratwohl, 2001). This taxonomy emphasizes that most information can be learned at different conceptual levels, from simple (e.g., facts) to complex (e.g., evaluating information). Most important, Bloom's taxonomy reminds teachers that, regardless of the topic, all students benefit from well-planned lessons.

## FIGURE 5.1 • BLOOM'S TAXONOMY FOR TEACHING, LEARNING, AND ASSESSING (REVISED)

**Cognitive Process Dimension**

Remembering—Recalling information (listing, naming)

Understanding—Explaining ideas or concepts (summarizing, interpreting)

Applying—Using information in another situation (implementing, carrying out)

Analyzing—Breaking information into parts and exploring relationships (comparing, organizing)

Evaluating—Justifying a decision or course of action (checking, critiquing)

Creating—Generating new ideas or ways of viewing things (producing, inventing)

Source: Adapted from Anderson, L., & Krathwohl, D. (Eds.). (2001). *A taxonomy for learning, teaching, and assessing* (p. 31). New York: Longman.

## Universal Design for Learning

**REFLECTIVE EXERCISE**

**#2** What changes in current textbooks would be needed to address the needs of all (or almost all) students? How might creating textbooks in a digital format accommodate the varying reading and conceptual levels of students?

Instructional materials that support or enrich the general education curriculum have traditionally been designed with typical, or "average," learners in mind. Still, with many students unable to make adequate progress using standard instructional materials, educators have begun exploring options for making the curriculum accessible to all students, including those with disabilities. One powerful method, **universal design**, is all around us, most noticeably in architecture and product development (Center for Applied Special Technology, 2009; Hitchcock, Meyer, Rose, & Jackson, 2002; Orkwis & McLane, 1998). For example, architects use universal design to build in accommodations to buildings from their initial design phases, including ramps for wheelchair users as an essential part of the building's design rather than as an awkward afterthought. Closed captioning was intended to benefit people who cannot hear the sound from a television because they are deaf or hearing impaired. However, many others (e.g., those in noisy bars, health clubs, or bedrooms when another person is sleeping) find closed captioning useful.

When applied to the development of curriculum, universal design builds in accommodations and makes differences among students an ordinary part of the school day (Kurtis, Matthews, & Smallwood, 2009; McLeskey & Waldron, 2000). In many instances, technology plays a critical role. For example, readability cannot be altered using traditional hard copies of textbooks, but digital versions allow many options for accommodating student reading levels (and other needs). Digital textbooks contain multiple representations (e.g., image, text, video) of content and can transform one medium to another (e.g., text-to-speech or speech-to-text) or modify the characteristics of a presentation (e.g., size and color of text, loudness of the sound) (Hitchcock et al., 2002).

These modifications have the potential to benefit all students, particularly those whose primary language is not English, those who have difficulty maintaining attention to materi-

Technology plays a critical role in classroom-based universal design accommodations.

als for long periods of time, students who have reading difficulties, persons who lack the motor skills to write or type, or those with intellectual disabilities. As recently as the mid-1990s, universal design for learning was the distant, far-fetched dream of a few instructional technology experts. However, given the dramatic improvements in technology that have occurred during the past decade, universal design is a reality that will soon be a mainstay of most curriculum materials.

## Planning Pyramids

Many teachers use grade-level textbooks that align with state content standards as their primary planning tool for instruction. These textbooks meet the majority of students' instructional needs in a relatively straightforward fashion. However, instruction based largely on textbooks is often too difficult for students who do not read well, lack subject-specific knowledge of vocabulary, lack background knowledge regarding the content, or have disabilities that limit their access to the material (Schumm, 1999).

One way teachers can plan instruction to meet the diverse needs of all students in a classroom is by using *planning pyramids* (Schumm, 1999; Vaughn, Bos, & Schumm, 2007). Built on the concept of "degrees of learning," planning pyramids help teachers analyze both the content and instructional practices as they plan lessons or units of instruction. Similar to Bloom's taxonomy, the fundamental idea is that while "all students are capable of learning, not all students will learn all the content covered" (Vaughn et al., 2007, p. 190). Key concepts and skills to be learned for the specific lesson are first identified and then categorized based on three levels of learning:

1. Content all students will learn (the base of the pyramid)
2. Content that most (but not all) students will learn (the middle of the pyramid)
3. Content that a few students will learn (the top of the pyramid)

Figure 5.2 illustrates a sample middle school science pyramid lesson plan addressing weathering and erosion. The base of the pyramid includes content important for all students to learn, such as the forces that change the Earth's crust. At the

FIGURE 5.2 • **THE PLANNING PYRAMID UNIT PLANNING FORM**

| UNIT PLANNING FORM | **Date:** Sept. 1 – 30   **Class Period:** 1:30 – 2:30 |
|---|---|
| | **Unit Title:** Weathering and Erosion |
| What some students will learn. | • How Earth looked during Ice Age<br>• Disasters caused by sudden changes<br>• Geographic examples of slow and fast changes | **Materials/Resources:**<br>Guest speaker on volcanoes<br>Video: erosion and weathering<br>Rock samples<br>Library books — disasters, volcanoes, etc.<br>Colored transparencies for lectures |
| What most students will learn. | • Compare and contrast weathering and erosion<br>• How humans cause physical and chemical weathering<br>• Basic types of rocks | **Instructional Strategies/Adaptations:**<br>Concept maps<br>Cooperative learning groups to learn material in textbook<br>Audiotape of chapter<br>Study buddies to prepare for quizzes and tests |
| What ALL students should learn. | • Basic components of Earth's surface<br>• Forces that change crust are weathering and erosion | **Evaluation/Products:**<br>Weekly quiz<br>Unit test<br>Learning logs (daily record of "What I learned")<br>Vocabulary flash |

Source: Vaughn, S., Bos, C., & Schumm, J. (2007). *Teaching students who are exceptional, diverse, and at-risk in the general education classroom* (4th ed.), p. 218. Boston: Allyn & Bacon.

next level is content that most but not all students will learn, including how humans cause weathering. Finally, the top of the pyramid includes content that only a few students will learn, including how the Earth looked during the Ice Age. In addition to planning content, the unit planning form prompts decisions regarding materials and resources; instructional strategies and adaptations; and evaluation/products to meet the needs of all students. Students are not slotted permanently into one part of the pyramid, and the amount of content a student will learn will vary over time and across content and lessons.

## REFLECTIVE EXERCISE

#3 How can you justify the fairness of using adaptations for some students and not others? How could you determine which adaptations are best for individual students?

## Adapting Curriculum and Instruction

To facilitate student participation in the general education curriculum, teachers can choose among nine types of instructional adaptations (see Table 5.1). The most frequently used tend to be the more obvious—adaptations in size (e.g., the number of items that a student is expected to complete) and time (e.g., time allocated for completing a task). However, creative teachers consider variable ways to (1) adjust the difficulty level of lessons; (2) structure how students participate and provide

**TABLE 5.1 • NINE TYPES OF ADAPTATIONS**

| Adaptation | Definition | Example |
|---|---|---|
| Input | The instructional strategies used to facilitate student learning | Teachers use videos, computer programs, field trips, and visual aids to support active learning. |
| Output | The ways learners can demonstrate understanding and knowledge | Students write a song, tell a story, design a poster or brochure, or perform an experiment. |
| Size | The length or portion of an assignment, demonstration, or performance learners are expected to complete | Reduce the length of report to be written or spoken, reduce the number of references needed, or reduce the number of problems to be solved. |
| Time | The flexible time needed for student learning | Individualize a time line for project completion; allow more time for test taking. |
| Difficulty | The varied skill levels, conceptual levels, and processes involved in learning | Provide calculators; tier the assignment so that the outcome is the same but with varying degrees of concreteness and complexity. |
| Level of support | The amount of assistance to the learner | Students work in cooperative groups or with peer buddies, mentors, cross-age tutors, or paraeducators. |
| Degree of participation | The extent to which the learner is actively involved in the tasks | In a student-written, -directed, and -acted play, a student may play a part that has more physical action rather than has numerous lines to memorize. |
| Modified goals | The adapted outcome expectations within the context of a general education curriculum | In a written language activity, a student may focus more on writing some letters and copying words rather than composing whole sentences or paragraphs. |
| Substitute curriculum | Significantly differentiated instruction and materials to meet a learner's identified goals | In a foreign language class, a student may develop a play or script that uses both authentic language and cultural knowledge of a designated time period rather than reading paragraphs or directions. |

Source: Adapted from Cole, C., et al. (2000). *Adapting curriculum and instruction in inclusive classrooms: A teachers' desk reference* (2nd ed., p. 39). Bloomington, IN: Indiana Institute on Disability and Community.

responses; (3) provide support; and (4) recognize an individual student's success in large-group lessons. As you review the nine types of adaptations, keep in mind that some are intended for use with all students. Others are intended for students who may not learn the same content as others but who may learn adapted or alternative content (Cole et al., 2000).

# DELIVERING INSTRUCTION

In general, the majority of students, approximately 50% to 80%, seem to easily learn required content in their general education classrooms. The remaining students do not learn this content easily as they move from one grade level to the next. These students may or may not be identified as having a disability. Nonetheless, they share a struggle to learn academic content and to pass state-mandated accountability tests. These students require teachers like Bobby Biddle who recognize alternative approaches to teaching and use evidence-based techniques and methods for systematically teaching well-defined content.

## Approaches to Teaching

Since the passage of the first IDEA in 1975, special education has been dominated by one approach to instruction: a behavioral approach. The behavioral approach emphasizes explicitly identifying content or objectives and systematically teaching this content to students. This approach has been the foundation for numerous instructional practices that have been effective for students with disabilities. Arguably the most common behavioral method, **direct instruction** has explicit guidelines for beginning a lesson, presenting information during the lesson, guiding student practice after instruction, correcting student work and providing feedback, planning and carrying out student seat work, and following up the lesson (Carnine, Silbert, Kame'enui, & Tarver, 2003; Rosenshine & Stevens, 1986). Chapter 8 contains detailed information on how to apply direct instruction.

The behavioral approach to instruction is most effective when teaching students fundamental types of information (e.g., basic skills such as vocabulary or math facts). However, it is not always sufficient to meet many of the higher-order needs of students with learning problems or disabilities. In such cases a cognitive approach to instruction is necessary. Cognitive approaches view students as active, strategic learners who can solve problems when provided with appropriate supports and accommodations. Specific teaching methods within the cognitive approach are not as explicitly structured as those found within the behavioral approach. However, common instructional techniques include (1) comparing and contrasting; (2) concept formation and exemplar selection; (3) informed guessing; and (4) development of specific problem-solving sequences.

These approaches to teaching are not mutually exclusive. Effective instruction is often a blend of techniques and methods. A widely applied example of a successful combination of the cognitive and behavioral approaches is the **strategies intervention model (SIM)**, conceptualized and developed at the University of Kansas Center for Learning. The cognitive component of the model focuses on the teaching of learning strategies—techniques, rules, and generalizations that guide students in the acquisition, integration, storage, and retrieval of curriculum content (Rogan, 2000). Behavioral principles are used to directly teach the strategies through an explicit instructional sequence. Specifically, using a structured series of learning activities, targeted strategies are described, modeled, rehearsed, practiced, and, if successful, generalized to other areas of instructional content (Deshler & Schumaker, 2006). We have an in-depth discussion on SIM in our presentation of learning disabilities.

**PEARSON my education lab**

Go to the Assignments and Activities section of Topic 7: Instructional Strategies in the MyEducationLab for your course and complete the activities entitled *Learning Strategies* and *Differentiating Instruction for All Students*.

**PEARSON my education lab**

To learn more about how direct instruction is used in a classroom, go to the Building Teaching Skills and Dispositions section of Topic 8: Learning Disabilities and complete the learning unit entitled *Using Direct Instruction to Assist Struggling Readers*.

## REFLECTIVE EXERCISE

#4 Think back to your days as an elementary and secondary student. What content were you taught using a behavioral approach? A cognitive approach? Which of these approaches were most effective for you?

## Systematic Teaching

How do effective teachers deliver instruction? What do teachers need to know to deliver instruction to diverse and sometimes challenging groups of students? We focus on five elements of effective teaching: grouping for instruction, presenting content, providing opportunities for practice, monitoring student progress, and using technology to support instruction.

### Grouping for Instruction

How were you grouped for instruction during your years in school? You may remember instances of small-group work and working in collaborative teams. However, it is more likely you will recall a teacher at the front of the room providing instruction to all students in your class. There are advantages to this type of large-group instruction: Information is quickly and efficiently conveyed to a large number of students, and many students learn this information and can respond correctly to questions on a test when asked about the content. Still, many students cannot learn academic content in whole groups and require some instruction that uses alternative grouping arrangements. We focus on three alternative grouping strategies that are designed to allow teachers to provide more focused instruction to students who struggle when faced with whole-class instruction.

**Ability grouping** allows teachers to focus on students' common learning characteristics and instructional needs. When used judiciously, this type of instructional arrangement can be highly effective, allowing struggling learners to benefit from the intensive and targeted instruction they need to make adequate academic progress. Unfortunately, the overuse of ability grouping can be detrimental academically and socially, with low-performing students spending most of their school day separated, and eventually alienated, from high-achieving peers (Freeman & Alkin, 2000; Good & Brophy, 2008; Salend & Duhaney, 1999, 2007).

Mixed ability grouping is an approach in which small groups of students (usually three to six) work in cooperative groups to learn and to ensure that others on their team learn as well (Slavin, 1990a). Validated by years of research (e.g., Good & Brophy, 2008; Johnson, Johnson, & Holubec, 1993; Slavin & Madden, 2006), cooperative learning groups vary widely in type yet share some common beneficial characteristics (Putnam, 1998):

- **Positive interdependence.** The accomplishment of the group goal depends on heterogeneous, diverse group members working together *and* each individual attaining his or her goal.
- **Individual accountability.** All students are held individually accountable for their own learning as well as for their contributions to the group.
- **Cooperative skills.** Students practice social and cooperative skills that are commonly used in group activities, such as sharing materials, turn taking, helping one another, and encouraging others.
- **Student reflection and goal setting.** At the end of a cooperative activity, students evaluate how the group functioned and whether the group's goals were met.

Individual tutoring is generally recognized as the optimal instructional method for meeting the needs of students who are struggling academically (D'Agostino & Murphy, 2004; Ehri, Dreyer, Flugman, & Gross, 2007; Vaughn, Gersten, & Chard, 2000). Of course, the drawback to this method is that it is very labor intensive and expensive. To reduce costs, some schools have rearranged the school day to allow teachers to provide tutoring just before or after school. Others have trained tutors (e.g., parent volunteers, teacher education students from local universities) to work with students during or after school hours.

**Peer-tutoring** programs, widely used and cost-effective, often focus on after-school tutoring in subject areas for middle or high school students or tutoring in basic skills areas (e.g., reading and math) for elementary students. These programs use same-age peers or cross-age arrangements, typically older students tutoring younger students. Interestingly, well-designed tutoring programs result in improved educational outcomes for both the tutor and the tutee who is struggling to learn academic content (Elbaum, Vaughn, Hughes, & Moody, 1999; Fuchs, Fuchs, & Burish, 2000; Mathes, Howard, Babyak, & Allen, 2000; Vaughn et al., 2000).

Well-designed peer-tutoring activities result in improved outcomes for those who both give and receive assistance.

### Presenting Content

The effective presentation of new content typically begins with an overview, or **advance organizer**, of the activities students will do and how they fit contextually with previous and future lessons and units. Once this initial review is completed, instruction on new content begins with an explicit demonstration of target concepts, facts, skills, or principles. Lecturing is a primary way of presenting information in content classes. However, effective teachers often introduce demonstrations from students and frequently check for student understanding by providing opportunities to respond (e.g., unison and individual responding).

To engage students during instruction, it is critical that teachers question students in ways that match the specific goals of the lesson for the individual student (Rosenberg et al., 2006). For example, depending on the goal of the lesson for the student, questions range from factual knowledge and comprehension to higher-order demands such as application, analysis, integration, and evaluation of information. Equally important is how teachers provide feedback to students. Effective teachers typically respond to students' correct answers with statements that paraphrase or elaborate on the content. When responses are incorrect, teachers provide additional cues and corrective feedback.

## Opportunities for Practice

**Guided practice** is characterized by closely supervised activities in which the teacher uses prompts, cues, and feedback to shape fluent student performance. However, as students begin to acquire the content of a lesson, teachers begin to fade their level of prompts and focus on fast, accurate, and fluent responding. In many lessons, the shift from presenting content to guided practice is often indistinguishable; the most important factor is that students have numerous opportunities to practice the content of the lesson. Examples of effective guided practice activities include unison responding (groups of students responding to a single request simultaneously), having several students solving a problem on the board, and having groups of students working together cooperatively to illustrate a specific concept or operation (Rosenberg et al., 2006).

**Independent practice** follows success with guided practice, when students are ready to work toward greater fluency through activities such as seatwork and homework. Although independent practice can be addressed through instructional games and cooperative learning activities, seatwork is the most frequently used form of independent practice; students spend as much as 70% of their day in such activities.

## FIGURE 5.3 • HOMEWORK: GUIDELINES FOR TEACHERS TO ENSURE EFFECTIVE PRACTICE

1. The amount of homework should differ based on the student's grade level.
   Grades 1–3: three or four assignments per week, lasting 10–30 minutes each
   Grades 4–6: three or four assignments per week, lasting 40–60 minutes each
   Middle school: four or five assignments per week, lasting 70–90 minutes each
   High school: four or five assignments per week, lasting 100–120 minutes each
2. Homework for students with disabilities should be similar to homework completed by others.
3. The purpose of homework should be clear to students and their parents:
   Practice information already learned
   Elaborate on information already learned
   Prepare to learn new information
4. Homework should be work that the student can complete independently and include both mandatory and voluntary assignments.
5. The role of the parent in homework is to create a positive home environment for completing homework.
6. Feedback should be provided for all homework that is completed.

Source: Adapted from Cooper, 2001; Cooper & Nye, 1994; Marzano et al., 2001.

Consequently, it is essential that teachers prepare independent seatwork effectively. According to Gaffney (1987), successful teachers

- Develop and assign independent seatwork activities that are age-appropriate, attractive, organized, and directly related to the goals and objectives of their lessons
- Preface seatwork with instructions that are clear and succinct
- Design seatwork with multiple response formats
- Ensure that the activities can be completed with a high degree of success and that provisions are made for students to check the accuracy of their responses

Once students demonstrate proficiency with specific concepts and operations, independent practice activities can be given as homework assignments. Like seatwork, homework is most helpful when teachers adhere to certain guidelines (Cooper, 2001; Marzano, Pickering, & Pollock, 2001). However, when assigning homework, keep in mind that for younger students homework is a method to foster positive attitudes toward school and to develop desirable work habits; for older students the main goal is to provide additional practice opportunities to reinforce skills acquired in class. Consequently, homework should not be used to punish students or to replace school-based instruction (see Figure 5.3).

## Monitoring Student Performance

When teachers monitor student academic progress and make changes in instruction based on this progress (or lack of progress), student academic achievement improves (L. Fuchs, 2004; Jenkins, Graff, & Miglioretti, 2009). Teachers monitor their students by directly observing them performing academically (e.g., reading orally, completing math problems, conducting a science experiment), administering quizzes and exams, and analyzing independent assignments and homework. Teachers also receive summative, long-term

Teachers who monitor student academic work and adjust instruction accordingly typically see improvements in student performance.

feedback from standardized tests. Unfortunately, many teachers do not have readily available information to monitor the effectiveness of instruction on a daily or weekly basis, data needed to make decisions about changes in instruction (e.g., reteaching a basic skill or concept).

A system of classroom assessment called **curriculum-based measurement (CBM)** can help address this shortcoming (Deno, 1985, 2003; L. Fuchs, 2004). CBM is a simple, easy-to-use approach for assessing student progress in academic content areas over time. Compared to other procedures that monitor student progress, CBM has the following advantages (Deno, 2003; L. Fuchs, 2004; Overton, 2009):

- It allows teachers to select skills measured based on the curriculum being taught.
- It is quick and efficient, taking 1 to 3 minutes.
- It is used to plan student instruction (e.g., identifying specific skill deficits to reteach).
- It compares the progress of students as needed.
- Teachers can modify instructional methods to facilitate better academic achievement.

## Using Technology to Support Instruction

Technology continues to greatly influence instruction at all levels of education. Two types of technology are commonly used in educational setting: instructional technology and assistive technology. **Instructional technology (IT)** is hardware- and software-designed to enhance teaching and learning in your current courses (Edyburn, 2000). Instructional technology is so pervasive (applications of Blackboard, PowerPoint presentations, etc.) that some teachers view it as distracting, overwhelming, and a "solution in search of a problem." To avoid such a situation, teachers should evaluate each piece of hardware or software, keeping the following questions in mind (Edyburn, 2000; Higgins, Boone, & Williams, 2000):

1. Is the IT easy to use and based on the principles of effective teaching?
2. Has research been conducted to support the effectiveness of the IT?
3. Does the IT address the objectives that guide your instruction and address the needs of students at different skill levels?
4. Is the IT accessible for students with different types of disabilities (e.g., cognitive, sensory, physical)?

**Assistive technology (AT)** refers to "any item, piece of equipment, or product system, whether acquired commercially off the shelf, modified, or customized, that is used to increase, maintain, or improve the functional capabilities of a child with a disability" (IDEA, 2004, Sec. 620[1]). Recall that IDEA requires that teachers consider AT when planning IEPs for students with disabilities. AT devices used to enhance the performance of students with disabilities include communication boards for persons with limited mobility and devices that translate written words into tactile symbols for persons who read braille (Edyburn, 2002; Westling & Fox, 2009). (Features on how technology is applied to the education of students with specific disabilities, "Technology for Access," appear in Chapters 6 through 15.)

## MANAGING STUDENT BEHAVIOR

Interesting, well-planned, evidence-based lessons are necessary but not sufficient to ensure that students learn required content. Perhaps you recall an instance from your own school experience when a teacher was attempting to teach an interesting lesson, but student disruptions prevented the lesson from proceeding. Situations like this are frustrating to teachers and students alike. Successful teachers recognize that well-planned and motivating lessons reach students only if they are complemented by efficient and positive strategies for managing student behavior.

The following scenario illustrates the importance of classroom management. You are teaching a very interesting lesson on the characteristics of American society that contributed to the birth of rap and hip-hop music. You observe that most of the 10th graders are engaged in the lesson. Why not? You spent more than 3 hours preparing the lesson, carefully selecting a series of recordings by musicians who have influenced generations of adolescents. Moreover, you have tied the music to a time line of significant historical events ranging from civil rights marches to demonstrations against the persistent poverty in urban centers such as Los Angeles and Detroit. Most of the students are truly motivated by the lesson. Still, as he has for several weeks, Sammy Tisch has refused to settle down and attend to the lesson. Even when he chooses to participate in the discussion, he does so in a most inappropriate fashion. He tries to upstage his classmates by ridiculing their opinions, acting like the class clown, and denigrating aspects of your teaching. Sammy disrupts the flow of class by frequently talking out of turn and using suggestive and sometimes profane language. Even more significant, he has yet to hand in an acceptable assignment.

In one form or another, situations like this occur in classrooms. Consequently, teachers' level of anxiety and concern about behavior management, particularly if they are beginning teachers, is quite high. Teachers often report that the lack of discipline is a serious problem in their local school and that student misbehavior interferes with their teaching (Gonzalez, Brown, & Slate, 2008; Langdon, 1999; National Center for Education Statistics, 2002). This need not be the case: Along with teaching students to acquire content, teachers can minimize classroom disruptions by managing and directing the complex interrelationships among structure, expectations, and student behaviors.

Fortunately, most school and classroom misbehavior is related to a few well-defined factors, including inattention to task, crowd control issues during transitions, getting work accomplished in a timely fashion, and students' trying to be cool by testing the limits (Ashford, Queen, Algozzine, & Mitchell, 2008; Jones & Jones, 2004; Kottler, 2002). Common misbehaviors include tardiness, disrespect, being unprepared, talking, calling out, and mild, infrequent varieties of verbal and physical acting out. Many of these behaviors can be prevented through proactive structuring of the school and classroom environment; behaviors that are not prevented typically stop when they are brought to the attention of teachers, administrators, and/or parents. However, some students go beyond these mild forms of challenging behavior and repeatedly disrupt the flow of school and classroom events, respond defiantly when asked to participate appropriately in activities, and hurt others both physically and emotionally when frustrated. The number of such students and the frequency of their behaviors often vary according to the levels of structure and consistency in the school and individual classrooms.

Just as they plan and provide academic supports for instruction, teachers like Bobby Biddle take an active role in ensuring that student behavior is managed in a systematic, proactive, and positive fashion. When we use the term *systematic,* we mean that discipline and behavior-management activities

## REFLECTIVE EXERCISE

#5 Discipline and behavior-management issues tend to elicit considerable anxiety among beginning teachers. Think of a teacher you have observed who managed the classroom in a calm, positive, and effective manner. Do you have dispositions that will help you manage student behavior in your classroom?

Behavior management is a major anxiety-producing concern for many beginning teachers.

are well-planned interrelated actions within the complex and complicated ecosystems of schools and classrooms. There is no easily accessed bag of tricks for managing schools and classrooms; effective discipline and behavior management require logical, logistical, and careful thinking in a comprehensive fashion.

Being *proactive* refers to specific actions taken to prevent or minimize the frequency or intensity of problem behaviors. Proactive measures can be as simple as organizing high-traffic areas of the classroom to minimize disruptions or as sophisticated as developing and prompting specific procedures to maintain order in the lunchroom or during recess.

Finally, when we talk of being *positive,* we are addressing the attitude that accompanies discipline and behavior-management activities. Rather than emphasizing the punitive side of a classroom discipline, having a positive behavior-management system—often referred to as positive behavior support (PBS)—allows the teacher to encourage appropriate student behavior by providing explicit standards, supports to assist students in meeting those standards, and recognition for doing what is expected.

## The Three Tiers of Systematic Behavior Management

The first step in developing a systematic, proactive, and positive behavior-management system in your school and classroom is recognizing the three tiers of behavior management (Lewis & Sugai, 1999; Robertson & Lane, 2007; Rosenberg & Jackman, 2003; Walker et al., 1996). The first level, *inclusive proactive management activities* (see Figure 5.4), focuses on enhancing preventive and protective factors in a way that encourages students to meet behavioral expectations. At this inclusive or universal level, the learning environment is organized by developing a statement of purpose, rules, procedures, and consequences for appropriate and inappropriate behavior. Moreover, parent and family involvement, crisis procedures, and the physical environment are structured in ways that promote student success. By having a consistent set of rules, expectations, procedures, and consequences, consistency in the application of discipline procedures is increased, and the frequency of students requiring more intensive interventions is reduced.

Even with the best plan and activities for this first inclusive level of behavior management, some students cannot or will not respond with appropriate behavior. Students with chronic and sustained levels of problem behaviors will require more intensive and targeted interventions and support. Typically, these targeted secondary interventions require specialized academic enhancements and accommodations as well as individually tailored behavior-change initiatives, including social skills instruction, self-monitoring, and the teaching of appropriate replacement behaviors. Interventions at the third tier of the model are most appropriate for students whose behaviors are severely involved, frequently antisocial, and very difficult to change. Teachers are not alone with these students: Collaborative, wraparound, interagency cooperation is at the core of these interventions, and a major goal of educators is connecting students and their families with the appropriate community-based social service agencies (Walker et al., 1996).

Keep in mind that the implementation of systematic, comprehensive behavior-management systems is a prime example of an evidence-based intervention that is a suggested practice for our nation's schools and classrooms. In fact, both *Early Warning, Timely Response: A Guide to Safe Schools* (Dwyer, Osher, & Warger, 1998) and *Safeguarding Our Children: An Action Guide* (Dwyer & Osher, 2000), two federally funded guides for violence prevention in schools, strongly recommend that schools build a supportive school-wide foundation to meet the behavioral needs of all students. This is due in large part to the positive outcomes reported by program developers in large numbers of project schools.

**REFLECTIVE EXERCISE**

#6 Why is it important to begin systematic behavior management efforts at the primary or universal level? Why not start with intensive interventions that address the needs of students who are acting out?

FIGURE 5.4 • **INCLUSIVE SUPPORT MODEL**

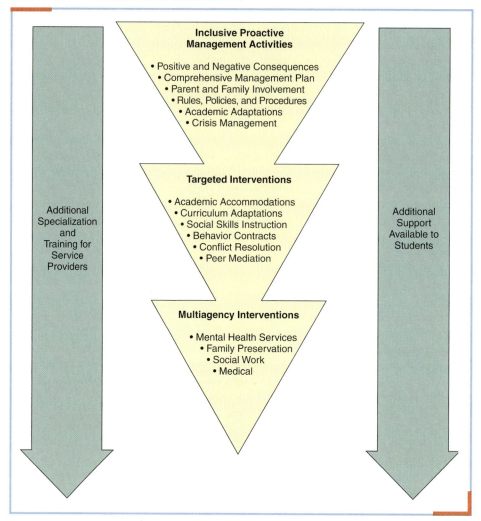

Source: Adapted from Nelson, 1996; Rosenberg & Jackman, 1997; and Walker et al., 1996. Reprinted with permission of PRO-ED, Inc.

## Inclusive Behavior-Management Practices

Three factors are at the core of effective inclusive management practices: (1) the design of the physical environment; (2) the quality of classroom organization and instruction; and (3) the elements of the tangible management plan.

### Design of Physical Environment

Where we place students' desks, how we organize frequently used materials, and where we designate free-time zones all impact student behavior. Moreover, the relationship between the physical environment and student responses is especially pronounced for students with disabilities, because they typically require additional structure in all aspects of their education. Guides, strategies, and checklists (e.g., Algozzine, Ysseldyke, & Elliot, 1998; Evertson et al., 2005; Paine, Radicci, Rosellini, Deutchman, & Darch, 1983; Rosenberg et al., 2006) have been developed that focus on specific areas including (1) arranging public and private space; (2) ensuring easy line of vision; (3) access, care, and storage of materials; and (4) aesthetics. Table 5.2 contains strategies for arranging the classroom to facilitate appropriate behavior.

TABLE 5.2 • ARRANGING THE CLASSROOM TO MINIMIZE PROBLEM BEHAVIORS

| Areas | Strategies and Actions |
|---|---|
| Arrange public and private space | • Provide areas for group work, individual work, and free activity time.<br>• Limit exposure to potential distracters such as windows, free-time area, and displays, particularly for those with attention-deficit issues.<br>• Keep high-traffic areas free of unnecessary congestion by locating commonly visited stations (e.g., pencil sharpener, lavatory pass, assignment in-box) in separate areas of the classroom.<br>• Use furniture, bookcases, and dividers to facilitate flow of student movement.<br>• Have a fixed yet flexible seating arrangement for students, and make sure that low-ability students are close to the action.<br>• Open spaces with no clear purpose should be avoided. |
| Ensure easy lines of vision | • Ensure that students can see key elements of instruction (e.g., the teacher, aide, chalkboard).<br>• Arrange the classroom to keep all areas of the room in full view. |
| Materials and supplies: Access, care, and storage | • Allow for easy access to supplies and materials to facilitate transitions between and among activities.<br>• Keep frequently used materials within easy reach by making use of learning centers, activity stations, or other similarly designated areas. |
| Aesthetics | • Post content-appropriate bulletin board displays.<br>• Provide ample opportunities to showcase student work.<br>• When possible, ensure that lighting is appropriate and that the room is not uncomfortably hot or cold.<br>• Highlight a policy of room care by regularly scheduling opportunities for students to keep the room neat and clean.<br>• Allow students to make part of the room their own; designate specific areas of the room for students to share their hobbies and interests. |

Source: Adapted from Evertson et al., 2005; Paine et al., 1983; and Rosenberg et al., 2006.

## Organization and Effective Instruction

When a teacher is well organized, seemingly trivial matters are less likely to escalate into time-consuming classroom-management challenges. Consider how key teacher-based organizers, such as transition cues, routines and procedures, and coordination of resources, can minimize misbehavior. Transitions, the unavoidable by-products of busy classrooms, tend to cause disruptions because students, required to switch locations and activities, are not engaged in a specific task. Organized teachers facilitate efficient transitions by directly teaching students how to transition: (1) breaking the transition down into specific steps or components; (2) modeling appropriate ways of moving step-by-step through the transition; (3) asserting control in various transition activities; and (4) using a range of group and individual cues to signal transitions (Rosenberg et al., 2006).

**Routines and procedures** help teachers orchestrate everyday tasks and activities with efficiency and effectiveness. When taught, prompted, and reinforced, explicit guides for morning arrival, dismissal, going to the lavatory, and entering the cafeteria decrease minor disruptive behaviors. As with transitions, specific steps for routines and procedures guide students through the often complicated processes associated with completing a task. Moreover, supports such as self-monitoring sheets and peer-buddy systems help those students who have difficulty following established procedures (see Figure 5.5).

To enhance your understanding of how a teacher can set and maintain rules and procdeures in the classroom, go to the IRIS Center Resources section of Topic 6: Classroom/Behavior Management in the MyEducationLab for your course and complete the Case Study entitled *Norms and Expectations*.

FIGURE 5.5 • **SAMPLE PROCEDURES FOR AVOIDING DISRUPTIVE EVENTS**

*Cafeteria Procedures*
**C**ARE **A**BOUT **F**OOD & **E**NJOY lunch!
- Join the END of ONE line, ONE time.
- Sit in your assigned area.
- Respect each other's space, feelings, and property.
- Use appropriate language and tone.
- Dispose of waste correctly when you're finished eating. (Remember to recycle your aluminum cans in the bins!)
- Remain silent during dismissal.
- Follow hallway procedures when returning to class.

*Morning Arrival Procedures*
- Go directly to your locker.
- Take all supplies needed for your morning classes.
- Put hats and other personal items in your locker.
- If you eat breakfast in school, report directly to the cafeteria.
- Report directly to homeroom by the warning bell.
- Upon arrival to homeroom, complete your morning log.
- Listen quietly to morning announcements.

*Arrival to and Dismissal from Class Procedures*
- Be seated when bell rings, and begin working on warmup.
- After completing warmup, wait quietly for teacher to begin.
- The teacher directs preparation for dismissal.
- When given the signal, clean up your workspace and pack your book bag.
- When bell rings, wait for teacher to dismiss the class.
- Walk safely, quickly, and quietly to your next class.

When we speak of coordinating resources to prevent the occurrence of misbehavior, we are referring to several organizational, up-front procedures that increase the opportunities for disruption-free instruction. Two of these resources help during particularly stressful times: (1) Keep a list, complete with names and phone numbers, of the school and community resources available to assist you when faced with difficult behavior-management situations; and (2) prepare a substitute-teacher packet that includes building-policy information, behavior-management plans, daily lesson plans, alternative activities, specific student information, and classroom procedural information (Platt, 1987).

A major prerequisite to the success of any systematic approach to behavior management is that motivating, effective instruction is occurring on a consistent basis. Some students, such as Sammy Tisch, described earlier, encounter repeated frustration with academic content and how it is presented, and may find it more acceptable to act out rather than "act dumb." For understandable developmental reasons, it is much easier for unsuccessful learners to tell peers that they are goofing on a teacher rather than explaining that they are clueless about how to respond to the content presented. So what does this mean in terms of a teacher's behavior-management system? Clearly, a catalog of specific instructional accommodations, supports, and content enhancements, like the ones presented in the first part of this chapter, are part of a management toolkit. Those students who can access and interact with the instructional content are less likely to act up because they will be able to "act smart" and receive the internal satisfaction that accompanies a task well done. Moreover, with an emphasis on instruction, classroom management is directed at the modification of educational factors that directly influence academic productivity, sustaining the role of teachers as specialists in learning responsible for promoting academic gains in the classroom (Witt, VanDerHeyden, & Gilbertson, 2004).

## Elements of the Tangible Management Plan

What should be included in a comprehensive behavior-management plan, and how should these elements be presented to students, their family members, and our related-service colleagues? Five core elements contribute to successful plans: (1) mission or statement of purpose; (2) explicit rules, procedures, and supports; (3) consequences for appropriate and inappropriate behavior; (4) a crisis-management plan; and (5) a document that describes the plan (Curwin & Mendler, 1988; Lewis & Sugai, 1999; Nelson, 1996; Rosenberg & Jackman, 2003; Walker, Colvin, & Ramsey, 1995).

**Mission, or Statement of Purpose.** When we speak of a mission, or statement of purpose, we are referring to a brief declaration that asserts an approach to teaching and learning with a particular emphasis on expected school and classroom behavior. The statement should have a positive focus and reflect a respect for the dignity of all students and a commitment to helping students perform to their highest level (White, 1996).

**Explicit Rules, Procedures, and Supports.** Explicit rules and procedures allow us to communicate behavioral standards and expectations to all in the school or classroom community. Rules define what is and is not acceptable behavior; procedures delineate the specific steps required for the successful completion of a task, activity, or operation. We cannot overstate the importance of well-articulated rules and procedures, particularly for students with disabilities who need supports. Well-defined, succinct rules and procedures promote positive behavior, and teachers who make use of them are regarded as effective classroom managers (Smith & Rivera, 1995).

Teachers have found the following general guidelines useful for developing rules and procedures (Curwin & Mendler, 1988; Evertson et al., 1983; Paine et al., 1983; Rosenberg et al., 2006; Walker et al., 1995).

- Identify behaviors expected of students. Use action-based terminology to define behaviors necessary for success in your school and classroom.
- Limit the number of rules, and keep the language positive and jargon-free. Typically four to six jargon-free rules are enough to cover the range of typically desired behaviors.
- Generate a menu of procedural events. Conduct a task analysis, and develop step-by-step, student-based actions for successful completion of daily events (lavatory, cafeteria, entry to class, dismissal).
- Have a solid rationale for each of your rules and procedures. Relate the need for each rule and procedure back to how following the rules and procedures promotes success.
- Involve students in the development and teaching of rules and procedures. Let students illustrate positive and negative examples of rule and procedure compliance.
- Keep rules posted in several visible areas. Displays of rules and procedures are powerful cues for desired behavior and often prompt students to exhibit positive behaviors with limited teacher direction.
- Teach, practice, reteach, and practice again. Rules and procedures need to be taught just like content material in the curriculum. Teachers should model instances of rule compliance and the performance of specific procedures.
- Provide supports for those students who have difficulty meeting expectations. Rather than changing expectations for those students who have difficulty with rule and procedural compliance, provide accommodations that increase the probability that students will succeed.

**Surface Management and Consequences.** A systematic approach to behavior is built on the foundation that students choose to either comply or not comply with the stated expectations. Not surprisingly, how we respond to their choices has an

### REFLECTIVE EXERCISE

#7 How can a mission statement set the tone for high expectations in a school or classroom? What values and beliefs would you wish to convey in a mission or statement of purpose to the students in your classroom?

PEARSON
**myeducationlab**

Go to the Building Teaching Skills and Dispositions section of Topic 6: Classroom/Behavior Management and complete the learning unit entitled *Establishing Classroom Rules and Routines* to deepen your understanding of this concept.

### REFLECTIVE EXERCISE

#8 Identify student behaviors you believe are essential for success in your classroom. How would you develop these expectations into a set of positive rules and procedures?

enormous impact on the quantity and quality of future student behavior. Typically, teacher responses to student behavior fall into three major categories: surface management techniques, consequences for rule and procedure compliance, and consequences for noncompliance.

**Surface management techniques** refer to a range of measures for dealing with minor instances of misbehavior quickly, efficiently, and, for the most part, with little disruption of ongoing instruction. Although the names for these techniques may seem novel and unusual, in action they will seem recognizable. As you review several of the surface management techniques presented in Table 5.3, consider which of the techniques would work best for common disruptive behaviors.

Consequences are planned, teacher-based actions that follow students' behaviors, both appropriate and inappropriate (Curwin & Mendler, 1999). Therefore, consequences are not used exclusively as punishment for rule infractions; effective consequences also allow for recognition of students when they follow rules and procedures. Effective consequences are functional, meaning that they should result in changes in student behavior. Unfortunately, some consequences, particularly those that address student misbehavior, are applied out of anger and frustration, with little thought for their impact on student behavior.

Why is it important to look at the impact of consequences on the frequency and intensity of student behavior? Consider the common situation of sending students to the office for one of any number of possible rule infractions. Although it may be difficult to fully grasp, some students may feel better off with a trip to the office than having to complete assignments in class. Consider what goes on while they are in the office. While waiting to see the assistant principal in charge of discipline, they get to observe the administrative activities and events as well as interact with the many people who come and go. And, if they can time it correctly, they might even be able to meet friends and

### TABLE 5.3 • SURFACE MANAGEMENT TECHNIQUES

| Technique | How It Works |
| --- | --- |
| Planned ignoring | Similar to the behavioral technique of extinction, planned ignoring is the conscious attempt not to feed into the student's need for immediate gratification. This technique works best for minor behaviors that will fade away if not reinforced. |
| Signal interference | Signal interference is the use of nonverbal gestures, eye contact, noises, and body postures that communicate to students that their behavior is not appropriate. |
| Proximity control | Proximity control is when the adult uses close presence to deter behaviors of concern. |
| Interest boosting | Interest boosting is a direct intervention used to reenergize a student's flagging interest by noting the challenging nature of the activity or indicating personal interest in the content. |
| Tension decontamination through humor | This involves the diplomatic use of humor, often the self-deprecating type, to reduce a tense or anxiety-filled situation. When in doubt of the value of the humorous comment to be made, don't make it. |
| Antiseptic bouncing | Antiseptic bouncing is a technique used to safely remove a student from a potentially serious behavioral event in a nonpunitive fashion (e.g., delivering a message, washing up). Care should be taken not to use antiseptic bouncing so often as to allow students to realize that, by acting up, they can get out of ongoing activities. |

fool around even more in the bustling office! How does all of this relate to consequences? In brief, if office referrals are not planned correctly, it is possible they can actually increase instances of negative behavior rather than decrease them.

One more cautionary note regarding consequences: When delivering consequences, it is essential to maintain an educative rather than vindictive disposition. Sometimes events in the classroom anger and frustrate teachers. Instead of presenting consequences in a thoughtful manner, they are delivered in a vengeful, almost menacing fashion. Rather than looking to alter student misbehavior, a teacher's immediate reaction may be to get back at the student. These situations can be minimized by sustaining a professional manner, attending to feelings regularly, and recognizing that it is part of your responsibility to keep frustration and resentment in check (Curwin & Mendler, 1999).

Effective teachers respond to student misbehavior in an educative and thoughtful manner, keeping any frustration and resentment in check.

Many teachers choose to recognize appropriate behavior with tangible yet natural recognitions such as certificates, notes home, phone calls home, free time, and homework passes. Students can also be recognized by having the honor of being the first to go for lunch, helping the teacher grade papers, tutoring younger students, and serving as a messenger for the librarian. In other cases, teachers can use a series of novel techniques to recognize the entire class based on the behavior of all of its members. For example, "gotta have it" cards (see Figure 5.6), mystery motivators, and lottery systems allow teachers to respond to positive behavior in a strong, intermittent fashion. Still, when selecting positive consequences, you should exercise caution and choose recognitions that are age appropriate, correspond to students' levels of functioning, and do not inadvertently deprive students of their basic rights (Rhode et al., 1998). No student should have to earn access to lunch, the lavatory, or, in some cases, field trips that are provided to all students.

To decrease the frequency and intensity of problem behaviors, effective teachers develop a hierarchy of negative consequences. Consider the following negative-consequence hierarchy developed collectively by the teachers of Stratford Landing Elementary School in Fairfax, Virginia:

- **Level 1.** Surface management techniques (see Table 5.3).
- **Level 2.** Class reminders, restate rules, praise those complying.
- **Level 3.** Verbal reminder specific to individual student.
- **Level 4.** Take-a-break within classroom. (Allow the student to have quiet time and rejoin group when ready; work missed is to be made up.)
- **Level 5.** Teacher-directed time-out. (The student makes up all missed work during portion of recess or free time.)
- **Level 6.** Reflection time in class or in buddy teacher's room. (Student [1] completes an age- or grade-level-appropriate reflection sheet, [2] has a private conference with teacher, and [3] completes a back-to-class activity that focuses on work missed when out of class. Parent will be contacted after a second reflection-time consequence during each marking period.)
- **Level 7.** Administrative/office referral. (The student brings the referral sheet and any previous reflection forms to the office. The parent is contacted, and an action plan for change in behavior is generated.)
- **Note.** Some inappropriate behaviors (e.g., fighting, bullying, bringing contraband to school) will result in immediate referral to the office and possible suspension from school.

FIGURE 5.6 • **GOTTA HAVE IT CARD**

Have you got IT? - No?
Well, here's how to get IT?
Why? Because you Gotta

Students will be rewarded for a variety of behaviors on a school-wide basis through the "Gotta Have It Cards":

- Get your Gotta Have It Card from your homeroom teacher.
- Immediately write your full name and homeroom on the back of the card to make it valid.
- Students are responsible for holding onto their cards and presenting them on request. (Stay alert for teachers asking for the Gotta Have It Card throughout your school day.)
- Collect teacher stamps by showing all teachers how well you follow the rules.
- Once your card is filled it can be deposited in drawing containers or used to purchase admission to a variety of activities that will be announced.

Examples of behaviors that the Gotta Have It Card may be used for:

**Hallway behaviors:** - Teachers recognizing compliance with rules during hallway movement will stamp the card of students and verbally acknowledge the behavior.

**Attendance:** - Monthly, homeroom teachers will stamp the cards of students who have had perfect attendance for that month.

**Uniform compliance:** - Teachers tracking compliance of wearing the school uniform daily will stamp cards on Fridays to indicate compliance for an entire week. Attendance is necessary.

Source: Adapted from Deer Park Middle School (1998) PAR manual.

The presence of a hierarchy does not mean that every step must be used every time a student acts out. Successful teachers usually apply the least intrusive, most natural intervention that matches the student's behavior. The hierarchy serves as a guide and allows for a graduated response to differing rates and intensities of behavior.

**Crisis Management.** Consider the saying "An ounce of prevention is worth a pound of cure." Although most teachers will not have to deal with behaviors that threaten the safety of staff or students, having basic information on how to address such rare occurrences can be valuable. The most frightening part of a crisis situation is that the student involved appears to have little or no control over his or her behavior. Consequently, surface management techniques and consequences have little or no effect. When a crisis occurs, the teacher's initial task is to help get the student through the crisis in a safe, nonthreatening, and nonpunitive fashion and maintain the safety of others. When dealing with the crisis, you should not exceed your level of expertise. Note that crisis intervention differs from crisis management in that it requires a series of actions from counselors, psychologists, and certified crisis personnel. Nonetheless, all teachers should know how to manage a crisis situation. The ideal course of action is for each school to develop a crisis response team of four or five people trained in both verbal intervention techniques and safe, nonaversive methods of physical restraint (Johns & Carr, 1995). However, you may be in a school without a proper-functioning team. When required to manage crisis situations, do the following (Albert, 2003; Johns & Carr, 1995; V. Jones & Jones, 2004):

- Remain calm and send someone for assistance.
- Guard against body language and punitive, confrontational verbalizations that can escalate the situation.
- Be aware of the safety needs of other students.
- Have a plan for reentry after the crisis.

**Promoting Access to the Plan.** Once a comprehensive behavior-management plan is conceptualized, you will want to disseminate it to students, their families, administrators, and related-service providers. Some school-wide teams and individual teachers create full-sized manuals that articulate rather completely the major components (mission statement, rules, procedures, consequences) of the management plan. Others have developed user-friendly brochures that highlight the major components of the plan. Figure 5.7 provides an example of a brochure produced by the teachers of William Halley Elementary School as part of their participation in the PAR project at Johns Hopkins University (Rosenberg & Jackman, 2003).

## Targeted and Wraparound Interventions

To address the needs of students who do not respond to inclusive management structures, teachers and school personnel apply targeted interventions and wraparound interventions. **Targeted interventions** are powerful, school-based actions

FIGURE 5.7 • **HALLEY BROCHURE**

| Halley School Rules STARS | Positive Behavior Recognition | Hierarchy of Consequences |
|---|---|---|
| **S**ucceed<br>Stay on task. Try your best and put forth your best effort. Be prepared for class.<br><br>**T**hink<br>Think safety first. Think of how others feel. Think of yourself. Think before you act.<br><br>**Attitude**<br>Follow directions the first time they are given. Use appropriate language and tone. Be on time. Build up, no put-downs.<br><br>**R**espect<br>Respect each other's space, feelings, and property. Show respect for adults. Respect yourself. Take responsibility for your own actions.<br><br>**S**oar<br>Set goals. Go beyond expectations. Reach for the stars. | • Smiles<br>• Stickers<br>• Happy Notes<br>• Star Bookmarks<br>• Character awards<br>• Specialist awards<br>• Bus awards<br>• Cafeteria awards<br>• Happy phone call home<br>• Special privileges<br>• Lunch with an adult<br>• Special treats<br>• Tokens<br>• Games or activities<br>• Each teacher has developed a specific plan to reward positive behavior in his or her classroom. Be sure to ask your teacher about the reward program in your child's classroom. | • Nonverbal Cues<br>• General Classroom Reminders<br>• Student-Specific Warning<br>• Time-out in Classroom<br>• Time-out in Another Classroom<br>• Parent Contact<br>• After-School Detention<br>• Guidance Referral<br>• Office Referral*<br>• CT Button*<br><br>* Parents may be notified at any level, depending on the severity of the situation or problem.<br><br>* Some inappropriate student behavior may warrant immediate use of more severe consequences. |

Source: Adapted from William Halley Elementary School (2001) brochure.

directed toward the chronic, repetitive, and pervasive problem behaviors of individual students (Scott et al., 2009; Walker et al., 1995). These interventions are typically dynamic, simultaneously strengthening appropriate behavior as they weaken the presenting challenging behaviors. **Wraparound interventions** are even more intensive, typically requiring the structured, coordinated, and integrated efforts of a team of professionals (Eber, Sugai, Smith, & Scott, 2002). How are targeted and wraparound interventions designed? The most direct method is to complete a three-stage process that includes (1) conducting functional behavioral assessments (FBAs.), (2) developing behavior intervention plans (BIPs), and (3) evaluating the effectiveness of intervention. Details on conducting an FBA and specific applications of these processes are illustrated in subsequent chapters of this text.

When developing interventions to address the needs of students who exhibit extreme problem behaviors, remember that you are not alone. Typically, the school will convene a team of specialists from human service backgrounds to develop a comprehensive intervention. Many schools have administrators, behavior specialists, counselors, social workers, psychologists, and behavior-support teams that implement specialized programs of outreach and intervention. For example, it is not unusual for counseling and guidance personnel to deliver family-support interventions or for school psychologists to have social-skills training groups and short-term individual therapy sessions for high-need students. Outside the school, students can be "wrapped around" by services from physicians, mental health service providers, family-preservation personnel, and state protective-service officers, juvenile justice personnel, and even law-enforcement officers. Services should be grounded in values that emphasize family empowerment, cultural competence, flexibility, and the strengths of the child and family. (We provide descriptions of wraparound programs in Chapter 7.)

# PREVAILING ISSUES, CONTROVERSIES, AND IMPLICATIONS FOR THE TEACHER

Although considerable progress has been made on how to effectively address the academic and behaviors needs of students with disabilities (and their peers without disabilities), several critical issues continue to challenge educators and policy makers. In this section, we discuss two of the more prominent issues—teaching content to students with severe disabilities and disproportionate behavior management referrals for certain groups of students.

## Content Area Instruction for Students with Severe Disabilities

Should students with severe disabilities participate in the general education curriculum and be provided content area instruction? Cognizant of the many academic, behavioral, and functional challenges these students experience, many teachers are not supportive of their increased participation in the general education curriculum. In fact, until recently, many educators assumed that individuals whose measured intelligence fell below an IQ of 55 were incapable of content area learning. For an increasing number of teachers, this thinking has changed: Although students with severe disabilities will not acquire academic skills approximating the level of students without disabilities, research has shown that many can benefit from access to the general education curriculum and strategically enhanced content instruction (Browder & Spooner, 2006). Access to such instruction broadens curriculum options, increases expectations for achievement, develops academic skills, and promotes important social opportunities with their peers who do not have disabilities. Encouraged by recent research and spurred on by federal legislation requiring an increased focus on academic instruction, teachers now are expected to provide content area instruction at some level for students with severe disabilities (Westling & Fox, 2009).

# THE REAL WORLD challenges and solutions

## What is an evidence-based practice?

*After successfully implementing school-wide positive behavior support procedures (e.g., Lewis & Sugai, 1999; Rosenberg & Jackman, 2003; White et al., 2001), Mr. Sal Piscano and the professional development committee of Land of Lakes Middle School decided to focus on ways to support students who were not responding to the universal interventions. Land of Lakes had been approached by a group urging adoption of a character education curriculum. Although it sounded great, Mr. Piscano and his team were reminded by their principal that any new program implemented in the district had to be evidence based. The professional development team wanted to select a program that worked but were unsure about several important details. What does the term evidence based really mean in relation to curriculum and educational practices? Who makes these decisions, and how are such determinations made? More important, are any resources available that list and describe evidence-based practices?*

Many teachers adopt programs and employ practices based more on fads, bandwagons, and anecdote, usually with dismal results (Yell & Drasgow, 2005). Consequently, policy makers have urged educators to use scientific-based research to guide decisions on interventions. Unfortunately, many teachers share the uncertainty of Mr. Piscano: They are unaware of how best to distinguish evidence-based practices from those that are not, and they do not know where to turn for descriptions of effective interventions. Fortunately, the Institute of Education Sciences of the U.S. Department of Education (2003) provides advice. In general, an intervention is considered backed by strong evidence if there is a clear description of intervention components and participants in the research are randomly assigned to experimental and control groups. The research should also contain valid outcome measures that assess sustained changes in performance, typically in multiple sites. Finally, conventional statistical measures including indices of effect size should be included in the data analyses.

Six user-friendly questions developed by the Johns Hopkins University Center for Data-Driven Reform in Education (CDDRE, 2009) can help teachers determine if an intervention program is evidence based:

1. Was the program compared to a control group? ( ) yes ( ) no
2. Was the study at least 12 weeks in duration? ( ) yes ( ) no
3. Were the program and control groups equivalent in performance at the time of the pretest? ( ) yes ( ) no
4. Was the posttest a valid test (e.g., standardized or state accountability) rather than inherent to the intervention? ( ) yes ( ) no
5. Were positive effects found in at least two studies with a sample of at least 5 classes and 125 students per treatment group? ( ) yes ( ) no
6. Across all studies, was the average advantage of the intervention group at least 20% of 1 standard deviation over the control group? ( ) yes ( ) no

In addition to conducting an evaluation, teachers can also access Website listings of interventions that have been found to be supported by evidence. Among the more useful listings are:

- **The What Works Clearinghouse** (www.w-w-c.org): Established by the U.S. Department of Education to serve as an independent and trusted source of scientific information.
- **The Best Evidence Encyclopedia** (www.bestevidence.org): A free Website created by the Johns Hopkins University School of Education's CDDRE designed to provide educators with fair and useful information about the strength of the evidence supporting a variety of programs available for students in grades K–12.
- **Promising Practices Network** (www.promisingpractices.net): Operated by the Rand Corporation, the Website provides evidence-based information about what works to improve the lives of children, youth, and families.

### Valuable Resources for the Teacher

For more information on determining evidence-based practices, consult the following resources:

Cook, B. G., Tankersley, M., & Landrum, T. J. (2009). Determining evidence-based practices in special education. *Exceptional Children, 75*(3), 365–383.

Slavin, R. (2008). Perspectives on evidence-based research in education—What works? Issues in synthesizing educational program evaluations. *Educational Researcher, 37*(1), 5–14.

U.S. Department of Education. (2003). *Identifying and implementing educational practices supported by rigorous evidence: A user friendly guide*. Washington, DC: Author.

### Final Thoughts

Educators generally accept that increased awareness and use of evidence-based practices have the potential to substantially improve educational practice (Slavin, 2008). Knowledge of user-friendly guides and published descriptions of evidence-based practices can assist teachers like Mr. Piscano as they seek out and evaluate specific programs and interventions to meet the needs of their students. Keep in mind, however, that what makes an intervention evidence based is complicated and not without limitations. Under the best of conditions, randomized controlled experiments are difficult to conduct in school settings. Consider the logistical difficulties in randomly assigning students in several grades to different programs. Moreover, interventions geared to low-incidence populations of students with disabilities are nearly impossible to conduct using randomized designs and often require specialized single-subject quasi-experimental research. Reliance on overly rigorous randomized trials as the only standard creates the risk that very few special education practices will have the opportunity to demonstrate strong evidence (Cook et al., 2009). What does all of this mean for teachers like Mr. Piscano and for you? Be an educated consumer of educational interventions, and look for the presence of high-quality research-supported programs. Look for randomized controlled evidence, but also be aware that legitimate factors may necessitate the use of alternative methods of determining effectiveness.

**PEARSON**
**myeducationlab**

After reading the Real World feature on evidence-based practice, go to the Assignments and Activities section of Topic 7: Instructional Strategies in the MyEducationLab for your course and complete the activity entitled *Evidence-Based Practices in Instruction* to deepen your understanding of this concept.

This type of instruction is not without controversies and challenges. Specifically, no clear understanding exists of what elements of the content instruction must be taught to students with severe disabilities, and methods for delivering content—in both inclusive settings or in separate classrooms—have yet to be validated (Browder & Spooner, 2006). What is known is that teaching content to students with severe disabilities requires many of the same processes used with other students with disabilities. Units and lessons need to be designed and delivered with an understanding of curriculum, collaboration, and instructional methods if all students are to benefit from the instruction. Universal design principles that employ multiple means of presentation, expression, and engagement are necessary if students are to truly participate during lessons (Wehmeyer & Agran, 2006). Finally, working with peer tutors or friends without disabilities increases involvement with the content as well as fosters greater opportunities for social interaction (Carter, Cushing, Clark, & Kennedy, 2005).

## Disproportionate Behavior-Management Referrals

Despite decades of national attention, disproportionately high rates of disciplinary office referrals and suspensions among students who are culturally and linguistically diverse (CLD) are still prevalent (e.g., Day-Vines & Day-Hairston, 2005; Kewal-Ramani et al., 2007). Specifically, an African American student in elementary school is 2.65 times more likely than a white student to receive out-of-school suspension for a minor discipline infraction such as disrespect, work refusal, or classroom disruption; Latino students are 4.68 times more likely than white students to receive a suspension. Unfortunately, many teachers have difficultly recognizing and discussing the possibility of cultural conflicts in their own schools and classrooms (e.g., Gay, 2002; Greenman & Kimmel, 1995), a clear indication that low levels of cultural responsiveness may contribute to some problem behaviors.

Instances of problem behaviors among referred students may be the result of a lack of correspondence between expectations for student behavior and the diverse cultural orientations students bring to their classrooms. In some cases, teachers have only a superficial knowledge of the cultural values of their students, which may lead to a misinterpretation of the intent of behaviors among those who differ in terms of race, sexual orientation, or disability. In other situations, teachers may simply be unaware of how to improve their culturally responsive practices (Scott, Alter, Rosenberg, & Borgmeier, 2009). From the student perspective, students who are CLD may be unable to fully comprehend the culture of their school.

What can be done to enhance cultural understanding? A number of researchers have reported promising practices that integrate culturally responsive pedagogy into school and classroom behavior-management practices (King, Harris-Murri, & Artiles, 2006; Richards, Brown, & Forde, 2006; Weinstein, Tomlinson-Clarke, & Curran, 2004). Still, the major hurdle may not be a shortage of approaches or techniques. Many educators consider discussions of race and culture to be uncomfortable and difficult, and simply avoid them. It may be necessary for teachers and teacher educators to face their discomfort and defensiveness, taking a long hard look at their own values and expectations for their diverse students. Only then can schools make progress in improving the cultural synchronization between teachers and students and in reducing behavioral misunderstanding that leads to referrals and suspensions (Monroe, 2006; Vavrus, 2001).

# 5 SUMMARY

A teacher's major responsibility is to deliver effective instruction in a safe and orderly classroom. To meet this challenge, you must know what to teach, how to apply evidence-based instructional techniques, and how to choose and implement strategies for managing student behavior.

## Communicating Instruction and Behavior Management

- The manner in which we communicate to students, colleagues, and families is equally as important as the technical aspects of instruction and behavior management.
- Strategies that contribute to effective communication of instruction and behavior management include the development of authentic relationships; civility and respect; maintaining credibility and dependability; and being a response-to-intervention (RTI) problem solver.
- Keep things in perspective, and realize that, even with the best of plans, problems occur. How one behaves during stressful situations is a public display of competence.

## General Education Curriculum and Tools Used to Adapt Instruction

- State governments are increasing their influence over the development of the curriculum—that is, the content taught in local schools.
- Most students with disabilities are expected to participate and make progress in some aspects of the general education curriculum.
- Effective teachers use different strategies and tools to adapt curriculum and instruction, including taxonomies, universal design for learning, planning pyramids, and instructional accommodations.

## Major Approaches to Instruction and Systematic Teaching

- Three common approaches for delivering instruction are behavioral, cognitive, and a combination of the two.
- The behavioral approach is most useful for teaching basic skills; cognitive and combined approaches such as the strategies intervention model (SIM) are

useful for teaching problem solving and higher-order content.
- Effective teachers make use of evidence-based practices in the areas of instructional grouping, presenting content, providing opportunities for practice, monitoring student progress, and using technology to support instruction.

## Systematic, Proactive, and Positive Behavior Management

- Well-planned, supportive lessons will fail if behavior-management concerns are neglected; fortunately, most student misbehavior can be addressed by focusing on inattention to task, crowd control, and general testing of limits.
- Effective teachers make use of three tiers of behavior management:
  - Inclusive classroom management practices focus on the prevention of problem behaviors, including the careful design of the physical environment, the quality of instruction, and the clarity of the management plan.
  - Targeted intervention plans are made available for those students who do not respond positively to the universal interventions.
  - Wraparound interventions are for students whose severe and intractable behaviors require community and interagency intervention.
- Well-designed management plans include five elements: a mission statement; rules, procedures, and supports; consequences for appropriate and inappropriate behavior; a crisis plan; and a document that presents the plan.

## Prevailing Issues

- Although many students with severe cognitive disabilities will not acquire academic skills at the levels of students with less severe disabilities, they can benefit from enhanced content instruction.
- A major hurdle in addressing the disproportionate representation of behavioral referrals among culturally diverse students may be the result of educators avoiding these uncomfortable discussions and self-reflections.

## ADDRESSING THE PROFESSIONAL STANDARDS

Council for Exceptional Children (CEC) Knowledge Standards addressed in the chapter:

ICC5K1, ICC5K2, ICC5K3, ICC5K4, ICC5K6, ICC5S10, ICC5S13, ICC7K1, ICC7K3

Appendix B: CEC Knowledge and Skill Standards Common Core has a full listing of the standards referenced here.

## myeducationlab

Now go to Topic 6: Classroom/Behavior Management and Topic 7: Instructional Strategies in the MyEducationLab for your course, where you can:

- Find learning outcomes for the broad concepts covered in this chapter along with the national standards that connect to these outcomes.
- Complete Assignments and Activities that can help you more deeply understand the chapter content.
- Examine challenging situations and cases presented in the IRIS Center Resources.
- Apply and practice your understanding of the core concepts and skills identified in the chapter with the Building Teaching Skills and Dispositions learning units.

- Check your comprehension on the content covered in the chapter by going to the Study Plan in the Book-Specific Resources section for your text. Here you will be able to take a chapter quiz, receive feedback on your answers, and then access Review, Practice, and Enrichment activities to enhance your understanding of chapter content.
- Access video clips of CCSSO National Teachers of the Year award winners responding to the question, "Why Do I Teach?" in the Teacher Talk section.

# Meeting the Multiple Needs of Students with Exceptionalities:

## What Is Effective Practice?

part three

# chapter

# 6

# Learning Disabilities

**REFLECT UPON**

- How are learning disabilities defined?
- What are the characteristics of students with learning disabilities?
- How many students are identified with learning disabilities, and what are the major causes?
- How are students with learning disabilities identified?
- What principles guide effective instruction for students with learning disabilities?
- What are the prevailing controversial issues related to learning disabilities?

Carol Sprague began teaching after completing an undergraduate degree in elementary education. She loved school as a child, always knew she wanted to be a teacher, and has never questioned her decision to become a teacher. She entered teaching because every day is different and a challenge. Teaching for Carol Sprague is not a job but a career.

Carol has taught at both elementary and secondary levels, as both a general and special education teacher. Many of her assignments have been in inclusive settings. For several years Carol has taught in an inclusive elementary classroom.

A typical day in Carol Sprague's classroom begins with a morning meeting in which students share things that have happened to them, learn to know and appreciate one another socially, and get excited about learning. Throughout the day, she strives to connect academic content across the curriculum and make this information applicable to the students' lives. She asks questions to make these connections as well as to encourage students to think deeply and learn about small things in their lives. Carol notes that learning is more fun for students and the teacher and students retain more information if learning is made real for them.

Carol describes her greatest successes as a teacher in relation to individual students. She describes several students, some of whom had learning disabilities, who made significant progress in learning to read during their time in her class and learned to feel successful and confident as readers when they left her class. Interestingly, when asked about the positive impact she has had on her students, she emphasizes the classroom climate and sense of community she has worked to develop. She notes that when she develops a good classroom climate, all students, including low, middle, and high achievers, are supported and make progress in learning the academic content.

An effective teacher for students with learning disabilities, from Carol's perspective, is a teacher who views students as individuals and takes responsibility for each student's learning. She emphasizes that a lack of academic progress should *never* be viewed as the student's fault. Rather, an effective teacher closely monitors student progress, reflects on her practice, examines what could have been done differently, and adapts instruction until the student does make progress. Carol notes that a large part of meeting students' needs relates to how the teacher organizes instruction. Small groups, cooperative groups, peer tutoring, and related activities provide more individualized instruction that focuses on the specific skills the student needs.

A final quality of an effective teacher that Carol emphasizes is the need to understand what children need to learn and monitor their progress as they learn this content. She notes that state standards have been quite helpful in that teachers know what students need to learn and when. She states that an effective teacher systematically monitors student progress toward learning content, especially students who are struggling, and organizes her class to ensure that all students reach benchmarks.

While Carol loves to teach, some aspects of teaching nonetheless frustrate her. Two major sources of frustration are paperwork and giving students grades. She makes every attempt to limit paperwork that doesn't support student learning but has little control over it. However, she does have control over student grades. From her perspective, teachers vary greatly in the criteria they use for grading students, emphasizing some combination of effort, mastery of material, and progress related to others. She recently developed a new report card at her school to ensure that she was using grades

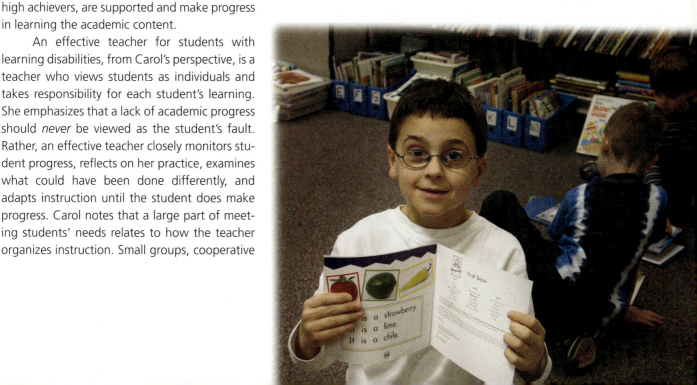

to support students and to communicate clearly with parents. Carol emphasizes that grading should be fair to all students, which means that grading should vary depending on the student's needs.

Carol notes that certain characteristics have helped her continue to improve as a teacher, including the fact that she works hard and doesn't give up easily. She also emphasizes the need for all teachers to continue to learn throughout their educational career. She emphatically states that most "sit and get" professional development has not been useful for her. The source of the most beneficial learning for Carol has come from a network of friends who are also teachers. They meet frequently to discuss teaching issues and how to improve as a teacher. She also notes that she benefited from teaching in a school with a well-developed learning community. This school supported continual teacher learning by providing retreats, time for teachers to plan together, book studies, and so forth.

Carol's advice to a beginning teacher is to view teaching as a career, not just a job. She also encourages new teachers to "find a way to feed yourself and continually learn. The best way to do this is to surround yourself with other teachers who share a similar philosophy, who will challenge and feed off each other."

## REFLECTIVE EXERCISE

#1 Did you know a student in your classes when you were in school who struggled to learn academic content in a specific content area? How did the student react to these academic struggles? How did you and other students react?

**PEARSON**
## myeducationlab

To check your comprehension on the content covered in Chapter 6, go to the Book-Specific Resources in the MyEducationLab for your course, select your text, and complete the Study Plan. Here you will be able to take a chapter quiz, receive feedback on your answers, and then access Review, Practice, and Enrichment activities to enhance your understanding of chapter content.

If you think back on your school experience, you will probably remember students who seemed typical on the playground or when you interacted with them socially. However, in the classroom these students struggled greatly to learn academic content in reading or mathematics, resulting in a high level of frustration for both student and teacher. In this chapter, we consider a group of students who, by virtue of their disability, struggle in school and require special supports to make **adequate yearly progress (AYP)** academically, as mandated by the No Child Left Behind Act (NCLB). These students are identified with a learning disability.

Students with learning disabilities are often perplexing to parents and teachers because they have difficulty in some academic areas but not others. This uneven pattern of development is a primary characteristic of these students. Moreover, students with learning disabilities are sometimes said to have a *specific* learning disability because they tend to struggle to learn academic content in one or two specific academic areas and have strengths in other areas (Torgesen, 2002).

What sets these students apart from others in general education classrooms who struggle to learn academic content is that they often continue to struggle, even when given highly effective, intensive instruction, and are typically the lowest of the low achievers in general education classrooms (Fuchs, Fuchs, Mathes, Lipsey, & Roberts, 2002). These students need a highly effective teacher, much like our featured teacher in this chapter, Carol Sprague. Carol's persistence, use of varied grouping strategies, and application of effective instructional strategies are all vital if the needs of students with learning disabilities are to be met and these students are to make adequate yearly progress in core academic areas.

## DEFINITIONS AND CLASSIFICATION CRITERIA FOR LEARNING DISABILITIES

### Definition of Students with Learning Disabilities

Students with learning disabilities, at least superficially, do not seem to differ from their typical peers yet struggle to learn academic content in particular academic areas. Since the passage of the original Individuals with Disabilities Education Act in 1975, children with learning disabilities have been defined and identified based on "unexpectedly" low achievement (J. Fletcher, Morris, & Lyon, 2003). That is, their measured level of intelligence suggests that they should learn academic content with little difficulty; but for some unexplained reason, they do not readily learn this information.

The most widely accepted definition for learning disabilities has been provided by the U.S. Department of Education in the regulations for IDEA 2004, the Individuals with Disabilities Education Act:

> A) In general—The term "specific learning disability" means a disorder in one or more of the basic psychological processes involved in understanding or in

using language, spoken or written, which disorder may manifest itself in the imperfect ability to listen, think, speak, read, write, spell, or do mathematical calculations.

    B) Disorders included—Such term includes such conditions as perceptual disabilities, brain injury, minimal brain dysfunction, **dyslexia, and developmental aphasia.**

    C) Disorders not included—Such term does not include a learning problem that is primarily the result of visual, hearing, or motor disabilities, of mental retardation, of emotional disturbance, or of environmental, cultural, or economic disadvantage. (IDEA 2004, H.R. 1350, Sec. 602 [30])

The definition of learning disabilities has four primary components. First, *learning disability* is defined as low academic achievement in one or more of several academic areas. Second, educators assume that these academic problems exist because of some form of psychological processing disorder, which causes a student to have difficulty in acquiring academic knowledge and skills in certain areas. For example, many students with learning disabilities who have difficulty learning to read have trouble using sound–symbol correspondences to sound out words they have not previously seen; this is referred to as a **phonological processing** problem (Torgesen, 2002).

Students with learning disabilities often continue to struggle in certain academic areas, even when given highly effective, intensive instruction.

Third, learning disability is considered to be synonymous with several labels used in the past (*perceptual disabilities, brain injury, minimal brain dysfunction*) or terms presently used by some educators (*dyslexia, developmental aphasia*). Finally, students with other disabilities (e.g., mental retardation, visual impairment) or who have learning problems because of environmental factors (e.g., living in poverty) are excluded from being identified with a learning disability. The law includes this so-called **exclusion clause** in the definition to ensure that the primary reason the student has difficulty progressing academically relates to a learning disability and not to another type of disability or to environmental conditions (e.g., poor teaching).

The federal definition of learning disabilities was a model to states in the late 1970s as they developed definitions and identification criteria of their own. In spite of most states' widespread acceptance of the federal definition of learning disability (Ahearn, 2003), much controversy surrounds use of the definition to identify students with learning disabilities (J. Fletcher, Lyon, Fuchs, & Barnes, 2007). This has resulted in significant differences across states in the identification rates for these students and practices that have been characterized as "confusing, unfair, and logically inconsistent" (Gresham, 2002, p. 467). To illustrate, data from the U.S. Department of Education (2009) reveal that, in 2007–2008, 4.9% of school-age students in the United States were identified with learning disabilities. However, across states, the identification rate varied from 1.90% to 7.21%, with the result that some states (i.e., Iowa, Oklahoma, Pennsylvania) identified twice as many students with learning disabilities as did other states (i.e., Georgia, Idaho, Kentucky, Louisiana).

In addition to inconsistent identification of students with learning disabilities, another controversial aspect of this category is that students often must fail before they can be identified with a learning disability. This wait-to-fail approach to identification has led to frustration for many educators and parents and a desire to develop an approach to learning disability identification that allows the use of more preventive measures (Ahearn, 2003). These concerns regarding the learning disability definition and identification criteria were significant factors that led to the inclusion of a **response-to-intervention (RTI)** approach to identifying students with learning disabilities in IDEA 2004. We described RTI in detail in Chapter 4. In this chapter, we describe the application of RTI to identify students with learning disabilities (see the following section).

## REFLECTIVE EXERCISE

\#2 Have you been in a class with a student with a learning disability? How did the teacher react to this student's academic difficulty? How did the teacher support the student?

# FAQ Sheet

## STUDENTS WITH LEARNING DISABILITIES

| | |
|---|---|
| Who are they? | • Students with learning disabilities have an intelligence level in the normal range (i.e., above the cutoff for intellectual disabilities) and unexpectedly low achievement in one or more academic areas, most often in reading.<br>• Students with learning disabilities have also been labeled with terms such as *dyslexia* (reading disability), **dysgraphia** (handwriting or written expression disability), and **dyscalculia** (math disability). |
| What are typical characteristics? | • Low achievement<br>• Inattention/distractibility<br>• Information-processing deficits<br>• Social-skills deficits<br>• Poor motivation<br>• A heterogeneous category |
| What are the demographics? | • 4.9% of students ages 6 to 17 (approximately 2.42 million) have been identified with learning disabilities.<br>• Approximately 43% of all school-age students with disabilities have a learning disability.<br>• The percentage of the school-age population identified with learning disabilities grew twice as fast as the overall school population between 1990 and 2000, but began to decline thereafter.<br>• 80% of students identified with learning disabilities have reading problems.<br>• Approximately 75% are male. |
| Where are students educated? | • 51% of students identified with learning disabilities spend most of the school day in general education classrooms.<br>• The proportion of students with learning disabilities who are educated in highly segregated separate settings declined by approximately 42% between 1990 and 2003. |
| How are students identified and assessed for intervention? | • Until recently, the primary criteria for identification were a severe discrepancy between expected and actual achievement levels and exclusion of students who have other disabilities and those who have not had adequate opportunities to learn.<br>• Increasingly, school districts are using a response-to-intervention (RTI) approach to identify students with learning disabilities. This approach is designed to ensure that a student has had high-quality instruction before being identified.<br>• Curriculum-based measures are used to determine current academic level in the classroom curriculum as well as to monitor student progress as interventions are used. |
| What are the outcomes? | • Reading problems tend to become more severe as students with learning disabilities move through school.<br>• Learning disabilities tend to persist into adulthood.<br>• Many adults with learning disabilities have difficulty finding good employment, living independently, and finding satisfaction in life. |

## Classification Criteria for Learning Disabilities

The passage of IDEA 2004 resulted in significant changes in the criteria and related procedures that educators use to identify students with learning disabilities. In this section, we initially address traditional identification criteria. We then discuss the changes in classification criteria included in IDEA 2004 and how these changes have influenced identification practices in most states. Finally, we describe an alternative, the RTI approach to the identification of students with learning disabilities that is now used in most states (Spectrum K12, 2009).

## Identification Criteria

Educators traditionally have used four criteria to identify students with learning disabilities, and some states continue their use. The most widely used criterion is a **severe discrepancy** between how well the student is achieving in an academic area and how well the student is expected to achieve based on ability. (Ability is typically determined by using an intelligence test.) Thus, a student in the fifth grade who has an average level of intelligence (i.e., a measured IQ of 100) and is reading on a second-grade level (as measured by a standardized achievement test) would have a severe discrepancy between expected and actual achievement levels and would most likely meet this severe discrepancy criterion.

It is important to note that, to meet the severe discrepancy criterion, a student must fall significantly behind grade-level peers in academic achievement. Thus, the severe discrepancy criterion is difficult to meet in the early elementary grades (first or second grade), when all students are learning basic academic skills, have completed only 1 or 2 years of school, and can be only 1 or 2 years behind grade level. Moreover, a student must often fail academic subjects and perhaps be retained in a later grade before the discrepancy is large enough to merit identification of a learning disability.

A second criterion that has traditionally been used to identify students with learning disabilities is the exclusion clause, which ensures that students with learning disabilities do not have another disability, such as a mild intellectual disability or a visual impairment, which causes the learning problem. The exclusion clause is also used to ensure that learning problems do not result from environmental, cultural, or economic disadvantages. This criterion is intended to ensure that the learning disability is the primary reason that a learning problem exists (e.g., the underachievement should not be the result of a visual impairment or the student's cultural background) and is an attempt to ensure that the learning disability category does not overlap with other disability categories.

A third criterion for identifying students with learning disabilities addresses the extent to which the student has been provided with appropriate learning experiences. This criterion relates to the student's opportunity to learn and suggests that students who have a learning problem that is the result of poor teaching should not be identified with a learning disability. Until recently, this criterion has not been widely used in identifying students with learning disabilities. However, this has changed as many states have moved to the use of an RTI approach to identifying students with learning disabilities (discussed later in this section).

The final criterion requires demonstrating that the student needs special education services and that the identified academic problem cannot be overcome in the general education classroom without these services. This criterion extends upon and strengthens the exclusion from the learning disability category of students who have not had appropriate or sufficient opportunity to learn as a result of not attending school or poor instruction while in school.

## IDEA 2004 Changes in Identification Criteria

As we have noted, several changes in IDEA 2004 have significantly influenced procedures that states use to identify students with learning disabilities (U.S. Department of Education, 2006b). These changes include the following:

- States cannot require that a severe discrepancy be used to identify students with learning disabilities in local schools. As a result, some local school districts have continued to use this criterion, while others have begun to use an alternative approach to student identification based on an RTI model.
- States must permit the use of the child's response to scientific, research-based interventions for identifying students with learning disabilities. (We describe the use of this RTI approach to student identification later in this section.)
- Limited English proficiency is added to the exclusion clause. That is, limited English proficiency must be eliminated as a possible cause of the learning disability.

**PEARSON myeducationlab**

To learn more about response to intervention, go to the IRIS Center Resources section of Topic 8: Learning Disabilities in the MyEducationLab for your course and complete the module entitled *RTI (Part 1): An Overview.*

Students with learning disabilities who struggle learning to read often benefit from intensive, small-group instruction.

## Response to Intervention

School districts across the United States are increasingly using an alternative, RTI approach to identify students with learning disabilities. For example, a national survey indicated that about one half of all school districts reported having a defined process for RTI, which is being used mostly at the elementary level (Spectrum K12, 2009). As we described in Chapter 4, RTI uses the child's response to scientific, research-based interventions and does not require the use of a severe discrepancy.

Use of an RTI model for student identification assumes that a student should be identified with a disability only if the student continues to struggle after receiving high-quality, research-based instruction (see Figure 6.1). High-quality instruction includes core instruction in the general education classroom (typically referred to as Tier 1 instruction), instruction in small groups (Tier 2), and intensive, individualized instruction that focuses on specific student needs (Tier 3) (L. Fuchs & Fuchs, 2007; Gersten et al., 2009).

When educators have delivered tiers of instruction and students continue to struggle learning academic content, lack of quality instruction has been eliminated as a possible cause. These students are typically referred to a multidisciplinary team for further evaluation, more intensive intervention, and possible identification with a disability.

While many professionals contend that the use of RTI is an improvement over traditional wait-to-fail approaches to the identification of students with learning disabilities, others are not convinced that this approach will be an improvement over current practice (L. Fuchs, 2003; L. Fuchs, Fuchs, & Speece, 2002; Gersten et al., 2009; Scruggs & Mastropieri, 2002). We address the controversy regarding RTI later in this chapter.

FIGURE 6.1 • **AN ALTERNATIVE APPROACH TO IDENTIFYING STUDENTS WITH LEARNING DISABILITIES**

(6) Specific learning disabilities
(A) In general—Notwithstanding section 607(b), when determining whether a child has a specific learning disability as defined in section 602, a local educational agency shall not be required to take into consideration whether a child has a severe discrepancy between achievement and intellectual ability in oral expression, listening comprehension, written expression, basic reading skill, reading comprehension, mathematical calculation, or mathematical reasoning.

(B) Additional authority—In determining whether a child has a specific learning disability, a local educational agency may use a process that determines if the child responds to scientific, research-based intervention as a part of the evaluation procedures described in paragraphs (2) and (3).

Source: IDEA 2004, P.L. 108–446, Sec. 614(b).

# PRIMARY CHARACTERISTICS OF STUDENTS WITH LEARNING DISABILITIES

## Heterogeneity

The only common characteristic shared by all students with learning disabilities is uneven development of academic skills. That is, these students achieve at significantly lower levels in some academic areas than in others. Indeed, other than low achievement in reading, which occurs in approximately four of every five students with learning disabilities (McMaster, Kung, Han, & Cao, 2008), most characteristics occur in a small number of students (i.e., often 25% or fewer). This has led some to conclude that one of the major characteristics of the learning disabilities category is its heterogeneity (Mercer & Pullen, 2009) and that it should be separated into several categories or subtypes of learning disabilities (i.e., students with reading problems, those with mathematics disabilities, students with language difficulties, etc.). Thus, as you review the following characteristics, keep in mind that, in most cases, they relate to only a small group of students identified with learning disabilities.

## Academic Difficulties

The academic area in which most students with learning disabilities have difficulty is reading: approximately 80% of these students struggle in this area (McMaster et al., 2008). Research conducted since the 1980s has provided significant insight regarding why many students with learning disabilities fail to make adequate progress as they are learning to read.

As students begin to learn to read, those who progress with ease

Students with learning disabilities have difficulty in some academic areas and not in others.

- Understand how the sounds of speech are represented in letters
- Apply this information rapidly and fluently in decoding words
- Have sufficient vocabulary and language abilities to quickly connect what they are reading to their experiences and background knowledge (Lyon et al., 2001)

Research has demonstrated that many students with learning disabilities lack these language skills, which contributes to their difficulty in learning to read. To illustrate, students with the most severe reading problems often have difficulty decoding words rather than comprehending text (J. Fletcher, Lyon, Fuchs, & Barnes, 2007). A major contributing factor to this difficulty is a problem with phonological processing (i.e., the association of sounds with letters in oral language and when reading). Fortunately, research has shown that explicitly teaching beginning readers skills related to sounds in oral language and letter–sound relationships as well as how to translate this information into words can help to reduce the impact of a reading disability for many students (Siegel, 2003).

As you will readily recognize, reading is a foundational skill that is necessary if students are to progress throughout the school years. Thus, as students move through elementary school, reading becomes more and more important in other academic areas. For example, early mathematics skills depend heavily on recognizing numbers and learning math facts and basic operations, and reading skills are of little consequence. However, as students move to later elementary school, word problems become increasingly important in mathematics. Thus, the reading problems of students with learning disabilities tend to cause difficulty in a range of academic content areas as they progress through the school years.

Slightly more than one of every four students with learning disabilities has problems in mathematics (Lerner & Johns, 2009). Students with learning disabilities most often have difficulty with one of four areas related to mathematics (Bryant & Dix, 1999):

1. Learning math facts to allow quick, automatic response
2. Learning strategies to complete math calculations (e.g., regrouping)
3. Comprehending word problems
4. Learning strategies for completing word problems

The first two of these problems reflect learning disabilities specifically in the area of mathematics. The difficulties related to word problems may also result from these initial difficulties in learning the basic skills required for higher-level math. However, as we've noted, many students learn these basic skills with little trouble, but word problems present difficulty because of students' related learning disabilities in reading or language (i.e., understanding the word problems, especially as they become more complex). Thus, the teacher's instructional intervention will differ depending on the cause of the mathematics disability and whether the student has difficulty learning math facts or operations or cannot read and understand math word problems.

The other academic area in which many students with learning disabilities have difficulty is written expression (Graham & Harris, 2003). Reading disabilities may contribute to difficulties students with learning disabilities face in written expression as reading skills tend to develop before comparable writing skills. Thus, a student who lags behind peers in learning to read will invariably do the same in the area of written expression. However, some students with learning disabilities have problems with written expression in spite of reading well.

For students with good written expression skills, writing involves three basic processes (Graham & Harris, 2003): "planning what to say and how to say it, translating plans into written text, and reviewing to improve existing text" (p. 323). Graham and Harris note that students with learning disabilities related to written expression tend to use a simplified or condensed version of this process: They rely on generating ideas and place little emphasis on planning, organization, or reviewing the text. Thus, the goal of teaching students with written expression disabilities should often be to develop a more sophisticated approach to writing, including each of the previously described steps.

## Cognitive Skill Deficits

### Memory Problems

Students with learning disabilities are often characterized by certain cognitive problems that contribute to the difficulties they have learning academic content. One of the most frequently noted of these problems is a memory deficit. Many students with learning disabilities have difficulty with long-term memory and experience great frustration in attempting to learn basic information and rapidly retrieve this information during school activities. For example, many students with learning disabilities who have problems with math have difficulty learning math facts. Moreover, they may remember facts one day and forget them the next. Much the same can be said about learning to spell for a significant number of students with learning disabilities.

The most frequently investigated aspect of memory for students with learning disabilities is **working memory** (Siegel, 2003). Working memory is the ability to see something, think about it, and then act on this information. For example, when reading, students see a word they do not know, retrieve information from long-term memory regarding the letters in the word and the sounds they represent, blend these

Go to the Assignments and Activities section of Topic 8: Learning Disabilities in the MyEducationLab for your course and complete the activity entitled *Characteristics of Learning Disabilities.*

sounds into a word, and then say the word while retaining information regarding the context of what is being read. Obviously, this is a complex process and is made more difficult by the fact that a fundamental problem that many students with learning disabilities face is a deficit in working memory. Evidence indicates that working memory problems contribute to learning disabilities in the areas of reading, mathematics, and written expression (Swanson & Saez, 2003).

### Attention Problems

A second cognitive factor that may contribute to many learning disabilities is attention problems. Available evidence suggests that as many as 25% of students with learning disabilities are identified with attention-deficit/hyperactivity disorder (DuPaul, 2007), while many more of these students have some level of attentional difficulty. Attentional problems for students with learning disabilities may relate to three types of attention:

Some students with learning disabilities are not well accepted by their peers.

- Orienting toward important activities in the classroom (i.e., the teacher provides an example of regrouping on the board, while the student looks out the window at children playing on the playground)
- Sustaining attention for an appropriate period of time (i.e., paying attention for a sustained period of time without distraction)
- Selectively attending to material that is most important (e.g., attending to directions before responding to math problems on a worksheet)

### Metacognitive Deficits

Students with learning disabilities may also have difficulty with metacognitive skills. **Metacognition** relates to an awareness of thinking processes and how these processes are monitored. Scott (1999) has more simply characterized this phenomenon as "knowing what you know and how you know it" (p. 55). Students with learning disabilities often have difficulty monitoring their thinking, and these difficulties contribute to academic problems. Teachers have used many strategies to support students with metacognitive difficulties, including providing advance organizers before presenting material, use of mnemonic devices to assist in remembering information (e.g., HOMES is a device to remember the names of the Great Lakes), and procedures for planning and organizing study time in a content area.

## Social and Motivational Problems

Although not all students with learning disabilities have social-skills deficits, research has revealed that some do manifest difficulties getting along with peers and teachers as a result of deficits in this area. For example, some students with learning disabilities lag behind others in social skills: They have difficulty helping others, accepting authority, and expressing feelings (Lerner & Johns, 2009).

Some research suggests that social-skills deficits among students with learning disabilities may result, at least in part, from the inability to read social cues and interact successfully in conversations (Lerner & Johns, 2009). These deficits may lead to low social status of some of these students in school. This low status also may be influenced by factors related to the students' low achievement level (e.g., student placement in classes with other low-achieving students, low status in a school of

#4 Do you have an academic area or other skill area (e.g., music) in which you have not been successful? How did you react to this lack of success? What did you learn from this experience that can make you a better teacher, especially for students who struggle academically?

low-achieving students). Regardless of the cause, this low status often leads to a negative self-concept and emotional maladjustment and increases the potential for dropping out of school (Vaughn et al., 1999).

With the academic, cognitive, and social issues faced by students with learning disabilities, much potential exists for these students to become frustrated with school. Indeed, as many students with learning disabilities progress through school, they face increasing difficulty in successfully completing school tasks and making passing grades; and this may result in avoidance of academic activities, frustration, behavior problems, and, ultimately, disengagement from school. Maintaining student motivation becomes a key issue in ensuring that students with learning disabilities continue to adjust to school and make adequate academic progress. The most important factors in maintaining a high motivation level for students with learning disabilities involve recognizing when these issues arise and addressing them by providing effective instruction that is appropriate to the students' needs.

## PREVALENCE, COURSE, AND CAUSAL FACTORS

### Prevalence

Learning disability is commonly referred to as a *high-incidence disability*. In a typical classroom of 25 students, at least one is likely to have a learning disability. In a nontechnical sense, *high-incidence disability* refers to a condition that a lot of people have. In fact, in 2007, more than 2.42 million students were identified with learning disabilities, representing 4.9% of the school-age population in the United States (U.S. Department of Education, 2009). Students with learning disabilities account for more than 43% of all school-age students with disabilities, by far the largest disability category.

#5 Why has the number of students with learning disabilities grown so rapidly? What factors have contributed to this growth? Is this growth a good thing or not?

The number of students identified with learning disabilities has grown dramatically since the 1970s. In 2000, more than three times as many students with learning disabilities were identified than in 1976–1977. Much of the early growth of the learning disability category could be attributed to its newness: Students who had not previously been eligible for special education were now identified. For example, in Indiana in 1976, only 5,422 students were identified with learning disabilities (Indiana Department of Education, 2005). Ten years later, in 1985, this number had grown to 33,558, an increase of more than 500%. Similar growth occurred in many states across the United States during this time.

At a national level, the learning disability category grew twice as fast as the overall population during the 1990s and peaked at 2.71 million school-age students in 2000. However, since that time, the number of students identified with learning disabilities has declined by approximately 9%, to 2.42 million in 2007 (U.S. Department of Education, 2009). The prevalence of students with learning disabilities may be further affected by the use of an RTI approach to identification; however, it will be several years before we determine the nature of these changes.

#6 While many of the academic difficulties of persons with learning disabilities persist into adulthood, many of these individuals compensate for these difficulties and achieve success in life. How do adults with learning disabilities overcome or compensate for their disability? What can you as a teacher learn from these successful adults to better prepare children with learning disabilities for life after school?

### The Course of Learning Disabilities

As students with learning disabilities progress through school, a gap often widens between the performance of students with and without disabilities (Deshler et al., 2001; Mercer & Pullen, 2009). A major contributor to this widening gap for many students with learning disabilities is reading deficits that influence progress in academic content areas as well as the development of language skills (e.g., vocabulary development).

Extensive research has documented that the effects of learning disabilities persist into adulthood (Wagner, Newman, Camero, Garza, & Levine, 2005). For example, adults with learning disabilities continue to have difficulties similar to those they experienced during their school years in areas such as reading, mathematics, language, interpersonal interactions, and so forth. While it is important to note that a substantial proportion of students with learning disabilities are quite successful in adulthood, many adults with learning disabilities (perhaps as many as one in four) have difficulty finding good employment, living independently, and experiencing satisfaction regarding their lives (Mercer & Pullen, 2009).

## Causal Factors

For most students identified with learning disabilities, we do not know the particular cause of the disability. Research points cautiously to multiple contributing factors, implicating abnormal brain function, genetic predispositions, and poor teaching.

### Abnormal Brain Function

The most widely studied cause of learning disabilities has been abnormalities in brain function. Recent advances in how the brain is studied have resulted in much progress in understanding the relationship between brain function and learning disabilities, especially those in the area of reading. For example, extensive research has documented that children with reading disabilities often differ from typically developing peers in brain structure and function (Miller, Sanchez, & Hynd, 2003).

While brain anomalies and learning disabilities are intriguing topics for many educators, it is important to recognize that this causative information tells us little about how to teach students with learning disabilities. Furthermore, it is unclear whether the brain dysfunctions cause the reading disability or the reading problem causes the brain anomaly (Miller et al., 2003). Moreover, some research has shown that brain function may improve with effective academic intervention (Shaywitz et al., 2004). While the study of brain function may provide useful information in the future regarding how to prevent or intervene with learning disabilities, to this point these findings have few implications for more effective instruction.

### Genetic Factors

A second frequently cited factor that may contribute to or cause learning disabilities is genetic factors. Research conducted with students with reading disabilities has established that reading and writing disabilities tend to run in families (Thomson & Raskind, 2003). For example, parents with reading disabilities have been found to be eight times more likely to produce children with reading disabilities (J. Fletcher et al., 2002).

It is unclear whether genetic factors cause reading disabilities or result in a predisposition for a disability that is influenced by environmental conditions. Some have speculated that genetic factors may be an inherited susceptibility to a reading disability that will be manifested given certain environmental circumstances (J. Fletcher, et al., 2002). For example, some parents with a reading disability may be less likely to read to their children or provide other reading and language experiences that are critical for success in early reading. When this occurs, the quality of reading instruction in the early school years becomes critical for preventing the development of a reading disability.

### Lack of Effective Instruction

A final factor that is widely believed to contribute to the identification (and likely overidentification) of students with learning disabilities is the lack of access to effective instruction. Moreover, it is likely that many students are referred for possible identification with a learning disability because of poor teaching. Research on this issue has contributed significantly to the movement toward the use of an RTI approach to the identification of students with learning disabilities, as discussed previously in this chapter.

Researchers who have provided high-quality instruction for students with learning disabilities have found that up to 50% of these students can overcome their learning problems and succeed in school (L. Fuchs et al., 2005; Torgesen et al., 2001; Vellutino et al., 2006). For example, after providing kindergarten and first-grade interventions consisting of small-group and individualized tutoring for students who were at risk for reading problems, Vellutino and colleagues found that well over one half of these students were no longer at risk and continued to achieve at this level through third grade. Similarly, Torgesen and colleagues (2001) provided high-quality instruction for 2 years for students with severe reading disabilities. One year after the completion of the intervention, 40% of these students were no longer in need of special education services.

These studies reveal that the lack of high-quality instruction is a frequent cause of learning disabilities in reading and mathematics in the early elementary grades. Moreover, high-quality instruction may reduce, at least temporarily, the prevalence of learning disabilities in the early elementary grades up to 50%. L. Fuchs and colleagues (2005) caution, however, that additional research is needed to determine if these effects are lasting. Moreover, as these students progress through school, some are likely to reemerge with learning disabilities unless they continue to receive high-quality instruction.

**REFLECTIVE EXERCISE**

**#7** Many parents and some teachers are very interested in what causes a learning disability. Why is there a high level of interest in this information? How might this information be useful for improving educational outcomes for these students?

## IDENTIFICATION AND ASSESSMENT

Educators use two approaches to identify students with learning disabilities. One approach is based on the previously described definition of learning disabilities and identification criteria. The primary criterion used in this approach is a severe discrepancy. A second approach to student identification is the use of an RTI model. We subsequently provide descriptions of these approaches to the identification of students with learning disabilities.

### Severe Discrepancy Approach to Identification

Most students who currently have a learning disability were identified using an approach based on the previously described definition and identification criteria. These students were typically identified after they entered school and were referred by their classroom teacher or parent to determine their eligibility for services. They were then administered several tests by a school psychologist or other professional with expertise in test administration and interpretation, typically including an intelligence test and a test of academic achievement. Educators then used these test results to determine if the student met the primary criteria for learning disabilities.

When this approach to identification is used, the primary criterion is a severe discrepancy between expected and actual achievement levels. A severe discrepancy is determined by administering an intelligence test and an achievement test. The first step in establishing if a severe discrepancy exists is to administer an intelligence test to determine a student's expected level of achievement. Intelligence tests that are most frequently used include the Stanford Binet Intelligence Scale (5th ed., Roid, 2003) and the Wechsler Intelligence Scale for Children (4th ed., Wechsler, 2003).

A standardized, norm-referenced achievement test is administered to determine the student's current achievement level in core academic areas. Achievement tests that are often used for this purpose include the Woodcock-Johnson Tests of Achievement-III (Woodcock, McGrew, & Mather, 2001) and the Wechsler Individual Achievement Test-II (WIAT-II) (Psychological Corporation, 2001). The tests include separate subtests that address language, reading, writing, and mathematics. Subtest scores are used to determine student achievement level in the academic area or areas in which the student is having difficulty making progress.

Intelligence and achievement test scores are then compared to determine if the student's actual achievement level is significantly below expected achievement—that is, if a severe discrepancy exists. For example, a student with an average IQ (i.e., a standard score of 100) in the fifth grade is expected to achieve in an average range and therefore obtain achievement scores commensurate with the IQ level. If this student obtained a below-average score (i.e., a standard score of 75) in reading, a severe discrepancy would be evident. A multidisciplinary team typically makes a decision regarding whether or not a severe discrepancy exists through the use of statistical procedures that are generally specified in state regulations and guidelines (Mercer & Pullen, 2009).

While a severe discrepancy is the primary criterion when this approach is used, the multidisciplinary team also looks at other information (e.g., results of an observation in the general education classroom, a review of the child's previous educational experiences) to ensure that each of the classification criteria for learning disabilities is met. This includes ensuring that the student does not have another disability (e.g., an intellectual disability or visual impairment), has had appropriate opportunities to learn, and that the academic problem cannot be overcome in the general education classroom without special education services.

## Response-to-Intervention Approach to Identification

As described earlier, many school districts currently identify students with learning disabilities using RTI, which is built on the assumption that students should be identified with a learning disability only after they have been provided high-quality instruction and continue to struggle to learn academic content.

One approach a multidisciplinary team may use to determine if the student has a learning disability is called a dual-discrepancy approach (J. Fletcher et al., 2007; Fuchs, Fuchs, & Speece, 2002). If a multidisciplinary team uses a dual-discrepancy approach, they would likely proceed using the following steps (J. Fletcher et al., 2007; Fuchs, Fuchs, & Speece, 2002). First, the student must have been provided high-quality instruction and continue to struggle learning to read (or in another academic area). "Continue to struggle" means that the student is not making adequate progress so that he is not catching up with peers or making expected progress toward doing grade-level work. This illustrates a discrepancy between the student's progress and that of other students. Second, the student should be administered an achievement test, which may be curriculum based or norm referenced to determine if he is significantly behind peers in reading (or another academic area).

If both of these discrepancies exist (the student is not progressing at a rate commensurate with grade level, and is significantly behind grade-level benchmarks and peers on an achievement measure), further tests may be administered, as appropriate, to address other factors that may cause the underachievement (e.g., another disability, language or cultural difference). The multidisciplinary team would then review all available information and make a decision regarding whether the student has a learning disability. Thus, if the student has not responded to high-quality instruction and continues to struggle, lags behind peers on a standardized achievement measure, and other causes of the underachievement are not found, he would be identified with a learning disability.

To learn more about how response to intervention can be used to identify students who may have learning disabilities, go to the IRIS Center Resources section of Topic 8: Learning Disabilities in the MyEducationLab for your course and complete the module entitled *RTI (Part 2): Assessment*

## EDUCATIONAL PRACTICES

Extensive research has been conducted regarding evidence-based practices that are effective with students who have difficulty progressing academically, including those with learning disabilities. Some of this evidence has been obtained from classes much like Carol Sprague's, the featured teacher in this chapter. This research reveals that, while a student identified with learning disabilities may take more time to learn

Most students with learning disabilities spend most of the school day in general education classrooms.

a skill than a typical peer, good teaching methods persistently applied by an effective teacher work well with them.

## Service Delivery

Research has revealed that students with learning disabilities benefit from spending a large proportion of the day in general education classrooms with appropriate supports (e.g., Salend & Duhaney, 2007). Through the 1980s and much of the 1990s, many students with learning disabilities were educated for a substantial portion of the school day in separate settings (McLeskey, Henry, & Axelrod, 1999; McLeskey & Pacchiano, 1994). However, recent data indicate that most students with learning disabilities now spend the majority of the school day in general education classrooms (McLeskey, Hoppey, Williamson, & Rentz, 2004).

Table 6.1 illustrates that increasing numbers of students with learning disabilities have been educated in more inclusive settings from 1990 to 2005 (U.S. Department of Education, 2009). For example, in 1990–1991, only 22.6% of all students with learning disabilities spent most of the school day in the general education classroom. This percentage increased to 43.2% in 1998 and continued to climb to 51.2% in 2004–2005 (the most recent year for which least restrictive environment data are available from the U.S. Department of Education for school-age students). While the growth in placements of students with learning disabilities in general education settings has slowed somewhat in recent years (McLeskey et al., 2004), we anticipate that the trend toward educating increasing numbers of students with learning disabilities in general education classes will continue in the coming years.

While placements of students with learning disabilities in general education classrooms have increased, placements in highly restrictive settings have declined. For example, in 1990–1991, approximately 24% of all students with learning disabilities

**TABLE 6.1** • PERCENTAGE OF SCHOOL-AGE STUDENTS WITH LEARNING DISABILITIES TAUGHT IN DIFFERENT PLACEMENT SETTINGS, 1990–1991, 1998–1999, AND 2004–2005

| School Year | Placement Settings | | | |
| --- | --- | --- | --- | --- |
| | General Education[a] | Resource[a] | Separate Class[a] | Separate Setting[b] |
| 1990–1991 | 22.6 | 53.6 | 22.4 | 1.5 |
| 1998–1999 | 43.2 | 40.4 | 15.5 | 0.9 |
| 2004–2005 | 51.2 | 35.8 | 12.0 | 1.1 |

[a]Students in general education settings spend 80% or more of the school day in general education classrooms. Those in resource settings spend 21% to 60% of the school day in a separate special education resource class. Students in a separate class spend more than 60% of the school day in a separate special education class.

[b]Separate setting combines several categories reported by the U.S. Department of Education, including public separate facility, private separate facility, public residential facility, private residential facility, and home/hospital environment.

Source: U.S. Department of Education, 2009.

were segregated from their peers for most or all of the school day in separate classes or separate schools. This percentage had declined to approximately 16% in 1998–1999 and still further to 13% in 2004–2005. These highly segregated placements are likely to continue to decline in the coming years as the movement toward educating students with learning disabilities in general education settings for much of the school day continues (McLeskey et al., 2004).

If increasing numbers of students with learning disabilities are to be included in general education classrooms, several activities are needed to ensure that these students have appropriate supports to succeed. These supports include, perhaps more than anything else, well-prepared general and special education teachers who are knowledgeable about providing effective instruction for these students as well as adapting instruction and curriculum to meet student needs. McLeskey and Waldron (2000, 2006) suggest that the provision of adequate supports for these students in general education classrooms requires school-wide change that addresses how schools are organized, how they plan and deliver instruction, and what roles teachers play in addressing student needs.

REFLECTIVE EXERCISE

#8 What are the potential benefits for students with learning disabilities who are placed in inclusive general education settings as compared to placements in highly segregated separate class settings? What are the potential negative factors associated with inclusive placements? How might you as a teacher address these factors?

## Early Intervention

Only within the past 20 years have educational programs for preschool children with disabilities been developed and widely available. This has occurred primarily for two reasons. First, research has documented that the early experiences of children have a significant impact on their later growth and development. Moreover, effective preschool programs have been shown to positively influence students' intelligence levels, academic achievement, and social competence (Beirne-Smith, Patton, & Kim, 2006; Lerner & Johns, 2009).

Providing early intervention for students with learning disabilities can be complex. For example, it is difficult to accurately identify students with learning disabilities before they enter school. As we have noted, most students with learning disabilities are identified because they struggle while learning to read. In schools, students are not expected to begin learning to read until kindergarten or first grade. Thus, identification of students with learning disabilities before they enter kindergarten or first grade requires hypothesizing that the student will fail in the future or is at risk for a learning disability.

Research has revealed that most students who are identified with learning disabilities before entering school have problems with language (Mann, 2003). More specifically, as students learn about the world by talking and listening, the information they obtain provides a foundation for reading and writing (Lerner & Johns, 2009). These early oral language experiences allow children to build vocabulary (semantic knowledge) and develop an awareness of sentence structures (syntactic knowledge) that they will use in learning to read and write (Lerner & Johns, 2009). Early language problems prevent children from obtaining the language skills needed in early reading and writing.

Young children who are at risk for learning disabilities because of language problems benefit from early intervention programs that include rich experiences with oral language. These experiences should address activities that enhance listening comprehension, phonological awareness of language sounds, building a listening vocabulary,

Early intervention programs for students with learning disabilities often emphasize rich oral language experiences.

understanding sentences, listening comprehension, critical listening, and listening to stories (Lerner & Johns, 2009). For example, listening comprehension entails focusing on activities that allow students to learn to follow directions, understand a sequence of events, listen for details, get the main idea, make inferences, and draw conclusions. Research reveals that early intervention for preschool children with language problems can significantly influence a child's development and reduce or prevent later school failure (Wolery & Bailey, 2002).

Early intervention programs have proven very beneficial for students with learning disabilities, especially those students with reading problems. Early in this chapter, we discussed the use of interventions with students with reading problems that included explicitly teaching phonemic awareness skills, the alphabetic principle, and other skills that are necessary for early reading (Torgesen, 2000). Success with these early intervention programs has precipitated the movement toward the RTI approach to the identification of students with learning disabilities, which ensures that evidence-based instruction is provided to children who are at risk for reading failure at an early age (kindergarten and first grade) before these students experience failure in school.

## Classroom Interventions

The discussion of effective instruction in this chapter is primarily based on the work of Kame'enui and colleagues (Coyne, Kame'enui, & Carnine, 2007; Kame'enui & Carnine, 1998; Kame'enui & Simmons, 1999). Extensive research has documented that these principles are effective guiding practices for teaching students who struggle to learn academic content. Figure 6.2 defines the four principles of effective curriculum design and instruction that we address here.

### Big Ideas

Information has proliferated at an unprecedented pace since the 1970s. What students are expected to learn in school reflects this explosion of knowledge, resulting in curricula in many schools that are so broad that only the highest-performing students can begin to learn all of the information. The most widely used approach to address this information explosion is to superficially expose students to a broad range of information. This results in very little in-depth learning for many students, especially those with disabilities.

A more effective strategy is needed to ensure that students, especially students with disabilities, learn academic content. "Big ideas" offers such an alternative. This approach entails examining the curriculum to determine key skills, knowledge, and concepts and focusing instruction on this information. *Big ideas* are "concepts, principles, rules, strategies, or heuristics that facilitate the most efficient and broadest acquisition of knowledge" (Coyne et al., 2007, p. 10). These big ideas serve as anchoring

Go to the Assignments and Activities section of Topic 8: Learning Disabilities in the MyEducationLab for your course and complete the activity entitled *Instructional Strategies for Students with Learning Disabilities*.

FIGURE 6.2 • **PRINCIPLES THAT GUIDE EFFECTIVE CURRICULUM DESIGN AND INSTRUCTION**

1. *Big ideas*—key concepts or principles that facilitate the most efficient and broadest acquisition of information
2. *Mediated scaffolding*—temporary instructional support provided until the student can solve a problem or understand a concept independently
3. *Judicious review*—opportunities to practice or apply information that was previously taught
4. *Conspicuous strategies*—steps used to accomplish a task or solve a problem

Source: Adapted from Coyne, Kame'enui, & Carnine, 2007.

concepts as students learn smaller ideas. The primary assumptions underlying big ideas are (1) not all curriculum objectives contribute equally to academic development and (2) important information should be taught more thoroughly than less important information (Kame'enui & Simmons, 1999).

Using big ideas to guide curriculum planning and instruction ensures that all students learn the most important information and have basic skills and anchoring concepts necessary for acquiring higher-level knowledge and skills. Furthermore, this approach allows students who quickly learn curriculum to assist others in learning basic skills, anchoring concepts, and higher-level concepts. Two examples of big ideas follow, one in elementary school and a second at the high school level.

**Beginning Reading for Elementary Students.** Most researchers agree that three big ideas are needed to ensure that beginning readers succeed: (1) phonemic awareness, which is the awareness of sounds in letters and words; (2) the alphabetic principle, which is an awareness of letter–sound relationships and a facility with mapping sounds to letters; and (3) automaticity with the code, which ensures that beginning readers can rapidly translate letters to sounds and sounds to words (Coyne, et al., 2007).

**Written Expression in High School.** Research has demonstrated that good writing requires students to progress through a sequence of steps as they learn to write increasingly complex narratives or expository passages. These steps include planning to write, drafting an initial version of the passage, revising the draft, changing plans as deemed necessary, modifying drafts as plans change, and editing the final version (Kame'enui & Carnine, 1998).

Focusing on big ideas provides a good framework for addressing certain aspects of academic problems. For an example of a first-grade student with a reading problem, and how these ideas might be applied, see "Can You Help Me with This Student?"

## Mediated Scaffolding

**Scaffolding** is the support that teachers give students as they learn content. When learning math skills, some students are presented information once from the teacher and can then independently solve problems, apply this information in other settings or to other material, and retain the information over time. Those students who do not learn this information immediately need more steps in instruction and more support. Effective teachers build this support into the curriculum by scaffolding instruction. Effective teachers have support available for students as they need it and withdraw the support when it is no longer necessary.

In math, scaffolding may be built into the curriculum through partially solved examples, or it may take the form of peer or teacher support for solving problems. For example, instructional materials that are scaffolded with partially solved problems might include the following:

$$1/2 + 1/3 = 3/6 + 2/6 = \underline{\hspace{1cm}} /6$$

$$1/4 + 1/3 = 3/12 + \underline{\hspace{1cm}} /12 = \underline{\hspace{1cm}} /12$$

$$1/5 + 1/2 = \underline{\hspace{1cm}} /10 + \underline{\hspace{1cm}} 10 = \underline{\hspace{1cm}} /10$$

Notice that the prompts or hints gradually fade as the student learns the material. There are no set rules regarding when to use scaffolding, how long it should be used, or how many problems of the first type should be solved before proceeding to the problems with less scaffolding.

Scaffolding can also be used to support reading instruction and instruction in other content areas. For an excellent example of the use of technology to support reading instruction by using scaffolding, see "Technology for Access."

Kame'enui and Simmons (1999) suggest that mediated scaffolding should vary according to student needs, be used only as needed by the student, and be removed

PEARSON
**myeducationlab**

Go to the Building Teaching Skills and Dispositions section of Topic 8: Learning Disabilities in the MyEducationLab for your course and complete the learning unit entitled *Scaffolding Learners* to enhance your understanding of this concept.

| To… | Todd Boniface, School Psychologist |
|------|-------------------------------------|
| From… | Tanya Suarez, First-Grade Teacher |
| Subject: | Possible learning disability in a first-grade student |

Mr. Boniface, I have a student in my first-grade class, Juan, who began attending Southside Elementary in kindergarten. Although Spanish is the primary language Juan and his parents speak in the home, Juan speaks both English and Spanish fluently. He has two siblings, a sister in third grade and a brother in fourth grade. Juan's parents are very involved in his education. They have read books to him in both Spanish and English since infancy. They also have been very involved in school activities at Southside since their older son entered school here and have become leaders in the parent–teacher organization. I checked with Juan's kindergarten teacher, and she was very impressed by his excellent vocabulary and facility with oral language. However, she was concerned that he was having difficulty with phonological awareness and letter knowledge, as well as recognizing words by sight. She said that she was aware that these difficulties are often related to reading problems in young children, but felt that Juan's excellent language skills and strong parent support would help him overcome this delay. After Juan entered my class, I noted that he has problems understanding how oral language is represented in print and has a very limited sight vocabulary. I suspect that Juan has a learning disability and plan to refer him to special education. In the meantime, could you provide suggestions regarding what I can do to help Juan now?

Thanks,

Tanya

---

To:      Tanya Suarez
From:    Todd Boniface
Subject: RE: Possible learning disability in a first-grade student

Tanya, I'm most pleased to provide feedback regarding what might be done to support Juan. Based on the information you've provided, it is a good idea to refer Juan for possible special education services, as I also suspect that he may have a learning disability. The delays you've described are often indicative of reading problems among first-grade students, and I advise that you use evidence-based practices in reading to ensure that he does not continue to fall behind his peers in reading. Elements of effective reading instruction that are especially important to emphasize with Juan include the following (Foorman & Torgesen, 2001):

- *Provide explicit instruction in phonological processing.* Most children in the early elementary grades learn to associate sounds and symbols and recognize sight words with ease and require very little explicit instruction. However, when students do not make adequate progress in learning these skills, explicit, systematic instruction will help them learn these skills, which are needed to decode words.

- *Instruction in reading must be more intense.* If Juan is to successfully learn the phonological processing skills needed to progress in reading and also catch up with peers in learning sight vocabulary, he will require more intense instruction than is typically offered to first-grade students. More intense instruction is required because Juan will likely learn these skills more slowly than other children and will thus require more repetition of skills to ensure that they are learned to a level at which he can apply them automatically. Either increasing the time Juan is engaged in reading in the general education classroom or including more small-group instruction can be used to provide more intense instruction.

- *Instruction should be very supportive cognitively and emotionally.* Instruction must be very supportive cognitively because Juan has not learned the skills needed for early reading spontaneously and thus requires teacher instruction and support to learn these skills. This is often done by using approaches such as scaffolding and entails breaking a task down and teaching the student manageable parts of the task and then leading the student in putting the parts together to create a whole. Scaffolding may be done with Juan as he learns oral sounds, the names of letters, how oral and written sounds relate, how these sounds are blended into words, and so forth.

If you'd like additional information on strategies to address the needs of early elementary students with reading disabilities, consult the following resources:

Foorman, B., & Torgesen, J. (2001). Critical elements of classroom and small-group instruction promote reading success in children. *Learning Disabilities Research and Practice, 16*(4), 203–212.

Mercer, C., & Mercer, A. (2005). *Teaching students with learning problems* (7th ed.). Upper Saddle River, NJ: Merrill/Pearson Education.

---

**EXTEND AND APPLY**

- If you were Juan's teacher, what type of emotional support would you offer alongside his intensive instruction to learn to read?

- How could Juan's teacher use one or more of the principles that guide effective curriculum design and instruction that were discussed previously to support Juan's reading instruction?

---

gradually as learner proficiency increases. Questions to ask regarding scaffolding as instruction begins and proceeds might include the following:

1. Does the teacher provide sufficient guided examples before students are expected to begin solving problems?
2. As students begin to solve problems, does the teacher provide multiple, partially solved examples of the problem before the students must solve the problem without support?
3. Do the problems proceed from easy to more difficult?
4. Does the sequence separate potentially confusing information (e.g., addition of fractions from multiplication of fractions) during initial instruction?
5. Does the sequence of examples provide a manageable amount of instruction for the student?

## Judicious Review

Every content area contains some information that simply must be practiced and learned. The most common example that comes to mind is math facts, but every content area has basic information or facts that students must learn and then combine to produce higher-level learning. These are the essential building blocks within a content area. Simple repetition does not ensure that the facts are learned (Kame'enui & Simmons, 1999). Rather than dull, often mindless review, Coyne, Kame'enui and Carnine (2007) have identified dimensions of "judicious review," which include the following.

1. Review should be distributed over time, not massed into a brief time.
2. It should be varied to provide the students with a wide understanding and application of the information and prevent boredom.

Englert, Wu, and Zhao (2005) provide an excellent, research-based example of how technology may be used to improve the effectiveness of instruction and enhance learning for students with disabilities. These educators developed a software program called TELE-Web, which incorporates several features of effective instruction to facilitate the learning of written expression by students with disabilities. This software is designed to provide students with support (scaffolding) as they engage in the writing process.

As a student begins writing, she is given a prompt via the appearance of a "Topic Sentence Box" at the top of the computer screen. This reminds the student to write a topic sentence as she begins her work. Immediately following this information is a prompt to write "Supporting Details" about the topic sentence. The student may continue to add as many paragraphs as she desires; but with the addition of each paragraph, a "Topic Sentence Box" appears, followed by a "Supporting Details Box." Finally, a "Concluding Statement" box appears at the bottom of the computer screen in which the student writes a summary statement to wrap up her written work.

In addition to these basic prompts, TELE-Web also has reminders prepared by teachers regarding specific topical content and questions, strategies, or key words for a particular text structure (e.g., narrative, expository, persuasive). To support and enhance student work, teachers might provide prompts such as "Use *who, what, when, where, how* to help you" or "Repeat your topic sentence at the end in a different format to cover your main idea again." Finally, TELE-Web includes a spellcheck function, students can check their text by having the computer read it back, and students may share their work with others and receive editorial feedback from selected peers or the entire TELE-Web community.

As you review the components of the TELE-Web support system for writing, it becomes obvious that Englert and colleagues have built into this system many aspects of effective instruction related to writing. To further support the effectiveness of this instructional technology, Englert and colleagues conducted research regarding the use of the TELE-Web to enhance writing of students with disabilities in upper elementary school. They found that the use of TELE-Web significantly enhanced student writing performance when compared to less scaffolded instruction, particularly with respect to the students' ability to produce organized text.

Source: Adapted from Englert, C.S., Wu, X., & Zhao, Y. (2005). Cognitive tools for writing: Scaffolding the performance of students through technology. *Learning Disabilities Research and Practice, 20*(3), 184–198. Adapted by permission.

## REFLECTIVE EXERCISE

**#9** Do you remember learning information in school that seemed painless? Or information that was learned in a boring way and seemed to take forever? What did the teacher do to facilitate the learning of the information that was learned painlessly? Why was the information that took forever so painful?

3. It should be sufficient to enable the student to perform a task without hesitation.
4. It should be cumulative over time, and information should be integrated into more complex tasks.

Research has long revealed that students who study material for 10 minutes a day over 5 days retain more information than students who study for 50 consecutive minutes during 1 day. It is often more effective to provide brief presentations (e.g., 10 minutes) of material spread over time rather than packing these presentations into a single time period (e.g., 60 minutes). Brief presentations ensure that students attend to more of the information, provide students with repeated opportunities to review and remember the information, and thus often result in improved learning outcomes.

Kame'enui and Carnine (1998) suggest that teachers review curriculum materials and textbooks to determine if opportunities for judicious review exist. Some curriculum and textbook developers provide for distributed, judicious review, while others do not. For example, some particularly difficult skills in beginning reading such as reading words that end in *ing* or *ed* require more practice than many other skills. If sufficient opportunities are not provided, then the teacher needs to build these opportunities into lessons across time with a variety of activities. This is a time-consuming task for teachers and illustrates the need to carefully select curriculum materials that build in judicious review with a variety of tasks that are distributed over time.

### Conspicuous Strategies

Once big ideas have been identified, effective teachers use conspicuous strategies to ensure that complex cognitive information has been conveyed to the learner effectively and efficiently. To effectively and efficiently solve problems or learn information, students need strategies for learning. These are likely to be strategies you have used in school to learn or to remember information or solve problems.

While some students develop these strategies independently, students who struggle to learn academic content often do not develop them unless they are explicitly taught. Experts in content areas succeed because they have developed strategies for solving problems, perhaps strategies that they cannot articulate. Kame'enui and Carnine (1998) note that there is an intuitive appeal to the idea of letting students who struggle in school (and others, for that matter) in on trade secrets that experts know and use. They also note that research evidence supports the perspective that students in general, and those who struggle to learn academic content in particular, benefit from instruction in the use of good strategies.

Several approaches to strategy instruction have been developed for use with students who struggle in school. For example, mnemonic devices have been developed across content areas to facilitate learning for students who have difficulty remembering important information. Mastropieri and Scruggs (2007) note that mnemonic devices have proven very effective in improving or aiding memory of students with disabilities as well as other students as they learn new information. For example, letter strategies can be used to learn material in science. "FARM-B" is a letter strategy mnemonic that is used to facilitate memory related to classes of vertebrate animals, which include F—Fish, A—Amphibian, R—Reptile, M—Mammal, B—Bird.

Keyword strategies are another approach to facilitating memory in areas such as learning a new language. For example, *strada* is the Italian word for "road." The keyword strategy uses a word that is familiar to the learner, which sounds like *strada* and is easily pictured, such as *straw*. Then a picture of straw lying in a road is used to strengthen the connection between the new word (i.e., *road*) and *strada* (Mastropieri & Scruggs, 2007).

Deshler and colleagues have developed the most comprehensive set of strategies for adolescents who struggle in school (Deshler, 2005; Deshler & Schumaker, 2006). These strategies are designed to support students in solving problems and completing tasks independently. Deshler and colleagues have developed strategies for study skills, test taking, writing paragraphs, monitoring errors, following instructions, teamwork, self-advocacy, assignment completion, text comprehension, and many other areas. For more information regarding these strategies, see "Can You Help Me with This Student?"

## REFLECTIVE EXERCISE

**#10** Can you name the five Great Lakes? (a hint—HOMES). Which months have 30 days? (another hint, use your knuckles or "Thirty day hath September . . ."). What are strategies you have used to remember information? Would these strategies be useful for students who are struggling to learn in your classroom?

## REFLECTIVE EXERCISE

**#11** In the teacher feature at the beginning of this chapter, Carol Sprague highlights developing a positive classroom climate in her classroom, where students work together and support one another to ensure that all learn. How might a teacher implement the principles described in this section in a classroom with the type of positive classroom climate that Carol describes?

## CAN YOU HELP ME WITH THIS STUDENT?

| To... | Jenny Hodges, High School Special Education Teacher |
|---|---|
| From... | Tom McCoy, High School History Teacher |
| Subject: | RE: Supporting a student with a learning disability in history class |

Dear Ms. Hodges,

I need your thoughts regarding how to help a student in my 12th-grade history class. Dylan has a reading problem and has been identified with a learning disability since elementary school. He is now a senior and has aspirations to attend the local community college, then transfer to the state college and complete his degree in building construction.

Dylan is having problems in my history class. While he works hard, participates in class discussions, is always well prepared for class, and completes all homework assignments and projects on time, he is having difficulty on tests. I have examined Dylan's test responses, and he has difficulty on tests that include material from an entire chapter. He also has problems with informational items, such as names of historical figures and events.

Dylan will likely fail my class unless I do something to provide him with support so he can get passing grades on tests. If he could learn test-taking and study skills, this could also benefit him in college. Any recommendations you can provide would be most appreciated.

—Tom McCoy

---

To:          Mr. McCoy
From:        Jenny Hodges
Subject:     RE: Supporting a student with a learning disability in history class

Mr. McCoy, as you know, many secondary students, especially those with learning disabilities, do not spontaneously develop learning strategies for taking tests, studying, and doing other academic work (Schumaker & Deshler, 2006). Deshler, Schumaker, and colleagues have developed instruction for several types of learning strategies to help students gain these skills (Deshler, et al. 2001; Schumaker & Deshler, 2006). This work has focused on directly teaching adolescents learning strategies, which are "an individual's approach to a task" (p. 122), and include "how a person thinks and acts when planning, executing, and evaluating performance on a task and its outcomes" (p. 122). This work has been based on five assumptions (Schumaker & Deshler, 2006):

1. Research has shown that a major contributing factor to the learning problems exhibited by adolescents is a failure to obtain the necessary strategies to succeed in the secondary curriculum.

2. Many adolescents with learning problems do not automatically produce strategies as they address novel tasks. Thus, these strategies must be explicitly taught.

3. Adolescents are more proficient in acquiring strategies for learning than are younger children.

4. Adolescents need to acquire learning strategies so that they will be in a position to learn independently in secondary school and beyond.

5. A learning strategies approach requires students to take responsibility for their own learning.

I have several books I will lend you that have more specific information regarding these strategies, including the following:

Deshler, D., & Schumaker, J. (Eds.). (2006). *Teaching adolescents with disabilities.* Thousand Oaks, CA: Corwin Press.

Deshler, D., Schumaker, J., Lenz, K., Bulgren, J., Hock, M., Knight, J., et al. (2001). Ensuring content-area learning by secondary students with learning disabilities. *Learning Disabilities Research and Practice, 16*(2), 96–108.

Lenz, K., Deshler, D., & Kissam, B. (Eds.). (2004). *Teaching content to all: Evidence-based inclusive practices in middle and secondary schools.* Boston: Allyn & Bacon.

Reid, R., & Lienemann, T. (2006). *Strategy instruction for students with learning disabilities.* New York: Guilford Press.

Schumaker, J., & Deshler, D. (2006). Teaching adolescents to be strategic learners. In D. Deshler & J. Schumaker (Eds.), *Teaching adolescents with disabilities* (pp. 121–156). Thousand Oaks, CA: Corwin Press.

I hope you find this information useful.

# TRANSITION TO ADULT LIFE

As we have noted, the symptoms of learning disabilities persist into adulthood. Of course, this disability category is populated by a broad range of students, with varying needs for support as they transition to adult life. The support that any particular student with a learning disability will need depends on the severity of the deficits that the individual has relative to academic and social-behavioral skills. Some of the students with the mildest of disabilities learn to compensate for these deficits and are very successful in life with no support. Others with severe reading or language problems that persist into adulthood may have great difficulty succeeding in postsecondary education or getting and keeping a job.

## Vocational Support

Research has documented relatively high levels of employment for persons with learning disabilities immediately after high school. For example, Goldstein, Murray, and Edgar (1998) found that persons with learning disabilities worked more hours per week and earned more than peers without learning disabilities during the first 4 years after high school. This finding reflects the fact that the relatively mild disabilities that characterize learning disabilities did not serve as a major barrier to obtaining entry-level (and relatively low-paying) jobs.

While this finding is cause for some optimism regarding the employment prospects for persons with learning disabilities, which are better than those for people in other disability categories (Mellard & Lancaster, 2003), the long-term employment prospects are not so positive. More specifically, Goldstein and colleagues (1998) found that after 4 years, persons *without* learning disabilities earn much more than persons with learning disabilities, with no significant difference in hours worked. Mellard and Lancaster (2003) speculate that this trend in earnings occurs because "adults without learning disabilities are finishing college or specialized training and receiving promotions during and following the 5th year of employment, while adults with learning disabilities are experiencing career stagnation" (p. 360). This career stagnation occurs primarily because a large proportion of persons with learning disabilities do not participate in postsecondary education. Thus, the vocational success of students with learning disabilities, as with students without learning disabilities, is strongly related to participation in postsecondary education. Engaging these students in a discussion of the value of postsecondary education and the range of postsecondary options that exist is critically important to ensuring that students with learning disabilities are well prepared to make decisions about their life after school (Mellard & Lancaster,

Many students with learning disabilities attend college, and some will need accommodations to succeed in college courses.

2003). Furthermore, careful selection of postsecondary options that provide the necessary supports for persons with learning disabilities to succeed is an important consideration.

### Support in Higher Education

Many students with learning disabilities will attend some form of postsecondary education, often a 2- or 4-year college. Many colleges and universities make special accommodations and provide supports for students with learning disabilities through student services offices on campus. Information regarding colleges and universities that offer comprehensive programs for students with learning disabilities are described in *Colleges with Programs for Students with Learning Disabilities or Attention Deficit Disorders* (Peterson's Guide, 2003).

It is noteworthy that some states have made significant efforts to develop support systems for students with learning disabilities in postsecondary settings. For example, the California community college system has developed supports for students with learning disabilities, including extensive in-class assistance as well as support in other areas (e.g., counseling, assistive technology, support in transitioning to a 4-year institution of higher education) (Mellard & Lancaster, 2003).

## PREVAILING ISSUES, CONTROVERSIES, AND IMPLICATIONS FOR THE TEACHER

Great progress has been made since the 1970s in addressing the educational needs of students with learning disabilities. Although researchers generally agree about educational interventions for these students, several areas of controversy remain regarding who is identified with learning disabilities and where the education of these students should occur.

## Is an Alternative Approach Needed to Identify Students with Learning Disabilities?

Much controversy continues to surround the identification of students with learning disabilities. Major problems related to the learning disability category include the following:

- The discrepancy criterion, which has often been used as a primary criterion for identifying students with learning disabilities, is not educationally meaningful (i.e., students who are behind grade level in reading but who do not have a discrepancy are taught using the same methods as students with a severe discrepancy) (Bradley, Danielson, & Doolittle, 2007).
- Children must wait to fail before a severe discrepancy exists and they are eligible for identification with a learning disability (Bradley et al., 2007).
- The number of students identified with learning disabilities grew rapidly during the 1990s, and some contend that too many students are identified with learning disabilities. Currently, students with learning disabilities make up about 43% of all students with disabilities.

As noted, the controversy surrounding the identification of students with learning disabilities led to language in IDEA 2004 that allows states to use an alternative approach to identify these students that does not require the use of a severe discrepancy. While many professionals support the alternative, RTI approach to student identification (L. Fuchs, 2003; Reschly, 2005; Vaughn & Fuchs, 2003), others question its feasibility (Gerber, 2005; Kavale, Holdnack, & Mostert, 2005; Mastropieri & Scruggs, 2000).

Some contend that RTI has advantages over more traditional approaches to the identification of students with learning disabilities (L. Fuchs, 2003; L. Fuchs et al., 2005; L. Fuchs, Fuchs, & Speece, 2002; Reschly, 2005). Perhaps most important, RTI provides assistance to students in a timely fashion and does not require that students wait to fail before assistance is provided (D. Fuchs et al., 2004). A second advantage of this approach is that it ensures that the student's learning problem does not result from poor instruction (L. Fuchs et al., 2005). Finally, the assessment data that are collected to identify students who are at risk and monitor their progress provide useful information for the teacher regarding how to improve instruction.

Several disadvantages to using RTI have also been identified (Gerber, 2005; Kavale et al., 2005; Mastropieri & Scruggs, 2005). Perhaps most important, the roles and responsibilities of teachers and school psychologists who will implement RTI procedures have not been clearly defined. For example, who will be responsible for implementing scientifically based methods of instruction? Second, it is unclear how local school systems will implement scientifically based practices in classrooms district-wide. Research evidence suggests that implementation of these practices in special education classrooms has been limited and that many general education teachers may lack the necessary skills to implement them (Gerber, 2005; Mastropieri & Scruggs, 2005). Finally, while a significant number of students are initially identified with learning disabilities at the secondary level, it is unclear how educators will use RTI to identify these older students.

Although the implementation of RTI remains unclear, and much controversy exists regarding technical aspects of this approach, RTI procedures are being widely adopted in states and local school systems across the United States (Spectrum K12, 2009). Whether this approach will result in improved practice regarding the identification of these students and reduce some of the problems related to a traditional approach to identification remains to be seen.

## Are Students with Learning Disabilities Appropriately Included in General Education Classrooms Across the United States?

Since the 1960s, controversy has reigned regarding the extent to which students with learning disabilities should be educated in inclusive settings (Dunn, 1968; D. Fuchs & Fuchs, 1994; McLeskey, 2007). Much of this controversy has addressed whether students should spend all of the school day in general education classrooms (i.e., what some call *full inclusion*). Most professionals who work with students with mild disabilities have not called for full inclusion but have recommended that students with learning disabilities be educated in general education classrooms for much of the school day, with small-group intensive instruction provided in separate settings as needed (e.g., McLeskey & Waldron, 2000, 2002).

This perspective is based on two areas of research regarding these students. First, research on the effectiveness of highly restrictive separate-class placement has demonstrated that these settings are generally not more effective than placements in general education for much of the school day for students with learning disabilities (Carlberg & Kavale, 1980; Salend & Duhaney, 2007). Thus, most professionals have taken the perspective that students with learning disabilities should spend much of the school day in general education classrooms.

Second, while students with learning disabilities should spend most of the school day in the general education classroom, they may need to receive brief, intensive instruction in a separate setting. The research on effective reading instruction has revealed that students with learning disabilities and reading problems need instruction that is more explicit and intense than instruction that is typically provided in the general education classroom (Foorman & Torgesen, 2001). This type of instruction is often delivered individually or in small groups (two or three students) and thus may be provided within the general education classroom or in a separate setting.

National data regarding the inclusion of students with learning disabilities in general education classrooms reveal that most states are moving toward educating students with learning disabilities for much of the school day in general education classrooms (McLeskey et al., 2004). We anticipate that this movement toward more inclusive placements for students with learning disabilities will continue in the future, although several states continue to educate large numbers of students with learning disabilities in highly restrictive settings. However, we believe that the emphasis that has been placed on student achievement outcomes in recent years will result in less emphasis on full inclusion and more emphasis on settings in which research-based practices can be delivered that result in improved outcomes for students with learning disabilities.

A key to providing successful inclusive programs that improve student outcomes is collaboration between special and general education teachers. For further information regarding how teachers work collaboratively to support students with learning disabilities in general education classrooms as part of inclusive programs, see the "Real World" feature.

Challenges and Solutions

## Working collaboratively with a general education teacher

*For several years, Mr. Berg spent most of the school day teaching high school students with learning disabilities learning strategies and study skills in his separate, special education classroom. He has been very successful in these activities and has worked with several content area teachers to make sure that the students use their learning strategies in the general education classroom. Beginning next year, Mr. Berg will work with general education content area teachers to adapt instruction and differentiate instruction in their classrooms. He is excited about his new role but is concerned because he has heard that some general education teachers do not like to collaborate with other teachers. Mr. Berg wants to learn more about how to be a successful collaborator with general education teachers. He has several questions about this work. How do his collaborators view collaboration? How should he and his collaborators prepare to make sure their collaboration is successful? What are critical considerations to ensure that collaboration succeeds?*

Most students with learning disabilities spend some or much of the school day in the general education classroom. Special and general education teachers often work collaboratively to support these students. At times these teachers work as co-teachers, sharing responsibility for instruction and student learning. At other times, special education teachers work as consultants, providing ideas about adapting instruction and curriculum to better meet student needs.

As he read about consultation, Mr. Berg found that many teachers view collaboration as a natural skill, something that they should just know how to do (Friend & Cook, 2010). Upon further investigation, he found that this is often not the case (Dettmer, Thurston, Knackendoffel, & Dyck, 2009). Some teachers may be natural collaborators, but many must learn key skills if they are to work effectively with others (McLeskey, Rosenberg, & Westling, 2010). In examining the experience and perspective of his fellow high school teachers who are potential collaborators, Mr. Berg found that few of these teachers had been involved in collaboration, and most were wary of having another in their classroom or sharing responsibility for planning and student outcomes.

In reading about effective collaboration, Mr. Berg found that he and his collaborators would benefit from implementing several steps before beginning to collaborate. These steps include (Friend & Cook, 2010; McLeskey et al., 2010):

1. Prepare for collaboration by participating in professional development with collaborators to develop the necessary knowledge and skills for success.
2. Make sure that collaborative roles of all participants are clearly defined and that all understand their roles. For example, will Mr. Berg work with teachers to develop lesson plans and adapt instruction in their classrooms? Or will he work with teachers on testing accommodations to make sure tests measure content accurately?

3. Understand the importance of role parity. That is, no matter what roles teachers play in collaboration, all should feel that they are important contributors and equal partners as decisions are made.
4. Develop key skills for collaboration related to communication, especially active listening skills.
5. Evaluate the success of collaboration frequently, as the nature of collaborative relationships change over time, making it necessary to determine how a collaborative relationship might be changed to work better.

### Valuable Resources for the Teacher

For more information on how to successfully collaborate with others, you may want to consult the following resources:

Dettmer, P., Thurston, L., Knackendoffel, A., & Dyck, N. (2009). *Collaboration, consultation, and teamwork for students with special needs.* Upper Saddle River, NJ: Merrill/Pearson Education.

Friend, M., & Cook, L. (2010). *Interactions: Collaboration skills for school professionals* (6th ed.). Boston: Allyn & Bacon.

Kochhar-Bryant, C. (2008). *Collaboration and system coordination for students with special needs.* Upper Saddle River, NJ: Merrill/Pearson Education.

### Final Thoughts

Teachers who are effective collaborators are those who continue to gain skills and dispositions to support their work and make it successful. Collaborators must be flexible and open to new ideas, even when those ideas contrast with their own. For example, teachers often bring different perspectives to important classroom issues, such as how reading should be taught, how a test should be used to measure student knowledge of content, or how students should be grouped for learning particular content. Being open-minded about possibilities for changing and improving a classroom is a way of demonstrating respect for other collaborators and can prevent potential problems with collaborative interactions. Several essential behaviors to consider when working toward a respectful, equal partnership with a collaborator include (Dettmer et al., 2009):

- Really listen, and talk, together with collaborators
- Describe your perspectives, but give objective examples whenever possible
- Work toward resolutions or compromises together
- Provide a collective summary of discussion points and tentative agreements
- If the process is stalled, seek input from others
- Talk after completing a plan, to reflect on outcomes and how to improve collaboration next time

# 6 SUMMARY

Students with learning disabilities are often perplexing to parents and teachers. These students have difficulty in some academic areas but not others. What all students with learning disabilities have in common is that they tend to struggle to learn academic content in one or two specific areas and have strengths in other areas.

## Definitions and Classification Criteria for Students with Learning Disabilities

- The primary criterion used to identify students with learning disabilities has traditionally been a severe discrepancy between expected achievement level and actual achievement level in one or more academic content areas.
- Other criteria used to identify these students include ensuring that another disability (the exclusion clause) or lack of opportunity to learn did not result in the severe discrepancy and documenting that the student needs special education services.
- An alternative approach used to identify students with learning disabilities is response-to-intervention, which is based on the assumption that students who are struggling academically should only be identified with a learning disability if they do not respond to effective instruction. The use of this approach is rapidly growing across the United States.

## Characteristics of Students with Learning Disabilities

- The only characteristic that is shared by all students with learning disabilities is uneven development of academic skills. This category is thus very heterogeneous.
- The most common area in which students with learning disabilities have difficulty is reading, which is a problem for approximately 80% of these students.
- Many students with learning disabilities also have difficulty with oral expression, written expression, and mathematics.
- Students with learning disabilities also often have cognitive difficulties in areas such as memory, attention, and metacognitive skills and problems with social skills.

## Prevalence, Course, and Causes of Learning Disabilities

- Learning disability is the largest special education category, with a prevalence of more than 4.9%.

- The prevalence of learning disabilities differs significantly across states and ranges from approximately 2% to more than 7%.
- Although research documents that learning disabilities persist into adulthood, many persons with learning disabilities compensate for their disability and are successful as adults. However, one in four adults with learning disabilities has difficulty finding good employment and living independently.
- In most instances, we do not know what causes a learning disability. Several factors have been implicated as contributing factors, including abnormal brain function, genetic factors, and lack of access to effective instruction.

## Identification and Assessment of Students with Learning Disabilities

- Students with learning disabilities are typically identified after they enter school and fail to make appropriate progress in one or more academic areas.
- A severe discrepancy has traditionally been the primary criterion used to identify students with learning disabilities in most states. Increasingly, states are using a response-to-intervention (RTI) approach to identify students with learning disabilities.

## Effective Educational Practices for Students with Learning Disabilities

- Research indicates that most students with learning disabilities spend most of the school day in general education classrooms.
- The number of students with learning disabilities who are educated in separate classrooms or separate school settings has decreased significantly over the past decade.
- To ensure that students with learning disabilities receive high-quality instruction, researchers have recommended that teachers focus on four principles to guide instruction.
- Successful inclusion of students with learning disabilities is highly dependent upon general and special education teachers working collaboratively to provide needed supports.

## Prevailing Issues

- Controversy has surrounded the identification of students with learning disabilities because many professionals contend that the primary criterion used to identify these students (i.e., the severe discrepancy)

As teachers, we often marvel at how our students develop: Motor skills mature; sophisticated (and sometimes shocking) language skills emerge; abstract thinking develops, and creativity is expressed, often with passion. Stunning changes occur in the areas of social and emotional development. Over time, students develop friendships based on common interests and engage in cooperative, satisfying play. These same students also test limits and experience the consequences of their growing independence. The behaviors associated with the social and emotional development of children and adolescents are challenging to parents and teachers. These behaviors are, for the most part, developmentally appropriate. In this chapter, however, we focus on students whose affect and behavior differ significantly from their typically maturing peers. These students with differences are a varied group, with some bearing little resemblance to others. For example, some of these students are extremely withdrawn and unable to make friends due to high levels of anxiety or a lack of social competence. Others, like the adolescents taught by Steve Kennedy and Steve Williams, behave aggressively and want attention so much that they disrupt instructional activities.

Educators use many terms to refer to these extreme student behaviors, including *emotional disturbance, emotional handicap, mental illness,* and *social maladjustment,* to name just a few. Some professionals use these different terms to distinguish subtle differences in the nature or severity of the presenting behavior problems, while others use the terms interchangeably (Rosenberg, Wilson, Maheady, & Sindelar, 2004). We use the term ***emotional and behavioral disabilities (EBD)*** because it is consistent with language used in federal and state regulations. More important, it reflects our belief that the primary goal of teachers is to influence specific behaviors that impede student achievement.

## REFLECTIVE EXERCISE

Many students with EBD exhibit high-risk acting-behaviors. What dispositions person considering these students possess?

## FAQ Sheet
### STUDENTS WITH EBD

| | |
|---|---|
| ...they? | • Children and youth whose behavioral and emotional responses are so different from appropriate age, cultural, or ethnic norms that their educational performance is affected adversely. |
| ...typical ...istics? | • Aggression<br>• Rule breaking<br>• Anxiety<br>• Depression<br>• Social skills deficits<br>• Social withdrawal<br>• Attention deficits |
| ...the ...phics? | • 458,000 students ages 6–21 (0.69% of all school-age students)<br>• 7.6% of all students with disabilities<br>• Approximately 80% male<br>• Approximately 60% white, 26% African American, 11% Hispanic<br>• Approximately 50% receive medication |
| ...e students ...? | • Approximately one third are educated in general education facilities but are outside general education classes 60% of the day.<br>• Students with EBD are four times more likely than all others with disabilities to be educated in separate facilities. |
| ...students identified ...sed for intervention? | • Common methods used for identification include direct, systematic observation of specific behaviors and commercially prepared behavior rating scales.<br>• Functional behavioral assessments provide the most useful information for instructional and behavioral planning. |
| ...the outcomes? | • Approximately one third are arrested during their school years.<br>• Approximately one half are unemployed 3 to 5 years after leaving school. |

is not educationally meaningful and that children must wait to fail before being identified.

• An alternative approach to the identification of students with learning disabilities, RTI, is being used in many school districts across the United States, and offers much promise for improving identification it practices for students with learning disabilities.

• Controversy exists regarding the extent to which students with learning disabilities should be included in general education classrooms.

• Available evidence suggests that most students with learning disabilities should spend much of the school day in general education classrooms with appropriate support.

## ADDRESSING THE PROFESSIONAL STANDARDS

Council for Exceptional Children (CEC) Knowledge Standards addressed in the chapter:

ICC1K5, EC1K1, EC1K2, ICC2K1, ICC2K2, ICC2K5, ICC2K6, ICC3K2, ICC5K3, ICC7K4, ICC8K1, ICC8K2.

Appendix B: CEC Knowledge and Skill Standards Common Core has a full listing of the standards referenced here.

**myeducationlab**

Now go to Topic 8: Learning Disabilities in the MyEduationLab for your course, where you can:

• Find learning outcomes for the broad concepts covered in this chapter along with the national standards that connect to these outcomes.

• Complete Assignments and Activities that can help you more deeply understand the chapter content.

• Examine challenging situations and cases presented in the IRIS Center Resources.

• Apply and practice your understanding of the core concepts and skills identified in the chapter with the Building Teaching Skills and Dispositions learning units.

• Check your comprehension on the content covered in the chapter by going to the Study Plan in the Book-Specific Resources section for your text. Here you will be able to take a chapter quiz, receive feedback on your answers, and then access Review, Practice, and Enrichment activities to enhance your understanding of chapter content.

• Access video clips of CCSSO National Teachers of the Year award winners responding to the question, "Why Do I Teach?" in the Teacher Talk section.

# chapter

# 7

# Emotional and Behavioral Disabilities

## REFLECT UPON

- How are emotional and behavioral disabilities (EBD) defined and classified?
- What are the primary behavioral characteristics of EBD?
- How many students have EBD, and what causal factors are associated with the disability?
- How do we identify and assess students with EBD?
- What educational practices improve academic, social, early childhood, and transition outcomes for students with EBD?
- What are two prevailing and controversial issues associated with the education of students with EBD?

## MY PROFESSION, MY STORY: **STEVE KENNEDY AND STEVE**

Steve Kennedy and Steve Williams, known affectionately as "the Steves," coordinate the "school within a school (SWAS)" behavioral support program at Heritage High School in Loudon, Virginia. SWAS is a dynamic, comprehensive program that employs a range of service-delivery arrangements and evidence-based strategies to successfully support students with EBD in the general education environment. Being experienced athletic coaches (Steve Williams is currently a football coach at HHS), the "Steves" recognize that teamwork, organization, and persistence are essential if the goals of any worthwhile endeavor are to be met. Consequently, their SWAS "game plan" is direct and straightforward: Students have opportunities to participate in all school activities—required and extracurricular. Teachers also provide positive behavior support and instructional accommodations to enhance and sustain participation. Mr. Kennedy and Mr. Williams work closely with teams of general educators to make instructional accommodations as well as develop and maintain behavior intervention plans. Focused instruction in social skills, immediate recovery room services for crisis management, and personalized content area instruction in a self-contained setting are available for those with more intensive needs. Most important, all services are provided in a climate of commitment, collaboration, and respect.

Mr. Kennedy and Mr. Williams are sensitive to challenges and stressors associated with teaching students with EBD. They have seen how the behaviors of students with EBD can be volatile and threatening to others. They have learned that positive behavior support is energizing but can, at times, result in frustration and exhaustion. To navigate the tough days, endurance and motivation come largely from the empathy both men feel for the students and their families. By recognizing the perspectives of these stakeholders, they humanize the process of education, going beyond the often-distant, jargon-filled talk of placements, levels, and hours of service delivery. Like successful coaches addressing the individual characteristics of their players, Mr. Kennedy and Mr. Williams remind themselves that these are real kids, with real families, and not merely a collection of behavioral difficulties or goals in an individualized education program (IEP). They remind themselves that their program—their game plan—must provide hope and success in an environment of fairness and respect.

The rewards come when instructional efforts result in well-earned Heritage High team victories. The most heartfelt moments are when students who initially presented high rates of inappropriate behaviors earn their diplomas and transition successfull[...] pendent living. These are the occasio[...] Steve Williams, in their roles as teac[...] that they positively impact the lives [...] for those who plan on teaching st[...] prepared, adapt lessons for succes[...] team, and remember your commitr[...] sensitive to student and family nee[...] propriate behaviors personally. Pos[...] teachers to assess and address the f[...] haviors, without becoming too i[...] emotions of tense situations. Fina[...] teachers of students with EBD requ[...] emotionally. Teachers must include[...] of the overall "game plan" and e[...] ing) that allow for rewarding dive[...] classroom.

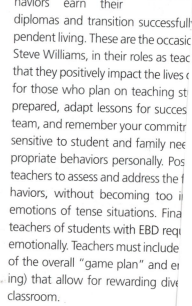

REFL[...]

#1[...]
out beha[...]
should a[...]
teaching[...]
Why?

Who are[...]

What are[...]
character[...]

What are[...]
demogra[...]

Where a[...]
educated[...]

How are[...]
and asses[...]

What are[...]

# DEFINITIONS AND CLASSIFICATION CRITERIA

## Defining Emotional and Behavioral Disabilities

What do we mean when we say that a student has an emotional and behavioral disability? Specifically, how do the behaviors of those with EBD differ from the behaviors of students who engage in mischief? How do we measure these differences? Such questions continue to challenge personnel involved in the identification and education of students with EBD. Let's consider the definition of emotional disturbance in the Individuals with Disabilities Education Act (IDEA), and assess the usefulness of the definition in answering these questions.

> The term emotional disturbance means a condition exhibiting one or more of the following characteristics over a long period of time and to a marked degree that adversely affects a student's educational performance: (A) An inability to learn which cannot be explained by intellectual, sensory, or health factors; (B) An inability to build or maintain satisfactory interpersonal relationships with peers and teachers; (C) Inappropriate types of behavior or feelings under normal circumstances; (D) A general pervasive mood of unhappiness or depression; (E) A tendency to develop physical symptoms or fears associated with personal or school problems. The term includes children who are schizophrenic. The term does not include children who are socially maladjusted, unless it is determined that they have an emotional disturbance. (U.S. Department of Education, 2005)

Interestingly, the IDEA definition is not new to the field of special education. Eli Bower published the original version in the 1960s; and with a few minor changes, it has been included in all reauthorizations of the law. However, does this definition with its long history help identify students with EBD? On the positive side, the definition is descriptive and contains likely manifestations of the disability. Unfortunately, the descriptions are general, and some terms are not defined. For example, the initial qualifying terms "to a marked extent" and "over a long period of time" are not quantified and are subject to arbitrary interpretation. Moreover, it is unclear what is meant by "satisfactory interpersonal relationships" or "inappropriate behaviors and feelings." These vague terms are subject to wide interpretation and, as we will discuss later, have resulted in certain groups of students being overrepresented in this disability category. Moreover, the exclusion of those with social maladjustment from the definition invites confusion, because it is difficult to distinguish if certain patterns of behavior are antisocial or the manifestation of an emotional disorder (Merrell & Walker, 2004).

Many people who are active in the field have been trying to strengthen the definition of EBD. Consider the definition that has been proposed by National Mental Health and Special Education Coalition, a group of 30 different education, mental health, advocacy, and parent organizations.

- The term "emotional or behavioral disorder" means a disability that is: characterized by behavioral or emotional responses in school programs so different from appropriate age, cultural, or ethnic norms that the responses adversely affect educational performance, including academic, social, vocational or personal skills; more than a temporary, expected response to stressful events in the environment; consistently exhibited in two different settings, at least one of which is school-related; and unresponsive to direct intervention applied in general education, or the condition of a child is such that general education interventions would be insufficient.
- The disability can co-exist with other disabilities.
- The term includes schizophrenic disorder, affective disorder, anxiety disorder, or other sustained disorders of conduct or adjustment, affecting a child if the disorder affects educational performance as described in paragraph (1). (*Federal Register*, February 10, 1993, p. 7938)

To check your comprehension on the content covered in Chapter 7, go to the Book-Specific Resources in the MyEducationLab for your course, select your text, and complete the Study Plan. Here you will be able to take a chapter quiz, receive feedback on your answers, and then access Review, Practice, and Enrichment activities to enhance your understanding of chapter content.

Is this definition an improvement over the IDEA version? In some respects, it reflects considerable progress in that it focuses on school-based behavior and considers contextual factors such as age and cultural norms (Forness & Kavale, 2000). Moreover, the coalition definition requires multiple sources of data for eligibility and recognizes that EBD coexists with other disability conditions. Still, like the IDEA definition, it includes many vague terms that are difficult to quantify (e.g., "so different from appropriate . . . norms"), and methods for measuring key aspects of the definition are not provided (Cullinan, 2004).

However, before we become too critical, let's conduct a brief reality check: It is possible that an objective, fail-safe definition of EBD is impossible to develop (Rosenberg et al., 2004). Consider the following problems. First, defining a disability requires a reliable and valid assessment of behaviors. For example, validated intelligence tests are common in the identification of students with developmental disabilities, and reliable measures of academic achievement are central to the identification of learning disabilities. With EBD, however, no single trusted measure of social or emotional functioning is equivalent to those used for assessing intelligence or achievement. Second, the range of behaviors presented by those with EBD often overlaps with the behaviors of those without disabilities. Indeed, many who work with such students are startled to find that the behaviors of those with EBD are not totally unlike their own behaviors (Rhodes, 1967). Finally, the variety of theories that attempt to explain the development and maintenance of EBD often directly conflict. Consequently, it is unlikely that any single definition could satisfy those who approach EBD from differing perspectives.

Despite these formal problems in definition, most teachers believe that they can recognize social and emotional problems when they see them. These teachers are usually correct, especially when facing extreme instances of student behavior. Unfortunately, a large gray area of behavior cannot be reliably categorized as either typical or problematic. Consequently, students are often identified as having EBD based on individual and imprecise tolerance levels of teachers, administrators, related-service providers, and parents. Because of this subjectivity, you will find that students with EBD vary in characteristics both among and within schools and classrooms.

## Classification Criteria

It is likely that you will come into contact with the two systems used to classify EBD: **statistically derived dimensional** and **clinically derived.** In the statistically derived system, EBD is viewed as a cluster of extreme forms of typical behaviors and emotions. Classification is based on how much an individual differs in rate and frequency from normative samples of the population. The most researched dimensional system is the Achenbach System of Empirically Based Assessment (ASEBA) (Achenbach & Rescorla, 2001), in which teachers, parents, and children themselves rate behaviors associated with eight dimensions: aggressive behavior, rule breaking, anxious/depressed, withdrawn/depressed, somatic complaints, attention problems, social problems, and thought problems. Those classified as having EBD would have extreme ratings in one or more of the categories.

Clinically derived systems evolved from the work of psychologists who observed that certain patterns of behavior occur regularly among specific groups of individuals. These patterns of behaviors evolved into distinct diagnostic entities. The most widely used clinically derived system for classifying behavioral issues is the *Diagnostic and Statistical Manual* (4th ed.) (DSM-IV-TR), published by the American Psychiatric Association (2000). DSM-IV-TR (the "TR" stands for text revision) provides descriptions and diagnostic criteria for psychological disorders and associated problems such as physical and communication disorders. Keep in mind that not all psychological problems affect educational performance and not all children and adolescents with DSM-IV-TR diagnoses will qualify for special education services.

FIGURE 7.1 • **WHAT IS DSM-IV-TR?**

DSM-IV-TR (American Psychiatric Association, 2000) is the most current iteration of the American Psychiatric Association's classification system of mental disorders. The original DSM system was developed in 1952 as a way for psychiatrists to systematically classify the symptoms, etiologies, and progressions of the variety of mental diseases. DSM-IV-TR, the fifth revision of the system, uses a comprehensive and systematic multi-axial framework to characterize disorders. Since mental disorders are not singular events that occur in isolation, the multi-axial framework allows for assessment of different domains of information relevant to diagnosis and treatment. Both Axis I and Axis II are used to report specific clinical disorders. Some of the more common DSM disorders that can be applied to children and adolescents with EBD include mental retardation, learning disorders, attention-deficit and disruptive behavior disorders, mood disorders, anxiety disorders, psychotic disorders, and adjustment disorders. Axis III is used for noting general medical conditions (e.g., diseases of the blood or nervous system) that may be relevant in fully understanding the disorder; Axis IV is used to identify associated psychosocial and environmental factors such as family legal, social, or legal issues. Finally, Axis V is a clinical assessment of the individual's global or overall level of functioning.

It is important for educators to have a working knowledge of DSM-IV-TR (Cullinan, 2004; Mattison, 2004):

- DSM diagnoses are often found in students' records and presented at various team meetings.
- Clinical personnel often use DSM terminology and information when suggesting possible treatment interventions.
- DSM is the official classification system of many mental health organizations, government agencies, and medical providers.
- Services and insurance reimbursements are often contingent on a clinical DSM diagnosis.
- Teachers can help families obtain necessary supplemental community-based mental health services that require clinical rather than educational diagnoses.
- DSM emphasizes that many students with EBD have multiple behavior problems that require comprehensive solutions.

Which of these two classification systems will you find most useful? The major advantage of statistically derived systems is that categories of behavior can be quantified and compared among students. The use of quantitative rating scales tends to be more authentic and reliable than the judgments typical in clinical systems. Moreover, listings of behavioral indicators assist in the formulation of educational goals and the design of interventions. Most important, the statistically derived system reinforces that most patterns of EBD are extreme forms of typical behavior that can, under the right conditions, be modified (Gresham & Gansle, 1992; Gresham & Kern, 2004; Lambros, Ward, Bocian, MacMillan, & Gresham, 1998). Still, when working with students with EBD, you will come into contact with clinically derived classifications such as DSM-IV-TR and should have a working knowledge of how that system works (see Figure 7.1).

# PRIMARY BEHAVIORAL CHARACTERISTICS

## Externalizing Behaviors

Externalizing behavior problems are the defiant, aggressive, and noncompliant student actions that disrupt school and classroom activities. Because teachers have a low tolerance for such behaviors, externalizing behaviors are the most frequent reasons for disciplinary removals as well as referrals for psychological, psychiatric, and juvenile justice services (Cullinan & Sabornie, 2004; Tobin, Sugai, & Colvin, 1996). Three of the more common types of externalizing behaviors are aggression, rule breaking, and noncompliance.

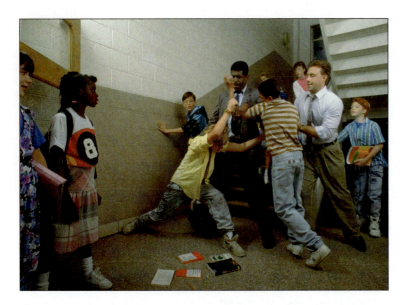

The anger and explosiveness of aggressive behaviors are frightening for both students and teachers.

## Aggression

Because they are violent, abusive, and destructive, aggressive behaviors are easily identified in our schools and classrooms. Aggressive behaviors have three elements—an observable behavior, intent to do harm, and an identifiable victim—and are usually divided into two discrete categories: verbal aggression and physical aggression. Verbal aggression includes yelling, teasing, whining, tantrums, and using profanity as well as verbally threatening or humiliating another person. Physical aggression includes abusive and violent actions such as hitting, kicking, grabbing, and biting (Patterson, Reid, Jones, & Conger, 1975; Rosenberg et al., 2004).

Aggressive behaviors are frightening. They jar us with their anger, volatility, and explosiveness. Students who use aggression appear to understand shock value and use their extreme behaviors to intimidate and coerce others. In fact, students identified as having EBD threaten others at significantly higher rates than do other students (Kaplan & Cornell, 2005). Peers and, not surprisingly, many adults acquiesce to aggressive students' demands in order to avoid confrontations and the resulting flare-ups that accompany threatening behaviors. An unfortunate consequence of this chain of events is that other students learn that aggression (or the threat of aggression) can result in desired outcomes.

## Rule Breaking

Many students who break rules believe that established boundaries do not apply to them. Their rule breaking ranges from minor offenses such as tardiness to class and running in the hallways to more extreme behaviors such as substance abuse, truancy, theft, cheating, and vandalism. Keep in mind that most young people—up to 95%—engage in some misconduct that could bring them into contact with school administrators or juvenile legal authorities. Therefore, when describing rule breaking, it is critical to focus on (1) the frequency of the act, (2) the seriousness of the act, and (3) the attitude of the offender (Simonsen & Vito, 2003). Single angry or impulsive acts accompanied by remorse are not indicators of EBD, and they require different interventions than do repetitive, premeditated acts committed with little guilt or regret.

## Noncompliance

Noncompliance, a situation in which students actively choose not to respond to instructions or requests, disrupts academic and social development and often leads to more serious patterns of antisocial behavior (Walker, Ramsey, & Gresham, 2004; Walker & Walker, 1991). Left unaddressed, noncompliance can have a detrimental effect on postschool vocational, personal, and social outcomes. An individual who fails to respond to requests and blames others would be unable to maintain employment. Similarly, an individual who responds to social requests with hostility and derision would have a difficult time developing and maintaining friendships.

## Internalizing Behaviors

Internalizing behavior problems are inwardly directed actions that often result in the same debilitating degree of destruction associated with externalizing problems. However, the relatively covert nature of internalizing behavior problems makes them

**PEARSON**
**myeducationlab**

To enhance your understanding of these types of externalizing behaviors, go to the IRIS Center Resources section of Topic 10: Emotional/Behavioral Disorders in the MyEducationLab for your course and complete the Module entitled *Addressing Disruptive and Noncompliant Behaviors (Part 1): Understanding the Acting-Out Cycle.*

difficult to identify. Consequently, in sharp contrast with externalizing problem behaviors, teachers underrefer students with suspected internalizing behavior problems (Gresham & Kern, 2004). Three major internalizing behavior problems are social withdrawal, anxiety disorders, and depression.

## Social Withdrawal

Students who are withdrawn share three common characteristics (Odom & DeKlyen, 1986; Rubin, Coplan, & Bowker, 2009):

- An excessive amount of time in solitary play
- Infrequent positive social interactions with peers
- Low rates of verbalization

Why is it important to identify these students and improve their frequency and quality of socialization? First, children learn from their interactions with one another, and low rates of interpersonal exchanges limit opportunities to learn important social, communicative, and cognitive behaviors. Exchanges with peers also provide opportunities for children to try out strategies, receive feedback, and refine essential elements of how best to communicate and get along with others (Kennedy & Shukla, 1995). Second, the failure to develop appropriate peer relationships in childhood is predictive of social adjustment and psychological problems in adolescence and adulthood, most notably for depression and loneliness (Gresham, Lane, MacMillan, & Bocian, 1999; Rubin et al., 2009). Finally, students who are socially withdrawn engage in important and related academic behaviors (e.g., attention to task, conversing about assignments) at lower rates than do their peers, conditions that often result in diminished academic achievement (Rosenberg et al., 2004).

**REFLECTIVE EXERCISE**

**#2** Although internalizing behavior is difficult to identify, teachers must learn to recognize it. How might teachers informally screen their students for excessive withdrawal, anxiety disorders, or depression as part of the instructional routines?

## CAN YOU HELP ME WITH THIS STUDENT?

| To... | Dr. Sandy Ludwig, District Psychologist |
|---|---|
| From... | Clara Hart, Fourth-Grade Teacher |
| Subject: | Addressing the needs of a student with depression |

Dear Dr. Ludwig,

I have been teaching fourth-grade students for 2 years. For the past several weeks, I have seen a significant change in Tanika's behavior. Although she was never what is considered an extrovert, her interactions with the rest of my fourth-grade class have decreased to the point that she rarely interacts with others during cooperative group work. Tanika seems to have lost weight and appears tired and sad, with a look that indicates that her attention is elsewhere. She rarely attends during direct instruction, and her completion rate of assignments, once quite high, is now infrequent. When I ask about her assignments, Tanika says little and tears up, saying only that she wishes to be alone. I suspect that Tanika may be depressed. What can I, as a teacher, do to help this student?

Sincerely,

Clara Hart

To:         Clara Hart
From:       Sandy Ludwig
Subject:    RE: Addressing the needs of a student with depression

Dear Clara,

You were correct in contacting me. The changes in Tanika's behavior may be related to depression, and you can help. Although the clinical treatment of depression in children and adolescents requires considerable training in psychology and psychiatry, several interventions may help in the classroom. Following is a sample of strategies (Clarizo, 1994; Maag, 2002; Willis, 1996; Wright-Strawderman & Lindsay, 1996):

- **Check for the presence of environmental stressors.** Assess if alterable events in the immediate environment may be contributing to the student's behaviors, and make necessary adjustments.

- **Encourage more, and judge less.** Observational research has demonstrated that teachers tend to respond negatively to children who are depressed, actually exacerbating the problem. Establish rapport, and make a special effort to recognize and interact with these students.

- **Combat low self-esteem.** Provide students with special jobs such as helping an academically challenged peer in a lower grade. Provide frequent public praise for even the smallest accomplishments.

- **Reinforce responsibility for one's own feelings.** Develop activities that make explicit how we are responsible for the development of our own feelings. Use stories, case studies, or even contextually based directives (requirements to engage in troublesome symptoms associated with depression at different times, locations, and situations) that illustrate how our feelings are a direct result of both the events in our lives and our responses to those events.

- **Increase students' attention to positive things in their lives.** Have students create a pleasant-events diary, and record each time they participate in an enjoyable activity or have a pleasant thought. When a student is feeling especially down, suggest a review of the diary.

- **Encourage and model hopefulness, helpfulness, and self-reinforcement.** Demonstrate explicitly how students' behaviors influence events in their lives and show that they can make substantial changes in their current situations. Teach students effective ways to self-reinforce when good things are accomplished.

- **Promote group work and teamwork.** Develop student teams that encourage group work requiring the interdependence and cooperation of all participants. Have students complete a task, and describe the processes used to ensure that all members of the team are involved and valued.

More information on strategies can be found in the following resources:

Maag, J. (2002). A contextually based approach for treating depression in school-age children. *Intervention in School and Clinic, 37*(3), 149–155.

Wright-Strawderman, C., & Lindsay, P. (1996). Depression in students with disabilities: Recognition and intervention strategies. *Intervention in School and Clinic, 31*(5), 261–265.

Hope this helps!

Sandy Ludwig

---

**EXTEND AND APPLY**

- Try to develop an activity that will allow a student who appears to be depressed to see that he can be responsible for the development of his own feelings.
- How could you integrate this activity into the general flow of instructional and social assignments?
- How would you assess the impact and effectiveness of your activity?

## Anxiety

Although uncomfortable, the feelings, thoughts, and physiological responses associated with anxiety are an essential part of being human. Anxiety is the signal for concern, thought, and action toward daily physical and emotional challenges and has likely aided in our survival as a species. The majority of child and adolescent anxiety is transitory and does not interfere with typical development. However, approximately 8% of children experience severe anxiety, characterized by excessive worry occurring for a significant amount of time and often requiring clinical intervention (Kauffman, 2001).

Five patterns of severe anxiety are experienced by students. With *generalized anxiety* the symptoms of restlessness, fatigue, irritability, muscle tension, sleep disturbances, and difficulty concentrating are so severe that they interfere with daily activities. **Separation anxiety,** excessive worry about being separated from primary caretakers and the home, is typical of younger children. **Obsessive-compulsive disorder (OCD)** is characterized by ritualistic and repetitive behaviors (e.g., hand washing, excessive checking on events) and thoughts (counting, praying, sequencing numbers) to reduce distress or avoid a feared situation. These behaviors are debilitating in that they are overly time-consuming, impair functioning, or cause màrked distress (American Psychiatric Association, 2000). *Social anxiety* is extreme fear of social or performance situations. Students tend to respond with a situational panic attack or contrived methods of avoidance, or they endure the situation with extreme discomfort. Finally, **posttraumatic stress** is reexperiencing fear that was originally the result of an extremely threatening traumatic event. Students may have recurrent recollections of the event that interfere with social and academic functioning and try to avoid any events, activities, or situations associated with the initial trauma.

Students with severe generalized anxiety are often restless, tired, and irritable, symptoms that make learning difficult.

## Depression

We all experience periods of "feeling blue," times when we feel sad, hurt, tired, or just low and out of sorts. Like anxiety, these feelings are part of the human condition and are usually short in duration. However, extreme and persistent symptoms indicate a more serious condition. More than just a transitory gloomy affect, *depression* is defined as a pervasive and insidious group of symptoms that affects a person's mood, thoughts, and carriage. Although precise incidence rates are unknown, researchers estimate that between 2% and 21% of all students experience some symptoms of depression; estimates among students with special education needs range from 14% to 54% (Maag & Reid, 2006; Montague, Enders, Dietz, Dixon, & Cavendish, 2008; Newcomer, Barenbaum, & Pearson, 1995). Frequently overlooked is the high degree of **comorbidity** of depression with other disorders, including conduct disorders and anxiety disorders. What makes depression particularly frightening is that it is a contributing factor in more than half of all suicides. Although depression is generally viewed as a psychiatric condition requiring clinical intervention, teachers are, arguably, in the best position to identify symptoms because they see students in many social and academic situations.

What does one look for to detect depression in students, and how do we determine risk factors from the moody and emotional behaviors typical of developing children and adolescents? Wright-Strawderman and Lindsay (1996) suggest that teachers be aware of students who manifest extreme and persistent affective disturbances such as a depressed mood, low self-esteem, withdrawal, emotional mood swings, and negative expressions about the future. Teachers should also be aware of significant changes in social behavior and academic performance. Students with depression often have difficulty forming and maintaining relationships with others, and they give little attention to social problem solving. In the academic area, teachers may see changes in energy, with assignments not being completed and increased levels of distractibility. Obviously, any suspicion of suicidal behavior should be addressed immediately.

## Other Behaviors

### Attention Deficits

Students who are inattentive go to great lengths to avoid tasks that require sustained mental effort and concentration, have difficulty staying in their seats, and act hurriedly and unsystematically with little regard for consequences. Seemingly impatient, they blurt out comments, talk out of turn, have short-term memory gaps, and interrupt others excessively (Henley, Ramsey, & Algozzine, 2006; Schworm & Birnbaum, 1989). It is easy to understand how such patterns of behavior, when frequent, intense, and sustained, can be viewed as a behavior disorder. Keep in mind that for some students, attention deficits are severe enough to be considered indications of attention-deficit/hyperactivity disorder (ADHD). We discuss fully the essential features of ADHD in Chapter 9.

### Social Skills Problems

When we speak of social skills deficits, we are referring to shortcomings in social competence. Although it often means different things to different people, social competence is best viewed as a set of interpersonal behaviors that parents, teachers, and students consider important for success. Recent data indicate that students with EBD have consistently and significantly lower social skills than peers with and without disabilities (Wagner, Kutash, Duchnowski, Epstein, & Sumi, 2005). According to Gresham and colleagues (e.g., Gresham, 1988; Gresham, Sugai, & Horner, 2001), the three types of social skills deficits are skills deficits, performance deficits, and fluency deficits. Students with skills deficits have not acquired the knowledge or skills required to perform the social behavior. In contrast, students with performance deficits have the social skills in their repertoire but, for one reason or another, do not exhibit those behaviors consistently. Either the student does not have the opportunity to perform the behavior, or she makes an active decision not to perform the behavior because of particular circumstances (e.g., not motivated to do so, considerable secondary gain in misbehavior, etc.). Finally, fluency deficits are the result of inadequate exposure to models of social skills and/or too few opportunities to rehearse or practice appropriate behaviors.

Being aware of the different types of social skills deficits helps teachers select or design interventions. For example, it would not be effective to teach social skills or behaviors to students who already have them in their repertoires but who actively choose not to use them. It would be better to consider an approach designed to increase the performance of that skill. Similarly, an

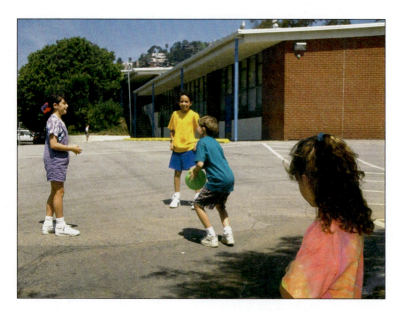

Students with social skills deficits have shortcomings in the interpersonal behaviors that sustain relationships with peers.

intervention to increase performance would have limited utility with a student who had not acquired the targeted social skill.

## Cognitive and Learning Characteristics

In addition to significant problems with social-emotional and behavioral functioning, students with EBD tend to have IQ scores in the low-average range, with scores represented disproportionately in the mild developmental disability range. Relatively few students tend to fall in the upper ranges, and verbal subtest scores tend to be higher than performance scores (Kauffman, 2001; Mattison, 2004). Similarly, when compared to the academic profiles of typically developing peers, students with EBD present moderate-to-severe academic difficulties in multiple areas that do not improve over time. Reports on the academic characteristics of students with EBD (Lane, Carter, Pierson, & Glaeser, 2006; Wagner et al., 2005) indicate that they earn lower grades and fail their courses more often than do students in any other disability group. Consequently, they are retained in grade at more than twice the rate (16%) of their general education peers. Dropout rates for students with EBD are a tragic 58.6%, more than three times that of their peers (Osher, Morrison, & Bailey, 2003; Wagner & Blackorby, 1996) (see Figure 7.2).

The presence of academic deficits among students with EBD is not surprising. The students engage in behaviors incompatible with learning—not attending to instruction, disrupting class repeatedly and aggressively, responding impulsively—that ultimately result in academic underachievement. In some cases, students act out to mask their inability to complete difficult tasks. Researchers also speculate that the academic deficits of some students with EBD may be the result of concomitant learning disabilities. Although the precise prevalence of concomitance is uncertain, studies of students with EBD have found that between 38% and 75% were also identified as having learning disabilities (Mattison, 2004; Rock, Fessler, & Church, 1997).

**myeducationlab**

Go to the Assignments and Activities section of Topic 10: Emotional/Behavioral Disorders in the MyEducationLab for your course and complete the activity entitled *Characteristics of Students with Challenging Behaviors.*

FIGURE 7.2 • **STUDENT VOICES: THE CHALLENGES OF HIGH SCHOOL COMPLETION**

Why do so many students with EBD fail to complete their high school education? Unfortunately, we know more about the number of students with EBD who leave school than we do about the reasons that precipitate such a devastating decision. To shed some light on the issue, Kortering, Braziel, and Tompkins (2002) surveyed students with EBD to learn why school completion is challenging. In one-on-one interviews with 33 high school students who received special education services, researchers solicited opinions regarding (1) the best and worst parts of school, (2) changes that would help them and others stay in school, and (3) the characteristics of teachers who had helped them learn. What follows is a synthesis of their responses:

- Best classes were those that allowed physical activity, provided vocational tasks (e.g., auto mechanics), and socialization.
- Worst situations were difficult and boring classes as well as frequent negative encounters with teachers.
- Students recognize the importance of education in making a successful transition to adulthood and believe they need more academic supports to acquire high-level content material and strategies for getting along with teachers and peers.
- Students respond best to those teachers who remain positive and who provide individual help, encouragement, and curricular accommodations.

What do we learn from these responses? Clearly, students with EBD have distinct preferences for specific classroom environments and teacher behaviors as well as equally strong feelings about those practices they find aversive. The authors of the study suggest that alterations in the ways we design programs and the manner in which we interact with students would impact rates of school completion.

# PREVALENCE, COURSE, AND CAUSAL FACTORS

## Prevalence

The prevalence, or frequency of occurrence, of students with EBD is less than 1% (0.69%) of the school-age population (U.S. Department of Education, 2008). This represents approximately 458,000 students, 7.6% of all students identified as having a disability. Although this low rate of occurrence has been stable for three decades, many (e.g., Kauffman, Mock, & Simpson, 2007) believe that the percentage of students who need services (3% to 6%) far surpasses the number who actually receive them. Compared to students with other disabilities, students with EBD continue to be the most neglected and underserved group of students in our schools. Numerous national reports have documented how "we" in the educational and social service establishments have failed collectively to adequately address the needs of this challenging population (Rosenberg et al., 2004).

Issues surrounding the prevalence of students with EBD are complex and controversial. Although researchers agree that students with EBD remain underidentified and underserved, great concern remains that certain groups of students are overrepresented. For example, compared to White students, African Americans are approximately 1.7 times more likely to be identified. Native Americans are also overrepresented, while Asian/Pacific Islander and Hispanic students are underrepresented (Coutinho, Oswald, & Forness, 2002). Compounding these racial differences are data indicating that identification rates vary by state and local school district. African American students are twice as likely to be identified as white students in 29 states. Locally, African American students were likely to be overidentified in districts in which they had minority status and underidentified in those districts in which they were a majority (Osher et al., 2003). Keep in mind that disproportional representation is probably the result of many factors (e.g., poverty and family status) and that these factors are not equally distributed across ethnic groups. Consequently, we must be cautious that efforts to achieve equal identification rates do not overlook the need for necessary interventions (Coutinho et al., 2002).

Analyzing several large national databases of students with disabilities in schools, Wagner et al. (2005) found additional demographic data regarding students with EBD:

- More than three fourths of those classified with EBD are boys.
- Students with EBD are more likely than other students to live in households with several risk factors, including poverty, a single parent, an unemployed head of household, and a peer with a disability.
- Students with EBD are more likely than other students to change schools often.

## Course of Disability

The outcomes for students with EBD continue to be among the most dismal of any disability group. Consider the results of several key longitudinal studies summarized by Henderson and Bradley (2004). Although identified later than students with other disabilities, approximately three quarters of students with EBD are suspended or expelled from school compared with 32.7% of students with disabilities and 22% of students in the general population. This typically leads to excessive involvement with the justice system, with more than a third (34.8%) of students with EBD being arrested during their school years. Among those who drop out, 70% are arrested within 3 years of leaving school.

Unfortunately, the outcomes do not improve over time. Over their lifetimes, people with EBD experience high unemployment and occupational adjustment problems. Approximately one half of students with EBD are unemployed 3 to 5 years after leaving school, and only 40% of those with EBD live independently (Corbett, Clark, & Blank, 2002; Wagner, Blackorby, Cameto, Hebbeler, & Newman, 1993). The antisocial behavior from childhood and adolescence remains debilitating and durable. Students with EBD face mental health challenges and incarceration at higher rates than that of any other population, with drug abuse and addiction contributing greatly to these problems (Bullis, 2001; Newman, Wagner, Cameto, & Knokey, 2009).

## Causal Factors

What causes students with EBD to behave in such extreme and disparate ways? Because the complex behavioral patterns of EBD are a function of interrelated, interacting factors rather than singular events (e.g., Crews et al., 2007), it is difficult if not impossible to identify definitive causes of the disability. For our purposes, it is more productive to consider the range of influences that may contribute to the cause and maintenance of the disorder (Kauffman, 2001) and then focus on what can be modified.

### Biophysical Influences

While a range of possible biophysical factors may influence behavior problems, they are tied together by one common theme: EBD is considered a manifestation of some underlying physiologic disturbance, disease, or disorder. Consider the three major types of biophysical causal factors. *Biochemical abnormalities* are disruptions of the body's central nervous system or metabolism. **Brain injury** and *neurological dysfunction* are indications of specific injury or damage to the brain or central nervous system, resulting in improper functioning. *Genetic transmission* refers to the role of heredity in the development of problem behaviors.

Historically, because medical-model explanations fall outside our areas of expertise, special educators have deemphasized their relevance. In fact, it has been suggested that biophysical explanations of EBD actually create negative expectations for students and are a convenient excuse for why some interventions do not work. For example, you may hear a colleague say, "Of course, I can't get Brad to stop yelling out; he has been diagnosed with brain and central nervous system damage."

How should we view biophysical factors associated with EBD? Obviously, as educators, we must recognize that our responsibility to teach students does not end with the identification of a biophysical causal factor or the prescription of a medical intervention (Kauffman, 2001). However, this does not mean ignoring biophysical factors. Recent advances in the study of psychiatric medications with children have been significant enough to suggest that screening for biophysically based psychiatric problems should be part of educators' assessment and planning repertoire (Konopasek & Forness, 2004).

### Psychodynamic Influences

Psychodynamic explanations of EBD center on disturbances among the components of an individual's personality structure. According to the classic work of Redl and Wineman (1957), some children with EBD have underdeveloped or deficient internal, or intrapsychic, structures (e.g., ego, id, superego), making them unable to control their impulses. Others have delinquent structures in which elements of the personality develop adequately but are used to rationalize misconduct. These and other psychodynamic theories provide a structure to understand actions and emotions. However, little empirical evidence supports their hypotheses, and they arguably have little utility for classroom teachers.

### Familial and Home Influences

In the classic Russian novel *Anna Karenina,* Tolstoy observes that all happy families resemble each other, yet each unhappy family is unhappy in its own way. Clearly, family structure and dynamics influence attitudes, emotions, behaviors, and, to some degree, our happiness. But how much do such factors contribute to the development of EBD? According to Kauffman (2001), most family factors predispose or increase risk but do not alone account for EBD. For example, factors such as physical and psychological abuse increase substantially the risk that children will learn from their childhood experiences and view violence as appropriate responses to daily events. Such maltreatment also increases the risk of acquiring many of the characteristics associated with EBD, such as aggression, rule breaking, and depression. However, risk is not synonymous with inevitability. Many children are resilient and remain psychologically healthy even in the most abusive of situations (Feldman, 2000).

Family structural factors such as being a member of a single-parent family or a blended family do not by themselves influence the development of behavior problems. However, when the level of stress increases in the family unit, typical parenting practices are disrupted, and behavior in the home may become inconsistent and unpredictable. Such events can result in an inability to meet the basic psychological needs of children, resulting in behaviors reflective of inadequacy and low self-worth. Household stress can also increase the rate of coercive interactions among family members, with all members of the home engaging in high rates of negative, aggressive, and aversive attempts at control. Not surprisingly, children and adolescents from such environments are at high risk for developing many of the antisocial behaviors associated with EBD (Walker, Severson, & Feil, 1995).

## Societal/Environmental Influences

Several radical psychologists of the 1960s, such as R. D. Laing (1967) and Thomas Scheff (1966), asserted that disturbed behavior is a natural reaction to the mad world around us. Moreover, those who do not develop disturbed patterns of behavior are the ones who are truly deviant. Although this is an extreme proposition, let's consider the possibility that the development of emotional and behavior problems is influenced by social and environmental events. First, many researchers (e.g., Walker et al., 1996) contend that our society is caught up in an epidemic of violence—acts including road rage, mean-spirited bullying, sexual harassment, and the use of weapons to settle disagreements—and that this violence is spilling over into the daily lives of our children. Correspondingly, aggressive, antisocial, impulsive, and destructive acts are increasingly typical of students in our schools and classrooms. Second, children with EBD are more likely to live in dilapidated and crowded areas in which they experience extreme rates of poverty, violence, and crime. These types of environments provide far too few positive exemplars of adaptive behavior and contribute to feelings of fear, stress, helplessness, and alienation (Cullinan, 2002).

Third, the constant barrage of media influences the behavior of children and adolescents. In addition to high rates of television viewing, with estimates as high as 35 hours per week for many children, the quality of what is viewed has been linked to social and emotional difficulties. For example, violent programs, some with as many as 20 violent acts per hour, can make children afraid, worried, or suspicious and may increase aggressive behavior. Moreover, television often portrays sexual behavior and the use of alcohol, cigarettes, or drugs in inviting terms (Kidsource, 2000).

## School Influences

Can schools, the social institutions charged with the education and emotional development of young people, contribute to the onset and maintenance of EBD? Unfortunately, the answer is yes, but the extent of the influence often depends on the characteristics of individual students. First, some students, particularly those with multiple risk factors, react negatively to the overcrowding, disorder, vandalism, and incivility found in far too many large, impersonal, comprehensive schools. Clearly, these climate factors contribute additional risks to those who enter with vulnerabilities.

Second, some teachers inadvertently contribute to risk by being insensitive to students' individuality, providing inadequate instruction, being inconsistent in behavior management, failing to teach and model appropriate social skills, as well as having unreasonable expectations for their students (Kauffman, 2001; Mayer, 2001; Sprague & Walker, 2005). When having lower expectations, teachers treat students differently by staying physically and psychologically distant, assigning less challenging assignments, and providing fewer indications that success is possible to attain. A **self-fulfilling prophecy** occurs, and students behave in ways that meet rather than exceed their teachers' low expectations. With exceedingly high, unreasonable expectations, students become frustrated and depressed because they are unable to meet the standards set by their teachers. Not surprisingly, inappropriate behaviors such as class disruptions, immaturity, and aggression increase when students are given tasks that are too far outside their threshold for success.

**REFLECTIVE EXERCISE**

#4 Now that you have reviewed the range of causal influences associated with EBD, comment on how useful knowledge of such factors would be in your planning of classroom-based interventions.

## IDENTIFICATION AND ASSESSMENT

A number of methods are available for identification and assessment of EBD. Regardless of methods used, the process typically follows a three-step approach: screening, identification, and instructional/behavioral planning.

### Screening

When screening for EBD, the teacher determines if a student has the broad set of characteristics suggesting risk for the disability. If the screening is positive, more intensive assessment is necessary to determine the actual presence or absence of the disability. Most teachers, through their daily interactions and observations, informally screen for behavioral difficulties on a regular basis. When inappropriate behavior patterns such as hostility, aggression, and disruptions persist over time and escalate, students are typically referred for a more in-depth examination. Although this informal screening appears practical and straightforward, recognize that it has several shortcomings. First, students who exhibit externalizing and disruptive behaviors are overrepresented, and those with internalizing problems are rarely recognized. Second, teachers vary greatly in their tolerance levels for certain externalizing behaviors. Specifically, teachers with low tolerance levels will likely refer large numbers of students, while those with high tolerance levels will identify few students and actually fail to identify a significant proportion of students at risk (Rosenberg et al., 2004).

To address these limitations, formalize the screening process. One approach is to actively rank students on categories of functioning such as appropriate classroom behavior, social competence, and withdrawal. Those ranked at the problematic extreme ends of the distributions would be considered for additional evaluation. A second, more structured, approach is to use commercially prepared systems of screening such as the Systematic Screening for Behavior Disorders (SSBD) (Walker & Severson, 1992) and the Early Screening Profile (ESP) (Walker et al., 1995). Both the SSBD and the ESP are multistep screening systems (see Figure 7.3) designed for students between the ages of 3 and 11. Teachers initially rank every student in their classes in terms of their internalizing and externalizing behaviors. The top three students on each list proceed to the second step, in which teachers analyze these students' behaviors against typical classroom behavioral standards and expectations. Those who exceed normative criteria proceed to the third step, where teachers conduct direct observations during instruction and independent work periods.

### Identification

Those students screened as possibly having EBD are referred to multidisciplinary or child study teams for more intensive evaluation. This evaluation is conducted to determine if a disability is present and, if so, the intensity of special education services

PEARSON
**myeducationlab**

Go to the Assignments and Activities section of Topic 10: Emotional/Behavioral Disorders in the MyEducationLab for your course and complete the activity entitled *The Role of the Teacher in Determining EBD*.

## FIGURE 7.3 • MULTIPLE-STEP SCREENING SYSTEM

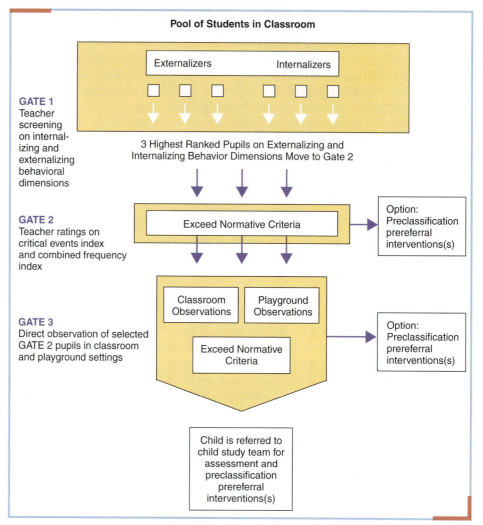

Source: Walker, H. M., Severson, H., Stiller, B., Williams, G., Haring, N., Shinn, M., & Todis, B. (1988). Systematic screening of pupils in the elementary age range at risk for behavior disorders: Development and trial testing of a multiple gating model. *Remedial and Special Education, 9,* 8–14. Reprinted with permission from Pro-Ed.

necessary for academic and social success. Two types of assessment methods are most often used: behaviorally based methods and personality-oriented methods.

## Behaviorally Oriented Methods

Direct measurement using behavior rating scales is the most common method for identifying EBD. Behavior rating scales are relatively easy to administer, can be used repeatedly across settings and sources (teachers, parents, and students), and serve as efficient summaries of different types of behaviors (Elliott & Busse, 2004). Among the more frequently used checklists are the Child Behavior Checklist (CBCL) (Achenbach & Rescorla, 2001), the Walker Problem Behavior Identification Checklist (Walker, 1983), the Behavioral and Emotional Rating Scale (BERS) (Epstein & Sharma, 1998), and the Social Skills Rating System (SSRS) (Gresham & Elliott, 1990).

To illustrate the essential components of behavior rating scales, consider the CBCL, regarded as the most comprehensive and technically sound. There are two forms of the CBCL, one for ages 1.5 to 5 and one for ages 6 to 18. In both forms, parents, guardians, or close family members consider 118 problem behaviors and rate how true each item is for their child (see Figure 7.4 for sample items). The CBCL

FIGURE 7.4 • ITEMS FROM CBCL

*Please print. Be sure to answer all items.*

Below is a list of items that describe children and youths. For each item that describes your child **now** or **within the past 6 months,** please circle the **2** if the item is **very true or often true** of your child. Circle the **1** if the item is **somewhat or sometimes true** of your child. If the item is **not true** of your child, circle **0.** Please answer all items as well as you can, even it some do not seem to apply to your child.

**0 = Not True (as far as you know) 1 = Somewhat or Sometimes True 2 = Very True or Often True**

| | |
|---|---|
| 0 1 2   1. Acts too young for his/her age | 0 1 2   32. Feels he/she has to be perfect |
| 0 1 2   2. Drinks alcohol without parents' approval (describe): _____ | 0 1 2   33. Feels or complains that no one loves him/her |
| | 0 1 2   34. Feels others are out to get him/her |
| 0 1 2   3. Argues a lot | 0 1 2   35. Feels worthless or inferior |
| 0 1 2   4. Fails to finish things he/she starts | 0 1 2   36. Gets hurt a lot, accident prone |
| 0 1 2   5. There is very little he/she enjoys | 0 1 2   37. Gets in many fights |
| 0 1 2   6. Bowel movements outside toilet | 0 1 2   38. Gets teased a lot |
| 0 1 2   7. Bragging, boasting | 0 1 2   39. Hangs around with others who get in trouble |
| 0 1 2   8. Can't concentrate, can't pay attention for long | 0 1 2   40. Hears sound or voices that aren't there (describe): _____ |
| 0 1 2   9. Can't get his/her mind off certain thoughts; obsessions (describe): _____ | |
| | 0 1 2   41. Impulsive or acts without thinking |

Source: Achenbach, T. M., & Rescorla, L. A. (2001). *Manual for the ASEBA school-age forms and profiles.* Burlington: University of Vermont, Research Center for Children, Youth, and Families. Reprinted with permission.

also has 20 competence items covering the child's activities, social relations, and school performance. The CBCL results in normative comparisons on the broad dimensions of externalizing and internalizing behaviors as well as on several specific factors such as aggression, delinquency, and anxiety/depression.

## Personality-Oriented Methods

Although less frequently used in education settings, personality-oriented methods remain prevalent among clinicians who work with children and adolescents. When measuring personality, the goal is to capture how an individual thinks, behaves, and feels across situations and over periods of time. The two major categories of personality measurement are objective and projective (Cullinan, 2002). Objective instruments, such as the Piers-Harris Self-Concept Scale (Piers & Harris, 1984), present items in a standard fashion, use a protocol for scoring, and employ normative data to determine the presence of a disability. Projective measures, such as the Rorschach Ink-Blot test (Rorschach, 1932), require that individuals interpret or project meaning onto ambiguous pictures, images, or statements. Interpretations of responses are believed to reveal an individual's innermost thoughts, feelings, needs, and motives. These methods can yield interesting information about students. However, be aware that the technical adequacy of these instruments, particularly in the areas of validity and reliability, is questionable.

## Instructional/Behavioral Planning: The Functional Behavioral Assessment

The measurement of student performance for instructional and behavioral planning is arguably the most important aspect of the assessment process. Following the determination of EBD, this process involves the identification of instructional and behavioral problems as well as the generation of a plan to address them. The most effective and comprehensive method for instructional/behavioral planning is a functional behavioral assessment (FBA; Lane, Weisenbach, Phillips, & Wehby, 2007). The logic behind conducting an FBA is that much of an individual's behavior is supported by the environment, occurs within a particular context, and serves a specific purpose. Specifically, all individuals behave in ways to satisfy needs or achieve desired outcomes. In most situations, students use appropriate methods to get what they want. However, some students, particularly those with EBD, use extreme, inappropriate methods to reach their goals. Students who employ disruptive and unproductive academic behaviors typically require guidance in seeking alternative ways, or *replacement behaviors,* to address their legitimate social and instructional needs.

FBAs are most useful when you consider the following. First, behaviors, both appropriate and inappropriate, are learned and can be reduced (Chandler & Dahlquist, 2002). Second, all behaviors are purposeful. There is a reason why the individual is engaging in a behavior. Because many behaviors arise from and are maintained by environmental factors, FBAs allow educators to determine those factors that influence an individual's behaviors.

Third, multiple behaviors can serve one function; and correspondingly, one behavior can serve multiple functions. For example, a student may sit for 5 or 10 minutes; begin to fidget, doodle, get up to sharpen a pencil, and talk with others on the way back to the table; and openly defy attempts to redirect him to his assignment. These multiple behaviors may have one purpose: to escape difficult or confusing work. One behavior can also have multiple purposes: A student may loudly defy a teacher's attempts to have her complete an assignment, which may result in a referral to the office. The purpose of student's behavior may be to escape difficult work and gain an opportunity to chat with other students and even staff about pleasant topics. Finally, an FBA is most effective when members of a team collaborate in assessing the behavior, planning the intervention, and evaluating the treatment.

Effective FBAs are developed through a user-friendly, six-step process (Center for Effective Collaboration and Practice, 1998; McConnell, Hilvitz, & Cox, 1998; Ryan, Halsey, & Matthews, 2003; Scott & Kamps, 2007; Shippen, Simpson, & Crites, 2003):

- **Step 1: Describe and verify the seriousness of the problem.** Judge the significance of the behavior problem by considering the following: (a) Does the student's behavior differ significantly from classmates? (b) Is the behavior chronic and a threat to others? (c) Is the behavior an excess or deficiency rather than a cultural difference?
- **Step 2: Refine the definition of the problem behavior.** Narrow the defining characteristics of the problem behavior by noting (a) the times when the behavior occurs; (b) where the behavior occurs and who is present; (c) the conditions (e.g., during large-group instruction, during unstructured time) in which the behavior occurs; (d) events and conditions that occur both before and after the behavior; and (e) common setting events (e.g., when late to school, after missing breakfast).
- **Step 3: Collect information on the environment, setting demands, and possible functions of the problem behavior.** Employ multiple methods to collect information on the behavior and the student, including review of records and academic products, interviews with parents and relevant school personnel, and direct observations. Describe the environment, the time, and what is expected of the student. Characterize the behavior as either functional or as a skill or performance deficit. (As mentioned earlier, functional behaviors involve getting something such as attention or revenge, or avoiding something such as difficult assignments or interactions with certain peers. Students who exhibit skills deficits do not know how to behave, and those who have a performance deficit know how to behave but do not perform it under specific conditions.)
- **Step 4: Analyze the information.** Synthesize the data collected, focusing on the sequence of observed behaviors.

- **Step 5: Generate a hypothesis statement, and plan for replacement behaviors.** Develop a concise summary of information, focusing on factors surrounding the student's behavior and including both the antecedents and consequences. The hypothesis is a best guess as to why the behavior is occurring.
- **Step 6: Develop, implement, and evaluate an intervention plan.** Develop an intervention plan that includes positive behavior-change strategies, program modifications, and behavior supports necessary to address the problem behavior. Remember that the plan should directly address replacement behaviors, those functionally equivalent actions that allow students to meet their needs but in a more socially acceptable manner. Implement the plan with fidelity, and collect data consistently on the targeted behavior in order to evaluate the efficacy of your intervention plan.

**REFLECTIVE EXERCISE**

#5 Although most educators agree that FBAs provide a wealth of information about behavior, teachers do not use FBAs with great frequency. What factors contribute to their limited use? What can be done to increase their use?

## EDUCATIONAL PRACTICES

Several **evidence-based practices** are appropriate for addressing the instructional and behavioral needs of students with EBD. We begin with the controversial area of service delivery and then focus on several of the more common interventions and techniques that, regardless of setting, are successful in improving academic and social/behavioral performance.

### Service Delivery

Students with EBD are educated in restrictive settings more often than any other students with disabilities. In fact, approximately one third of all students with EBD between the ages of 6 and 21 spend more than 60% of their time outside general education classes in their neighborhood schools, 11.1% are served in separate day treatment facilities, and 1.4% are educated in their homes or in hospitals (Henderson & Bradley, 2004).

What are the implications of these data? Educators continue to debate how best to deliver the variety of special services needed by students with EBD. The debate is the result of the tension between the desire to provide essential services and the need to maintain these students in the least restrictive environment. As we have noted elsewhere in this text, the rationale for inclusive education is compelling. All children, even those with challenging behaviors, should garner the benefits of inclusive programming (e.g., attending one's neighborhood school, interacting with appropriate peer role models, participating in shared content-rich educational experiences). Unfortunately, the intense needs of many students with EBD make such programming challenging if not unrealistic. Teachers often believe they lack the expertise and skills to address the extreme behaviors of these students. Moreover, it has been argued (e.g., Kauffman, Bantz, & McCullough, 2002) that education provided in separate settings more effectively addresses the intensive needs of some students with EBD (e.g., support, individualization, and monitoring) than does education delivered in the typical environment. The consensus in the field is that students with EBD require individually tailored programs that make use of the full

Techniques that can facilitate the inclusion of students with EBD include cooperative learning and peer tutoring.

REFLECTIVE EXERCISE

#6 Students with EBD present many behaviors that general education teachers feel unprepared to manage. How do you feel about students with extreme problem behaviors being included with the general population of students?

continuum of placement and service options, like Heritage High School's SWAS program coordinated by Steve Kennedy and Steve Williams (described in "My Profession, My Story," in the beginning of this chapter).

A series of activities can maximize efforts to support students with EBD in less restrictive environments. From a school-wide perspective, co-teaching by general and special education teachers, adult mentors, and peer facilitators; flexibility in training; integration of socials skills instruction into curriculum; positive behavior support; and opportunities for out-of-school activities have facilitated the inclusion of students with challenging behaviors. Specific in-class curricular techniques that are effective tools for inclusion include **self-management,** cooperative learning, peer tutoring, and problem-solving training (Guetzloe, 1999; Hendley, 2007; Shapiro, Miller, Sawka, Gardill, & Handler, 1999; Wilkinson, 2005).

## Early Intervention

Almost universal agreement exists among educators that early childhood is the most opportune time to intervene in the challenging behaviors associated with EBD (Kendziora, 2004). Although many developing young children exhibit episodic troublesome behaviors, approximately 4% to 6% of preschool-age children have serious emotional and behavioral issues that require immediate and intensive action. Consider what happens without intervention. Left unserved, young children with EBD attend, participate, and learn less than their peers and have difficulty being accepted by both classmates and teachers. Not unexpectedly, their difficulties stabilize or escalate, and they are frequently held back in early grades (Raver & Knitze, 2002).

For early intervention efforts to succeed, young children with EBD must be provided with environments that teach and actively support prosocial behaviors. Consequently, programs typically focus on two areas: (1) center-based programs address the child's acquisition of cognitive skills required for appropriate social behavior, and (2) home-based programs provide families with strategies to promote and maintain appropriate behavior. Reviews of center-based, home-based, and combined alternatives indicate that five factors affect program outcomes (Kendziora, 2004; Ramey & Ramey, 1998):

- **Developmental timing.** Programs started early in a child's development result in the most benefit.
- **Program intensity.** Programs with higher concentrations of home and center contact time produce larger positive developmental outcomes than do less-intensive alternatives.
- **Direct delivery of instruction.** For acquisition of cognitive skills, direct instruction to the child is more effective than indirect methods of instruction (e.g., teaching parents to provide social skills instruction).
- **Breadth of program.** Programs that include a wide range of services (e.g., education, health, social services) are more effective than alternatives with a narrow focus.
- **Maintenance of outcomes.** Without environmental supports, program benefits are lost.

Three factors limit the success of early intervention for students with EBD (Conroy, Hendrickson, & Hester, 2004; Kendziora, 2004). First, no universal, systematic screening program identifies those who would benefit from early intervention programs. The selection of a student for services is often a function of highly variable eligibility criteria of community social service programs or the clinical judgment of health care professionals. Second, the majority of students identified for early intervention tend to be children with externalizing behavior problems. Although large numbers of students suffer from internalizing problems such as anxiety and depression, manifestations of these problems tend not to bother others and remain largely ignored. Finally, because young girls tend to exhibit fewer externalizing behavior problems, they tend to be underrepresented in early intervention programs. However, in later years, a higher proportion of girls does act out, in part because of internalizing problems developed in early childhood. Arguably, early intervention efforts could have altered the development of these behaviors.

## Academic and Social/Behavioral Interventions

Although the selection of specific interventions should be driven by the results of an individual student's FBA, certain practices have a history of effectiveness for students with EBD. Next we highlight several common interventions for both academic and social/behavioral deficits.

### Academic Interventions

With extreme social and emotional behaviors being the defining characteristics of the disability, it is not surprising that educators pay little attention to the academic needs of students with EBD. This lack of attention is prevalent in classrooms—some teachers in self-contained EBD settings devote only 30% of the school day to instruction—as well as in many teacher preparation programs (Wehby, Lane, & Falk, 2003). Comprehensive reviews of academic interventions (e.g., Coleman & Vaughn, 2000; Kostewicz & Kubina, 2008; Lane, 2004; Pierce, Reid, & Epstein, 2004) indicate that both teachers and peers can contribute to efforts that improve the academic performance of students with EBD. Specific teacher-based actions, typically guided by the results of an FBA, include consideration of task difficulty, instructional modifications, learning strategies, providing choices, and content enhancements. Peer-mediated approaches include structured tutoring programs in which higher-performing readers are paired with their lower-performing classmates to supplement reading instruction.

Consider how these techniques come together in the classroom. Employing the results of a functional assessment, Penno, Frank, and Wacker (2000) applied several accommodations that resulted in both improved academic productivity and reduced behavior problems among several students who exhibited severe and chronic behavior problems. Among the accommodations employed for the adolescent boys during their reading and math assignments were (1) working with a peer tutor, (2) shortened work assignments, (3) self-monitoring worksheets, and (4) completing assignments on the computer. Before the application of the academic supports, the students' high rates of inappropriate behavior were due to a desire to escape from difficult academic tasks. By making assignments less aversive to the students and easier to accomplish, Penno et al. observed discernible changes in academic performance and classroom behavior.

### Social/Behavioral Interventions

**Behavioral Techniques.** The most common approaches for addressing the social/behavioral needs of students with EBD involve the simultaneous strengthening and reducing of targeted behaviors through the use of behavioral techniques. Techniques exclusively intended to reduce or eliminate challenging behaviors are often ineffectual because they fail to strengthen appropriate replacement behaviors. To avoid this situation, behavioral interventions are typically dynamic, simultaneously strengthening appropriate behavior as they weaken the challenging behaviors.

The **token economy** is the behavioral technique that best manages the gamut of behaviors associated with EBD as well as incorporates the range of techniques used to increase and decrease behavior. The fact that more than 90% of teachers of students with EBD use some form of token economy is testament to its acceptance and efficacy (Rosenberg et al., 2004). The classic study by O'Leary and Becker (1967) illustrates why these procedures are replicated in many of our classrooms today. In their study, tokens were awarded for intervals of time in which students acted appropriately (i.e., did not

**PEARSON**
**myeducationlab**

Go to the Assignments and Activities section of Topic 10: Emotional/Behavioral Disorders in the MyEducationLab for your course and complete the activity entitled *Strategies for Managing Challenging Behavior.*

More than 90% of teachers of students with EBD use some form of token-based behavior management system, a testament to its efficacy and user-friendliness.

disrupt classroom activities); inappropriate behaviors were ignored. Disruptive behaviors decreased from a baseline of 76% of the time intervals to 10% of the intervals following introduction of the token economy.

In some circumstances, token economies are complemented by a *levels system,* a structure in which students progress through varying token or point-based systems as their behavior changes. As the student moves to a higher level, expected behaviors and responsibilities typically increase in difficulty and/or demand; correspondingly, potential privileges also increase. In many settings for students with EBD, progression through levels continues until the behaviors suggest that movement to a less restrictive environment is warranted.

**Teaching Self-Control.** The ultimate goal of any intervention is for a student to regulate his or her own behavior independently. How do we move students to such levels of independence? Self-control is one technique that has demonstrated positive outcomes, allowing students with EBD to assume larger roles in their behavior change efforts. Most self-control programs consist of three components: self-assessment, goal setting, and self-determination of reinforcement (Polsgrove & Smith, 2004). In self-assessment, a student reflects on her own behavior and recognizes that the behavior of interest is inadequate or inappropriate. The student then recognizes the behaviors required, sets goals, and selects strategies that help regulate behavior. Finally,

## CAN YOU HELP ME WITH THIS STUDENT?

| To... | Sue Sperling, School Behavior Specialist |
|---|---|
| From... | Edie LoDucca, Sixth-Grade Math Teacher |
| Subject: | Improving rates of participation and academic success |

Dear Sue,

I hope you can provide a tangible suggestion for dealing with the inappropriate behaviors of one of my sixth-grade math students. Some details: When I assign independent seat work, Taquon begins a series of disruptive and oppositional behaviors. Today, for example, after taking a quick look at the fraction problems, he tried to engage his neighbor, Corey, in an argument over which basketball team would win the NBA championship. When directed to return to work, Taquon swore under his breath and began to doodle on his worksheet. After a few moments, Taquon put his head on the desk and screamed for all to hear that he was "on strike," refusing to do any work involving fractions. Although on strike, Taquon continued to speak out loudly and inappropriately. I am at a loss; during the past few weeks, I have assigned Taquon to the time-out area, withheld recess, and sent him to the office with a disciplinary referral. None of this seemed to get him back on task. Help!!

—Edie

To: Edie LoDucca
From: Sue Sperling
Subject: RE: Improving rates of participation and academic success

Dear Edie,

Stay calm. This situation is an unfortunate yet familiar scene in a number of classrooms serving students with EBD. However, I have seen some success by explicitly offering students choice-making opportunities. Here is a protocol for implementing the technique:

- When Taquon chooses not to participate, provide him with two or more options regarding the completion of an assignment, allow him to independently select an option, and then provide him with that option.

- Provide choices either before or during the task. You can provide Taquon with the opportunity to decide when he will begin the assignment, if he requires any mini-breaks during the assignment, the number and order of problems to be completed, and under what kind of conditions he would like to complete the task (e.g., type of writing utensil, color of paper, area of room to move desk, etc.).

- Ensure that you and his other teachers reinforce Taquon's choice making. Taquon will learn that positive outcomes are possible when he honors his choices.

I am confident that providing Taquon with choices can work. First and foremost, the available research (e.g., Kern & State, 2009) indicates that it increases academic achievement and reduces inappropriate behaviors. Second, I have seen how use of the technique improves the classroom climate with enhanced teacher-to-student and student-to-student relationships. Finally, the technique allows students with EBD to assert decision-making power in the classroom, a process that increases the motivation to succeed. More information on applying choice making to academic activities is available in the following resources.

Jolivette, K., McCormick, K. M., & Lingo, A. S. (2004). Embedding choices into the daily routines of young children with behavior problems: Eight reasons to build social competence. *Beyond Behavior, 13*(3), 21–26.

Kern, L., & State, T. M. (2009). Incorporating choice and preferred activities into classwide instruction. *Beyond Behavior, 18*(2), 3–11.

Let me know how it works.

Sue

---

**EXTEND AND APPLY**

- Why does choice making improve student participation in class activities?

- In general, having the opportunity to make choices provides predictability, consistency, and, most important, a sense of control over behavior. Unfortunately, students like Taquon do not always see relationships between their actions and environmental events. Can you think of other student behaviors that teachers can improve through providing choice-making opportunities?

- What types of choices would be appropriate to present to students in those situations?

---

through the process of self-determination, the student evaluates her performance and considers the nature and scope of reinforcement that should be received for performance of the target behavior.

**Social Skills Instruction.** Because large numbers of students with EBD have social skills deficits, logic dictates that direct instruction in behaviors associated with social competence should be a priority. Social skills instruction activities typically include

Many adolescents with EBD have difficulty finding success during their academic careers and after they leave school. Many of these difficulties have been linked to a lack of self-control rather than a lack of vocational knowledge or cognitive ability. One strategy that has been successful in improving social behaviors is self-monitoring. Unfortunately, many students with EBD are resistant to intrusive behavior interventions that make them appear different from their peers; others find it particularly difficult to reflect on their own behavior using traditional pen-and-paper methods.

The use of handheld computers shows promise in supporting self-monitoring for such students. During a 12-week intervention, Kramer (2004) taught eight adolescent males with EBD to monitor their behavior using handheld computers such as Palm Pilots. The handheld computers were programmed to sound a signal every 10 minutes that would prompt students to answer if they were performing five prosocial behaviors, including respecting peers and following directions. The devices were included in one class and gradually introduced into a total of three classes over the length of the study. By the end of the intervention phase, all of the participants were two to four times more likely to demonstrate the targeted behaviors. An unexpected benefit was that, after the third week of the study, social behaviors increased in classes where the handheld devices were not present. This trend intensified over the duration of the study; and by the study's conclusion, the social skills demonstrated in the intervention and nonintervention classes were nearly equal. Additionally, the students were able to maintain the positive behavior change in all classes as the use of the handheld devices was faded and eventually discontinued.

Why did the students improve in such dramatic fashion? For the most part, the use of the handheld devices reduced the resistance to behavior-change interventions common among students with EBD. All of the participants reported that they enjoyed using the handheld computers and preferred it to being verbally reminded by staff members, suggesting that the intervention device was considered socially appropriate by the students. The students' feedback and improvement in social skills performance suggest that the infusion of technology into self-monitoring is a potentially powerful method to increase student participation and appropriate behavior.

Note: Charles Kramer contributed to this feature.

(1) identification of social skills needing improvement, (2) modeling and explaining the identified skills, (3) providing opportunities for practice while being coached, (4) delivering feedback and reinforcement during practice, and (5) identifying real situations where the skills can be applied (Kavale, Mathur, & Mostert, 2004).

How do we actually teach social skills? Many teachers look first to commercially prepared social skills curricula. Two of the more popular treatment packages are ACCEPTS (A Children's Curriculum for Effective Peer and Teacher Skills) (Walker et al., 1983) and the Skillstreaming series (Goldstein & McGinnis, 1997; McGinnis & Goldstein, 1997). In both programs, specific skills are clustered in groups or domains (e.g., dealing with feelings, friendship-making skills, coping skills) and instructional sequences for teaching the skills are provided. It is extremely useful to know what to look for when selecting a social skills curriculum. Sugai and colleagues (Carter & Sugai, 1989; Sugai & Lewis, 1996) suggest that a program should include instructional components such as direct instruction, modeling, coaching, reinforcement, and positive practice. Moreover, one should ensure that the program includes assessment instruments and has the flexibility to address the needs of individual students as well as small groups. Finally, one should consider the level of training needed to administer the program, the cost of the program, and the emphasis placed on generalization and maintenance of program outcomes (S. W. Smith & Gilles, 2003).

Teachers who design their own methods and activities for teaching social skills often make use of instruction in replacement behaviors (also known as the teaching of alternative behaviors). **Replacement behaviors** are a series of actions that achieve the same intent as the problem behaviors (Neel & Cessna, 1990). Determining what behaviors to replace is very similar to conducting an FBA. We first determine the intent or functions of the inappropriate behaviors and then focus our instructional efforts on teaching appropriate ways to achieve the desired outcomes. Subsequent instruction focuses on when and under what conditions students are to perform the replacement behaviors (Meadows & Stevens, 2004).

## REFLECTIVE EXERCISE

# 7
Many social skills interventions have resulted in only modest improvements and limited generalization across settings. What factors contribute to the poor showing of social skills teaching efforts? Can you think of strategies that can enhance our efforts to teach social behaviors that generalize and maintain over time?

**Life-Space Interview.** The **life-space interview (LSI)** is a technique used when students with EBD are in crisis or in response to severe acting out and violent behaviors. Originally developed as a therapeutic tool to aid in the rehabilitation of students in residential treatment programs, LSI is based on the assumption that verbal mediation following an extreme behavioral event can result in enduring behavioral change. Consider the logic of the approach. When students with EBD are in crisis or engaged in intense emotional acting-out situations, their perception of reality is distorted, and they need emotional support. At such times, the usual impenetrable defensive barriers to behavioral change are weakened, and the student is unusually open to intervention. At such times therapeutic actions can accomplish two major goals: Emotional First Aid on the Spot (EFAS) and Clinical Exploitation of Life Events (CELE) (Redl & Wineman, 1957). Specific LSI activities associated with each of these goals are highlighted in Figure 7.5.

Keep in mind that, while the use of LSI has considerable intuitive appeal, logistical challenges can limit its applicability to certain settings. First, LSI is time-consuming and requires considerable coordination of efforts. Because it is essential to conduct LSI immediately at the time of the crisis and to administer LSI by a trained individual who is familiar with the student, staffing patterns must allow for flexibility in scheduling and coverage of classrooms. Second, teachers who conduct LSIs often uncover complex problems, many of which

At times of crisis, the usual impenetrable defensive barriers to behavioral change among students with EBD are weakened and unusually open to intervention.

FIGURE 7.5 • **COMPONENTS OF THE LSI**

The goals of the LSI are predicated on the psychodynamic assumption that intensive emotional life events and crises can be opportunities to influence a student's behavior. Developed by Fritz Redl and David Wineman (1957), these techniques have been applied in a range of educational and clinical settings serving students with EBD. The first goal—emotional first aid on the spot—is a series of short-term procedures designed to prevent excessive damage caused by delusional perceptions accompanying the crisis situation. Specific actions include the following:

- *Drain off frustration.* Encourage the student to vent anger and hostility in an acceptable way.
- *Support the management of panic, fury, and guilt.* Help the child put things back into perspective with a minimum of guilt over the outburst.
- *Communication maintenance.* Sustain meaningful interactions to prevent the child's withdrawal into a fantasy world.
- *Regulate behavioral and social traffic.* Remind the student that rules were broken and that there are consequences for such actions.
- *Provide umpire services.* Assist and reinforce the student's efforts at self-control and decision making.

The clinical exploitation of life events is the process of using the student's current outburst or crisis for the purpose of long-term therapeutic gain. Key techniques for exploiting these events include the following:

- *Reality rub-in.* Stress the facts surrounding the current behavioral situation, and dispel the denial and/or delusional misinterpretation presented by the student.
- *Symptom estrangement.* Stress that inappropriate actions have limited secondary gain and that there are many negative consequences associated with the presenting behaviors.
- *Massaging numb value areas.* Reach out to seemingly dormant value areas in the student to develop a sensitivity to the feelings of others.
- *New tool salesmanship.* Assist the student to develop new coping skills to replace counterproductive inappropriate behaviors.
- *Manipulation of boundaries of self.* Help students see how their behaviors affect others in the immediate environment.

contain deep-seated psychological issues that are beyond the scope of school or classroom interventions and require clinical expertise.

**Wraparound Services.** Due to the extreme, pervasive, and multifaceted nature of problems faced by students with EBD, a highly structured, coordinated, and integrated system of service delivery is often necessary. As we noted in Chapter 5, educators use the term *wraparound* to describe service coordination because it reflects that intervention plans are family- and child-centered. Wraparound is not a specific program or type of service but a definable planning process that results in a unique set of community services and supports designed to meet the unique needs of children and families (Burns & Goldman, 1998). Teachers involved in this process embrace families as full partners in the intervention process and stay involved with the range of service providers both within and outside the school system.

What does it take to integrate wraparound services in schools? Eber, Sugai, Smith, and Scott (2002) recommend that school-based teams do the following:

To enhance your understanding of behavioral interventions discussed in this section, go to the IRIS Center Resources section of Topic 10: Emotional/Behavioral Disorders in the MyEducationLab for your course and complete the Module entitled *Addressing Disruptive and Noncompliant Behaviors (Part 2): Behavioral Interventions.*

- **Engage in initial conversations with family.** Family members discuss their ideas, values, views, frustrations, and dreams regarding their child. The information accessed assists in developing interventions that relate directly to the goals of the family.
- **Focus on student strengths, and articulate a mission.** Develop a strength profile of the child across multiple life domains, and construct a mission statement focusing on what the team is to accomplish.
- **Identify and prioritize needs.** Summarize the needs of student and family, and develop goals that help the student function effectively in the school and community. Prioritize the goals, allowing those with greatest direct responsibility (e.g., teachers, family members) to have most impact on the list.
- **Develop an action plan, and assign tasks.** List the steps to address the prioritized needs, and note the persons responsible for implementing the task to completion.
- **Monitor, evaluate, and refine.** Review and evaluate actions proposed at previous meetings. If needs have not been met to the team's satisfaction, reexamine available data and revise the plan.

## Transition to Adult Life

Previously in this chapter, we discussed the dismal postschool outcomes for students with EBD. When compared to peers with and without disabilities in longitudinal studies, these students underperform in nearly every important transition to adulthood variable. Initially, the employment outcomes experienced by young adults with EBD are comparable to those achieved by the general population of young adults leaving school. Both groups find relatively low-status, high-turnover jobs, and approximately 60% are employed at any given time. Four to five years after leaving school, however, the general population of young adults makes a significant shift to higher-status, family-wage jobs, an indicator of being on a stable career path. Young adults with EBD typically do not make this same upward shift. The following interventions can alter this situation and assist students to make a more successful transition to adulthood.

### Vocational Education and Work Experience

Reviews of the research (Cheney & Bullis, 2004; Sample, 1998; Sitlington & Nuebert, 2004) indicate that vocational education and work experience, alone or in combination, are linked to positive postschool outcomes for students with EBD. Vocational education, one of the more common interventions for adolescents with EBD, is effective because it centers on the development of work-based competencies such as occupational skills, interpersonal skills, technological literacy, and employability skills associated with particular occupations. The impact of interpersonal skills in the workplace should not be underestimated: surveys of employers indicate that social skills, working as members of teams, and the absence of antisocial behaviors are major factors in the retention of employees (Heal & Rusch, 1995). Paid work experience during high school, particularly when combined with vocational education, decreases dropout rates and has a significant positive impact on postschool earnings. There is no substitute for the real-life experiences gained through placements in work settings (Bullis, 2001). In fact, students with EBD who work while in school continue to be workers once they leave school.

### Supported Employment and Service Learning

Supported employment is a process in which a vocational specialist assists students in finding an appropriate job and then provides on-the-job coaching in the skills necessary for success in the work environment (Drake, Skinner, Bond, & Goldman, 2009; Inge & Tilson, 1994). To meet the intensive needs of students with EBD, the role of the vocational specialist, or job coach, often goes beyond workplace issues and includes a full range of case-management activities. Specifically, the vocational specialist must have knowledge of and facilitate collaboration among social service agencies, juvenile justice personnel, schools, and potential employers. The ultimate goal of supported employment for students with EBD is to help them succeed in paid employment and begin achieving personal goals that lead to success in the community (Lehman, 1992).

Another option for providing work experience is service learning. **Service learning** consists of (1) direct experience in working with communities or organizations that promote the public good and (2) lessons that allow for reflection of the experiences, with particular emphasis on how the service benefits both the community and the student. Because students with EBD have limited social skills, a high need for structure, and tendencies to think of self rather than others, service-learning projects need to be designed carefully. Activities need to be organized and well supervised as well as provide opportunities for students to develop and practice intrapersonal and interpersonal skills (Frey, 2003; Muscott, 2000).

### Family and Demographic Factors

Keep in mind that, while the interventions just discussed are powerful, they do not alone account for successful transitions to adulthood. Students with EBD who have involved parents and families make the transition to adulthood with greater speed and effectiveness than do those whose parents are not active in the process. Also, demographic and socioeconomic characteristics such as family socioeconomic position, minority status, suburban living environment, low unemployment rate in the local labor market, and gender have been found to influence post–high school success (Wagner, D'Amico, Marder, Newman, & Blackorby, 1992).

## PREVAILING ISSUES, CONTROVERSIES, AND IMPLICATIONS FOR THE TEACHER

Although great strides have been made in delivering services to those with EBD, some critical issues continue to challenge the field. Next we discuss two of the more pressing issues—physical restraint and medication.

### Physical Restraint

Should educators ever physically restrain a student? When working with students who engage in volatile, violent, and dangerous behaviors, it may become necessary to keep a student from injuring himself or others. Physical restraint is often regarded as a tool of restrictive placements such as psychiatric hospitals and residential treatment

REFLECTIVE EXERCISE

#8 How do you feel about the possibility of having to use physical restraint with one of your students? What preparation do you believe you would need to safely restrain a student who had lost control of herself?

facilities, and many do not believe that its use has a place in general education settings. Nonetheless, the increase in the numbers of inclusive programs for students with EBD has thrust the issue of restraint into discussions of teaching. Although the research is limited, policy makers generally believe that educators commonly use physical restraint with students with EBD.

Consequently, teachers working with violent and volatile students should be aware of guidelines regarding the safe and appropriate use of restraint. According to Ryan and Peterson (2004), restraint should be used only by trained personnel who know how to apply it safely using the minimal amount of force. Moreover, procedures for reporting, data collection, and parent notification should be in place. Obviously, nonphysical options to diffuse crisis situations are available and can minimize the need for restraint.

## Medication

Drug or pharmacological treatment is one of the most frequently used and controversial methods for managing behavior problems. Consider the recent data: Approximately 2% to 4% of students in general education, 15% to 20% of children in special education, and 40% to 60% of students in residential settings receive medications for behavioral issues. Moreover, the rate of students using medications has tripled over the past 10 years, with increased use of stimulants and antidepressants leading the way (Konopasek & Forness, 2004). The popularity of psychotropic medications for students with behavioral issues is not surprising. For many students, medications work effectively with few if any side effects. Moreover, medications for all types of psychological diagnoses are advertised throughout the media, and we are arguably a society that demands fast, convenient solutions to problem situations. As educators, we have an important role in our students' medical interventions. We are well positioned to ensure that students receive their prescriptions on schedule as well as to observe and report on the effects, both intended and unintended, of the medication (Quinn et al., 2000).

The frequent and increasing use of psychotropic medications, particularly among the preschool population, raises concerns regarding both the long-term health and the social impact of these controversial interventions (R. A. Barkley, 1981; Diller, 2000; Miller, 1999). Specifically:

- How ethical is it to treat children with medications of little-known long-term safety and efficacy?
- Are too many children being given drugs without appropriate management and supervision?
- Are physicians equipped with enough data to prescribe proper dosages of medications that children will use in educational settings?
- Are children, parents, and policy makers viewing medications as an exclusive solution to social problems?

# THE REAL WORLD Challenges and Solutions

## Managing the stress associated with teaching students with EBD

*Alana Faroque, the eighth-grade special education specialist at Vandelay Middle School, had another challenging day. Right at the start of the day, three of her students with EBD got into a fight as they were entering the building. Although no one was hurt, she was responsible for handling the paperwork and contacting parents. The parents were not pleased and, in no subtle way, they let Ms. Faroque know it. Two of the parents were downright nasty and seemed indignant that they had to come to school and develop a collaborative behavioral plan. Although she had considerable experience working with frustrated parents, Ms. Faroque was dreading the meeting. As the day progressed, things did not get any better. During the second period—a co-taught social studies class—several of the students tried repeatedly to disrupt the lesson. She was able to manage their behavior effectively but was exhausted as the period ended. Hopes for recharging her batteries during her planning period came to a quick end when she was called into a new student/parent orientation to explain how special education services are delivered at Vandelay. The student had behavior problems in her previous two schools, and the parents had many questions. Due to the long meeting, she had only 5 minutes to literally swallow her lunch. Then it was a race to the fourth-period co-taught math class. Driving home at the end of the day, Ms. Faroque was frazzled and exhausted and felt a headache coming on. She loved her job but knew she was going to have to make some changes to address the stress associated with it.*

Many jobs and careers are stressful. However, being a professional educator who works with students with behavioral issues can be especially challenging. Generally, when we speak of stress, we are referring to a series of physiological and psychological responses that occur when one senses that coping resources are inadequate (Wood & McCarthy, 2004). In manageable doses, stress can motivate an individual to enhanced performance. However, too much stress, like the intensity of circumstances experienced by Alana Faroque, can lead to health issues, burn-out, and in extreme circumstances leaving the profession. To reduce the stress associated with teaching (Lapp & Attridge, 2000; Rosenberg et al., 2006):

- **Recognize the warning signs and signals of stress:** Indications of high stress levels include:
  - Apathy toward students, families, and colleagues
  - Experiencing physical symptoms such as fatigue, headaches, and stomach pains before, during, after work hours
  - Lower productivity and avoidance of productive workplace initiatives
  - Engaging in negative self-statements regarding effectiveness
- **Engage in self-control strategies that minimize stress:**
  - Employ relaxation techniques, and engage in physical activity regularly.
  - Get support: Develop and sustain relationships with peers and mentors.
  - Have realistic goals, and minimize self-initiated demands.
  - Reward yourself for what you do well.
- **Employ realistic time-management strategies:**
  - Be proactive rather than reactive.
  - Plan work activities, and identify time for tasks requiring sustained attention.
  - Organize, prioritize, and simplify.

### Valuable Resources for the Teacher

Abrams, B. J. (2005). Becoming a therapeutic teacher of students with emotional and behavioral disorders. *Teaching Exceptional Children, 38*(2), 40–45.

Fore, C., Martin, C., & Bender, W. N. (2002). Teacher burnout in special education. *High School Journal, 86*(1), 36–45.

Kabat-Zinn, J. (1991). *Full catastrophe living: Using the wisdom of your body and mind to face stress, pain, and illness.* New York: Delta.

### Final Thoughts

Be aware of potential administrative supports and interventions, and do not be apprehensive about seeking assistance whenever possible. Most school administrators recognize that stress is common among teachers of students with challenging behavior and want to provide assistance before situations reach crisis proportions. Specific types of support that may be available include scheduled breaks during the school day, increased paraprofessional assistance, and peer groups that address concerns and exchange ideas to minimize tense situations.

# 7 SUMMARY

Students with EBD exhibit affect and behavior that differ significantly from those of age-related peers. The primary goal for teachers is to influence those behaviors that impede learning and improve student achievement.

## Definitions and Classification Criteria for Emotional and Behavioral Disabilities

- The field of education has two major definitions of EBD, each with its relative strengths and weaknesses.
- It is difficult, if not impossible, to develop an objective, fail-safe definition of EBD.
- Educators use two classification systems—statistically derived and clinically derived—to categorize possible emotional and behavioral problems.

## Primary Behavioral Characteristics of Emotional and Behavioral Disabilities

- Two broad classes of behavioral characteristics—externalizing and internalizing—typically indicate EBD.
- Common external behaviors are extreme rates of aggression and rule breaking; internalizing behaviors include pronounced social withdrawal, anxiety, and depression.
- Other behaviors associated with EBD include attention and social skills deficits.
- Students with EBD tend to have low average IQ scores, earn low grades, and drop out of school at alarmingly high rates.

## Prevalence, Course, and Causal Factors

- The official prevalence of students with EBD is less than 1%, yet most believe that up to 6% of students require special education services for EBD.
- Students with EBD are underidentified, yet there is considerable concern that certain groups, particularly African American students, are overrepresented in the disability category.
- Students with EBD have dismal postschool outcomes, with almost 50% unemployed 3 to 5 years after leaving school.
- Many theories are used to explain EBD, including biophysical, psychodynamic, familial/home, societal, and even school factors. Still, EBD is more a function of interrelated, interacting factors rather than any single cause.

## Identification and Assessment

- Educators identify students with EBD using a series of objective and projective instruments, yet the most useful tool for instructional/behavioral planning is a functional behavior assessment (FBA).
- FBAs help identify events, activities, and situations associated with a student's problem behaviors and guide environmental adjustments to alter such behaviors.

## Educational Practices

- Typical interventions for students with EBD include behavioral techniques, instruction in self-control and social skills, as well as life-space interviews (LSIs).
- Students transitioning to the world of work often require vocational education, work experience, and supported employment. For students with extreme, pervasive, and multifaceted behavior problems, educators coordinate community services and supports and deliver services in a wraparound fashion.

## Prevailing Issues

- Although great strides have been made in how we teach students with EBD, prevailing issues include the use of physical restraint and the role of medications.

 **Council for Exceptional Children**

## ADDRESSING THE PROFESSIONAL STANDARDS

Council for Exceptional Children Knowledge Standards addressed in the chapter:

ICC1K5, GC1K1, GC1K2, GC2K1, ICC2K2, ICC2K3, ICC2K5, ICC2K6, ICC3K1, ICC3K2

Appendix B: CEC Knowledge and Skill Standards Common Core has a full listing of the standards referenced here.

 **PEARSON myeducationlab**

Now go to Topic 10: Emotional/Behavioral Disorders in the MyEducationLab for your course, where you can:

- Find learning outcomes for the broad concepts covered in this chapter along with the national standards that connect to these outcomes.
- Complete Assignments and Activities that can help you more deeply understand the chapter content.
- Examine challenging situations and cases presented in the IRIS Center Resources.
- Apply and practice your understanding of the core concepts and skills identified in the chapter with the Building Teaching Skills and Dispositions learning units.

- Check your comprehension on the content covered in the chapter by going to the Study Plan in the Book-Specific Resources section for your text. Here you will be able to take a chapter quiz, receive feedback on your answers, and then access Review, Practice, and Enrichment activities to enhance your understanding of chapter content.
- Access video clips of CCSSO National Teachers of the Year award winners responding to the question, "Why Do I Teach?" in the Teacher Talk section.

# Intellectual Disabilities

**REFLECT UPON**

- What are the primary criteria used to identify students with intellectual disabilities?
- What are the major characteristics of students with intellectual disabilities?
- How many students are identified with intellectual disabilities, and what are the major causes?
- What educational practices improve outcomes for students with intellectual disabilities?
- What are the prevailing controversial issues related to students with intellectual disabilities?

# MY PROFESSION, MY STORY: **ANDREA CRAINE**

Andrea Craine wanted to be a special education teacher since she worked at a camp for people with physical and cognitive disabilities during college. "I always knew I wanted to work in an area affecting kids' lives. I fell in love with working with these children." She then completed her bachelor's and master's degrees, obtained certifications in special education and elementary education, and began teaching students with intellectual disabilities at Fort Clark Middle School in Gainesville, Florida.

Andrea felt well prepared when she began her job as a special educator. "One of the most important things I learned (in my teacher education program) was how to differentiate the curriculum by creating different activities or lessons for kids based on their ability and skills." This provided her with the skills to implement lessons so that everyone is engaged and learning. She also noted that she learned important techniques to manage behavior, using positive behavior supports, which were important as she began teaching.

A typical day for Andrea Craine starts out with getting her students ready for school. Often some of her students don't sleep well or eat well before coming to school. "I want to be a positive presence to start out the day." She also noted that most middle school students at her school spend about 30 minutes in loosely structured activities before school starts. She sees this as a time to make sure that the students with intellectual disabilities are engaged socially with other students and not isolated. "This allows them to mingle and have natural social interactions with other kids before school and throughout the day." During the school day, Andrea spends much of her time co-teaching with general education teachers, providing small-group instruction, working with students using direct instruction materials and activities, and supervising independent work. She tries to break up tasks during the day to keep students motivated, and she often pairs preferred tasks with those that students don't enjoy as much to improve work completion.

There are very few negatives related to teaching for Andrea Craine. However, one concern she has is "not having enough time for planning during the day, especially during my first couple of years as a teacher. By my fourth year, I was better at this and it wasn't quite as big a problem." She feels that planning time is a key to providing highly motivating lessons that result in improved student outcomes. Planning time is also important for working with general education teachers when students are included in their classes.

One thing that Andrea Craine is insistent upon is that students with intellectual disabilities should be included in general education classroom. She notes that these students learn so much more when they are included, at least in part because they have so

many good models for learning and behaving appropriately. They're also exposed to more ideas and information, and challenged by the higher academic expectations. She emphasizes that students with intellectual disabilities "want to be part of the school community—that's a big thing for them. Once they're included, I see other students starting conversations with them, saying 'hi' in the hallways, making friends. It's so much more natural, and if we exclude them, they're not going to know how to interact with other students. Socialization is a huge thing!"

One frustrating part of inclusion for Andrea is that some teachers have trouble seeing how much students with intellectual disabilities can do. "At times when I try to include a student in seventh-grade social studies, the teacher raises her eyebrows, and asks, 'How am I going to grade her?' I see so many strengths in these students. I have trouble seeing how everyone doesn't see that too. But teachers get better, and I know it's just a learning process for them that takes them time to see these students' strengths."

Many things keep Andrea Craine in teaching. Most important are "building relationships with students, seeing students grow, and knowing you have a positive influence on their lives. They know they can turn to you if they have a concern or need. It's really the kids that keep you in teaching."

An effective teacher from Andrea Craine's perspective is one who "is always reflecting on her work. After they do their work, they reflect on what they've done, and how to do it better. An effective teacher is always trying to do better than they did the last time." Effective teachers also must be flexible, good listeners, and willing to work with others as part of a team.

Andrea has improved each year as a teacher by continuing to seek out new ideas and effective practices from others. In particular, she mentions a principal and mentor teacher who have helped her become a better teacher by encouraging her to try new things and think outside the box. Andrea has been recognized as an outstanding teacher by the Council for Exceptional Children, who awarded her with the state's rookie of the year teaching award for her excellent work.

For beginning teachers, Andrea suggests that they "reach out to teachers within your school. You can have an ally, and someone you can turn to for help or support, and this is huge. Also, don't be afraid to invite people into your classroom. It helped me feel more confident about teaching. In your work, you can reflect on what you're doing, but sometimes you need to rely on input from other teachers. Sometimes you just need to just hear that you're doing a great job, keep it up!"

Andrea Craine was recently selected by her district to work with teachers from other schools in developing strategies for successfully including students with disabilities. She enjoys working in other teachers' classrooms, as she learns from them and also can provide them assistance in meeting the needs of students with disabilities.

## REFLECTIVE EXERCISE

# 1 The words we use make a difference. Think of a word that has been used to describe you or some real or imagined characteristic you possess. This word may relate to your race, ethnicity, gender, body shape or type, hair color, religion, and so forth. How did you feel when this word was used? Is this word socially acceptable (or politically incorrect)?

If you have had direct contact over time with persons with **intellectual disabilities** (formerly called **mental retardation**), you know that these individuals vary dramatically in the characteristics they exhibit. This includes how they communicate and get along with others, how quickly they learn academic material, how much support they need in school, and a range of other variables.

To illustrate, consider for a moment the differences between students who have mild intellectual disabilities and those with severe intellectual disabilities. Most students with mild intellectual disabilities appear very similar to others in school, except for the fact that they learn academic material much more slowly than most other students. The President's Committee on Mental Retardation (1969) called these students the "**six-hour retarded child**" because they were labeled as intellectually disabled during the school day but adapted well and were often not readily distinguishable as intellectually disabled at home or in the community. As Andrea Craine suggests in the opening interview in this chapter, these are students who, with some support, can successfully interact with other middle school students and become active participants in the school community. While students with mild intellectual disabilities may need support as they transition from school to work, they can often succeed in work settings with real paying jobs.

In contrast, students with severe intellectual disabilities are often readily distinguishable from other students in schools. These students have significant difficulties in communicating, learning, and interacting socially with others. Many students with severe disabilities also have significant weaknesses in sensory and physical development. As a result of these characteristics, limitations are placed on the level of independence of persons with severe disabilities, and they need supports (e.g., assistive technology, a paraeducator) in school and at home.

Perhaps in part due to the complexity of the category, intellectual disabilities are widely misunderstood. Many persons, especially those who have had little contact with individuals with intellectual disabilities, have narrow, stereotyped perspectives about the persons in this special education category. One thing that most professionals and the general public agree on is that intellectual disability is the most stigmatizing disability category. This stigma is vividly illustrated by the casual use of the word *retard* among school-age students and the frequent lack of reaction from teachers or parents when this term is used. For a quick overview of the category of intellectual disabilities, you might want to examine the critical information about these students that is included in the FAQ Sheet.

## FAQ Sheet

### STUDENTS WITH INTELLECTUAL DISABILITIES

| Who are they? | • Students with intellectual disabilities have a measured IQ that is lower than 98% of the school-age population (i.e., below approximately 70).<br>• These students have adaptive behavior skills that are significantly below average. Adaptive behavior includes conceptual, social, and practical skills that people learn so that they can function in their everyday lives. |
|---|---|
| What are typical characteristics? | • Mild to significant weaknesses in general learning ability<br>• Low achievement in all academic areas<br>• Deficits in memory and motivation<br>• Inattentive/distractible<br>• Poor social skills<br>• Deficits in adaptive behavior<br>• Some may exhibit uncommon characteristics (self-stimulatory or self-injurious behavior).<br>• Some may have serious medical conditions. |
| What are the demographics? | • 0.76% of students ages 6 to 21 (approximately 498,000) are labeled with intellectual disabilities.<br>• Approximately 348,000 students are labeled with mild intellectual disabilities.<br>• The percentage of the school-age population identified with intellectual disabilities declined by approximately 18% between 1998 and 2007. |
| Where are students educated? | • 16% of students labeled with intellectual disabilities spend most of the day in general education classrooms.<br>• 57% spend most of the school day segregated from typical peers. |
| How are students identified and assessed for intervention? | • The primary criteria for identification are significantly subaverage intellectual functioning existing concurrently with deficits in adaptive behavior and manifested during the developmental period that adversely affects a child's educational performance.<br>• A score of approximately 70 or below on an intelligence test is considered to be subaverage intellectual functioning.<br>• A standardized test of adaptive behavior is used to determine if the child has deficits in conceptual, social, and practical skills that are significantly subaverage.<br>• A standardized achievement test is used to determine if the child's educational performance is adversely affected (i.e., if the student's achievement is well below grade level). |
| What are the outcomes? | • Intellectual disabilities persist through the school years and into adulthood.<br>• Adults with intellectual disabilities are often employed in occupations with low status and low pay.<br>• Many students with intellectual disabilities continue to need support into adulthood in employment and independent living, although some of these students need no support.<br>• Most students with severe intellectual disabilities live with their families or in community-based residential settings after high school.<br>• Some students with severe intellectual disabilities may work in supported employment or in sheltered workshop settings. |

The use of terminology for this category has changed in the last few years. For example, in the late 1990s, *mental retardation* was widely used by states for this category of students. However, in January 2007, the American Association of Mental Retardation (AAMR) changed its name to the American Association on Intellectual and Developmental Disabilities (AAIDD). This change occurred largely because the term *mental retardation* had become highly stigmatizing. Now the term *intellectual disabilities* is rapidly coming into general use in the United States and is already the term of choice for this category in Europe (Shalock, Luckasson, & Shogren, 2007). We discuss the controversy surrounding the terminology used in this category in more detail as a prevailing issue at the end of this chapter.

### REFLECTIVE EXERCISE

#2 Have you ever used the word *retard* in casual conversation? Did others react negatively to your use of this word? Is this word considered politically incorrect? Have you heard others use it? How did you react? Why are reactions to the use of the words discussed in Reflective Exercise #1 so different from reactions to the word *retard*?

**PEARSON**
**myeducationlab**

Go to the Assignments and
Activities section of Topic 9:
Intellectual Disabilities in the
MyEducationLab for your course
and complete the activity entitled
*From Mental Retardation to
Intellectual Disabilities.*

# DEFINITIONS AND CLASSIFICATION CRITERIA

The definition of intellectual disability in IDEA 2004 (the term *mental retardation* is still used in this law) stipulates that these students have "significantly subaverage general intellectual functioning, existing concurrently with deficits in **adaptive behavior** and manifested during the developmental period, that adversely affects a child's educational performance" (Sec. 300.8[c][6]). Educators use four criteria to identify students with intellectual disabilities based on this definition. First, these students must have a measured IQ that is significantly below average. This typically is defined as an IQ of approximately 70 or below, which means that the student scores lower than approximately 98% of all school-age students. Second, the student must have deficits in adaptive behavior. This criterion is used to ensure that intellectual functioning is not the exclusive criterion used to identify persons with intellectual disabilities. Thus, to be identified with an intellectual disability, students must also have significant limitations in adaptive behavior, which includes practical and social skills that students use to function effectively in their everyday lives. Third, the student must have manifested the intellectual disability during the developmental period, thus indicating that the disability is a long-term problem. This criterion is used to differentiate intellectual disabilities from other disabilities, such as traumatic brain injury, which may occur in adulthood. Finally, the intellectual disability must adversely affect the student's educational performance. This includes low levels of academic achievement, difficulty adapting to classroom or other school settings, poor social skills, and so forth.

Levels of intellectual disability are often differentiated based on a student's IQ level (APA, 2000). For example, Table 8.1 provides IQ ranges for students with differing levels of intellectual disability. Students with **mild intellectual disabilities** typically have an IQ that ranges from 50 or 55 to 70. These are students who can attend to their personal needs, are largely independent in school settings, and in many cases can interact successfully with other students with limited assistance from teachers or other educators. In addition, the disability of students with mild intellectual disabilities is typically not readily noticeable and is only identified upon examining the student's learning and adaptive skills.

Students with **moderate intellectual disabilities** score above 35 to 40 and below 50 to 55 on traditional intelligence tests. Generally, they can learn many basic skills in areas such as communication, self-help, functional academics, domestic skills, community functioning skills, and vocational skills. Many adults with a moderate intellectual disability can manage all of their own daily self-care needs, prepare food, participate in conversations, interact appropriately with others, use money correctly, and hold different kinds of jobs in the community (Westling & Fox, 2009).

If a person with **severe intellectual disabilities** has received a good education and has had adequate support, by adulthood she may have learned several

**TABLE 8.1 • LEVELS OF INTELLECTUAL DISABILITY BASED ON IQ**

| Label | Range of IQ Scores |
| --- | --- |
| Mild intellectual disability | 50/55 to approximately 70 |
| Moderate intellectual disability | 35/40 to 50/55 |
| Severe intellectual disability | 20/25 to 35/40 |
| Profound intellectual disability | Below 20/25 |

Source: American Psychiatric Association, 2000.

useful skills. These could include being able to eat with a fork or spoon, dressing and bathing with some supervision, using the toilet independently, and washing hands and face without help (although she may have to be told or reminded to do so). The individual's physical ability will probably be fair to good, and she will probably be able to walk, run, hop, skip, dance, and maybe skate, sled, or jump rope. The person with a severe intellectual disability probably will not learn many academic skills, such as reading, but may be able to recognize some words and common signs and enjoy books read aloud. The person may know that money is of value but may not be able to state the specific value of coins. Most adults with severe intellectual disability will be able to communicate using signs, symbols, or words (McLean, Brady, & McLean, 1996).

Often individuals with **profound intellectual disabilities** are referred to as having "the most severe" or "significant" disabilities. Their developmental levels will often be comparable to that of a child under 12 months of age. It is difficult to provide a typical profile of an individual at this functioning level because such an extreme degree of variability exists among them. Some are capable of near-independent functioning in common self-care activities, such as eating and toileting, and they may also possess functional skills in other domains such as vocational and domestic skills. Others may not speak, may have very limited sensory and motor abilities, might be nonambulatory, and may only minimally attend or respond to environmental stimuli. Still, many of these persons demonstrate the ability to learn and are capable of at least "partial participation" in normal daily activities (Westling & Fox, 2009).

The **American Association on Intellectual and Developmental Disabilities (AAIDD)**, the leading professional organization in the field of intellectual disabilities, has published a widely used definition of intellectual disability. This definition expands on some of the concepts provided in the IDEA definition (Luckasson et al., 2002): "[Intellectual disability] is . . . characterized by significant limitations in both intellectual functioning and in adaptive behavior as expressed in conceptual, social, and practical adaptive skills. This disability originates before age 18" (p. 13).

Luckasson and colleagues note five factors that should be considered when determining if a person should be identified with an intellectual disability:

1. Limitations in present functioning must be considered within the context of community environments typical of the individual's age peers and culture.
2. Valid assessment considers cultural and linguistic diversity as well as differences in communication, sensory, motor, and behavioral factors.
3. Within the individual, limitations often coexist with strengths.
4. The purpose of describing limitations is to develop a profile of needed supports.
5. With appropriate personalized supports over a sustained period, the life functioning of the person with mental retardation generally will improve. (2002, p. 13)

This definition extends the IDEA definition in three noteworthy ways. First, it defines the developmental period as occurring before age 18. Thus, an intellectual disability should be manifested during the school years and is most often identified before school entry for students with more severe intellectual disabilities and early in elementary school for students with mild intellectual disabilities.

Second, this definition extends the concept of adaptive behavior to include conceptual, social, and practical skills that people use to function in their everyday lives. When these skills are significantly limited, a person's ability to respond to specific situations and the environment is affected (Luckasson et al., 2002). Areas in which adaptive behavior deficits occur are listed in Figure 8.1.

Third, and perhaps most significantly, rather than identifying students based on the severity of their disability (see Table 8.1), as currently occurs in most states, the AAIDD recommends an emphasis on identifying students based on the **level of supports** needed to function effectively (see Figure 8.2). For example, using this approach, most students who have traditionally been identified with a mild intellectual disability would probably be identified as students needing intermittent support

FIGURE 8.1 • ADAPTIVE BEHAVIOR SKILLS USED TO IDENTIFY PERSONS WITH INTELLECTUAL DISABILITIES

**Conceptual Skills**
Receptive and expressive language
Reading and writing
Money concepts
Self-direction
**Social Skills**
Interpersonal
Responsibility
Self-esteem
Gullibility (likelihood of being tricked or manipulated)
Naïveté
Following rules
Obeying laws
Avoiding victimization
**Practical Skills**
Personal activities of daily living such as eating, dressing, mobility, and toileting
Instrumental activities of daily living such as preparing meals, taking medication, using the telephone, managing money, using transportation, and doing housekeeping activities
Occupational skills
Maintaining a safe environment

Source: Adapted from AAIDD. (2009). *FAQ on Intellectual Disability*. Retrieved August 4, 2009, from http://www.aamr.org/content_104.cfm.

FIGURE 8.2 • LEVELS OF SUPPORT FOR PERSONS WITH INTELLECTUAL DISABILITIES

*Intermittent.* Supports on an "as needed basis." Characterized by episodic nature, person not always needing the support(s), or short-term supports needed during life-span transitions (e.g., job loss or acute medical crisis). Intermittent supports may be high or low intensity when needed.
*Limited.* An intensity of support characterized by consistency over time, time-limited but not of an intermittent nature, may require fewer staff members and less cost than more intense levels of support (e.g., time-limited employment training or transitional supports provided during the school to adult period).
*Extensive.* Supports characterized by regular involvement (e.g., daily) in at least some environments (such as work or home) and not time-limited (e.g., long-term support and long-term home living support).
*Pervasive.* Supports characterized by their constancy and high intensity; provided across environments; potential life-sustaining nature. Pervasive supports typically involve more staff members and intrusiveness than do extensive or time-limited supports.

Source: Adapted from Luckasson et al., 2002, *Mental retardation: Definition, classification, and systems of support* (10th ed.), p. 152.

(episodic need), while perhaps a few would need limited support for specific periods of time. In contrast, the needs of students with severe disabilities would range from limited, to extensive, to pervasive support in most instances.

*Supports* are defined as "resources and strategies that aim to promote the development, education, interests, and personal well-being of a person and that enhance individual functioning. Services are one type of support provided by professionals" (Luckasson et al., 2002, p. 145). This approach to the identification of persons with intellectual disabilities is a radical departure from past practices and is intended as a first step in "forcing the field to think differently about mental retardation and how we intervene in the lives of people with that label" (Wehmeyer, 2003, p. 273).

Most students with mild intellectual disabilities need intermittent supports.

More specifically, while past definitions have emphasized the student's deficits in intellectual development and adaptive behavior, the levels-of-support approach emphasizes how a person's needs can be met within a particular setting (e.g., school, home, work). Thus, rather than viewing an intellectual disability as solely a problem that resides within the student, this approach recognizes the need to consider how the environment can be altered so that the student receives appropriate supports and can succeed.

The extent to which professionals in the field of intellectual disabilities will accept this change in practice remains in question. While the levels-of-support approach to identification was originally proposed in 1992 (Luckasson et al., 1992), by the late 1990s, few states had adopted the definition (Polloway, Chamberlain, Denning, Smith, & Smith, 1999). Moreover, this definition has generated much controversy among professionals in the field (Macmillan, Siperstein, & Leffert, 2006). While the levels-of-support approach to student identification is designed to reduce the stigma associated with *intellectual disabilities* and place more emphasis on the supports that students need to be successful, it will likely take many years to determine whether this approach can be successfully implemented in schools.

### Intellectual Disabilities Syndromes

Another way professionals categorize persons with severe disabilities is according to specific syndromes. A *syndrome* is a condition signified by a cluster of similar physical and behavioral characteristics having a common etiology, or origin. Table 8.2 lists several syndromes that might result in a "severe disability" classification.

## PRIMARY CHARACTERISTICS OF STUDENTS WITH INTELLECTUAL DISABILITIES

In the following section, we describe these students based on key learning, cognitive, and social characteristics. While we discuss several characteristics that are often seen when a student is identified with an intellectual disability, we do not mean to suggest that all students with this disability are alike. Indeed, as with any group of people, students with intellectual disabilities vary widely in their ability to do

### REFLECTIVE EXERCISE

#3 Have you had contact with a person with an intellectual disability? How was this person different from others? How was he or she the same? Can you identify behaviors indicating that the person needs intermittent supports to function independently? Behaviors indicating that the person needs extensive or pervasive support?

**TABLE 8.2** • SYNDROMES ASSOCIATED WITH SEVERE INTELLECTUAL DISABILITIES

| Name | Etiology | Key Features | Sources of Information |
|---|---|---|---|
| Down syndrome | Chromosomal anomaly (trisomy 21) | Mild-to-severe intellectual disabilities. Physical characteristics: a flattening of the back of the head; slanting eyelids; small folds of skin at the inner corners of the eyes; depressed nasal bridge; small ears, mouth, hands, and feet; decreased muscle tone; 60% to 80% have hearing impairments; 40% to 45% have congenital heart disease; a tendency toward obesity. Hypothyroidism affects 15% to 20%. Frequent skeletal problems, immunologic concerns, leukemia, Alzheimer's disease, seizures, sleep disorders. | National Down Syndrome Society (http://www.ndss.org/); National Association for Down Syndrome (http://www.nads.org/); Roizen (2001) |
| Fragile-X syndrome | X-linked transmission | Physical characteristics: a long, narrow face; large ears, jaw, and forehead. Common characteristics: an unusual style of social interaction; may avoid direct eye contact; sometimes hand flapping or hand biting; may speak fast and repetitiously; can have short attention span and hyperactivity. | National Fragile-X Foundation (http://www.fragilex.org/); Fragile X Research Foundation (http://www.fraxa.org/); Meyer & Batshaw (2001) |
| Fetal alcohol syndrome | Consumption of alcohol during pregnancy | General developmental delay, growth problems, and other physical problems. Intellectual disabilities may range from mild to severe. May have a small head, narrow eye slits, a flat midface, and a low nasal bridge. Babies may have sleeping problems, be restless and irritable, and have sucking problems. | FASlink (http://www.acbr.com/fas/); Wunsch, Conlon, & Scheidt (2001) |
| Prader-Willi syndrome | Chromosomal anomaly on chromosome 15 | Often results in a moderate mental disability, but measured IQs have ranged from 40 to more than 100. Between ages 1 and 3, will develop insatiable appetite, become very preoccupied with food, want to eat continuously, and develop life-threatening obesity. Begin to show delayed psychomotor activity, intellectual delay, and emotional/behavioral problems. | Prader-Willi Syndrome Association (http://www.pwsausa.org/); Scott, Smith, Hendricks, & Polloway (1999) |
| Angelman syndrome | Chromosomal anomaly (a portion of chromosome 15 is missing) | Usually severe-to-profound intellectual disabilities. Tend to have jerky body movements and stiff-legged walking. Common facial features such as a wide smiling mouth, a thin upper lip, and deep-set eyes. Often have fair hair and skin and light blue eyes. About 80% of the time they will have epilepsy. | Angelman Syndrome Foundation (http://www.angelman.org/angel/) |

schoolwork and adjust to social situations in school and other locations. However, in contrast to most other disability categories, students with intellectual disabilities tend to have more general, delayed development in academic, social, and adaptive skills. This delayed development is reflected in low achievement across content and skill areas as well as significantly lower scores on measures of intelligence and adaptive behavior when compared with students who are not identified with intellectual disabilities. In addition, many students with more severe intellectual disabilities tend to have health problems.

## Academic Performance

As Andrea Craine notes in the interview at the beginning of this chapter, students with intellectual disabilities can learn many academic skills, especially if they are exposed to this information in the general education classroom. However, even with high-quality instruction, students with intellectual disabilities lag significantly behind grade-level peers in developing academic skills. Students with mild intellectual disabilities are likely to be significantly delayed in learning to read and learning basic math skills (Taylor, Richards, & Brady, 2005). This delay in developing foundational skills in reading and math, coupled with delays in language skills, then results in delays in other academic areas that require the use of these skills (e.g., writing, spelling, science).

Although it is possible for students with substantial intellectual disabilities to learn many skills, the number and type (e.g., complexity) of academic skills they learn are not comparable to those learned by most students. The skills that these students learn are often very functional and applicable to their current and future needs (e.g., learning words such as *exit*).

Students with intellectual disabilities continue to lag behind age-level peers in academic achievement throughout their school years. However, many students with mild intellectual disabilities develop basic literacy skills and functional mathematics skills. For example, most students with mild intellectual disabilities learn basic computational skills and functional arithmetic skills related to money, time, and measurement. However, most of these students continue to have difficulty with more advanced skills related to content, such as mathematical reasoning and applying concepts to solve problems (Beirne-Smith et al., 2006; Browder, Spooner, Ahlgrim-Delzell, Harris, & Wakeman, 2008).

## Cognitive Performance

Students with intellectual disabilities are characterized by general delays in cognitive development that influence the acquisition of language and academic skills. Moreover, while these students can learn information that is part of the general education curriculum, they learn more slowly than do typical students, require more time to learn, and have difficulty learning more complex skills. Deficits in specific cognitive skill areas also contribute to this delay. Three of the most important cognitive skill deficits that contribute to these difficulties relate to attention, memory, and generalization.

### Attention

Students with intellectual disabilities have difficulty with different types of attention, including orienting to a task, selective attention, and sustaining attention to a task (Merrill, 2005; Wenar & Kerig, 2006). Orienting to a task requires a student to look in the direction of the task (e.g., a teacher demonstrating how to solve a math problem on an overhead projector in the front of the room). Selective attention requires that the student attend to relevant aspects of the task and not to unimportant task components (e.g., attending to one type of math problem on a page and completing the appropriate operation). Finally, sustained attention requires that the student continue to attend to a task for a period of time.

### Memory

Students with intellectual disabilities also have difficulty remembering information (i.e., short-term memory). Major problems in this area are related to not being adequately exposed to the learning condition initially, having insufficient opportunity to practice or use the information or skill after it is initially learned, and then not using strategies adequately to pull the information from long-term memory for use when needed (Westling & Fox, 2009).

**PEARSON**
**myeducationlab**

Go to the Assignments and Activities section of Topic 9: Intellectual Disabilities in the MyEducationLab for your course and complete the activity entitled *Learning Characteristics.*

Students with intellectual disabilities often need support to make friends and get along with peers in general education classrooms.

## REFLECTIVE EXERCISE

#4 What skills do you and your friends need to get along socially? What characteristics of students with intellectual disabilities might negatively affect their ability to get along with others? What could a teacher do to reduce the effect of these characteristics and support students with intellectual disabilities in getting along with others?

### Generalization

A final area in which many students with intellectual disabilities have difficulty relates to the generalization of information to other material or settings (Wenar & Kerig, 2006). For example, a young man with a severe intellectual disability might know it is okay to hug his mom but not realize it is inappropriate to hug another woman. Similarly, a student with a mild intellectual disability may have difficulty generalizing material learned in one setting to another (e.g., from school to the community).

## Social Skills Performance

Many people with intellectual disabilities have full lives. They have friends, enjoy various leisure and recreational activities, and, as teenagers or adults, may have jobs in the community. However, as Andrea Craine points out in the interview at the beginning of this chapter, these outcomes do not occur as easily as they do for persons without disabilities, and usually some intentional planning is necessary. For example, some students with intellectual disabilities may need support in getting along and making friends with their peers during loosely structured opportunities for social interaction.

Many of the cognitive characteristics of students with intellectual disabilities may contribute to difficulty interacting socially. For example, a low level of cognitive development and delayed language development may cause a student with intellectual disability to have difficulty understanding the content of verbal interactions and understanding expectations (e.g., when to listen, when and how to respond) during verbal interactions. Similarly, difficulty with attention and memory impedes social interactions, as students with intellectual disabilities have difficulty attending to important aspects of social interactions, maintaining attention over time, and holding important aspects of what they observe in short-term memory.

As you will see in a later section on placement practices for students with intellectual disabilities, most of these students have little opportunity to interact with age-level peers in school settings, due to the fact that they spend a large proportion of the school day in segregated school settings with other students with disabilities (Williamson, McLeskey, Hoppey, & Rentz, 2006). Extensive research evidence reveals that the social skills of students with intellectual disabilities tend to improve when they receive appropriate supports and attend a general education classroom with age-appropriate peers for a large part of the school day (Freeman & Alkin, 2000; Westling & Fox, 2009).

## Physical Characteristics

Individuals with severe intellectual disabilities often have serious medical or physical conditions. Cerebral palsy and epilepsy are two conditions that are often present. Other conditions can also limit normal physical development and activities. Common medical conditions include gastrointestinal disorders, inadequate ventilation of lungs, kidney and heart problems, sensory problems, and frequent infections (Thuppal & Sobsey, 2004).

In the classroom, teachers of students with severe disabilities will typically work with school nurses as well as physical and occupational therapists to address students' physical and medical needs. On a regular basis, students may have nutritional problems, **anemia**, dehydration, skin irritation and pressure sores, **respiratory infections**, asthma, ear infections, and **contractures** (Heller, 2004).

# PREVALENCE, COURSE, AND CAUSAL FACTORS

## Prevalence

During the 2007–2008 school year, more than 498,000 U.S. students were classified as having intellectual disabilities, or 0.76% of the school-age population (U.S. Department of Education, 2009). Researchers have estimated that 70% to 85% of all children with intellectual disabilities have mild-to-moderate intellectual disabilities (Murphy, Yeargin-Allsopp, Decoufle, & Drews, 1995; Taylor et al., 2005). Our best estimate of the number of students with mild-to-moderate intellectual disabilities is about 348,000, resulting in a prevalence rate for these students of approximately 0.70%. This results in approximately 150,000 students with more severe intellectual disabilities.

It is important to note that the number of students in the intellectual disabilities category declined between 1998 and 2007, by approximately 18% (U.S. Department of Education, 2009). It is unclear why this decline occurred, although Beirne-Smith and colleagues (2006) have speculated that it could relate to factors such as (1) reticence to label students from culturally diverse backgrounds because of their overrepresentation in the mild intellectual disabilities category, (2) identifying high-functioning students with the less stigmatizing learning disability label; and (3) the positive effects of early intervention efforts that reduced the occurrence of mild intellectual disabilities.

A final consideration regarding the prevalence of students with intellectual disabilities is the extent to which students in this category represent the racial and ethnic population of students in the United States. Table 8.3 presents data from the 2007–2008 school year regarding the percentage of students from each of five racial groups who were identified with intellectual disabilities and the percentage of each of these groups in the population of school-age students in the United States. It is noteworthy that the group that is most significantly **overrepresented** in the intellectual disability category is African American students. Based on their representative proportion in the school-age population, these students are more than twice as likely to be identified with an intellectual disability as one would predict. Furthermore, African American students have been significantly overrepresented in the intellectual disability category since at least the 1960s (Skiba, et al., 2008).

## The Course of Intellectual Disabilities

As students with intellectual disabilities move through school and into adulthood, the performance gap when compared to persons without disabilities becomes greater. This occurs in relation to both academic and social/adaptive skills. Thus, persons with intellectual disabilities enter adulthood at a significant disadvantage with respect to academic

**REFLECTIVE EXERCISE**

#5 How will your learning about intellectual disabilities influence your expectations for these students in your classroom? How will this information influence what you teach these students? How will you guard against having expectations that are too low, which is difficult for any teacher to avoid?

**TABLE 8.3 •** PERCENTAGE OF ALL SCHOOL-AGE STUDENTS LABELED INTELLECTUALLY DISABLED BY ETHNICITY, 2007–2008

| Race/Ethnicity | Intellectually Disabled[a] | Total Population[b] |
|---|---|---|
| American Indian and Alaska Native | 1.32 | 0.96 |
| Asian and Pacific Islander | 2.21 | 4.22 |
| Black | 31.92 | 15.07 |
| Hispanic (not Black) | 15.05 | 18.88 |
| European American | 49.50 | 60.87 |

Source: U.S. Department of Education, 2009.

Most adults with intellectual disabilities are employed in less skilled jobs.

and social skills when compared to their peers who are not identified with disabilities.

Three outcomes are viewed as critically important for adults with intellectual disabilities (and other adults as well): productive employment, participating successfully in postsecondary education, and psychological well-being (Patton et al., 1996). While some persons with intellectual disabilities struggle greatly with each of these outcomes, others are relatively successful and are generally satisfied with their lives.

### Productive Employment

Research has shown that persons with intellectual disabilities are typically employed in jobs requiring fewer skills with lower take-home pay than are typical peers and attain limited advancement in their employment (Seltzer et al., 2005). However, some research has shown that adults with mild intellectual disabilities are "equally likely to be employed as their higher IQ siblings, [have] greater job stability, and [are] equally satisfied with their jobs" (Seltzer et al., 2005, p. 465). Some adults with severe intellectual disabilities work in **supported employment** settings that provide pay for work by adults who may need support or supervision (Westling & Fox, 2009). However, most of these adults continue to work in settings with other adults with similar disabilities, such as sheltered workshops or adult activity centers, and do not engage in competitive employment.

### Postsecondary Education

A major factor that impedes the success of many adults with intellectual disabilities is their lack of opportunity to participate in postsecondary education. Patton and colleagues (1996) note that a critical step toward successful involvement in postsecondary education for persons with intellectual disabilities is the extent to which they are welcomed into these settings and accommodations are provided for their disability. Until recently, postsecondary education was largely limited to persons without disabilities. This has changed dramatically in recent years, as large numbers of persons with disabilities, including those with mild-to-severe intellectual disabilities, have begun to attend postsecondary education institutions to network, learn social and academic skills, and obtain job skills (e.g., Pearman, Elliott, & Aborn, 2004; Zafft, Hart, & Zimbrich, 2004). As increasing numbers of adults with intellectual disabilities continue their education, it is likely that employment will improve, as will other critical life outcomes.

### Psychological Well-Being

Finally, some research indicates that adults with intellectual disabilities seem to be most at risk in the area of psychological well-being (Neece, Kraemer, & Blacher, 2009; Seltzer et al., 2005). More specifically, adults with intellectual disabilities often have less of a sense of purpose in life, fewer opportunities for personal growth, a higher rate of depressive symptoms, and less personal autonomy than do their peers without intellectual disabilities (Seltzer et al., 2005). Unfortunately, mental health services are often lacking for adults with intellectual disabilities (Neece et al., 2009). One strategy that is being used to address these concerns, at least to some degree, is the increasing use of approaches that provide persons with intellectual disabilities with the core skills needed for **self-determination** (Sands & Wehmeyer, 2005). These skills have been shown to correlate with "an improved quality of life for adults with disabilities, particularly those outcomes [such] as employment, community living, and post-secondary education" (Thoma & Getzel, 2005, p. 234). We provide further information regarding self-determination later in this chapter.

# CAUSAL FACTORS

For almost all students identified with mild intellectual disabilities, we do not know the particular cause of the disability. However, we do know that many of these students come from families who live in poverty and that a disproportionate number of such families are members of non–European American groups (Wenar & Kerig, 2006). We more often know the cause of more severe intellectual disabilities. Most of these causes occur prenatally (or before birth), while some are peri- or postnatal (during or after birth).

## Family Factors

A disproportionate number of students who live in poverty and who are from non–European American groups are identified with mild intellectual disabilities. Because of the strong family and cultural factors involved, this type of intellectual disability was originally called "cultural-familial" but now is referred to as "intellectual disability that results from psychosocial disadvantage" (Beirne-Smith et al., 2006, p. 162).

As we discuss these issues, it is important to note that most children who grow up living in poverty are not identified with mild intellectual disabilities, nor are most children from non–European American groups (often called "minority" groups) who grow up in these settings. Moreover, most students who grow up living in poverty have measured IQs that fall within the normal range. However, family factors do seem to be related to living in a low-socioeconomic-status home, especially for children from non–European American groups, which put a student at greater risk for being identified with a mild intellectual disability.

Many professionals have speculated that a combination of risk factors may exist in high-poverty settings and contribute to the high incidence of mild intellectual disabilities in these settings. For example, risk factors may include the amount of stress in the environment (e.g., inadequate housing, inadequate nutrition, inadequate health care), the family's resources for addressing this stress, the number of children in the family, the education level of the parent(s), head of household in an unskilled occupation, mental health and education level of the mother, and the family's flexibility in addressing children's needs (Sameroff, 1990).

## Pre-, Peri-, and Postnatal Causes

Several factors have been identified that may contribute to the development of intellectual disabilities (The ARC, 2005; Wenar & Kerig, 2006; Westling & Fox, 2009). These factors include:

- Problems during pregnancy, such as use of alcohol or drugs, malnutrition, exposure to environmental toxins (e.g., radiation), or maternal illnesses such as rubella or syphilis. Severe intellectual disabilities may be also be caused by genetic conditions (e.g., Tay-Sachs disease) and chromosomal anomalies (e.g, Down syndrome).
- Perinatal factors, such as prematurity and low birth weight, or difficulties during delivery, such as birth injuries or temporary oxygen deprivation.
- Postnatal factors, such as infections (e.g., meningitis, encephalitis), injuries (e.g., a blow to the head), or exposure to environmental toxins (e.g., lead or mercury).

# IDENTIFICATION AND ASSESSMENT

The primary criteria used to identify students with intellectual disabilities are subaverage scores on tests of intelligence and adaptive behavior. A school psychologist often administers a test of intelligence and interprets the results for the multidisciplinary team. The multidisciplinary team determines if the student's level of intelligence falls below the cutoff for an intellectual disability, and, if the IQ score is below 70, which

**REFLECTIVE EXERCISE**

**#6** How does knowledge regarding the causes of intellectual disabilities influence how you perceive these students? Will this information influence how you interact with and teach these students in your classroom? What will you expect of these students?

Many factors during pregnancy, at birth, or during the early years of a child's life may contribute to the development of an intellectual disability.

level of intellectual disability is indicated. (See Table 8.1 for cut-offs for different levels of intellectual disability.) Intelligence measures that are widely used to identify students with intellectual disabilities are the Stanford-Binet Intelligence Scale (5th ed.) (Roid, 2003) and the Wechsler Intelligence Scale for Children (4th ed.) (Wechsler, 2003).

While an IQ score of 70 or below is a major criterion for identifying a student as intellectually disabled, it is not sufficient. The student also must have significant limitations in adaptive behavior. To make this determination, a team member administers a measure of adaptive behavior. Tests that are most often used in this area include the AAMR Adaptive Behavior Scale—School (Lambert, Nihira, & Leland, 1993), the Adaptive Behavior Assessment System (2nd ed.) (ABAS-II) (Harrison & Oakland, 2003), and the Vineland Adaptive Behavior Scales (2nd ed.) (Sparrow, Cicchetti, & Balla, 2005). See Figure 8.1 for a list of the adaptive behavior skills that educators use to identify persons with intellectual disabilities.

Finally, if a student's IQ and adaptive behavior measures fall within the range that indicates significant limitations, the multidisciplinary team determines if the child's educational performance has been adversely affected. Measures of academic achievement, such as the Woodcock-Johnson Tests of Achievement (Woodcock, McGrew, & Mather, 2001) and the Wechsler Individual Achievement Test (3rd ed.) (WIAT-III) (Psychological Corporation, 2009), are typically administered to provide this information. These tests provide achievement scores in the areas of language, reading, writing, and mathematics.

## EDUCATIONAL PRACTICES

Extensive research has been conducted regarding evidence-based educational practices that are effective with students with intellectual disabilities. This evidence reveals that these students can learn far more than we anticipated in the past but need more time to learn and benefit from effective instructional practices. Students with severe disabilities also benefit from effective instruction, but it is very important that this instruction begins when they are very young and continues throughout life. Even though these students may not achieve the level of learning and development reached by individuals without disabilities, overwhelming evidence indicates that good instruction can promote skill development and a better quality of life (Snell & Brown, 2005; Westling & Fox, 2009). In the sections that follow, we review placement practices regarding students with intellectual disabilities and follow this with a discussion of educational practices that are effective for these students as they progress through school and transition to adult life.

### Service Delivery

While students with intellectual disabilities have been provided with an education in primarily segregated, separate settings for the past 100 years, researchers have questioned the effectiveness of these placements for more than 70 years (Bennett, 1932; Carlberg & Kavale, 1980; Johnson, 1962; Polloway, 1984). Much of the research that has been conducted on this issue reveals that students with intellectual disabilities benefit from spending at least some—and, in many instances, a large—proportion of the school day in general education classrooms. For example, after reviewing research related to the effectiveness of **separate class placements** for students with intellectual disabilities, Freeman and Alkin (2000) concluded, "children with milder mental levels of intellectual disabilities achieve more positive results in the integrated classroom than do their counterparts in segregated settings." They also note that the placement of students "with mental retardation in general education classrooms tends to improve their social skills and competence" (p. 15).

In spite of the support from research to place these students in general education classes for at least part of the school day, many students with intellectual disabilities are taught in segregated, separate settings for most of the day (McLeskey, Henry, & Hodges, 1999; Smith, 2007; Williamson et al., 2006). For example, overall, approximately 57% of students with disabilities spend most of the school day in general education classrooms, compared to about only 16% of students with intellectual disabilities (see Table 8.4). Similarly, only 21% of all students with disabilities spend most of the school day segregated from peers, compared to 57% of students with intellectual disabilities.

It is important to note that changes have occurred over the past two decades indicating that significant progress has been made in including increasing numbers of students with intellectual disabilities in general education classrooms (Williamson et al., 2006). For example, in 1989–1990, approximately 8% of students with intellectual disabilities were educated in general education settings for most of the school day. By 2007, this figure had increased to 16% (U.S. Department of Education, 2009). Similarly, in 1989–1990, 70% of students with intellectual disabilities were educated in settings where they were segregated for 60% or more of the school day. By 2007, this figure had dropped to 57%. Even with these changes, however, most students with intellectual disabilities do not spend sufficient time with general education peers and in general education classrooms to realize the benefits of inclusive placements that Andrea Craine describes in the interview that opens this chapter.

## Early Intervention

Research has revealed that the early experiences of children have an important influence on their later development and that effective early intervention programs can have a significant positive influence on a student's intelligence level, academic achievement, and social competence (Taylor et al., 2005). Children with severe intellectual disabilities will almost always participate in these programs, as their disabilities are often obvious early in life, and their parents will seek these services. While these programs do not eliminate the need for later services, they can maximize

**REFLECTIVE EXERCISE**

**#7** In spite of evidence that many students with intellectual disabilities benefit from placement in well-supported general education classrooms for much of the school day, few of these students are educated in such settings. Why do you think this is the case? What challenges would these students present for teachers? What types of support would teachers need to successfully include more students with intellectual disabilities?

TABLE 8.4 • PERCENTAGE OF STUDENTS AGES 6 TO 21 WITH INTELLECTUAL DISABILITIES AND ALL DISABILITIES TAUGHT IN DIFFERENT PLACEMENT SETTINGS, 2007–2008

| | Placement Settings | | | |
|---|---|---|---|---|
| | % Time Outside General Education Classroom | | | |
| Disability Category | <21%[a] | 21–60%[a] | >60%[a] | Separate Setting[b] |
| Intellectual disability | 15.8 | 27.6 | 49.0 | 7.6 |
| All disability | 56.8 | 22.4 | 17.4 | 3.4 |

[a] These percentages represent the time students spend outside the general education classroom. Thus, the first category, <21%, indicates that these students spend less than 21% of the school day in a separate, special education setting and is thus the most inclusive setting.
[b] Separate setting combines several categories reported by the U.S. Department of Education, including public separate facility, private separate facility, public residential facility, private residential facility, and home/hospital environment.

Source: U.S. Department of Education, 2009.

Well-designed early intervention programs are very beneficial for children with intellectual disabilities.

the child's development, prevent secondary disabilities, and provide important support for the child's family.

Early intervention programs for children with intellectual disabilities should be family centered, and teaching should be based on developmentally appropriate practice (Allen & Cowdery, 2009). Family-centered programs are those that provide services directly to the family, addressing the family's needs and increasing their ability to provide support. Developmentally appropriate practices means that instructional activities are individually appropriate, age appropriate, and reflective of the social and cultural conditions of the child's life.

## Classroom Interventions

As you will recollect from the previous discussion of the characteristics of students with intellectual disabilities, these students take longer to learn academic content than do other students and lag behind age-level peers in basic skills. They also do not automatically generate strategies for learning and remembering academic content, as many students do. In the sections that follow, we discuss what should be taught students with intellectual disabilities and the use of systematic instruction and technology to address their instructional needs.

### Functional Curriculum Versus the General Curriculum

Since the 1970s, teaching functional skills has been the primary curricular philosophy guiding the education of students with intellectual disabilities (L. Brown, Nietupski, & Hamre-Nietupski, 1976; L. Brown et al., 1979). Such a curriculum includes skills that are necessary for living day to day and for participating in daily life as much as possible. Whether students are in the general education classroom or a special classroom, the functional curriculum model is supposed to prepare them for living, playing, and working in the same world that everyone else lives in.

A functional curriculum includes a broad group of skills that range from learning to feed oneself and use the toilet to learning to cross the street and shop for groceries. Westling and Fox (2009) suggest several preferred practices for teaching functional skills:

- Teachers should not teach skills in isolation but as integrated clusters that build on each other.
- All objectives should focus on increasing the independence, participation, or self-determination of the individual or on making the individual less dependent and less isolated.
- Students should not be excluded from instructional activities because they cannot learn a complete skill independently. Instead, meaningful *partial participation* should be a target.
- The teacher should identify the most important skills as instructional objectives and develop instructional programs and data-collection systems to better ensure learning.
- Objectives should be written so that they describe specific observable behaviors and include criteria so that the student's skill level on a particular objective can be readily determined.

- The teacher should teach important skills that contribute to all life domains (e.g., language, ambulation and mobility, motor skills, and social skills) within functional routines and contexts.

In addition to other functional skills, teachers often teach students with intellectual disabilities functional academic skills. Functional academics include areas such as sight word reading, basic arithmetic operations, counting money, and telling time. Since 1997, however, IDEA requires that students with intellectual disabilities have access to the general curriculum as much as possible and be assessed on end-of-grade tests using alternate assessment systems. The intent is for their progress to be evaluated like that of other students in public schools based on state curriculum standards. Research evidence reveals that students with mild-to-severe intellectual disabilities can benefit from this instruction in reading and mathematics, especially when systematic instruction is used (Browder, Ahlgrim-Delzell, Courtade, Gibbs, & Flowers, 2008; Browder, Spooner, Ahlgrim-Delzell, Harris, & Wakeman, 2008; Carnine, Silbert, Kame'enui, & Tarver, 2003; Stein, Silbert, & Carnine, 1997).

One strategy to increasing participation in the general curriculum is to design a universal curriculum from which all students can learn. There are three essential aspects of a universal curriculum (Wehmeyer, Lance, & Bashinski, 2002):

1. **Multiple means of representation.** This means presenting the curriculum material in a variety of ways so that each student can grasp something relevant from it.

2. **Multiple means of expression.** This means that students can respond in their preferred way. For example, instead of giving a written or oral response, they might respond through the use of an alternative or augmentative communication (AAC) device.

3. **Multiple means of engagement.** All students do not need to participate in the learning activity in the same way. Involvement may mean, for example, working with a peer instead of working alone.

## Systematic Instruction

While systematic approaches to instruction are highly effective for students with and without disabilities (Browder et al., 2008; Coyne, Kame'enui, & Carnine, 2007), these approaches are especially useful for students with intellectual disabilities. Several assumptions underlie this approach to learning (Shuell, 1996):

- Instruction is organized into well-defined units.
- Mastery of each unit is expected of each student before proceeding to the next unit.
- Tests are administered to determine mastery.
- If mastery has not been achieved, supplemental materials and activities are used to teach the information again.
- Under appropriate conditions, all students can learn well or master most of the content.
- Time is used to individualize instruction. (Some students take more time to master content than others do and may have to repeat the instructional cycle more than once.)

See the "Can You Help Me with This Student?" feature for more information regarding the use of systematic instruction.

Various programs and approaches to instruction have been developed based on mastery learning, and these programs have generally been proven effective (Coyne et al., 2007). The approach that has the strongest research to support its effectiveness and is the most widely used is **direct instruction** (Carnine et al., 2003; Coyne et al., 2007).

| To... | Sandra Ellis, District Special Education Supervisor |
|---|---|
| From... | Susan Kerns, Special Education Teacher |
| Subject: | Addressing a learning objective for a student with a profound intellectual disability |

Sandy, I need your assistance regarding how to address a learning objective for one of my students. Jesus has a profound intellectual disability. One of the learning objectives I have for him this year is:

Jesus will shake his head up and down to indicate when he wants an offered item or activity 90% of the time that something is offered. He will do this throughout the school day in different locations with different people for 5 consecutive days.

Could you provide suggestions regarding how I might support Jesus in reaching this objective? Many thanks for any assistance you can provide.

—Susan

---

To:        Susan Kerns
From:      Sandy Ellis
Subject:   RE: Addressing a learning objective for a student with a profound intellectual disability

Susan, I'm glad to provide some ideas about teaching Jesus. As you're teaching to the objective you've described, here are some things I would recommend keeping in mind:

- Because the skill needs to be taught and learned in different locations, you will need to think of the locations that are most appropriate. Where are the natural places where a student would need to say whether or not he wants something? If the skill is taught in only one location, by one person, at a certain time, then Jesus will not generalize it. This means that he may learn to do the skill but only in a very limited way.

- You need to find out the kinds of things Jesus might like to have. To do this, you need to do a preference assessment. Basically, a preference assessment is a systematic way to learn what a person with a severe disability likes or desires. Because individuals such as Jesus often cannot tell us verbally what they like or dislike, we must present them with items that may be of interest and then carefully monitor their interactions with these items. As they choose which they prefer, we need to make records so we will remember what they like and dislike.

- You need to use systematic instruction. If you look at the references provided below, you will find information on systematic instructional approaches.

- You might use peers to help Jesus learn this skill. For many reasons, peers without disabilities can be very effective instructors for students such as Jesus.

- Students who have significant disabilities often progress very slowly. Special education teachers therefore often record their progress quite frequently, even daily. To do this, you'll need to address the following questions. What kind of data would you collect to see if Jesus is making progress toward achieving his objective? How often would you measure his performance? What kind of information do you think you could glean from the data? Let me know if you need assistance addressing any of these questions.

If instruction of students such as Jesus is to succeed, we need to use very precise, systematic instructional methods. Research suggests that, if we do, many students can learn skills that will allow them to participate more meaningfully in their personal environments.

For more information on how you might teach Jesus, see the following sources:

Snell, M. E., & Brown, F. (2005) *Instruction of students with severe disabilities* (6th ed.). Upper Saddle River, NJ: Merrill/Pearson Education.

Westling, D. L., & Fox, L. (2009). *Teaching students with severe disabilities* (4th ed.). Upper Saddle River, NJ: Merrill/Pearson Education.

**EXTEND AND APPLY**

- What do you think about the process of systematic instruction? Is this something you might want to apply sometime? You may find it very effective!

- Teachers working with a student like Jesus might react in different ways. One might be, "This is a real challenge, and I think it would be exciting to try to achieve it." Another could be "Is it really worth the time and effort to teach such a basic skill?" What would your reaction be? Why?

Direct instruction is based on extensive research regarding what a teacher should do to begin a lesson, present information during the lesson, guide student practice after instruction, correct student work and provide feedback, plan and carry out student seat work, and follow up the lesson. A well-designed direct instruction lesson includes the following steps:

1. Review and reteach previously taught information that is directly relevant to the current lesson. Teach any necessary prerequisite skills.
2. Clearly state the purpose of the lesson, and provide an advance organizer so the students will understand what content the lesson will address and what activities will be included.
3. Present the information in small steps, providing illustrations, modeling any necessary skills, and providing varied examples.
4. Provide clear and detailed instructions or explanations regarding the content being taught.
5. Provide students with a high level of practice on the content being learned after each step.
6. Ensure that all students understand the content. The teacher should closely monitor student practice, and ask many questions to check for student understanding.
7. Reteach the content as necessary.
8. Provide students with teacher-guided practice of newly learned content.
9. Provide students with the opportunity to practice the newly learned skill with peers or independently, with feedback and correction as necessary.
10. Provide explicit instruction for seat-work activities and monitor student seat work.

While some educators have provided extensive information regarding how to apply the principles of direct instruction to reading (Carnine et al., 2003) and math (Stein et al., 1997), others have developed entire instructional programs that apply these principles. For example, Reading Mastery (Engelmann & Bruner, 2003) is

## REFLECTIVE EXERCISE

#8 Based on what you have read in this chapter about the characteristics of students with intellectual disabilities, why do you think systematic approaches to instruction have been so effective with these students? What characteristics of systematic instruction lead to this effectiveness?

## REFLECTIVE EXERCISE

#9 What goals might a fifth-grade teacher have for students with mild intellectual disabilities when teaching Aesop's fables? How would these goals differ from the goals for students who read on grade level in the class? Advanced students? How could the teacher use UDL to accommodate the needs of all these students?

a complete instructional program in reading that includes highly structured material for students in grades K–6, with related instructional scripts for teachers. Similar programs are available to teach reading to older students and to teach mathematics: Corrective Reading (Engelmann, Hanner, & Johnson, 2008) for students in grades 4–12, Connecting Math Concepts (Engelmann, Carnine, Bernadette, & Engelmann, 2003) for grades K–8, and Corrective Math (Carnine, Engelmann, & Steely, 2003) for grade 4 to adult.

### Assistive Technology

Assistive technology has great potential for improving instruction for students with intellectual disabilities and other disabilities (Edyburn, 2002). **Assistive technology (AT)** means "any item, piece of equipment, or product system, whether acquired commercially off the shelf, modified, or customized, that is used to increase, maintain, or improve the functional capabilities of a child with a disability" (IDEA 2004, Sec. 620[1]). It is important to note that language in IDEA requires that educators consider AT when planning individualized education programs (IEPs) for students with disabilities.

Many types of devices have been used to enhance the learning of students with disabilities and to address student needs in a multitude of areas (Edyburn, 2002; Westling & Fox, 2009). Areas addressed by assistive devices include writing, communication, reading, studying, math, recreation and leisure, mobility, vision, and hearing. For example, a motorized wheelchair is considered a relatively low-tech assistive technology device. Other AT devices include communication boards for persons with limited mobility and devices that translate written words into tactile symbols for persons who read braille.

For students with intellectual disabilities, AT has enormous potential for providing support in general education classrooms and access to the general education curriculum. For example, teachers can use AT to provide students with additional practice on information or skills that are not yet mastered; provide feedback to the student through prompts, reminding, and reteaching skills; and monitor student responses and provide additional information to support the student in achieving mastery (Foshay & Ludlow, 2005). For an example of the potential use of these strategies, see the "Can You Help Me with This Student?" feature that addresses the needs of Ernest.

Technology can be used to provide access to the general education curriculum.

Perhaps the approach to assistive technology that has the most potential to benefit persons with intellectual disabilities is built upon the concept of **universal design for learning (UDL)**. One of the most important applications of UDL entails the use of technology to provide all students with access to the general education curriculum. For example, textbooks and other materials designed to facilitate learning of the general education curriculum have traditionally been designed with typical or "average" learners in mind. Thus, these materials are usually written at a level that is reasonable for a student who can readily read and understand grade-level material, and such students often make adequate progress in the curriculum using these materials and learn the material to mastery. However, for students with mild intellectual disabilities and others with reading problems (e.g., most students with learning disabilities), the material is often too difficult to read independently. Publishers of textbooks and curriculum materials are beginning to design these materials to accommodate a broad range of student skill levels. For more information regarding universal design for learning, see the "Technology for Access" feature.

| To... | Charles McDuffie, Middle School Special Education Teacher |
| --- | --- |
| From... | Jasmine Eastrich, Middle School Social Studies Teacher |
| Subject: | **Supporting a student with mild intellectual disabilities in a general education social studies class** |

Charles, one of my students, Ernest, is just beginning here at McArthur Middle school. In elementary school, he was educated in an inclusive program, where he was taught in a general education classroom for most of the school day. As you know, we have only recently begun our inclusive program here at McArthur, and students with mild intellectual disabilities such as Ernest are now educated in general education classrooms for most of the school day.

Ernest has been assigned to my social studies class. As you know, I've worked with many students who have learning problems, and I do many things in my class to support students (e.g., cooperative learing) and engage them in discussions of critical historical issues and current events. However, I'm not sure if I will be able to meet Ernest's needs. He is interested in history (a big plus!) and is well behaved, but he tends to sit quietly in class and not participate unless I call on him. He has shown that he is quite capable of participating in class discussions when he has knowledge of the historical or currents events that are being addressed. He also works well with others, although he does not attempt to take the lead during group activities. I suppose what I'm getting at is that the major barriers to Ernest's participation in class discussions and group activities are his inability to read class material and his hesitation to speak unless called upon. He is reading on a second-grade level, while the material in class is on the seventh-grade level. We're beginning a unit on the Civil War and the contributions of important people to the war. Do you have suggestions regarding how I can better engage Ernest in this content and provide him with the support that he needs?

—Jasmine

---

To:      Jasmine Eastrich
From:    Charles McDuffie
Subject: RE: Supporting a student with mild intellectual disabilities in a general education
         social studies class

Jasmine, as you probably know, Ernest's difficulty in reading is common among students with mild intellectual disabilities as they begin middle school. Furthermore, your concerns regarding how to address Ernest's needs are well founded and reasonable. Inclusion is a new experience for many of us here at McArthur, and assistance will often be needed in devising instructional approaches to address student instructional needs.

You should note that some of the instructional strategies that you already use with students who are not labeled with disabilities may be useful for Ernest, including books on tape, movies and television movies related to the Civil War, and cooperative group activities. Additional elements of effective practice that you may choose to use with Ernest include the following:

*Design instruction using the principles of systematic instruction.* As you plan instruction, you should use the principles of systematic instruction that we discussed in a professional development session earlier this semester. This approach would be beneficial for Ernest, as well as for some of the other students in your class.

*Adapt curriculum and instruction using the nine types of adaptations.* To facilitate student participation in the general education curriculum, you can choose among nine types of instructional adaptations (Cole et al., 2000). For example, the most frequently used adaptations tend to be adaptations in size (e.g., the number of items that a student is expected to complete) and time (e.g., time allocated for completing a task). However, for Ernest, you may want to adjust the difficulty level of lessons, structure how students participate and provide responses, and provide peer support for learning material.

*Use assistive technology to provide access to the curriculum.* I have several computer programs that may be useful to provide support for Ernest as he learns information regarding the Civil War. I'd be glad to talk with you about these programs and provide a demonstration of their use if you'd like. You may use these programs to provide Ernest with practice on knowledge he needs to master, or to monitor his responses so you will know the type of support he needs to achieve mastery.

For more information on strategies to address the needs of middle school students with mild intellectual disabilities in inclusive classrooms, consult the following resources:

Cole, C., Horvath, B., Chapman, C., Deschenes, C., Ebeling, D., & Sprague, J. (2000). *Adapting curriculum & instruction in inclusive classrooms: A teachers' desk reference* (2nd ed.). Bloomington: Indiana Institute on Disability and Community.

Deshler, D., & Schumaker, J. (Eds.). (2006). *Teaching adolescents with disabilities.* Thousand Oaks, CA: Corwin.

Foshay, J., & Ludlow, B. (2005). Implementing computer-mediated supports and assistive technology. In M. Wehmeyer & M. Agran (Eds.), *Mental retardation and intellectual disabilities: Teaching students using innovative and research-based strategies* (pp. 101–124). Washington, DC: AAIDD.

McLeskey, J., Rosenberg, M., & Westling, D. (2010). *Inclusion: Highly effective practices for all students.* Upper Saddle River, NJ: Merrill/Pearson Education.

**EXTEND AND APPLY**

- How would you respond to Ms. Eastrich if she asked why Ernest is being included in her classroom?
- How would you assure her that she will be able to meet Ernest's instructional needs?

Two important goals for students with intellectual disabilities are to include them in general education classrooms and to prepare them to be lifelong learners. UDL has great potential for providing the supports that are needed to realize these goals, as persons with disabilities are provided with access to increasingly complex content in school and job settings.

## TRANSITION TO ADULT LIFE CONSIDERATIONS

Students who have varying needs for support as they transition to adult life are included in the intellectual disability category. These supports are determined, in large part, by the severity of individual deficits in academic skills, adaptive behavior, and social/behavioral skills. Some students with very mild intellectual disabilities can be successful in living and work settings with little support as they learn to compensate for these deficits. In contrast, individuals with more significant disabilities will have difficulty getting and keeping a job and functioning independently in society. We begin this section with a critical concept that is important to ensure the success of any student with disabilities: self-determination. This is followed by a review of supports that many of these students will need in postsecondary and vocational settings.

Recognition of the shortcomings of currently available curriculum materials has led some educators and textbook publishers to explore options for designing materials using universal design for learning (UDL) that are more accessible to all students. A critical feature of universal design when it is applied to the development of curriculum is that this framework builds in accommodations and makes differences among students in a classroom an ordinary part of the school day (McLeskey & Waldron, 2000) rather than requiring that changes be built in as an afterthought. Such a design feature for the curriculum would save the teacher much planning time, reduce the stigma that is attached to some adaptations and accommodations for students, and ensure that more students could be successfully included in a general education classroom.

While many UDL features may be designed into written materials (e.g., differing instructional goals for students), technology plays a critical role in ensuring that a curriculum is universally designed. For example, using a traditional hard copy of a textbook, reading levels cannot be changed. However, the use of digital content for a textbook or other classroom material allows many options for accommodating student reading levels (and other needs) by building in multiple representations (e.g., image, text, video), transforming one medium to another (e.g., text-to-speech or speech-to-text), or modifying the characteristics of a presentation (e.g., size and color of text, loudness of the sound) (Hitchcock, Meyer, Rose, & Jackson, 2002).

UDL is intended for use by all students and should benefit students who already know much of the information presented in the curriculum and who are ready to move beyond this information, those whose primary language is not English, students who have difficulty maintaining attention to materials for long periods of time, or persons with intellectual disabilities who may lack the reading and conceptual skills to successfully master the material being presented.

Following is an illustration of the application of UDL using a typical lesson from a general education classroom (Hitchcock et al., 2002):

### TEACHING AESOP'S FABLES

Suppose the teacher assigns a student to read an Aesop's fable. The goal of this assignment determines the appropriate steps for making the fable accessible. The teacher will ask, is the goal

> To learn to decode text?
>
> To learn comprehension strategies?
>
> To build vocabulary?
>
> To learn the moral or point of the fable?
>
> To learn the common elements of any fable?
>
> To learn how to compare and contrast fables with news reports?
>
> To articulate the relationship between the fable and the overall culture?

The scaffolds and supports that might be appropriate depend entirely on the purpose of the assignment.

If, for example, the purpose of the fable assignment were to become familiar with the elements commonly found in fables, then supporting word decoding, vocabulary, and comprehension of the story itself would not interfere with the learning challenge. Supports such as text-to-speech, linked vocabulary, or animations illustrating interactions between characters would support different students but still leave the appropriate kind of challenge for all learners.

But if the goal were to provide practice in decoding and reading fluency, providing those same supports could undermine the learning challenge and actually impede access to learning. The reading support would eliminate the students' opportunity to practice and work toward reading independence.

This task provides an example of the need for the teacher to clearly determine the goals of instruction for all students in the classroom. Furthermore, the teacher may have different goals for different students in the classroom for this task, depending on the skills that students have to address this fable.

## Self-Determination

Self-determination has been defined as "volitional actions that enable one to act as the primary causal agent in one's life and to maintain or improve one's quality of life" (Wehmeyer, 2006, p. 117). An action is thus self-determined if the individual acts autonomously, the behaviors are self-regulated, the individual initiates the action and responds in a psychologically empowered manner, and the individual acts in a self-realizing way (Wehmeyer & Field, 2007).

Historically, persons with intellectual disabilities have had decisions made for them, often by teachers, parents, or other caregivers. Thus, the basic tenets of a democratic society, including autonomy, independence, empowerment, and self-determination, were often overlooked for these people (Sands & Wehmeyer, 2005).

Go to the Assignments and Activities section of Topic 9: Intellectual Disabilities in the MyEducationLab for your course and complete the activity entitled *Self-Determination.*

Student-led IEP meetings can increase a student's self-advocacy and skills for self-determination.

This probably occurred because most professionals, parents, and caregivers underestimated the capacity of persons with intellectual disabilities to make these decisions (Wehmeyer & Fields, 2007).

This has changed in recent years as increasing numbers of parents and professionals have recognized the importance of involving persons with intellectual disabilities in decisions regarding their own lives (Pierson, Carter, Lane, & Glaeser, 2008). Research has shown that persons with intellectual disabilities who develop the core skills of self-determination have an improved quality of life and improved outcomes with regard to community living, postsecondary education, and employment (Pierson et al., 2008; Thoma & Getzel, 2005). In addition, the process of self-determination provides persons with intellectual disabilities with the opportunity to take more ownership for their lives, and

> helps students become more persistent, productive, and motivated. Their self-confidence increases, and, with it, their self-esteem and comfort in attempting difficult tasks. In some cases, behavior problems decrease once students are allowed to exercise personal preferences within their daily activities and routines. Students have made academic gains when goal-setting activities are integrated into lessons in subjects such as reading, writing, and math. (Sands & Wehmeyer, 2005, p. 274)

If students with intellectual disabilities are to be self-determined when they exit school and enter adult life, they need certain skills and dispositions that may be developed while in school. The skills that lead to self-determination include knowledge about how to access resources that are needed as an adult; communicating interests, preferences, and needs; setting and monitoring goals; planning and managing time; identifying and solving problems; and self-advocating (Wehmeyer & Fields, 2007). Developing these skills and an increased level of self-determination will ensure that individuals have significant influence and control over their own lives, are less dependent on others, and have a higher-quality life (Westling & Fox, 2009).

Sands and Wehmeyer (2005) have developed a framework for teaching the key skills related to self-determination: goal setting and decision making. This framework includes guidelines for teaching students (1) to identify a goal, (2) to explore options for reaching the goal, (3) to choose and act on an option for reaching the goal, and (4) to evaluate and revise goals and decisions. For more information on one approach a teacher might use to address some aspects of self-determination, see the "Real World" feature.

## Vocational Support

Some individuals with mild intellectual disabilities can succeed in competitive employment with little or no support in job settings. However, many individuals with intellectual disabilities, especially those whose academic, adaptive, and social-behavioral skills are most severely delayed, will probably have difficulty meeting the demands of a job setting and will require support, especially if they do not have strong family support (Neece, Kraemer, & Blacher, 2009). For example, individuals with intellectual disabilities may need assistance on jobs that require reading or

# THE REAL WORLD Challenges and Solutions

## A teacher's search to support student self-advocacy and self-determination: The student-led IEP

*Ms. Vasquez has taught high school students with mild intellectual disabilities for many years. One of her areas of responsibility is the development of plans for transition services, and working with the students and their teachers to carry out these plans. Many of Ms. Vasquez's students have successfully transitioned to employment or postsecondary education settings (e.g., vocational schools). Over the last several years, however, Ms. Vasquez has noted that many of her students lack sufficient knowledge regarding their disability and have difficulty self-advocating. She is concerned that if students leave the high school without knowledge of their disability and skills for self-advocating, they will have difficulty succeeding.*

*These concerns led Ms. Vasquez to seek information regarding self-advocacy from colleagues in other schools and by searching the Web and the professioinal literature. She discovered many useful resources regarding this topic. Many of these publications also addressed self-determination (the student's ability to act as a decision maker and make choices free from undue influence), a concept that is strongly related to self-advocacy. Ms. Vasquez found that many educators recommend student-led IEP meetings as an excellent approach to increasing a student's knowledge of his disability, as well as his self-determination skills, including self-advocacy. She then determined that she would begin to use student-led IEP meetings in her high school.*

### What Is a Student-Led IEP Meeting?

Ms. Vasquez located several resources related to student-led IEP meetings. She found that if these meetings are to be effective, they require many changes on the part of teachers and other professionals, as well as preparation for the student. She noted that in these meetings the student is not just a participant but takes the lead in the meetings and in determining goals, accommodations, and so forth that are part of the IEP. Research has shown that student-led IEP meetings can be quite successful if students are prepared well before the meeting (Hammer, 2004; Martin, Van Dycke, Christensen, Greene, Gardner, & Lovett, 2006; Mason, McGahee, Johnson, & Stillerman, 2002). Ms. Vasquez found that she should address several areas of preparation with her students (Hammer, 2004; Mason et al., 2002):

1. The student and teacher review the student's areas of interest, strengths, concerns, and needs. They also discuss the student's rights, the purpose of the IEP, and the nature of the student's disability.
2. The teacher and student read the student's most recent IEP, and the student determines goals, accommodations,

and other sections of the IEP that he agrees with and those that he feels need to be changed.
3. The student meets with his teachers and parents to discuss goals in the current IEP that have been met and new goals that are needed.
4. The student and teacher review and revise the goals for the IEP and other relevant information.
5. The student and teacher discuss and prepare the student to address his postschool plans and transition needs (for students age 14 and over).
6. The teacher provides feedback and further preparation regarding specific skills (e.g., listening skills) that are useful to ensure the success of the IEP meeting, and provides feedback to the student regarding these skils as the student practices his presentation for the IEP meeting.

Ms. Vasquez found that there are many benefits of student-led IEP meetings, including (1) improved student knowledge regarding his disability; (2) increased student awareness regarding accommodations that are used in the classroom; (3) more student ownership for the goals of the IEP; (4) increased student self-confidence and self-advocacy; and (5) increased parent involvement in their child's education (Martin et al., 2006; Mason et al., 2002; Test, Mason, Hughes, Konrad, Neale, & Wood, 2004).

### Valuable Resources for the Teacher

For more information on the use of student-led IEP meetings, the following resources may prove useful:

Hawbaker, B. (2006). Student-led IEP meetings: Planning and implementation strategies. *Teaching Exceptional Children Plus, 3*(5) Article 4. Retrieved April 8, 2009, from http://escholarship.bc.edu/education/tecplus/vol3/iss5/art4/

Martin, J., Marshall, L., Maxon, L., & Jerman, P. (1997). *The self-directed IEP.* Longmont, CO: Sopris West.

McGahee, M., Mason, C., Wallace, T., & Jones, B. (2001). *Student-led IEPs: A guide for student involvement.* Arlington, VA: CEC.

### Final Thoughts

As Ms. Vasquez reflected on her experience with IEP meetings, she realized that students with a wide range of disabilities can participate in and benefit from taking a leadership role in IEP meetings (Test et al., 2004). However, she also discerned the importance of having the student assume the leadership role and ensuring that he is well prepared to assume this role. Research has revealed that students with disabilities who attend their IEP meetings mathematics skills, or that require complex response patterns. A job coach can work with the individual and employer to ensure that supports are in place so that these issues are addressed.

Another issue that is important to address in job settings that employ individuals with more significant delays is the training of co-workers. Job settings for persons with disabilities are more successful if co-workers understand how disabilities affect job performance. Training for co-workers is best achieved in small groups rather than in formal training sessions and should include information regarding the specific supports needed by an individual rather than more general information regarding disabilities (Westling & Fox, 2009).

## Residential Options

When students with intellectual disabilities enter adulthood, their goals and aspirations are similar to any adult, and most desire to leave their parents' home and live on their own. While some persons with intellectual disabilities can live independently, many need support to achieve this goal. Unfortunately, many persons with intellectual disabilities continue to live at home with their parents, often not by choice, but by necessity because of lack of planning or limited alternatives for residential living (Larson, Doljanac, & Lakin, 2005). Planning for residential living for adults with intellectual disabilities should be guided by the principles of normalization and self-determination, which call for the adult to guide decisions about residential arrangements, and for these arrangements to be as typical as possible.

The most desired form of residence for adults with intellectual disabilities is the same as for all adults, a privately owned residence. Approximately 12% of adults with intellectual disabilities own their own residence (Larson, Scott, & Lakin, 2008). This represents a 20% increase in the proportion of adults owning private residences in the last 10 years. A more common living arrangement for many adults with intellectual disabilities is a supported living arrangement based on a person-centered plan. With either of these options, natural supports (e.g., supports from roommates or family) are used as much as possible, while professional supports are used as needed, depending on availability. Ideally, persons with intellectual disabilities who move into a residential setting will enjoy choices of location and type of home and roommates and will have significant input on decisions about both services and living arrangements.

## Support in Higher Education

While the majority of high school graduates go on to some form of postsecondary education, higher education opportunities are very limited for students with more pervasive developmental delays, such as students with intellectual disabilities. Recently, this has begun to change, and several states have developed dual-enrollment programs in community colleges (i.e., students enroll in the community college while still in high school) for students with intellectual disabilities and other developmental disabilities (Hart, Mele-McCarthy, Pasternack, Zimbrich, & Parker, 2004; Pearman et al., 2004; Zafft et al., 2004). Most of these programs provide some form of life-skills preparation and community-based employment training. Many of the programs also emphasize educating students with disabilities with typical peers.

For example, the College Career Connection (CCC) is designed to assist persons with intellectual disabilities and autism to choose, gain admission, and successfully complete an inclusive postsecondary experience in a local community college (Zafft et al., 2004). Practices include the use of a student-centered approach to identify student strengths and preferences and the development of an interagency planning team that works with the student to develop individualized services and supports. The CCC model is based on the following guiding principles:

1. The vision of the student sets the direction and controls decision making.
2. Options explored for the student are inclusive and occur in settings with a natural proportion of persons with disabilities.
3. Options do not include any special programs or specially designated, segregated classes.
4. Supports are based on individual student needs and are not "one size fits all."
5. Collaboration is a necessary component for a successful program.

Evaluation of this model for the adults with intellectual disabilities who completed the postsecondary experience revealed that they were more likely to gain competitive employment and were less likely to need ongoing supports as they moved into employment than were peers who did not complete such a program. In addition, Zafft and colleagues (2004) note that the postsecondary experience resulted in positive perceptions and raised the expectations of parents, teachers, and prospective employers regarding the individual who had "been to college." While additional research is needed to better understand how postsecondary programs may be used to improve outcomes for persons with intellectual disabilities, it is clear that such programs have the potential to offer persons with intellectual disabilities many opportunities to improve their lives with respect to employment and social involvement in the community that have not been available in the past.

**REFLECTIVE EXERCISE**

#10 Based on what you have read in this chapter, what role can you play, and what activities can you engage in as a teacher to increase the value of persons with intellectual disabilities in your classroom? In your school? In the community?

# PREVAILING ISSUES, CONTROVERSIES, AND IMPLICATIONS FOR THE TEACHER

Great progress has been made in the past 30 to 40 years in addressing the educational needs of students with intellectual disabilities. In spite of this progress, several areas of controversy remain, including what students with intellectual disabilities should be taught and concerns regarding the stigma associated with the category of intellectual disabilities.

## What Should Students with Intellectual Disabilities Be Taught?

Since the 1970s, special education teachers have used a functional curriculum (i.e., teaching functional skills related to daily living) for most students with intellectual disabilities. This type of curriculum appeals to many teachers, as it is designed to prepare students with intellectual disabilities to successfully participate in work and leisure activities in as typical a manner as possible. Areas addressed include managing money, employment skills, community participation, travel and mobility training, personal care, and home living skills, among others (Wehman & Kregel, 2004). These skills are often taught in a meaningful way in real-world settings to increase the possibility that the skills will be retained and generalized across settings (Beirne-Smith et al., 2006).

A functional curriculum has typically been viewed as alternate curriculum, separate from what is taught to other students (Kearns, Burdge, & Kleinert, 2005). This changed with the requirements in IDEA and NCLB that all students with disabilities must have access to the general education curriculum and must be included in state assessments to determine how much of the curriculum they have learned. These changes have caused special educators to rethink what and how persons with intellectual disabilities are taught.

To respond to these changes in policy, some states have added practical living and vocational skills to the standards required of all students. However, these standards are often not included in state-wide assessments (Kearns et al., 2005). Recently, some states have begun to modify standards to accommodate the needs of students with significant disabilities. For example, Florida has developed Access Points, which are expectations for students with significant cognitive disabilities as they access the general education curriculum (Florida Department of Education, 2009). The Access Points address the core intent of state standards but with reduced levels of complexity. Levels of access include participatory (the least complex), supported, and independent levels.

These changes have been welcomed by many special education teachers, as they have led to renewed interest in curriculum and in research and development activities to improve instruction and achievement outcomes for students with intellectual disabilities. For example, research by Browder and colleagues (Browder, Ahlgrim-Delzell, et al., 2008; Browder & Spooner, 2006; Browder, Spooner, et al., 2008) has demonstrated that students with moderate-to-severe intellectual disabilities can learn more than educators had anticipated, especially in the areas of reading and mathematics. These researchers have also affirmed that effective instructional practices should include systematic instruction and instruction in applied, or real-world, settings.

In the coming years, additional changes likely will occur in curriculum and instruction for students with intellectual disabilities. For example, questions remain about the balance between functional and academic skills that these students should learn. In addition, it remains unclear just what students with intellectual disabilities are capable of learning and how these skills might be best taught. These changes require that special education teachers stay abreast of the newest developments, as educators continue to develop improved approaches to meet the needs of students with intellectual disabilities.

## How Should Teachers Address the Stigma That Students with Intellectual Disabilities Face?

Teachers, parents, advocates, and other professionals have expressed much concern regarding the use of the term *mental retardation*, primarily because it is the most stigmatizing of disability labels. In addition, the negative colloquial use of the term ("He's a retard" or "That's retarded") has become so widespread that it seems likely that the term will soon be discarded for a more neutral but descriptive one.

As mentioned earlier in this chapter, *intellectual disability* seems to be emerging as a preferred term for labeling persons rather than using the term *mental retardation* (Shalock et al., 2007), a trend the AAMR affirmed when it changed its name to the American Association on Intellectual and Developmental Disabilities. However, at this point, *mental retardation* remains the term that appears in federal legislation, is used in many states, and is used by most professionals and the general public.

Changes in terminology have occurred several times over the years. Persons with intellectual disabilities were originally labeled using terms such as *feebleminded, moron, imbecile,* and *idiot.* Later, the term *mental deficiency* was used, while the term *mental retardation* was adopted in 1961 by the AAMR (Heber, 1961). These changes at least temporarily reduced the stigma associated with persons who were so labeled. While teachers recognize that changing terminology in response to identified needs and stigma attached to labels is important, some question whether this is enough.

Bogdan and Biklen (1977) first used the term *handicapism* to describe "assumptions and practices that promote the differential and unequal treatment of people because of apparent or assumed physical, mental, or behavioral differences" (p. 59). These authors contend that people with disabilities are subjected to stereotyping, much as members of some racial groups are subjected to racism or women are subjected to sexism. Beirne-Smith and colleagues (2006) have changed this term to *disablism* and suggest that it is comprised of three elements—stereotyping, prejudice, and discrimination. They note that "Many people view adults with retardation as childlike (stereotyping), which leads to the belief that they are incapable of making decisions for themselves (prejudice), which in turn results in others making decisions for them without their input or knowledge (discrimination)" (pp. 47–48). This stereotyping was addressed by Andrea Craine in the interview that opened this chapter, as she noted that some teachers have very low expectations for students with intellectual disabilities and have concerns about having these students in their classrooms.

Discrimination against persons with disabilities, particularly those with intellectual disabilities, seems to emerge from the low value we place on these persons. Wolfensberger (1985) contends that a strong connection exists between how we perceive a person and how that person is treated. He identified socially devalued groups in society based on the extent to which they were treated with pity, viewed as a menace, ridiculed, perceived as childlike, and so forth. Wolfensberger found that only persons with mental illness were more negatively perceived than persons with intellectual disabilities.

What should be done about disablism and the low value society places on persons with intellectual disabilities? This will remain a controversial issue for teachers and others in the foreseeable future. However, progress is being made as more persons with intellectual disabilities are being included with typical peers for much of the school day, have jobs in competitive work settings, and interact with persons without disabilities in typical, day-to-day settings (e.g., health clubs, restaurants, grocery stores). This contact will serve to dispel many of the misconceptions regarding persons with intellectual disabilities and should increase the value many persons place on these individuals. Furthermore, the emphasis that has been placed on self-determination for persons with intellectual disabilities and other disabilities will serve to better prepare these individuals for self-advocating and improving their status in society. Obviously, you as a teacher play a key role in ensuring that persons with intellectual disabilities are valued and are not the victims of discrimination in schools.

Go to the IRIS Center Resources section of Topic 9: Intellectual Disabilities in the MyEducationLab for your course and complete the module entitled *What Do You See? Perceptions of Disability.*

# 8 SUMMARY

### Definitions and Classification Criteria

- Intellectual disabilities have two major definitions, one from IDEA 2004 and the other from the American Association on Intellectual and Developmental Disabilities.
- The primary criteria used to identify students with intellectual disabilities are significantly subaverage functioning in general intellectual development and adaptive behavior (including practical and social skills that students use in their everyday lives).
- The American Association on Intellectual and Developmental Disabilities (AAIDD) has suggested that a levels-of-support approach be used to identify students with intellectual disabilities, but this approach has not been widely accepted.

## Characteristics of Students

- The primary characteristics of students with intellectual disabilities relate to significant delays in the development of academic, cognitive, and social skills.
- All academic skills tend to be delayed. Cognitive skills that are delayed include attention, memory, and generalization skills.
- Delays in developing social skills seem to be related, at least to some degree, to delays in developing language and cognitive skills.
- Students with intellectual disabilities have difficulty interacting with peers and may need to be directly taught social skills.

## Prevalence, Course, and Cause

- Approximately 0.76% of students aged 6 to 21, or one student in every five general education classrooms, is identified with an intellectual disability.
- African American and American Indian/Alaska Native students tend to be significantly overrepresented in the intellectual disabilities category.
- Intellectual disabilities persist through school and into adulthood. While some adults with intellectual disabilities struggle greatly, others are relatively successful and generally satisfied with their lives.

- While we can often identify the causes of severe intellectual disabilities, we do not know the causes of mild intellectual disabilities for most students.
- A major risk factor for intellectual disabilities is growing up in a home where several risk factors exist, such as limited financial resources, low education level of parents, and a high level of stress in the environment.

## Identification and Assessment

- Several changes have occurred in the primary criteria used to identify students with intellectual disabilities (i.e., intellectual functioning and adaptive behavior) over the past several decades.
- Changes in the identification criteria have occurred primarily because of the overrepresentation of certain non–European American groups in this category as well as the stigma that is associated with this category of disability.
- An IQ score of 70 or below and a similar score on a measure of adaptive behavior are the primary criteria used to identify students with intellectual disabilities.

## Educational Practices

- Early intervention services for students with intellectual disabilities should be built on the principles of developmentally appropriate, family-centered practices.
- Students with intellectual disabilities benefit from being taught using systematic, teacher-directed instruction.
- An instructional approach that has proven to be highly effective for students with intellectual disabilities is direct instruction.
- The use of assistive technology (AT) to support instruction is also an effective instructional approach for these students.

## Prevailing Issues

- While educational opportunities for students with intellectual disabilities have improved significantly since the passage of IDEA in 1975, controversial issues remain, including the curriculum that should guide instruction for these students, and the stigma that continues to be attached to this category.

 **Council for Exceptional Children** **ADDRESSING THE PROFESSIONAL STANDARDS**

Council for Exceptional Children Knowledge Standards addressed in the chapter:

ICC1K5, EC1K1, ED1K2, ICC2K1, ICC2K2, ICC2K3, ICC2K5, ICC2K6, EC2K3, EC2K4, ICC3K1, ICC3K2, ICC5K3, ICC6K1, ICC6K4, ICC7K4, ICC8K1, ICC8K2

Appendix B: CEC Knowledge and Skill Standards Common Core has a full listing of the standards referenced here.

**PEARSON myeducationlab**

Now go to Topic 9: Intellectual Disabilities in the MyEducationLab for your course, where you can:

- Find learning outcomes for the broad concepts covered in this chapter along with the national standards that connect to these outcomes.
- Complete Assignments and Activities that can help you more deeply understand the chapter content.
- Examine challenging situations presented in the IRIS Center Resources.
- Apply and practice you understanding of the core concepts and skills identified in the chapter with the Building Teacher Skills and Dispositions learning units.

- Check your comprehension on the content covered in the chapter by going to the Study Plan in the Book-Specific Resources section for your text. Here you will be able to take a chapter quiz, receive feedback on your answers, and then access Review, Practice, and Enrichment activities to enhance your understanding of chapter content.
- Access video clips of CCSSO National Teachers of the Year award winners responding to the question, "Why Do I Teach?" in the Teacher Talk Section.

# chapter 9

# Attention-Deficit/ Hyperactivity Disorders

**REFLECT UPON**

- How is attention-deficit/hyperactivity disorder (ADHD) defined and classified?
- What are the primary characteristics of ADHD?
- How many students are identified with ADHD, and what are the causes of this disability?
- How are students with ADHD identified?
- How effective is medication in addressing the symptoms of students with ADHD?
- What interventions are effective in improving academic and social outcomes for students with ADHD?
- What prevailing controversial issues are related to students with ADHD?

## MY PROFESSION, MY STORY: MERIDITH TAYLOR-STROUT

Meridith Taylor-Strout became interested in teaching students with disabilities when she volunteered to work with students with physical disabilities at a summer camp when she was 15. This experience created a passion for working with students with disabilities, as she felt that these students were not given the opportunities they deserved and needed in order to be successful in life. She felt that she could be an advocate for these students as well as their teacher.

After high school, Meridith entered a special education teacher education program in a small private school in Virginia. She speaks highly of the excellent preparation she received, as she began working in schools during her freshman year, received extensive feedback from professors and field supervisors regarding her work in schools, and exited the program with a well-stocked toolbox for addressing students' needs. The one area in which she felt less well prepared related to student discipline and behavior management. She notes that it took her a couple of years as a teacher to learn to successfully manage difficult student behaviors.

After completing her undergraduate program in special education, Meridith took her first teaching position with the Multidisciplinary Diagnostic and Training Program (MDTP) at the University of Florida. Her position with the MDTP consisted of working intensively with small groups of students with academic problems for 6 to 12 weeks and then following up with the students and their classroom teacher as they returned to a general education classroom full-time. Many of the students with whom she worked were identified with ADHD and tended to be quite active, impulsive, and inattentive.

For Meridith, the most rewarding aspect of teaching has been helping students with disabilities gain the skills they need to succeed in the general education classroom. She feels that it is important for these students to interact with peers without disabilities, which provides them with opportunities for academic and social development they would not have in a separate special class. One of her greatest successes was working with a third-grade girl who had low self-esteem and difficulty with math. After Meridith worked with this girl intensively for 12 weeks, the child returned to the general education classroom, completed math on grade level, felt successful, and became a leader in her class.

Meridith feels that a key quality of an effective teacher, especially for students with ADHD, is a well-structured classroom. This includes having clear rules for behavior, teaching the rules to all students, reminding students of the rules, and ensuring that consequences are attached to the rules. She goes on to note that, to work effectively with students with ADHD, the teacher must provide explicit instruction, break down tasks into manageable parts, and vary the approach used to present information (using multiple senses). In a well-structured class,

students know exactly what is expected of them, and transitions from one task to another are quick and smooth. Finally, Meridith notes that the teacher must always be "with it" when monitoring student behavior—moving around the room, redirecting student behavior as necessary, and using a variety of strategies to keep students on task (e.g., proximity control, a tap on the shoulder, visual reminders).

Meridith is passionate about teaching but finds some aspects of teaching frustrating. One major source of frustration is teachers' lack of voice in changing and improving schools. She feels that, all too often, it is very challenging to change and improve a school to better educate students with disabilities. For example, her students were not included in general education classes as much as she thought they should be, but achieving this change was very challenging. A second frustration Meridith has faced as a teacher is the lack of a school-wide discipline plan in her school. She feels that every school should have a consistent plan for addressing student behavior, but she has found that often this does not occur. As a result, students, especially those with disabilities, have a difficult time adjusting to different sets of rules in different places in the school.

Several personal characteristics have served Meridith well as a teacher. For example, she is a very positive person with lots of energy, who enjoys working with others. She is also very well organized, manages time well, and is highly strategic in working with students. She has found that she has become a better teacher through professional development, which has included observing in other teachers' classes, meeting with other teachers to discuss student issues, and taking college classes. She notes that teachers must continue to improve because children are always changing; teachers need to keep up by learning new things. Meridith's teaching expertise has been recognized in Florida; she received a rookie of the year award in her first year as a special education teacher and later won the state's teacher of the year award.

Meridith's advice to beginning teachers is that, while teaching is very rewarding, it is a long journey with ups and downs. She notes that, if you as a teacher put a lot of effort into teaching and respect your students, the students will return this respect, and you will develop a bond like no other.

It is very difficult for parents to control the behavior of a child with ADHD, even under the best of circumstances.

## REFLECTIVE EXERCISE

# 1 Media coverage of ADHD has been widespread, often controversial, and has influenced public opinions regarding this disability. What controversial issues have you heard about through the media or other sources? How have these issues influenced your perspective on ADHD?

We have all seen a child, most often a boy, in a department store or a supermarket who seems driven by a motor, responding to everything he sees, unable to maintain attention for more than a minute or two (if that), then moving on to the next source of interest. If we pay close attention, we notice that this child doesn't seem to listen when spoken to by his parents or store clerks, talks excessively, has difficulty waiting his turn, interrupts or intrudes on others, and generally makes a nuisance of himself. In short, he is energetic, overactive, impulsive, and difficult to handle and may be a child with **attention-deficit/ hyperactivity disorder (ADHD)**.

Perhaps our first thought when seeing such a child is to blame his parents for his poor behavior. Some might think, "Why do his parents let him get away with that behavior?" Those of us who have had close contact with a child with ADHD, whether as a parent, sibling, or close friend, look at this issue differently. The same is true for a teacher who has one or two of these students in a classroom with 25 others. Parents often have to develop creative strategies for addressing the behavior of these children. Similarly, as Meridith Taylor-Strout notes at the beginning of this chapter, teachers must have a toolbox of strategies to ensure the success of students with ADHD.

While children identified with ADHD pose a significant challenge for their parents and teachers, with appropriate support (including many of the ideas Meridith Taylor-Strout has suggested), they can and often do grow up to lead highly successful lives. In this chapter, we address students who manifest some combination of overactive behavior, impulsive responses, and inattention. While we see these behaviors at some level in most children and youth, the students we address in this chapter exhibit them at such an extreme level that they may have difficulty fitting in and learning well at school and be labeled with ADHD.

## DEFINITION AND CLASSIFICATION CRITERIA

### Defining ADHD

The definition of ADHD is unique among all the categories of disability that are defined in this book. While the majority of the definitions of categories in special education are taken from federal law (i.e., IDEA 2004), the definition of ADHD has been developed and disseminated by professionals in medicine—pediatrics and psychiatry in particular (Reiff, 2004).

While this medically based definition is widely accepted and used in medicine, psychology, and education, educators have resisted accepting ADHD as a category of disability in IDEA. Moreover, some parent advocates, educators, and others have questioned whether the category should exist (Zentall, 2006). ADHD, to say the least, has been a category embroiled in controversy. We will discuss the particulars of this controversy later in the chapter. Suffice it to say for now that the controversy has not been settled and will give you much food for thought about the ADHD category as you proceed through this chapter.

One of the most difficult issues facing those who must compose a definition of ADHD is the fact that many children, youth, and adults manifest some of the characteristics that are part of this disorder under certain circumstances. For example, we all tend to occasionally manifest some level of inattentive behavior in particular situations. (Remember that dull history lecture in college?) We all have been distracted by stimuli in a setting rather than focusing attention on the subject at hand. Some of those distractions were minor (tapping a pencil); others were major ("There's a firetruck in front of the school!"). At times we all respond without thinking ("Yes, I'll buy that convertible!") and make foolish decisions.

The behaviors that characterize ADHD are even more common in young children before they enter school or as they progress through the early elementary grades. If you've observed a group of these students in preschool or kindergarten or first or second grade, you have surely noted widespread inattentive behavior,

To check your comprehension on the content covered in Chapter 9, go to the Book-Specific Resources in the MyEducationLab for your course, select your text, and complete the Study Plan. Here you will be able to take a chapter quiz, receive feedback on your answers, and then access Review, Practice, and Enrichment activities to enhance your understanding of chapter content.

## FAQ Sheet

### STUDENTS WITH ADHD

| | |
|---|---|
| Who are they? | • Children with ADHD manifest "a persistent pattern of inattention and/or hyperactivity–impulsivity that is more frequently displayed and more severe than is typically observed in individuals at a comparable level of development" (American Psychiatric Association, 2000, p. 85). |
| What are typical characteristics? | • Impulsivity<br>• Hyperactivity<br>• Inattention<br>• Coexisting conduct problems<br>• Coexisting academic problems |
| What are the demographics? | • 3% to 7% of school-age children (between 1.9 and 4.5 million students) are identified with ADHD.<br>• Approximately 3% receive stimulant medication.<br>• Less than 1% are identified under IDEA as *other health impaired*.<br>• Approximately 75% are male. |
| Where are students educated? | • 59% of students identified with ADHD under IDEA spend most of the day in general education classrooms.<br>• Placement settings are similar to those for students with learning disabilities. |
| How are students identified and assessed for intervention? | • Criteria from DSM-IV-TR are used for identification (see Figure 9.1).<br>• Multiple methods are used to document ADHD, including interviews with parents and teachers, rating scales, and observations in multiple settings.<br>• Functional behavioral assessments provide the most useful information for instructional and behavioral planning. |
| What are the outcomes? | • Approximately 30% have no symptoms of ADHD as adults.<br>• Approximately 25% have conduct disorders that continue as adults.<br>• Approximately 25% develop major depression as adults. |

## REFLECTIVE EXERCISE

#2 Given the fact that many children (and adults, for that matter) exhibit some level of the symptoms of ADHD (i.e., inattention, impulsivity, or overactivity), what approach could educators use to ensure that children are appropriately identified with ADHD?

frequent impulsive decision making, and high levels of activity, all behaviors used to identify ADHD. This is to be expected: Over time, children learn to sustain their attention for increasingly longer periods. They also learn to monitor and control their behavior to reduce the level of impulsive responses and control their activity level in situations where this is necessary.

So how can a definition be developed that accounts for the common occurrence of the major characteristics of the disorder? Those who have defined ADHD have addressed this dilemma by focusing on the frequency and severity of the behaviors and how a person exhibiting these behaviors compares to her same-age peers. The American Psychiatric Association developed the definition for ADHD as part of the ***Diagnostic and Statistical Manual (4th ed.) (DSM-IV-TR)*** (American Psychiatric Association, 2000). ADHD is defined as "a persistent pattern of inattention and/or hyperactivity–impulsivity that is more frequently displayed and more severe than is typically observed in individuals at a comparable level of development" (p. 85). The specific DSM-IV-TR criteria that educators and health-care workers use to identify students with ADHD are included in Figure 9.1.

## Classification Criteria for ADHD

As you can see in Figure 9.1, three primary behaviors are the basis of the definition of ADHD. These behaviors are **inattention**, **hyperactivity**, and **impulsivity**. Students who are inattentive are those who cannot sustain attention for age-appropriate periods of time. Teachers often characterize inattentive students as those who are careless in their work, disorganized, easily distracted, unable to follow directions, forgetful, and poor at listening to directions and completing tasks.

The second major characteristic of ADHD is hyperactivity, which is generally defined as a high level of activity that is not appropriate in a setting and is not age-appropriate. Teachers often characterize these students as fidgety, incessantly talkative, and constantly on the go at inappropriate times. Impulsivity is the third major characteristic of students with ADHD. This behavior is generally defined as responding without thinking at a level that is not age-appropriate. According to teachers, students who are impulsive blurt out answers, interrupt others, intrude on the activities of others, and have difficulty waiting their turn.

Students need not exhibit all of these characteristics to be identified with ADHD, as Figure 9.1 reveals. Moreover, three major types of ADHD are common among school-age students and are identified by particular behaviors in the ADHD criteria. These are a **predominately hyperactive–impulsive type (ADHD-PHI); a predominately inattentive type (ADHD-PI); and a combined type (ADHD-C)**, characterized by both hyperactive–impulsive and inattentive behavior.

Other key factors included in the definition of ADHD for preschool and school-age children and youth are the student's age when the behaviors initially occurred, the duration of the behaviors, the importance of the settings in which the behaviors occur, the level or severity of the behaviors, and the impact of the behaviors on academic and social outcomes. For students identified with ADHD, some symptoms should appear before the age of 7, and the behaviors should last for at least 6 months. Thus, behaviors that occur for a short period of time due to illness, stress in a family (e.g., divorce), or transition into a new setting (e.g., beginning school) should not result in identification as ADHD.

To further ensure that a student has ADHD, the symptoms must appear across two or more settings, such as at school and at home. This ensures that the behaviors are pervasive and do not appear only as a reaction to a stressful or demanding situation or in a setting where good principles of behavior management are lacking. Similarly, the behaviors of students who are identified with ADHD must be significantly more extreme than their age-level peers and must significantly impair the

## REFLECTIVE EXERCISE

#3 Think of times you have observed preschool children. Did many of these students exhibit characteristics similar to those used to identify students with ADHD? Have you observed a young child (e.g., in a grocery store, on a playground) who exhibited these behaviors at such an extreme level that you thought she might be identified with ADHD?

FIGURE 9.1 • **DSM-IV-TR CRITERIA FOR IDENTIFYING ADHD**

A. Either (1) or (2):

(1) six (or more) of the following symptoms of inattention have persisted for at least 6 months to a degree that is maladaptive and inconsistent with developmental level:

*Inattention*

    (a) often fails to give close attention to details or makes careless mistakes in schoolwork, work, or other activities

    (b) often has difficulty sustaining attention in tasks or play activities

    (c) often does not seem to listen when spoken to directly

    (d) often does not follow through on instructions and fails to finish schoolwork, chores, or duties in the workplace (not due to oppositional behavior or failure to understand instructions)

    (e) often has difficulty organizing activities

    (f) often avoids, dislikes, or is reluctant to engage in tasks that require sustained mental effort (such as schoolwork or homework)

    (g) often loses things necessary for tasks or activities (e.g., toys, school assignments, pencils, books, or tools)

    (h) is often easily distracted by extraneous stimuli

    (i) is often forgetful in daily activities

(2) six (or more) of the following symptoms of hyperactivity–impulsivity have persisted for at least 6 months to a degree that is maladaptive and inconsistent with developmental level:

*Hyperactivity*

    (a) often fidgets with hands or feet or squirms in seat

    (b) often leaves seat in classroom or in other situations in which remaining seated is expected

    (c) often runs about or climbs excessively in situations in which it is inappropriate (in adolescents or adults, may be limited to subjective feelings of restlessness)

    (d) often has difficulty playing or engaging in leisure activities quietly

    (e) is often "on the go" or often acts as if "driven by a motor"

    (f) often talks excessively

*Impulsivity*

    (a) often blurts out answers before questions have been completed

    (b) often has difficulty awaiting turn

    (c) often interrupts or intrudes on others (e.g., butts into conversations or games)

B. Some hyperactive–impulsive or inattentive symptoms that caused impairment were present before age 7 years.

C. Some impairment from the symptoms is present in two or more settings (e.g., at school [or work] and at home).

D. There must be clear evidence of clinically significant impairment in social, academic, or occupational functioning.

E. The symptoms do not occur exclusively during the course of a Pervasive Developmental Disorder, Schizophrenia, or other Psychotic Disorder and are not better accounted for by another mental disorder (e.g., Mood Disorder, Anxiety Disorder, Dissociative Disorder, or a Personality Disorder).

*Code based on type:*

314.01 Attention-Deficit/Hyperactivity Disorder, Combined Type: if both Criteria A1 and A2 are met for the past 6 months

314.00 Attention-Deficit/Hyperactivity Disorder, Predominantly Inattentive Type: if Criterion A1 is met but Criterion A2 is not met for the past 6 months

314.02 Attention-Deficit/Hyperactivity Disorder, Predominantly Hyperactive-Impulsive Type: if Criterion A2 is met but Criterion A1 is not met for the past 6 months

Source: Reprinted with permission from the *Diagnostic and Statistical Manual of Mental Disorders,* Fourth Edition, Text Revision, Copyright 2000. American Psychiatric Association.

students' social adjustment (e.g., getting along with peers, making friends) and/or academic achievement.

As we have noted, ADHD is not a separate special education category that is included in federal legislation (i.e., IDEA 2004). In 1991, the U.S. Department of Education issued a "policy clarification" memorandum indicating that students with ADHD could be identified if they met the *other health impaired* (OHI) criteria in IDEA. However, this policy was not fully and effectively implemented (IDEA Law and Resources, 1999). This led to the formal inclusion of ADHD in the reauthorization of IDEA in 1997 as one of several disorders that could form the basis of identification for the OHI category. Thus, students with ADHD may receive services under IDEA if they meet criteria in the OHI category. OHI is defined in IDEA as follows:

> Other health impairment means having limited strength, vitality or alertness, including a heightened alertness to environmental stimuli, that results in limited alertness with respect to the educational environment, that—
>
> (i) Is due to chronic or acute health problems such as asthma, attention deficit disorder or attention deficit hyperactivity disorder, diabetes, epilepsy, a heart condition, hemophilia, lead poisoning, leukemia, nephritis, rheumatic fever, sickle cell anemia, and Tourette syndrome; and
>
> (ii) Adversely affects a child's educational performance. [PL 108-446 Regulations, Sec 300.8(c)(9)(i)]

You will note that while **ADD** (an acronym formerly used to identify children with predominantly inattentive behaviors [ADHD-PI]) and ADHD are mentioned in Section (i) of this definition, a specific definition for ADHD is not provided. This is also the case (i.e., no definitions are provided) with the other medical conditions included in the OHI category because all of these conditions require a medical diagnosis. Thus, the medical definition and criteria for identification provided in DSM-IV-TR are used to determine if a student has ADHD, and a physician typically makes this determination.

Once a determination is made that a student has ADHD, the school-based multidisciplinary team addresses Section (ii) in the OHI definition and determines if this condition adversely affects the child's educational performance. If it is determined that this is the case, the student is then eligible for special education services as part of IDEA.

You should be aware that some students who have been identified with ADHD are not eligible for special education services, usually because they do not meet the IDEA criterion related to whether the condition adversely affects educational performance. This could occur because the ADHD condition is relatively mild, or the symptoms of the ADHD may be controlled by medication, and the ADHD does not adversely affect educational performance. (We will provide more information about the use of medication as an intervention for ADHD later in this chapter.) Students who do not meet the educational performance criterion in IDEA may still be eligible for accommodations in the general education classroom as part of **Section 504 of the Rehabilitation Act of 1974**.

Section 504 is a civil rights act, not legislation that provides educational support for students (e.g., IDEA). Moreover, this law was enacted to prevent discrimination against persons with disabilities and ensure that these students receive reasonable accommodations (Zirkel, 2009). Thus, students who have been identified with ADHD and are eligible under Section 504 must receive reasonable accommodations in a general education classroom to ensure that they are not discriminated against because of the disability. Accommodations might include activities such as changing the location of the student's seat (e.g., nearer to a student who is a good role model or to a quiet area of the classroom); allowing the student to move about the room at appropriate times; allowing extended time for taking a test, with breaks as necessary; or providing support to the student to improve his organizational skills.

## Major Characteristics of Students with ADHD

A review of Figure 9.1 will provide you with a good overview of the major behaviors that characterize ADHD, the symptoms that are used to identify these behaviors, and the subtypes of this disorder. We will not discuss these characteristics

**PEARSON**
**myeducationlab**

Go to the Assignments and Activities section of Topic 11: ADHD in the MyEducationLab for your course and complete the activity entitled *Characteristics of ADHD*.

further in this section but will address two major characteristics of students with ADHD: social and behavioral problems and academic difficulties. These difficulties often adversely affect educational performance and may result in eligibility for the OHI label. Moreover, when the academic or behavior problems are extreme, the student with ADHD may also be identified with a learning disability or emotional and behavioral disability.

## Social and Behavioral Difficulties

If you consider the characteristics of ADHD that we have discussed to this point, it is apparent that many students with this disorder will have difficulty getting along with peers. Consider the behaviors that are used to identify these children (included in Figure 9.1). As you can see, children with ADHD have difficulty sustaining attention during play activities, often do not listen when spoken to, run and climb excessively in situations where this behavior is inappropriate, have difficulty with turn taking, and often interrupt or intrude on others. These are behaviors that most do not want in friends and many find unacceptable and wish to avoid in others.

Research has confirmed these difficulties. Students with ADHD tend to interact with peers in a more negative and unskilled manner than do other students (Wenar & Kerig, 2006). "Moreover, when introduced to a peer with ADHD, children take only minutes to notice and react negatively to the ADHD child's behavior" (p. 189). This is not to say that every student identified with ADHD has difficulty getting along with peers, but many children who are so identified have social problems.

Some students with ADHD also cause disruptions in classrooms as a result of their inattentive, impulsive, and/or hyperactive behaviors. In more extreme cases, these behaviors include problems with stubbornness, defiance, verbal hostility, and temper tantrums (Barkley, 2006a). As these behaviors suggest, a strong relationship exists between ADHD and emotional and behavioral disabilities (EBDs), as approximately 60% of students with EBD are also identified with ADHD (DuPaul, 2007; Reiff, 2004).

## Academic Difficulties

As with social and behavioral difficulties, many of the behaviors that are used to identify students with ADHD have the potential to have a negative influence on academic achievement. For example, symptoms of ADHD included in Figure 9.1 include inability to pay close attention to details, carelessness in schoolwork, difficulty sustaining attention, difficulty organizing tasks, and many additional behaviors that will likely lead to academic difficulties.

As you might expect, many students identified with ADHD have difficulty progressing academically in school. Research has revealed that approximately 70% of students with ADHD will probably have a learning problem in reading, mathematics, writing, or spelling (Mayes & Calhoun, 2006). A smaller but still substantial proportion of these students, about 20%, are likely to have a learning disability in reading or mathematics (DuPaul, 2007; Schnoes, Reid, Wagner, & Marder, 2006).

It has been suggested that two potential factors contribute to academic problems among children with ADHD (Rapport, Scanlan, & Denney, 1999). First, as we have noted, the behaviors associated with ADHD increase the probability that students will have conduct problems, which contribute to lowered academic achievement. That is, students who are disruptive and inattentive frequently do not attend to and learn academic content that is addressed and reviewed in class. The second pathway connecting ADHD and academic problems is through cognitive deficits

**REFLECTIVE EXERCISE**

#4 Discuss with a peer how the symptoms of ADHD might lead to social problems for a student. How might a teacher address these behaviors to reduce the social adjustment problems?

**REFLECTIVE EXERCISE**

#5 Students who are impulsive or inattentive to classroom activities are highly frustrating for some teachers. How can teachers ensure that these student behaviors do not have a negative influence on their interaction with or instruction to a student with ADHD?

associated with ADHD. For these students, behaviors such as lack of organizational skills, lack of sustained attention to tasks, and problems with monitoring and controlling their behavior may lead to academic skills deficits.

# PREVALENCE, COURSE, AND CAUSAL FACTORS

## Prevalence

While educators generally agree that ADHD is the most common behavior disorder among children (Barkley, 2006b; Gureasko-Moore, DuPaul, & Power, 2005; Tsal, Shalev, & Mevorach, 2005), estimates of the prevalence of this disorder vary widely. The most frequently cited, and probably the most accurate, estimate of prevalence for ADHD is 3% to 7% of the school-age population (Barkley, 2006b).

These prevalence rates mean that anywhere from 1.9 to 4.5 million school-age students are identified with ADHD in the United States. The vast majority of these students are served in general education classrooms (U.S. Department of Education, 2009), which means that general educators will see approximately one or two students with ADHD in their classrooms each year.

One aspect of prevalence that is clear is that boys are as much as three times more likely to be identified with ADHD than are girls (B. Smith, Barkley, & Shapiro, 2006). Some evidence also indicates that ADHD is more common among children from low socioeconomic backgrounds; however, it is unclear whether differences exist across different racial groups (Bussing, Gary, Mills, & Garvan, 2007; Wenar & Kerig, 2006).

Researchers estimate that between 50% and 60% of students with ADHD have a coexisting disability (Reiff, 2004; Schnoes et al., 2006). The approximate percentages of students with ADHD by disability category include learning disabilities, 20%; intellectual disabilities, 20%; EBD, 60%; OHI, 66%; and autism spectrum disorder, 25% (DuPaul, 2007; Reiff, 2004; Schnoes et al., 2006).

The prevalence estimates for ADHD vary for several reasons. Perhaps the major reason is the difference among individuals, including well-trained professionals, in defining terms such as *sustained attention, inattention, impulsive,* and *hyperactive.* A second issue related to varying prevalence levels is the fact that the behavior of children with ADHD varies depending on the measurement procedures that educators use to assess the existence of the condition. For example, the use of parent reports to determine if a child meets the behavioral criteria for ADHD results in lower prevalence rates, while teacher reports result in higher prevalence rates (up to twice as high) (Barkley, 2006a).

A final factor that contributes to variation in prevalence rates relates to the context within which the behaviors of concern occur. Barkley (2006a) has reviewed research related to contextual factors that influence the ability of students with ADHD to sustain their attention, perform tasks, control impulses, regulate their activity level, and consistently produce work. He concludes that the performance of children with ADHD is worse

Later in the day

With greater task complexity

When restraint is needed

With tasks that are not highly stimulating

Under variable schedules of immediate task consequences

Under conditions with a long delay before reinforcement

In the absence of adult supervision during task performance

Thus, the prevalence rates of children identified with ADHD vary widely. You will see the manifestation of these differences in schools: Some schools and school districts tend to have a high prevalence rate for students with ADHD, while others have a much lower rate.

## The Course of ADHD

Parents often observe the first hint of ADHD when they note excessive motor activity as toddlers begin to walk and explore the world around them (American Psychiatric Association, 2000). This is only a hint, because the vast majority of very active toddlers are not later identified with ADHD. Moreover, only a few students with ADHD are identified before entering school. These students typically have very high levels of hyperactive and inattentive behavior as well as more negative temperaments and greater emotional reactivity to events (American Psychiatric Association, 2000; B. Smith et al., 2006).

Most students with ADHD are identified in early elementary school, as increasing demands are placed on children to fit into the rules and structure of school. These demands often create a context in which behaviors such as a high activity level and impulsiveness become apparent and result in teacher and parental concern about disruptive behavior and, for a substantial portion of these students, lack of academic progress (Barkley, 2006a).

Researchers generally recognize that hyperactive and inattentive behaviors decline as students enter adolescence (B. Smith et al., 2006; Wenar & Kerig, 2006). However, these behaviors also decline in students without ADHD (i.e., typical students become more attentive and less active). The sum of these changes is that students with ADHD remain significantly more active and inattentive than do typical students in adolescence (B. Smith et al., 2006). Research has also revealed that during adolescence, the manifestation of ADHD symptoms change for some students, as high levels of motor activity are replaced by an inner feeling of restlessness, while reckless behavior on a bicycle may be replaced by reckless behavior while driving an automobile (Wenar & Kerig, 2006).

For a substantial portion of adolescents, ADHD persists into adulthood in a somewhat altered form. Symptoms related to hyperactivity seem to significantly decline or disappear for most adults, while inattentiveness and impulsive behavior decline both for adults with ADHD and those who are not so labeled (Barkley, Fischer, Smallish, & Fletcher, 2002). Overall, researchers estimate that, as adolescents with ADHD enter adulthood, 30% outgrow ADHD; 40% continue to have symptoms of restlessness, inattention, and impulsivity; while 30% develop additional problems (e.g., substance abuse, antisocial behavior) (Wenar & Kerig, 2006).

## Causal Factors

What causes the behavior of students with ADHD to develop as it does? Why do some preschool children have symptoms of ADHD that disappear as they grow older, while these behaviors persist in others? Are these behaviors a function of parents' child-rearing practices, heredity, neurological anomalies, exposure to toxins, or intake of food additives? These are some of the questions that arise for parents and teachers regarding students with ADHD. The short answer to why students develop ADHD is, for the vast majority of these students, "We don't know." It is apparent that ADHD is a function of a complex interaction of many factors that contribute to the development of this disorder, including brain injury, brain abnormalities, hereditary influences, and family issues.

### Brain Injury

The one cause of ADHD that we can be sure of is brain injury. A long history of research, dating to the study of brain-injured World War I veterans, reveals that traumatic brain injury, especially to the frontal area of the brain, often results in

Some adolescents with ADHD exhibit inner feelings of restlessness.

**REFLECTIVE EXERCISE**

**#6** Have you observed an adult who might have been identified with ADHD? How did the behavior of this adult differ from the behavior of children with ADHD? Why do you suspect that the identification of adults with ADHD has grown rapidly in recent years?

hyperactive, impulsive, and inattentive behavior (Strauss & Lehtinen, 1947). You should note that most children with ADHD do not have brain damage. Only 5% to 10% of these children have documented brain damage that results from trauma (e.g., an auto accident or a fall), toxins, or disease (Barkley, 2000).

### Brain Abnormalities

While 90% to 95% of students with ADHD do not have documented brain injury, a significant amount of evidence has accumulated suggesting that these students do have certain abnormalities in brain function that relate to ADHD. For example, the brain chemistry of children with ADHD often differs from those who do not have ADHD (DuPaul, Barkley, & Connor, 1998). In particular, research has shown that children with ADHD have a deficiency of the neurotransmitters dopamine and norepinephrine, which are chemicals in the brain that influence the transmission of signals between nerve cells. This relationship was initially recognized when researchers found that stimulant medications, which are effective in reducing the symptoms of ADHD, act by increasing the amount of these neurotransmitters in the brain (DuPaul et al., 1998).

Additional research has been conducted with neuropsychological tests and medical tests that measure brain activity, which have resulted in evidence that abnormalities primarily in the frontal areas of the brain contribute to ADHD (B. Smith, Barkley, & Shapiro, 2006; Wenar & Kerig, 2006). These abnormalities are not brain damage but differences that exist when comparing children with ADHD with those who do not have this disorder.

### Hereditary Influences

Compelling evidence supports the perspective that heredity plays a major role in ADHD. Research with families has shown that, if the mother, father, or a child has ADHD, the chances of another child having ADHD are five times as high as in a family with no previous evidence of ADHD (Biederman, Faraone, Keenan, & Tsuang, 1991). Studies of twins provide even more persuasive evidence. This research has revealed that, if one identical twin has ADHD, the odds that the other twin will have this disorder are between 67% and 81% (Barkley, 2003). This evidence suggests that heredity explains at least 80% of the range of behaviors related to ADHD, which is similar to the heritability of height (B. Smith et al., 2006).

### Family Influences

Early theories regarding the causes of ADHD contended that poor parenting was a major cause of the disorder. Research has not supported this perspective (Barkley, 2006a). While poor parent management skills can make the behaviors associated with ADHD worse, and extreme levels of stress in a family (e.g., an acrimonious divorce) can temporarily result in some of the symptoms of ADHD, no evidence indicates that parenting practices or a dysfunctional family situation can cause the extreme behaviors associated with ADHD.

Parents play an important role in determining how the symptoms of ADHD will be manifested when the child is not in school.

This is not to say that a parent's behavior isn't important in determining how the symptoms of ADHD will be manifested in the home and, to some degree, in school. Indeed, parents, siblings, teachers, and peers are all crucial in influencing the extent of negative behaviors exhibited by children with ADHD (American Psychiatric Association, 2000). As we will discuss later in this chapter when we address interventions, well-managed programs to support these students, which often include well-designed instructional settings, use of good behavior-management practices, and, in many cases, the use of medication, can provide a very effective approach to treatment for these students.

## IDENTIFICATION AND ASSESSMENT

### Screening and Identification

The first step in identifying a student with ADHD is screening (DuPaul, 2004). In a school, a teacher will typically be the first to observe that a student exhibits inattentiveness, hyperactivity, and/or impulsiveness at levels that are greater than peers' and that these behaviors interfere with the student's academic progress and/or social adjustment in the classroom. Once a teacher determines that a student may have ADHD, the teacher should seek the assistance of a psychologist to determine if further evaluation is needed. The psychologist will interview the teacher to screen for the severity and frequency of symptoms that might indicate ADHD.

It is important to note that a teacher should not recommend to a parent that a student be referred to a physician for evaluation for ADHD or that a student might be a good candidate for medication. The multidisciplinary team should be involved in any decision regarding whether a referral to a physician will be recommended to the parent. Moreover, the physician, in consultation with the psychologist, teachers, other relevant school professionals, and the child's parents, will make any decision regarding whether the student should be identified with ADHD and the use of any medical intervention that may be needed.

Despite efforts to standardize the criteria for ADHD (see Figure 9.1) in DSM-IV-TR, these criteria "remain subjective and may be interpreted differently by different observers" (American Academy of Pediatrics, 2000, p. 1163). Because of this subjectivity in the identification process, the multidisciplinary team should use multiple measures and multiple methods to collect data regarding the student's behavior across a range of settings and sources (Salend & Rohena, 2003). These methods should include interviews with parents and teachers, a review of the student's school records and medical history, observation of the child's behavior in multiple school settings (e.g., classroom, lunchroom, playground), and assessment of academic functioning (DuPaul, 2004; Office of Special Education Programs [OSEP], 2003). Behavior rating scales may also be used to collect information from parents and/or teachers regarding the student's behavior. Frequently used measures include the Conners' Parent Rating Scale—3 (Conners, 2008a); Conners' Teacher Rating Scale—3 (Conners, 2008b); and Behavior Assessment System for Children (BASC-2) (Reynolds & Kamphaus, 2004).

While a physician ultimately makes the decision regarding whether a student has ADHD, the multidisciplinary team is responsible for conducting an educational evaluation to determine the extent to which the behaviors associated with ADHD might have influenced the child's academic achievement and social adjustment. The team may use both standardized norm-referenced tests and criterion-referenced measures of

**REFLECTIVE EXERCISE**

#7 Now that you have reviewed the range of causal influences associated with ADHD, discuss with a peer how useful knowledge of such factors would be in your planning of classroom-based instructional and behavioral interventions.

Parent interviews are often an important component of the identification of students with ADHD.

academic achievement as well as curriculum-based measures that address the child's progress in the general education curriculum. In addition, the team should use observations of the student in the general education classroom, examination of test scores and report-card grades, and interviews with teachers and parents to collect this information.

### Determining Eligibility for Services

**PEARSON**
**myeducationlab**
Go to the Assignments and Activities section of Topic 11: ADHD in the MyEducationLab for your course and complete the activity entitled *Assessment of Students with Special Needs.*

Once the student has been identified as having ADHD and information has been collected from multiple sources regarding the student's academic progress, behavior, and social adjustment, the multidisciplinary team examines and discusses these data to determine if the student is eligible for special education services. To be eligible for special education services, the student must be identified with ADHD, and the ADHD must adversely affect educational performance.

Another important consideration for students with ADHD is whether they have a coexisting disability. When the multidisciplinary team suspects that the student may have another disability, additional information should be collected to determine whether the student is eligible for special education services based on a disability other than ADHD. As we have noted, a substantial proportion of students with ADHD also have intellectual disabilities, learning disabilities, and EBD.

Finally, the multidisciplinary team may decide that the student has ADHD but is not eligible for special education services because the disability does not adversely affect educational performance (e.g., result in an academic achievement level that is significantly below grade level). As mentioned earlier in this chapter, a student who has ADHD but is not eligible for special education services may be appropriate for evaluation under Section 504. The same type of data is collected for making this determination. If the data collected demonstrate that the child's ADHD adversely affects his learning (which is a major life activity), the student may qualify under Section 504 for services (OSEP, 2003). Students who are eligible under Section 504 do not have an IEP but "must be provided regular or special education and related aids or services that are designed to meet their individual needs as adequately as the needs of non-disabled students are met" (p. 5).

## EDUCATIONAL PRACTICES

In the past decade, extensive research has been conducted regarding practices that are effective in addressing the needs of students with ADHD. We begin with a review of placement practices regarding students with ADHD and then focus on major approaches that educators use to address the needs of these students from preschool through the school years and into vocational settings.

### Service Delivery

Most students identified with ADHD spend the majority of the school day in a general education classroom. Separate data are not available from the U.S. Department of Education regarding placement settings for students with ADHD, as these students are included in the OHI category. However, data for the OHI category reveal that approximately 59% of these students spend the majority of the day (80% or more) in general education classrooms, while an additional 29% spend 40% to 79% of the school day in general education classes. These placements are similar to data for students with learning disabilities (U.S. Department of Education, 2009). Students who are identified as ADHD under Section 504 are also educated primarily in general education classrooms.

Of course, these data also reveal that some students with ADHD are educated in more restrictive settings (approximately 11% of students identified as other health impaired). Furthermore, students with ADHD who are identified with other disabilities, especially intellectual disabilities and EBD, are likely to be educated in more restrictive settings for much of the school day.

What are the implications of these data? Most students with ADHD have mild disabilities that are typically addressed in general education classrooms. Educators' success in addressing these students' needs depends on the use of effective interventions. Many of the interventions developed for students with ADHD are effective in any setting.

## Early Intervention

The symptoms of ADHD are typically noted before the child enters school (i.e., before age 7) (American Psychiatric Association, 2000). Furthermore, children who are identified with ADHD before entering school tend to have more severe symptoms and are often identified with ADHD-PHI or ADHD-C. Many of these children present significant challenges for their parents and preschool teachers and are at a high risk for developing academic difficulties and oppositional and defiant behaviors. This makes it especially important to intervene early to address current behavior difficulties as well as to prevent or reduce the severity of academic skill deficits, aggression, opposition, and defiance (DuPaul & Stoner, 2003).

One strategy that has been proven effective in addressing the needs of young children with ADHD is the use of parent-mediated interventions. Parent-mediated interventions that have proven effective include (DuPaul & Stoner, 2003)

1. Use of brief, direct commands
2. Positive parent attention to appropriate child behavior
3. Implementation of contingency management strategies in which children earn token reinforcers (e.g., poker chips) for compliance with parent directives
4. Use of response cost and time-out from positive reinforcement strategies to reduce noncompliant and aggressive behavior

If early intervention efforts are to succeed, it is important that teachers develop home–school partnerships with families. These partnerships are largely based on gaining trust of the family; addressing the diverse needs, backgrounds, and experiences of the family; and offering a range of usable, flexible services that address the changing needs of the family (Salend & Rohena, 2003). These partnerships also offer parents and teachers the opportunity to share information about the child, monitor the effectiveness of medications that may be administered, coordinate assignments, and develop behavior modification plans (Bos, Nahmias, & Urban, 1999).

Barkley (2000) has recommended the use of home-based reward programs as part of home–school partnerships in addressing the needs of students with ADHD. One such program is the behavior report card (Reiff, 2004). The behavior report card consists of a structured form that the teacher completes daily as an evaluation of the student's behavior in targeted areas, such as class participation, performance of classwork, and following class rules. The parents then use this report card to give or take away rewards, depending on the child's behavior. Report cards are initially sent home daily; but as the child's behavior improves, the report cards are sent home less frequently.

In the case of young children with extreme hyperactive and impulsive behavior, it is likely that even with intensive interventions and close cooperation between home

REFLECTIVE EXERCISE

#8 Most students with ADHD are included in general education classrooms. What challenges might the impulsive and inattentive behaviors of these students present to classroom teachers? What types of support do classroom teachers need to ensure that these students succeed?

It is important that teachers and parents work together to ensure that early intervention efforts succeed for children with ADHD.

and school, the behaviors will continue to interfere with the child's development. Under these circumstances, medication will often be prescribed to control the child's behavior. When this occurs, it is especially important that teachers and families work together closely to monitor the effects of medication on the child's behavior and continue to use effective interventions to ensure the child's academic and social progress.

## Classroom Interventions

Many of the classroom intervention strategies that are useful for students with emotional and behavioral disabilities have proven effective for students with ADHD. In particular, the use of behavior modification, a token economy, social skills training/teaching replacement behaviors, functional behavior assessments, and teaching self-control have been shown to be effective with students with ADHD (Gureasko-Moore, DuPaul, & White, 2006; Harlacher, Roberts, & Merrell, 2006; Reid, Trout, & Schartz, 2005; Rosenberg, Wilson, Maheady, & Sindelar, 2004).

Similarly, effective instructional practices that are used to teach students who struggle to learn academic material (e.g., students with learning disabilities) may be used with students with ADHD. This may include the principles that guide effective curriculum design and instruction, the use of strategy instruction, and highly effective instructional strategies such as systematic instruction and classwide peer tutoring (Coyne, Kame'enui, & Carnine, 2007; Deshler & Schumaker, 2006; DuPaul, 2007; McMaster, Kung, Han, & Cao, 2008).

An intervention that holds much promise for addressing the needs of students with ADHD is the use of strategies that help these students regulate their own behavior. **Self-regulation strategies** have been the topic of much research in recent years. Reid and colleagues (2005) reviewed this research and concluded that self-regulation strategies have been proven effective for use with students with ADHD to decrease inappropriate behaviors, increase on-task behaviors, and increase academic accuracy and productivity. These "self-regulation" strategies are "used by students to manage, monitor, record, and/or assess their behavior or academic achievement" (Reid, et al., 2005, p. 362). For more information regarding these interventions, see "Can You Help Me with This Student?"

In addition to these interventions, Barkley (2000) has provided general principles for structuring and managing a classroom that are particularly important in addressing the needs of students with ADHD:

1. The presentation of rules and instructions should be brief, clear, and (whenever possible) presented visually in the form of charts, lists, and other visual reminders. Relying on a child's memory and verbal reminders will often be ineffective.
2. The approach to consequences must be well organized, thoroughly planned, and systematic. Feedback, rewards, and punishment used to manage a child's behavior must be delivered immediately.
3. Frequent feedback when the child follows rules is crucial for maintaining the child's compliance.
4. Children with ADHD are often less sensitive to social praise and reprimands. The consequences for good and bad behavior must be more powerful than those needed to manage the behavior of other children.
5. Rewards and incentives should be used before punishment is incorporated. More rewards should be used than punishments, by a ratio of at least 3 to 1.
6. Token reinforcement systems can be effective over an entire school year as long as rewards are changed frequently.
7. Anticipation is a key for students with ADHD, especially during classroom transitions. Ensure that students know rules and procedures that are used for transitions before the transition occurs.

**PEARSON**
**myeducationlab**

Go to the Assignments and Activities section of Topic 11: ADHD in the MyEducationLab for your course and complete the activities entitled *Instructional Strategies for Students with ADHD* and *Self-Monitoring*.

## REFLECTIVE EXERCISE

#9 At the beginning of this chapter, Meridith Taylor-Strout describes several classroom strategies that are effective for meeting the needs of students with ADHD. Considering the behaviors frequently exhibited by students with ADHD, which of these strategies do you feel would be most effective? Why?

| To... | Gloria Rogers, School Psychologist |
| --- | --- |
| From... | Sean Brice, High School Math Teacher |
| Subject: | Helping an 11th grader with ADHD to monitor and manage his behavior in math class |

Gloria, a student in my math class, Roberto, is a bright, hard-working 11th grader. He enjoys math and is very cooperative in class. However, I've noticed that Roberto often has difficulty monitoring his responses when doing math problems, resulting in mistakes on work he does in class, on homework, and, most importantly, on his test responses. I want to find a way to help Roberto learn to better monitor and manage his behavior during math class. I'm convinced that if we could do this, he could learn more, improve his grades, and significantly increase his score on the state-wide test of math skills. Roberto understands that he has difficulty monitoring and managing his behavior, and he is anxious to learn a strategy that will improve his performance.

I look forward to hearing your suggestions.

—Sean

---

To:      Sean Brice
From:    Gloria Rogers
Subject: RE: Helping an 11th grader with ADHD to monitor and manage his behavior in math class

Sean, as we have discussed previously, Roberto's difficulty in math is not unusual for a student with ADHD. Many of these students have difficulty monitoring their behavior. This makes self-monitoring especially important, given the accuracy of responses that are required in math. I have some ideas about strategies that will help Roberto regulate his own behavior.

A lot of research has been done on self-regulation strategies, which can be used to decrease inappropriate behaviors, increase on-task behaviors, and increase academic accuracy and productivity (Reid, Trout, & Schartz, 2005). These strategies are "used by students to manage, monitor, record, and/or assess their behavior or academic achievement" (p. 362). Two of these interventions that you might find useful with Roberto are described below.

**Self-monitoring:** To use this intervention, the student self-monitors an academic task (e.g., practicing math facts), determines the amount of work completed and the accuracy of the work, and produces a graph that he uses to monitor accuracy or work completion. Self-recording provides the student with an immediate consequence for his behavior, which may be sufficient in some instances to result in improvement in the student's behavior. For students whose behavior is more difficult to change, reinforcement is provided to improve accuracy or work completion to a predetermined level. The teacher may provide reinforcement, or the student may have this responsibility, after meeting a predetermined level of performance.

Self-monitoring can also be used with student behavior such as attention to task. When self-monitoring is used with attention to task, the teacher periodically provides the student with a reminder to record whether or not he is paying attention to a classroom task. The student then graphs the behaviors, and the teacher may provide reinforcement based on predetermined criteria.

**Self-management:** This intervention requires that a student "monitor, rate, and compare some aspect of his or her behavior to an external standard" (Reid et al., 2005, p. 363). While self-management is similar to self-monitoring, it adds a step that requires the student to evaluate accuracy, and the student's results are compared to an external evaluator (e.g., teacher, paraprofessional). The teacher then provides reinforcement based on the extent to which the student's self-evaluation closely matches the external evaluator.

Using self-regulation strategies with students with ADHD (Reid et al., 2005) has several advantages, including:

- The goal of these interventions is to teach students to self-regulate their behavior, a key difficulty for students with ADHD.
- These interventions have been shown to consistently improve behavior commonly exhibited by students with ADHD, including on-task behavior, amount of work completed, and accuracy of work.
- The interventions have also been shown to be effective in reducing inappropriate and disruptive behaviors.

For more information on self-regulation strategies, consult the following resources:

Deshler, D., & Schumaker, J. (Eds.). (2006). *Teaching adolescents with disabilities.* Thousand Oaks, CA: Corwin.

Reid, R., & Lienemann, T. (2006). *Strategy instruction for students with learning disabilities.* New York: Guilford Press.

Reid, R., Trout, A., & Schartz, M. (2005). Self-regulation interventions for children with attention deficit/hyperactivity disorder. *Exceptional Children, 71*(4), 361–377.

These strategies should prove useful for Roberto.

—Gloria

**EXTEND AND APPLY**

- Can you think of other strategies that could help Roberto learn to monitor his responses in math class?
- What strategies might students use in other content area classes (e.g., science, social studies)?
- Why do you think using external feedback helps in learning to manage your own behavior?

Computer technology is a potentially useful approach for addressing the needs of students with ADHD. In spite of this great promise, surprisingly little research is available regarding the use of technology with these students. The "Technology for Access" feature provides information about this topic, including suggested characteristics of software to ensure engagement and motivation of students with ADHD.

## Interventions and the Use of Medication

### Research on Medication

The use of medication to address the behaviors associated with ADHD has had a long and controversial history. You have probably seen or heard of some of the attacks in the media on the use of medication to control ADHD. Much of the controversy has centered on the overidentification of students with ADHD and the increasing use of medication to address this disorder (Connor, 2006a, 2006b; Scheffler, Hinshaw, Modrek, & Levine, 2007). Given the nature of the behaviors used to determine if a student should be identified with ADHD, there is little doubt that some students are misidentified. However, with the appropriate use of assessment procedures and multidisciplinary team decision making, the overidentification of these students should be the exception rather than the rule.

The controversy surrounding the use of medication for ADHD has led to extensive research regarding the effectiveness of medication in reducing the symptoms of ADHD. The vast majority of this research has revealed that low-to-moderate doses of **stimulant medication** (e.g., methylphenidate [Ritalin or Concerta]) or **amphetamine** (Dexedrine or Adderall) are the most effective treatments for children with ADHD (Connor, 2006a).

Xu, Reid, and Steckelberg (2002) reviewed research regarding the use of technology with students with ADHD. They found only two studies that evaluated the effects of computer-assisted instruction (CAI) for these students. While both of these investigations resulted in positive outcomes, too few studies have been conducted to reach definitive conclusions regarding the use of CAI with students with ADHD. With this caveat in mind, Xu and colleagues reviewed the characteristics of many CAI software packages and suggest that many of the recommended strategies for effective teaching of students with ADHD (and other students, for that matter) are often built into CAI. Thus, this software may be especially beneficial for students with ADHD.

Xu and colleagues' review of research suggests that, as teachers choose software for CAI with students with ADHD, several considerations should guide selection to ensure student engagement and motivation. Software should have characteristics such as the following:

- Provide step-by-step instructions.
- Wait for student responses, then provide immediate feedback and reinforcement following responses.
- Allow students to work at their own pace.
- Actively involve students in learning.
- Organize content into small, manageable chunks of information.
- Offer repeated trials using variable formats, as needed, when students are learning content.
- Offer novel, attention-grabbing approaches when addressing critical content. For example, introduce new material with graphics, words, and sounds within game formats, animation, or color, or use software to simulate real-world situations with images and sounds.

Source: Adapted with permission from Xu, C., Reid, R., & Steckelberg, A. (2000). Technology applications for children with ADHD: Assessing the empirical support. *Education and Treatment of Children, 25*(2), 224–228.

---

The largest study conducted regarding the effectiveness of medication and behavioral interventions with ADHD was sponsored by the National Institute of Mental Health and completed in the late 1990s. This study, called the Multimodal Treatment of ADHD (MTA) study (MTA Cooperative Group, 1999), compared the use of medication to behavioral interventions, community-based programs, and the combined use of medication and behavioral interventions. The results revealed that medication was the most effective intervention in reducing the symptoms of ADHD. However, the behavioral interventions and combined medication/behavioral interventions treatments were rated higher on parent satisfaction than other treatments, and the behavioral intervention was as effective as medication in addressing some behaviors of students with ADHD.

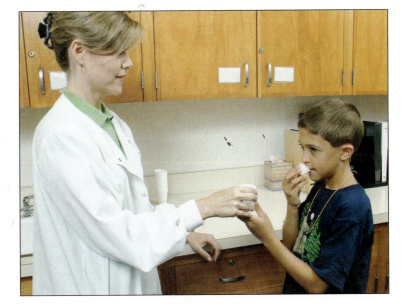

Medication is often highly effective in reducing the symptoms of ADHD.

This research reveals that medication is a very effective treatment for reducing the symptoms for approximately 70% to 85% of students with ADHD (Connor, 2006a; Wenar & Kerig, 2006). These symptoms include increased vigilance, impulse control, fine motor coordination, and reaction time; improved social interactions with peers and adults; and reduced hostile and negative behavior toward peers and adults (Connor, 2006a). However, it is important to recognize that medication controls negative behavioral symptoms of ADHD but does not directly address academic and social adjustment problems. Indeed, once medication is used to control negative student behavior, teachers find behavioral interventions to be most helpful in addressing

**TABLE 9.1** • MEDICATIONS USED WITH ADHD

| Medication Name | Dosage/Schedule | Duration |
|---|---|---|
| *Methylphenidate* (generic name) | | |
| Short-acting: | | |
| Ritalin, Methylin, Focain | 2 times per day, 2.5–20 mg | 3–5 hr |
| Intermediate-acting: | | |
| Ritalin SR, Metadate ER, Methylin ER | 1 or 2 times per day, 20–60 mg | 3–8 hr |
| Extended-release: | | |
| Concerta, Metadate CD, Ritalin LA | 1 time per day, 18–72 mg | 8–12 hr |
| *Amphetamine* (generic name) | | |
| Short-acting: | | |
| Dexedrine, Dextrostat | 2–3 times per day, 5–15 mg | 4–6 hr |
| Intermediate-acting: | | |
| Adderall, Dexedrine Spansule | 1–2 times per day, 5–30 mg | 6–8 hr |
| Extended-release: | | |
| Adderall-XR | 1 time per day, 10–30 mg | 10 hr |

Source: Conner, 2006a, 2006b; Reiff, 2004.

academic needs and social adjustment of students with ADHD. For more information regarding the use of interventions to address a student's academic needs, see "Can You Help Me with This Student?" addressing Jerome's inattentive behavior.

### Considerations About Medication and ADHD

About 3% of preschool and school-age students are prescribed stimulant medications to treat the symptoms of ADHD (Connor, 2006a; Gureasko-Moore et al., 2005). Table 9.1 provides information regarding the two major types of medications prescribed to control the symptoms of ADHD.

Research has shown that methylphenidate is effective for most children and accounts for about 90% of prescribed medications for ADHD (Konopasek & Forness, 2004). However, the particular type of medication and dosage level that a student will respond to is unpredictable. Thus, it may be necessary to begin with one stimulant, closely monitor the effects (teachers may be asked to provide some of this feedback), and perhaps alter the dosage level or stimulant until an optimal response is achieved (Reiff, 2004).

Another consideration for physicians in selecting a medication relates to whether a short-acting or slow-release form of medication will be prescribed. As Table 9.1 indicates, both methylphenidate and amphetamine come in short-acting, intermediate-acting, and extended-release forms. Some students respond more favorably to an extended-release form of methylphenidate or amphetamine. Furthermore, longer-lasting forms of these medications reduce issues related to taking medication during the school day (e.g., forgetting to take the medication or interrupting school activities).

While stimulant medications are prescribed to treat the vast majority of students with ADHD, other medications are used in some cases, including antidepressants or antianxiety medications. One of these medications, Strattera, is being used increasingly with school-age children and adults with ADHD. Strattera has side effects that are similar to stimulant medications, although they may be somewhat milder, and this medication lasts longer (up to 12 hours) than most stimulants (Connor, 2006b).

When using medications to control the symptoms of ADHD, it also important that the child's parents and teacher closely monitor potential side effects. Educators are in a unique position because they can monitor the effects of medication on classroom behavior and academic achievement and also note how different dosage levels influence student behavior and achievement (Rosenberg et al., 2004). For example, in some instances when the level of the medication is too high, the child may behave "like a

**REFLECTIVE EXERCISE**

**#10** Research strongly supports the effectiveness of medication for reducing the symptoms of ADHD. Given this research, why do you feel that some parents strongly oppose the use of medication for their children? How should you as a teacher respond to these parents?

zombie" in class and be largely unresponsive to academic work and other school activities. Potential side effects of medications used to treat ADHD may include insomnia, decreased appetite, stomachache, headache, dizziness, and motor tics (Kollins et al., 2001).

In sum, a critical role for teachers and parents is to monitor the effect of medication on the child's behavior as well as any side effects that occur as a result of the use of medication. Moreover, the American Academy of Pediatrics (2001) in guidelines for the treatment of ADHD recommends the use of a sustained monitoring system to ensure that medication is prescribed appropriately. In particular, these guidelines recommend that parents and teachers gather information, monitor student outcomes, and track any adverse effects of medication. To ensure that these responsibilities are effectively addressed, teachers should have a basic understanding of the use of medications to control the symptoms of ADHD.

## Transition to Adult Life

As we have noted, the extent to which the symptoms of ADHD persist into adulthood depends, to a large degree, on the severity of the hyperactive–impulsive behaviors in childhood, the coexistence of oppositional-defiant behavior or conduct disorders, and the nature of the family relationship (Barkley, 2003). Up to 30% of students identified with ADHD have few or no symptoms of this disorder when they become adults (Wenar & Kerig, 2006). Individuals with ADHD who have the most difficulty adjusting as adults are those who are identified with conduct disorders or other major psychiatric disorders. Up to 25% of adults with ADHD have conduct disorders that continue into adulthood, while 25% develop a major depression as an adult (Fischer et al., 2002).

For others with ADHD, the transition to adulthood is much more promising. For these individuals, major barriers to success include overcoming continuing symptoms of ADHD, which include inattentiveness, poor inhibition, poor self-regulation or self-discipline, restlessness, and difficulty resisting distractions (Barkley, 2000). In addition, many of these persons were identified with learning disabilities during their school years and will continue to have academic difficulties as adults. These difficulties may require supports for some persons with ADHD as they enter the workforce or move into higher education.

### Vocational Support

Many adults with ADHD can succeed with little or no support in job settings. However, those with more extreme manifestations of ADHD symptoms, such as distractibility and lack of self-regulation, will likely have difficulty with the demands of many work settings. In addition, many adults with ADHD have difficulty working independently, meeting deadlines, persisting in completing work, and/or getting along with co-workers (Barkley, 2000). These adults may need the support of a job coach to assist them in getting a job that is appropriate to their skills and abilities. For example, jobs demanding close attention to detail for sustained periods of time will not be appropriate for most adults with ADHD, while jobs requiring physical movement and frequent change in the focus of work may be a better fit for many of these adults.

In addition, the job coach may provide assistance on the job to ensure that the job demands and supervision are appropriate to the needs of the adult with ADHD. For example, Barkley (2000) has suggested that adults with ADHD may need a range of adjustments in the work settings, including (1) accountability to a supervisor on a more frequent and immediate basis than others, (2) work responsibilities that are broken down into smaller tasks, (3) a supervisor who states goals each day and provides close supervision to ensure goals are met, and (4) consequences that are contingent on meeting goals.

### Support in Higher Education

Many students with ADHD are quite capable of going to college or taking advantage of other appropriate postsecondary opportunities. Moreover, many colleges and universities provide accommodations to maximize the opportunities of students with

| To... | Addie Sams, Middle School Special Education Teacher |
|---|---|
| From... | Yvette Yon, Middle School Math Teacher |
| Subject: | Supporting a middle school student with suspected ADHD in math class |

Addie, I have a new student, Jerome, who transferred into my eighth-grade math class at the beginning of January. Initially, he seemed to adapt well and appeared to be making good progress in adjusting socially and academically, although he seemed a bit disorganized and forgetful about homework assignments. After a couple of weeks, I noticed that Jerome did not do well on pop quizzes that I use to determine students' understanding of material that we've covered during a class period. In preparation for a chapter exam, I worked with Jerome and several other students after school and was impressed with his grasp of the material. When the exam was administered and scored, I was very disappointed to find that Jerome responded correctly to only 45% of the items. I reviewed the test with Jerome and found that he had trouble with multiple items on a single page and seemed to have difficulty switching algorithms when moving from one math problem to the next. Over the next several classes, I observed Jerome's on-task behavior and determined that he spent much of the class period off task, was easily distracted by unimportant activities, and had difficulty sustaining attention for more than a couple of minutes on a task.

I suspect that Jerome may have ADHD-PI. I'm planning to talk with the school psychologist next week about a possible referral for testing; but in the meantime, can you give me some ideas about what to do?!!

Thanks,

Yvette

---

To:      Yvette Yon
From:    Addie Sams
Subject: RE: Supporting a middle school student with suspected ADHD in math class

Yvette, you provided an excellent description of Jerome and the difficulty he is having in your class. As you note, it is important to address both his attention in class as well as his performance on exams and tests. While his behaviors may result in a label of ADHD-PI, I agree that it's important to immediately determine strategies for providing support to Jerome. Strategies that may be useful include the following (Zentall, 2006):

- *Use shorter, more frequent tasks or tests.* Determine if it is possible to break classwork down into smaller tasks that are more manageable for Jerome. Similarly, administer an exam over a longer period of time (two to four sessions), with fewer items per page and fewer types of problems per session.

- *Use distributed practice rather than massed practice.* Practicing for short periods of time and spreading these sessions over several classes is a more effective means of ensuring that students retain information. This strategy may be useful for Jerome as well as other students in your class.

- *Increase novelty.* Presenting information using novel means will help to ensure more attention to task. This may include the use of technology, presenting real-world problems involving math, incorporating student interests in tasks, or alternating low- and high-interest tasks.

- *Increase opportunities for motor responding during or after task performance.* This may entail allowing students time to manipulate materials being used in class, providing opportunities for task-related talking, or allowing students to work in small groups using a method such as class-wide peer tutoring.

- *Increase opportunities for self-monitoring and self-control.* Jerome may benefit from opportunities to monitor his own behavior. This may be done in collaboration with another student or with your assistance in developing a plan for self-monitoring. Self-monitoring consists of three components: self-assessment, goal setting, and self-determination of reinforcement (Polsgrove & Smith, 2004). In self-assessment, Jerome should be asked to reflect on his behavior and recognize that the behavior of interest is inadequate or inappropriate. He will then recognize the behaviors required, set goals, and select strategies that help regulate behavior. Finally, Jerome should evaluate his performance and consider the nature and scope of reinforcement that he should receive for performance of the target behavior.

For more information on strategies to address the needs of students with ADHD-PI, you may find the following sources useful:

Polsgrove, L., & Smith, A. W. (2004). Informed practice in teaching self-control to children with emotional and behavioral disorders. In R. B. Rutherford, Jr., M. M. Quinn, & A. R. Mathur (Eds.), *Handbook of research in emotional and behavioral disorders* (pp. 399–425). New York: Guilford Press.

Rief, S. (2005). *How to reach and teach children with ADD/ADHD* (2nd ed.). San Francisco: Jossey-Bass.

Zentall, S. (2006). *ADHD and education: Foundations, characteristics, methods, and collaboration.* Upper Saddle River, NJ: Merrill/Pearson Education.

Hope these help,

Addie

---

**EXTEND AND APPLY**
- If you were Jerome's teacher, how would you use the strategies just described or other strategies to ensure that he had the opportunity to demonstrate on exams what he has learned in class?
- How would you address Jerome's problem with pop quizzes?

---

ADHD and learning disabilities for success in higher education. Information on institutions of higher education that offer comprehensive programs for students with disabilities are described in *Peterson's Guide: Colleges with Programs for Students with Learning Disabilities or ADD* (*Peterson's*, 2003).

In addition to this information, the National Resource Center on ADHD (2005) provides information for students with ADHD who are planning to attend college. For example, students with ADHD who attend college and continue to have difficulty with inattention, impulsivity, and/or hyperactivity may benefit from class scheduling and classroom organization strategies such as these (Amenkhienan, 2003):

**Class Scheduling**
1. Schedule classes at times when you feel you are most alert.
2. Avoid taking back-to-back classes whenever possible.
3. Avoid taking several classes with especially demanding reading or writing requirements during a single semester.
4. Be aware of drop/add dates. Consider dropping a class if reasonable accommodations cannot be arranged.

**Classroom Strategies**
1. Do not sit by a window.
2. Audio-record class lectures or use notes from another dependable student or the professor.
3. Participate in class discussions as much as possible to enhance your concentration.

4. Seek accommodations (e.g., note takers, extended time for tests, support from the writing center) and supports as needed.

5. Take medication as prescribed by a physician if it helps. Symptoms of ADHD do not disappear upon high school graduation, and medication can help.

## PREVAILING ISSUES, CONTROVERSIES, AND IMPLICATIONS FOR THE TEACHER

Although great progress has been made in developing interventions and delivering services for students with ADHD, controversial issues continue to challenge the field. Two of the most important of these issues are the overidentification of students with ADHD and the use of medication as an intervention.

### Are Too Many Children Identified with ADHD?

A major concern of many professionals and advocates is the potential to significantly overidentify students with this disorder. The rapid growth of the OHI category over the past decade (a growth of almost 700%) has further fueled these fears. While criteria and evaluation procedures are in place that should largely prevent this problem (American Academy of Pediatrics, 2000; American Psychiatric Association, 2000), evidence supports the perspective that some children are identified as having ADHD who should not be (Barbaresi et al., 2002; DuPaul & Stoner, 2003; Gureasko-Moore et al., 2005).

Research has confirmed that the application of recommended practices to identify children with ADHD that were described previously in this chapter will result in reliable identification and reduce the risk for overidentification (DuPaul & Stoner, 2003). However, research has also revealed that the people identifying students with ADHD often do not use these practices. For example, one investigation (Wasserman, et al., 1999) revealed that only 38.3% of physicians used the DSM-IV-TR standards to identify these students, while 36.9% used behavioral questionnaires as part of the identification process.

It is important to note that there is another side to this controversy. Some parents and advocates have reacted to the mis- or overidentification of children with ADHD by refusing to accept this label or refusing to use medication as a treatment (Carey, 2004; Leslie, 2004). This has led, in some areas, to the underidentification of children with ADHD and very limited use of medication as a treatment for these children (Barbaresi et al., 2002; Rowland et al., 2002). Dr. Laurel Leslie (2004) eloquently addresses this issue of over- versus underidentification:

> My own experience mirrors these contradictory perspectives. Recently, I sat next to a teacher on a plane who commented that 9 children in her class of 30 in a suburb of New Jersey were taking a stimulant medication for ADHD. Yet, in my own community clinic setting, children and adolescents [who] present with blatant signs of ADHD and co-existing mental health disorders and learning disabilities have gone unrecognized by the medical and the educational professions. So is there an ADHD epidemic? Like many clinicians and researchers, I suspect that the truth falls somewhere in between. (p. 1)

We, too, suspect that this is the case. This controversy comes down to the particular child and the person or persons who are making the identification. Adherence to good practice will result, in the vast majority of cases, in the appropriate identification of children with ADHD (American Academy of Pediatrics, 2000; American Psychiatric Association, 2000), and you as a teacher will play a central role in collecting data to ensure that this occurs.

### Should Medication Be a Major Intervention for ADHD?

Another controversy regarding ADHD relates to the extent to which medication should be used to control symptoms of this disorder. The use of medication to control symptoms of ADHD has increased dramatically in the past decade (Barbaresi et al., 2002; Jensen et al., 1999; Konopasek & Forness, 2004; Zito et al., 1999, 2000). Moreover,

**REFLECTIVE EXERCISE**

#11 Review the symptoms used to identify children with ADHD in Figure 9.1. Which symptoms are common among children in kindergarten and first grade? Given the common occurrence of ADHD symptoms and what you've learned in this chapter, how can professionals ensure that children with ADHD are not overidentified?

# THE REAL WORLD Challenges and Solutions

## Addressing parent concerns about treatments for ADHD: Which treatments are effective?

*Ms. Marie is a fourth-grade teacher who has a reputation for successfully addressing the needs of a wide range of students in her classroom. Parents are very appreciative of Ms. Marie's fine teaching but are also very involved in the education of their children, often question her about the methods she uses for instruction, and closely monitor the academic progress and social status of their children. While this level of involvement is sometimes a bit trying, Ms. Marie realizes that much good comes from parent involvement, especially for her students.*

*Ms. Marie has developed a reputation for working effectively with students with ADHD. She has been successful teaching most of these students, many of whom took medication to control the symptoms of ADHD. Recently, one of Ms. Marie's parents read news reports that addressed concerns regarding the use of medication with students with ADHD. Upon reading about these concerns, this parent began searching for alternatives and located many such treatments on the Internet and from other sources. After completing this research, the parent e-mailed Ms. Marie about a meeting to talk about the use of medication and alternative treatments for students with ADHD.*

### What Evidence Is Available Regarding Alternative Treatments for ADHD?

To begin to address this parent's concern, Ms. Marie searched the Internet and other sources and found many concerns regarding the overidentification of students with ADHD and the use of medication with so many students. As she reflected on her own experience, she became convinced that the students who were identified in her classroom clearly met the criteria for ADHD, and overidentification was not an issue. Furthermore, when a student in her class takes medication for ADHD, Ms. Marie works closely with the school psychologist and child's pediatrician to monitor the effects of the medication, making sure that the student's symptoms are reduced and the side effects of the medication do not negatively influence student performance in the classroom. These experiences have shown Ms. Marie that the type of medication and dosage level must be carefully tailored for a particular student, and that while medication works for most students, it does not work for all.

Ms. Marie continued her search and found many alternative treatments for ADHD. These included reducing the child's intake of food additives (particularly certain food colorings) and preservatives; addressing ADHD by treating the child's vestibular system in the inner ear, which controls balance and movement; and other treatments that include giving children large doses of vitamins and minerals and reducing the intake of sugar. Ms. Marie found that little research evidence exists for the effectiveness of these treatments (DuPaul, 2007; Pfiffner, Barkley, & DuPaul, 2006; Zentall, 2006). Moreover, she found that research was available to support only two interventions for ADHD: the use of medication and behavioral interventions.

### Valuable Resources for the Teacher

For more information on the effectiveness of treatments for ADHD, the following resources may prove useful:

Reiff, M. (2004). *ADHD: A complete and authoritative guide.* Elk Grove Village, IL: American Academy of Pediatrics.

Pfiffner, L., Barkley, R., & DuPaul, G. (2006). Treatment of ADHD in school settings. In R. Barkley (Ed.), *Attention deficit hyperactivity disorder: A handbook for diagnosis and treatment* (3rd ed., pp. 547–589). New York: Guilford Press.

Zentall, S. (2006). *ADHD and education: Foundations, characteristics, methods, and collaboration.* Upper Saddle River, NJ: Pearson Education.

### Final Thoughts

How would you react to a parent who was seeking an alternative treatment for ADHD? Ms. Marie's experience with highly involved parents caused her to never take such inquiries personally, because she knows her parents are always motivated by their child's best interest. When a parent brings up any alternative treatment, she treats the inquiry respectfully, and provides the parent with information regarding the effectiveness (or lack of effectiveness) of the treatment. The parent inquiry and controversy regarding ADHD led Ms. Marie to learn all she could about possible treatments, and she now routinely shares this information with parents of students with ADHD to ensure that they are well informed about both the positives and negatives of these interventions.

evidence reveals that stimulant medication is used with approximately 3% of preschool and school-age children to treat the symptoms of ADHD (Connor, 2006a).

Perhaps the major concern regarding the use of medication to treat ADHD relates to the previously described controversies. That is, parents are hesitant to use powerful medication to control the behavior of their child when so many questions and controversies swirl around the overidentification of children with the disorder. A substantial number of these parents have sought alternative treatments for ADHD that do not require medication. For more information regarding these treatments, see the "Real World" feature.

Another issue that is frequently cited by those who oppose the use of medication for students with ADHD is the concern that its use may result in an increased risk for substance abuse later in life. Well-designed research that has been conducted to study this issue has revealed that the use of stimulant medication to treat ADHD does not increase the student's risk for substance abuse later in life (Barkley, Fischer, Smallish, & Fletcher, 2003; Wilens, Faraone, Biederman, & Gunawardene, 2003). Moreover, some evidence suggests that some students who receive stimulant medication to treat ADHD during the school years may experience a reduced risk of substance abuse (Wilens et al., 2003).

We contend that caution in using stimulant medication to treat ADHD is a good thing, very justifiable, and should help to reduce overidentification of this disorder. Indeed, parents, physicians, psychologists, and teachers (to the extent to which they are consulted about these decisions) should be very cautious in labeling a child with ADHD and using medication to treat the child's symptoms.

# 9 SUMMARY

Students with ADHD are often frustrating for parents and teachers. These students have some combination of impulsive, inattentive, and/or hyperactive behavior that often is difficult to control. Students with ADHD may or may not have behaviors that interfere with their educational performance.

## Definition and Classification Criteria

- Students with ADHD are identified based on the extent to which they exhibit some combination of inattentive, hyperactive, and impulsive behaviors.
- Some students are predominantly hyperactive and impulsive (ADHD-PHI) and do not exhibit the other symptoms (i.e., inattentive behaviors), while some students are predominantly inattentive (ADHD-PI), and still others combine all three of the major characteristics (ADHD-C).
- These behaviors should last for at least 6 months and should occur across at least two settings (e.g., school and home).

## Characteristics of Students

- The characteristics of students with ADHD often lead to difficulty getting along with others at school, and a significant proportion of these students develop behavior problems (e.g., oppositional-defiant disorder, anxiety disorder, conduct disorder).
- The symptoms of ADHD often influence the academic achievement of these students, as the impulsive, inattentive, and hyperactive behaviors cause difficulty in learning academic material, and the difficulty may develop into a learning disability over time.

## Prevalence, Course, and Causes

- ADHD is the most common behavior disorder. Its prevalence has been estimated as 3% to 7% of the school-age population.
- Significantly more boys than girls are identified with ADHD.
- Many students with ADHD are also identified with another disability, most commonly an intellectual disability, learning disability, or emotional and behavioral disability.
- Students with ADHD remain significantly more active and inattentive than typical students in adolescence, and these behaviors more often result in behavior problems.
- For most individuals, ADHD persists into adulthood in somewhat altered form, as 40% continue to have symptoms of restlessness, inattention, and impulsivity; while 30% develop additional problems (e.g., substance abuse, antisocial behavior).
- While we don't know what causes ADHD in most cases, contributing factors to this disorder may include brain injury, brain abnormalities, hereditary influences, and family issues.

## Identification and Assessment

- It is difficult to identify students with ADHD because the criteria used for identification are somewhat subjective and many students exhibit at least some of these behaviors.
- To ensure that students are appropriately identified, multidisciplinary teams should use multiple measures across settings to ensure that the severity of the student's symptoms is sufficient to be identified as ADHD.

## Educational Practices

- Extensive research has demonstrated that stimulant medication is the most effective intervention for reducing the symptoms of ADHD for most students.
- Medication should be closely monitored to ensure that the appropriate medication is used to reduce the symptoms of ADHD.
- Behavioral interventions, such as the use of behavior modification, a token economy, and teaching self-regulation, are effective interventions to support the students in learning appropriate classroom behaviors and making progress learning academic content.

## Prevailing Issues

- Many parents and professionals have expressed concern that students with ADHD are overidentified.
- The use of stimulant medications to control the symptoms of ADHD has led to controversy regarding whether students are overmedicated.

 **Council for Exceptional Children**

## ADDRESSING THE PROFESSIONAL STANDARDS

Council for Exceptional Children (CEC) Knowledge Standards addressed in the chapter:

ICC1K5, EC1K2, ICC2K1, ICC2K2, ICC2K5, ICC2K6, ICC2K7, ICC3K1, ICC3K2, ICC8K1, ICC8K2

Appendix B: CEC Knowledge and Skill Standards Core has a full listing of the standards referenced here.

**PEARSON myeducationlab**

Now go to Topic 11: ADHD in the MyEducationLab for your course, where you can:

- Find learning outcomes for the broad concepts covered in this chapter along with the national standards that connect to these outcomes.
- Complete Assignments and Activities that can help you more deeply understand the chapter content.
- Examine challenging situations presented in the IRIS Center Resources.
- Apply and practice your understanding of the core concepts and skills identified in the chapter with the Building Teaching Skills and Dispositions learning units.

- Check your comprehension on the content covered in the chapter by going to the Study Plan in the Book-Specific Resources section for your text. Here you will be able to take a chapter quiz, receive feedback on your answers, and then access Review, Practice, and Enrichment activities to enhance your understanding of chapter content.
- Access video clips of CCSSO National Teachers of the Year award winners responding to the question, "Why Do I Teach?" in the Teacher Talk section.

# chapter
# 10

# Autism Spectrum Disorders

**with Sunil Misra**
*Johns Hopkins University*

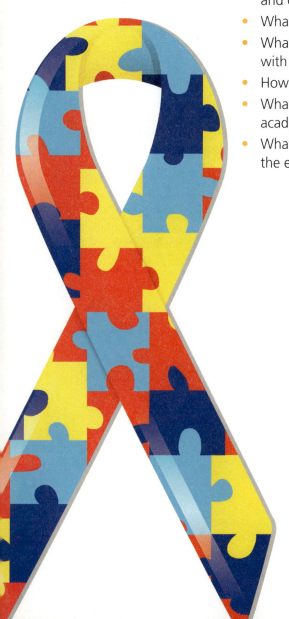

## REFLECT UPON

- How are the two most prevalent forms of the autism spectrum disorders (ASD)—autistic disorder and Asperger's disorder—defined and classified?

- What behavioral characteristics are universal and specific to ASD?

- What are the prevalence rates for and causal factors associated with ASD?

- How do we screen, identify, and assess students with ASD?

- What educational practices are effective in improving early childhood, academic, social, and transition outcomes for students with ASD?

- What are three prevailing and controversial issues associated with the education of students with ASD?

## MY PROFESSION, MY STORY: **KIM THOMAS**

Kim Thomas, a teacher of students with severe autism spectrum disorders (ASD), believes you can always learn new ways to help students. A 2005 Model of Excellence Award–winning teacher and a former president of her student council of the Council for Exceptional Children, Kim believes that if a teacher thinks he or she knows it all, that person should get out of the business. Motivated by her experiences with an uncle who had an intellectual disability, Kim has been teaching at the Heartspring School, a small specialized school for students with intensive needs in the Wichita, Kansas, area.

Kim works with students who are on the extreme or severe side of the autism spectrum. For her students to be served in more inclusive environments, their daily living skills must be strengthened and made more independent. Also, the frequencies of their maladaptive behaviors need to be decreased. Not surprisingly, Kim's day begins early, teaching and reinforcing adaptive living skills in the natural setting of her students' homes. To help her students get ready for the day, Kim often employs structured teaching methods during bathing, grooming, and eating breakfast. The classroom part of her day begins at 8:25, when her 14 students post their picture schedules for the day. Instruction is based on the Syracuse Community-Referenced Curriculum for Students with Moderate and Severe Disabilities (Ford et al., 1989), a curriculum for preparing students to function in the world. The major areas of emphasis are community-living domains, functional academics, and life-embedded skills designed for students whose learning needs are well beyond the offerings of traditional general education programs. However, Kim has to address maladaptive behaviors among her students, including aggression and property destruction.

The part of teaching Kim views as most satisfying is seeing her students grow. Most enter school wholly dependent on staff and after intensive instruction learn to perform tasks with greater independence. Consider one of her most positive experiences: After much work with an extremely aggressive student, Kim's behaviorally based intervention program reduced the frequency and intensity of problematic behaviors to levels that now allow the student to work in a sheltered

workshop with coaching. Kim gets frustrated with teachers and administrators who do not adhere to a student's individualized education program as well as educators who do not recognize the importance of developing relationships with their students. The only part of her job that she doesn't like is dealing with the politics and actions of people who do not understand special education.

Kim has some advice for people who are thinking of a career spent teaching students with ASD: Make sure that this is something you really want to do. As Kim knows firsthand, working with students with disabilities is not easy and is often physically exhausting. However, the opportunity to make a difference in a child's life makes all of the hard work worthwhile. Kim believes that, to be successful, a teacher must remain patient, positive, and enthusiastic; have high expectations for students; and make every effort to assist students to believe in themselves.

**Autism spectrum disorders (ASD)**, also known as pervasive developmental disabilities (PDD), are among the most mysterious and vexing of the disabilities that teachers encounter. Very little is known about these disabilities, not the least of which is what causes them and how best to overcome them. Many children with ASD appear to be in a world of their own, often exhibiting extreme behaviors and facial expressions that separate them from activities, events, and interactions that enrich everyone's lives. Often, people who are close to children with ASD look for cures and quick fixes, seeking a dramatic lift from the apparent social isolation. However, as teachers like Kim Thomas observe every day, ASD are lifelong, all-encompassing conditions that involve difficulties in social interaction skills, deficiencies in communication skills, and the presence of extreme and rigid interests and behaviors (American Psychiatric Association, 2000; Heflin & Alaimo, 2007).

Interestingly, the number of children who are being identified with ASD (most often **autistic disorder** and **Asperger's disorder**) is increasing greatly. Not coincidentally, interest in these children has also grown: They are now the subjects of television features, stories in the popular press, and even Academy Award–winning films. Although such attention raises awareness of the intensive needs of these children, it can also create and reinforce mistaken stereotypes. Therefore, as we discuss these disabilities, keep in mind that the spectrum of behaviors that characterize ASD is wide and variable. For example, a rare few individuals with ASD are **savants** who display special talents such as being able to calculate complex equations in their heads (like the character Raymond in the film *Rain Man*) or re-create intricate melodies on musical instruments with little or no practice. Most people who have ASD have no unusual talents but do exhibit limited eye contact and repetitive hand movements. As with other children and youth, those with ASD are ever-changing individuals whose behaviors evolve in unique ways over time. As you read this chapter, keep in mind that behaviors associated with ASD exist on a continuum, from so-called "lower" functioning to "higher" functioning. For example, most students with Asperger's disorder do not have extreme delays in language, cognitive development, and acquisition of age-appropriate self-help skills, as do many of those with autistic disorder.

## DEFINITIONS AND CLASSIFICATION CRITERIA FOR STUDENTS WITH ASD

When we speak of ASD, we are referring to five clinical conditions: autistic disorder, Asperger's disorder, **Rett's disorder**, **childhood disintegrative disorder**, and **pervasive developmental disorder—not otherwise specified (PDD-NOS)** (see Table 10.1). Because autistic and Asperger's disorders are by far the most prevalent, we focus our discussion on these two conditions.

### Autistic Disorder

Autistic disorder, routinely referred to simply as *autism,* is a severe developmental disability characterized by an early age of onset, poor social development, impairments in language development, and rigidity in behavior (Heflin & Alaimo, 2007; Phelps & Grabowski, 1991). Leo Kanner initially identified autism as a distinct diagnostic category in 1943. In his classic paper, "Autistic Disturbances of Affective Content," he presented detailed descriptions of 11 children "whose condition differs so markedly and uniquely from anything reported so far, that each case merits . . . a detailed consideration of its fascinating peculiarities" (Kanner, 1943, p. 217).

As with many other cognitive disabilities, clinicians rely on the definitions in the DSM-IV-TR (American Psychiatric Association, 2000) to identify autistic disorder

## FAQ Sheet

### STUDENTS WITH ASD

| | |
|---|---|
| Who are they? | • Individuals with ASD have pervasive, lifelong difficulties in social interaction skills and deficiencies in communication skills as well as extreme and rigid interests and behaviors. |
| What are typical characteristics? | • Low rates of eye contact, or gaze, to others<br>• Lack of attention to multiple dimensions of a task (joint attention)<br>• Restricted range of interests<br>• Stereotypical and repetitive movements and behaviors<br>• Social isolation<br>• Limited receptive and expressive language skills<br>• Difficulties in understanding their own and others' behaviors and emotions |
| What are the demographics? | • Estimates range from a low of 2 cases per 10,000 persons to a high of 67 per 10,000 children.<br>• Approximately 225,000 children receive special education services under the IDEA autism classification, a 500% increase in the past 10 years.<br>• Four times as many boys as girls are identified. |
| Where are students educated? | • General education classrooms<br>• Specialized programs in public or private schools<br>• Residential programs |
| How are students identified and assessed for intervention? | • Common methods for screening and identification include rating scales, observation protocols, and semi-structured interviews.<br>• Transdisciplinary functional behavioral assessments provide information for instructional and behavioral planning. |
| What are the outcomes? | • The course of the disability is lifelong and chronic, and most people have ongoing problems with social aspects of life, jobs, and independence.<br>• Success depends on early intervention, the quality and stability of the network of supports, the person's cognitive ability, and symptom severity. |

**TABLE 10.1** • THE FIVE TYPES OF ASD

| Type | Definition |
|---|---|
| **Autistic disorder** | Severe developmental disability characterized by an early age of onset, poor social development, impairments in language development, and rigidity in behavior |
| **Asperger's disorder** | Sustained and often lifelong impairments in social interactions and the development of restricted, repetitive patterns of behavior, interests, and activities |
| **Rett's disorder** | Following typical development during first year of life, a genetic deficit, almost exclusively affecting girls; characterized by rapid deterioration of behavior, language, and purposeful hand movements as well as mental retardation and seizures |
| **Childhood disintegrative disorder** | A rare condition in which a typically developing 3- to 15-year-old child experiences a rapid loss of language, social, motor, and toileting skills |
| **Pervasive developmental disorder—not otherwise specified (PDD-NOS)** | A vague designation used to describe children who resemble those with autistic disorder or Asperger's disorder but differ in a diagnostically significant way (e.g., age of onset) |

Source: Adapted from Towbin, Mauk, & Batshaw, 2002; Van Acker, Loncola, & Van Acker, 2005; and Volkmar & Klin, 2005.

FIGURE 10.1 • **DSM-IV-TR**

**Diagnostic criteria for 299.00 Autistic Disorder**
A.  A total of six (or more) items from (1), (2), and (3), with at least two from (1), and one each from (2) and (3):
  (1) qualitative impairment in social interaction, as manifested by at least two of the following:
    (a) marked impairment in the use of multiple nonverbal behaviors such as eye-to-eye gaze, facial expression, body postures, and gestures to regulate social interaction
    (b) failure to develop peer relationships appropriate to developmental level
    (c) a lack of spontaneous seeking to share enjoyment, interests, or achievements with other people (e.g., by a lack of showing, bringing, or pointing out objects of interest)
    (d) lack of social or emotional reciprocity
  (2) qualitative impairments in communication as manifested by at least one of the following:
    (a) delay in, or total lack of, the development of spoken language (not accompanied by an attempt to compensate through alternative modes of communication such as gesture or mime)
    (b) in individuals with adequate speech, marked impairment in the ability to initiate or sustain a conversation with others
    (c) stereotyped and repetitive use of language or idiosyncratic language
    (d) lack of varied, spontaneous make-believe play or social imitative play appropriate to developmental level
  (3) restricted repetitive and stereotyped patterns of behavior, interests, and activities, as manifested by at least one of the following:
    (a) encompassing preoccupation with one or more stereotyped and restricted patterns of interest that is abnormal either in intensity or focus
    (b) apparently inflexible adherence to specific, nonfunctional routines or rituals
    (c) stereotyped and repetitive motor mannerisms (e.g., hand or finger flapping or twisting, or complex whole-body movements)
    (d) persistent preoccupation with parts of objects
B.  Delays or abnormal functioning in at least one of the following areas, with onset prior to age 3 years: (1) social interaction, (2) language as used in social communication, or (3) symbolic or imaginative play.
C.  The disturbance is not better accounted for by Rett's Disorder or Childhood Disintegrative Disorder.

Source: Reprinted with permission from the *Diagnostic and Statistical Manual of Mental Disorders,* Fourth Edition, Text Revision (Copyright 2000). American Psychiatric Association.

(Towbin et al., 2002). As Figure 10.1 illustrates, the diagnostic criteria that define the disorder include markedly abnormal or impaired development in social interaction and communication as well as rigidity in activities and interests. The definition and classification of autism, as it relates to eligibility for special education services, has changed. Earlier iterations of IDEA included it with physical and other health impairments (Rosenberg, Wilson, Maheady, & Sindelar, 2004). In more recent reauthorizations, autism received a category of its own and is defined as

> a developmental disability significantly affecting verbal and nonverbal communication and social interaction, generally evident before age 3, that adversely affects a child's educational performance. Other characteristics often associated with autism are engagement in repetitive activities and stereotyped movements, resistance to environmental change or change in daily routines, and unusual responses to sensory experiences. The term does not apply if a child's educational performance is adversely affected primarily because the child has an emotional disturbance. (34 C.F.R., Part 300.7[c] [1][i][1997])

## Asperger's Disorder

Asperger's disorder is characterized by severe, sustained, and often lifelong impairments in social interactions and the development of restricted, repetitive patterns of behavior, interests, and activities (American Psychiatric Association, 2000). If you detect that these descriptors resemble those that define autism, you are correct. The presenting behaviors of Asperger's disorder are similar to high-functioning autism, except that people with Asperger's do not have the same intensity of impairment in language, cognition, and self-help skills. Hans Asperger, an Austrian pediatrician, documented the disorder one year after Kanner (1943) described autism. Although his research was based on investigations of more than 400 children, Asperger's efforts received little attention due to the difficulties of sharing information across borders during World War II. Today, Asperger's disorder is widely known, in large part because of its increased prevalence (Smith-Myles & Simpson, 2001).

Although specific diagnostic criteria continue to be debated, Asperger's disorder is defined as a disability characterized by a qualitative impairment in social interaction as well as restricted behavior patterns. Other criteria are an absence of clinically significant delays in (1) language development, (2) cognitive development or the development of age-appropriate adaptive behavior (other than social interaction), and (3) self-help skills. The final criterion is a failure to meet the diagnostic criteria for **schizophrenia** and other ASDs.

**PEARSON myeducationlab**

Go to the Assignments and Activities section of Topic 13: Autism in the MyEducationLab for your course and complete the activities entitled *Characteristics of Autism Spectrum Disorders* and *Behavioral Characteristics of Students with Autism Spectrum Disorders.*

## PRIMARY BEHAVIOR CHARACTERISTICS OF ASD

Three categories of characteristics are universal and specific to ASD: (1) impairments in social reciprocity; (2) deficiencies in communication skills; and (3) repetitive, stereotypical, and ritualistic behaviors. By *universal* and *specific,* we mean that these behaviors are found in nearly all youngsters with ASD and are relatively infrequent in children who do not have the disability (Rutter, 1978).

### Impairments in Social Reciprocity

When we speak of **social reciprocity**, we are referring to the complex, multifaceted process of interacting with another person. Consider what is involved in this process: Simultaneous and instantaneous awareness of one's own interests and state of mind as well as a "reading" of the emotions and motives of others. Reciprocity involves having a degree of social perception—being able to understand and act upon the verbal nuances and nonverbal cues expressed by another person.

Because of their reduced ability to understand or make use of the basic implicit rules that govern social exchanges, children and adolescents with ASD do not usually experience success in social situations (American Psychiatric Association, 2000; White, Keonig, & Scahill, 2007). These implicit rules are unwritten and unstated, yet they wield considerable influence on speech, gesture, posture, movement, eye contact, choice of clothing, proximity to others, and many other aspects of behavior (Wing, 1981). How does the absence of these implied yet expected social behaviors appear to family, teachers, and peers? Infants with autistic disorder do not respond to familiar faces with a warm, social smile and exhibit little pleasure in the presence of their parents. Even when they age, children with autistic disorder appear aloof, do not turn to their parents when hurt, and rarely engage in affectionate activities like a good-night hug and kiss. The children avoid direct eye contact, and they do not attain

Children with ASD have problems communicating and are often left out of social activities.

many of the usual developmental benchmarks such as friendships, play, and expressions of empathy (Rutter, 1978).

For people with Asperger's disorder, problems in socialization are less severe yet still problematic. Students with Asperger's disorder engage others socially, but the quality of their interactions tends to be awkward, one-sided, and filled with contextually inappropriate verbalizations (Linn & Smith-Myles, 2004; Paul, Orlovski, Marcinko, & Volkmar, 2009). Rather than feeling engaged in meaningful dialogue, adults and peers interacting with students with Asperger's disorder sense that they are objects being talked at in blunt, rote fashion, with little attention given to their needs or input. This rigidity is also evident in the application of social skills. Unlike most students who can gauge the utility of social rules in specific situations, students with Asperger's disorder often apply rules to all situations uniformly, regardless of settings and people involved (e.g., tattling on a student who mutters a bad word under his breath when striking out during a playground ball game). Consequently, family members and peers characterize people with Asperger's disorder as lacking common sense and being unaware of the subtle unspoken messages typical of social interactions (Smith-Myles & Simpson, 2001).

As a result of failing to consider **situational specificity** (adjusting behavior to conform to varying circumstances) and to comprehend verbal and nonverbal nuances associated with social interaction, the individual with Asperger's can become a target of ridicule and be distanced from peers. Most unfortunate is that in the face of repeated unsatisfactory interactions, students with Asperger's disorder fail to recognize their odd missteps and persist in their awkward, rigid, self-centered, and emotionally blunted modes of social engagement (American Psychiatric Association, 2000; Sigman & Capps, 1997; Tager-Flusberg, Paul, & Lord, 2005).

## Deficiencies in Communication Skills

Deficits in communication skills are characteristic of all students with ASD, although, like deficits in social reciprocity, levels of severity vary considerably. For those with autistic disorder, impairments in communication skills are pervasive, involving most aspects of expressive and receptive language development. Approximately 50% of those with autistic disorder fail to acquire **functional language;** many, like Kim Thomas's students, are nonverbal or suffer **echolalia**, a response in which all or part of what is heard is repeated. Those who do speak often use speech in a monotonous tone accompanied by unusual pitch, rhythm, and syntax. Students with autistic disorder typically do not use speech for social communication. Consequently, their gestures, body movements, and eye contact are infrequent; and their verbalizations tend to be overly literal, filled with reversals, and lacking in abstract, metaphorical terms. Students with autistic disorder also have problems understanding spoken language. This is likely the result of their inability to process nonverbal cues when encountering verbal input.

For people with Asperger's disorder, deficits in communication are not as severe. Most have difficulty, however, in comprehending and making use of **figurative language**—idioms, metaphors, analogies, slang, and jokes that enhance and add emotion to communication. How important is figurative language? Review the examples of figurative language in Table 10.2, and consider how often figurative language is used in the media and during daily interactions with others.

As you have probably noted, the use of figurative language pervades most aspects of our lives. When people with Asperger's disorder encounter figurative phrases, they interpret words literally and have difficulty deciphering the communicative intent of the message. Along with difficulties in reading faces and understanding the interplay of voice (e.g., rhythm, intonation, stress, volume, and cadence), these students suffer other consequences from misunderstanding figurative language, especially when an immediate understanding of another person's

| To... | Josh Peters, District Behavior Specialist |
| --- | --- |
| From... | Ada Kadinsky, Middle School Science Teacher |
| Subject: | Social supports for students with Asperger's disorder |

Dear Josh,

I hope you can help me with this challenging and frustrating situation. Alexander G., a 13-year-old student in my fourth-period biology class, continues to be the brunt of jokes and pranks among his peers. As you know, Alex is an A student who tends to be a popular partner when monthly group-lab assignments are due. Unfortunately, Alexander seems to be unaware that some students are tricking him into behaving in ways that violate typical rules of social functioning. For example, his male "friends" convinced him to compliment several of the girls in his class on certain aspects of their physical appearance and then touch them, words and actions that were unusual and bordered on sexual harassment. Moreover, they baited him repeatedly into speaking of personal family matters that are best left private. Alex is a nice kid who enjoys attention and wants to make and keep friends. Nonetheless, he doesn't understand much of his peers' slang and sarcasm and will act out when he is overwhelmed by the stress associated with keeping up social interactions. He wants so much to please his peers, many of whom don't always have his best interests at heart. What can I do to help Alexander?

—Ada

---

To: Ada Kadinsky
From: Josh Peters
Subject: RE: Social supports for students with Asperger's disorder

Dear Ada,

The situation you describe is one of the major challenges facing students with Asperger's disorder who are included in general education settings: difficulty in understanding the hidden or implicit rules that govern social interactions. Here are some techniques (e.g., Safran, 2002; Smith-Myles & Simpson, 2001) that should help Alex deal with his peers and succeed in your classroom:

- Carefully structure group work and seating arrangements. Since Alex, like many other students with Asperger's, is an easy victim of pranks and bullies, place him with understanding peers who are willing to serve as social translators.

- Establish safe-haven procedures. During times of extreme anxiety, allow Alex to decompress in a private area or make use of a previously designated support person (either another adult or a trusted peer).

- Help Alex save himself. Come up with a way—perhaps a signal—to prompt Alex when his verbalizations and behaviors border on the inappropriate; peer "social translators" can help Alex interpret his social actions.

- Provide accommodations and supports. A "power card," just one type of visual support, can prompt Alex to stop, think, and reflect on elements of social interactions.

- Promote positive peer interactions. Use creative ways to promote productive conversations between Alex and his peers without disabilities. Particularly useful are discussions of hidden social agendas and what people may be thinking during social interactions.

You can get more information on how to address the social needs of students with Asperger's from the following resources:

Safran, J. S. (2002). Supporting students with Asperger's syndrome in general education. *Teaching Exceptional Children, 34,* 61–65.

Smith-Myles, B., & Simpson, R. L. (2001). Effective practices for students with Asperger's syndrome. *Focus on Exceptional Children, 34,* 1–16.

Hope this helps.

Josh

**EXTEND AND APPLY**

- Develop an instructional activity that will allow a student with Asperger's disorder to explore critical components of implicit social behavior.
- What aspects of the "hidden social curriculum" would you prioritize?
- How could you motivate students without disabilities to participate in these activities?
- How would you assess the impact and effectiveness of these activities?

**TABLE 10.2 • EXAMPLES OF FIGURATIVE LANGUAGE**

| Form | Definition | Example | Meaning |
|------|-----------|---------|---------|
| **Idiom** | An expression whose meaning cannot be understood by analyzing its elements | A fine kettle of fish | A real mess; a really bad situation |
| **Simile** | An expression that compares two unlike things | As brave as a lion | To be brave |
| **Metaphor** | An expression that takes the attributes of one thing and transfers them to another in an implicit manner | To possess ideas is to gather flowers; to think is to weave them into garlands. | Thinking is composed of many ideas, just as a garland is woven from many flowers. |
| **Allusion** | Referring to a related thing or situation that requires prior knowledge | Pandora's box | A source of many problems, troubles |
| **Analogy** | A comparison of a like characteristic of two different things, generally one known and one less known | Food is to farming as laughing is to joking. | A person farms to produce food just as she tells jokes to produce laughter. |
| **Understatement** | An expression that intentionally deemphasizes a thing in order to emphasize it | Hitler was not a nice person. | Of course |
| **Hyperbole** | An exaggeration or extravagant overstatement | I could eat a horse. | I could eat a lot. |
| **Oxymoron** | A figure of speech that combines two terms that normally contradict each other | Deafening silence | Complete silence |
| **Slang** | Language used by particular social groups to exclude others from the conversation; words may be standard but with encrypted meanings or may be unique | Fly right | To be honest and dependable |

motives and intentions is required. Impairments in communication are also evident when these individuals try to express themselves. Words and phrases are typically enunciated in an odd, robotic fashion accompanied by a limited range of gestures, facial expressions, and eye movements.

## Repetitive, Stereotypical, and Ritualistic Behaviors

The most obvious behaviors observed among individuals with ASD are the repetitive, stereotypical, and ritualistic actions that typically interfere with everyday activities. Several of the more extreme motor behaviors—rocking, spinning, arm flapping, and finger flicking—are high-frequency actions typical of those with the most severe manifestations of the disability. Along with an unusual fascination with innocuous objects, people with ASD bring a rigidity and seemingly obsessive consistency to their actions. For example, while other children often have favorite dolls or blankets, students with autistic disorder may cling to pieces of string, repeatedly flush a toilet, or spend hours lining up toys in a carefully designed, elaborate pattern. Although less extreme, people with Asperger's disorder present their own unusual forms of ritualistic behavior (American Psychiatric Association, 2000). Many have intense interests in weather systems, maps, or the telephone book as well as schedules for trains, airlines, and television shows (Loveland & Tunali-Kotoski, 2005). Teachers report that it is not unusual for such students to be preoccupied with obscure dialogue from movies and television shows and to be extremely anxious and upset when daily routines are changed due to unforeseen circumstances.

Many of the ritualistic and repetitive actions appear to be unpredictable, with little purpose. However, researchers suspect that these behaviors fulfill a specific need for people with ASD. Early theorists speculated that the ritualistic and repetitive behaviors were attempts to control episodes of **generalized anxiety** (Bettelheim, 1967; Kanner, 1943). More recently, researchers have hypothesized that the behaviors are mini-experiments conducted by the individual to figure out cause-and-effect relationships in the environment (Baron-Cohen, 2005). These behaviors also may serve a range of functions that are specific to an individual, perhaps satisfying the person's perceived needs for attention, to engage in a particular activity, or to escape or avoid an unpleasant situation or task demand (Kennedy, Meyer, Knowles, & Shukla, 2000). As such, teachers need to be aware of how environmental events can influence the development, frequency, and intensity of repetitive and ritualistic behaviors.

# SECONDARY BEHAVIORAL CORRELATES

Recall that when we speak of secondary behavioral correlates, we are referring to those characteristics that often occur in conjunction with the primary characteristics of a disability. Regarding ASD, three factors—age of onset, intellectual functioning, and self-injurious behavior—are of particular interest to teachers.

## Age of Onset

For a diagnosis of autistic disorder, evidence of its universal and specific characteristics must be present before a child reaches 3 years of age. Parents generally report concerns when their child is between 15 and 22 months of age, usually because of a lack of speech and the emergence of ritualistic and repetitive behaviors. However, retrospective videotape analysis studies have found that infants with autism can be distinguished from typical children as early as 6 to 8 months of age (Chawarska & Volkmar, 2005; Robins, Fein, Barton, & Green, 2001). Compared to their age mates, infants with autistic disorder exhibit diminished visual attention to people, are less likely to have early social communicative exchanges, and tend not to respond differentially to personal verbalizations such as the sound of their own names.

## REFLECTIVE EXERCISE

# 2 Hyperbole, idioms, and metaphors are essential elements of satisfying social interactions. Try describing a favorite sports or entertainment event or a memorable meal without using abstract or figurative language.

## REFLECTIVE EXERCISE

# 3 What would be your course of action to determine the functions of repetitive, stereotypical, and ritualistic behaviors?

REFLECTIVE EXERCISE

#4 Why does it take so long to identify students with Asperger's disorder? Are there behavioral characteristics that parents and teachers can look for to secure early diagnosis and intervention?

Compared to autistic disorder, Asperger's disorder tends to be diagnosed at a later age. Because most children with the disorder do not have clinically significant delays in language acquisition, cognitive development, or self-help skills, differences in functioning are not apparent until the child is in social situations with peers. In fact, compared to most children with autistic disorder who have diagnosis confirmed by about 5 years of age, children with Asperger's disorder are not typically diagnosed until they are 11 years of age (Howlin & Asgharian, 1999).

## Variable Intellectual Functioning

Although most children with ASD have below-average IQ scores, their measured intelligence ranges from superior to profound mental retardation (American Psychiatric Association, 2000). Historically, estimates of intelligence of children with ASD indicated that only 15% to 30% of those with the disability had IQ scores outside the range of intellectual impairment, a score of 70 or above. But measures of the intelligence of children with ASD have changed over time, and it appears that 38% to 48% have scores outside the intellectual impairment range. Consider two explanations for this change. First, the number of students with Asperger's disorder and higher-functioning autism included in epidemiological studies of those with ASD has increased sharply (e.g., Autism Information Center, 2009). Although these students have difficulty comprehending abstract materials, they typically have average intellectual abilities. Second, the increases in IQ scores may be a function of the increased frequency of beneficial early intervention efforts provided to students with ASD. Comprehensive and intensive programs have resulted in important positive outcomes in cognitive areas assessed by intelligence tests. For example, in an evaluation of a preschool educational and behavioral program, children with high-functioning autism had increases in IQ scores by approximately 19 points after 1 year of participation (Harris, Handleman, Gordon, Kristoff, & Fuentes, 1991).

Keep in mind that increases in IQ scores do not mean that other challenging characteristics of ASD are no longer present. Increases in measured intelligence do not usually result in corresponding gains in adaptive skills and improvements in the social use of language. However, students with higher IQ scores are less likely to exhibit (1) gross deficits in social interaction and emotional expression; (2) inappropriate play; (3) self-injurious behavior; and (4) delays in motor and language development (Yirmiya, Sigman, Kasari, & Mundy, 1992).

## Self-Injurious Behavior

**Self-injurious behavior (SIB)** is self-directed aggression manifested by severe head banging, punching, scratching, and/or biting. More common in children with autistic disorder than those with Asperger's disorder, SIB can result in serious injury and, needless to say, elicit extreme levels of stress among those who love and care for these children. Not surprisingly, elimination of these behaviors is a priority for families and educators. In addition to the obvious health issues, self-injury precludes placement in the least restrictive environment and limits access to most learning, working, and leisure opportunities (Symons, 1995). Keep in mind that SIB is not universal and specific to individuals with ASD. Approximately 10% to 20% of those with the disability do display it; however, a sizable proportion of individuals with severe developmental disabilities and psychiatric conditions also engage in these behaviors (Rosenberg et al., 2004).

Why would a person engage in behaviors that inflict pain and suffering on himself or herself? Intuition, common sense, and what we know about typical functions of behavior dictate that most people go to great lengths to avoid unpleasant physical stimuli. Although researchers have developed theories regarding the development and maintenance of self-injury, no definitive explanations have been made. For example, from the biophysical perspective, SIB is believed to be a function of abnormal physiological development or impaired biological functioning (Filipek, 2005). The psychodynamic perspective views SIB as the result of experiences in infancy and early childhood, when the child's attempts to reach out to others were blocked or frustrated. The child avoids danger by retreating from reality, not using language common to others, and refusing to react, preferring instead to turn aggression inward (Bettelheim, 1967; Bloch, 1978). Finally, from the behavioral perspective, SIB is believed to be a learned response reinforced by positive and/or negative stimuli. Examples of positive reinforcement include others' attention and sensory gain; negative reinforcement takes the form of escape from demands or situations the individual with autism wishes to avoid.

For teachers, the behavioral theory is most useful. Considerable evidence shows that interventions based on functional assessment or functional analysis of behaviors can reduce self-injury, and many behaviorally based techniques and programs have been developed to do so (Rosenberg et al., 2004).

# PREVALENCE, COURSE OF DISABILITY, AND CAUSAL FACTORS

## How Many Students Have ASD?

Determining the number of students with ASD is controversial and unfortunately inconclusive. Some have suggested that we are in the midst of an autism epidemic. According to the DSM-IV-TR (American Psychiatric Association, 2000), the prevalence of autistic disorder ranges from 2 to 20 cases per 10,000 persons. However, recent epidemiological data suggest that the prevalence of ASD is many times higher than rates reported in the 1980s and early 1990s, a considerable 34 to 67 per 10,000 children (Autism Information Center, 2009; National Alliance for Autism Research, 2005; Yeargin-Allsopp et al., 2003).

Are these sharp differences over time a function of some environmental threat, vaccine, or genetic agent, or can they be explained by methodological factors associated with the nature of the studies? Issues surrounding the increased prevalence rates remain controversial, and no one is certain of the cause or causes. Nonetheless, several factors need to be considered when comparing prevalence rates of ASD over time. First, recent measures of prevalence have included all forms of ASD (e.g., Asperger's disorder), while previous studies employed a more narrow definition of autism. Second, in the past many students, because of their low IQ scores, were identified as having intellectual impairments. Currently, as a result of improved diagnostic systems and the increased competence of professionals who use them, many of these students are identified correctly as having ASD (Fombonne, 2003). Finally, as public awareness of ASD increases, parents and clinicians are probably looking earlier and more intensively for signs of the disability.

Consider other useful demographic information (Volkmar, Szatmari, & Sparrow, 1993; Yeargin-Allsopp et al., 2003): ASD occurs throughout the world and affects males four times more often than females. Unlike several other disabilities in which certain racial groups are overrepresented, prevalence rates among African American and White students are comparable. Finally, if a family already has one child with autism, they have a 5% to 10% chance that they will have another with ASD.

## Course of ASD

Although the course of ASD is lifelong and chronic, outcomes vary depending on the level of severity of the disability. For example, the prognosis for students with autistic disorder is bleak. Identification of problems occurs in early childhood, and specialized treatments and supports are required through childhood and adolescence. Only a small percentage of people with autistic disorder can transition to work and living situations without support. Approximately one third of those with the disability can sustain some level of supported or partial independence, and a full two thirds remain severely disabled and fail to develop independent living skills (American Psychiatric Association, 2000). Follow-up studies of people with the disability indicate that most have ongoing problems with social aspects of life, jobs, and independence (Howlin, Mawhood, & Rutter, 2000; Lotter, 1978). Those who achieve appropriate levels of adjustment and maintain the greatest amount of independence tend to have intelligence levels that are above the intellectual impairment range and have developed functional language skills.

Because they do not have significant delays in cognitive or language development, people with Asperger's disorder tend to have better outcomes than those with autistic disorder. Although many experience socialization and behavioral adjustment problems during their school years, many adults with Asperger's disorder obtain jobs that are related to their interests. Some students with the disability successfully complete college and pursue graduate studies. Still, their social problems persist: Rigidity, awkwardness, self-centeredness, and emotionally dulled social engagement continue to make interactions with others difficult. Not surprisingly, many require the services of mental health providers for depression and anxiety (Shea & Mesibov, 2005).

## Causal Factors

One of the many frustrations associated with the study and treatment of ASD is that we don't know for certain what causes these disorders. What is clear, however, is that the disabilities are probably the product of one or more nature-based factors such as genetic, neurochemical, and neurobiological abnormalities (Towbin et al., 2002). Nonetheless, nurture-based explanations from both behavioral and psychodynamic perspectives have also been forwarded as factors that contribute to the development and maintenance of ASD.

### Nature-Based Factors

Increasingly, genetic influences are viewed as major contributors to the development of ASD. Studies on the occurrence of autism in twins and the presence of ASD-like behaviors in families suggest that a strong heritability of the traits is associated with the entire autism spectrum (Gillberg & Cederlund, 2005; Segal, 2005). Unfortunately, the specific genes susceptible to ASD have not been identified (Hu-Lince, Craig, Huentelman, & Stephan, 2005).

From the neurochemical perspective, abnormally high and low levels of certain chemicals in the brain and central nervous system have been linked to ASD. In particular, researchers have found elevated levels of serotonin—an amino acid–based neurotransmitter that most likely contributes to the regulation of sleep, appetite, and mood—in a significant percentage of children with autistic disorder (Anderson & Hoshino, 2005). Irregular serotonin levels are associated with other conditions such as depression, anxiety, and obsessive-compulsive disorder. ASD has also been linked to certain physical aspects of brain development. The brains of some children with autistic disorder are larger and heavier than those of individuals without disabilities (Redcav & Courchesne, 2005). Moreover, research using magnetic resonance imaging has found structural irregularities in sections of these brains that are responsible for language, facial recognition, and social cognition (Akshoomoff, Pierce, & Courchesne, 2002). The reasons for these structural problems remain the subject of considerable inquiry and speculation.

## Nurture-Based Factors

Consider the feelings expressed by Catherine Maurice (1993), a parent of a child with ASD, in her memoir *Let Me Hear Your Voice:*

> It was I who had created this nightmare. I was sure of it. Either I had made Anne-Marie autistic by not giving her enough attention, or I had made everyone believe she was autistic by reading about it and talking about it too much. (p. 28)

Clearly, parents do not "cause" autism by their actions toward their child or by the child's perception of parental behavior. Nonetheless, you should be aware that parents of children with ASD question themselves regularly, from their selection of diet and lifestyle choices to their spirituality, the locations of their homes, and the vaccinations of their children.

Be aware that damaging generalizations of parent causality persist. Several prominent psychologists from both the psychodynamic and behavioral models have hypothesized that parents of children with ASD contribute to the development and maintenance of the disability (Rosenberg et al., 2004). Although these models are now dismissed as being misguided, fraudulent, and malicious, Bruno Bettelheim, for example, a Freudian psychiatrist, claimed that autism was a child's response to extreme parental rejection. Based on initial positive responses to his book, *The Empty Fortress,* in 1967, generations of devastated mothers—actually referred to as "refrigerator mothers"—doubted their ability to bond with their children. Although Bettelheim's view has been disproved, it remains shocking that it took decades for the psychiatric community to disavow the counterproductive theory of maternal blame.

Interestingly, parent unresponsiveness is also part of the behavioral explanation of ASD. According to Ferster (1961), the child with autism fails to develop communicative language and appropriate social behaviors because early, unsophisticated attempts at such behaviors are not reinforced. Because parents either ignore or respond only intermittently to appropriate behavior, initial attempts of **prosocial behaviors** are extinguished, and the foundation for more complex skills do not have the opportunity to develop adequately. To secure the attention of others, the child engages in increasingly bizarre behaviors. The result is that the attention actually serves to increase the frequency and intensity of the inappropriate behaviors. What are we to make of this seemingly logical explanation of ASD? Clearly, consideration of reinforcement contingencies when designing intervention strategies is essential. However, Ferster's use of basic stimulus–response explanations as an explanation for this pervasive spectrum of behaviors is a misguided overgeneralization of behavioral principles. More important, it is counterproductive for enlisting the essential support of parents and other primary caregivers.

What do these misguided speculations mean for teachers? The most important implications for the educator regarding knowledge of possible causal factors is realizing that (1) the student with ASD is not being obstinate when displaying behaviors of concern; (2) the parents and family members are not to be blamed; and (3) regardless of causal factors, students can make great strides in their education when presented with effective research-based practices.

## REFLECTIVE EXERCISE

#5 What are the ramifications of theories that implicate parents in the cause of their children's disabilities? How can such theories influence the outcomes of early intervention efforts that rely on intensive family involvement?

Rather than focus on misguided generalizations surrounding parental causality of ASD, it is more productive for teachers to secure parental support and involvement in home–school partnerships.

# IDENTIFICATION AND ASSESSMENT

Because ASD is pervasive across developmental domains, identification and assessment require measurement of functioning across disciplines, including pediatrics, neurology, psychiatry, speech-language, and education. These processes are comprehensive and require time and collaboration among health-care and educational professionals as well as families (Towbin et al., 2002). Numerous diagnostic instruments and clinical protocols have been developed to help determine the existence of ASD, its impact on functioning, and how best to treat aspects of the disability. Recall that identification and assessment of students suspected of having a disability typically follows a three-step process: screening, identification, and instructional/behavioral planning.

## Screening

When **screening** for ASD, we are determining if a child has the broad set of behavioral characteristics suggesting risk for the disability. Quite simply, the purpose of screening for ASD is to identify children who require further evaluation. The process requires less time, training, and experience to administer, and the results of screening indicate levels of risk rather than a specific diagnosis. Nonetheless, screening for ASD is critical. Although elements of the disability can be seen in children as young as 18 to 24 months, children who are not diagnosed or treated until they are older—and there are far too many—lose valuable early intervention opportunities (Coonrod & Stone, 2005).

Coonrod and Stone (2005) have outlined two approaches for screening young children for ASD: nonspecific and autism-specific. Nonspecific approaches screen for deficits in a wide range of developmental areas, including language, behavior, cognitive skills, and motor skills as well as social and self-help skills. Because children suspected of having ASD present deficits in some of these areas, they will be identified as at risk. Examples of nonspecific screening instruments include the Ages and Stages Questionnaire (ASQ) (Bricker & Squires, 1999) and the Brigance Diagnostic Inventory of Early Development (Brigance, 1991). Autism-specific screening devices specifically target symptoms of ASD and include the Checklist for Autism in Toddlers (CHAT) (Baird et al., 2000) and the Modified Checklist for Autism in Toddlers (M-CHAT) (Robins et al., 2001). Each of these nonspecific and specific instruments includes questionnaires (which parents or teachers fill out); interview protocols; observational rating scales; and scales that measure specific areas of functioning.

## Identification

Children screened as possibly having ASD are referred to multidisciplinary or child-study teams for more intensive evaluation. Typically, these teams include a physician with expertise in ASD, a developmental psychologist, a speech–language specialist, a social worker, and an educator. The content of the clinical evaluation should include a psychological evaluation and a developmental history of the child; tests of hearing, speech, language, and communication; intelligence testing; medical and neurological exams; and an evaluation of current family functioning (Klin, McPartland, & Volkmar, 2005; Towbin et al., 2002). Evaluators should take care to ensure that indicators of performance are assessed over time and in a cross-section of settings.

Multidisciplinary teams commonly use four classes of standardized measures in determining the presence of ASD. **Core deficit scales** focus on individual, specific deficit areas associated with ASD (e.g., social responsiveness, language, affect, and cognition), allowing for precise assessment of symptoms and functioning. **Autism rating scales** combine the many elements of ASD into a single instrument and use cutoff scores to signal the probability of the disability. **Diagnostic interviews** are semi-structured narrative methods of gaining information from families and caregivers regarding patterns of development and needs of individuals with ASD. Finally, **direct**

**observation scales** provide a structure for observing the social and communicative behaviors of people suspected of having ASD.

Most available instruments are intended for use with children suspected of having autistic disorder. A great need remains to develop valid instrumentation and identification protocols for individuals with higher-functioning ASD such as Asperger's disorder. Currently, the lack of standardized measures along with the difficulty of defining Asperger's disorder make it critical that the assessment methodologies used for identification of the disability be as comprehensive and detailed as possible (Klin et al., 2005).

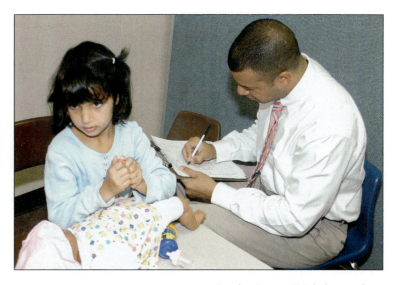

### Instructional/Behavioral Planning

The role of the teacher in measuring student performance for instructional planning is critical. Educators use information gathered from direct observations, structured data collection, and diagnostic tests to assess students' strengths and needs as well as to generate intervention plans. Because applied behavior analysis serves as the instructional foundation for most interventions, educators typically use **functional behavioral assessment (FBA)** for educational planning. As we have noted throughout this text (and detailed in Chapter 7), conducting an FBA involves three steps: (1) operationally define the behavior of interest; (2) identify events, antecedents, and consequences that may influence the behavior; and (3) develop, implement, and evaluate the effectiveness of a specific intervention plan. FBAs are conducted in the child's natural environment, integrating diagnostic information received from psychologists, speech–language therapists, and specialists in the areas of sensory and motor development.

Conducting an FBA helps teachers identify events, antecedents, and consequences that may maintain inappropriate behavior.

## EDUCATIONAL PRACTICES

Evidence-based educational practices for students with ASD range from specific instructional components and techniques to highly prescriptive comprehensive programs.

### Service Delivery

As with other students with disabilities, those with ASD should receive educational services in the least restrictive environment. For high-functioning students, such as those with Asperger's disorder, the least restrictive environment often includes inclusive programming in the general education classroom, typically with academic and behavioral supports. For those with more intensive instructional and behavior-management needs, such as Kim Thomas's students, programming is provided in more restrictive settings with supplemental opportunities for social inclusion.

What factors are considered in programming and placement decisions? According to Handleman, Harris, and Martins (2005), competence in social skills is an essential prerequisite for including students with ASD in general education classrooms. Because they are not affectionate, responsive to greetings, assertive in conversation and play, or purposeful when interacting with others, students with ASD stand out and are prone to rejection by classmates. However, meaningful contact with normally developing peers augments direct instruction in these social skills; peers serve as models of appropriate behavior and can be enlisted to initiate, prompt, and reinforce important social responses of students with ASD (Owen-DeSchryver, Carr, Cale, & Blakely-Smith, 2008).

PEARSON **myeducationlab**

Go to the Assignments and Activities section of Topic 13: Autism in the MyEducationLab for your course and complete the activity entitled *Educational Approaches for Students with Autism Spectrum Disorders*.

Positive peer actions toward students with ASD can influence the success of inclusive programming.

Do not underestimate the influence of those without disabilities on the success of inclusion efforts. Consider the results of a **naturalistic study** of 16 students with high-functioning autism included in general education classrooms (Ochs, Kremer-Sadlik, Solomon, & Sirota, 2001). The students who experienced negative experiences were in classrooms where teachers and classmates either disregarded or paid little attention to their special needs. Because their peers were not made aware of the behavioral characteristics of ASD, the included students were often scorned, rejected, or simply left alone. In sharp contrast, students with ASD who had positive inclusion experiences had nondisabled classmates who were told explicitly about their peers' special needs. Armed with this awareness, nondisabled classmates were able to clarify instructional requirements, correct inappropriate behaviors, minimize displays of certain symptoms, and include the students with ASD in social events.

A second component of successful inclusion involves academic benefit. Decisions regarding placement in the general education classroom should be based on the ability of the student with ASD to participate in academic activities with increasing independence with and without supports. Examples of participation include acquisition of new skills, generalization of acquired skills, and attention to group instructions (Simpson, de Boer-Ott, & Smith-Myles, 2003). Determining if there is a match between student and environmental characteristics requires careful observation and analysis in (1) curriculum delivery and reception; (2) environmental arrangements; (3) participation levels; (4) interaction types and amounts; and (5) attitudes of teachers, paraeducators, and peers.

## Early Intervention

Because early interventions usually result in better outcomes, they are essential (Woods & Wetherby, 2003). For students with ASD, early interventions typically focus on (1) sensory issues—helping the young child process and integrate visual, auditory, touch, gustatory, olfactory, and kinesthetic input; (2) communication skills—developing functional communication, preverbal communication, and verbalizations; and (3) social behaviors—improving attention, initiation, and response frequency. Educators most often use **applied behavior analysis (ABA)** techniques to improve young children's functioning in these areas (Howlin, Magiati, & Charman, 2009). ABA (as we have noted throughout this text and review in subsequent sections) is the application of behavior change procedures involving functional relationships among antecedent events, specific behaviors, and actions that occur after behaviors of interest.

Infants and toddlers with ASD usually receive ABA interventions at home or in school- or center-based programs (Harris & Delmolino, 2002). In addition to working directly with the child, professionals involved in the home-based approach teach parents and family members the skills necessary to enhance and maintain the benefits of the behavioral techniques. Services delivered at home have the advantage of minimized time and effort when compared with

Professionals involved in home-based early intervention help families learn the skills necessary to generalize and maintain educational improvements.

travel to a center. Most important, the effects of interventions, because they are generated in the child's natural environment, have a higher probability of generalizing across family members and home activities. Unfortunately, the expectation that family members will, with fidelity, follow up with components of interventions is not always realistic. Time constraints and competing demands contribute to this slippage.

School- or center-based programs offer the advantage of easier access to a multidisciplinary team of professionals who can work together and coordinate services in a comprehensive, or wraparound, fashion. Moreover, center-based programs give young children with ASD opportunities to interact with other children, situations that are critical for social development. Which of these approaches is best? According to Harris and Delmolino (2002), school- or center-based alternatives tend to be more cost-efficient than home-based methods because a range of specialists can see a child over the course of the day. However, when implemented properly, home-based interventions allow for the greatest intensity of treatment and generalization of benefits.

## Academic and Social/Behavioral Interventions

The intensity and complexity of the academic and social challenges faced by students with ASD require comprehensive and programmatic interventions across a range of overlapping domains. Educators typically align interventions with results of an individual student's assessment data and functional needs. However, due to the multiplicity of needs and limitation of time, educators commonly apply interventions to improve academic performance, social/behavioral functioning, and language skills simultaneously.

## Curriculum Content

### Academic Content

No one particular academic curriculum exists for students with ASD. The standard school district curriculum, assessments of students' needs, and, to some degree, common sense dictate the individualized academic program for students with autistic and Asperger's disorders (Olley, 2005). Some students with ASD learn academic skills readily, while others struggle with basic preacademic skills. Regardless of their level of functioning, students with ASD have difficulty remembering and organizing information and do not always attend to all critical elements of a task. Consequently, students with ASD require supplemental cognitive and problem-solving strategies to learn academic concepts and skills. Higher-functioning students with Asperger's disorder included in general education settings also benefit from individualized supports and accommodations (e.g., Hart & Whalon, 2008), particularly in content-rich areas that require large amounts of comprehension of verbal material and written expression. In many cases, the content-enhancement supports (e.g., graphic organizers, mnemonics, note taking, self-monitoring) are similar to those provided to students with learning disabilities. Keep in mind that strategies for teaching academics to students with ASD are similar to those that benefit students with learning disabilities and attention-deficit/hyperactivity disorder. You will find detailed information on academic supports and accommodations in the "Educational Practices" section of Chapters 6 and 9.

### Social/Behavioral Content

Instruction in social/behavioral functioning typically focuses on age-appropriate behaviors that students must learn to survive and ultimately thrive in the real world. Although instruction is individualized and based on assessed strengths and needs, lesson content typically involves daily living skills, self-care skills, functional communication skills, and those intangible social graces that enable one to be integrated into the world at large. Many students with ASD require explicit instruction in how to play with peers and, as they get older, deal with the emotions and anxiety of being "different." Typically, these students need instruction in interpretative skills such as understanding facial expressions and gestures, comprehending nonliteral figurative language (i.e., idioms and metaphors), discriminating when others' intentions do not match their words, and understanding the implicit rules of social functioning—those ways of behaving that are not acquired through direct instruction (Smith-Myles & Simpson, 2001).

### Language Content

Educators determine the content of language instruction based on the student's ability to verbalize along with his corresponding intelligence level. Students who are nonverbal may be taught to communicate through the use of pictures, symbols, communication boards, sign language, and electronic devices. Using these devices, students can press a button representing a symbol that is produced verbally. For students who are verbal, instruction often focuses on aspects of language production, including pragmatics, syntax, semantics, and articulation. *Pragmatics,* the social use of language, is the area that requires the greatest intensity of intervention for verbal, higher-functioning students with ASD. Specific instruction is typically required in recognizing the purpose of communication, speaking in a conversational manner, and understanding and being sensitive to the needs of the listener (Paul, 2005). Moreover, subtle skills such as beginning, sustaining, and ending conversations in a socially appropriate fashion are essential if students are to succeed among those without disabilities. For detailed information on the content of instruction in areas of language production, see Chapter 11.

## Instructional Methods

Educational programs commonly used for improving the academic, social, and language skills of students with ASD include **applied behavior analysis (ABA)**, **augmentative/ alternative communication (AAC)** strategies, and **social skills instruction**.

### Applied Behavior Analysis

At its most basic level, ABA is a highly structured behavior-change process that involves (1) conducting a baseline assessment of a targeted behavior, (2) implementing a behavior-change intervention, (3) collecting ongoing data on changes in the targeted behavior during intervention, (4) modifying the intervention based on the data, and (5) generalizing the effects of the intervention to untreated conditions and individuals (Arick, Krug, Fullerton, Loos, & Falco, 2005). Typically, an FBA guides the selection or development of the intervention plan.

One technique commonly employed as an intervention for students with severe ASD is discrete trial instruction (DTI). DTI is a carefully organized, deliberate, and monitored structuring of antecedent and consequent sequences designed to influence the frequency and/or intensity of a targeted behavior (Harris & Delmolino, 2002). Because it is most effective in teaching basic preacademic and receptive language skills, it is the most commonly used ABA procedure with young children with ASD. Antecedents, often referred to as discriminative stimuli, are presented, often with prompts, to elicit a specific behavior. When the child responds with the desired behavior, a consequence, usually a reinforcer, is presented to strengthen that behavior. Incorrect responses are often met with a punisher—usually a neutral "no" or a withdrawal of attention—designed to decrease the frequency and intensity of the behavior. Careful data collection allows for the monitoring of progress and, when necessary, changes in programming (e.g., providing more prompts, increasing the rate of reinforcement).

## Augmentative/Alternative Communication Strategies

Unaided and aided AAC strategies and devices can help nonverbal students with ASD learn to communicate. With unaided strategies, the communicator's own body is the means of communication; aided systems make use of supplemental tools such as picture boards and computers (Paul, 2005). Early on, sign language, an unaided system, was the mainstay of communication training. Unfortunately, too many students failed to acquire the signs, most likely due to challenges associated with teaching students with severe ASD to attend to and imitate symbols. Moreover, for many people unfamiliar with this mode of communication, little opportunity exists for practice and generalization outside clinical settings (Schreibman & Ingersoll, 2005).

Picture boards and picture-exchange procedures are iconic aided systems that require students to identify a visual representation of a desired item or activity. These are low-cost systems that enable students to rely on recognition rather than recall to receive and express common communicative functions. The **Picture Exchange Communication System (PECS)** (Frost & Bondy, 2000), one of the most commonly used symbol-exchange programs, teaches students to initiate requests by exchanging an icon for a desired object or activity. The program effectively accommodates student growth by being able to expand language functioning from merely requesting things to higher-order communication skills such as labeling and commenting (Sulzer-Azaroff, Hoffman, Horton, Bondy, & Frost, 2009).

With the growth of lower-cost digitized technology-based devices, augmentative devices that make use of synthesized speech are commonplace. **Voice output communication aids (VOCA)** are portable devices that allow messages to be accessed through graphic symbols and words on computerized displays. With the capacity to store endless combinations of spoken and written text, students have the opportunity to develop more normalized, natural interactions (National Research Council, 2001).

## Social Skills Instruction

For students with ASD who present severe deficiencies in social skills, teachers use ABA techniques to help develop important prerequisite behaviors such as functional communication skills, initiating interactions, and responding to others' attempts at engagement. For higher-functioning students with ASD, instruction focuses on interpretative social skills, the process of understanding the implicit, or hidden, rules of social functioning.

PEARSON
**myeducationlab**

Go to the Assignments and Activities section of Topic 13: Autism in the MyEducationLab for your course and complete the activity entitled *Visual Supports and Social Stories*.

Students with ASD require explicit instruction in the implicit, or hidden, rules of social functioning.

Teachers can illustrate, teach, and provide practice in interpreting the unspoken and typically untaught subtleties of implicit social functioning. Smith-Myles and Simpson (2001) suggest the following:

- **Situation-options-consequences-choices-strategies-simulation (SOCCSS).** Students explicitly interpret a difficult social interaction by identifying salient features of the situation, brainstorm response options, evaluate the options by considering consequences of each choice, select an option, develop a plan, and implement the plan in a role-play situation.
- **Cartooning.** Cartoon figures are used to illustrate everyday social encounters. The visual representation of the characters' inconsistent actions, verbalizations, and thoughts help students analyze the social exchanges.
- **Social stories and autopsies.** Social stories are short, simple narratives written from the perspective of the child. They explicitly highlight a course of action to take when encountering challenging social situations. According to the originators of the technique (Gray, 2000; Gray & Garand, 1993), the stories consist of concrete, developmentally appropriate cues, thoughts, and responses typical of targeted social situations. During instruction, students dissect social-situation errors to assess the causes and damage. Teachers and students discuss strategies to prevent errors and develop plans to minimize occurrences of the errors (Sansosti, Powell-Smith, & Kincaid, 2004).

## Comprehensive Program Models

Comprehensive program models are an efficient alternative for providing specialized educational supports to children with ASD and their families. Most programs have a unique conceptual framework that guides service delivery, employ highly trained staff applying evidence-based practices, and allow for services to be delivered in a consistent and concentrated fashion (Harris, Handleman, & Jennett, 2005). The National Research Council (NRC, 2001) has identified 10 specific comprehensive program models. Although approaches differ (some are developmentally based, others more behaviorally oriented), elements that contribute to each model's success tend to outweigh conceptual differences. Common elements among the programs identified by the NRC include

- Intervention beginning as early as possible
- Intensive amounts of intervention ranging from 20 to 45 hours per week
- Families actively involved in interventions
- Highly trained staff specializing in ASD
- Continual assessment of children's progress
- Custom-designed curriculum focusing on communication, social engagement, play, self-help, motor skills, and academics delivered in a systematic and predictable fashion
- Teaching methods that emphasize generalization and maintenance of skills
- Individualized education plans to accommodate the wide range of children's strengths and needs
- Transitions between and among programs that are planned and supported

One of the more prominent model programs is Treatment and Education of Autistic and Related Communication Handicapped Children (TEACCH), a statewide program in North Carolina that emphasizes consultation and training for parents, schools, and daycare centers (NRC, 2001). TEACCH maintains a holistic philosophy based on an understanding of the characteristics of autism, strong parent–professional collaboration, the need for individualized environmental adaptations to enhance skills, and accepting deficits in children and their parents (Gresham, Beebe-Frankenberger, & MacMillan, 1999; Schopler, 2005). The program

| To... | Dr. Alan LaRoche, Professor of Education |
|---|---|
| From... | Irene Lee, Second-Year Special Education Teacher |
| Subject: | Increasing levels of communication, interaction, and participation in a student with autistic disorder |

Dear Professor LaRoche,

I hope this e-mail finds you well and that you can help me with this challenging situation.

Owen Patel, a 10-year-old nonverbal student with autistic disorder, has been transferred to our self-contained classroom for students with moderate-to-severe disabilities. For several years, Owen had been abroad and moved frequently among schools that did little to address his special needs. We have been told that, because of his relentless acting-out behavior, Owen spent considerable time isolated from others. Moreover, his records do not mention any systematic efforts at assessing the functions of his behaviors. After a few weeks of conducting our standardized behavioral assessments, we suspect that many of Owen's inappropriate behaviors—hand flapping, tantrums, and some SIB—are the result of his inability to understand the communicative intent of others or make his needs known in an appropriate fashion. Clearly, a naturalistic, socially appropriate method of communication must be developed if Owen is to progress. Do you have any ideas on how to best accomplish this? Evidence-based protocols would be much appreciated.

Thanks in advance,

Irene

---

To:     Irene Lee
From:   Dr. Alan LaRoche
Subject: RE: Increasing levels of communication, interaction, and participation in a student with autistic disorder

Dear Irene,
So nice to hear from you! Here are my thoughts on this: Because of their inability to communicate with others in the natural environment, students like Owen are unable to benefit fully from participation in their educational programs. As you likely remember from class, limited receptive and expressive language skills can be enhanced by visually aided natural language simulation. According to Cafiero (1998), aided language is easy to learn, inexpensive to implement, and readily generalized across settings. To communicate with the student, a partner points or touches a communication symbol—usually a picture on a board or a computer screen—as the word is spoken. These receptive language opportunities eventually expand into expressive language activities in which the student initiates communication by pointing to symbols. Cafiero suggests the following steps for implementing communication programs:

- *Create environmentally specific language boards.* Language boards are most effective when they are associated with one specific environment or activity. Observe activities to determine the vocabulary that is most relevant for inclusion on the board.

- *Determine the number of symbols.* The number of symbols included on a board depends on students' level of functioning; those who can point and have joint attention (the ability to focus on multiple aspects of a task) can handle as many as 50. Those without should be presented with approximately six symbols.

- *Arrange symbols logically.* Organize symbols on the board as the English language is organized: subjects, verbs, etc.

- *Embed use of the board in the activity.* So that the student can link language to activities, introduce the language simulation as part of ongoing, natural educational activities.

- *Evaluate the effectiveness of the board.* Use copies of the communication board to assess levels and quality of use.

You likely have the following resources that address how best to develop visual language and augmentative communication systems for students with autistic disorder:

Cafiero, J. (1998). Communication power for individuals with autism. *Focus on Autism and Other Developmental Disabilities, 13,* 113–122.

Miranda, P. (2001). Autism, augmentative communication, and assistive technology: What do we really know? *Focus on Autism and Other Developmental Disabilities, 16,* 141–152.

Best of luck with your new student! Let me know how things work out.

Al

---

**EXTEND AND APPLY**

- Develop a visual-aided language board that will allow Owen to begin functioning in his new classroom.
- What symbols do you think would best familiarize him with the students, teachers, and routines of his classroom?
- How would you motivate Owen to focus on the language board?
- How would you assess the impact and effectiveness of this intervention?

---

is based on behavioral methodologies; however, it relies more on routine and consistency than on conditioning. The hallmark of TEACCH is structured teaching, an approach designed to make the learning environment understandable and predictable and assigned tasks meaningful to the individual. Implementing structured teaching involves the following (Marcus, Kunce, & Schopler, 2005; Schopler, 2005):

- **Design the physical environment.** Provide ample space for play, individual work, and practicing self-help skills, while minimizing distracting stimuli.
- **Organize and schedule activities.** Provide explicit prompts and cues to help students organize and predict daily events; make use of individualized sequences of events to illustrate to the student how she is accomplishing daily tasks.
- **Use supportive and explicit teaching methods.** Make use of strengths in visual processing, rote memory, and special interests when providing supports and accommodations during instruction; liberally use graphic and visual structures to organize lessons, tasks, and procedures.

According to the NRC (2001), comprehensive programs in general have positive effects on children with ASD and their families. Individual treatment components used in most programs have been validated, and the available outcome data indicate gains in IQ scores, language functioning, social behavior, and success in future school placements. However, to date, few research efforts have assessed the overall efficacy of individual comprehensive programs, and no data compare one model with another or compare the effectiveness of programs in addressing individual differences among students with ASD.

## TRANSITION TO ADULT LIFE

Given the rather bleak outcomes for persons with ASD—underemployment, unemployment, social and emotional isolation, and even victimization—the need for supports and services does not disappear as students approach young adulthood. When a student graduates from high school, the protections of IDEA end; and school, as the single point of service, no longer exists. Transition planning should begin early in the teen years and should not assume that family members will be able to support the individual with ASD. Planning must build in wraparound community services and service providers. Depending on the level of severity transition planning must include vocational training and employment, postsecondary education, living arrangements, and emotional supports (Hendricks & Wehman, 2009; Howlin, 1997).

## Vocational Training and Employment

Educators use three major approaches to vocational training and employment for students with ASD (Gerhardt & Holmes, 2005). **Supported employment** is a process that recognizes that an individual with ASD can function in the general workforce with ongoing support. Options of supported employment range from intensive one-to-one job coach assistance models to group-oriented cluster support arrangements. **Entrepreneurial supports** are business entities that are built on the skills and interests of those with disabilities. A self-sustaining, for-profit corporation is formed to pay the salaries of workers with disabilities and support staff. **Sheltered workshops**, segregated facilities designed to provide training and employment opportunities for individuals with severe disabilities, are often final placements. Although common and designed to be transitional, sheltered workshops, by nature of their design, may not work in the best interests of many individuals with ASD. Working surrounded by large numbers of individuals with disabilities, isolated from normative events with limited supervision, and working on repetitive tasks with little feedback are not effective ways to promote personal growth and foster quality of life.

Effective practices in planning for the employability of students with ASD include the following (Gerhardt & Holmes, 2005):

* Consider all persons with ASD as viable candidates for employment.
* View first jobs as learning experiences rather than final placements.
* Task-analyze complex jobs, and combine components into doable tasks that match the strengths of students.
* Provide co-workers with training and support.
* Develop cooperative relationships with the local business community.

## Postsecondary Education

An increasing number of students with high-functioning ASD are transitioning to postsecondary or higher education settings. Now that you are aware of their patterns of behavior, consider these students' experiences as they begin college. Moving from a small, supportive high school environment to the independence and demands of a large college campus can be overwhelming, challenging, and anxiety producing. For students with ASD, the organizational, functional, and social aspects of college life tend to be problematic, outweighing the challenges of acquiring advanced academic content. To best address these issues of daily living, peer mentors and college disability services personnel can (1) help students with ASD expand their social circles; (2) provide guidance in ways to integrate interests into social opportunities; and (3) coach on explicit strategies in time management, independent living, speaking with professors, and stress management. Students with ASD who attend residential colleges should also have their own rooms—private places where they can reflect, decompress, and reduce the stress associated with managing their idiosyncratic behaviors (Shea & Mesibov, 2005).

## Living Arrangements

Without support and assistance, few adults with ASD can live independently. Accordingly, family members worry endlessly about how their relatives with special needs will live if, or when, family members are unable to take care of them.

**REFLECTIVE EXERCISE**

**#6** To what extent should college personnel provide specialized academic and social supports to students with ASD? What types of supports should professors provide to facilitate learning in their classrooms?

In the past, most adults with ASD were institutionalized; today a range of community-based, specialized, supported living facilities are available. Parents of children with ASD want to see an adult child live a rewarding life away from home. Consequently, transition planning and education, like the efforts of our featured master teacher, Kim Thomas, help shape independent living behaviors. Targeted education and training can help parents guide children in household maintenance, money management, and skills associated with **self-advocacy** and social self-protection. As adolescents approach early adulthood, educators should provide opportunities for sampling or practicing independent living—in either group homes or supervised apartment complexes (Marcus et al., 2005; Shea & Mesibov, 2005).

## Emotional Supports

We all experience stress and anxiety as we grow into our adult roles, relationships, and responsibilities. However, when faced with these natural transitions, adolescents with ASD experience higher rates and greater intensities of anxiety and depression, often alone, without the benefit of peer or professional support. The pressure of having to do the correct things in social situations causes exhausting anxiety, much like a feeling of constant stage fright (Arick et al., 2005; Grandin, 1992). Moreover, the increasing opportunities for romantic and sexual relationships, brimming with subtle and implied communications, result in fear and confusion.

Unfortunately, the frequency and intensity of observable challenging behaviors masks the need for emotional support. Methods for providing emotional supports for people with ASD do not differ significantly from those provided to people without disabilities. First and foremost, students need a support person, perhaps a trained counselor, with whom they can discuss their fears and anxieties and plan a hopeful, socially appropriate course of action. Second, activities for diverting or reducing stress, including exercise, recreation, and relaxation techniques, must be available. Finally, students with ASD must be empowered with a mechanism for taking a self-directed time-out. After being taught to recognize when an anxiety or panic attack is near, students need an explicit procedure for regaining composure and emotional equilibrium (Arick et al., 2005).

# PREVAILING ISSUES, CONTROVERSIES, AND IMPLICATIONS FOR THE TEACHER

As the incidence of children identified with ASD increases and the interest in this mysterious group of disabilities heightens, controversies and critical issues continue to challenge the field. Following are three topical issues.

## Role of Vaccines in ASD

Is Thimerosal, a mercury-based preservative used in vaccines, responsible for the considerable increase in the incidence of ASD and other neurological disorders? A number of organizations, independent physicians, and muckraking investigative journalists claim that scientific evidence indicates the existence of cases of vaccine-induced autism, most likely caused by Thimerosal (National Vaccine Information Center, 2005). Moreover, some of these same sources suggest that government officials, conspiring with the pharmaceutical industry, are covering up damaging data that, if exposed, could dramatically reduce the profitability of the vaccine industry. Consider the evidence: In the 1990s, introduction of several new universal vaccines for infants, containing Thimerosal, was accompanied by dramatic increases in the incidence of ASD.

A number of large, well-controlled studies, however (e.g. Stehr-Green et al., 2003), have found no evidence of a relationship between vaccines and/or their mercury-based preservatives and the rise in incidence of ASD. Many experts (e.g., Paul, 2009) believe there is no reason for parents to deny their children the protections provided by vaccines. Still, several states are taking no chances and have banned Thimerosal; scores of others are considering such action. Based on the available scientific evidence, the Centers for Disease Control and Prevention (CDC) do not support the hypothesis that vaccines cause autism. Because of considerable public concern, however, particularly among parents who must decide if they should vaccinate their children, the CDC supports additional research on this issue. The fact that vaccines prevent measles, mumps, and rubella makes it inevitable that a cost–benefit debate will follow.

**REFLECTIVE EXERCISE**

#7 What does "consideration of the cost-benefits of vaccination" mean? What levels of safety are required before an intervention should be approved for public consumption?

## Facilitated Communication

Is it possible that trapped beneath the symptoms of ASD are individuals with hidden potential and creativity waiting to be heard? Facilitated communication (FC) is an emotionally charged technique that claims to assist individuals with ASD to express themselves. Originally developed by Rosemary Crossley in Australia in the 1970s, FC was touted as a method that assisted people with severe communication impairments to communicate and was eventually attempted with persons with autism. Due to compelling outcomes, interest in the technique spread (it is frequently highlighted when popular news periodicals focus on autism), and centers for the study and application of the process were developed across the world.

According to Biklen (1990), a founder of the Facilitated Communication Institute at Syracuse University, FC involves supporting the hand, typically at the wrist or forearm, and providing backward resistance to assist in the selection of letters from either a keyboard or a letter board. Proponents of FC claim that the technique allows many with ASD to communicate with complex language filled with abstract and emotional content. Based on these claims, FC has been used to administer intelligence tests and other standardized educational assessments. In some cases people previously found to function in the severe–profound range of mental retardation have been reclassified as having normal intelligence.

Unfortunately, the empirical evidence for FC does not match the excitement or enthusiasm expressed in anecdotal reports. Several independent reviews of the FC literature (e.g., Howlin, 1997; Mostert, 2001) have noted that facilitators influence responses of clients and that too many claims of communication remain unsubstantiated. Researchers have since labeled FC a fad (Frith, 2003), and some professional organizations have adopted a formal resolution opposing the technique as a valid mode of enhancing expression.

## Ongoing Pressures and Demands on Families

As we have noted throughout this chapter, developing and maintaining family involvement is critical in the education of students with ASD. Teachers facing their own ongoing classroom challenges and demands often overlook or underestimate the continual and sometimes exhausting social, emotional, and economic responsibilities associated with supporting a high-maintenance family member. Beyond the obvious physical demands, families perceive ASD as a confusing and frightening disability. They are often at a loss as to how to engage their child, worry about ill-timed public displays of inappropriate behavior, and experience an almost constant roller coaster of hopefulness and frustration based on the uneven and often unusual developmental progress of their loved one. Moreover, they serve multiple roles: teachers, advocates, and loving (and sometimes resentful) family members (National Research Council, 2001).

# THE REAL WORLD Challenges and Solutions

## Helping families discern evidence-based practices from fads and media frenzy

*Bonnie Green is the special educator for fourth- and fifth-grade students at Wellwood Elementary School. In her third year of teaching, Bonnie fulfills a number of roles including consultation with her general education teacher colleagues; co-teaching during reading and math lessons; and responding to the needs of families of the students in her caseload. Although most of her interactions with family members are positive and productive, Bonnie finds that one set of parents are particularly challenging: The Sequins are the parents of Austin, a 10-year-old student with ASD. Highly educated and well read, the Sequins are—thankfully in Bonnie's view—actively involved in all aspects of Austin's education. However, the Sequins are constantly advocating for unusual approaches to intervention. For example, the Sequins often call or write lengthy e-mails about controversial educational "cures" that are featured on cable news programs. At IEP meetings they advocate for interventions that are expensive and labor intensive, but these approaches lack empirical evidence of positive outcomes. Bonnie is sensitive to the pressures faced by the Sequins, and she recognizes that they are seeking to improve their family's quality of life. However, Bonnie is a firm believer in using evidence-based practices in her teaching and is reluctant to integrate techniques and approaches that make excessive claims of success with no valid outcome data. Moreover, Bonnie is bound by the requirements of NCLB to use only scientifically based approaches in her teaching. Bonnie welcomes the involvement of the Sequins—indeed, she wishes some of her other students' families would follow their lead. However, she wonders how she can convey to the Sequins the importance of employing evidence-based practices.*

Families of children and youth with ASD experience an almost constant roller coaster of hopefulness and frustration. Friends, relatives, and a seemingly unending blitz of media contribute to the volatility by suggesting a range of actions to deal with the challenging and mysterious behaviors (Heflin & Alaimo, 2007). Understandably, family members (and some professionals) often engage their children's teachers by advocating for methods that appear useful but lack adequate scientific evidence. Teachers and administrators, legally and ethically charged to employ evidence-based practices, are often put in the uncomfortable situation of having to decide the suitability of such practices (Simpson, McKee, Teeter, & Beytien, 2007).

Heflin and colleagues (Heflin & Alaimo, 2007; Heflin & Simpson, 1998) have generated a set of questions that can guide all stakeholders through these challenging methodology and strategy discussions:

- **What are the anticipated outcomes of the intervention?** Are the outcomes relevant, and does the intervention consider the individual profile of the student?
- **What are the potential risks associated with the approach?** What are the potential immediate and long-term risks, and what are the implications if the intervention fails?
- **What proof is available that the intervention is effective?** What is the quality of information indicating intervention efficacy? And are the outcome data published in respected peer-reviewed journals?
- **How will the intervention be evaluated for the individual student?** What criteria will be used to determine if the approach is effective for the individual student? Are generalization and maintenance effects considered? Who is responsible for evaluation, when will it take place, and how will it be completed?
- **What other activities would be excluded if the intervention is implemented?** What is the possible impact on the student's educational program if the new intervention is implemented, and how does the program impact placement in inclusive settings?

### Valuable Resources for the Teacher

American Speech-Language-Hearing Association. (2009). Guidelines for speech-language pathologists in diagnosis, assessment, and treatment of autism spectrum disorders across the life span. Retrieved July 5, 2009, from http://www.asha.org/docs/pdf/GL2006-00049.pdf

Heflin, L. J., & Alaimo, D. F. (2007). *Students with autism spectrum disorders*. Upper Saddle River, NJ: Pearson.

National Research Council. (2001). *Educating children with autism*. Washington, DC: National Academy Press.

### Final Thoughts

It is generally accepted that no single best or universally effective intervention is appropriate for all students with ASD (Simpson et al., 2007). Clearly, some interventions result in better outcomes than others. However, anecdotal advocacy for specific programs and contradictory information appearing in the mass media make informed program decision making by educators and families challenging and controversial. Teachers like Bonnie Green can best serve families like the Sequins by listening to their suggestions and using accepted scientific guidelines to assess the viability of new and promising educational interventions.

How can teachers support and assist families of students with ASD? First, educators must demonstrate awareness and sensitivity to the developmental life cycle of the family and adjust their roles accordingly (Marcus et al., 2005). For example, during early childhood, assistance is best pointed toward direct assessment of functioning, emotional support for grieving family members, and parent counseling/training. As the child enters the elementary school years, the teacher should emphasize supports for maintaining home–school relationships, addressing learning problems, and providing strategies for improving adaptive behavior. During adolescence, efforts focus on independent living skills and work opportunities.

Other strategies for supporting parents and families include the following (Marcus et al., 2005):

- Stress that ASD is a long-term developmental disorder that is adapted to rather than removed.
- View inappropriate behaviors of the child as attempts to cope with the environment.
- Assist families to structure their environments by helping to establish predictable routines and structured teaching processes.
- Model mutual respect in the family–professional partnership.
- Focus on the needs of the total family.

# 10 SUMMARY

Students with ASD exhibit an extreme range of behaviors that separate them from activities and interactions that enrich everyone's quality of life.

## Definition and Classification of ASD

- The two most common forms of ASD are autistic disorder and Asperger's disorder.
- Autistic disorder is characterized by an early age of onset, poor social development, impairments in receptive and expressive language development, and rigidity.
- Asperger's disorder is characterized by severe and sustained impairments in social interactions and restricted, repetitive patterns of behavior and interests.

## Characteristics of ASD

- Students with ASD share three categories of characteristics: (1) impairments in social skills; (2) deficiencies in communication skills; and (3) stereotypical, ritualistic behavior.
- Many students with autistic disorder fail to acquire functional language, and students with Asperger's disorder have difficulty comprehending and making use of figurative language.
- Secondary behavioral correlates of ASD include early age of onset, variable intellectual functioning, and self-injurious behavior.

## Prevalence Rates, Course, and Causal Factors

- Prevalence rates range from 2 to 67 cases per 10,000; and some have suggested that we are in the midst of an autism epidemic.
- The course of ASD is lifelong and chronic, with outcomes depending on the level of severity of the disability.
- The cause of ASD remains unknown, although researchers generally accept that the disorders are the result of one or more nature- or biophysically based factors.
- Damaging and counterproductive etiological theories implicating parents have been disavowed.

## Identification and Assessment

- Identification and assessment of ASD require measurement across disciplines.
- Initially, educators use screening devices to determine if a child has either the specific or nonspecific behaviors suggesting risk for the disability.
- Children deemed at risk are referred to multidisciplinary teams that conduct intensive clinical evaluations.
- After identification, educators use the results of functional behavioral analyses (FBAs) for educational planning.

## Educational Practices

- Factors used for making educational placement decisions include competence in social skills and the ability to benefit from instruction.
- The focus of early educational efforts is on sensory issues, communication skills, and social behaviors. As students enter school, interventions focus on academic content, language, and social/functional material.

- Applied behavior analysis (ABA) techniques, including discrete trial instruction (DTI), are frequently used practices for basic skills.
- Various techniques, including social stories and cartooning, are used to teach higher-functioning students.
- The need for supports and instruction does not disappear once the student with ASD finishes school. Vocational training, supported employment, and help securing assisted living arrangements are essential.

 **ADDRESSING THE PROFESSIONAL STANDARDS**

Council for Exceptional Children (CEC) Knowledge Standards addressed in the chapter:

ICC1K5, GC1K1, ICC2K2, ICC2K4, ICC2K5, ICCEK6, ICC2K7, GC2K4, ICC3K1, ICC3K2, ICC6K4, ICC6S1

Appendix B: CEC Knowledge and Skill Standards Common Core has a full listing of the standards referenced here.

**myeducationlab**

Now go to Topic 13: Autism in the MyEducationLab for your course, where you can:

- Find learning outcomes for the broad concepts covered in this chapter along with the national standards that connect to these outcomes.
- Complete Assignments and Activities that can help you more deeply understand the chapter content.
- Examine challenging situations presented in the IRIS center Resources.
- Apply and practice your understanding of the core concepts and skills identified in the chapter with the Building Teaching Skills and Dispositions learning units.

- Check your comprehension on the content covered in the chapter by going to the Study Plan in the Book-Specific Resources section for your text. Here you will be able to take a chapter quiz, receive feedback on your answers, and then access Review, Practice, and Enrichment activities to enhance your understanding of chapter content.
- Access video clips of CCSSO National Teachers of the Year award winners responding to the question, "Why Do I Teach?" in the Teacher Talk section.

# Communication Disorders

**REFLECT UPON**

- What are communication disorders? Language disorders? Speech disorders?
- What are the main types of language and speech disorders?
- How are communication disorders related to other disabilities?
- How often do different communication disorders occur, and what causes them?
- What kinds of assessment do speech–language pathologists (SLPs) use to plan interventions for students with communication disorders?
- What are the major features of interventions for communication disorders and the service delivery options that may be used? What are some ways that teachers can collaborate with SLPs?
- What are the major issues today with regard to providing services to students with communication disorders?

## MY PROFESSION, MY STORY KATHLEEN LANCE MORGAN

To look at the degrees, certificates, and licenses held by Kathleen Lance Morgan, you would think that she knows just about everything there is to know about speech–language pathology. She has bachelor's and master's degrees in speech–language pathology and an educational specialist (Ed.S.) degree. Along with her degrees, she has the "three Cs" (CCC, the certificate of clinical competence) from the American Speech-Language-Hearing Association (ASHA) as well as a license in speech–language pathology from the North Carolina Board of Examiners and teaching certificates in speech–language pathology and severe/profound disabilities from the North Carolina Department of Public Instruction. Still, Kathleen sometimes worries that she doesn't know enough. That's why she is always on the lookout for new ways to expand her knowledge and skill repertoire.

Kathleen learned about speech–language pathologists (SLPs) when she was a little girl and had a sister with an articulation disorder. The SLP working with her sister recruited Kathleen to practice with her to hasten improvement. When Kathleen went away to college, she talked to her father about the career she might pursue. He told her she should consider speech pathology because it would let her "help a lot of children." In the end it was her dad's influence that led her into the field of speech–language pathology. Now Kathleen is in her ninth year working as an elementary school–based SLP in Waynesville, North Carolina, and she finds the work to be just as rewarding and challenging as it was when she first began.

As you might expect, Kathleen's day is very full. Before and after she sees students, she meets with parents, teachers, and/or administrators; attends staff meetings, reevaluations, or individualized education program (IEP) meetings; and answers phone calls and e-mails. In formal and informal settings, she seems to be in constant contact with teachers about students' communication needs and how best to meet them. Her direct service begins at 8:30, when she starts seeing a mix of students with a variety of communication disorders. Most of the time, she works with groups of three or four students in her small therapy room for 30 minutes at a time, but sometimes, though rarely, she will work one on one with a student. Always she tries to work with teachers so that the skills the students are learning will generalize to the classroom and beyond.

Sometimes Kathleen's efforts to collaborate with other professionals are successful, and sometimes they are not. For example, at the beginning of the school year, she introduces herself to the teachers in her school by putting a "welcome back" note in their boxes. In the note she tells them that she is working on the speech–language schedule and encourages the teachers to look at the IEP speech–language goals of students in their classes. She also lets them know that she will meet with

them individually so that she can discuss students' goals. The idea is for the teachers to be aware of the goals so that they can reinforce them in the classroom. Kathleen says, "Sometimes I have teachers come forth, and they are anxious to review the records, and then there are others who look at the letter and disregard it." It is this latter group, of course, that seems to have little knowledge of the communication needs of their students or why Kathleen is working with them. As you might expect, Kathleen finds this very frustrating. On the other hand, she says, there are many who are "very good about following through, and they are willing to collaborate, and they are very diligent and will want to know what they can do in the classroom to help the student." Teachers like this, in Kathleen's opinion, make an important difference in kids' communication abilities.

Another challenge for Kathleen is the scope of her work. Students have so many communication needs, and they are all so different and important. She says, "We deal with kids who have traumatic brain injury, who have cleft palate, kids with pediatric feeding problems, besides the traditional articulation problems, kids with all kinds of language problems and processing disorders. I mean there's a huge range!" She adds,

"When I started out I thought I had a good foundation, a good basis, but because the field is so broad, there was still a lot of knowledge that I wanted to acquire. That really resounded with the low-incidence population because I felt like I had not had enough preparation for that area." Because of the variety of needs, Kathleen feels that she must constantly work to acquire new knowledge to work effectively with her students.

What is it about Kathleen that makes her an effective SLP? It's hard for her to say. Certainly, she's had extensive professional preparation and a lot of hands-on experience. But she also thinks there are other significant traits. She says you need to be compassionate so that you can understand "where your kids are coming from," creative in order to "think of ways to help them with the maximum effect," and flexible so that you can work well with other teachers and understand their point of view. Most important, you must be willing to seek out additional knowledge and information because "you are never fully prepared" for all that you need to face.

Kathleen also offers important advice for teachers who want to work effectively with SLPs: "Really think about walking a mile in the other person's shoes. Speech pathologists wouldn't be in a school setting if they didn't have something very valuable to offer students. Just keep in mind that working collaboratively with a speech pathologist can be beneficial for everybody. Everybody has strengths to share and different ideas." Kathleen clearly has her strengths, and she's always willing to add to them by taking advantage of the strengths of others.

### REFLECTIVE EXERCISE

#1 Although we are focusing on the communication disorders of students, can teachers also have communication challenges? What kind have you seen or heard among teachers you have had?

To realize the significance of Kathleen Lance Morgan's role, think about the frequency of your communication. We talk to each other so often and in so many different ways that it's hard to think of life without effective verbal communication. From muttering over the first cup of coffee to bidding a congenial good night, we are in nearly a constant state of communication. Thinking, saying, hearing, and understanding—the major elements of communication—occur continuously and help make our lives what they are. Teachers, of course, must be master communicators. To be a good teacher, you must be able to explain to your students what you want them to learn, what they must do, how they must do it, whether they are doing it correctly, how they can improve on what they are doing, and many other things. You must also be able to listen to their ideas, their questions, their answers, their concerns, and everything else they would like you to know about. The way you and your students communicate with each other will often determine the quality of your teaching and their learning.

For most students, communication will not be a problem, although you might not always like what they are communicating. On the other hand, some students have communication problems that interfere with learning and other life activities. From both a personal and a professional perspective, these students will be a concern to special educators, to general education teachers, and certainly to speech–language pathologists (SLPs) like Kathleen Lance Morgan.

Communication is commonly described as sharing information between two or more persons. We use communication to make requests or to respond to them, provide information and ideas, or comment on virtually any topic. To participate in an act of communication, one person has to formulate a thought and transmit it, while the other (or others) must receive it and comprehend its meaning. If a person has significant difficulty with one or more of these processes, we may consider her to have a communication disorder. The term *significant* means that the difficulty is serious enough to impact the person's daily life at home, at school, or in the community (Justice, 2006).

There will be days in many of your students' lives, as there are in your own, when they will have a hard time saying what they mean. Even in your college courses, you will sometimes see students having a hard time formulating the question they want to ask or the idea they want to contribute. If these episodes just come and go—that is, if they are not permanent—they are not communication disorders. But if constant problems affect the way a person verbally interacts with other people and the way other people respond, then the person is experiencing a communication disorder.

Students need to communicate to express their ideas, their questions, their answers, and their concerns.

## FAQ Sheet

### STUDENTS WITH COMMUNICATION DISORDERS

| | |
|---|---|
| Who are they? | Students with communication disorders include those with language disorders, speech disorders, or sometimes a combination of both. |
| What are typical characteristics? | Language disorders include (1) form disorders (difficulty making correct sounds, constructing words, or connecting the words correctly); (2) content or semantic disorders (lack of word–meaning knowledge); and (3) use or pragmatic disorders (application of language in social contexts). Speech disorders include (1) phonological/articulation disorders (distortions, substitutions, or omissions of speech sounds); (2) fluency disorders (the most common is stuttering); (3) voice disorders (e.g., speaking with a harsh or raspy voice); and (4) motor speech disorders (difficulty using the physical components of speech, often due to a neuromuscular disorder such as cerebral palsy). |
| What are the demographics? | About 2.3% of children enrolled in public schools are classified as having speech or language disabilities. This does not include other students with speech or language disabilities served under other disability categories. Totally, about 5% of school-age individuals have speech disorders, and between 2% and 8% have specific language impairments. |
| Where are students educated? | Most students with speech disorders are served in general education classrooms and receive speech therapy provided by speech–language pathologists (SLPs). Many students with communication disorders are also in general education classrooms; but communication disorders are common among many students with disabilities, and these students may be served in various settings, including the general education classroom or a special classroom. |
| What are the outcomes? | Many language and speech disorders improve either without therapy (especially with young children) or with therapy. Some individuals with these disorders have them throughout life. |

**REFLECTIVE EXERCISE**

#2 Have you or anyone you've known ever had a communication disorder? Would you say it was a language disorder or a speech disorder? What was its impact?

# DEFINITIONS AND DESCRIPTIONS OF COMMUNICATION DISORDERS

According to Justice (2006), "Individuals are normal and effective communicators when they are able to formulate, transmit, receive, and comprehend information from other individuals successfully. A communication disorder or impairment is present when a person has significant difficulty in one of more of these aspects of communication when compared with other people sharing the same language, dialect and culture" (pp. 21–22).

In this chapter we will discuss two major types of communication disorders: language disorders and speech disorders. Although an individual may have both, the terms are not synonymous. Language disorders include problems in formulating and comprehending spoken messages, whereas speech disorders consist of problems related to the verbal transmission of messages. Additionally, some individuals who have difficulty receiving verbal messages are classified as being deaf or having a hearing impairment. This is another type of communication disorder, but we discuss it separately in Chapter 13.

## Language Disorders

Language is a formal communication system that is shared by its users. Although we can communicate without language, language facilitates our communication by making it more effective. In order for language to be most effective, its users must all use the same symbols (i.e., words having the same meanings) and the same rules to connect the symbols (i.e., putting the words in the right order to convey the intended meaning). When people are effective language users, they can clearly share their thoughts with each other.

An individual may have generally good speaking ability yet have a language problem. For example, an elementary school student may have a language disorder if he has a difficult time finding and using the right word or combinations of words; using words in the right order; or using the correct words, phrases, or sentences at the right time. Your ability to understand his individual words may be fine, but you may still have a difficult time comprehending what he is trying to say.

Experts usually divide language disorders into three major categories. These are disorders of (1) form, (2) content (also called **semantics**), and (3) use (also called **pragmatics**) (Justice, 2006; Owens, Metz, & Haas, 2007; Peña & Davis, 2010). We discuss each of these in the following sections.

### Form Disorders

In language, we define form by three aspects: the sounds used to make words and word parts **(phonology),** the rules for constructing words and parts of words **(morphology),** and the rules for connecting the words together **(syntax).**

The sounds of the language are referred to as its *phonology*, and the phonological components are called **phonemes.** Phonemes are the smallest unit of sound that can affect word meaning. The word "mat" has three phonemes: the "m" sound, the "a" sound (which is written by language specialists as "æ" to distinguish it from other "a" sounds), and the "t" sound. Most English speakers can both produce and comprehend these sounds when they are linked together (m-æ-t) to conjure an image of an item lying on the floor to wipe our feet on or on a table to put a plate on. The meaning changes, however, if we change just one phoneme. For example "mat" could become "sat," "met," or "map" by changing the first, middle, or last phoneme, respectively, and any of these changes would change the meaning of the word.

You should not confuse phonemes with letters, because some phonemes are created through letter combinations, such as "th" or "sh," which make the difference

## FIGURE 11.1 • THE PHONEMES OF STANDARD AMERICAN ENGLISH

| | Consonants | | | | | Vowels | | | |
|---|---|---|---|---|---|---|---|---|---|
| /p/ | pat | /t/ | tip | /g/ | go | /i/ | feet | /ɪ/ | fit |
| /b/ | bat | /d/ | dip | /ŋ/ | sing | /e/ | fate | /ɛ/ | fret |
| /m/ | mat | /n/ | not | /h/ | hop | /u/ | food | /u/ | foot |
| /f/ | fit | /s/ | sun | /ʔ/ | uh-oh | /o/ | phone | /ɔ/ | fought |
| /v/ | vat | /z/ | zoo | /l/ | lose | /æ/ | fan | /a/ | hot |
| /θ/ | think | /c/ | chew | /r/ | rose | /ʌ/ | cut | /ə/ | bathtub |
| /ð/ | those | /j/ | jeep | /j/ | young | /aɪ/ | fight | /au/ | found |
| /s/ | shop | /k/ | kiln | /w/ | week | /ɔɪ/ | toy | | |
| /z/ | measure | | | | | | | | |

*Source:* From L. Justice, *Communication Sciences and Disorders* (2006), p. 15. Published by Merrill/Prentice Hall. Copyright © by Pearson Education. Reprinted with permission.

between "bath" and "bash." **Standard American English (SAE)** uses about 40 phonemes (25 consonant sounds and 15 vowel sounds) to make more than 100,000 words. Figure 11.1 shows the phonemes that make the sounds of SAE.

A person who has a phonological disorder may not have developed an adequate mental representation of the phoneme or may not be able to adequately produce some phonemes with enough distinction from other phonemes. Usually children go through their early development with many errors in developing and using correct phonemes—for example, saying "ovah deyah" for "over there" or "dats mine" for "that's mine." Phonological disorders such as these usually disappear as the child grows older, but not always. Speech disorders called *articulation disorders* sometimes occur as a product of phonological disorders. We discuss these disorders later in the chapter.

Another language form disorder occurs when an individual doesn't use the correct internal structure of words, instead using the meaningful components of words, which are called "morphemes," erroneously. For example "walk" is a **morpheme** and so is "-s," "-ed," and "-ing." When we attach any of these last three morphemes to the first one, "walk," we are using them to change word meaning. Like the person who cannot articulate the appropriate phoneme, a person who has difficulty using the correct morpheme to convey what she intends would also have a language form disorder.

Finally, form disorders can include syntax disorders. Language syntax consists of the rules used by a speaker to connect words appropriately so that the listener can accurately comprehend what the speaker intends. For example, in English, if we are talking about someone doing something, like "The girl threw the Frisbee," we must put the words in a certain order so that all knowledgeable English language users will agree about the meaning of the statement. If we don't arrange the words correctly, the listener may not comprehend what the speaker is trying to say. Although we could also say, "The Frisbee was thrown by the girl" (using the passive voice instead of the active voice), we would not say, "The Frisbee threw girl" or "Girl the Frisbee threw." Were we to do so, this would be evidence of an English syntax problem.

You can see that if someone has difficulty producing acceptable language form, either using the correct sounds (phonology), word parts (morphology) or word arrangements (syntax) or maybe a combination of these, he would likely have a significant problem in effective language usage. In such cases, intervention might be necessary to help the individual improve his language form.

## REFLECTIVE EXERCISE

**#3** If you have ever tried to learn a foreign language, you probably had some problems with the language's form. Have you heard someone with an English language form problem? How did it affect that person's communication?

A child's early environment can affect learning opportunities and language development.

## Content Disorders

We call the second major type of language disorder *content disorder,* which is also called a *semantics disorder.* The semantics of a language are the rules that dictate the meanings applied to specific words or word combinations. For example, if a person consistently uses words or phrases that are not meaningful to other people who use the same language, or uses words or phrases that are not valid for the situation, the person is experiencing a content or semantics problem.

Language content is often affected by life and learning experiences. Some children who grow up in very impoverished environments and, as a result, lack many of the opportunities for exploring an array of social and literary conditions may have limited language content. As a result, you may find that they often have difficulty finding the right words to express themselves or they may use words that are inappropriate for their communication needs. Individuals who have trouble finding the right words, who have a hard time understanding or using more abstract language, or who have a vocabulary that is inadequately developed for their age are considered to have a language content disorder.

## Use Disorders

The real value of language is its potential to allow us to communicate more precisely than if we did not have it. So an important component of a person's language is the adequacy with which she can *use* the language, that is, how well she can apply language skills when communicating with others in daily social situations.

Language use disorders, which are also referred to as *disorders in pragmatics,* are characterized by individuals who do not use language that is appropriate for their current social context. A child who has a problem in pragmatics might have difficulties initiating conversations, taking turns with partners, engaging in extensive dialogues, or engaging in a wide range of other language uses in specific situations (e.g., greetings, making requests, or commenting). This person may have adequate language form and content but be deficient when using language for social purposes.

## Manifestation of Language Disorders

Although we presented the different language disorders as discrete conditions, different types of disorders often occur together. In fact, children may exhibit combinations of language form, content, and use disorders, sometimes even with all three of the disorders occurring together. When this happens, the child is said to have a diffuse language disorder. What's more, the language disorders displayed by a child can change over time. Changes can occur because of maturation, speech–language intervention, or educational experiences. Additionally, a child may experience a particular type of language disorder at one time and another disorder at another time.

Appropriate use of language is a critical skill for toddlers and preschoolers to develop. Many young children, who will ultimately be classified as having disabilities, such as learning disabilities or mild intellectual disabilities, will show problems in language use during the preschool years. These problems will also occur for other children, but many of them will develop adequate language skills as they get older. If you visit or work in a program for toddlers or preschoolers, especially those who are developmentally at risk, you will see the teachers placing a great deal of emphasis on children's appropriate language use.

**PEARSON myeducationlab**

Go to the Assignments and Activities section of Topic 12: Communication Disorders in the MyEducationLab for your course and complete the activity entitled *Describing Language Impairments.*

# Speech Disorders

Before discussing speech disorders, we will review how speech is normally produced. This will help you appreciate the different ways in which speech may be adversely affected. Speech relies on the coordinated use of four building blocks: **respiration, voice, articulation,** and **fluency.**

- **Respiration.** An essential need for speaking is being able to produce enough air pressure from our lungs. Our breathing, or respiration, produces a consistent and even breath stream that provides the power for speech. Just as air is used to produce sound in a pipe organ, it is the basic ingredient necessary for people to speak.
- **Voice.** As we exhale, voice is used to create sound and to vary the sound in volume, pitch, and resonance. We use our **larynx** and **oral** and **nasal cavities** to modify the sounds we produce.
- **Articulation.** The sounds are further refined into phonemes through articulation. Articulation is conducted by using our mouth parts, including our lips, tongue, teeth, jaws, and soft palate. These are referred to as the articulators.
- **Fluency.** Finally, fluency is used to produce effortless and smooth speech so that the speaker's intention is easy to understand. Fluency allows us to speak hurriedly or slowly, transitioning smoothly from word to word and stopping and continuing at appropriate places in our speech.

## Speech Production

Justice (2006) provides this simple description to help us comprehend the complex process of speech:

> To better understand the processes involved with speech, say the word "eat" slowly and deliberately and think about the process as you do so. You will see that the speech process begins with the intake of a breath of air, which is then exhaled; this is the basic fuel needed for all speech. The exhalation travels up from the lungs through the windpipe (trachea) and over the vocal chords, which begin to vibrate and create the "eeeee" sound. This "eeeee" sound is then sent into the oral cavity, which is open and marked by a big toothy smile with the lips pulled wide. Notice that the upper and lower jaws are held fairly close together, but are not closed; the tongue sits low in the mouth, with the tip tucked behind the lower row of teeth and the middle rounded up on the sides to touch the upper teeth. Once the "eeeee" sound is in the oral cavity, a brief "ea" escapes and then the tongue comes quickly up behind the teeth to produce the "t" sound following the "ea." (p. 16)

When you understand that this is the process required for producing a *single* word, you have a good idea of what we mean when we say that speech is an extremely complex activity.

In the following sections, we will describe speech disorders that can sometimes occur. As you will see, these disorders can interfere significantly with the speaker's ability to say something that can be easily understood and comprehended. At the same time, the speech disorder can call attention to the speaker and sometimes cause personal discomfort.

## Phonological and Articulation Disorders

If speech is to be an effective way to produce language, a speaker must generate speech sounds (specifically, phonemes) that a listener can understand and attach meaning to. Phonological (knowledge of sounds) and articulation (production of sounds) disorders impair a person's ability to clearly create speech sounds. Instead of producing standard speech sounds, the speaker produces sounds that include distortions, substitutions, omissions, or additions. A distortion occurs when a nonstandard phoneme, like a lisp, is produced. A substitution is when one phoneme is replaced

#4 Have you ever been in a situation in which you had to communicate but could not speak? What did you do? Do you recall the extra effort required to get your message across?

with another, such as "shair" for "chair." An omission is the deletion of a phoneme such as saying "chai" for "chair," and an addition is when an extra phoneme is added such as "chuh air" for "chair" (Owens et al., 2003).

As we mentioned earlier, one type of form disorder was called a *phonological disorder*. As we explained, a phonological disorder is a language disorder that occurs when an individual has a faulty perceptual representation of a particular phoneme. This means that, although the person has the physical ability to produce the correct phoneme, he constantly produces an incorrect phoneme. The problem is attributed to having an inadequate mental representation of this aspect of the language sound. An example would be a person who can distinguish between a "ch" sound and a "sh" sound but doesn't make a distinction between the two sounds when speaking (Davis & Bedore, 2010).

Phonological disorders (a perceptual problem) produce what sounds like an articulation disorder that is actually a speech-production problem. However, articulation problems can also be attributed to structural problems, such as a cleft palate, or faulty control of the articulators, such as incorrect placement of the tongue in relation to the teeth to produce an "r" sound. A common example of an articulation problem would be the child who says "wed" instead or "red." In such a case we might say that the child simply has not had enough experience to correctly form the desired speech sound.

In some cases phonological disorders and articulation disorders can both occur. Davis and Bedore (2010) offered an example of a child who had a history of chronic otitis media (middle ear infection) that led to a mild hearing loss. Because of the hearing loss, the child may not have been able to develop a correct mental representation of some speech sounds, which would lead to a phonological disorder. At the same time, the child would not be able to monitor his own speech sounds and thus might not know whether the sounds are correct.

### Fluency Disorders

Although less frequent than phonological or articulation disorders, fluency disorders are typically much more noticeable. The most common fluency disorder, and the one with which you are likely to be most familiar, is **stuttering.** Stuttering can draw a great deal of attention to the speaker and often causes much stress. Because it is often affected by environmental and circumstantial conditions, teachers can play an important role in creating conditions to reduce the likelihood that a child will stutter.

Stuttering has been defined by using descriptions and explanations of the condition. Descriptive definitions usually note that stuttering consists of producing an abnormally high number of sound and syllable repetitions, prolongations, or blocks. Explanatory definitions try to address the question "Why does the person stutter?" and tend to speculate that stuttering occurs due to psychological or neurological conditions. In fact, the true cause of stuttering is unknown.

Shapiro (1999) offered this definition: "stuttering refers to individualized and involuntary interruptions in the forward flow of speech and learned reactions thereto interacting with and generating associated thoughts and feelings about one's speech, oneself as a communicator, and the communication world in which we live." He further noted, "Stuttering occurs within the context of communication systems, thus affecting and being affected by all persons who communicate with the person who stutters" (p. 14).

When you observe the person who stutters, you will typically see both primary, or core, behaviors and secondary behaviors. The primary behaviors are the speech characteristics that we normally think of as stuttering—that is, the repetitions, prolongations, and blocks. The secondary behaviors are the person's reaction to stuttering as she tries to deal with the uncomfortable verbalizations or

**PEARSON**
**myeducationlab**

Go to the Assignments and Activities section of Topic 12: Communication Disorders in the MyEducationLab for your course and complete the activity entitled *Describing Speech Impairments.*

avoid them altogether. Commonly you will see the person doing things like blinking her eyes, opening her jaws, pursing her lips, substituting easier words for those that are more difficult, or inserting "uh" before a difficult word (Byrd & Gillam, 2010).

Stuttering behavior demonstrates a great deal of variability. In other words, if you carefully observe people who stutter, you will see that they do not do so in the same way (Byrd & Gillam, 2010). Generally, however, we know that different circumstances tend to increase the probability that a person who stutters will stutter. Usually this happens when the person tries to put more pressure on himself to be fluent. For example, talking on the phone, trying to communicate briefly or quickly (e.g., giving your name or ordering in a restaurant), or speaking to an authority figure (e.g., a teacher or a principal) are all situations when stuttering is more likely to occur.

In contrast, in some conditions a person who stutters is less likely to stutter. Some of these include during choral reading, when speaking in a low volume, when speaking slowly, when speaking in a rhythmical way, and when singing. In fact, as Shapiro (1999) points out, most people who stutter do so only 15% to 20% of the time they speak. He suggests that, by focusing on conditions related to fluent speech, therapists and others in the students' communication environment (e.g., teachers) can be more successful in increasing effective speaking.

Have you known someone who stutters? Perhaps a child, an adolescent, a friend, or a colleague? What if you were a teacher of a child who stuttered? What could you do? Take a look at the student described in "Can You Help Me with This Student?" and the suggestions that are listed. You might find them useful.

## Voice Disorders

One of the key human characteristics that distinguishes us from each other is our voice. Like facial features and bodily shapes, we know each other by how we sound. Before you see your friend coming up behind you in the hall, you know who it is when she calls your name or yells for you to wait a minute.

Our unique voices are a result of the physical components that allow us to produce them. The voice begins as air is pushed out of our lungs. It then passes into our larynx and through the larynx's two **vocal folds** (or **vocal chords**). By vibrating our vocal folds as the air from our lungs passes through them, we begin to create our voice. The voice is further modified as it passes through the pharynx (or throat) and then into the oral and nasal cavity where it is given resonation (Justice, 2006).

One of the most salient variations in our voices is that which exists between mature males and females. But as you know, there are many, many more variations. This, of course, is why we can distinguish each other by our voices. The interaction of three vocal characteristics creates our unique voice: frequency, intensity, and phonatory quality. **Frequency** (or pitch) refers to how high or low our voice is. It is controlled by the physical characteristics of our vocal folds. Vocal folds that are longer and thicker produce lower sounds, whereas those with greater tension produce higher sounds. **Intensity** describes how loudly or softly we normally speak and can be reported in terms of **decibels (dB).** We produce more intense or louder speech by forcing more air over the vocal folds as they increase in their resistance. When the folds open suddenly and widely, they produce a louder sound. As we all know, we can control our loudness, but it is also true that every person has a baseline loudness level. This is what you typically hear during normal conversation. The third determinant of voice, **phonatory quality,** is a little more difficult to explain; but we know it varies a lot between people, and we usually can easily describe it. Typically, this voice characteristic is described as mellow, velvety, rich, harmonious, whispery, harsh, and so on (Justice, 2006).

**REFLECTIVE EXERCISE**

#5 Many people who stutter are able to control their stuttering, but sometimes they lose their control in different situations. What types of conditions might contribute to such loss of control?

| To... | Madeline Jacobson, Speech–Language Pathologist |
|---|---|
| From... | Denise Sommers, General Education Teacher |
| Subject: | What should I do when my student stutters? |

Hi, Madeline,

I was wondering if you could help me with one of my sixth graders. His name is Travis, and he has a pretty noticeable stutter. I am trying to find a way for him to participate like the other students, but I don't want to embarrass him about his speech disorder. Do you have some strategies that might be helpful?

—Denise

---

To:       Denise Sommers
From:     Madeline Jacobson
Subject:  RE: What should I do when my student stutters?

Denise,

It was good to hear from you, and I'm glad to try and help you with Travis. Many students like Travis will stutter in certain situations but will be more comfortable in others. The main thing you can do is try to avoid putting pressure on Travis to speak. Here are a few ideas that should be helpful.

1. Talk with Travis in private, and show your support. Explain to him that when talking, just like when learning other skills, we sometimes make mistakes. Explain that you are his teacher and that his stuttering is okay with you. By talking to Travis in this way, you help him learn that you are aware of his stuttering and that you accept it—and him. You can also ask him if there are any particular accommodations that might be helpful.

2. When you are asking questions in the classroom, you can do certain things to make it easier for Travis. For example, ask him questions that can be answered with relatively few words. If everyone is going to be asked a question, call on Travis early. Tension and worry can build up the longer he has to wait his turn. Assure all students that they will have as much time as they need to answer questions and that you are interested in having them take time and think through their answers, not just answer quickly.

3. Many students who stutter can handle oral reading tasks in the classroom satisfactorily, but some will stutter severely even while reading aloud in class. If Travis stutters while reading, rather than not calling on him to read, let him have his turn with one of the other children. In fact, if you let the whole class read in pairs, Travis might not feel so "special."

4. If one of your other students teases Travis, talk with Travis to help him understand why others tease and brainstorm ideas for how to respond. If a certain student or students are doing most of the teasing, talk to them alone, and explain that teasing is unacceptable.

5. When you are talking to Travis, never say "slow down" or "relax" or complete words or talk for him. Don't make stuttering something to be ashamed of. Talk about it just like any other matter.

6. Always speak with Travis in an unhurried way, and pause frequently. Wait a few seconds after Travis finishes speaking before you speak. This slows down the overall pace of conversation. You can also help the other kids to learn to take turns talking and listening.

7. Use your facial expressions, eye contact, and other body language to convey to Travis that you are listening to the content of the message and not how he is talking.

8. You should expect the same quality and quantity of work from Travis as from the others. Definitely, do not let his speech disorders affect your expectations of him.

[Adapted from Lisa Scott (2006). *The Child Who Stutters at School: Notes to the Teacher.* Copyright 1991–2009 by the Stuttering Foundation of America. (www.stutteringhelp.org). Used with permission.]

For more information on stuttering and how to deal with it, go to the websites of the Stuttering Foundation, http://www.stutteringhelp.org/. You will also find useful information at the National Institute on Deafness and Other Communication Disorders, http://www.nidcd.nih.gov/health/voice/stutter.asp.

Good luck with Travis. Hope this information is helpful.

—Madeline

**EXTEND AND APPLY**

You can see that certain situations can increase the likelihood that a person will stutter. As a teacher, you will need to consider how you will deal with this condition if it occurs. If one of your students stuttered, do you believe you could be supportive? How? Also, what do you think is the most effective way to deal with children or adolescents who tease? Would you talk to them directly or to their parents? Would you punish them? Think about your response.

Voice disorders occur when a person's, pitch, loudness, or phonatory quality differs significantly from others with the same gender, age, ethnicity, and cultural background. In other words, when compared to one's peers, the person with a voice disorder will have an unusually high- or low-pitched voice, one that is too soft or too loud, or one that has unusual phonatory qualities. In order to be considered a "disorder," the condition of the voice has to be different enough to draw attention to the person or to adversely affect performance in school, at home, or in the community.

Voice experts use a variety of terms to describe a person's voice, but the most commonly used are a *harsh or strained* voice, a *breathy* voice, and a *hoarse* voice (Dalston & Marquardt, 2010). A harsh voice sounds like the voice of a person who is very angry but is trying to control his temper. The person may appear to be making a great deal of effort to speak, and her neck and jaw might appear tense. A breathy voice sounds like a partial whisper or a confidential voice. It is caused by an excessive amount of air escaping through the vocal folds, which are separated too much to vibrate appropriately. A hoarse voice is a combination of harshness and breathiness and is caused when the vocal folds have an irregular vibration. The irregular vibration is caused when the two folds have a different mass (Dalston & Marquardt, 2010; Justice, 2006).

Voice disorders can result from several reasons, including vocal abuse, neurological or psychological conditions, or the surgical removal of the larynx. Among the children and adolescents you are likely to encounter as a teacher, the most common voice problem will be due to vocal abuse. Figure 11.2 shows some of the most common voice misuses and abuses.

Vocal abuse leads to the development of **vocal nodules.** Nodules are small tissue formations on the vocal folds that are somewhat like calluses. They often develop because of misuse of the voice such as screaming or loud talking (Dalston &

## FIGURE 11.2 • COMMON MISUSES AND ABUSES OF THE VOICE

| | |
|---|---|
| Yelling and screaming | Alcohol use |
| Hard glottal attack | Speaking during menstrual cycle |
| Abusive singing | Excessive speaking |
| Hydration concerns | Inadequate breath support |
| Speaking over noise | Laughing hard |
| Coughing/throat clearing | Aspirin (drugs) |
| Grunting in exercise | Cheerleading, aerobics instruction, pep clubs |
| Calling at a distance | Making toy/animal noises |
| Inappropriate pitch | Athletic activity (coaching, etc.) |
| Excessive talking with allergy or upper respiratory infection | Intense personality |
| Muscular tension | Arguing |
| Smoking factor | |

*Source:* From *Clinical Management of Voice Disorders* (4th ed.), by G. L. Case, 2002, Austin, TX: Pro-Ed. Copyright 2002 by Pro-Ed. Adapted with permission.

Voice disorders can occur for a number of reasons, including vocal abuse.

Marquardt, 2010). Justice (2006) notes, however, that nodules can also develop because of physiological problems like **gastroesophageal reflux,** low blood circulation, dehydration, and **laryngeal tension.**

### Motor Speech Disorders

All of our day-to-day actions require us to use our muscles so we can move or act as we desire. When we make these movements, we are exercising our motor skills. Motor skills and specific movements originate within the neurological system, including our central and peripheral nervous systems. Even though we do not consciously realize it, to make even a relatively simple movement such as flicking a finger or kicking a ball, we must first go through a neurologically based programming and planning process (sort of like "get ready . . . set") and then execute the movement ("go!").

The activities involved in speaking, which we have described as the building blocks of speech, are the most complex motor movements that a person undertakes, requiring well-coordinated movements of very small muscles in order to produce speech sounds. Because these movements have a neurological origin, when neurological insult or trauma occurs, one or more of the building blocks of speech may be adversely affected (Maas & Robin, 2006).

### Manifestation of Speech Disorders

Speech disorders, especially phonological/articulation disorders and fluency disorders, usually originate during the early years of life. Sometimes they disappear, and sometimes they continue. Stuttering is a good example. As we have said, the cause of stuttering is not known. What is known, however, is that at some point in their lives, usually during the early childhood years, many individuals will stutter, perhaps as much as 5% of the population. In about 80% of these cases, the stuttering disappears, either as a result of normal development or because of therapeutic intervention. This leaves about 1% of the population who will stutter at any given time.

In terms of relative frequency, most children who have speech disorders have phonological or articulation disorders. During the school years, these students comprise the largest proportion of the SLP's case load. For example, most of Kathleen Lance Morgan's students (in the beginning of this chapter) have articulation problems. A smaller number of students have a fluency disorder, and relatively few children have other speech disorders.

The occurrence of both speech and language disorders tends to be higher among students with other disabilities. A defining characteristic of children with autism is their weak communication skills. Individuals with intellectual disabilities also have a relatively high incidence of language and speech disorders, with the number of cases of communication disorders directly related to the severity of the intellectual disabilities. Speech and/or language disabilities also occur with higher-than-average frequency among individuals with other disabilities, including learning disabilities, emotional/behavioral disabilities, traumatic brain injury, and physical disabilities.

**REFLECTIVE EXERCISE**

#6 Many teachers have students who have communication disorders. What are some ways a teacher and an SLP can collaborate to help students improve their communication?

## COMMUNICATION DIFFERENCES VERSUS COMMUNICATION DISORDERS

Before we continue with other issues in this chapter, it is critical that you understand that not all people who communicate differently from you are exhibiting communication disorders. In many cases you may be seeing a *communication difference* rather than a *communication disorder*. What's the difference?

Our speech and language characteristics are very much products of our culture, and our culture reflects our communication characteristics. This is extremely important to note in a society as diverse as the United States. For example, verbal communication generally differs among people who have grown up in the mountains of western North Carolina, people from Baltimore, and people who are natives of Houston. In different regions of our country, vocabulary differs, idioms vary, and speech is often distinguishable by dialects. Southern White people often sound different from northern White people, who often sound different from African American people, who often sound different from Hispanic people, and so on and so on. In the most extreme cases of communication differences, people have little or no knowledge or experience with the predominant language, which greatly impairs their ability to communicate effectively.

Do such people have a communication disorder? Most often the answer is no. Usually, it is more correct to say that they have a different form of communication. This is not a small matter. Many children have been inappropriately placed in special education programs because of their language differences. It is critical, therefore, that we recognize that not all uncommon communication patterns are communication disorders.

To establish that a student has a communication disorder as opposed to a communication difference, the student must have a discrepancy between her verbal communication and the communication of others who have the same culture, language, and dialect. To differentiate communication *differences* and communication *disorders,* Justice (2006) notes that the latter is present only when the person's communication ability is

- Outside the norms of the person's language or cultural group
- Considered by members of that group to be disordered
- Interferes with communication within the language or cultural group

# CHARACTERISTICS OF STUDENTS WITH COMMUNICATION DISORDERS

The challenges associated with communication disorders can sometimes be complex. In the following sections, we consider communication disorders as they may relate to other conditions.

## Cognition and Learning

From the perspective of the SLP and the teacher, generally speaking, students who have communication disorders fall into two broad groups: those without other disabilities (i.e., their challenges are limited only to rather specific communication disorders) and those with other disabilities (i.e., their communication problems result from other disabilities, lead to other disabilities, or are associated with other disabilities).

### Students Who Have Only Speech or Language Disorders

In the first group (those without other disabilities), you will usually find children or adolescents with speech disorders such as articulation problems or fluency disorders. These students form the largest group of students receiving services from an SLP and are distributed across the academic spectrum. A student can have a speech disorder and be just as capable as the student sitting next to him. In fact, many notable historical figures have experienced speech disorders, especially stuttering, yet have been very successful (see Figure 11.3).

In addition to students with specific speech disorders, you will also find students who have language disorders but no other disabilities. These students may be classified as having **specific language impairments (SLI)** (Justice, 2006). The cause of their language disorder is unknown, and they may have different types of language disorders. Children with SLI do not have hearing impairments; intellectual disabilities; or obvious neurological, sensory, or motor impairments. Nevertheless, after about their third birthday, children with SLI begin to show signs of language disorders beyond simply being a late talker. Although children with SLI have significant variety in their language profiles, you are likely to see the following characteristics:

- Inconsistent skills across language domains (e.g., being strong in phonology but weak in syntax and morphology)
- A history of slow vocabulary development
- Word-finding problems
- Difficulty with grammatical production and comprehension, particularly with the use of verbs
- Problems with social skills, behavior, and attention (Justice, 2006).

Table 11.1 shows language difficulties that might appear at different ages for an individual who has SLI.

### Students Who Have Communication Disorders and Other Disabilities

Many children who exhibit language disorders at the preschool level successfully overcome them due to intervention or language growth spurts. However, about 50% of these children continue to have language disorders during elementary school and

FIGURE 11.3 • **FAMOUS PEOPLE WHO STUTTER**

*20/20's* **John Stossel** still struggles with stuttering, yet has become one of the most successful reporters in broadcast journalism today.

**Robert Merrill**, world-famous baritone, was the first American to sing 500 performances with the Metropolitan Opera.

NBA All Star and Hall of Famer **Bill Walton** is recognized as a well-known NBC Sports commentator.

Explorer, conservationist, and zoologist **Alan Rabinowitz** works tirelessly to protect endangered species as described in his new book, *Beyond the Last Village.*

Singer **Carly Simon**, winner of an Oscar and a Grammy, not only has many hit records but is also an author of children's books.

Basketball star **Kenyon Martin** has been a two-time member of basketball's Team USA and was elected to the 2004 NBA All Star Team.

NFL star **Darren Sproles** is a football running back and return specialist for the San Diego Chargers. He was twice named *The Kansas City Star* Player of the Year.

Author **John Updike** enjoyed a long and successful career with best-sellers *Rabbit at Rest, Brazil,* and *Villages.*

Country music star and recording artist **Mel Tillis** has entertained audiences across the country and around the world.

Actor **James Earl Jones**, a Broadway and television star, is well-known for his voice as "Darth Vader" in *Star Wars* and his book, *Voices and Silences.*

**Annie Glenn**, wife of astronaut John Glenn, was grounded for years by a stuttering problem. Speech therapy, hard work and determination helped to turn it around.

**Bob Love**, legendary star of the Chicago Bulls, now heads up Community Affairs for the championship team.

**John Melendez**, announcer for the *Tonight Show*, is a talented musician, actor, and comedian.

**Marilyn Monroe** captivated movie audiences and fellow performers alike throughout her legendary career.

Legendary golfer **Ken Venturi**, U.S. Open Champion, is a successful commentator for CBS Sports.

Congressman **Frank Wolf** of Virginia feels that meeting the challenge of stuttering helped prepare him to meet other challenges in life.

As "Xander" in the popular TV series, *Buffy the Vampire Slayer,* **Nicholas Brendon** has won fans of all ages.

**Winston Churchill** captured the attention of millions during WWII with his inspiring speeches.

Source: *18 Famous People Who Stutter.* Copyright 2001–2009 by the Stuttering Foundation of America. Used with permission. Retrieved from: http://www.stutteringhelp.org/portals/english/18_famous_people_2008.pdf

**TABLE 11.1** • LANGUAGE DIFFICULTIES ASSOCIATED WITH SPECIFIC LANGUAGE IMPAIRMENT

| Age | Language Difficulties |
|---|---|
| Infancy and toddlerhood | Late appearance of first word (average age of 23 months); delayed use of present progressive (-*ing*), plural (*s*), and possessive ('*s*); late use of two-word combinations (average age of 37 months); less frequent use of verbs and less variety in verbs; slow development of pronouns; longer reliance on gestures for getting needs met; difficulty initiating with peers; difficulty sustaining turns in conversation |
| Preschool | Use of grammar that resembles that of younger children (e.g., pronoun errors, as in *me want dolly*); late use of verb markers (e.g., third person singular *is* as an auxiliary); frequent errors of omission (e.g., leaving out key elements of syntax); shorter sentence length; problems forming questions with inverted auxiliaries; difficulty with accurate use of *be* as an auxiliary or copular verb form; slow development of pronouns; requests similar to those of younger children; difficulty with group conversations (i.e., conversing with more than one child); difficulty with verbal resolution of conflict |
| Early and later elementary | Word-finding problems accompanied by circumlocutions and pauses; naming errors (e.g., *shoes* for *pants*); slower processing speed; use of earlier-developing pronoun forms; low sensitivity to the speech of others (e.g., difficulty responding to indirect requests); difficulty maintaining topics; difficulty recognizing need for conversational repair |
| Adolescence | Difficulty expressing ideas about language; inappropriate responses to questions and comments; poor social language; insufficient information for listeners; redundancy; inadequate sense of limits or boundaries; difficulty expressing needs and ideas; difficulty initiating conversations with peers; immature conversational participation |

Source: From L. Justice, *Communication Sciences and Disorders* (2006), p. 224, published by Merrill/Prentice Hall. Copyright © by Pearson Education. Reprinted with permission.

even into high school and adulthood. When language disorders continue beyond the preschool years, the children who exhibit them are likely to be ultimately classified as having learning disabilities, intellectual disabilities, or emotional and behavioral disabilities (Owens et al., 2003).

Language disorders are prevalent among students with learning disabilities. Gillam and Petersen (2010) note,

> To read, children must decode sequences of letters into language. To write, they must encode their language into sequences of letters. It only makes sense that children who have difficulty comprehending and producing spoken language are at a significant disadvantage when they begin to learn how to read and write. Therefore, it should not be surprising that most children with language disorders have significant difficulties with the development of literacy.

When you note the definition and major characteristics of learning disabilities that we presented in Chapter 6, you can see that language weakness in this population is significant. Furthermore, scholars have come to recognize the strong relationship between communication skills and academic success (Thatcher, Fletcher, & Decker, 2008). Schoenbrodt, Kumin, and Sloan (1997) reported that, in various studies, estimates of the co-occurrence of language disorders and learning disabilities is 35% to 60%.

**REFLECTIVE EXERCISE**

#7 What experiences have you had with students with learning disabilities? Have you noticed any particular language difficulties?

For another example of the relationship between communication disorders and individuals with other disabilities, consider a student with cerebral palsy (CP). (We describe this condition in Chapter 14.) CP is a neuromuscular condition that results from brain damage that occurs before, during, or soon after birth. Individuals with CP have physical and sometimes intellectual disabilities and also often have dysarthria, a speech motor disorder. Persons with CP often have difficulty speaking because of general weakness and a lack of coordination of muscles involved in different parts of the speech process. They may have difficulty with respiration, voice, articulation, and fluency. Their overall speech development takes longer than usual and is usually challenging throughout their lives.

As these two examples suggest, very often speech or language problems affect students who have other disabilities. Regardless of their identified disability, very often communication disorders will be one of their major challenges.

## Social Behavior

Just as communication disorders can co-occur with conditions related to cognitive and learning challenges, a person's communicative abilities may be related to social skills development. It should be obvious that our communication skills are used primarily in our social relations. If we lack adequate speech or language skills, our social position can be affected in different ways. We may become withdrawn and avoid others; we may interact inappropriately with others, causing them to avoid us; or we may try to compensate for our lack of communication skills by interacting with others in ways that are undesirable, such as through aggression or disruptive behavior. A couple of examples help make this point.

People who stutter typically develop secondary behaviors as a result of their stuttering. They may purse their lips, blink their eyes, look away, fidget, or engage in other behavior as they try to force out what they want to say. Take a look again at Travis, the boy described earlier in "Can You Help Me with This Student?" How do you think he felt standing in front of his teacher and classmates trying to recite his poem? Would you guess that his social adjustment might be adversely affected? Do you think that the laughter of his classmates might have made him want to

withdraw? Or maybe it would have challenged him to excel like some of the people noted in Figure 11.3. Regardless, we think it is safe to conclude that the speech disorder exhibited by this young man would lead him to be a different person than he would have otherwise been.

Although a person with a speech disorder such as stuttering might experience a degree of emotional stress, can communication disorders, including language and speech disorders, lead a child to engage in challenging behavior or become behaviorally or emotionally disabled? It is almost impossible to answer such a question. Given the complexity of human beings, we don't always know what causes what. However, we do know that communication disorders occur very frequently among students who have disciplinary problems and those classified as emotionally disturbed or behaviorally disordered. For example, Ross, Neeley, and Baggs (2007) found that second-grade children with language disorders had significantly more disciplinary office referrals than did their classmates without language disorders. Furthermore, Benner, Nelson, and Epstein

Can communication disorders lead a student to become emotionally disturbed or behaviorally disordered?

(2002) reviewed 26 studies that looked at the relationship between emotional and behavioral disabilities and language disorders. They found that 71% of students identified with emotional and behavioral disability had language deficits, and 57% of the students diagnosed with language deficits also were classified as having emotional and behavioral disabilities.

## PREVALENCE AND TRENDS

In the United States, slightly more than 1.1 million students are served in public schools as students with speech or language impairments. This is nearly 19% of all students served under IDEA and represents about 2.3% of the individuals between 6 and 17 years who were enrolled in school (U.S. Department of Education, 2009).

In addition, as we have noted, many students are classified as having other disabilities who have communication disorders as secondary conditions. These students are counted in addition to the 1 million just mentioned. The National Institute on Deafness and Other Communication Disorders (NIDCD, 2008) reported that 8% to 9% of preschool-age children have speech disorders and that, by the first grade, approximately 5% have "noticeable speech disorders." Other data reported by NIDCD include the following:

- Approximately 7.5 million people in the United States have trouble using their voices.
- More than 3 million Americans stutter. Stuttering occurs most frequently in young children between the ages of 2 and 6 who are developing language. Boys are three times more likely to stutter than girls. Most children, however, outgrow their stuttering, and fewer than 1% of adults stutter.
- Between 6 and 8 million people in the United States have some form of language disorder, and this includes 2% to 8% of school-age students.

## CAUSES OF COMMUNICATION DISORDERS

Sometimes the cause of a communication disorder can be tied to a specific physiological etiology; sometimes it cannot. A recognizable etiology is an organic cause for the condition. When the cause is unknown, the communication disorder is referred to as a functional disorder. Organic causes of speech disorders can be congenital (present from the time of birth), or they may be acquired later in life. Some commonly recognized organic causes of speech disorders include the following:

- Apraxia: Neurological damage that affects speech planning and production
- Brain trauma: Injuries of the brain that result in various communication disorders
- Cerebral palsy: A neurological condition that can result in articulation and voice disorders associated with abnormal muscle function
- Cleft lip and palate: A prenatal malformation that can result in very nasal speech even after surgical correction
- Dysarthria: Neuromuscular condition that can affect respiration, phonation, articulation, resonance, and prosody
- Otitis media: A middle ear infection that can result in delays in speech development (Davis & Bedore, 2010; Dalston & Marquardt, 2010)

For most of the speech disorders that you are likely to observe in school settings (primarily articulation disorders and fluency disorders), the cause is not readily identifiable, even by the SLP. Likewise, it is also difficult to pinpoint the cause of most language disorders. As noted, specific language impairments are defined as such by the fact that no specific cause can be fingered.

# IDENTIFICATION AND ASSESSMENT

Communication delays are one of the earliest indicators of a possible disability. Children as young as 12 to 18 months old may show signs that their language development is not on target. For some of these children, the delays evolve into disorders that continue into the preschool and school years and perhaps beyond. The communication challenges exhibited by children may range from relatively mild to more severe. Parents, pediatricians, and preschool or elementary school teachers may identify communication problems and refer the child to an SLP for formal evaluation.

As you have seen, many different types of communication disorders exist, so the SLP must use an assessment procedure that will best identify the type of disorder and its relevant characteristics. The diagnostic information that is collected will help the SLP develop the most appropriate treatment or intervention. The SLP will be able to evaluate communication and related conditions including language, speech, cognition, voice, fluency, hearing, feeding, and swallowing disorders.

Assessment procedures in the area of communication disorders attempt to answer several questions. Some of the more important are these (Justice, 2006; Owens et al., 2003):

- Is there a communication problem?
- Is there a diagnosis for the problem?
- What communication skills and deficits does the person exhibit?
- How severe is the problem?
- What is the probable cause of the problem?
- What form of treatment or intervention should be provided?
- What is the likely outcome (prognosis) if intervention is or is not provided?
- Does the individual meet eligibility requirements to receive services for a communication disorder?

The SLP will use an assessment protocol when attempting to answer these questions. This protocol will include several types of procedures for gathering information. Usually, it will begin with a chart review. This is an examination of the target person's developmental, educational, and medical history as contained in records collected by different professionals and agencies. Additionally, the SLP will interview the student, parents, caregivers, teachers, and other professionals to acquire relevant information about the person's communication history and current condition. In addition to the interview, the SLP might also ask these people to fill out questionnaires about the student's communication characteristics.

To determine how the student is currently communicating in real day-to-day conditions, the SLP will conduct a systematic observation. This might occur in different settings in the school and maybe also at home and in the community. During the observation, the SLP will look for characteristics such as difficulty paying attention, understanding abstract concepts, answering questions, seeking help, or explaining complex details (Justice, 2006).

The SLP may conduct a speech or language sampling procedure with the student. This is usually done in a preplanned session, either with the SLP or between the student and a parent or a peer. During this session, the SLP will make an audio recording and later transcribe it for analysis. This analysis will help the SLP get a clearer picture of the student's key communication characteristics (Owens et al., 2003).

Sometimes the SLP will use formal tests to learn more about the student's speech and language characteristics. The following types of formal communication disorders tests are available (Owens et al., 2003):

- **Articulation tests.** The SLP asks the child to name different objects such as a shoe, hat, pencil, and so on.

PEARSON
**myeducationlab**

Go to the Assignments and Activities section of Topic 12: Communication Disorders in the MyEducationLab for your course and complete the activity entitled *Working with a Speech Language Pathologist.*

## REFLECTIVE EXERCISE

#8 Which of the assessment questions will be most important to the teacher? Are there other questions you would ask?

- **Complex phonological naming tasks.** The SLP asks the child to name pictures such as elephants, encyclopedias, valentines, and so on.
- **Grammatical understanding.** The SLP asks the child to point to the correct picture when given a particular sentence, such as "The boy is getting dressed," "The boy is dressed," "The boy is undressed."
- **Grammatical production.** The examiner asks the student to complete sentences such as "This is a picture of one shoe. This is a picture of two_____." "The boy is putting on his sock." "The boys are putting on_____."
- **Pragmatic language use.** The SLP might ask a student what he would say in certain circumstances, such as when a person gives him a present or he meets a friend.

## EFFECTIVE INTERVENTION

After sufficient information has been gathered, the SLP interprets the results; and if it is clear that the student has a language or speech disorder, she develops an intervention plan. The best plan is effective, efficient, and easy for the student to follow. In developing the plan, the SLP uses her theoretical knowledge of communication and how a disorder affects it, empirical knowledge based on research, practical knowledge based on experience, and personal knowledge based on the student and his communication needs (Gillam & Petersen, 2010; Justice, 2006; Peña & Davis, 2010).

The SLP's primary objective is either to remediate the disorder or, if that is not possible, to help the student to develop compensatory skills. A remedial intervention attempts to correct the problem, whereas a compensatory intervention recognizes that the disorder cannot be remedied but provides the student with a skill to counter the condition. For example, the SLP may help a child improve a hoarse and breathy voice by retraining her to use her voice correctly (remediation) or assist a student with autism who is trying to comprehend directions by teaching him to use a picture schedule (compensation).

### Setting Goals

The first step of an intervention, whether to remediate or compensate for communication disorders, is to establish one or more long-term goals. The goals should represent the best-possible realistic outcome that the student can achieve over a period of time, such as 6 months or a year. For example, "Heather will be fully intelligible during conversations," or "LeShawn will use his voice properly in all speaking situations."

For each long-term goal, the SLP will develop short-term goals or objectives that should lead to achieving the long-term goal. The best short-term objectives address the student's real-world communicative needs as well as build skills necessary for reaching the long-term goal. Finally, for each short-term goal, the SLP establishes objectives for each therapy session or for daily achievement. These will be very observable communication behaviors that the SLP can record (Roth & Worthington, 2000).

## INTERVENTION PROCEDURES

The SLP uses specific intervention procedures to address specific communication disorders. He develops a procedure that he believes will remediate the communication disorder or help the student compensate for it. Once the procedure is determined and implemented, the SLP carefully monitors the progress of the student during each therapy session and also in real-world contexts. The SLP relies on direct observation data as well as feedback from key persons, including the student, the teacher, and the parents, to determine if the intervention plan is working. If the performance is improving sufficiently, the intervention plan continues until the student achieves the short-term and long-term objectives. If the data indicate that performance is not improving, the SLP develops a new intervention plan.

Just as there are different theoretical approaches to teaching and learning in general and special education, so there are different approaches used to address communication disorders. Justice (2006) described the following four models:

- The *behavioral* approach is based on classical learning theory. It emphasizes the importance of the environment in shaping behavior, especially the influence of behavioral antecedents and consequences.
- The *linguistic-cognitive* approach is based on developmental psychology and cognitive science. It focuses on helping the student develop an understanding of the rules that structure normal language production.
- The *social-interactionist* approach incorporates the theories of developmental psychology, which emphasize the importance of social interactions between people as a key element of learning. Scaffolding is provided within the learner's zone of proximal development to help achieve improved communication skills.
- *Information processing* models are based on theories of cognitive science and focus on how the brain processes information. This model holds that communication disorders are best treated by determining the processing deficit that is affecting communication.

## Supporting Students Using AAC Devices

Some students, especially those with physical or multiple disabilities, require **alternative or augmentative communication (AAC) devices** to help compensate for their lack of verbal communication ability. Many speech therapists, like Kathleen Lance Morgan, have received specific training in this area and can support students who have such needs. A variety of AAC devices are available for students to use. We include some examples in "Technology for Access." You can see how much they vary and the different levels of intellectual and physical ability that are required for their use.

As you can see in "Technology for Access," AAC devices can be characterized by the type of speech output that they produce, the way the message is represented, and the access or required input from the user. Speech output is digitized or synthesized. Digitized output is speech that is recorded by a human voice and stored on a computer chip. Only the recorded words or phrases can be expressed. Synthesized speech is generated by the computer and resembles the human voice. A device with synthesized speech can produce more varied messages. DEC-Talk is the most common speech synthesizer used in communication devices (Coping.org, 2006).

Message representation includes the symbols, words, pictures, or phrases that the user has available to produce his message. Sometimes this array can be very extensive, and sometimes it can be very limited. The breadth of the symbols available to a user for communication depends largely on his intellectual functioning and language development.

All AAC devices require some form of input from the user, and this can also be varied. At the least complex level, the user touches one part of the board, and a message is produced. Many devices at this level use switches, head pointers, or joysticks. At a more advanced level, one requiring both better physical and cognitive ability, students can use a keyboard to type specific words.

When supporting a student who uses an AAC device, the SLP must consider several important factors. These include the specific communication needs of the student; her cognitive, physical, and sensory abilities; the student's preference for the device; where the device will be used; and the attitude of the family or caregiver toward the use of the device. The SLP, along with other professionals, is responsible for teaching the student how to use the device, teaching other key persons how to interact with the student, and maintaining the device so that it operates effectively (Best, Reed, & Bigge, 2005).

PEARSON
**myeducationlab**

Go to the Assignments and Activities section of Topic 12: Communication Disorders in the MyEducationLab for your course and complete the activity entitled *Instructional Accommodations for Students with Communications Disorders.*

**REFLECTIVE EXERCISE**

**#9** Some conditions make it very difficult for a student to use an AAC device even when the student might benefit from one. What do you think these conditions might be?

# TECHNOLOGY for ACCESS

## EXAMPLES OF AAC DEVICES

| Device and Company | Speech Output | Message Representation | Access (User Input) |
|---|---|---|---|
| AlphaTalker II (Prentke Romich Company) | Digitized speech | Combine symbols to create messages | Direct selection |
| Dec-Aid (Aptivation, Inc.) | Recorded speech | 10-switch capacity | Direct switch |
| DigiVox 2 (DynaVox Systems) | Digitized speech | Can use symbols, words, pictures, etc. | Direct selection |
| DynaVox 3100 (DynaVox Systems) | Synthesized speech and/or digitized speech | Dynamic display | Direct touch on the panel |

| Device | | Speech | Features | Selection method |
| --- | --- | --- | --- | --- |
| LightWRITER (Zygo Industries) | | Synthesized DECtalk | Type messages on the keyboard | Direct selection keyboard sensitivity can be adjusted |
| Macaw Series (Zygo Industries) | | Digitized speech | Add your own symbols/message overlays; up to 128 messages | Direct selection using the membrane keyboard |
| SuperHawk (ADAMLAB) | | Digitized speech | Up to 72 message cells per page | Direct selection by the touch panel or plug in up to four remote switches |
| Vanguard (Prentke Romich Company) | | DECtalk synthesized speech and digitized speech | Fully customizable; can use symbols, words, pictures, etc.; uses Minspeak technology | Direct selection with the touch panel, optical head pointing, or scanning with switches/joysticks |

Source: From Coping.org. (2006). Tools for coping with life's stressors. Retrieved on July 14, 2006, from http://www.coping.org/specialneeds/assistech/aacdev.htmDECtalk. Coping.org is a public service of James J. Messina, Ph.D., and Constance M. Messina, Ph.D. Reproduced with permission.

## Service-Delivery Models

Traditionally, school-based SLPs have used a pullout model as their primary approach. With this model, the SLP removes one or a few students from the classroom and provides treatment sessions in a separate office or therapy room. Santos (2002) referred to this approach as the "black hole" or "den of mystery" model, because students with speech or language needs are often taken out of the classroom and returned to the teacher with little or no explanation of why they were being seen or what they were doing while they were gone. When they return, the students are sometimes in a quandary about what they have missed in class.

The pullout model is considered appropriate in many cases; but according to the American Speech-Language-Hearing Association (ASHA, 1999), the SLP has several other service-delivery options.

According to ASHA (1999),

> Service delivery is a dynamic concept and changes as the needs of the students change. No one service delivery model is to be used exclusively during intervention. For all service delivery models, it is essential that time be made available in the weekly schedule for collaboration/consultation with parents, general educators, special educators and other service providers. (p. III–273)

## Collaboration Between Teachers and SLPs

More than ever, SLPs and teachers need to cooperate with each other in order to provide better services to students with communication disorders (Sunderland, 2004). The need for cooperation is based on effectiveness and efficiency. The SLP is not with the student as much as the teacher is. Therefore, the teacher has a much greater opportunity to reinforce a student's communication skills, which the SLP has targeted. In fact, authorities on communication disorders have proposed that collaboration with teachers, parents and other family members, and counselors is a critical part of service delivery for students with communication disorders and an important factor in the success of the intervention (Hampton, Whitney, & Schwartz, 2002; Santos, 2002). Teachers have the opportunity to collaborate in numerous ways with SLPs to improve students' communication skills. The second "Can You Help Me with This Student?" shows some ways in which this collaboration can occur.

# PREVAILING ISSUES, CONTROVERSIES, AND IMPLICATIONS FOR THE TEACHER

School-based SLPs are likely to have very busy days, mixing their time among providing direct services to students, consulting with teachers on specific cases, and sometimes providing professional development information to teachers and other staff members. Not only are they concerned about providing remediation or developing compensatory skills, but they are also interested in preventing future communication disorders whenever possible.

## Interacting with Parents Who Want More Services

A great number of parents of students with communication disorders feel that the best way for their child to be served is to receive direct therapy from the SLP. This is especially true when a student has a communication disorder existing as part of another disability, such as an intellectual and/or physical disability. In such cases, parents often do battle with the SLP, the teacher, and the school administration to modify the individualized education program (IEP) to increase the direct contact time between the SLP and their child.

| To... | Andrea Fox, Speech–Language Pathologist |
| --- | --- |
| From... | Krystal Oliver, Second-Grade Teacher |
| Subject: | What should I do to collaborate with the SLP? |

Dear Ms. Fox,

I have some concerns about the speech and language of several of my second graders. I know that you work with many of them, but I was wondering if there might be some ways I could work more closely with you. I really think their communication is a central issue in both their academic and social development. What are some ways I can work effectively with you to help my students communicate better?

—Krystal

---

To: Krystal Oliver
From: Andrea Fox, Speech–Language Pathologist
Subject: RE: What should I do to collaborate with the SLP?

Krystal, I am so happy to hear from you. So many times teachers and SLPs seem to be operating in two different worlds, and this is not an efficient way for either to work. Here are some ideas that a number of SLPs have suggested that might improve our collaboration.

1. Teachers should discuss with the SLP any students who appear to be having trouble communicating, whether the problem is with speech or with language. You should ask for ways to screen students to help you find those whose communication difficulties might not be readily apparent.

2. Teachers should also talk to the SLP about ways to build speech and language exercises into the daily routine, both for your students who are receiving SLP services and as ways to improve the communication skills of your all your other students. The teacher and the SLP should look at lesson plans together to look for ways to build appropriate communicative exercises into them.

3. All teachers should make sure they know the specific targeted skills the SLP is working on with individual students and ask how to help students achieve these skills and generalize them. Teachers should especially know some specific do's and don'ts of how to intervene with students with communication disorders.

4. It is very important for the SLP to know how students with communication disorders are progressing. So you should find a good way to communicate this information, maybe even offer to keep some type of performance data.

5. Finally, you should keep the SLP informed about behavioral challenges that students may exhibit and work together to find effective communication skills for students who exhibit such behaviors.

Here are some reference materials you might find useful for more information on collaboration among professionals:

Cook, L., & Friend, M. P. (2007). *Interactions: Collaboration skills for school professionals* (5th ed.). Boston: Allyn & Bacon.

Hampton, E. O., Whitney, D. W., & Schwartz, I. S. (2002). Weaving assessment information into intervention ideas: Planning communication interventions for young children with disabilities. *Assessment for Effective Intervention, 27*, 49–59.

Pugach, M. C., & Johnson, L. J. (2002). *Collaborative practitioners, collaborative schools* (2nd ed.). Denver: Love.

Reed, V. A., & Spicer, L. (2003). The relative importance of selected communication skills for adolescents' interactions with their teachers: High school teachers' opinions. *Language, Speech, and Hearing Services in Schools, 34,* 343–357.

Ritzman, M. J., Sanger, D., & Coufal, K. L. (2006). A case study of a collaborative speech-language pathologist. *Communication Disorders Quarterly, 27* (4), 221–231.

Santos, M. (2002). From mystery to mainstream: Today's school-based speech-language pathologist. *Educational Horizons, 80,* 93–96.

Thanks again for bringing this issue up. . . . Let's plan to get together to discuss some specifics.

—Andrea

---

**EXTEND AND APPLY**

To be an effective professional, you must reflect on the challenges your students face and work collaboratively with others to address them. Besides those just suggested, what are some other ways in which teachers and SLPs can work together effectively? Do you believe that there are some personal characteristics that are necessary for collaboration? Do you have these characteristics, or do you believe you need to develop them?

---

**PEARSON**
**myeducationlab**

After reading the "Can You Help Me with This Student?" and "The Real World" features on working with SLPs, go to the Building Teaching Skills and Dispositions section of Topic 12: Communication Disorders in the MyEducationLab for your course and complete the learning unit entitled *Collaborating with the Speech Language Pathologist.*

School personnel often resist this push from parents for two reasons. First, as you have seen, schools provide services to individuals with communication disorders in various ways, and ASHA (1999) maintains that an SLP has a professional obligation to offer services suitable to the needs of the student. Sometimes this involves direct services, sometimes services of a less direct nature. Second, although not often discussed, there is a serious shortage of SLPs working in public schools. Therefore, their caseloads tend to be very heavy. From a practical point of view, then, most schools simply cannot provide the intensity of services that many parents would like. Unfortunately, the parents sometimes feel that the school isn't meeting their child's communication needs. In some cases it may be because the student will really benefit from collaborative consultation; in others it may be due to the lack of a sufficient supply of SLP services. In either case the parent may not be satisfied, and the special education teacher or the classroom teacher might get caught in the middle.

## Developing Positive Relationships Between Teachers and SLPs

A related critical issue is the ability of both special education teachers and classroom teachers to work in a collaborative relationship with SLPs. Many SLPs, like Kathleen Lance Morgan, express concern about the fact that some teachers don't really understand the role of the SLP and, worse, fail to realize that some children require active intervention to improve their communication skills. Without teachers' willingness and ability to work collaboratively with SLPs, the collaborative-consultation model will not be effective. Because of this concern, we encourage you to look at the suggestions "Can You Help Me with This Student" regarding ways for teachers and SLPs to work cooperatively and also suggest that you learn as much as possible about being a productive team member.

# THE REAL WORLD Challenges and Solutions

## Should I talk to the SLP?

*Marissa Harrison thought that Dom was probably one of her smarter students. What really impressed her was that while he definitely had some reading issues, he excelled in math, he got along great with the other first graders, he seemed to be on top of a variety of current cultural issues, and most important, he was always in a good mood. He could tell you who was doing what on just about any HBO show, who was batting well and who was crummy on the Rays, and even who was going with whom. He was such a great kid, that Marissa didn't really think the learning disabilities label fit him very well, except for that problem he had in reading. And there was one more thing. She couldn't quite understand everything he was saying.*

*It wasn't anything she could put her finger on. He didn't stutter, he didn't have a lisp or anything like that, and if you asked him to repeat what you said, like, "Dom, let me hear you say 'zebra,'" he would usually say it just fine. If she listened carefully, she could almost always make out what he was saying, and when she couldn't, she would just ask him to say it again, say it in another way, or explain what he was talking about, and then, most of the time, she could figure out what he was trying to get across. But there were times when she just wasn't certain.*

*His speech, or was it his language, wasn't exactly like the other kids. Of course he was only in the first grade, and Marissa thought there was a chance that he could outgrow any real problem that he might have, but still she wondered whether or not she should look into getting some help for him in the speech–language area.*

*Marissa did not know Mrs. Gonzalez, the SLP, very well, and she wasn't really sure what she could do for Dom, if anything. Some of the other teachers had told her about the SLP, but she had never been formally introduced, and Marissa had never gone out of her way to meet her. What Marissa knew was that the SLP always seemed to be in a hurry and didn't hang out with the other teachers and school employees in the lounge or at other times, probably because she was only half-time at Sea Breeze. So not only was Marissa unsure what she should do about Dom, she also wasn't exactly comfortable talking to Mrs. Gonzalez informally. She wasn't really sure what her next move should be.*

What do you think about Marissa's situation? What would you do? It seems she has three problems. First, she doesn't know if Dom really has a problem or what to do about it if he does. Second, she doesn't fully know what an SLP does. And third, she has not developed any type of relationship, formally or informally, with a key team member who can provide assistance for students with special needs.

Several signs could indicate a student *may* need speech or language therapy. Although it is not the teacher's job to decide if intervention is necessary or what type of intervention should be offered, teachers should be aware of what is worth reporting. Teachers should ask themselves four questions to decide if a student might need to see an SLP for evaluation:

1. **How is the student's intelligibility?** You should be able to understand most speech. Do you find yourself saying "wow!" or "oh no!" or "really?" a lot of the time? Do you sometimes pretend to understand? A good guide to use with a young child to judge the adequacy of speech is to divide the child's age by 4. The result should equal the percent of speech a stranger should be able to understand. For example at 1 year, 25% of the speech should be intelligible; at 2 years, 50%; at 3 years, 75%; and at 4 and older, 100%. So for school-age students, if you are not able to understand all of their speech, a referral for evaluation is warranted.

2. **How easy is it to communicate with the student?** For school-age students, you should be able to have a normal conversation with an easy, back-and-forth, turn-taking pattern of communication. If the student cannot complete a thought, if the student struggles to find the right words, or if the student has trouble with pronouncing words that others who are the same age can pronounce clearly, then the student may have a problem, and a referral would be appropriate.

3. **What is the student's general manner of interacting?** Is the student outgoing in about the same way as other students, or is he shy and quiet most of the time? Does the student seem to avoid talking in class by not asking or answering questions or commenting during class discussions? If so, the student may be trying to hide a speech or language problem.

4. **Does the student have notable speech characteristics?** Do you hear the student substituting sounds, deleting sounds, stuttering, speaking with a hoarse voice, or anything else that might be uncommon? In general, if a student's speech is different enough from other students of about the same age and cultural background, so much so that it draws attention to itself, then the student should be evaluated for a speech disorder.

**SLPS can intervene to improve speech or language disorders in the following ways:**

- Help individuals with articulation disorders to learn how to say speech sounds correctly.
- Assist individuals with voice disorders to develop proper control of the vocal and respiratory systems for correct voice production.
- Assist individuals who stutter to increase their fluency.
- Help children with language disorders to improve language comprehension and production.
- Assist individuals with aphasia to improve comprehension of speech and reading and production of spoken and written language.

# 11 SUMMARY

Children with communication disorders are a relatively large group of students who receive services under IDEA.

## Definitions of Communication Disorders, Language Disorders, and Speech Disorders

- Communication disorders include both language disorders and speech disorders. Although a student may have both, they are not the same thing.
- A language disorder can be a disorder of form (including phonology, morphology, or syntax), content (also called *semantics*), or use (also called *pragmatics*). These can appear individually or in combination.
- Sometimes students with language disorders also have other disabilities.
- Speech disorders include articulation disorders, fluency disorders, voice disorders, and motor speech disorders.
- Like language disorders, speech disorders sometimes occur along with other disabilities, and sometimes they do not.

- It is important to be aware of the difference between a communication disorder and a communication difference. Some individuals may be erroneously assumed to have a communication disorder when actually their communication is appropriate within their own cultural milieu.

## The Relation Between Communication Disorders and Other Disabilities

- Students who have learning disabilities, intellectual disabilities, emotional and behavioral disabilities, physical disabilities, or traumatic brain injury often have communication disorders associated with their disabilities.

## The Prevalence and Causes of Different Communication Disorders

- Almost one in five students served under IDEA is served because he or she exhibits a speech or language disorder.
- The cause for many communication disorders is unknown, and the causes that are known are usually

associated with other disabilities such as intellectual disabilities, autism, or cerebral palsy.

- When the cause cannot be identified, it is called a *functional disorder*.

### Types of Assessment Used to Plan Interventions for Students with Communication Disorders

- SLPs use different types of assessment procedures to assess the nature of the communication and develop an intervention plan. These may include direct methods, such as taking a speech or language sample, and indirect methods, such as interviewing other persons about the student's communication characteristics.

### Major Features of Interventions for Communication Disorders and Service-Delivery Options

- Using the diagnostic information, the SLP develops an intervention plan that includes long-term, short-term, and session goals.
- The SLP monitors the student's progress during the intervention and continues providing services until the student achieves the goals. If adequate progress is not occurring, the SLP modifies the intervention and continues observing the student's progress.
- An SLP may develop interventions based on different theoretical models or approaches. The most common include the behavioral approach, the linguistic-cognitive approach, the social-interactionist approach, and the information-processing model.
- Students whose needs are more severe may benefit from AAC devices. The nature of the AAC device must be based on unique student characteristics, such as intellectual and physical abilities, and the student's communicative context.
- The SLP can use different service-delivery options depending on the student's needs. These range from providing direct therapy to offering consultation to teachers.
- The classroom teacher, the special education teacher, family members, and others can provide communication support for the student by collaborating with the SLP. For example, they may reinforce the intervention and give the SLP feedback on the student's progress.

### Major Issues in Providing Services to Students with Communication Disorders

- One major issue is how SLPs can deliver effective services when they often have many students in their caseload with different needs.
- Another is how teachers can work more collaboratively with SLPs to complement their services.

 **Council for Exceptional Children**

## ADDRESSING THE PROFESSIONAL STANDARDS

Council for Exceptional Children (CEC) Knowledge Standards addressed in this chapter:

ICC1K5, ICC1K10, GC1K5, GC1K7, ICC2K1, ICC2K5, ICC2K6, GC2K1, ICC3K1, ICC5K4, ICC6K1, ICC6K2, ICC6K3, GC6K3, GC7K4, GC8K1, ICC10K1, ICC10K2, GC10K2, IC1K1, IC2K3, IC2K4, IC8K3

Appendix B: CEC Knowledge and Skill Standards Common Core has a full listing of the standards referenced here.

 **PEARSON myeducationlab**

Now go to Topic 12: Communication Disorders in the MyEducationLab for your course, where you can:

- Find learning outcomes for the broad concepts covered in this chapter along with the national standards that connect to these outcomes.
- Complete Assignments and Activities that can help you more deeply understand the chapter content.
- Access video clips of CCSSO National Teachers of the Year award winners responding to the question, "Why Do I Teach?" in the Teacher Talk section.

- Apply and practice your understanding of the core concepts and skills identified in the chapter with the Building Teaching Skills and Dispositions learning units.
- Check your comprehension on the content covered in the chapter by going to the Study Plan in the Book-Specific Resources section for your text. Here you will be able to take a chapter quiz, receive feedback on your answers, and then access Review, Practice, and Enrichment activities to enhance your understanding of chapter content.

# chapter 12
# Traumatic Brain Injury and Multiple Disabilities

**REFLECT UPON**

- What do we mean by traumatic brain injury? What is the definition of multiple disabilities?

- What are the significant characteristics of students with traumatic brain injury, and what are the characteristics of students with multiple disabilities?

- How many students have traumatic brain injury, and how many have multiple disabilities? What are the causes of these conditions?

- What types of identification and assessment procedures are used with students with traumatic brain injury and those with multiple disabilities?

- What are some effective educational practices for teaching students with traumatic brain injury, and what are some effective practices for teaching students with multiple disabilities?

- What are some major issues related to educating students with traumatic brain injury and students with multiple disabilities?

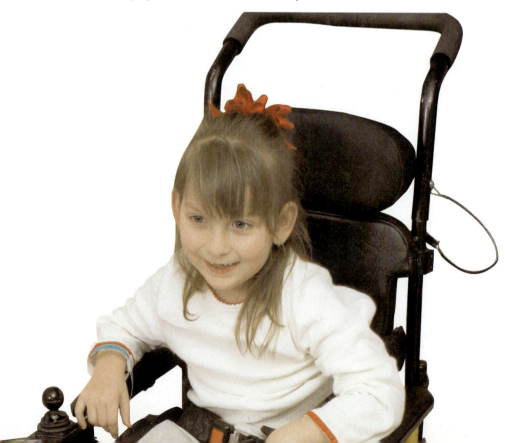

# MY PROFESSION, MY STORY: **SHANNON HUNT**

When Shannon Hunt was a little girl, she liked to play teacher and liked the idea of becoming a teacher. In her freshman year of college, she volunteered to work in a first-grade classroom, and she was hooked. She completed a bachelor's degree in English and then stayed an extra year to earn a master's degree in elementary education. Later she added an academically-intellectually gifted (AIG) certificate. She thought her preparation was about as good as it could be, but she also knew she still had a lot to learn.

On her first day, Shannon felt a tremendous sense of responsibility and wondered if she could handle it. It hit her when the kids came in, and the classroom door shut. All of a sudden she was the one in charge, the one who had to give the directions, and the one who had to answer all the questions. "I was, like, who hired *me* to do this job?"

But of course, Shannon hung in. She's had some ups and downs and has even thought about a career change from time to time, but now she is really having fun and hopes to make it for the long haul, minus the few years she wants to take to start her own family.

Shannon is a fourth-grade teacher at Ira Jones Elementary School in Asheville, North Carolina. She loves her class and, just as much, she loves her current working conditions. Her energy and enthusiasm are apparent, and she thinks they are a big part of being a successful teacher. "If you like the way things are going, it means you feel so much better about what you're doing and that, you know, affects the kids. They can see it."

What is it that Shannon likes so much? Well, of course, a big part of it is the kids. It's not that the kids are all that easy, but where they are in relation to each other, how they treat and understand each other really makes Shannon happy to be teaching them.

In Shannon's class, you will find four students with special needs: one with mild cerebral palsy; one with autism; one who has significant problems with speech, reading, and writing; and one with traumatic brain injury (TBI). To provide the best services for these students, Shannon works with a special education teacher, who spends about 2 hours a day in her classroom.

Of the four students, it is the child with TBI that Shannon finds most interesting . . . and also most challenging. We'll call him Josh. What Shannon knows is that, when Josh was very young, less than 2 years old, he had a very serious fall. From that point forward, he experienced various behavioral and learning problems that presented challenges to his parents and his teachers. In fact, this is the first year he has been in a general education classroom; and according to Shannon, he is doing fairly well. From her point of view, it's just as important for Josh to be with the group as it is for any other student. "Kids

want to belong," she says, and in this way Josh is no different.

But he *is* different in many ways. The biggest challenge for Shannon is his social immaturity and his lack of social perception. Dealing with his academics is difficult, she says, but at least you can prepare for that. She and the special education teacher work together to plan for Josh and the other students with special needs. But with Josh, there are times when he just has a hard time understanding what is going on. "For example," Shannon said, "today the kids were all running around outside, and there was a lot of goofing off, and they were all calling each other 'baby' and 'big baby,' and Josh just didn't get it. He got mad and started crying because he thought they were calling him a baby. He just didn't really get it."

Josh's parents really wanted him to be in a general education class this year, and Shannon wanted him there, too. So far his interactions with the other students have gone pretty well, and this makes Shannon happy. For now, anyway, she

thinks that things in her class are going well for everyone, including Josh, and she is very excited about how it has turned out.

In this chapter we will discuss two distinct groups of students: those with traumatic brain injury (TBI) and those with multiple disabilities. Both groups of students have unique characteristics, and as a teacher you are likely to find them interesting and challenging. Typically, like Shannon's student Josh, students with TBI have learning and social characteristics that set them apart from their peers. Importantly, the impact of their TBI can result in a lot of variability, both in how they differ from other students their age and how they themselves can fluctuate in their abilities and characteristics over time. The nature and extent of this variation will be related to the type of brain injury suffered and degree of its impact.

On the other hand, students with multiple disabilities usually have intellectual disabilities, often in the severe-to-profound range, that occur in combination with physical disabilities and health impairments. They are often included among students referred to as having "severe disabilities." They may be limited in areas such as language, academic, and motor skills, and may have various health impairments as well. Unlike students who may have acquired TBI later in life, students with multiple disabilities are likely to have had these conditions since birth or early childhood.

In comparison to most other students with disabilities, both groups of students, those with TBI and those with multiple disabilities, have a relatively low incidence of occurrence. Both are identified under IDEA as disability categories, although students from both groups may be classified under other disability categories by school districts. The FAQ sheet provides key information about both groups of students.

**REFLECTIVE EXERCISE**

**#1** What do you think would be most interesting and most challenging about teaching students with TBI or students with multiple disabilities? Which students do you think would benefit from your personal abilities and skills?

# FAQ Sheet

## STUDENTS WITH TBI AND MULTIPLE DISABILITIES

| | |
|---|---|
| Who are they? | *Traumatic brain injury* (TBI) is an acquired injury to the brain caused by an external force that can result in learning or behavioral disabilities or both. |
| | *Multiple disabilities* means concomitant impairments (e.g., intellectual and physical or medical disabilities) that result in severe educational needs. According to the Individuals with Disabilities Education Act (IDEA), the term does not include deaf-blindness. |
| What are typical characteristics? | Characteristics of students with TBI vary widely. They may have learning, social, and/or behavioral difficulties; and their abilities may vary from time to time. |
| | Students with multiple disabilities have significant weaknesses in general learning ability, personal and social skills, and sensory and physical development. Some may exhibit uncommon characteristics (self-stimulatory or self-injurious behavior) and most have serious medical conditions. |
| What are the demographics? | Students with TBI are only 0.04% of all school-age students, whereas students with multiple disabilities constitute about 0.23% of all school-age students. |
| Where are students educated? | Most students with TBI spend all or most of their time in the general education classroom, whereas most students with multiple disabilities are generally placed in special classrooms or schools but may also be included in general education classrooms. |
| What are the outcomes? | Individuals with TBI may continue to face challenges into their adult years, which may impact their postsecondary education and employment. Most individuals with multiple disabilities live with their families or in community-based residential settings after high school. Some may work in supported employment settings or in sheltered workshop settings. |

# DEFINITIONS AND CLASSIFICATION CRITERIA FOR STUDENTS WITH TBI AND STUDENTS WITH MULTIPLE DISABILITIES

## Traumatic Brain Injury

According to the definition of TBI in the Individuals with Disabilities Education Act (IDEA), the term applies to "open or closed head injuries resulting in impairments in one or more areas, such as cognition; language; memory; attention; reasoning; abstract thinking; judgment; problem-solving; sensory, perceptual, and motor abilities; psychosocial behavior; physical functions; information processing; and speech" (IDEA, Sec. 300.7). As you will recall from the discussion about Shannon Hunt and her student Josh, what struck her most about Josh were his immature social skills. Such characteristics, as well as learning challenges, may be seen in this group of students.

Different types of brain injury have varying degrees of seriousness and potential harm. Among the more common are these:

- **Skull fractures.** A linear fracture is a crack in the skull detectable by X-ray that does not usually cause significant neurological damage. In contrast, a depressed fracture means the skull is broken and pressing against the brain and is often associated with significant brain damage.
- **Contusion.** This is a bruise to a part of the brain. The degree of damage will depend on how extensive the bruise is. The symptoms of the contusion may worsen for a few days after it occurs.
- **Hematoma.** A hematoma is a blood clot. An epidural hematoma is one that forms between the skull and the outer covering of the brain. A subdural hematoma forms directly on the brain itself and is usually more serious than an epidural hematoma.
- **Concussion.** Any injury that can cause a loss of consciousness or amnesia is a concussion. It is caused by a slight injury to nerve fibers in the brain.
- **Diffuse axonal injury (DAI).** DAIs are similar to a concussion but much more severe. Nerve fibers (or axons) throughout the brain are injured through violent motion such as that caused by a car crash.

The severity of TBI is determined by the duration and severity of the **coma** that follows the injury. A coma is the loss of consciousness that sometimes occurs after a head injury, and it can last hours, days, or even months. Not all comas are equal in severity. They are considered to be minor, moderate, or severe based on the person's ability to open their eyes, move in response to verbal directions, and verbalize when asked. As the person is prompted to respond, his or her ability is rated using an instrument such as the **Glasgow coma scale**. Based on the overall rating, the severity of the trauma can be evaluated (Best, 2005b; Michaud, Duhaime, Wade, Rabin, Jones, & Lazar, 2007).

TBI was not recognized as a distinct disability category under IDEA until 1990, and today variation still exists across school districts and states in the identification of students with this condition. Many students who have sustained brain injury, and

**myeducationlab**

To check your comprehension on the content covered in Chapter 12, go to the Book-Specific Resources in the MyEducationLab for your course, select your text, and complete the Study Plan. Here you will be able to take a chapter quiz, receive feedback on your answers, and then access Review, Practice, and Enrichment activities to enhance your understanding of chapter content.

Unfortunately there are many ways children and adolescents can sustain traumatic brain injury, including automobile accidents.

### REFLECTIVE EXERCISE

#2 Have you ever known anyone whose day-to-day mood or interests or stamina changed unpredictably? Did this affect your interactions with the person? If you were teaching such a student, how would you try to stabilize his or her personal demeanor?

who may experience difficulty in learning or social behavior as a result, are not identified for special education services or are identified but are misclassified. Students with TBI may be identified as having learning disabilities, attention-deficit/hyperactivity disorder (ADHD), behavior disorders, physical disabilities, or communication disorders, but their educational characteristics and needs usually differ from these students' (McCaleb, 2006; Michaud et al, 2007). Michaud et al. noted that in contrast to other disabilities, "two hallmarks of TBI are highly variable performance within and across academic subjects and continued change over time. Depending on the time since the injury, recovery may still be proceeding rapidly, with abilities changing from month to month" (p. 468).

## Multiple Disabilities

As we noted previously, the category of multiple disabilities usually includes a combination of some degree of intellectual disability as well as physical disabilities, health impairments, and sometimes vision or hearing loss. According to IDEA, "Multiple disabilities are concomitant impairments (e.g., mental retardation–blindness, mental retardation–orthopedic impairment), the combination of which causes such severe educational needs that they cannot be accommodated in special education programs solely for one of the impairments. The term does not include deaf-blindness" (IDEA, Sec. 300.7).

Among students with multiple disabilities, the level of the intellectual disability is usually in the severe-to-profound range but may also fall into the mild-or-moderate range. In reality, the individual's intellect may actually be higher than what is sometimes estimated because the person's physical limitations may impair an evaluator's ability to determine a precise level of intelligence (Willard-Holt, 1998). The person will often have difficulty communicating effectively and may lack the opportunity to have many typical life experiences. As a result, the person's intellectual potential may be suppressed and it may be difficult to accurately assess it.

In addition to classification according to their identified or presumed intellectual status, students with multiple disabilities will often be classified according to the nature of their physical disabilities and other health impairments. Physical disabilities may be clinically defined according to the limbs that are affected and the specific form of the condition. Classification terms used include the following:

- Monoplegia: Only one limb is affected.
- Diplegia: The lower limbs are severely affected; the trunk and the upper limbs to a lesser extent.
- Paraplegia: Only the legs are affected.
- Quadriplegia: Major involvement of all four limbs, as well as the neck and the trunk.

One particular physical disability that often affects students with multiple disabilities is **cerebral palsy (CP)**, a neurologically based condition. Specific forms of CP include **spasticity**, which is characterized by muscle stiffness; **athetosis**, meaning unwanted or involuntary movement, and **ataxia**, which is characterized by a lack of balance and uncoordinated movement. **Epilepsy** is another condition often seen in individuals with multiple disabilities. The seizures that occur are generalized **tonic-clonic seizures**, complex **partial seizures** (known previously as *psychomotor, or temporal lobe, seizures*), and **absence seizures** (previously called *petit mal seizures*) (Westling & Fox, 2009). The classification process may also include other physical or health conditions.

It can be difficult to determine the true intellectual ability of a student with multiple disabilities.

# PRIMARY CHARACTERISTICS OF STUDENTS WITH TBI AND STUDENTS WITH MULTIPLE DISABILITIES

## Traumatic Brain Injury

The student with TBI will very likely have academic problems in areas such as literacy and math, but will also have difficulties in different areas of cognitive functioning such as concentrating and paying attention, remembering, carrying out complex cognitive tasks, problem solving, information processing, and communicating. Following are some examples of how you may see these conditions manifested in the classroom:

- Remembering: The student may fail to remember assignments or require a great deal of practice to remember tasks, activities, or procedures.
- Carrying out cognitive tasks: A student may be able to do math computations but may not be able to reason adequately to solve word problems.
- Problem solving: A student may become frustrated because of forgetting school materials and may not be able to work out a solution to compensate for the problem.
- Information processing: The student may become frustrated when given several bits of information or directions in a short period of time.
- Communicating: The student may have difficulty either expressing his thoughts or understanding others who are speaking.

In addition to these cognitive-academic limitations, students may show changes in their personality and exhibit behavioral issues such as being off task, increased or decreased activity levels, impulsivity, irritability, apathy, aggression, or social withdrawal.

An important characteristic that sets students with TBI apart from other students with disabilities is the variability that occurs in their performance and behavior and the changes that you may see over time. Most children (around 95%) survive brain injuries, but their future outcomes can vary based on the degree and severity of the initial coma, the type of brain injury, their age at the time of injury, and their level of functioning before the injury. All of these factors work into their overall future progress, which can vary in the time and level of recovery. For this reason, flexible planning for these students is imperative (Keyser-Marcus et al., 2002; Michaud et al., 2007).

## Multiple Disabilities

Individuals who have severe intellectual and multiple disabilities often are referred to as having "the most significant" disabilities. Their developmental levels will often be comparable to that of a child under 12 months of age, and they may only minimally attend or respond to environmental stimuli. They will have serious medical or physical conditions. As we noted above, cerebral palsy and epilepsy are two conditions that are often present. Other conditions can also limit normal physical development and activities. Common medical conditions include gastrointestinal disorders, inadequate ventilation of lungs, kidney and heart problems, sensory problems, and frequent infections (Thuppal & Sobsey, 2004). Even with these conditions, many of these students demonstrate the ability to learn and are capable of at least partial participation in normal daily activities (Westling & Fox, 2009).

In the classroom, teachers of students with multiple disabilities will typically work with school nurses as well as speech–language pathologists and physical and occupational therapists to address students' needs. On a regular basis, some of these students will have nutritional problems, **anemia**, dehydration, skin irritation and pressure sores, **respiratory infections**, asthma, ear infections, and **contractures** (Heller, 2004). These kinds of conditions can cause considerable discomfort for the student and imply that teachers and other professionals must collaborate as problem solvers in order to address them.

## REFLECTIVE EXERCISE

**#3** Some students with TBI may appear lazy and inattentive, and some may exhibit behavior problems. Do you think understanding these students' conditions could help you work more effectively with them without "blaming" them for the way they sometimes act?

## REFLECTIVE EXERCISE

**#4** Many teachers of students with multiple disabilities must devote a great deal of time to toileting, hygiene, and feeding. Do you suppose it is possible to do a good job at teaching when there are so many other needs you must address with these students? How would you do this?

# PREVALENCE, COURSE, AND CAUSAL FACTORS

## Prevalence of TBI

According to the National Center for Injury Prevention and Control in the Centers for Disease Control and Prevention (2009), every year TBIs to children between birth and 14 years old result in around 2,700 deaths, 37,000 hospitalizations, and 435,000 emergency department visits. This works out to mean that about 1 of 25 children is medically treated for head injuries. Of this group, about 1 of 500 suffers TBI, which means that more than a million school-age students acquire brain injuries each year. The condition has been established as the most common cause of death and disability among children (Best, 2005b; Keyser-Marcus et al., 2002).

However, according to the most recent data from the U.S. Department of Education (2009), only a little over 23,000 students between 6 and 21 years were classified as having TBI, which represents only about 0.04% of the school-age population. Based on these data, two points are important to note. First, many children who sustain brain injury are not provided services under IDEA, either because they are not recognized as having special needs, or their performance in school does not suffer enough to warrant special education. Second, many students who have sustained head injuries are likely to be found in other disability categories instead of being classified within the TBI category. In fact, one study found that most students who were reported as having brain injuries either were not being served in special education or were often being served as students with speech–language disorders or physical disabilities (McCaleb, 2006).

## Course of TBI

Several factors can influence the long-term outcomes that result from TBI. The location of the injury in the brain and the exent to which it is diffuse, or widespread, determine the amount of damage the person sustains. Generally the more localized the injury, the better the prognosis. When the damage is more diffuse, more areas of functioning are affected and often to a greater degree. The depth and the length of time the individual is in a coma also predict the ultimate outcome. Lower scores on the Glasgow Coma Scale, indicating less responsiveness, are generally predictive

Many students with traumatic brain injuries are not identified for special education services, and others are identified as having other disabilities.

of less favorable long-term outcomes. In contrast, children who become responsive within 6 weeks have a better prognosis for their recovery (Michaud et al., 2007).

The injured person will probably need medical treatment and therapy to aid rehabilitation in several areas. Brain injury may result in impaired motor functioning, feeding disorders, sensory impairments, communication impairments, cognitive disabilities, and emotional and behavioral disabilities (Best, 2005b; Keyser-Marcus et al., 2002; Michaud et al., 2007). The challenges that persons with TBI face as children and adolescents will probably remain with them throughout their adult lives. They may have happy and successful lives, but this will depend on how well they are able to compensate for the TBI and the vocational and social demands they encounter as adults.

## Causes of TBI

A head injury is considered to cause trauma to the brain when it is harsh enough to change the child's level of consciousness and/or to change the normal structure of the brain. Common causes of TBI during childhood include falls from heights, sports-and recreation-related injuries, automobile and other vehicle crashes, and assaults, including child abuse. As you would expect, the cause of the injury is likely to vary with age; young children are injured more in falls, whereas adolescents are injured more in car and motorcycle accidents (Michaud et al., 2007). TBI is most likely to occur at two critical times in a person's life: when a child is under 5, because that is when falls and child abuse are most common; and when he or she reaches adolescence, because that is when sports, recreation, driving, risk taking, and attempted suicide are most common (Best, 2005b).

Two kinds of forces—impact and inertial—can cause brain injuries. An impact force occurs when something hits the head with enough force to fracture the skull, bruise parts of the brain, or cause bleeding in the skull. Inertial damage happens when the brain experiences rapid and severe motion that is violent enough to damage nerve fibers and blood vessels. In most cases of TBI, both forms of damage occur simultaneously (Michaud et al., 2007).

## Prevalence of Multiple Disabilities

Students classified under IDEA as having multiple disabilities total approximately 132,000 according to the most recent data (U.S. Department of Education, 2009), and this comes to about 0.23% of the school-age population. Again, like students with brain injury, some students who have multiple disabilities may be found in other disability categories, most commonly, intellectual disabilities or physical disabilities.

## Course of Multiple Disabilities

The complex nature and characteristics of individuals with multiple disabilities make it difficult to identify a common path that most will follow through adolescents and into adulthood. Like other individuals with severe disabilities, the areas of future concern will be employment (or other meaningful adult activities), adult living arrangements, and, for some, postsecondary education. An overriding concern should be the opportunity to maintain an optimal quality of life.

Three key factors will influence the status of persons with multiple disabilities as adults. One will be their own personal needs, particularly their medical and health needs. The challenges faced during childhood will not abate as these individuals grow older and in some cases will become even more challenging. Therefore, the extent to which they may be able to live, work, and learn as an adult will largely depend on the level of supports they will require to do so.

The availability of personal resources to provide or secure necessary supports is a second factor. Individuals who may rely on the natural supports of those close to them, including family, friends, and co-workers, or who can secure the funds to help arrange for supports, are likely to enjoy a better life outcome. Development of

## REFLECTIVE EXERCISE

#5 How do you think you would react to a child becoming injured at school? If it were a head injury, would you know how serious it might be? This could be useful information for a new teacher.

## CAN YOU HELP ME WITH THIS STUDENT?

| To... | Jan Shook, Emergency Medical Technician |
| From... | Lauren Saunders, First-Year Second-Grade Teacher |
| Subject: | Deciding if a head injury is serious |

Hey, J., it's been a while. What are you and Josh doing for the holidays? I'm going to visit my parents for a couple of weeks and maybe get in some skiing.

You wouldn't believe what happened today. One of my kids, Sam, who really likes to show off for the girls, was hanging by his legs on the jungle gym and slipped off. It had been raining in the morning, and the playground was still wet, and I guess he slipped. But I nearly freaked. He hit right on his head, and for a few seconds I don't think he moved. I grabbed the nearest kid and sent her running to the office, and I went running over to see if Sam was moving. By the time I got to him, he was turning over and getting up, and the AP was running out. Sam got up and could walk, so they took him to the office and called his mom, and she picked him up. I guess he is OK, because I didn't hear anything else. But I was pretty upset. I guess I need to get some info on first aid or something, because I really didn't have a clue.

Have a good holiday, and let me know what's up with you and Josh sometime.

—Lauren

---

To:        Lauren Saunders
From:      Jan Shook
Subject:   RE: Deciding if a head injury is serious

Hi, Lauren,

It must be nice to get so much time off. I'm off on the 25th, and that's it. Josh and I are good, been talking about a date next fall. I'll let you know as soon as we decide.

Your little friend was lucky he didn't do more damage. I've seen some really bad stuff with kids, but it sounds like he got off pretty easy. You teachers need to keep an eye on those little ones, there are so many ways for them to get hurt. Usually, a head injury to a kid is mild and doesn't really have any long-term effects, but it could be bad. Here's what you have to look out for. The big thing is if the kid loses consciousness for more than a few minutes. This didn't happen to your little guy, which was a good sign. The other problem signs are if he becomes sluggish or confused or grumpy, or if there is a bad headache or any bleeding, or if vision or hearing is affected. Also, if the child starts to vomit, this should let you know you need to do something. Generally, if you see any of these, you need to take the child straight to the emergency room for a neurological exam. And here's the most important thing: If the kid remains unconscious for more than a couple of minutes, you need to call for emergency medical service right away.

Hope this helps. Here is some reading material you should get your hands on. Your little friend will probably be back after the holidays as good as new.

Batshaw, M. L., Pellegrino, L., & Roizen, N. J. (2007). (Eds.) *Children with disabilities* (6th ed.). Baltimore: Paul H. Brookes.

Johns Hopkins Children's Center. (2006). *First aid for babies & children fast.* London: DK Publishing.

National Institute of Neurological Disorders and Strokes. (2009). *Traumatic brain injury: Hope through research.* Retrieved from http://www.ninds.nih.gov/disorders/tbi/detail_tbi.htm?css=print

Traumatic Brain Injury.com. (2004). *What is traumatic brain injury (TBI)?* Retrieved from http://www.traumaticbraininjury.com/

Have a good break!

—Jan

transition plans as an integral part of the individualized education program (IEP) therefore should begin when the student enters adolescence, and the plans should focus on identifying or finding the supports that will be necessary. Finally, the extent to which the community in general, and specific community-based agencies in particular, can accept and support persons with significant disabilities affects their general outcome: the greater the support, the better their outcome.

## Causes of Multiple Disabilities

Multiple disabilities may be caused by prenatal, perinatal, or postnatal conditions (occurring before, around the time of, and after birth, respectively). Common **prenatal causes** of multiple disabilities include **genetic conditions**, **chromosomal anomalies**, **maternal infections**, the ingestion of harmful substances, and radiation. Rare genetic conditions can lead to children being born with syndromes characterized by severe intellectual and multiple disabilities. These genetic conditions may be recessive or dominant. If they are **recessive**, both parents of the child must be carriers of the condition, and each of their offspring will have a 25% chance of inheriting the condition. If the condition is due to a **dominant** genetic condition, only one parent must have the genetic information, and each child will have a 50% chance of inheriting the condition.

Chromosomal anomalies can occur in different ways. Sometimes a strand of chromosome may not join another during conception, or a strand may break off and/or attach itself to another strand in an uncommon way. These chromosomal anomalies are not genetically inherited disorders in the sense that the parents transmit them to their children. However, they do affect the development of the offspring in an adverse way because of the change in the chromosomal patterns.

Viral or bacterial maternal infections can occur during pregnancy that have little effect on the mother but may have more serious consequences for the developing fetus and result in multiple disabilities. **Rubella**, **cytomegalovirus**, **herpes**, **syphilis**, and **toxoplasmosis** are common types of infections. Most infections cause the greatest damage to the developing fetus during the first trimester of the pregnancy. At this time, the central nervous system of the fetus is developing rapidly, and the infection can cause inflammation and can damage brain tissue. The result is often severe intellectual disabilities and also physical and/or sensory disabilities.

Harmful substances, including alcohol, drugs, or other chemicals taken by the mother during pregnancy, can sometimes cause multiple disabilities. These substances can affect the development of the fetus by damaging the structure and functioning of cells. Physical growth, the developing brain, or both might be affected. For example, **thalidomide**, a drug developed in the 1950s to reduce morning sickness during pregnancy, was shown to lead to impaired limb development. Additionally, alcohol consumption has been found to result in brain damage. Anticonvulsant drugs and anticancer drugs are other agents that can lead to adverse development.

Multiple disabilities have various prenatal, perinatal, or postnatal causes.

Most of the conditions that cause a child to have multiple disabilities occur during the prenatal period. However, some perinatal conditions and postnatal conditions can affect the child's development as well. For example, difficult deliveries sometimes result in brain damage and cerebral palsy. Or if the mother has an acute illness at the time of birth, such as a viral infection, it may be transmitted to the infant. After birth, other conditions can affect development and lead to severe intellectual and multiple disabilities. One is **meningitis**. This condition is a bacterial or viral infection of the spinal cord and the fluid that surrounds the brain. The bacterial form is treatable through antibiotics, but there is no effective treatment for the viral form. If the condition is not effectively treated, it can result in severe intellectual and multiple disabilities.

## IDENTIFICATION AND ASSESSMENT

In most cases, physicians and other medical professionals will initiate evaluations for individuals who acquire brain injuries during their childhood or adolescent years and also for those who display multiple disabilities early in life. These evaluations will identify the medical conditions that will lead to a diagnosis of TBI, or the specific conditions associated with multiple disabilities such as intellectual disabilities, cerebral palsy, seizure disorders, or other related conditions. Following medical evaluations, psychological, educational, and related services professionals will assess the student to determine eligibility for special education, the student's educational goals and objectives, how and where the student will be provided instruction, and the related services necessary for the student to receive an appropriate education.

### Medical Evaluations

In the case of TBI, the student will need both immediate and long-term medical care and related medical services. Immediate care consists of addressing the injury through medical treatment, sometimes including neurosurgery. In some cases the child remains in a coma for an extensive amount of time—even days, weeks, or longer. During this time, doctors and health-care professionals provide medical treatment to prevent or treat complications and seizures. A physical therapist will provide passive range of motion exercises to stimulate the muscles and to help prevent contractures and pressure sores. Other therapeutic provisions might include the use of casts or splints and sensory stimulation. People who recover from a coma often do so at an uneven pace, and doctors monitor their recovery in order to determine when more intensive post-coma treatments should be provided (Best, 2005b). After medical treatment for the injury or when the person fully recovers from the coma, therapists provide rehabilitation to (1) counter conditions that can occur from immobilization and neurological dysfunction, (2) help the person regain abilities or teach him or her to adapt or compensate for any loss of function, and (3) help offset the effect of any form of chronic disability on learning or development.

We can also consider the initial medical evaluation of an individual who may develop multiple disabilities. For example, let's consider briefly how a child with CP, which is sometimes a condition of a child with multiple disabilities, is identified. The pediatrician or family physician is usually the professional who recognizes and

diagnoses the condition. The physician will first observe that the child's **primitive reflexes** are not disappearing according to a normal developmental timeline. These reflexes, including **asymmetric tonic neck reflex**, **tonic labyrinthine reflex**, and **positive support reflex**, are present in all newborns but usually disappear in the first year. When they do not disappear, they interfere with normal motor development and impede the child's ability to sit, stand, and walk. This is often the first symptom that the child has CP. When this condition is recognized, the physician continues to follow the child's development for a period of time. Ultimately, a medical diagnosis is made, and subsequent treatment is prescribed. The treatment may include medication, surgery, or physical therapy.

Continued planning and evaluation will be required for students with TBI and those with multiple disabilities, in order to allow them to participate in various life activities. They may require medication, surgery, therapy and rehabilitation to improve, maintain, or compensate for functioning in several areas including:

- Motor functioning, such as the use of their hands and arms for daily living skills and use of their legs for ambulation
- Eating abilities, which may be impaired by problems with swallowing, **gastroesophageal reflux**, or smelling or taste disorders
- Sensory abilities, including impaired vision, hearing, or both
- Communication skills, including speech or language impairments or receptive language abilities
- Cognitive abilities, which may be affected in various ways and to different degrees including severe intellectual disabilities (Michaud et al., 2007)

## Educational Evaluations

Educational evaluations for students with TBI and with multiple disabilities focus on four questions:

- What is the student's current ability in key areas including academics, social development, and physical and health needs?
- What general curriculum goals are appropriate for the student, and to what extent and in what ways can the student participate in the general curriculum?
- What additional areas of instruction must be addressed?
- What related services and supports will be required to provide the student with an appropriate education?

Planning the educational and related services for students with TBI is based on needs identified through physical, sensory, psychological, academic, and behavioral assessments. Planning for instruction must take the student's cognitive and learning characteristics into consideration, especially attention, visual and auditory perception, memory, and information-processing abilities. Information about the student's interests and abilities before the injury occurred is important in providing direction for future activities and instruction, but students with TBI will almost certainly lag significantly behind in all educational areas. Additionally, in some cases, students with TBI may exhibit **emotional lability** (or emotional "ups and downs") that may require functional behavioral assessments and behavior intervention plans. Teachers and parents must establish flexible and realistic short-term academic and behavioral goals and objectives and carefully monitor the student's progress to adjust them as necessary (Best, 2005b).

Educational planning for students with multiple disabilities must consider their learning needs as well as their physical and health-related needs. As with students with TBI and other disabilities, the general curriculum will provide a framework to identify academic learning needs. Beyond educational goals in the general curriculum, however, students with multiple disabilities may require additional goals related to

## REFLECTIVE EXERCISE

#6 What type of medical evaluation information do you think would be most useful if you were teaching students with TBI or multiple disabilities?

their needs to participate in multiple environments. Two effective ways to identify these goals are by conducting ecological inventories of important living environments and developing person-centered plans (Westling & Fox, 2009).

## Ecological Inventories

An ecological inventory approaches the question of what to teach a student with disabilities from the perspective of what skills the student needs to learn to live more fully in his or her current or future environments (L. Brown et al., 1979). Ecological inventories can provide a wealth of information about what students need to learn, what they can already do, and what might be done to help them learn certain skills.

An ecological inventory first looks at key environments such as the home, the school, and maybe different places in the community. Then it looks at subenvironments, such as the kitchen at home or the cafeteria at school. Then we ask, "What does a person normally need to do to function in here?" In the kitchen, someone might prepare a meal; in the cafeteria, someone might walk through a line to get a meal.

As you can see, many different skills might be identified for different environments. So the next step is to work with the parents or caregivers to identify skills that would be most useful for the student to learn. For example, maybe preparing a meal isn't the most appropriate thing for an 8-year-old to do, but helping to set or clear the table would be. These skills then become the key learning objectives for the student.

## Person-Centered Plans

Person-centered planning is not so much an assessment procedure as it is a process to help caring people develop a consensus about how to improve the quality of life for an individual with severe disabilities. Teachers use different approaches to person-centered planning, and some approaches have become fairly well recognized over the years. One, personal futures planning (Mount & Zwernik, 1988), is meant to provide a positive approach for life planning for persons with significant disabilities. Its purpose is to help friends and family members plan ways in which the individual can have a better life that includes personal relationships, an active life in the community, and more personal control. Personal futures planning doesn't focus on a person's deficits but on developing more positive opportunities for the person.

Making Action Plans (MAPs; Forest & Lusthaus, 1987; Vandercook, York, & Forest, 1989) is another person-centered planning process; but unlike personal futures planning, it focuses specifically on providing information for developing full-inclusion placements for students with significant disabilities. During a MAPs session, the individual with disabilities, family members, friends without disabilities, and teachers and other professional personnel gather to discuss the educational and life needs of the target individual. An important feature of MAPs is the inclusion of the targeted individual's chronological-age peers on the planning team.

As the session proceeds, a facilitator asks participants to respond to the following key questions:

- What is the individual's history?
- What is your dream for the individual?
- What is your nightmare?
- Who is the individual?
- What are the individual's strengths, gifts, and abilities?
- What are the individual's needs?
- What would the individual's ideal day at school look like, and what must be done to make it happen?

Answers to the questions are intended to help determine the learning goals for the student and how instruction should be provided in an inclusive environment throughout the school day.

# EDUCATIONAL PRACTICES

## Effective Practices for Students with TBI

Students with TBI present a unique challenge to both special educators and general educators. It is often difficult to know what they will remember from previous lessons, how well they will react emotionally to different situations, or how much their cognitive and learning abilities will vary from one day to another. When teaching a student with TBI, a teacher must be ready for progress to occur but also can expect some delays in learning and educational setbacks.

Providing instruction focused on specific academic needs and delivered in a structured manner will generally be the most effective educational approach for students with TBI. By enhancing the content of the material to appeal to the student's interest, the student will be more likely to remain engaged. Positive reinforcement for correct responding and correction of errors will also help the student make progress on appropriate academic tasks. Having a consistent, organized, predictable daily instructional routine will help the student re-learn forgotten material and advance in her academic progress. Additionally, a classroom that is well organized and free from distractive items and events will likely be helpful. Keyser-Marcus et al. (2002) present numerous useful suggestions for working with students with TBI including the following:

Go to the Assignments and Activities section of Topic 16: Multiple Disabilities & TBI in the MyEducationLab for your course and complete the activity entitled *Traumatic Brain Injury.*

- Use a multimodal approach (overheads, videos, hands-on activities) when presenting material and instructions for assignments. It is difficult to judge the way that many students with TBI will learn best. Having different ways to present material will better ensure that the student with TBI will comprehend the material.

- Teach compensatory strategies to students, and structure choices. Students with TBI may lack organizational abilities and may be somewhat confused by little structure in physical areas, routines, or activities. Help students to get organized and cope with classroom arrangements.

- Begin instruction with a review of previous material and overview of the topics to be covered in the coming class session. For students with TBI, this can be very useful. Memory lapses and confusion can make it difficult to cognitively organize information without putting it into a meaningful context.

- You can also promote better learning by providing students with a written or visual outline of the material. An advance organizer helps students comprehend the material.

- Students with TBI need to be able to see the big picture. Therefore, you should emphasize the main points of the topic you are covering and frequently explain the key ideas. You should also incorporate repetition into your instruction.

- Specific, frequent feedback on student performance and behavior are very useful. Students with TBI may have difficulty gauging their performance. Your feedback can help them do so more effectively.

- You should also encourage questions. Some students with TBI may be reluctant to ask about things they don't understand. They may fear that they will look silly or forgetful. Letting them know that their questions are important can help them get over these boundaries.

- Whenever possible, break down large assignments into smaller components. Assignments that are too lengthy can seem overwhelming and incomprehensible. Presenting them in smaller doses can often be helpful.

- Ask students how they could improve learning or how you might present printed material differently to aid in their comprehension. Too much material

REFLECTIVE EXERCISE

#7 Based on what you have learned about students with TBI, which of these teaching strategies seem to make the most sense? Would they be helpful for other students with disabilities?

may be in a small space; a different page layout may be beneficial. Student input might be valuable in determining a better format.

- You can use both open-ended and multiple-choice questions to encourage responding. Students may respond differently depending on the structure of the questions.
- Some difficult material can be made easier to understand if presented more simply. One way to do this is to use illustrations, diagrams, or other visuals, if possible.
- Sometimes students with TBI will not respond as others do to typical environmental actions or conditions. To help these students, you can provide them with additional verbal or visual cues.

Although instructional approaches such as these can be helpful when teaching students with TBI, often these students will need to use different ways to compensate for some impaired cognitive functions. "Technology for Access" shows how some assistive technology devices can assist in this compensation.

*Source:* Adapted with permission from Keyser-Marcus, L., Briel, L., Sherron-Targett, P., Yasuda, S., Johnson, S., & Wehman, P. (2002). Enhancing the schooling of students with traumatic brian injury. *Teaching Exceptional Children, 34*(4), 62–67.

## Effective Practices for Students with Multiple Disabilities

Unlike most students with TBI, most students with multiple disabilities are identified relatively early in life. Therefore, they have the opportunity to benefit from effective instruction and related services that can begin when they are very young and continue through the school years. Although they will not achieve the level of learning and development reached by individuals without disabilities, or even those with less severe disabilities, overwhelming evidence indicates that good instruction can promote skill development and enhance their quality of life (Westling & Fox, 2009).

### Preschool Programs

The younger the child, the more related his learning and development to the family's well-being. Early interventionists therefore work hard to support the family so that the family can support the child. This means that early intervention personnel will use a **family-centered approach**; the services provided to a child are directed by family needs and enhance the family's ability to support the child (Bailey et al., 1998). This implies that professionals who work with young children are more than teachers of children. They must also be consultants, resources, and aids to families. Support of the family is an integral component of early intervention, and this is why the family's strengths and needs must be identified on the individualized family service plan.

Complementary to the family-centered approach, the most effective early intervention programs for children with multiple disabilities use **developmentally appropriate practices**. Use of such practices means that instructional activities are individually appropriate, age-appropriate, and reflective of the social and cultural conditions of the child's life. Early interventionists must understand both typical child development and the influence of cultural settings and practices on child development. These professionals must also understand how the child's disability may affect learning and development.

Programs based on developmentally appropriate practices use relevant concrete materials, stimulate exploration, help the child make age-appropriate choices, and include a great deal of interaction with adults and peers. Adults prompt the child to communicate and socialize with other children as often as possible and respond to children immediately and directly when they see any effort made by the child. They also provide an array of interesting toys and activities to stimulate children's interest. Even though teaching and learning occur in a natural context using relevant materials, teachers use systematic instructional methods to better ensure the child's participation and success.

Individuals with TBI often have difficulty with tasks that require cognitive activities such as remembering, planning, and problem solving. One approach to these challenges is to provide instruction, exercise, and practice in an effort to remediate them. Another is to find strategies and mechanisms to compensate for weaknesses so that individuals who have survived brain injury can function in their daily lives as independently as possible.

According to Kirsch et al. (2004), "Assistive technology for cognition (ATC) is a class of compensatory interventions that typically utilizes some type of electronic device to facilitate performance of a functional tasks" (p. 200). By using these devices, the need for human intervention or support may be lessened, and thus more personal independence may be achieved.

## Types of Devices

Several ATC devices that have been demonstrated through research to be effective are listed below:

- **Pocket (or Palmtop) Computers.** These commercially available devices can be used as organizers to remind users with memory loss of certain activities. They can show time, sound alarms, and give directions or prompts for different required daily activities using visual and auditory cues.
- **Cell Phones.** Cell phones may use cuing systems functioning to prompt the user to engage in a specific activity in a certain way at a certain time.
- **NeuroPage.** This paging system sends audible or tactile signals to the wearer at specific times, prompting the individual to read the brief message displayed on a small screen.
- **WatchMinder.** This wristwatch has a built-in alarm to prompt activities at certain times. The alarm vibrates at preset times.
- **Voice Craft.** This digital voice recorder and alarm system beeps and verbally prompts the wearer to engage in a select activity at a certain time using a prerecorded message.
- **Personal Computers.** PCs can be used like mobile wireless devices, although they are not as portable.

## Use of the Devices

Devices such as these can help with different types of functional tasks. They are especially useful for tasks that require information that must be managed and tracked, such as a task like taking medications that must occur at certain times according to very specific directions. These devices can also be used to remind people to engage in (or refrain from) certain social behaviors at certain times like when to meet friends or when to take a shower. Some devices can be very helpful when decisions must be made based on complex information. For example, many tasks in the home, community, and workplace require decision making given some current contextual situation. For example, "if you have started the laundry, be sure to return in 45 minutes to put it in the dryer."

## Case Studies

Taking daily medication is a common need among many individuals with TBI. Often, however, remembering to do so is a problem, and so someone must prompt the individual to do so. Van Hulle and Hux (2006) reported using the WatchMinder and Voice Craft devices to help three young adults learn to take their medication independently. By the end of the study, two of the three participants learned to take their medication more independently.

In another study, Kirsch et al. (2004), attempted to teach a young man with TBI how to find his way around a clinic. He often got lost going from one location to another, and the order of the location changed daily, resulting in 30 different routes he had to take. The researchers placed colored stickers on the different rooms of the clinic and then transmitted the next location through a pocket computer. The audio and visual message said, "Look around for a circle like this one (showing a colored circle on the screen), and then walk over to it. Tap here when you are at this circle." Using the device, the man made significantly fewer errors when walking to the different locations.

## References

Kirsch, N. L., Shenton, M., Spirl, E., Rowan, J., Simpson, R., Schreckenghost, D., & LoPresti, E. F. (2004). Web-based assistive technology interventions for cognitive impairments after traumatic brain injury: A selective review and two case studies. *Rehabilitation Psychology, 49,* 200–212.

Van Hulle, A., & Hux, K. (2006). Improvement patterns among survivors of brain injury: Three case examples documenting the effectiveness of memory compensation strategies. *Brain Injury, 20,* 101–109.

## School Programs

Teaching school-age students with multiple disabilities presents teachers with many challenges and opportunities. The most effective practices include the following:

- Students are taught in inclusive schools and classrooms to the maximum extent possible. This results in greater levels of awareness and provides an opportunity to participate in meaningful academic, personal, and social learning events (Downing & Eichenger, 2003; Foreman, Arthur-Kelly, Pascoe, & King, 2004).

- Paraeducators and peers support students in inclusive settings in appropriate and judicious ways. Paraeducators do not serve to isolate students from their peers but instead use strategies and tactics as directed by the teacher to increase the students' involvement and inclusion. Peers also play an important role in supporting the inclusion of students with disabilities in both academic learning and social development (Carter & Kennedy, 2006; Giangreco, Edelman, & Broer, 2003).
- Students participate in the general curriculum adapted in ways so that the content of the curriculum is essentially the same as for students without disabilities, but adjusted or extended to allow students to participate (Browder, Spooner, Wakeman, Trela, & Baker, 2006; Spooner, Dymond, Smith, & Kennedy, 2006). As an important part of the general curriculum, students participate and develop literacy skills in accordance with their interests and abilities (Katims, 2000; Kliewer & Landis, 1999).
- In addition to academic skill instruction, functional and personal skill instruction are interwoven as a natural part of the daily routine in order for students to achieve important areas of growth (Billingsley & Albertson, 1999).
- Teachers use systematic instructional procedures to teach both academic skills and personal skills in order to ensure students are making the greatest degree of progress possible (Billingsley & Romer, 1983; Wolery, Ault, & Doyle, 1992).
- When necessary, students "partially participate" in those activities in which their disabilities inhibit complete participation (Ferguson & Baumgart, 1991; Wolery et al., 1992).
- Related services such as physical, occupational, and speech–language therapy are provided in a collaborative manner and in natural settings whenever possible. "Role-release" and "transdisciplinary" teaming increase support services to students (Orelove, Sobsey, & Silberman, 2004).
- Throughout the day and in all activities, students receive opportunities to gain as much independence as possible, to express preferences and choices, and to develop self-determination skills (F. Brown, Gothelf, Guess, & Lehr, 1998; Reid, Parsons, Green, & Browning, 2001; Wehmeyer, 1996).

For a good example of the challenges one teacher faced in teaching a student with multiple disabilities. See "Can You Help with This Student? Teaching a Student with Multiple Disabilities." Fortunately, an experienced colleague was able to provide her with assistance.

## Providing Physical Care and Supporting Hygiene Needs

As you have learned, students with multiple disabilities often have physical or medical conditions that require additional supports. Some, such as lacking toileting skills, are primarily due to the developmental level of the individual. Others are due to medical causes. For example, seizure disorders or cerebral palsy have neurological causes; not being able to swallow food and thus needing to be tube fed may be related to congenital abnormalities or other conditions. Still other conditions are secondary aspects of a primary disability. For example, respiratory infections often occur because a weak cough or a malformed chest or spine inhibits the student's ability to expel mucus (Heller, 2004; Thuppal & Sobsey, 2004).

The student with multiple disabilities will have objectives based on the general curriculum as well as objectives based on personal needs.

Regardless of the condition or the cause, school personnel often must provide a student with multiple disabilities additional physical assistance and adequate supports. While such tasks may initially seem daunting to a nonmedical professional, several strategies make accepting such challenges less threatening:

| To... | Joe Banks, Experienced Special Education Teacher |
| --- | --- |
| From... | Pamela Donahue, New Special Education Teacher |
| Subject: | Teaching a student with multiple disabilities |

Hi, Joe—good seeing you last weekend at the mall. Like I was saying, I really could use some advice with one of my students. If you have time, I'd appreciate your input. Here is some info about my guy Steve.

He is classified as having "multiple disabilities" and is in the "profound" mental disabilities range. He can't walk or talk, and his records say he is deaf and blind, but I'm not sure how much he can really see or hear. Obviously, he can't do much for himself in the way of daily living skills. His really big problem is that he cries most of the day, and I'm not sure why. He has to wear a body support jacket most of the day because he has scoliosis, and I think this might be really uncomfortable. The thing is, he can't talk or give me any other kind of clue about what the problem is. I also know from his mom that he doesn't sleep much at night, so that might be part of it, too. He gets occupational therapy, physical therapy, speech, and the vision teacher comes about twice a month, but no one really seems to know what he needs or how to help him. Any ideas you have would be great! I'd really like to make some progress with him this year.

Thanks,

Pam

---

To:       Pamela Donahue
From:     Joe Banks
Subject:  RE: Teaching a student with multiple disabilities

Hey, Pam. I know you have your hands full. Sue Tomlin had your guys last year, and she told me then about Steve and some of the others. I think she had made some pretty good progress, but then her husband got transferred to LA, . . . which I guess is why you are here now.

   Steve is going to be tough to figure out, but I have some ideas that might be helpful to you. My guess is that he's not happy about something, and he can't tell you what it is, and that is why he is crying so much. You might be right about that jacket. The best thing to do is conduct a functional behavior assessment. This will help you figure out why he is crying so much. I can give you some references that can help you with this. You might also talk to the physical therapist, and see about taking him out of the jacket and laying him down on the floor sometime. If his crying stops, then it might be because the jacket is uncomfortable, like you think. It could be other stuff, too, which is why the functional behavior assessment will be helpful. All in all, he can't tell you anything, so you will probably have to work on some kind of augmentative or alternative communication system. You need to find out if maybe he wants to sleep, or get something to eat or drink.

   I think I would go ahead and try to set up some kind of communication system, probably using little objects set on his wheelchair tray that he could touch when he wants to tell you something. Try to work with your speech therapist to set up a tactile communication board. I think I would have at least three or four little items that he can learn to touch to let you know what he wants (you can use something like a spoon for eating, a cup for drinking, and a piece of a blanket so he can let you know when he wants a nap). Then use a hand-over-hand approach to teach him to touch them. Then when he touches one, right away give him what he touches. When he touches the cup, give him something to drink. When he touches the other stuff, give him what he wants then, too. Always keep them in the same place, and try to gradually reduce how much help you're giving him. This could take awhile, but it could teach him how to let you know what he wants. You want him to learn to touch them by himself to let you know what he wants, then give him what he wants when he touches the item. If my hypothesis is right, once he can tell you what he wants and gets it, his crying will happen less often, maybe even stop.

Steve's challenges are certainly difficult but are not unlike those of most students who have multiple disabilities. You're really going to need to be inquisitive and creative in order to find some answers. Here are some references I can loan you that you will find helpful. I'll drop them at your house this weekend.

Best, S. J., Heller, K. W., & Bigge, J. L. (Eds.) (2005). *Teaching individuals with physical or multiple disabilities* (5th ed.). Upper Saddle River, NJ: Merrill/Pearson Education.

Beukelman, D. R., & Mirenda, P. (2006). *Augmentative & alternative communication: Supporting children & adults with complex communication needs*. Baltimore: Paul H. Brookes.

O'Neill, R. E., Horner, R. H., Albin, R. W., Storey, K., Sprague, J. R., & Newton, J. S. (1997). *Functional assessment of problem behavior: A practical assessment guide*. Pacific Grove, CA: Brooks/Cole.

Westling, D. L., & Fox, L. (2009). *Teaching students with severe disabilities* (4th ed.). Upper Saddle River, NJ Merrill/Pearson Education.

Good luck and let me know what happens.

—Joe

**EXTEND AND APPLY**

- What was Pam's greatest challenge? Was it Steve's sensory and physical disabilities? Was it his lack of skills? His challenging behavior?

- What personal characteristics do you have that might help you be an effective teacher of students like Steve?

- What particular strategy did Joe suggest Pam use that you would like to learn more about?

**You Are Not Alone.** First, you must remember that no one expects you to become a health-care expert overnight. Parents, school nurses, and physical and occupational therapists are all important sources of information about how to provide specific types of care and treatment. You will be able to rely on these individuals as long as necessary for your personal development before you are expected to take on any challenges without assistance. And then these persons will be able to continue to support you as necessary.

**Individual Health Care Plans.** Each student who requires special medical care or consideration will have his or her own individual health-care plan. You do not need to become an expert on all medical issues; you need only to be able to provide care or a response based on the unique needs of the student.

**Time Is an Ally.** The biggest challenge you may face is lack of understanding and familiarity with certain procedures. As time goes by and you become more accustomed to managing certain matters, they will become more commonplace to you. These unique challenges will then become part of your day-to-day routine.

**REFLECTIVE EXERCISE**

#8 Students with multiple disabilities have complex needs. Do you think teachers of these students need to be especially knowledgeable and creative to meet these needs? Do these students present the kind of challenge you would accept as a teacher?

# TRANSITION TO ADULT LIFE

When children with TBI or multiple disabilities grow into adolescence and adulthood, many of the challenges they faced as children continue or in some cases worsen. For individuals with TBI, this is especially true if their initial injuries occurred early, were relatively severe, their initial coma scores were low, and they were experiencing other developmental delays or disabilities before the injury (Michaud et al., 2007). For those with multiple disabilities, their cognitive, sensory, and physical conditions will persist, and they will continue to require support throughout their lives (Westling & Fox, 2009).

Adult life conditions of both groups of individuals often tend to be less than desirable, even when compared to other former students with different disabilities. According to one national study of young adults with disabilities who had been out of high school between 1 and 4 years, individuals classified as having TBI did not fare well in the areas of employment, postsecondary education, or independent living. Only 43% were employed when they were interviewed, and only 18% lived independently (Newman, Wagner, Cameto, & Knokey, 2009). An earlier study found similar conditions. This study followed 33 individuals who experienced brain injuries when they were in preschool into adulthood (Nybo & Koskiniemi, 1999). The researchers found that only 27% of the individuals worked full-time and that another 21% had subsidized employment. They also found that only 37% lived independently at home, and 15% needed help with basic daily activities. In a follow-up study of the same group, the outcomes did not vary considerably from the first report (Nybo, Sainio, & Müller, 2004).

Likewise, young adults who were classified in school as having multiple disabilities also do not tend to do well based on key indicators of adult life. Newman et al. (2009) found that at the time individuals with these conditions (or their parents or caretakers) were interviewed, only 48% were employed outside the home, and only 7% lived independently or semi-independently. In a measure of quality of life, only one third said they had communicated with a friend outside school or the workplace in the past year.

Conditions such as these highlight the need for well-developed transition plans. As you know, a transition plan must be a part of the IEP when the student becomes a teenager. The plan needs to consider the kinds of services the student will need after the school years, the agencies and organizations that might provide the services, and the preparations that are most important for the student and the family to prepare for young adulthood.

In the following sections, we discuss the needs of individuals with TBI and multiple disabilities as adults and how teachers can plan to address these needs. For both groups, three areas are most crucial: finding employment or purposeful adult activities, living as independently as possible, and experiencing a quality of life similar to others.

## Finding Employment and Adult Routines

Although many adults with TBI and multiple disabilities are still served in sheltered workshops or activities centers (Rusch & Braddock, 2004), many are employed in community-based jobs and given supports that help them to do those jobs. These supports include job coaches and natural supports, often available in the job setting. An important part of transition is to offer adolescents vocational training in real-world settings where they can learn essential job skills. Working in the community offers a chance to do meaningful work in exchange for fair wages in a natural context.

Of course, it is more than work that is important; it is the chance to have a life that includes co-workers and friends and the social connections that come with them. Persons with these disabilities have been able to learn a variety of jobs from groundskeeping and housecleaning to photocopying and data entry. Outside of paid employment, these individuals have other opportunities for meaningful daily activities, and a transition plan should explore these opportunities when necessary. These experiences can include various voluntary and social activities. Even if paid employment is not immediately available, adults with these disabilities should still be supported to have a purposeful lives.

## Living Options

Many young people leave their parents' home when they enter adulthood, and this is also important for many young adults with TBI and multiple disabilities. As research indicates, in reality, many of these individuals continue to live at home, often not by choice but by necessity or because of lack of planning. Planning for a place to live for a young adult with these disabilities should be guided by several values that have emerged during the postinstitutionalization era. These values are based on the principles of normalization, which call for lifestyles and routines to be as normal as possible.

The most desired form of residence is an independent or supported living arrangement based on a person-centered plan. Even for individuals with multiple disabilities, the model program is individually determined with necessary supports brought to the individual instead of placing the person in a restrictive setting simply because the supports are available in that setting (Racino, 1995). In addition to professional supports, the residence should use natural supports as much as possible, and the person should enjoy a choice of location, type of home, and roommates and, to the extent possible, should have input on decisions about all services and living arrangements.

## Quality of Life

Most important for any adult with disabilities, just as it is for you, is something that is hard to define: quality of life. The things we have talked about already—having a nice place to live and being employed or participating in a supportive environment—contribute to quality of life. Overall, though, quality of life for any adult is defined by being able to decide within reason what you want and then having a reasonable chance of getting it. Like everyone else, most adults with TBI and multiple disabilities want to have some choices in daily routine, friends, social and leisure activities, and a self-determined degree of participation in their community.

When school personnel develop transition plans, they tend to focus on supported employment or residential placements. But this isn't enough. Planning should also take into consideration the individual's personal future as well as the family's concerns and should support the individual's experiencing a quality of life similar to that of persons without disabilities (Kim & Turnbull, 2004).

## REFLECTIVE EXERCISE

#9 Do you think a person with TBI or multiple disabilities values as much independence and quality of life as an adult as do other people? What is important to you as an adult? Are people with disabilities significantly different?

Most adults seek a personally satisfying quality of life.

# PREVAILING ISSUES, CONTROVERSIES, AND IMPLICATIONS FOR THE TEACHER

From a historical perspective, students with TBI and multiple disabilities were the last group to receive services under the special education umbrella. Until the mid-1970s students with severe, multiple disabilities were excluded from most public schools, and it wasn't until 1990 when students with TBI were recognized as a unique disability category. In both cases, the changes in public school opportunities came about because of federal laws. Even today, many issues continue to be discussed and debated. Below we consider two issues: one pertaining to students with TBI and one about students with multiple disabilities.

## Should We Try to Improve the Identification of Students with TBI?

Before 1990, children or adolescents who suffered brain injury were not recognized as a distinct group of students with disabilities under IDEA. Because of this, students who had brain injuries either were not provided with special education services or were placed in other disability categories such as learning disabilities, emotional and behavioral disabilities, or intellectual disabilities (Graham, Tognazzini, & Lyons-Holden, 1996). As you saw at the beginning of this chapter, a clear definition of TBI is now provided in IDEA.

Despite these revisions, only a small percentage of school-age individuals who have TBIs are actually identified as TBI students under IDEA. As we discussed earlier, every year about 435,000 children under the age of 14 visit emergency rooms because of head injuries, 37,000 must be hospitalized, and 2,700 die! But in the most recent report to Congress, only 23,000 U.S. students were identified within the TBI category. This number represents only 0.04 % of the school-age population, one of the smallest categories of students identified for special education services. Furthermore, in a recent study, McCaleb (2006) found that many students reported to have experienced brain injuries were not receiving special education services, nor did they have 504 plans (for special medical considerations). Of those who were receiving special education services, McCaleb reported, "most of the students who had been identified as having brain injury and receiving special education services were not receiving those services under the disability category Traumatic Brain Injury. The majority of students who had identified brain injuries were receiving services under the disability categories of 'Other,' Speech-Language, and Physical Disabilities" (p. 71).

Should this be a concern? This is difficult to say. The real issue may be whether students are receiving adequate supports and educational services. Michaud et al. (2007) feel that the support for these students is questionable. They state that "although children with TBI may be identified as having behavior disorders . . . or learning problems, their patterns of cognitive impairment are actually quite different from those seen in children with ADHD or specific learning disabilities." They add that "flexibility and innovative approaches are needed to teach the child who is recovering from TBI" (p. 468).

But, we might ask, aren't flexibility and innovation important for all teachers, especially any who teach students with special needs? It may be important for students with TBI to be accurately identified, but the more important question may be whether or not teachers of these students, regardless of how they are classified, recognize their special needs and provide effective instruction to help meet them. Certainly, this is an issue that we as educators need to discuss and resolve.

For another look from a teacher's perspective, see the "Real World: Challenges and Solutions."

## REFLECTIVE EXERCISE

**#10** Some would argue that the exact classification of a student with disabilities doesn't matter as much as the quality of instruction. When it comes to students with TBI, what is your opinion on this issue?

*Three weeks into the school year, Carla Freer had mixed feelings about her new third-grade class. For one thing, on the whole, they seemed to be smarter than the group she had during her student teaching, and this pleased her. But they were awfully rambunctious, and she knew that she would have to plan a lot of fun and interesting activities to keep their attention. This was fine with her, but she knew it would require a lot of long days after school, some evenings, and no doubt a few weekends to develop her plans and line up her materials. Of course, there was also the group that she wasn't quite sure of what to do with. Those four boys and the one girl, Collette, already were taking up a lot of her time with their silliness, off-task behavior, and overall lack of interest in just about everything related to school. She knew she would have to get some really good advice on how to get this group to fall into line or, if they didn't, she was going to lose them. And she didn't want this to happen.*

*But all in all, Carla thought it was going to be a good year with a pretty good group of kids. Still, though, she was worried about Michael. As she thought about him now, she realized that she had several concerns. First, he was almost too good. He was very quiet and never had to be corrected for misbehavior. But he also didn't say very much. He smiled a lot, but he never seemed to know quite what to do. When she gave the class a direction such as "Put your journals away, and let's line up for the media center," Michael would always hesitate, look around, and not start to respond until most of the other kids were already moving to line up. Then when she would speak to him, "C'mon, Michael, let's go," he would smile at her and then just sit there a minute or get up and stand there, or maybe walk slowly over to the door. He wasn't like Jerome or that other bunch, who she just knew were testing her; it was more like Michael was in some kind of fog. He seemed to be this way most of the time, although sometimes he seemed to have it more together, still quiet, but doing what he was supposed to do. Then suddenly, when she thought he was doing fine, he might start crying about something someone said to him.*

*Carla knew she should look a little more into Michael's situation, but she hadn't had a lot of time. She had looked in his student folder, but nearly all the comments and data indicated he was just an average student. And quiet and moody. She really didn't see anything that helped her figure out what was going on with him. She spoke to Fran Mostovini, who had Michael last year, and Fran told her a few things that Fran knew to be true and a few that she thought might be true.*

*What Fran knew was that Michael had been adopted when he was under a year old. There was*

*some speculation that he had been abused by his biological parents, who were suspected of being heavy into meth. What was not clear were the circumstances of the adoption or whether or not the courts had forced the biological parents to give him up. She also knew that Michael had been tested for special education in the first grade but that he had not scored low enough and that his parents weren't too crazy about the idea of placing him even if he did qualify.*

*Carla found this interesting, but it still didn't help her to identify the current issue with Michael or what she could do to help him. She wondered if he might have a learning disability or even an intellectual disability or if he should be referred for speech. When she thought about the possible abuse, she thought maybe some kind of brain injury could be the problem. She decided that she would talk to Jean Freemont, the guidance counselor, on Monday to see what she might suggest.*

All teachers will have students about whom they feel a little bit lost. These students won't be among the best, and often, like Michael, they won't be among the worst. They may have conditions that the teacher knows little about, such as TBI, or they may simply have had early life experiences that have left them in a condition unlike many other children. What teachers can do in these kinds of situations may depend on their school and its services and governance system. But it is important that the teacher not simply ignore the child or the condition, because the long-term consequences might be serious. Here are some commonsense steps we suggest:

- **Do a thorough search of the student information you have access to.** Learn as much as you can about the student, including background information, interests, strengths, and weaknesses. Look for information in the student's folder, but also speak to other teachers and professionals who are knowledgeable about the student. Your goal should be to find information that explains the student's behavior and provides insight into effective instructional strategies.

- **Look for information on the Internet.** If you suspect the child has a particular condition, learn as much about it as possible. The Internet is certainly a source of information about many childhood diseases and disabilities. Websites that should be of value to you will be those of government agencies, advocacy organizations, and nonprofit groups. Two excellent starting points are the Centers for Disease Control and Prevention at http://www.cdc.gov/ and the National Institutes of Health at http://www.nih.gov/.

- **Talk to the chair of the student support team or the teacher assistance team.** There will be a student support team or a teacher assistance team in your school that can help you figure out ways to work with your student. These teams work well within the response-to-intervention model to help identify intervention strategies. It is not necessary for the student to be referred to special education in order to get assistance.

- **Talk to the parents; ask for their support.** Develop your rapport with the student's parents. Even if they are reticent to meet with you to discuss their child, maintain an open line of communication. It is not necessary that you say you believe the child has a disability or a special need, only that you want to ensure her maximum growth, development, and learning.
- **Develop a strong positive relationship with the student.** Obviously you should work hard to develop a healthy, trusting relationship with the student. Be honest, be open and be caring. Don't be patronizing, but do be supportive.
- **Teach using the most effective methods available to you.** Regardless of your concerns, the most effective thing you can be for your students is be a good teacher. For students about whom you have the greatest concerns, make sure your teaching approaches are most direct, explicit, and effective. The following resources will be helpful.

### Valuable Resources for the Teacher

McLeskey, J., Rosenberg, M. S., & Westling, D. L (2009). *Inclusion: Effective practices for all students.* Upper Saddle River, NJ: Merrill/Pearson Education.

Batshaw, M. L., Pellegrino, L. & Roizen, N. J. (Eds.). (2007). *Children with disabilities* (6th ed.). Baltimore: Brookes.

Institute for Educational Science. (2009). What Works Clearinghouse. Retrieved from http://ies.ed.gov/ncee/wwc/

National Reading Panel (NRP). (2000). *Teaching children to read: An evidence-based assessment of the scientific research literature on reading and its implications for reading instruction.* Washington, DC: National Institute of Child Health and Human Development. Retrieved from http://www.nationalreadingpanel.org/

### Final Thoughts

Even with so many services available today, many children with special needs slip through the cracks. Research suggests this is especially true about children who have had brain injuries. If you suspect a student has special needs, it will always be better to take proactive steps than to simply pass the student along. The impact of any condition will become more consequential the longer it is ignored.

## Should We Spend So Much on Teaching Students with Multiple Disabilities When Our Educational Budgets Are Always Stretched?

Everyone knows that our economy has been going through a rough period. Because of this condition, our state and local tax revenues have recently decreased, and some of our public services have been cut. In some places, teachers' or teacher assistants' positions have been eliminated, and class sizes have been increased in order to accommodate students. Even so, students with disabilities are guaranteed a "free and appropriate public education" under IDEA, a federal law. Furthermore, you should understand that local and state funds pay for most of special education, around 80% to 90%, and the federal government pays only the balance.

Because of the intensity of services provided, special education is much more expensive than general education. And among students with disabilities, students with multiple disabilities, especially those who have severe intellectual disabilities, are among the most expensive to provide an appropriate education. Based on data that is now somewhat dated, Parrish (2003) reported that the average cost per year to educate a student with multiple disabilities was about $20,000, more than most other students with disabilities and more than four times the cost to educate a student without disabilities.

Is this expense defensible for these students in this economy? First we should note that given the history of bipartisan political support for special education services, it is unlikely that services for these students will ever be suspended. But we suggest a more philosophical response can be made, and it is this: In a society as rich in resources and human acceptance as ours, the greater error would be to reject someone from participation because they may not benefit as much as someone else. If we are to make an error, let's make it on the side of inclusion and acceptance rather than on the side of exclusion and rejection. Of course, the answer that you give will have to be the one that makes most sense to you.

# 12 SUMMARY

Public schools in the United States have served individuals with multiple disabilities for about only 30 years and have recognized TBI as a disability for even less time. In this chapter, we have touched on some of the key points about these two distinct groups of students and how they are taught in public schools.

## Definitions of Students with TBI and Students with Multiple Disabilities

- Students with TBI have acquired open or closed head injuries that affect areas such as cognition, language, memory, attention, reasoning, abstract thinking, judgment, problem solving, sensory, perceptual, and motor abilities, psychosocial behavior, physical functions, information processing, and speech.
- Students with multiple disabilities are those who, in addition to intellectual disabilities, have physical or sensory disabilities. Their intellectual disabilities are usually in the range of severe to profound. The condition is a developmental disability.

## Significant Characteristics of Students with TBI and Students with Multiple Disabilities

- Students with TBI have academic problems in basic areas of literacy and math and have difficulties with concentrating and paying attention, remembering, carrying out complex cognitive tasks, problem solving, information processing, and communicating.
- Students with multiple disabilities usually have reduced intellectual development, severe physical disabilities, and medical problems associated with their disabilities.

## Prevalence and Causes of TBI and Multiple Disabilities

- According to the U.S. Department of Education (2009), only a little over 23,000 students between 6 and 21 years were classified as having TBI, which represents only about 0.04% of the school-age population. However, many more children are reported to suffer brain damage. Studies show that many are placed into other categories of special education or are not identified.
- Common causes of TBI during childhood include falls from heights, sports- and recreation-related injuries, automobile and other vehicle crashes, and assaults, including child abuse.
- Students classified as having multiple disabilities total approximately 132,000, which represents about 0.23% of the school-age population. Some students who have multiple disabilities may be found in other disability categories, most commonly, intellectual disabilities or physical disabilities.
- Multiple disabilities are usually caused by prenatal (occurring before birth) conditions. Common causes of multiple disabilities include genetic conditions, chromosomal anomalies, maternal infections, the ingestion of harmful substances, and radiation.

## Identification and Assessment Procedures Used with Students with TBI and with Students with Multiple Disabilities

- Medical personnel conduct initial evaluations for children and adolescents who have brain injuries. The focus is on stabilizing the individual and facilitating recovery.
- Medical personnel are also the first to evaluate children with multiple disabilities in order to determine appropriate diagnoses and the types of interventions required, including medications, surgery, therapies, or rehabilitation.
- Following medical evaluations, educational evaluations are conducted for students with TBI and students with multiple disabilities to determine their academic instructional needs in the general curriculum, other instructional needs, and the related services and supports they will need.
- Students with multiple disabilities may benefit from other forms of assessment and planning including ecological inventories and person-centered planning.

## Educational Practices Used with Students with TBI and with Students with Multiple Disabilities

- Providing instruction focused on specific academic needs and delivered in a structured manner is generally be the most effective educational approach for students with TBI.
- Having a consistent, organized, predictable daily instructional routine in a classroom that is well organized and free from distractive items and events is important for students with TBI.
- Most children with multiple disabilities can be identified early in life and participate in preschool programs that use a family-centered approach and developmentally appropriate practices.
- The most effective instructional practices during the school years are in inclusive settings and focus on participation in the general curriculum and instruction in other areas of personal needs.
- Paraeducators and peers provide supports in the classroom, and systematic instruction maximizes learning outcomes.

**Major Issues and Controversies Related to Educating Students with Severe Intellectual Disabilities and Multiple Disabilities**

- One issue related to educating many students with TBI is that many of them are either not identified for special education services or are misdiagnosed and placed in other categories of special education.

- One controversy related to teaching students with multiple disabilities is the expense. The cost per student per year may be up to four times the cost of students without disabilities.

## ADDRESSING THE PROFESSIONAL STANDARDS

Council for Exceptional Children (CEC) Knowledge Standards addressed in the chapter:

ICC1K: 1, 2, 4, 5, 7; IC1K: 1–8; ICC2K: 2, 4, 5; IC2K: 1–4; ICC3K: 1, 4; IC3K: 1, 3; IC4K: 2, 3, 4; IC5K: 5; ICC7K: 1; IC7K: 1; ICC8K: 1, 4; IC8K: 1; IC9K: 1, 2; ICC10K: 1, 3

Appendix B: CEC Knowledge and Skill Standards Common Core has a full listing of the standards referenced here.

**myeducationlab**

Now go to Topic 16: Multiple Disabilities in the MyEducationLab for your course, where you can:

- Find learning outcomes for the broad concepts covered in this chapter along with the national standards that connect to these outcomes.
- Complete Assignments and Activities that can help you more deeply understand the chapter content.
- Examine challenging situations presented in the IRIS Center Resources.
- Access video clips of CCSSO National Teachers of the Year award winners responding to the question, "Why Do I Teach?" in the Teacher Talk section.

- Apply and practice your understanding of the core concepts and skills identified in the chapter with the Building Teaching Skills and Dispositions learning units.
- Check your comprehension on the content covered in the chapter by going to the Study Plan in the Book-Specific Resources section for your text. Here you will be able to take a chapter quiz, receive feedback on your answers, and then access Review, Practice, and Enrichment activities to enhance your understanding of chapter content.

# chapter 13

# Sensory Impairments

**REFLECT UPON**

- What are the definitions and classifications for students with sensory impairments?
- What are the key characteristics of students with sensory impairments?
- What is the prevalence of different types of sensory impairments?
- What are appropriate educational approaches for students with sensory impairments, and what are some important curriculum areas?
- What are some major issues related to educating students with sensory impairments?

## MY PROFESSION, MY STORY: RYAN HESS

Like many who decide to teach students with sensory disabilities, Ryan Hess did so because of personal experience. A teacher of students who are blind or visually impaired, Ryan began his career as a school custodian at Franklin Elementary School in the rural West. He enjoyed his job and loved working with students, but never had any real desire to become a teacher. That is until Lorena entered his life.

Lorena was born prematurely; and as a result, her eyes were not fully and properly developed. Lorena was the only child in her school with a visual impairment, and none of the staff members were prepared to meet her educational needs. At first, there was a lot of whispering and wondering among the faculty about what would be done. Finally, the news came that a special teacher would come and help the teachers.

During Lorena's kindergarten year, she learned how to get around her school and community and how to read and write using enlarged print. The teacher who worked with her came into the school about 3 days each week and stayed for 45 minutes each time. After a while, Ryan befriended this teacher and learned that she was preparing to retire. Although his own retirement was coming soon as well, Ryan wanted to continue working and decided he would become a teacher. For the next 5 years, Ryan took courses part-time over the Internet to become certified both as a teacher of students with visual impairments and as an orientation and mobility specialist.

When Lorena's teacher retired, Ryan took her place. Ryan now works as an itinerant teacher, serving teachers and students in three districts and traveling nearly 1,000 miles per week. At each school, he varies his responsibilities based on the students' needs found in their individualized education program. Frequently, Ryan is asked to provide assessments and evaluations for students to determine whether they qualify for special education services. He provides information, support, and specialized materials to the general education teachers working with students who are blind or visually impaired. He trains students in orientation and mobility skills so that they can maneuver through their communities with ease. He teaches students to use adapted materials, such as braille or large print. He teaches students and teachers to use assistive or adaptive technology. Although it took a few additional years to get here, Ryan is now quite happy with the life he has found.

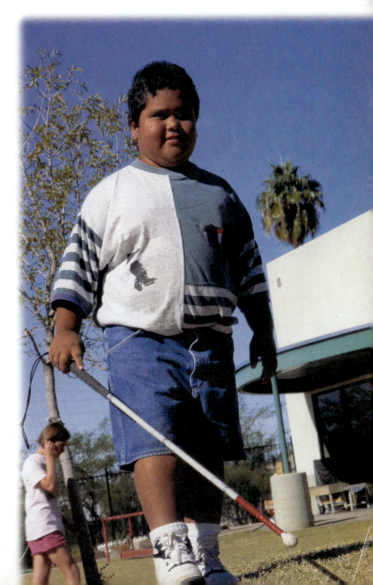

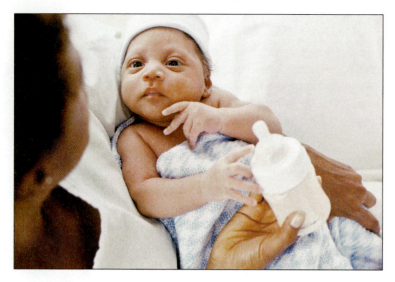

From the first moments of life, an infant begins to build the foundation for all learning.

From the first moments of life, an infant begins to build the foundation for all learning. She learns the feeling of a soft blanket, the sensation of light, the feeling of discontent, the taste of milk, the sounds of her mother's voice. To begin with, each experience is an isolated event, but quickly, children develop schemas and connections, learning, for example, that crying brings food to satisfy hunger. Within weeks, the child learns to turn and look toward a smiling face, and in just a few months, the child learns that making a sound causes another person to make a sound. By experiencing the world of sight, sound, taste, sensation, and smell, the child continues to build knowledge and understanding.

Now imagine an infant, cradled in her mother's arms, who turns to look at the smiling face but cannot find it. Or the one who makes a sound but hears nothing in return. Although learning continues when babies have sensory disabilities, their learning processes must be different. For them, no matter the source of the sensory impairment, the experiences that lead to learning must be accessed through methods that differ from those of most of us.

It is this issue of access to information and experience that is the core of services and interventions for students with sensory impairments, whether the nature of their disability is visual, auditory, or both. In this chapter, you will become familiar with basic characteristics and educational needs of students with sensory impairments. Basic information about these students is contained in the "FAQ Sheet."

## REFLECTIVE EXERCISE

#1 Would you consider teaching students who are blind or deaf? What about students who are both deaf and blind? What do you think you would find most challenging about this work?

## FAQ Sheet
### STUDENTS WITH SENSORY IMPAIRMENTS

| | |
|---|---|
| Who are they? | Classifications may include<br>• Blind or visually impaired<br>• Deaf or hearing impaired (also called hard of hearing)<br>• Deaf-blind |
| What are typical characteristics? | • Total or partial loss of vision<br>• Total or partial loss of hearing<br>• Loss of significant degree of both hearing and vision<br>• To qualify for special education, hearing and or vision loss must interfere with normal learning ability. |
| What are the demographics? | • In the total U.S. population, approximately 10,000,000 are blind or visually impaired; 42,000,000 are deaf or hearing impaired; and 50,000 are classified as deaf-blind.<br>• The number reported by the U.S. Department of Education receiving special education includes 29,000 who are blind or visually impaired, 78,000 who are deaf or hearing impaired; and 1,300 who are deaf-blind. |
| Where are students educated? | • Some students with sensory impairments are served in residential schools. Others are served in general classes or in special classes, often in general education schools. |
| What are the outcomes? | • Most persons with visual disabilities live as adults in integrated society.<br>• Many people who are deaf participate more in the Deaf culture but may also live in an integrated society.<br>• Persons with deaf-blindness usually require some degree of ongoing support. |

# DEFINITIONS AND CLASSIFICATION CRITERIA FOR SENSORY IMPAIRMENTS

Although sensory impairments are recognized, defined, and evaluated as medical conditions, the most important issue about these conditions under the Individuals with Disabilities Education Act (IDEA) is the extent to which they impact a student's ability to learn.

## Deafness and Hearing Impairment

Federal law provides distinct definitions for the categories of deafness and hearing impairment. Under IDEA, the educational definition of **deafness** is "a hearing impairment that is so severe that the child is impaired in processing linguistic information through hearing, with or without amplification, that adversely affects a child's educational performance" (IDEA, Sec. 300.8[c][3]). Additionally, a "**hearing impairment** means an impairment in hearing, whether permanent or fluctuating, that adversely affects a child's educational performance but that is not included under the definition of deafness in this section" (IDEA, Sec. 300.8 [c][5]). In general, the assumption is that more severe hearing loss is defined as *deafness*, while less severe hearing loss is defined as *hearing impairment* (also referred to as "hard of hearing").

Hearing is evaluated through an audiological examination. During this evaluation, the audiologist will present different levels of sounds and ask the examinee to respond when a sound is heard. Through this process, the audiologist determines the level of loudness required to hear certain sounds, the quietest level of speech the examinee can hear, and the ability to recognize words at a comfortable level of loudness. Together, these assessments help the audiologist measure hearing in terms of the degree of hearing loss, the type of hearing loss, and the configuration of the hearing loss, all of which provide a clinical assessment of hearing ability.

**Degree of hearing loss** is expressed in decibels (dB). The higher the decibel level required to hear a sound, the greater the hearing loss. Hearing loss is described in decibel levels as follows: normal hearing (0 to 20 dB), mild loss (20 to 40 dB), moderate loss (40 to 60 dB), severe loss (60 to 80 dB), and profound loss (80 dB or greater) (American Speech-Language-Hearing Association, 2009). **Type of hearing loss** describes the point in the auditory system where the loss is occurring (see Figure 13.1).

Types of hearing loss include conductive loss in the outer and/or middle ear; sensorineural loss in the cochlea, inner ear, or eighth cranial nerve; mixed loss of both conductive and sensorineural areas; and a central auditory processing disorder (a condition in which the brain has difficulty processing auditory signals that are heard). **Configuration of the hearing loss** describes qualitative aspects of hearing, such as whether both ears are affected (bilateral or unilateral loss) or whether different frequencies are affected differently (slope).

In addition to the educational and clinical definitions just described, there is also a **cultural definition of deafness**. Although from a clinical or professional perspective, the term *deaf* refers to those who cannot hear well enough to rely on their

To check your comprehension on the content covered in Chapter 13, go to the Book-Specific Resources section in the MyEducationLab for your course, select your text, and complete the Study Plan. Here you will be able to take a chapter quiz, receive feedback on your answers, and then access Review, Practice, and Enrichment activities to enhance your understanding of chapter content.

Go to the Assignments and Activities section of Topic 15: Sensory Impairments in the MyEducationLab for your course and complete the activity entitled *Hearing Impairment*.

FIGURE 13.1 • **PARTS OF THE EAR**

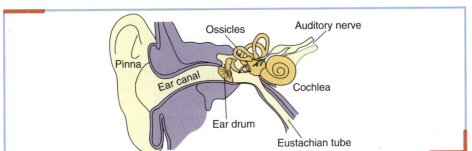

Members of the Deaf community do not consider deafness a disability.

hearing as a means of processing information, from a cultural perspective, the term **Deaf** (with a capital *D*) is used to describe a particular group of people (with hearing loss) who share a language and a culture. "The members of this group have inherited their sign language, use it as a primary means of communication among themselves, and hold a set of beliefs about themselves and their connection to the larger society" (Humphries & Padden, 1988, p. 2).

From the perspective of the Deaf community, the professional and clinical definitions of hearing and deafness reflect a pathological view. This pathological view accepts normal hearing as the standard and focuses on how deaf people deviate from that standard. This perspective has been traditionally held by a majority of non-deaf professionals, including teachers. In a sense, from the Deaf community's view, this is the outsider's view, focusing on how deaf people are different from (with the implication "inferior to") non-deaf people. It also perceives that deaf people have something wrong with them, something that can and must be fixed. The National Association for the Deaf (NAD, *http://www.nad.org/*) is the primary organization supporting Deaf culture and members of the Deaf community. It supports separate schooling for deaf children and promotes the use of American Sign Language (ASL) as the language of deaf people.

The Deaf cultural view recognizes that multiple factors must be considered when examining the issue of hearing loss. Those who hold a cultural view commonly define the Deaf community as a group of people

- Who share a common means of communication (gestural) that provides the basis for group identity,
- Who share a common language (ASL or other signed languages across the globe) and culture, and
- Whose primary means of relating to the world is visual.

The social support systems for the Deaf culture are frequently found in residential schools for deaf students. The Deaf community views residential or self-contained programs as important links in the transmission of Deaf culture and language because children are immersed in an environment rich in communication that is accessible to all. Still, the NAD recognizes that a student's placement should be individually determined: "There are diverse educational placements for deaf and hard of hearing children. There are residential schools, charter schools specializing in bilingual/bicultural education, day schools where sign language is used, day schools for deaf children that emphasize spoken language only, and neighborhood schools, some of which have programs for deaf and hard of hearing students. The NAD supports a continuum of alternative placements that will meet the needs of each individual child" (National Association of the Deaf, 2009c).

Even so, NAD and the Deaf culture strongly support residential or self-contained programs for deaf students. Parents who want their child to participate in the Deaf community usually select educational settings in which ASL is used and where Deaf adults are prominent throughout the school. These parents and students frequently discard the idea of deafness as a disability and embrace the notion of cultural and linguistic differences. For these families, the concept of classification under IDEA may be considered offensive and demeaning.

## REFLECTIVE EXERCISE

#2 Do you know a member of the Deaf community? How does this person view himself or herself within this community? Do you believe deaf people can be part of both their own community and the non-deaf community?

FIGURE 13.2 • **PARTS OF THE EYE**

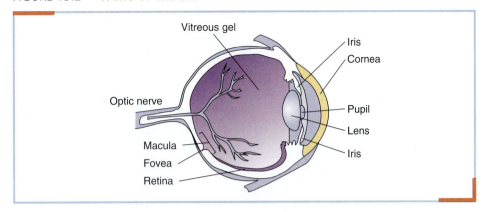

## Blind or Visually Impaired

Many people do not realize that the IDEA definition of blindness differs from the definition of legal blindness. Under IDEA, a **visual impairment**, including **blindness**, means "an impairment in vision that, even with correction, adversely affects a child's educational performance. The term includes both partial sight and blindness" (IDEA, Sec. 300.8[c][13]). In contrast, **legal blindness** is a degree of vision loss used to determine eligibility for various legal benefits, not for educational services.

Degree of vision loss is described according to a person's **visual acuity** and **visual field** (or peripheral vision). Visual acuity is reported as a fraction, such as 20/20. The top number states the distance the subject is standing away from the object or figure (i.e., 20 feet), and the bottom number states the distance at which a person with normal vision can see the same object or figure that is 20 feet away. Thus the larger the bottom number, the worse your visual acuity. A person with 20/200 visual acuity, when standing 20 feet from a figure or an object, would see it as well as a person with normal vision standing 200 feet away. A person is considered legally blind if his visual acuity is 20/200 or worse in the better eye with the best possible corrective lens.

A person can also be considered legally blind if she has a limited visual field. Along with visual acuity, vision can be evaluated according to visual field, which is the area in front of us that we can see while looking forward and not moving our head. The visual field for each eye is usually measured by a computerized assessment administered by an optometrist or ophthalmologist. No specific visual field is considered standard. However, a person is considered legally blind if she has a visual field of 20 degrees or less. Figure 13.2 is a diagram of the parts of the eye.

## Deaf-Blind

"**Deaf-blindness** means concomitant hearing and visual impairments, the combination of which causes such severe communication and other developmental and educational needs that they cannot be accommodated in special education programs solely for children with deafness or children with blindness" (IDEA, Sec. 300.8[c][2]). For most people, the term *deaf-blind* brings to mind the image of someone with no vision and no hearing, but this is not an accurate representation. Many students who are deaf-blind have some functional use of their vision or hearing or both.

In fact, only about 6% of children who are deaf-blind are totally deaf and totally blind (National Technical Assistance Consortium, 2004). Many children classified as deaf-blind have enough vision to be able to move about in their environments, recognize familiar people, see sign language at close distances, and perhaps read large print. Others have sufficient hearing to recognize familiar sounds, understand some speech, or develop speech themselves. Because deaf-blindness is a combination of vision and hearing losses, there are as many possible combinations as there are

**PEARSON**
**myeducationlab**

Go to the Assignments and Activities section of Topic 15: Sensory Impairments in the MyEducationLab for your course and complete the activity entitled *Defining Visual Impairments*.

**REFLECTIVE EXERCISE**

**#3** How do you think you would be able to support a child with visual disabilities in your classroom if you were a general education teacher? Do you think you might be able to work effectively with a visual disabilities teacher?

Many individuals who are deaf-blind are able to participate in meaningful life activities.

individuals. For this reason, no two children with deaf-blindness are alike, and educational programs for students who are deaf-blind are widely varied (National Consortium on Deaf-Blindness, 2008).

# CHARACTERISTICS OF STUDENTS WITH SENSORY IMPAIRMENTS

## Intelligence

Generally speaking, hearing or visual disabilities alone do not impact the cognitive skills of a child, but the mental processes required to learn new information differ for students with sensory impairments. You should not take this to mean, however, that all children with sensory impairments have normal cognitive skills, because this is not the case. For some students, a sensory impairment is only one aspect of their educational needs. Increasingly, infants who experience complications of pregnancy or birth have disabilities affecting both cognitive and sensory learning. The process of fetal development is very complex and can have a strong impact on sensory organ development. Sensory organs are formed so early in pregnancy that any change in the normal developmental process can have an impact on the sensory development while simultaneously impacting the brain.

## Learning

Overall, the impact of sensory impairments on learning is more a function of the lack of input than an inability to learn. It is very common for students with sensory impairments to have typical learning processes and learning modes; but their ability to access information may be restricted in some avenues, or the order in which they acquire new skills may vary. For these students, it becomes critical to present information in a variety of ways so that they can learn alongside their peers.

## Deaf and Hearing Impaired

Although most children who are deaf or hearing impaired have the cognitive ability to become proficient readers and expressive writers, this ability is often hampered by delays in language development. Typically, language is acquired as infants and toddlers hear and imitate the sounds produced in their environment. Eventually, they learn to form words, sentences, and conversations. As they enter school, children learn about the relationships between the words they hear in everyday conversation and printed text. Early literacy is especially focused on matching known words and sounds from speech to print, but this process of matching spoken and written language continues across grades. Language is so connected with literacy development that "learning environments that encourage the development of literacy also encourage the development of face-to-face language, and vice versa" (Schirmer, 2000, p. 131).

As students who are deaf or hearing impaired progress through school, literacy development typically does not proceed at a pace considered average for hearing students (Schirmer, 2001a). As a result of this slowed pace of literacy development (only one third the rate of same-grade peers per school year, according to Wolk and Allen [1984]), many students who are deaf or hearing impaired graduate from high school with a fourth-grade reading level (Schirmer, 2001b; Traxler, 2000). These educational results are not due to a lack of learning ability on the part of students who are deaf or hearing impaired; they are simply a result of the impact that language delay has on learning.

Because of the strong impact that language acquisition has on the learning process, the primary means of supporting learning is through language intervention. For some, language intervention is conducted in a visual format: ASL or a signed system patterned after English. For others, this means developing techniques for the mastery of spoken language.

## Blind/Visually Impaired

Most teachers engage their students by providing visual and auditory information. They convey their mood through facial expression, body language, and tone of voice. They give directions using gestures, pointing, and spoken words. If the students cannot receive this information, their ability to learn the presented material will be impacted. Students who are blind or visually impaired have equal ability to learn, but their ability to access the information presented is inhibited. To facilitate learning, the teacher must use a variety of presentation strategies.

The most common presentation strategies used with students who are blind or visually impaired are designed to convey information in an auditory or tactile format. Students are given opportunities to explore objects through touch whenever possible. For example, while other class members are viewing a cell through a microscope, the student who is blind or visually impaired may be exploring a model that contains all the parts of the cell.

The use of braille is another common method for tactile presentation. **Braille** is a code used to present text in a tactile format. Invented by Louis Braille in 1829, braille is presented as a rectangular six-dot cell, with up to 63 possible combinations using one or more of the six dots (see Figure 13.3). Braille is embossed onto thick paper and read with the fingers, which move across the top of the dots. The amount of space required to represent each letter is substantial (up to three times as much space as print!), so braille is typically contracted, with a small number of cells representing each word or morpheme.

Auditory presentation strategies are designed to convey visual information through sound. Auditory strategies are used in a greater variety of situations than most people realize. Individuals working with students who are blind or visually impaired frequently provide students with a verbal description of the environment around them. Orientation and mobility specialists teach students to recognize auditory cues

**REFLECTIVE EXERCISE**

#4 Individuals who are deaf or have hearing impairments rely a great deal on visual stimuli. What are some ways a general education classroom might be modified to accommodate the needs of these students?

**PEARSON**
**myeducationlab**

Go to the Assignments and Activities section of Topic 15: Sensory Impairments in the MyEducationLab for your course and complete the activities entitled *Life with Hearing Loss* and *Visual Impairment and Education–NCLB*.

FIGURE 13.3 • BRAILLE

## Braille Alphabet

The six dots of the braille cell are arranged and numbered:

| | a | b | c | d | e | f | g | h | i | j |
|---|---|---|---|---|---|---|---|---|---|---|
| | k | l | m | n | o | p | q | r | s | t |
| | u | v | w | x | y | z | Capital Sign | Number Sign | Period | Comma |

The capital sign, dot 6, placed before a letter makes a capital letter.

The number sign, dots 3, 4, 5, 6, placed before the characters a through j, makes the numbers 1 through 0. For example, a preceded by the number sign is 1, b is 2, etc.

Source: From National Braille Press Inc., 88 St., Stephen Street, Boston, MA 02115 www.nbp.org

REFLECTIVE EXERCISE

#5 Imagine describing a crystal-clear blue sky to a person without vision. This is the type of challenge that a special education teacher for students with visual impairments faces. How do you think you would handle such a challenge?

PEARSON
myeducationlab

Go to the Assignments and Activities section of Topic 16: Multiple Disabilities & TBI in the MyEducationLab for your course and complete the activities entitled *Small Group Instruction for Students with Deaf-Blindness* and *Language Lesson for Students with Dual Sensory Impairments*.

(along with physical and olfactory cues) to maneuver independently through the environment. Also, assistive technology is widely used to provide auditory information. Text-to-speech software programs read aloud any word on a page that is loaded onto a computer. Screen readers provide a verbal description of information presented on a computer screen, including Websites and e-mail. Students use note takers to type or braille their thoughts and then have their notes read aloud by the same machine. Students roll scanning pens across text in a book or magazine to read that text aloud.

Many individuals assume that students who are blind or visually impaired simply need to feel or hear everything in order to develop an understanding. But what can you feel or hear that will help you understand the concept of atoms? Even for students who use common adaptations such as braille, large print, assistive/adaptive technology, and audio, learning seemingly simple concepts can be a laborious process.

### Deaf-Blind

Approximately 63% of students who are deaf-blind have intellectual disabilities in addition to their sensory loss (NTAC, 2004). Depending on the specific nature of these additional disabilities, learning may be impacted to a greater or lesser degree. In these cases, the combination of factors impacting the child is likely to have implications for all aspects of life, including the learning, cognitive, social, emotional, and physical arenas.

Students who are deaf-blind face many learning challenges because they are reduced from five methods of receiving information to three. These students typically require a higher level of individualized instruction to provide the best access to the learning environment. Many students who are deaf-blind receive services similar to those preferred for students with severe intellectual and multiple disabilities.

## Social Behavior

Social behavior of students with sensory impairments may be impacted not because of an innate lack of social skills, but because sensory loss results in a loss of input. Without that input, children miss the opportunity for incidental learning. For example, a typical first-grade classroom always has a student who unabashedly engages in nose picking. Surrounding this child, several others will complain with a loud "Eeeew! Gross!" Imagine this experience for the child with sensory impairments.

Either the student does not hear the negative commentary, or the student knows something was gross but not what happened before that. Without both aspects of this social feedback, the child never learns that it is not socially appropriate to pick your nose.

The child with a sensory impairment must receive explicit instruction on social norms and behaviors, and several factors may ultimately influence the social behavior of students with sensory impairments. For example, at times, more restrictive educational settings result in atypical behaviors. This may be due to the isolation of both students and teachers from an awareness of age-appropriate behaviors. Vision or hearing loss can also result in social and behavioral problems because students may be missing a great deal of instruction and become bored in class. They may begin acting out as a way to draw attention to educational needs that are not being met.

Students with sensory impairments sometimes experience difficulty in developing social relationships. Young students may require assistance from adults to develop friendships. Participation in groups, clubs, and community classes can often be an unobtrusive way to provide structure to the development of social relationships.

## Physical Characteristics

Physical development of students with sensory impairments is similar to that of all other children, unless the student has an additional disability. Occasional malformation of the eyes or ears is possible and easily recognized. Blindness or visual impairment is sometimes physically recognizable, but this is usually more the result of the individual's social behavior than physical characteristics. Individuals who use sign language are identifiable while conversing but generally not at other times. Frequently, the ability to physically identify a person as blind or visually impaired or as deaf or hearing impaired requires personal contact with that individual.

## PREVALENCE AND CAUSAL FACTORS

Students with sensory impairments fall into the category of students with low-incidence disabilities. Table 13.1 includes data about students with sensory impairments (served within specific categories under IDEA) from the most recent report of the U.S. Department of Education (2009).

The National Consortium on Deaf-Blindness (NCDB, 2008) reported that in its 2007 census, a total of 10,174 infants, children, and young adults (0 to 21 or 22 years of age) were deaf-blind. As you will note, this number is much larger than the number of deaf-blind students reported under IDEA (see Table 13.1). According to NCBD (2008), the difference in the numbers is due to the criteria for including a student as deaf-blind. The U.S. Department of Education data include only those students who

**REFLECTIVE EXERCISE**

#6 What are some strategies a general education teacher might do to help a child who is deaf or one who is blind develop personal relationships with other children?

TABLE 13.1 • PREVALENCE OF STUDENTS WITH SENSORY IMPAIRMENTS SERVED UNDER IDEA[a]

| Disability Categories | Ages 3 to 5 | | Ages 6 to 21 | |
|---|---|---|---|---|
| | Number | % of Population | Number | % of Population |
| Hearing impairments | 7,702 | 0.07 | 71,712 | 0.11 |
| Visual impairments | 3,268 | 0.03 | 25,504 | 0.04 |
| Deaf-blind | 252 | 0 | 1,659 | 0 |

[a] Including the 50 states; Washington, DC; and the Bureau of Indian Affairs schools.

Source: U.S. Department of Education (2009).

have deaf-blindness as their only disability. In contrast, the NCDB count includes all individuals in public schools who are deaf-blind, including those classified in other ways, such as intellectually disabled or multiply disabled. The discrepancy clearly points out that many deaf-blind students can be classified in special education under categories other than deaf-blindness.

## Deafness and Hearing Impairments

Deafness and hearing loss can be caused by heredity, accidents, or illness; but in many cases the cause is unknown. Causes are frequently identified as being prenatal or post-natal. Genetics is attributed as the cause for about 50% of children with hearing loss, even though about 90% of these children are born to parents with normal hearing. Genetic factors include a history of hearing loss in the extended family or disorders arising during fetal development. Rubella, cytomegalovirus, or other illnesses of a pregnant mother may result in hearing loss in her unborn child.

Any time from birth onward, a child can have an experience that causes a hearing loss to develop. The educational implications vary according to how much linguistic competence the child has developed before the onset of hearing loss. Complications of birth, such as a sustained lack of oxygen, can have an impact on hearing. Hearing loss may result from traumatic brain injuries, tumors or lesions of the central nervous system, or medications that specifically harm the ear. Illness or infection, especially those with extremely high fevers (e.g., meningitis), may cause hearing loss in children.

Traumas to the ear including perforation of the eardrum, fractured skull, and changes in air pressure are all preventable causes of hearing loss. Another preventable cause is exposure to loud, constant noise. Loud noise damages the sensitive mechanisms of the inner ear, resulting in a progressive hearing loss.

## Blindness and Visual Impairments

Major causes of blindness or visual impairments in children include congenital cataracts, optic atrophy, albinism, retinopathy of prematurity, rod-cone dystrophy, cortical visual impairment, and optic nerve hypoplasia (Brilliant & Graboyes, 1999; Ferrell, 1998). Another critical factor used to describe visual impairment is timing, with a vision loss being described as congenital or adventitious.

Adventitious visual impairment is acquired after birth as the result of disease or accident. Children who are adventitiously blind or visually impaired may access their visual memory to help them develop conceptual understandings. Congenital visual impairment is present before or at the time of birth. Children who are congenitally blind have never experienced vision and do not rely on their visual memory to learn. Children who have experienced low vision since birth see the world differently from those with sight, and their visual memory and understanding may differ.

## Deaf-Blind

Many different syndromes and disorders result in deaf-blindness. As discussed, both the eyes and ears develop in the earliest stages of pregnancy. These organs originate from some of the same types of embryonic cells and tissue and have several anatomical similarities (Regenbogen & Coscas, 1985). Because of these similarities, various diseases and conditions result in damage to both organs. Deaf-blindness can be caused in an unborn infant by infection of the mother during pregnancy, including syphilis, toxoplasmosis, rubella, cytomegalovirus, and herpes. Whether the cause of deaf-blindness is the result of a syndrome, prematurity, low birth weight, or a congenital infection, bodily systems other than the sensory organs may be affected. Some of these complications include intellectual disabilities, shortened life span, poor body growth, motor abnormalities, and glandular disturbances such as thyroid problems or diabetes (Heller & Kennedy, 1994).

One major trend in providing effective instruction for students with sensory impairments is the importance of early intervention and preschool services.

# EFFECTIVE INSTRUCTIONAL PRACTICES

## Early Childhood Services

One major trend in providing effective instruction for students with sensory impairments is the importance of early intervention and preschool services. Intensive specialized services provided to young children with sensory impairments can lay an important foundation for continued development and later learning.

### Deaf and Hearing Impaired

During the first 3 years of life, children show incredible growth in language development. In these first months, the child learns to babble, form words, and finally form sentences. From this foundation, children's mastery of language grows throughout the elementary school years. Historically, this critical period of growth was missed by children with hearing loss. As recently as the late 1980s, the average age of identification for a child with hearing loss was just over 2 years old (Coplan, 1987; Mace, Wallace, Whan, & Steimachowicz, 1991; Yoshinaga-Itano, 1987). The linguistic development of children identified at such a late age was damaged to such an extent that they experienced difficulties and delays in all linguistic areas of learning, especially literacy. The link between age of identification and educational outcomes became clear in the early 1990s, and states began to implement programs to decrease the age of identification.

Today, most states use *universal newborn hearing screening programs* that are designed to assess infants' hearing before they leave the hospital (National Center for Hearing Assessment and Management, NCHAM, 2008). According to NCHAM, the average cost to screen a newborn for hearing impairments is between $10 and $50, depending on the procedure and the technology used. The benefit is referral of identified children and their families for early intervention services.

**Early Intervention.**   Early intervention services vary from state to state but generally focus on providing the family with support and resources, strategies for presenting linguistic information, and training for communication interventions. The result of this early interaction with the child is an improved outcome in speech and language development (Yoshinaga-Itano, Coulter, & Thomson, 2000). Children who receive early intervention services also show improved results in reading, arithmetic, vocabulary, articulation, social adjustment, and behavior (Watkins, 1987).

REFLECTIVE EXERCISE

#7 Note that some of the causes of severe intellectual disabilities can also lead to sensory impairments. Do you think effective instructional methods exist for students with both intellectual disabilities and sensory impairments?

A primary focus of early intervention services is the issue of language development. Families are presented with information about various communication and linguistic options, including spoken English, ASL, cued speech, and signed representations of English. Educators then apply this information to knowledge about family structure, the child's degree of hearing loss, and cultural expectations to determine the best communication method for that family and child. After selecting a communication method, specialists design services to the family to strengthen their implementation of this method. Families who prefer to use spoken English may select to use advanced amplification options or a cochlear implant to help in developing this communication method. For more information on this topic, see "Technology for Access."

**Preschool Services.**   As the infant grows into a toddler and then a young child, services provided in the home decrease, and children who are deaf or hearing impaired are more likely to receive services in a preschool class (U.S. Department of Education, 2003). Many preschool programs for students who are deaf or hearing impaired include individualized parent meetings in addition to small-group activities.

For students who are learning to use spoken language, the teacher or another certified professional may provide speech, language, or listening therapy for the child with the parent present. This model, used and promoted by Auditory-Verbal International, encourages parents to become actively involved in developing their child's spoken language skills by implementing professional techniques in the home.

For students who are learning to use sign language, a language mentor may come into the home to help both family and child develop sign language skills. This language mentor is generally an adult member of the Deaf community who is skilled in the use of ASL and has been specifically trained to support families in the language-acquisition process.

Preschool-age children who are deaf or hearing impaired also develop typical pre-academic skills. Activities are similar to those in community preschools and include counting, letter recognition, shapes, colors, patterns, and social activity. To develop these concepts, teachers rely heavily on experiential learning. Students are actively engaged in the world around them and frequently engage in physical play and field trips. Teachers and parents become proficient labelers, giving students the name and explanation for every object or activity they encounter. By filling the child's day with language, the adult develops linguistic skills while focusing on the curriculum of typical preschoolers.

### Blind/Visually Impaired

Identification of infants who are blind or visually impaired typically occurs through Child Find services. Pediatricians and eye care specialists are most likely to first diagnose a visual impairment in a child, but a time delay often occurs between diagnosis and referral to early intervention (Hatton, 2001). For families of children who are blind or visually impaired, access to early intervention services often depends on their health care professionals' knowledge of the Child Find system.

**Early Intervention.**   The majority of learning in the first years of life is acquired visually through imitation and exploration of events in the child's immediate environment. Without explicit instruction, infants who are blind or visually impaired may not learn to crawl or walk at an appropriate age, and gross- and fine-motor skills will not properly develop. They may not learn to accept solid foods or to feed themselves. Their language development may be delayed. Families of children with vision loss need specific strategies to support their children as they progress through normal developmental stages and build basic concepts as a foundation for future learning.

Early intervention programs are designed to help infants and children who are blind or visually impaired achieve early milestones and begin learning basic concepts. These infants and their families may receive services from teachers of students who are

**REFLECTIVE EXERCISE**

#8 What are some ways that Child Find programs could identify young children who are not easily found and referred for services?

In the United States, roughly 23,000 adults and 15,500 children have received cochlear implants (National Institute on Deafness and Other Communication Disorders, 2007). Children as young as 12 months are eligible for implantation, and many advocates suggest that children should receive the cochlear implant as early as 6 months of age.

A cochlear implant is a small, complex electronic device that can help provide a sense of sound to a person who is profoundly deaf or severely hearing impaired. An implant has four basic parts:

- A microphone, which picks up sound from the environment
- A speech processor, which selects and arranges sounds picked up by the microphone
- A transmitter and receiver/stimulator, which receive signals from the speech processor and convert them into electric impulses
- Electrodes, which collect the impulses from the stimulator and send them to the brain

The electrodes are the portion of the implant that is inserted within the cochlea. The other portions are worn externally. Cochlear implants work differently from hearing aids. Hearing aids amplify sound. To a person with severe-to-profound hearing loss, amplification won't provide much hearing, because sound is still being delivered through a damaged part of the ear. A cochlear implant doesn't make sounds louder; it bypasses the damaged part of the ear and sends sound directly to the auditory (hearing) nerve to provide a clearer understanding of sound and speech.

Even with this bypass system, an implant does not restore or create normal hearing. Instead, it can give individuals a useful auditory understanding of the environment and help them understand speech. For a simulation of what it sounds like to hear with a cochlear implant, visit *http://www.earinstitute.org/research/aip/audiodemos.htm.*

Because cochlear implants are specifically designed for use with individuals who have severe-to-profound hearing loss, their use has been questioned by the Deaf community. Historically, individuals with this degree of hearing loss have been users of ASL, but children who receive implants are much more likely to use spoken language instead of signed language. Many representatives of the Deaf community have questioned the use of cochlear implants with young children. They have expressed concerns about the safety and reliability of the implants; the variability of results (not all individuals with cochlear implants develop understanding of spoken language); the misrepresentation of implants in the mainstream media as a cure for deafness; and certainly the possibility that, if all parents choose implantation, the cultural use of ASL will diminish. The National Association of the Deaf (2000) encourages parents considering implantation to "meet and get to know successful deaf and hard of hearing children and adults who are fluent in sign language and English, both with and without implants."

The debates about whether to provide children with cochlear implants continue; but as information and technology advance, more and more parents are choosing implantation. School programs such as the Kendall Demonstration Elementary School at Gallaudet University are implementing programs designed to support students with cochlear implants in developing both spoken and signed languages.

### Cochlear Implant Resources

**Sound and Fury**
P.O. Box 2284
South Burlington, VT 05407
Voice: 1-800-336-1917
Website: http://www.pbs.org/wnet/soundandfury/index.html

**Alexander Graham Bell Association for the Deaf and Hard of Hearing**
3417 Volta Place, NW
Washington, DC 20007-2778
Voice: (202) 337-5220
Toll-free voice: (866) 337-5220
TTY: (202) 337-5221
Fax: (202) 337-8314
E-mail: info@agbell.org
Website: www.agbell.org

**Cochlear Implant Association, Inc.**
5335 Wisconsin Avenue, NW, Suite 440
Washington, DC 20015-2052
Voice: (202) 895-2781
Fax: (202) 895-2782
E-mail: info@cici.org
Website: www.cici.org

**House Ear Institute**
2100 West Third Street
Los Angeles, CA 90057
Voice: (213) 483-4431, 8:30 A.M.–5 P.M., Pacific time
TTY: (213) 484-2642
Fax: (213) 483-8789
E-mail: webmaster@hei.org
Website: www.hei.org

**PEARSON**
**myeducationlab**

After reading "Technology for Access: Cochlear Implants" go to the Assignments and Activities section of Topic 15: Sensory Impairments in the MyEducationLab for your course and complete the activity entitled *The Cochlear Implant*.

visually impaired, orientation and mobility instructors, occupational therapists, physical therapists, or all of these professionals. Teachers and therapists may provide services in the home, at a school or early intervention facility, or even in a daycare facility.

**Preschool Services.**   Preschoolers who are blind or visually impaired are likely to receive specialized preschool services, with most children spending at least part of their day in early childhood special education programs (U.S. Department of Education, 2003). Instruction in these settings is designed to specifically address the sensory needs of students who are blind or visually impaired. Characteristics of specialized programs are described by Bernas-Pierce and Miller (2005, pp. 7–8) as follows:

1. Pacing of program activities is slow and deliberate, allowing the child time to fully explore the physical and social environments.
2. Stress is one use of language to label objects and to describe activities in which the child is engaged.
3. Real objects are used in place of replicas.
4. Frequent repetition of common actions and activities helps the child who is blind/visually impaired internalize what sighted children see again and again and creates opportunities for hands-on practice.
5. A structured approach allows the child to function in a more predictable world and to generalize knowledge to all environments and situations.
6. Small child-to-teacher ratios assure ongoing access to information and the environment.
7. A process approach to learning fosters the development of compensatory skills of touch, hearing, residual vision, taste, and smell as tools to concept development and organization of the child's world and experiences.
8. Engagement in readiness activities involving pre-braille and early literacy experiences are integral parts of the program.
9. [Students have the] opportunity to develop and practice orientation and mobility skills in a safe and predictable environment.

Children who are blind or visually impaired do not learn incidentally and must be provided with direct instruction to learn the same concepts that other children develop naturally (Ferrell, 1997).

### Deaf-Blind

Professionals who work with infants who are deaf-blind should be highly trained. These individuals must master professional competencies in working with families from diverse backgrounds, coaching families in communication strategies with their infants, encouraging the use of hearing aids and glasses when prescribed, weaving intervention strategies into the family's routine, collecting data, and participating as a member of an interdisciplinary team. The multiple learning needs of infants who are deaf-blind require qualified professionals who can help families obtain appropriate medical treatments, hearing and vision evaluations, and other related services. Moreover, the complexity of these infants' learning needs demands a team approach. Service providers need to meet with each other and with families in order to plan how to best meet an infant's needs and the family's concerns. Families receiving services through home visits need regular contacts with other families and service providers. Although the home is a natural environment, some parents report feeling isolated and indicate that they appreciate opportunities for contact with other families who have children with similar learning needs (Chen, Alsop, & Minor, 2000).

## Elementary and Middle School Programs

### Deaf and Hearing Impaired

Students who are deaf or hearing impaired are likely to have educational experiences that differ somewhat from those of the general student population. Although the U.S. Department of Education (2009) reports that 86% of these students spend at least part of the day in general education settings, only 47% spend the majority of the day in a general education classroom.

**Consultation.**   Students who are deaf or hearing impaired and are educated primarily in the general education setting commonly receive special education services through an itinerant or consulting teacher. Itinerant teachers work with several students across several schools. They travel from building to building to meet with individual students and/or teachers. The itinerant teacher commonly focuses on supporting the student in accessing the general education curriculum, with occasional individual instruction or tutoring for particular skills. When working directly with the student, the focus of the itinerant teacher is often on developing speech, language, or listening skills as well as on instructing for the improvement of conceptual understanding, building background knowledge, or increasing vocabulary.

Itinerant teachers travel from building to building to meet with individual students and/or teachers.

Students receiving services from an itinerant teacher spend most of their instructional time with the general educator. The general educator collaborates with the itinerant teacher to be sure the student's individual needs are met, but some basic strategies such as the following can help a teacher make the student feel more comfortable in the class. A general education teacher should always do the following:

- Face the class when presenting information. Don't speak to the wall or blackboard! Even students who do not use speech-reading will benefit from your facial and body expressions, so make sure they can be seen.
- Allow the student to indicate his preferred seating. Many will request to be in the front of the room, but other factors such as lighting and ambient noise can impact this decision.
- The student may have paraprofessional assistance to present auditory information in a visual format. This could be a sign language interpreter, a captioner, an oral interpreter, or a cued speech transliterator. All these individuals have a common purpose: to facilitate communication, not to provide instruction.
- Provide visual aids to support information, especially when presenting a new concept. Charts, diagrams, posters, graphic organizers, pictures, and maps are great examples of visual aids that support learning.
- Take time to assess the student's background knowledge. Students who are deaf or hearing impaired may have unexpected gaps in their knowledge base because of limited incidental learning. Find out what they know and build from there.
- Do the best you can to reduce the noise distracters in the room. If available, classroom amplification systems benefit not only the student with hearing loss but the rest of the class as well.

**Resource or Special Classroom Services.**   Of those students educated within the general education schools, about 21% are outside of the general education classroom for at least 80% of the day. This implies that these students are served mostly in separate classrooms in the regular school (U.S. Department of Education, 2009). The Gallaudet Research Institute (2005) reported that 31% of students with hearing impairments receive their education in a self-contained classroom within a general education facility. Students served in this way may join the general education classroom for activities such as special projects, nonacademic subjects, assemblies, recess, or lunch. In the special classroom or resource room setting, the student receives more specialized instruction presented in ASL, other systems of signing, or orally. Regardless of the communication method used, teachers focus on developing language, literacy, and content knowledge.

PEARSON
**myeducationlab**

Go to the Assignments and Activities section of Topic 15: Sensory Impairments in the MyEducationLab for your course and complete the activity entitled *The Inclusion of Students with Hearing Loss.*

**Residential Services.** About 13% of students who are deaf or hearing impaired attend school in a separate facility (e.g., a day program or residential school) that specializes in educating these students (U.S. Department of Education, 2009). Residential schools are most likely to present a bilingual-bicultural educational philosophy in that students are taught to understand facets of Deaf culture and ASL, as well as facets of hearing culture and English. ASL is preferred as the first language, and English is taught through reading and writing. All teachers and students use ASL, and the communication environment is rich with open access. "Can You Help Me with This Student?" will give you an idea of the challenges a teacher can face when providing instruction to some students with hearing impairments.

Teachers address the content standards identified within their states as well as the language development of students on an individualized basis. With literacy skills

## CAN YOU HELP ME WITH THIS STUDENT?

| To... | Angela Liguori, District Consultant for Students with Hearing Impairments |
| --- | --- |
| From... | Matthew Hansen, Teacher of Middle School Students with Hearing Impairments |
| Subject: | Suggestions for helping an older student with a hearing impairment |

Dear Ms. Liguori,

My greatest challenge as a teacher of students with hearing impairments arrived this week, and his name is Miguel Sanchez. Miguel has traveled several thousand miles with his family in search of seasonal work. He is 14 years old and has never attended school before. I have been able to learn that in his hometown, there are no schools or services for students who are deaf or hard of hearing. His parents decided it would be best for him to attend school while he can. I was able to communicate a little with them (I speak a little Spanish) and learned that he has never had hearing aids, probably has a profound hearing loss, and most likely has not been able to hear the sounds of speech. He doesn't have any formal sign language, but his family does use some gestures with him about essential issues. For the most part, Miguel has lived for 14 years with very little communication and with no language. Any and all suggestions will be greatly appreciated!!!

—Mathew

---

To:       Matthew Hansen
From:    Angela Liguori
Subject: RE: Suggestions for helping an older student with a hearing impairment

Matthew,

I agree that Miguel presents a unique challenge, but there is a lot you can do. It will be essential for Miguel to learn more communication skills and for his family to be able to communicate with him better, so here are a few ideas.

First you need to promote language growth! To develop language skills, Miguel needs an immersion program. He should be in an environment where everyone around him will use ASL for all communications. Next you should try to support the family in their language development. It is important for the family to learn both English and ASL, and you can facilitate both these needs. You have a family literacy program available through the school (or your community center) that can also help them learn to read and write in English, not just speak.

As much as possible, you should provide opportunities for inclusion. Miguel is used to mingling with children he cannot communicate with and may miss this in a completely self-contained setting. Since he is 14, you should begin vocational/transition services immediately. Miguel is attempting to gain language and communication skills far beyond the ideal time frame. His delays in language development may impact other areas of learning, and the school can provide training and support so that he is prepared for the world of work when he leaves school.

It would be a good idea to use English language learner (ELL) teaching strategies. You and any other teachers working with Miguel may need more information on language learning, social integration, and educating students from diverse backgrounds. Teaching methods that work for students who are ELLs are often effective for students who are deaf or hard of hearing. The following resources will be helpful:

Easterbrooks, S., & Baker, S. (2002). *Language learning in children who are deaf and hard of hearing: Multiple pathways*. Boston: Allyn & Bacon.

Schirmer, B. R. (2000). *Language and literacy development in children who are deaf* (2nd ed.). Boston: Allyn & Bacon.

I hope this helps. Keep me informed of Miguel's progress.

—Angela

## EXTEND AND APPLY

What will you do to prepare for a student like Miguel in your school? Begin now by searching for resources in your community. First, find a beginning sign language class. Second, find an English class for adults. Does your community offer a class that teaches sign language to adults whose language is other than English? Are there family literacy programs in your community?

being essential to all academic learning and strongly emphasized in the No Child Left Behind Act (2001), the groundwork of language development takes priority as the primary emphasis of the teacher of students who are deaf or hearing impaired. To address the standards of the general education curriculum, teachers must have an understanding of the methods and expectations of the general education classroom (Luckner & Howell, 2002).

Literacy has a strong impact on the lives of individuals who are deaf or hearing impaired. Simple everyday events such as watching television, making a phone call to a friend, or asking a stranger for directions are often mediated through print. Many people believe that making something available in writing makes that information accessible for individuals who are deaf or hearing impaired. However, common adaptations such as closed captioning, text messaging, and telecommunication devices for the deaf and teletypewriters (TDD/TTYs) are effective only if individuals who are deaf or hearing impaired are literate. Therefore, teachers of students who are deaf or hearing impaired must provide literacy instruction in cooperation with their content instruction.

## Blind/Visually Impaired

Students who are blind or visually impaired are highly likely to have educational experiences similar to students without disabilities. The U.S. Department of Education (2009) reports that 87% of these students spend at least part of the day in general education settings (56% spend 80% of the day or more in general education classrooms), with only 13% educated in separate facilities. For students enrolled in the general education classroom, the focus of the general educator is on curriculum development. As determined by their individualized education program (IEP), most students receive services from an instructor with specialized training in educating students who are blind or visually impaired. Specialized instruction is commonly provided by an itinerant teacher or in a resource setting.

**Consultation Services.** Many people believe that the only assistance students who are blind or visually impaired need to access the curriculum is a different format of presentation. They expect braille or large-print materials to be the only necessary accommodation. However, this is not the case.

> Curriculum access is more than placement and providing books and materials in tactual modalities. Students who are blind still miss out on demonstrations conducted visually, metaphors without experiences, and other forms of incidental learning that assume the ability to see. The problem extends to students who use print but whose vision still limits their ability to see at a distance or in detail. Tactual diagrams, while often developed with the best of intentions, often assume a cognitive mapping not usually within the experience of blind and low vision students. The emphasis on educational modifications and adaptations often ignores the more subtle interplay that occurs in the classroom. (Ferrell, 2007, p. 3)

In consultation with the teacher of the blind and visually impaired, the general educator can incorporate a few simple strategies to be more effective with students with visual impairments:

- Provide opportunities for tactile exploration. When possible, bring real objects to class, or use models or other tangible representations to develop understanding.
- Allow space for specialized equipment. Students may use assistive/adaptive technologies to access printed information, and these items are often large. Plan a space in the room where they can be stored when not in use but easily accessed without disrupting others.
- Give verbal descriptions of visual information. Announce the obvious so that the student knows when someone comes and goes, when an unexpected event happens, or when a change in activity occurs. Describe any visual aids you use.
- Learn details about the implications of vision loss for your student. You may need to adjust lighting, colors of bulletin boards, papers, and so on to maximize what the student can see.
- Allow students to indicate their preferred seating. Many will request to be in the front of the room, but other factors such as field of vision or lighting preferences may impact this decision.

**Resource Classroom Services.** Resource teachers generally work within a public school and provide services to a small group of students with visual disabilities. Because the number of students requiring this type of service is small, this is a less common option. Resource arrangements for students who are blind or visually impaired frequently require students to be bused outside their local community to a central location where several students can be grouped in one classroom. In this setting, the student will join the public school for a portion of coursework and receive the rest of the instruction directly from the specialized teacher. The teacher may emphasize developing braille literacy skills or using assistive and adaptive technology. Concept development is conducted in a more hands-on, sensory-intensive format.

**Residential Services.** Very few students who are blind or visually impaired receive their full instruction in a separate or residential facility. Although residential schools were a common educational setting in the early years of educating students who were blind or visually impaired, the trend since the mid-1970s has been away from these separate facilities. Today, many students attending separate schools have disabilities in addition to their visual impairment. These additional disabilities make the constant presence of specialized instructors and paraprofessionals necessary.

In a residential school, students will receive intensive instruction in concept development, sensory integration, communication, orientation and mobility, life skills, and general academics. In "Can You Help Me with This Student?" you can see a description of how one student with visual impairments is served in a residential school.

## CAN YOU HELP ME WITH THIS STUDENT?

| To... | Marilyn Littlejohn, District Consultant for Students with Visual Impairments |
|---|---|
| From... | Wendy Kaufermann, Teacher of Students with Visual Impairments |
| Subject: | A young girl with complex needs |

Ms. Littlejohn,

I am working with a new little girl who as just started at the school. She lives with her parents but comes here every day, and I really would appreciate your advice. Julie Walker was born prematurely with very low birth weight. As a result of several complications surrounding her birth and early months of life, Julie has very limited control over her body. She spends most of her day in a wheelchair and communicates through gestures and vocalizations. Julie's parents noticed that she was not responding to much visual information, but her doctors were unable to find anything physically wrong with her eyes. The eyes were able to see quite clearly, but Julie could not process visual information. Eventually, a combination of characteristics led to the diagnosis of cortical visual impairment (CVI).

It seems that Julie frequently finds herself in a state of sensory overload. She does have favorite colors and patterns, and there are things she will look at for brief periods of time; but when she is presented with too much visual input, she simply stops using her eyes. I'm not sure what kind of strategies might be helpful. What would you suggest?

—Wendy

---

| To: | Wendy Kaufermann |
|---|---|
| From: | Marilyn Littlejohn |
| Subject | RE: A young girl with complex needs |

Wendy,
How exciting for you to have this opportunity to work with little Julie. Here is what I recommend:

- Limit the amount of sensory input. Julie needs to have times of day when she can focus on information from only one sense. She needs a classroom with a quiet area that has no distractions.

- Get family input to determine color, field preference, and communication needs. Like most students with CVI, Julie has developed a color that she loves and will look at. She also has an area where she sees best. By communicating with the family, you can make sure they are using materials that Julie will want to look at and placing them in the proper position.

- Use color, movement, and sound carefully to drive visual attending. Julie is highly sensitive to sensory input, which can be an advantage if you will carefully construct cues for behavior or activities based on her personal preferences.

- Add new sensory input slowly, one item at a time. Julie loves to look at multiple objects and to look at new objects, but she will need time to adjust to these changes. Introduce one new item at a time, and give her a chance to become familiar with it before adding others.

- Seek communication expertise. Julie is a strong communicator, but many adults are so dependent on spoken language that they do not notice her efforts. You and other teachers and Julie's parents should seek the expertise of a communication specialist who can observe Julie's nonverbal behaviors and give feedback about what kinds of messages she is sending. The school and family can then use these efforts at communication to increase her ability to access the world around her. See the following references:

Holbrook, C. (2006). *Children with visual impairments: A guide for parents.* Bethesda, MD: Woodbine House.

Lear, R. (1998). *Look at it this way: Toys and activities for children with visual impairment.* St. Louis, MO: Elsevier/Butterworth-Heinemann.

Niemann, S., & Jacob, N. (2000). *Helping children who are blind.* Berkeley, CA: Hesperian Foundation.

Good luck, and keep me up-to-date on Julie's progress.

—Marilyn

---

**EXTEND AND APPLY**

- Providing students who have CVI with materials that are controlled for sensory input is more difficult than it seems. To get a feel for the challenge facing these teachers, visit your local library, and search for a children's book that has only one picture or one color on each page.
- Visit a toy store, and search for items made of a single bright color that would be safe for a preschooler to handle, or search for a toy that has on/off switches for both the lights and the sounds.

---

**Short-Term Services.**   Many professionals working with students who are blind or visually impaired are concerned that the focus on inclusive educational settings may leave students without some of the specialized instruction they require.

> Although many school programs are providing the specialized instruction that visually impaired students need in addition to their academic instruction, there is much room for improvement. Too many visually impaired high school students graduate without having mastered the skills needed for higher education or economic survival. Others, for whom a standard high school diploma may not be achievable, lack the functional skills essential for meaningful participation in adult society. (Huebner, Merk-Adam, Stryker, & Wolffe, 2004, p. 14)

In an effort to meet these needs, many residential schools are beginning to offer short-term programs for students. These programs are designed to provide students with a particular set of skills in a defined time period. For example, a student whose vision is diminishing may spend 6 weeks in a residential program to learn braille skills, or another student may come in for 3 weeks to learn basic household skills such as laundering, washing, cooking, and shopping.

## Transition, Adolescence, and Adult Needs and Services

One of the most critical periods in the life of a young person is the transition from school to the world of work. Developing independence, exploring interests, and pursuing employment or additional schooling are just some of the challenges faced by young adults as they transition from school to adult life.

For the key postsecondary outcomes, many young adults with sensory impairments do not attain levels similar to young adults without disabilities. Drawing on the data collected by the National Longitudinal Transition Study 2 (NLTS2, 2009), we can see that for key outcomes, satisfactory achievement levels for individuals with sensory impairments is relatively small. Table 13.2 shows the results in three key areas: employment, postsecondary education, and social involvement.

**TABLE 13.2** • OUTCOMES FOR YOUNG ADULTS WITH SENSORY IMPAIRMENTS ONE OR MORE YEARS AFTER LEAVING HIGH SCHOOL

| Disability Category | Percent of Students who . . . | | |
| --- | --- | --- | --- |
| | Currently have a paid job outside the home | Attended a postsecondary institution | Get together with friends at least 2 or 3 days a week |
| Hearing impairment | 63.2 | 58.6 | 57.9 |
| Visual impairment | 40.9 | 57.7 | 61.3 |
| Deaf-blind | 31.8 | 33.7 | 48.8 |

Source: NLTS2 (2009).

In the following sections, we discuss some of the important educational and transitional needs for students in the distinct disability areas.

### Deaf and Hearing Impaired

The secondary educational needs of adolescents and adults who are deaf or hearing impaired are consistent with their earlier school experiences. Literacy remains a strong focus through high school and for those entering postsecondary programs.

Literacy is about learning how to learn, whether that learning is related to electrical engineering, auto mechanics, parenting, or science. According to previous studies, literacy outcomes for students who are deaf or hearing impaired are staggeringly poor. More than 30% of students who are deaf or hearing impaired leave high school functionally illiterate (Waters & Doehring, 1990). Holt (1993) reported that the average reading level of 18-year-old students who are deaf or hearing impaired was between third and fourth grade, which is not much different from 30 years earlier (Babbidge Committee Report, 1965). More recently, Traxler (2000) reported that students who are deaf or hearing impaired are *still* graduating from high school with a reading level just below fourth grade.

In a study conducted to learn more about the need for transition services for students with hearing impairments, the primary concern described by parents, caregivers, teachers, and other professionals was "the need for appropriate job behavior, opportunities for work-based learning, work exploration, and work experience including volunteer and paid work, prior to graduation from high school" (LeNard, 2001, p. 13).

### Blind/Visually Impaired

Career education activities for students with visual impairments should be directly tied to the school curriculum and integrated into family lives. Areas of instruction that will assist students as they prepare for the workplace include functional academics, work apprenticeships, cooperative education, and technology preparation. In addition to these skills, which are necessary for all students, Wolffe (1996) described five areas that educators must address for students who are blind or visually impaired: realistic feedback, high expectations, opportunities to work, compensatory skills, and exposure to visual input. In order to appropriately focus on career preparation, students with visual impairments and their families must begin early.

### Deaf-Blind

Employment opportunities are often limited for young people who are deaf-blind for various reasons. Many parents and professionals fear that students with deaf-blindness cannot work, partly because so many young adults who are deaf-blind also have other disabilities. Another reason for limited employment opportunities may be that children who are deaf-blind often have limited life experiences that have not allowed them to see and interact with a wide range of jobs.

Starting as early as possible, the child who is deaf-blind must build a knowledge and experience base regarding employment. Teachers can begin by exposing

**REFLECTIVE EXERCISE**

#9 Can you think of some ways in which the postschool outcome for students who are deaf or who have hearing impairments might be improved?

Some professionals and advocates believe that residential schools can provide an important service for students who are deaf or blind.

the child to a variety of community experiences so they have opportunities for interaction. As the child moves into adolescence, providing opportunities for paid employment is a vital component of building that knowledge base.

## PREVAILING ISSUES, CONTROVERSIES, AND IMPLICATIONS FOR THE TEACHER

Many professionals in the fields of education for students who are deaf and for students who are blind share a common philosophy that these students, at least for a portion of their lives, should be educated only with others who have the same characteristics. This philosophy is in contrast to the inclusion movement that has dominated the field of special education for the past 30 years (McLeskey, Rosenberg, & Westling, 2010).

### Should Deaf Students Learn ASL and Participate in the Deaf Culture?

As described earlier, NAD is an organization that supports the civil rights of people who are deaf and hearing impaired. It values humans with diverse abilities and backgrounds and believes all persons, including the deaf and hard of hearing, should be full participants in society. It also strongly defends the need for deaf people to learn ASL and to use this language as the essential element to maintain a culture of the Deaf.

> Established in 1880, the NAD was shaped by deaf leaders who believed in the right of the American deaf community to use sign language, to congregate on issues important to them, and to have its interests represented at the national level. These beliefs remain true to this day, with American Sign Language as a core value. (National Association of the Deaf, 2009a)

> The NAD recognizes that American Sign Language (ASL) is the backbone of the American deaf culture. The NAD values the acquisition, usage and preservation of ASL and is a recognized leader in promoting the acquisition, learning, teaching, and interpreting of ASL. The NAD was created in part to promote and preserve ASL as a legitimate language and an optimal educational tool for deaf children and adults. (National Association of the Deaf, 2009b)

The implication of maintaining a Deaf culture primarily through the use of ASL is that children who are deaf should be immersed in the language and culture of the Deaf from an early age. "Immersion" means that either they attend school primarily with other children who are learning ASL, or they live in a separate residential facility where ASL is the predominant language. Therefore, NAD opposes inclusion as an essential element of education for deaf students.

> Full Inclusion is the placement of all children with disabilities in their neighborhood schools, often irrespective of their unique abilities and needs. It is a concept rooted in ideology that differentiates from, and runs counter to, the provision of FAPE in the LRE. Full Inclusion is not a federal mandate that all children be placed in such settings. Full-inclusionists often call for the elimination of special schools and programs for all students with disabilities, including students who are Deaf and Hard of Hearing. In addition to full-inclusionists there are others who promote *inclusion* and advocate a less-radical approach, one that recognizes the continuum of alternative placement options. However, some advocates of this less-radical approach continue to push the notion that the regular classroom is always the option of first choice, in complete disregard for the provision of essential services,

based on a comprehensive assessment of each child. The NAD believes such approaches are in direct violation of the Individuals with Disabilities Education Act (IDEA). (National Association of the Deaf, 2009d)

## Should Blind Students Attend Residential Schools?

Just as NAD takes the position that deaf children should learn ASL and participate in the Deaf culture, many feel that a strong defense can be made for blind children to attend special residential schools. Kay Ferrell (2007) has written most clearly on this issue. She points out that residential schools for blind students were not developed to segregate them, but to bring into one location the necessary expertise so that these students could develop their maximum potential notwithstanding their visual disability:

> Schools for the blind were established in the United States during the first half of the 19th century not to segregate children who were blind, or to shelter them, or even to provide care for them. They were established with the belief that children who were blind and visually impaired were capable individuals who could become contributing members of society. . . . [Furthermore, one of the primary differences between the field of blindness and low vision and other special education fields is that the residential school system was never intended to separate blind students from society. It was established to provide an education that would prepare children with visual disabilities to take their places in society, as employees, family members, and taxpayers. (Ferrell, 2007, p. 1)

According to the U.S. Department of Education (2009), significantly higher percentages of students with hearing impairments (5.92%) and visual disabilities (5.69%) attend public residential schools as compared to the average for all other students with disabilities (0.30%). While the number of students with sensory disabilities in residential schools has decreased in recent years, the thought remains among some parents, professionals, and advocates that such placements can, for some, be beneficial. Consider the situation described in "The Real World" and how you might react.

## THE REAL WORLD Challenges and Solutions
### What should I tell a parent?

Joanna Maceland was enjoying her new part-time job as a childcare assistant. It was a job that required a lot of energy and focus, but it was always interesting, and her students ensured that every day would be a little different. But now Joanna was facing a somewhat difficult situation, one about which she had little knowledge and had never given much thought.

One of the mothers—a single parent—had just told Joanna that her 18-month-old son had survived a bout with meningitis. The disease was life-threatening and so awful, that when the boy survived, the mother was extremely thankful. But now the doctors had told her that, as a result of the disease, the boy had lost his hearing and was likely to be profoundly deaf. It was a condition the mom had never thought about when her baby was ill, and the diagnosis and its implications had still not completely sunk in.

As the boy's mother tried to learn more about deafness and what to do about it, she learned about different opinions. She learned about the cochlear implants and their benefits and some of their risks. She also learned about the community of deaf people that embraces the Deaf culture and encourages the use of American Sign Language. She learned that she could get early intervention and special education services from the local school district for her child. She also thought about later trying to get him in a residential school where he could be with more children who would also use ASL.

There was so much to think about, and time seemed to be going by too quickly. Although Joanna was only a childcare assistant, she was intelligent and the boy's mother valued her opinion. The only problem was, Joanna didn't know what to think.

If you teach or work with children in another capacity, your opinion will often be valued by parents, even though you may lack expertise. In this case, the mother is facing a dilemma. She has already started gathering information, but she is having a difficult time deciding which path to take. Here are some actions Joanna might take:

- Learn as much as you can about the alternatives. Use the Internet and other material available to you.

- Contribute the knowledge you develop to what the parent already has acquired. Share both your information and your sources of knowledge. Help the parent learn more.
- Don't purport to have expertise; don't make a recommendation. Such a decision must be made by the parents. Your job is only to try to make sure they have as many facts as possible.
- Always be supportive. Parents are often in a difficult position and are trying to make the best decision for their child. As a teacher (or an assistant), you should try to offer as much support as possible and respect the decision they ultimately make.

**Valuable Resources for the Teacher**

American Speech Hearing and Language Association (ASHA). (2009). *Information for the public.* Retrieved September 2, 2009, from http://www.asha.org/default.htm

Batshaw, M. L., Pellegrino, L., & Roizen, N. J. (Eds.). *Children with disabilities* (6th ed.). Baltimore: Brookes.

Centers for Disease Control and Prevention. (n.d.). National Center on Birth Defects and Developmental Disabilities. *What are developmental disabilities?* Retrieved September 2, 2009, from http://www.cdc.gov/ncbddd/dd/

National Institute on Deafness and Other Communication Disorders. (2009). *Health information.* Retrieved September 2, 2009, from http://www.nidcd.nih.gov/

**Final Thoughts**

All parents are faced with difficult choices, but parents of children with special needs must often make excruciatingly difficult decisions, decisions that can affect the kind of life their child will have. It is relatively easy for scholars and professionals to promote and debate certain approaches, but ultimately parents must determine the direction they will select for their child. We should help them in their decision making but should not pass judgment on their decisions.

# 13 SUMMARY

In this chapter, we have explored the education of students with sensory impairments and presented significant facts.

severe communication and other developmental and educational needs that they cannot be accommodated in special education programs solely for children with deafness or children with blindness.

## Disability Classifications for Students with Sensory Impairments

- A student may be eligible for special education if he has sensory impairments that have an adverse impact on learning.
- *Deafness* means the presence of a hearing impairment "so severe that the child is impaired in processing linguistic information . . . with or without amplification that adversely affects a child's educational performance."
- *Hearing impairment* means an impairment "that adversely affects a child's educational performance but that is not included under the definition of deafness."
- There is also a cultural definition of deafness through which a person identifies himself as part of the Deaf culture.
- *Visual impairment including blindness* means an impairment in vision that, even with correction, adversely affects a child's educational performance. The term includes both partial sight and blindness.
- *Legal blindness* refers to a central acuity of 20/200 or less in the better eye with the best possible correction as measured on a Snellen vision chart, or a visual field of 20 degrees or less.
- *Deaf-blindness* means concomitant hearing and visual impairments, the combination of which causes such

## Key Characteristics of Students with Sensory Impairments

- Hearing or vision disabilities alone do not impact cognitive skills of a child, but the mental processes required to learn new information differs for students with sensory impairments.
- A sensory impairment may be only one aspect of a student's educational needs. She may have other disabilities that affect learning ability. It can be difficult to distinguish between learning challenges caused by a lack of sensory input or by other conditions.
- It is very common for students with sensory impairments to have typical learning processes and learning modes; their ability to access information, however, may be restricted in some avenues, or the order in which they acquire new skills may vary.
- Social behavior of students with sensory impairments is impacted not because of an innate lack of social skills but because the sensory loss results in a loss of input.
- Physical development of students with sensory impairments is similar to that of all other children, unless the student has an additional disability.

## Prevalence of Students with Sensory Impairments

- According to the U.S. Department of Education (2009), about 79,000 children (3 to 21 years) have hearing impairments and about 29,000 have visual disabilities.

- The U.S. Department of Education (2009) counts 1,659 students as deaf-blind, but the National Consortium on Deaf-Blindness (NCDB, 2008) reported that in their 2007 census, a total of 10,174 students were deaf-blind.

## Educational Experiences for Students with Sensory Impairments

- Early intervention and preschool services are critical to the later learning and development of children with sensory impairments.
- Students with sensory impairments receive different forms of educational services, including consultation services, resource-room placements in regular schools, and residential schools. Sometimes students who are blind will go to residential schools for short periods of time to develop specific skills.
- Literacy skills of students who are deaf or have hearing impairments are often negatively affected, and both academic skills and functional living skills for students with visual impairments can be adversely affected.

## Important Curriculum Areas for Students with Sensory Impairments

- Teachers must address the needs of students that result from their sensory impairments as well as curricular areas in the general education curriculum.

## Major Issues Related to Educating Students with Sensory Impairments

- Many professionals, parents, and advocates for students who are deaf support students' learning American Sign Language (ASL) and participation in the Deaf culture and oppose inclusion in general education settings.
- Many professionals, parents, and advocates for students who are blind support the need for them to attend residential schools at least for brief periods of time.

 Council for Exceptional Children

## ADDRESSING THE PROFESSIONAL STANDARDS

Council for Exceptional Children (CEC) Knowledge Standards addressed in the chapter:

For teachers of students who are deaf and hearing impaired: DH1K1, DH1K4, DH2K1, DH2K2, DH3K1, DH3K2, DH6K2, DH6K3, DH6K5

For teachers of students who are blind or visually impaired: VI1K3, VI1K6, VI2K3, VI2K4, VI3K2, VI3K3, VI4K16, VI7K2

Appendix B: CEC Knowledge and Skill Standards Common Core has a full listing of the standards referenced here.

## PEARSON myeducationlab

Now go to Topic 15: Sensory Impairments in the MyEducationLab for your course, where you can:

- Find learning outcomes for the broad concepts covered in this chapter along with the national standards that connect to these outcomes.
- Complete Assignments and Activities that can help you more deeply understand the chapter content.
- Examine challenging situations presented in the IRIS Center Resources.
- Access video clips of CCSSO National Teachers of the Year award winners responding to the question, "Why Do I Teach?" in the Teacher Talk section.

- Apply and practice your understanding of the core concepts and skills identified in the chapter with the Building Teaching Skills and Dispositions learning units.
- Check your comprehension on the content covered in the chapter by going to the Study Plan in the Book-Specific Resources section for your text. Here you will be able to take a chapter quiz, receive feedback on your answers, and then access Review, Practice, and Enrichment activities to enhance your understanding of chapter content.

# chapter 1

# Physical Disabilities and Other Health Impairments

**REFLECT UPON**

- What are the definitions of physical disabilities and other health impairments as used in special education?
- What are the major characteristics of students with these disabilities?
- How often do physical disabilities and other health impairments occur?
- What are some important areas of assessment and planning for these students?
- What special considerations exist for these students with regard to instruction and related services?
- What are some major issues related to teaching and providing services to students with physical disabilities or other health impairments?

# MY PROFESSION, MY STORY: **MARGARET OTWELL**

The next time you are in a classroom, take a look around, and see if you can spot the students who have special needs due to physical disabilities or other health impairments. Because the prevalence of these students is relatively small, chances are, you won't see too many. But for Margaret Otwell, these are the students she sees the most.

After receiving her bachelor's degree in Exercise and Sports Science at the University of North Carolina in Chapel Hill, Margaret earned a master's in physical therapy at Western Carolina University. Then, after she passed both national and state exams, Margaret began working as a physical therapist (PT) for Asheville, North Carolina, City Schools.

The students Margaret works with are those whose physical needs require ongoing attention in order that they will be able to receive a free and appropriate education. Typically, Margaret has about 40 on her caseload. She works with these students directly and also with their teachers and parents in order to better ensure their success.

Margaret's job, like that of a teacher, entails many responsibilities. She explained, "My job consists of daily treatment sessions, evaluations, ongoing assessment of progress, goal setting [included in the individualized education program], IEP, patient and family education, documentation, multidisciplinary interaction, assessment and evaluation of current and needed adaptive equipment, and networking with related services providers and outside agencies."

The work of a PT begins early and continues throughout a long day. She told us that her typical day starts in her office, where she writes daily treatment session plans, checks e-mails, and communicates with other service providers. She also creates home and classroom exercise programs—so parents and teachers can continue therapies in the home and classroom—and completes necessary documentation including daily treatment notes, evaluation write-ups, billing, and IEP documentation.

After about 1 hour in the office, Margaret heads off to various schools to provide treatment, perform evaluations, and/or attend meetings. She serves all the schools in the Asheville City School System, from preschool to the high school. Margaret explained that "after each treatment session, I try to touch base with the child's teacher to communicate what we worked on in PT, [and to share] concerns and ideas to increase function within the school environment." On occasion she also conducts aquatic therapy and assists students on field trips if her support for them is important.

We asked Margaret to share an example of one of her successes with a student with a physical disability. "I worked with a student who when I first met him refused to participate in any PE activities other than propelling his wheelchair around

the perimeter of the gym the entire class period. Despite encouragement from his peers, teacher, and myself, he always refused and when asked why replied 'Because I can't.' After getting to know this student better, I tried hard to incorporate his personal interests into PE activities, worked with teachers to adapt activities to his capabilities, and practiced various PE activities one-on-one during our treatment sessions. Eventually, he slowly started to attempt more and more during PE class and became more independent and confident in his skills and abilities. Now PE is one of his favorite classes, and it means so much to see him succeed and believe in himself."

It is easy to see how a PT's effects on a student can extend beyond improving physical abilities. And it is also easy to see why Margaret Otwell loves her job. "The aspect of my job that I absolutely love is working with the kids, and specifically seeing them succeed and moreover enjoy themselves within their school environment. I enjoy that I am able to work with a wide age range and a diagnostically diverse caseload. My job both challenges and enriches me every day."

Of course every job has its challenges, and being a PT in a public school is no different. Margaret values providing therapy in natural settings, but at the same time finds it challenging. She says one of the most difficult parts of her job "is finding the best way to provide treatment in the natural school environment while not disrupting the teacher or other children. School-based PT is very functionally based, and it is ideal to provide treatment within the same setting as [a student's] peers." But, she says, "this can be difficult, as it may distract other students or the child being treated. However, I have found that communication with teachers, careful planning, and flexibility can help with this issue."

Some students with physical or medical conditions require special supports to receive an appropriate education.

As part of your day-to-day interactions with students, you, like other teachers, will see many illnesses, injuries, and the results of unexpected physical accidents and mishaps. From elementary school students with chicken pox to young girls who are pregnant, unexpected and often undesirable health and physical conditions are a notable part of school life.

Many of these conditions are transitory and have little significant bearing on the student or the teacher, at least in terms of public school education. A few might require short-term attention but will soon be forgotten. But as Margaret Otwell and many teachers know, some students have significant physical disabilities or chronic health conditions, and these students require extra attention to succeed. For these students, schools must provide special education services or, alternatively, develop a 504 plan for the student (DePaepe, Garrison-Kane, & Doelling, 2002; Zirkel, 2009).

In this chapter, we discuss those students whose physical or medical conditions are not short-lived and who, without special supports, may not receive an appropriate education. We will discuss two relevant groups: students with physical disabilities and those with chronic health impairments. Within each of these groups, great variation exists in the nature of the disability and its effects on the individual. We describe the major characteristics of some more common conditions and discuss how special education and related services can help students succeed.

## DEFINITIONS AND KEY CHARACTERISTICS OF STUDENTS WITH PHYSICAL DISABILITIES

Although we prefer the term *physical disabilities,* the U.S. Department of Education uses the term *orthopedic impairment* in its formal definition. "Orthopedic impairment means a severe orthopedic impairment that adversely affects a child's educational performance. The term includes impairments caused by congenital anomaly (e.g., clubfoot, absence of some member, etc.), impairments caused by disease (e.g., poliomyelitis, bone tuberculosis, etc.), and impairments from other causes (e.g., cerebral palsy, amputations, and fractures or burns that cause contractures)" (IDEA 2004, Sec. 300.7). Note that the condition must negatively affect the student's educational performance for the student to qualify for special education services. If the student is not eligible under the Individuals with Disabilities Education Act (IDEA), he may still qualify for a Section 504 plan.

Perhaps more important than the specific physical conditions of these students are some possible unique nonphysical characteristics of students with physical disabilities. Although you should never fall into the trap of stereotyping, you should know that the view of the world of persons with physical disabilities, and their interactions with others, are likely to be a bit different from those of people without physical disabilities. A person who has a physical disability, may—because of personal experiences—have a unique reaction to life events. For example, in one

## FAQ Sheet

### STUDENTS WITH PHYSICAL DISABILITIES AND OTHER HEALTH IMPAIRMENTS

| | |
|---|---|
| Who are they? | • *Physical disabilities:* Students with conditions such as cerebral palsy, spina bifida, or other conditions that affect their ability to walk or use their arms or legs <br> • *Other health impairments:* Students with chronic health conditions such as asthma, epilepsy, and HIV/AIDS, which may or may not be terminal, that cause weakness or fatigue or in some other way adversely affect school performance |
| What are typical characteristics? | • The conditions of students with physical disabilities may be relatively mild to more severe. Different body parts may be affected. Disabilities may be due to central nervous system damage or muscle or orthopedic impairments. <br> • Students with other health impairments may be weak and sometimes in pain. Lack of stamina may often be a debilitating factor. They may miss a lot of school due to their illnesses. |
| What are the demographics? | • Within the school-age population, approximately 0.14% have physical disabilities, and about 0.59% have other health impairments. |
| Where are students educated? | • The majority of students with physical disabilities and other health impairments are educated in general classes. |
| What are the outcomes? | • The physical, social, emotional, and health challenges faced by students with physical disabilities and other health impairments often continue into their adult years. <br> • Some conditions such as muscular dystrophy, HIV/AIDS, and cystic fibrosis lead to early death. |

study the authors interviewed seven high school students with physical disabilities to learn about their lives and how they fit in with others (Doubt & McColl, 2003). The researchers found that two types of factors, extrinsic and intrinsic, either caused the students with disabilities to be left out or helped them fit in to social groups.

*Intrinsic factors* are those conditions that the person can control. Based on what the students told the researchers, factors that helped the students be accepted included avoiding drawing attention to their disability; making fun of their own condition with self-deprecating humor; and finding a special niche among their peers, like serving in a support role on a sports team. Sometimes students also found it helpful to educate their peers about their condition. On the other hand, certain intrinsic factors tended to isolate them: mainly their own physical limitations and self-exclusion. In some cases, simply keeping up was a problem; in others, students excluded themselves because they felt they would not be accepted (Doubt & McColl, 2003).

The authors also reported that the students with disabilities could be limited by extrinsic factors such as the attitudes and behaviors of peers without disabilities. For example, their peers sometimes treated them as though they were younger or less competent. Inaccessible extracurricular activities, especially athletics, also restricted participation. The researchers stated that both intrinsic and extrinsic factors are unfortunate and suggested that teachers should try to reduce them (Doubt & McColl, 2003). Interestingly, in another study, the researchers found that the more that teachers integrate students with physical disabilities, the better the students' self-concept (Mrug & Wallander, 2002).

Because we cannot address all the physical disabilities that you may encounter, we will focus here on those that are relatively common. In Table 14.1 we describe four types of physical disabilities that teachers are likely to encounter, what causes them, and general considerations to consider when teaching students with these conditions. Then we discuss two of the four conditions—cerebral palsy and muscular dystrophy—in more detail in the following sections.

### REFLECTIVE EXERCISE

**#2** Do you have intrinsic factors that you control that either allow you to be better accepted or lead to you being more isolated by your peers?

### PEARSON
# myeducationlab

Go to the Assignments and Activities section of Topic 14: Physical Disabilities & Health Impairments in the MyEducationLab for your course and complete the activity entitled *Physical Disabilities in School-Age Children*.

TABLE 14.1 • PHYSICAL DISABILITIES TEACHERS ARE LIKELY TO ENCOUNTER

| Condition | Cause | Classroom Considerations |
| --- | --- | --- |
| **Cerebral Palsy (CP)**<br><br>CP is a neuromuscular disorder that results in the brain's inability to control some or all of the body's muscles. It may affect the person's limbs, making them tense (hypertonic) or flaccid (hypotonic). The person's head, neck, and trunk may also be affected. It may impair the person's ability to walk, use her arms and hands, chew and swallow, sit upright, and other abilities. Some persons with CP have intellectual disabilities, but many do not. Several different types of CP occur. | CP is caused by brain damage that occurs before, during, or after birth. It is a nonprogressive condition (the damage does not worsen over time). The area of the brain that is damaged and the extent of the damage determine the type of CP that will occur and its severity.<br><br>Several risk factors increase the chance that CP will occur. Some include prematurity, low birth weight, and illness during pregnancy. | A student's ability to physically engage in class activities depends on the severity and extent of CP. Many can easily participate, but some will require adaptations or accommodations. The PT and OT can help teachers design ways to include the student with CP in various learning activities. CP is not always accompanied by a severe intellectual disability, and teachers should not approach the student with this assumption. The motor limitations of students with CP often mask their intellectual ability. |
| **Muscular Dystrophy**<br><br>Muscular dystrophy is an inherited muscle disorder in which muscle tissue gradually degenerates. The most common type of the disease is Duchenne muscular dystrophy (DMD). Muscular dystrophy is a degenerative disease (it worsens over time). Fat tissue gradually replaces muscle tissue, and the child becomes weaker and weaker, with the weakness progressing from the legs upward. Ultimately, the child loses the use of all muscles. Death usually occurs during adolescence or young adulthood. | Muscular dystrophy is an inherited muscle disorder. Mothers carry the gene but do not have the disease. Instead, they can transmit it to their sons. The disease first appears during early childhood, between about 2 and 6 years of age. | The child with muscular dystrophy becomes gradually weaker throughout childhood. His intellectual ability does not decrease, but about one third of the boys with DMD have learning disabilities. Instructional activities must consideration both physical and academic characteristics. The longer the child can remain upright, active, and mobile, the better. Teachers should maintain positive attitudes about the value of the student as a participating member of the class. |
| **Spina Bifida**<br><br>Spina bifida is a break in the spinal cord. Different types of the condition exist. The most severe form, called *myelomeningocele,* results in a loss of sensation and muscle control in parts of the body below the lesion. Persons with myelomeningocele can't feel touch, temperature, pressure, or pain, and their lower body is very weak. They also do not have normal control over their bladder or bowels. | Spina bifida is a particular form of a neural tube defect (NTD). NTDs occur early in pregnancy when the vertebrae fail to fully grow around the spinal chord and instead leave a small opening in the protective bony structure. This opening, called a *bifida*, in some cases allows a part of the spinal cord and/or its covering, called the *meninges*, to pouch out of the vertebrae. The risk of spina bifida can be reduced if a woman takes folic acid before becoming pregnant. | The physical ability of the student with spina bifida varies based on where the lesion occurs, but most students require personal assistance to carry out daily activities. Adaptive devices are also commonly used. Many students with spina bifida are cognitively able but challenged by their physical limitations. Many students also experience social isolation from their peers, largely due to their bladder and bowel problems. Relations with the opposite sex can be especially trying. |
| **Orthopedic and Musculoskeletal Conditions**<br><br>Curvature of the spine (scoliosis), congenital hip dislocations, juvenile arthritis, osteogenesis imperfecta, and limb deficiencies are a few examples of orthopedic and musculoskeletal conditions. In these conditions, bodily structures involving the bones and muscles do not develop normally. Individuals may require surgery; may be fitted with prosthetic devices, such as artificial hands or legs; and usually have to use adapted approaches for accomplishing daily tasks. | Various causes lead to the different conditions in this category, but in many cases, the cause is idiopathic—(unknown). In some cases genetic conditions may be a factor; in other cases, drugs taken by the mother during pregnancy may be a factor (e.g., taking thalidomide resulted in limb deficiencies). Some conditions such as juvenile arthritis may result from a child's inefficient autoimmune system. | The biggest challenge for these students in the classroom, and for their teachers, is finding ways for them to be physically engaged and involved. Their prosthetic devices, body supports, wheelchairs, and other necessary supports may make it difficult for them to get close to instructional activities. OTs and PTs can help design classroom arrangements and conditions that increase physical closeness and participation. It is also important to address the discomfort that results from the devices so the student is not distracted from learning activities. |

## Cerebral Palsy

Cerebral palsy (CP) is a neurologic disorder caused by brain damage before, during, or after birth that affects a person's movement and posture. CP is considered a nonprogressive disability (the brain damage does not continue to worsen). However, treatment is necessary to prevent the person's posture from declining and to improve movement ability and independence (Best & Bigge, 2005; H. C. Griffin, Fitch, & Griffin, 2002; Pellegrino, 2007).

Cerebral palsy is commonly described by how it affects muscle tone. *Spastic CP* is the most common form. A person who has spastic CP has very stiff muscles, exhibits labored movement, and has limited range of motion due to severe muscle contractures that can affect the hands, elbows, hips, knees, and feet. This individual is also likely to have a malformed spine and hip dislocation. *Athetoid CP* is also referred to as *dyskinesia*, which means unwanted or involuntary movement. This form of CP is characterized by either slow, writhing movements or abrupt, jerky movements. These movements can occur in facial muscles, wrists and fingers, the trunk of the body, or one or more extremities. An uncommon type of cerebral palsy is *ataxic CP*. Ataxia is characterized by a lack of balance and uncoordinated movement (Best & Bigge, 2005). Some persons have *mixed* cerebral palsy, meaning they have more than one form of the condition (Pellegrino, 2007).

The medical classification of CP also describes the affected areas of the body. *Hemiplegia* means that one side of the body, such as the left leg and arm, are more affected than the other. *Diplegia* means the legs are more affected than the arms. *Quadriplegia* means that all four limbs are affected as well as the trunk and the muscles that control the neck, mouth, and the tongue. The terms *spastic hemiplegia*, *spastic diplegia*, and *spastic quadriplegia* all explain the characteristics of the muscle tone and the areas of the body that are affected.

Medical professionals also classify CP by its functional impact. A person who has *mild* CP can walk and talk, control head and neck motion, have unimpaired or only slight limitations in activities, and is independent regarding daily activities. Someone with *moderate* CP has some impairment in speaking and walking abilities and head and neck control and has some limits regarding activities. The person probably requires assistive technology devices, such as special controls for an electric wheelchair or a special mechanism for computer input. Persons with a *severe* level of CP are very incapacitated, have little or no head and neck control, have contracted and malformed limbs, and need assistance to take part in most of their daily activities (Best & Bigge, 2005).

Cerebral palsy can also be described according the location and nature of brain damage (see Pellegrino, 2007, for a medical explanation), and the brain damage that results in CP can sometimes lead to other problems as well. These may include visual impairments, hearing impairments, speech and language disorders, seizures, feeding problems, growth abnormalities, learning disabilities, emotional or behavioral disorders, and attention-deficit/hyperactivity disorder. Although about 50% of persons with CP may also have mild-to-profound intellectual disability (Pellegrino, 2007), it's very important to understand that persons with CP do not always have a cognitive deficit. In fact, determining the actual degree of cognitive ability in persons with severe CP is often difficult because standardized intelligence tests rely on a person's verbal and motor abilities (Best & Bigge, 2005; Willard-Holt, 1998; Pellegrino, 2007).

## REFLECTIVE EXERCISE

#3 Do you know or have you had any experiences with a person with CP? What did you see as this person's strengths? What challenges did this individual face?

PEARSON
**myeducationlab**

To learn more about another physical disability that teachers are likely to encounter, go to the Assignments and Activities section of Topic 14: Physical Disabilities & Health Impairments in the MyEducationLab for your course and complete the activity entitled *Raising a Child with Spina Bifida*.

Cerebral palsy does not necessarily mean that a person has an intellectual limitation.

## Muscular Dystrophy

When a child has muscular dystrophy, his muscle tissue gradually degenerates, turning into fatty tissue. The most common type of the disease is Duchenne muscular dystrophy (DMD), a disorder that is genetically transmitted by mothers to their sons. Although the mothers carry the disease, they do not themselves have any symptoms. Unlike CP, muscular dystrophy is a degenerative disease, meaning that it worsens over time. Unfortunately, it is a terminal condition, with death usually occurring during adolescence or early adulthood. (Escolar, Tosi, Rocha, & Kennedy, 2007).

Muscular dystrophy first appears during early childhood, between about 2 and 6 years of age, when the child's calves seem to be growing larger. (This condition is called *pseudohypertrophy*.) Actually, fat tissue is replacing muscle tissue in the legs. Gradually, the child's legs become weaker and weaker until, unable to stand up in a typical manner, he has to push with his hands against his own legs to climb to a standing position. When he walks, he may do so with a sway back to help compensate for the weakness in his legs. Gradually, the muscle weakness moves up the body, from the legs to the trunk and arms. Sooner or later, the child loses the ability to walk and has to use a wheelchair. Because of weak back muscles, scoliosis (curvature of the spine) is often a problem. To counter this, doctors may perform surgery to insert a metal rod to hold the back straight. As he becomes weaker, the child will no longer be able to power a manual wheelchair, and an electric wheelchair may become necessary for mobility control. Ultimately, early death occurs because of lung or heart failure (Escolar et al., 2007).

With a student who has muscular dystrophy or any similar terminal condition, the teacher's most important job is to make sure that the value of his life is maintained.

> It is important for teachers and others to maintain an attitude that the student is a valued, useful, and vital person. Demonstrating separate expectations for the student with DMD (e.g., altering classroom discipline or ignoring inappropriate behavior) heightens the risk of estranging the student from his peers and sends the undesirable message that he is not as important as others. Providing structure with the expectation of achievement to the best of one's ability provides good mental health. (Best, 2005b, p. 50)

## Definitions and Key Characteristics of Students with Other Health Impairments

Like physical disabilities, certain chronic health impairments can seriously affect a student's ability to receive an appropriate education. Sometimes these conditions occur in combination with other conditions (as when a student with cerebral palsy has epilepsy), but in other cases, the health impairment is the primary disability. According to IDEA (2004, Sec. 300.7),

> other health impairment means having limited strength, vitality or alertness, including a heightened alertness to environmental stimuli, that results in limited alertness with respect to the educational environment, that—(i) Is due to chronic or acute health problems such as asthma, attention deficit disorder or attention deficit hyperactivity disorder, diabetes, epilepsy, a heart condition, hemophilia, lead poisoning, leukemia, nephritis, rheumatic fever, and sickle cell anemia; and (ii) Adversely affects a child's educational performance.

Serious health impairments can be a significant detriment to a student's learning and can lead to the "other health impairment" classification. Even if this does not occur, the health impairment may still result in a Section 504 plan (Zirkel, 2009). With either classification, the school and teachers must take the necessary steps to help the student achieve an appropriate education.

In Table 14.2 we list some of the more common chronic health conditions that teachers might encounter and explain their characteristics and causes. In the

## REFLECTIVE EXERCISE

#4 Somewhat remarkably, many students with muscular dystrophy and similar degenerative diseases lead meaningful lives and maintain very positive attitudes. How do you suppose they maintain such attitudes?

TABLE 14.2 • CHRONIC HEALTH CONDITIONS TEACHERS ARE LIKELY TO ENCOUNTER

| Condition | Cause | Classroom Considerations |
|---|---|---|
| **Asthma**<br><br>Asthma is a chronic lung condition. Asthma attacks are characterized by difficult breathing, wheezing, coughing, excess mucus, sweating, and chest constriction. Attacks may result from different triggers, which may be allergens such as tiny dust particles, cigarette smoke, and pet dander or even cold, dry air, or physical exertion. | Asthma is caused by allergies or other physiological factors. Attacks do not occur as an emotional reaction, but a person may induce an attack by excessive crying or laughing. | Try to keep the classroom free of any antigens that may cause an attack or at least keep the child away from the source. Also be aware of the child's medication and help manage its appropriate use based on home and school guidelines. The child may miss many school days, so promote a supportive environment to help the child keep up with the other students. |
| **HIV/AIDS**<br><br>Children who have HIV/AIDS become progressively more ill as time passes. They may show signs of motor and cognitive delay, have neurological problems, have seizures, and often be nauseous. Most die before they reach age 10, some much sooner. | HIV is transmitted through sexual contact; through exposure to infected blood, blood products, or tissue; and from mother to fetus or infant. Most children with HIV/AIDS have acquired the condition from their mothers before birth, at the time of birth, or through breastfeeding. | Some children with AIDS have learning disabilities, while others may have ADHD and poor language skills. Individualize their instruction to meet their needs. Follow universal precautions to avoid contact with *anyone's* bodily fluid; acquiring the disease through casual contact is not known to occur. |
| **Sickle-Cell Disease**<br><br>Sickle-cell disease causes a block in normal blood flow, resulting in pain episodes in the arms, legs, chest, and abdomen as well as priapism (painful prolonged erection). It also causes damage to most organs, including the spleen, kidneys, and liver. Young children with sickle-cell disease can be easily overwhelmed by certain bacterial infections. | Sickle-cell disease is an inherited blood disorder. When sickle-shaped cells block small blood vessels, less blood reaches that part of the body. Tissue that does not receive a normal blood flow eventually becomes damaged, causing the complications of sickle-cell disease. | The student with sickle-cell disease may be absent often because of pain episodes and hospitalization, so extra support and homework might help him keep up. Plenty of access to water and the restroom and avoidance of overheating and cold temperatures are important. |
| **Epilepsy**<br><br>Epilepsy is a neurological condition that makes people prone to having seizures. Different types of seizures may occur. The most common is a tonic-clonic seizure (formerly called a grand mal seizure), during which the person loses awareness, ceases to engage in activity, and loses consciousness. She then becomes stiff (tonic), and then jerking (clonic) movements begin. | Epilepsy occurs because of an underlying brain abnormality. This abnormality may occur at some time during the development of the brain or as the result of later trauma. During a seizure, an abnormal hypersynchronous electrical discharge occurs in the brain. Different conditions can cause a seizure, but only when the seizures recur is epilepsy diagnosed. | When a student has a seizure, help her lie down, turn her to one side to prevent choking on saliva or vomit, loosen clothing around the neck, and place something soft under her head to prevent it from hitting a hard surface. Do not insert anything into the mouth. If the seizure lasts more than 5 minutes, call for emergency assistance. Also note when the seizure occurred and how long it lasted. |
| **Cancer**<br><br>Cancer is the spread of abnormal cells. The most common types of cancer among children are leukemia and brain tumors. Cancer and its treatment by chemotherapy can lead to numerous side effects, including impairment of the student's learning ability. Nausea, weight loss or gain, and growth retardation can occur. | For the most part, the causes of cancer are unknown. It appears more often alongside Down syndrome and other chromosomal and genetically based disorders, and environmental factors are suspected but difficult to prove. | The child with cancer is often in pain and fatigued, which interfere with concentration and learning ability. Many are diagnosed as having learning disabilities. The immune system may be suppressed, resulting in susceptibility to infections from other children. Some days are better than others. Encourage as much participation as possible, but reduced physical activities and shorter school days may be necessary. |

| Condition | Cause | Classroom Considerations |
|---|---|---|
| **Type 1 Diabetes** | | |
| Type 1 diabetes, also called juvenile diabetes or insulin-dependent diabetes, is an auto-immune disease that destroys the cells in the pancreas that produce insulin. Type 1 diabetes develops often in children or young adults but can occur at any age. Children with Type 1 diabetes require insulin shots. Without medication, the student may become very thirsty, need to urinate often, lose weight, and be very weak. | Type 1 diabetes is caused because the pancreas cannot produce insulin. Without insulin, the body can't use sugar and fat broken down from food. When sugar doesn't enter blood cells, blood sugar rises and causes damage to the body. | Students with diabetes can participate in most activities with other students but need a few special considerations. They may need privacy to test their blood sugar and inject insulin if necessary, may need access to the bathroom more frequently than others, and may need to have snacks more often than other students. In the case of hypoglycemia, the student may be sweating, pale, trembling, hungry, and weak, indicating the need for emergency treatment. |
| **Cystic Fibrosis** | | |
| Cystic fibrosis (CF) is a disease that affects major body organs that secrete fluids. CF primarily affects the lungs, where airway passages become blocked, and the digestive system, where the mucus interferes with the release of digestive enzymes. The secretions of normal fluids are blocked by the mucus and cause cysts to develop, which become surrounded by scar tissue. | CF is a genetically transmitted disease that occurs in 1 of every 2,000 live births. Both parents must be carriers of the condition for the child to inherit it, which occurs in 1 of 4 births to carriers. Boys and girls are equally affected. CF is a terminal condition, and death usually occurs between adolescence and early adulthood. | Students with CF undergo chest physiotherapy once or twice a day to loosen the mucus in their chests. This may occur before and after school; but while in school, they need to take digestive enzymes and other medications. Problems with digestion affect bowel movements, and privacy at this time is an important issue. Take steps if needed to improve social inclusion. |

Asthma affects millions of children, especially those in inner cities and poor countries.

following sections, we describe three conditions that may be of greatest concern for many teachers: asthma, epilepsy, and HIV/AIDS. (Note that for the sake of receiving special education services, ADHD is considered a health impairment. However, because of its relatively high incidence, we have discussed it in a separate chapter.)

## Asthma

Asthma is a chronic lung condition that affects millions of children in the United States and throughout the world, especially in inner cities and poor countries (American Lung Association, 2009). Because so many children have asthma, a teacher's chance of having one or more students with the disease is very high, especially in an urban area.

The signs of an asthma attack include difficult breathing, wheezing, coughing, excess mucus, sweating, and chest constriction. When a child is having an asthma attack, she is reacting to triggers in the environment. These triggers are antigens, or foreign bodies, that enter the lungs and cause the production of antibodies. As the antibodies respond to the antigens, they release chemicals that cause the lungs to swell, increase mucus secretion, and tighten the chest muscles. About half the people who have asthma have an allergic form of the disease. The antigens that affect them can be tiny dust particles, cigarette smoke, or pet dander. The disease can also occur because of non-allergic conditions, with attacks triggered by cold, dry air, or exercise (American Academy of Asthma Allergy and Immunology [AAAAI], 2009; Best, 2005a).

Besides being very dangerous, asthma can affect students' progress in school. According to the AAAAI (2009), children with asthma have about 13 million absences per year because of doctor visits and hospital admissions. A big problem, of course, is lost instructional time and fewer opportunities for social and recreational activities.

## Epilepsy

A seizure is an abnormal electrical discharge in the brain, a relatively uncommon occurrence. Several conditions can cause a seizure, such as a fever, an acute insult, or infection of the brain. In such cases, the seizure may occur once and never again. An example is a febrile seizure, which occurs in about 5% of all children before they are 5 years old; most children never experience another seizure (S. Weinstein & Gaillard, 2007). In contrast, epilepsy is a neurologic condition that makes people prone to having seizures. With epilepsy, an underlying brain abnormality periodically causes seizures (Epilepsy Foundation, 2009; Weinstein & Gaillard, 2007). However, as you may know, most people with epilepsy take antiepileptic drugs, and their seizures are generally well controlled. Different types of seizures occur; among the more common (and thus the type you are likely to encounter in schools) are absence seizures, tonic-clonic seizures, and status epilepticus (S. Weinstein & Gaillard, 2007).

- **Absence seizures.** Formerly called petit mal ("little bad") seizures, absence seizures are generalized (i.e., they come from broad regions of the brain), and they usually appear in children between the ages of 3 and 12. During an absence seizure, the child loses consciousness for about 30 seconds. Onlookers sometimes mistake the seizure for daydreaming, but the child is unable to respond until the seizure is over. Sometimes the absence seizure evolves into a tonic-clonic seizure. Without treatment, a child might have hundreds of absence seizures a day.

- **Tonic-clonic seizures.** During a generalized tonic-clonic seizure (formerly called a grand mal seizure), the first visible sign usually is that the person appears to lose awareness. He then ceases to engage in the current activity, loses consciousness, and falls to the floor. He becomes stiff (tonic), and then jerking (clonic) movements begin. The person becomes less rigid and shakes or jerks his arms, legs, or both. At some point during the seizure, the individual may lose control of his bowels or bladder, cry, or expel saliva from his mouth. After a few minutes, the person usually becomes drowsy and disoriented or falls into a deep sleep that may last from several minutes to several hours. Tonic-clonic seizures may be partial or generalized. A partial seizure may affect only a part of the body; a generalized seizure affects the whole body. Tonic-clonic seizures are the most common types of seizures among children.

- **Status epilepticus.** Status epilepticus actually is not a type of seizure but a condition in which a seizure continues to occur for a longer than usual amount of time. *Status epilepticus can require emergency action.* A tonic-clonic seizure usually ends after 2 or 3 minutes; and as we've said, an absence seizure is even briefer. But if a seizure does not end within a short time, status epilepticus is occurring, which may be life-threatening or lead to permanent brain damage. Any seizure that continues longer than 5 minutes should be considered status epilepticus and be treated as a medical emergency.

Because seizures can make the first-time observer uncomfortable, we display an e-mail conversation between two teachers in "Can You Help Me with This Student?" describing the appropriate actions to take during a student's seizure.

## HIV/AIDS

HIV/AIDS is a serious illness that we have certainly heard a lot about—and the medical community has learned a lot about—in the past 25 to 30 years. While we have made a great deal of progress in this country both in the prevention and treatment

## CAN YOU HELP ME WITH THIS STUDENT?

| To... | Elizabeth Craven, Special Education Teacher |
|---|---|
| From... | Doug Johnson, General Education Teacher |
| Subject: | What should a teacher do if a student has a seizure? |

Hi, Miss Craven. You said to get in touch if I needed your help, so there is something I would like to ask you about. I have one student in my class who has a history of epilepsy, and from time to time may have a "tonic-clonic" seizure. Is there anything special I need to do if this happens?

—Doug Johnson

---

To:         Doug Johnson
From:       Elizabeth Craven
Subject:    RE: What should a teacher do if a student has a seizure?

Doug, although medications can be very effective at managing seizures, you can still expect to see one from time to time, especially among students with disabilities. If you do, you may at first be a little nervous, but don't worry, everything will be fine. If, as a teacher, you must assist a student having a seizure, here is what you should do:

First, realize that there is nothing you or anyone can do to stop a seizure once it begins, so you shouldn't try. If it is an absence seizure (the person simply appears to lose contact with what is going on around him), there is not much to do unless the repeated seizures continue for more than 5 minutes. Then call for emergency medical assistance. For a tonic-clonic seizure (one in which the person loses consciousness, and falls to the floor and begins jerking and moving erratically), help the student to lie down and turn him to one side to prevent him from choking on excessive saliva or vomit. If possible, loosen any clothing around the neck to make breathing easier, and put a pillow or something soft under his head to keep him from banging it against the floor.

During the seizure, the person will bite down hard, but don't try to put anything into the mouth. Don't worry, he won't swallow his tongue! Just try to keep the head tilted to the side to prevent choking on saliva. Also, CPR is not necessary. Usually, you just need to let the seizure run its course. In some cases, status epilepticus can occur. This means the seizure will continue to occur for longer than usual. If the seizure lasts for more than 5 minutes, you should call for emergency assistance (i.e., dial 911 or call the school office).

After the seizure, let the student sleep in a quiet, private location. When he wakes up, comfort him and encourage him to resume normal activities. If the seizure and related conditions like loss of bowel or bladder control are embarrassing, try to provide some counseling. Explaining the nature of seizures to both the student and his classmates can help students understand the condition.

Finally, whenever a seizure occurs, you should keep a written record of it, including when it began and when it ended. Describe what happened as well as you can, including what preceded the seizure and what followed it. Give this information to the parents or directly to medical personnel.

Here are some sources of information that you will find helpful:

Batshaw, M. L., Pellegrino, L., & Roizen, N. J. (Eds.). *Children with disabilities* (6th ed.). Baltimore: Brookes.

The Epilepsy Foundation, http://www.epilepsyfoundation.org/

The National Institute of Neurological Disorders and Stroke, http://www.ninds.nih.gov/disorders/epilepsy/epilepsy.htm

I know this is a little long, Doug, but I hope it will help you.

—Elizabeth

of HIV/AIDS, in poorer developing countries, programs to prevent the disease and provide effective medical treatment are lacking, and the illness remains a major cause of death (National Institute of Allergy and Infectious Diseases [NIAID], 2004). In fact, it has become a chronic illness among many children. You should also realize that most children with HIV/AIDS have acquired the condition from their mothers before they were born, at the time of birth, or as infants through breastfeeding.

HIV can be transmitted from an infected person to another person in one of three ways: through sexual transmission; through exposure to infected blood, blood products, or tissue, which occurs when unclean needles are shared; and, as we have said, from mother to fetus or infant. Not all babies born to HIV-infected mothers will have the virus, especially if the mother is being actively treated using anti-AIDS medications and if the baby is delivered through a caesarian section. When doctors follow these medical precautions and when the baby is not breastfed, the baby's chances of getting HIV are much lower.

Slow physical growth and little weight gain are often the first indications of HIV in children. Delay may also occur in motor skills and cognitive development. Some children may have neurologic problems as shown by difficulty in walking and coordination. They may have seizures and perform poorly in their preschool or school activities. In school, some children with AIDS are classified as having learning disabilities, while others may have ADHD and poor language skills. The child is likely to often be nauseous, have episodes of vomiting, and be weak and in pain. During the final stage of the illness, when AIDS occurs, opportunistic infections such as pneumonia, certain types of cancer, or other diseases attack and cannot be rejected because of an ineffective immune system (Best, 2005a; NIAID, 2004).

The way in which HIV leads to AIDS is a complex process (see Figure 14.1), as is its treatment. However, a diagnosis of HIV does not necessarily mean that AIDS is inevitable. If you happen to become a teacher of a child with HIV/AIDS, it's better for you to think of it as a chronic illness rather than a terminal disease (Best, 2005a).

## PREVALENCE AND TRENDS

### Physical Disabilities

Within the population of school-age students, about 0.10% have physical disabilities (U.S. Department of Education, 2009). Cerebral palsy affects approximately 3 children in 1,000, or around 0.03% of the population. About 80% have the spastic form of CP, and around 60% have at least one additional developmental disability (National Center on Birth Defects and Developmental Disabilities, 2009). About 1 in every 3,500 live male births inherits the Duchenne type of muscular dystrophy (Batshaw, Pellegrino, & Roizen, 2007). The two most serious forms of spina bifida, meningocele and myelomeningocele, known together as "spina bifida manifesta,"

FIGURE 14.1 • **HOW HIV BECOMES AIDS**

Untreated HIV disease is characterized by a gradual deterioration of immune function. Notably, crucial immune cells called CD4 positive (CD4+) T cells are disabled and killed during the typical course of infection. These cells, sometimes called T-helper cells, play a central role in the immune response, signaling other cells in the immune system to perform their special functions. A healthy, uninfected person usually has 800 to 1,200 CD4+ T cells per cubic millimeter ($mm^3$) of blood. With untreated HIV infection, the number of these cells in a person's blood progressively declines. When the CD4+ T cell count falls below $200/mm^3$, a person becomes particularly vulnerable to the opportunistic infections and cancers that typify AIDS, the end stage of HIV disease. People with AIDS often suffer infections of the lungs, intestinal tract, brain, eyes, and other organs as well as debilitating weight loss, diarrhea, neurologic conditions, and cancers such as Kaposi's sarcoma and certain types of lymphomas.

Most scientists think that HIV causes AIDS by directly inducing the death of CD4+ T cells or interfering with their normal function and by triggering other events that weaken a person's immune function. For example, the network of signaling molecules that normally regulates a person's immune response is disrupted during HIV disease, impairing a person's ability to fight other infections. The HIV-mediated destruction of the lymph nodes and related immunologic organs also plays a major role in causing the immunosuppression seen in people with AIDS. Immunosuppression by HIV is confirmed by the fact that medicines that interfere with the HIV life cycle preserve CD4+ T cells and immune function as well as delay clinical illness.

occur in approximately 1 in every 1,000 births (National Dissemination Center for Children with Disabilities, 2009).

## Other Health Impairments

**REFLECTIVE EXERCISE**

#6 If you are or will be a general education teacher, how many students with physical disabilities or health impairments would you expect to have in your class? Do you think there would be more or fewer of these students than you might have seen 20 years ago?

About 0.77% of school-age students have other health impairments (U.S. Department of Education, 2009). Asthma is the most common chronic childhood disease, affecting about 6.7 million children under 18 years in the United States (American Lung Association, 2009). It is especially prevalent in urban areas. Almost 3 million Americans have epilepsy, and each year almost 200,000 Americans develop seizures and epilepsy for the first time (Epilepsy Foundation, 2009). At the end of 2003, an estimated 1,039,000 to 1,185,000 persons in the United States were living with HIV/AIDS. By 2006, an additional 56,300 cases were estimated to have occurred in the United States, but less than 1% of all new cases occur in children under 13 (Centers for Disease Control and Prevention, 2008).

## CAUSAL FACTORS

### Physical Disabilities

Physical disabilities can result from different causes. They may be congenital (i.e., the child is born with the condition) or acquired (i.e., something causes the condition that happens immediately before, during, or after birth or even later in life). Congenital physical disabilities may be due to a genetically transmitted condition, such as Duchenne muscular dystrophy; to some nongenetic factor, such as the mother's ingestion of a harmful substance such as **thalidomide** during pregnancy; or to unknown causes, as in the case of spina bifida.

Acquired physical disabilities may be due to an event occurring near the time of birth (which may be the case with CP) or to an accident or illness (e.g., the loss of a limb or having polio). Some physical disabilities are linked to central nervous system damage, like CP or spina bifida; some are degenerative, like muscular dystrophy; and some are musculoskeletal and orthopedic conditions, such as arthritis, limb deficiencies, or scoliosis (Best, 2005b).

If the condition is due to neurological damage, like CP, it may take different forms (i.e., spasticity, athetosis, mixed). The specific type of CP that occurs will depend on which part of the brain was damaged and the extent of the damage (Best & Bigge, 2005; H. C. Griffin et al., 2002; Pellegrino, 2007). Genetically transmitted conditions are inherited from one or both parents. For most genetic conditions, some of the children inherit the condition, some may become carriers, and some are unaffected.

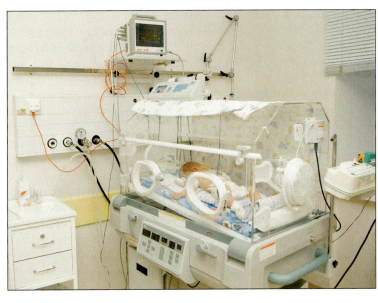

Many physical disabilities and health impairments occur early in life for different reasons.

People with physical disabilities continue to have the disabilities throughout their lives. For those with degenerative diseases, like muscular dystrophy, their lives are often relatively short, and their conditions deteriorate until death occurs. Persons whose conditions are nondegenerative, such as spina bifida or CP, will likely experience a typical span of life. Their disabilities, however, will continue to present physical challenges that may affect their vocational prospects and lead to social and emotional issues, depending on their milieu and a variety of personal characteristics.

## Other Health Impairments

The causes of health impairments are as varied as the causes of physical disabilities. Some, such as HIV/AIDS, are transmitted through viruses. Others, such as sickle-cell disease and cystic fibrosis, are genetically transmitted. Similarly, diabetes has a genetic basis but can be environmentally influenced through diet and exercise. For others, like asthma, epilepsy, and cancer, experts do not clearly understand the cause. The expected life outcomes for those with different health impairments range from premature death to a long and normal life that requires management of the disease through medication, diet, and other medical treatments.

## Transmission of Diseases to Teachers

For many teachers and other human services professionals who deal with children or adults with health problems, a common question is "How likely am I to get this disease from a student?" Most often, the answer is that you are not very susceptible. Diseases that children have genetically inherited pose no threat to you. One situation that many teachers worry about a great deal is the possibility of getting HIV/AIDS from a student. This is not likely. HIV/AIDS is transmitted through the exchange of bodily fluids or from mother to child. And except in the most extraordinary circumstances, most teachers will not be at risk for any of these occurrences with their students.

On the other hand, teachers should be concerned about contracting contagious diseases, such as cytomegalovirus (CMV) and hepatitis B. CMV poses little danger to you unless you are pregnant. A person who catches CMV has the symptoms of a cold

## REFLECTIVE EXERCISE

#7 Have you thought about the classroom as a place where contagious diseases can be transmitted? Does this concern you? Did you know this can easily be prevented?

or the flu for a couple of weeks. But if a woman is pregnant, the child may be born with severe, multiple disabilities. Hepatitis B is a serious disease caused by a virus that attacks the liver. The virus can cause lifelong infection, cirrhosis of the liver, liver cancer, liver failure, and death.

The best approach to protecting yourself against all contagious diseases is to use universal precautions. The Centers for Disease Control and Prevention developed universal precautions in 1987 in order to help control the spread of disease (Best, 2005a, Centers for Disease Control and Prevention, 1999; DePaepe et al., 2002). The precautions are referred to as "universal" because you should use them in any situation where the transmission of disease is possible, no matter how remote.

Universal precautions include proper handwashing (see Figure 14.2); use of personal protective equipment; safe methods for getting rid of waste, cleaning up spills, and handling laundry; and procedures for dealing with accidental contact to potentially infectious materials. You should use these precautions whenever you have contact with blood, semen, vaginal secretions, or other body fluids that may contain blood (Best, 2005a; DePaepe et al., 2002).

FIGURE 14.2 • **HANDWASHING PROCEDURE WHEN USING UNIVERSAL PRECAUTIONS**

1. Inspect your hands for any visible soiling, breaks, or cuts in the skin or cuticles.
2. Remove any jewelry. If you have a watch on, push it up your arm as high as possible. Also push up the sleeves of your blouse or jacket so that they are well above the wrist.
3. Turn on the water, and adjust water flow and temperature to ensure that it is not too hot or has too much flow. Warm water is needed to ensure proper action of the soap. Use cold water only if warm water is not available. Water that is too hot will remove the protective oils of the skin and will dry the skin, making it vulnerable to damage. Water that comes out of the tap with too much force is more likely to splash onto the floors and walls, possibly spreading the microorganisms.
4. With the water running, wet your hands and wrists. Ensure that your hands are lower than your elbows so that the water flows from the least contaminated areas (i.e., the wrists) to the most contaminated areas (i.e., the hands). Lather hands with soap. Liquid soap is preferable to bar soap, which can be a reservoir for bacteria. Use bar soap only when dispensed soap is not available.
5. Wash thoroughly for at least 30 seconds. If you have just handled a contaminated object (e.g., a dirty glass), wash for 1 minute. If you have been in direct contact with any type of bodily fluid (e.g., you have just changed a diaper), you should wash for up to 2 minutes. Use a firm, circular motion and friction and ensure that you wash the back of hands, palms, and wrists. Wash each finger individually, making sure that you wash between fingers and knuckles (i.e., interlace fingers and thumbs and move hands back and forth) as well as around the cuticles. Do not use too much pressure, as this may result in skin damage.
6. Rinse thoroughly with warm water. Use a fingernail file or orange stick and clean under each fingernail while the water is still running. If a file or stick is not available, use the fingernails of the opposite hand.
7. Shake hands to remove excess water. Dry your hands thoroughly using a paper towel, working upward from fingertips, to hands, to wrists, and finally to forearms. When drying, rather than rub vigorously, it is best to pat the skin. It is important that the hands be dried well to prevent chapping.
8. Turn off the taps using the paper towel you used to dry your hands. Use the paper towel to wipe the surfaces surrounding the sink. Dispose of the paper towel in a covered childproof receptacle with a disposable plastic liner.
9. Apply lotion, if desired, to keep skin soft, reduce the risk of chapping, and act as a barrier for invasion of microorganisms.

# IDENTIFICATION AND ASSESSMENT

## Medical Evaluation

Typically, physicians are the first to conduct evaluations of students with physical disabilities or other health impairments. They assess the students' physical status and determine the medical needs. The result of this process is to prescribe medications or medical interventions to improve physical status.

## Educational Evaluation

For some students with severe physical disabilities, such as CP, educators often are concerned about determining the student's actual intellectual ability through traditional approaches to assessment. Colleen Willard-Holt (1998) therefore attempted to identify key characteristics of students with CP who were also gifted. She studied two students with severe CP who showed extraordinary intellectual abilities. The students did not verbally communicate and had extremely limited mobility, so Willard-Holt spent 3 years observing, recording, and learning about them to identify their gifted characteristics. She found ample evidence that, even though they did not communicate in a typical fashion, they were gifted in terms of their academic abilities in most areas. In the accompanying "Can You Help Me with This Student?" we use our e-mail exchange format to share some suggestions for identifying students with severe CP who also have above-average intellectual abilities.

## Therapeutic and Health-Care Evaluation

For students with disabilities, the school must consider whether related services are necessary for the student to benefit from public education. For students with physical disabilities, this means that physical therapists (PTs) and occupational therapists (OTs) conduct evaluations and, if necessary, create intervention programs to meet a student's needs. In the case of CP, for example, the PT assesses and develops interventions for positioning the student to better align the spine, legs, and feet; fits and monitors orthotic devices for the student; and performs range-of-motion and post-operative exercises. The OT evaluates and works on areas such as eye–hand control, facilitating the use of hands and arms, fitting the child with hand splints to offset contractures, improving perceptual skills, evaluating sensory integration, and improving various daily skills (Best & Bigge, 2005).

For students with health-care needs, the school nurse plays a critical role. This person works with the student, parents, teachers and other school staff, the student's physician, and other health-care professionals to develop medical supports for the student while she is in school. The nurse seeks information from parents and medical personnel so that an *individualized health-care plan* can be developed for the student. This plan includes medical care information for both ongoing needs and emergency medical treatment. The student's health-care plan should be attached to the IEP and include information such as how medication should be delivered, skin care, catheterization procedures, gastronomy and respiratory care, and what to do in the case of an asthma attack or a seizure (DePaepe et al., 2002). Figure 14.3 shows an example of an individualized health-care plan.

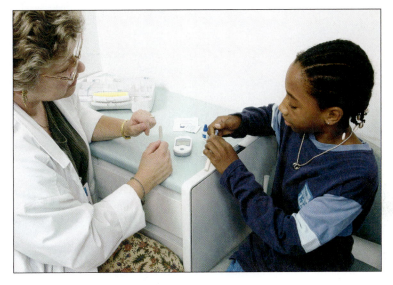

For students with health-care needs, the school nurse plays a critical role.

FIGURE 14.3 • SAMPLE STUDENT HEALTH-CARE PLAN

**Student Individualized Health-Care Plan**

☐ 504
☐ Special Education

Student's Name _____  Birth Date _____
Student's Teacher _____  School _____
Grade _____  School Year _____

Physician's Name _____
Address _____  Telephone Number _____
Parents/Guardians _____  Home Phone _____
Work Phone (Mother) _____  Emergency Phone _____
Work Phone (Father) _____  Emergency Phone _____
Work Phone (Guardian) _____  Emergency Phone _____
Hospital Health Care Coordinator _____  Phone _____
School Health Care Coordinator _____  Phone _____
Education Coordinator _____  Phone _____

**MEDICAL OVERVIEW**
Brief Medical History _____
_____
_____
_____

Known Allergies _____
_____
_____

Medications _____

Medication Authorization Form Attached for Each Medication   Yes ☐   No ☐
Specific Health Care Needs _____
_____
_____

Procedure Authorization Form Attached for Each Procedure   Yes ☐   No ☐

**ADDITIONAL NEEDS/PLANS**
Emergency Plan Attached   Yes ☐   No ☐
Recreational Activity Permission Form Attached   Yes ☐   No ☐

Transportation Plan Attached   Yes ☐   No ☐
Personnel Training Plan Attached   Yes ☐   No ☐
Entry/Reentry Checklist Completed   Yes ☐   No ☐
Other: _____

**ADDITIONAL INFORMATION**
Special Diet _____
_____
_____

Additional Information Attached   Yes ☐   No ☐
Special Safety Measures _____
_____

*Source:* From Best, S. (2005). Health impairments and infectious diseases. In S. J. Best, K. W. Heller, & J. L. Bigge (Eds.), *Teaching individuals with physical or multiple disabilities* (5th ed., pp. 59–85). Upper Saddle River, NJ: Merrill/Pearson Education. Reprinted with permission.

## CAN YOU HELP ME WITH THIS STUDENT?

| To... | Lawrence Freitag, Ph.D., School Psychologist |
|---|---|
| From... | Roseanne Parsons, Elementary School Teacher |
| Subject: | Testing a student with severe cerebral palsy |

Dear Dr. Freitag, I am writing you about my concern for a little boy in my second-grade class. He has a very severe physical disability (cerebral palsy) that seriously affects his speech and movement, but I think he may actually be gifted. I would like to get him tested, but I am afraid that he will not be able to perform well on the test because of his disability. Is there a way to find out if he really might be gifted?

Roseanne Parsons, Southside Elementary.

---

To:       Roseanne Parsons
From:     Lawrence Freitag, Ph.D.
Subject:  RE: Testing a student with severe cerebral palsy

Hello, Mrs. Parsons. It was nice to hear from you. This sounds like a very interesting little boy, and yes, he may be gifted. It may be possible to arrive at a reasonable estimation of his true intellectual ability in several ways. To begin, nonverbal tests such as the Peabody Picture Vocabulary Test will give a good estimate of intellectual ability. The child only has to look at or point to the picture that you name on the page. I am not really very familiar with nonverbal tests but would be willing to look into this approach in order to find out in a systematic way how much the student knows.

   There are also other sources of evidence about intellectual ability. Does the student have a special knack for any academic areas or any artistic abilities? Also watch how he reacts when certain people come into view. Does he seem to recognize them, and do they affect his emotions or behavior? Does he show a good sense of humor at appropriate times? Does he understand when certain activities are about to occur? Does he remember appointments or upcoming events; for example, does he remember when he is supposed to get some medication? What do his parents say? Do they think he is truly gifted? Does he sometimes surprise them with what he knows?

   Looking at the student in these ways might help you (and me) get a better picture of what's going on with regard to his real ability. I will schedule a time to come by and observe him. In the meantime, here are some reference materials you might find useful:

Overton, T. (2008). *Assessing learners with special needs: An applied approach* (6th ed.). Upper Saddle River, NJ: Merrill/Pearson Education.

Venn, J. J. (2006). *Assessing students with special needs* (4th ed.). Upper Saddle River, NJ: Merrill/Pearson Education.

Willard-Holt, C. (1998). Academic and personality characteristics of gifted students with cerebral palsy: A multiple case study. *Exceptional Children, 65,* 37–50.

I look forward to meeting with you.

—Lawrence Freitag

## EFFECTIVE INSTRUCTIONAL PRACTICES

To effectively educate students with physical disabilities or other health impairments, teachers and school personnel must address several important questions. Where should they serve the student, and what accommodations must they provide? What are the student's individual goals, and what is the appropriate curriculum for the student? What instructional methods will best meet the student's needs? Should adaptive devices be used; and, if so, what devices? How can school staff ensure that they address the student's physical and health-care needs as outlined in the individualized health-care plan? How can they interact most effectively with parents, families, and health-care professionals? Next we examine how educators address some of these issues at different stages of the student's school life.

### Preschool Years

Physical or medical conditions that occur relatively early in life may allow the child to be served in early intervention programs before the age of 3 or in public schools when he reaches the age of 3. As you know, the earlier interventions can start for children, the more effective they can be. Consider the importance of preschool programs for two conditions we have addressed in this chapter, CP and HIV/AIDS.

During the years of early physical growth, it is very important to maximize physical functioning while decreasing the impact of CP. Therapeutic intervention by pediatric PTs and OTs is essential. **Orthotic devices** can be applied to a very young child's body to provide support for weak muscles, improve posture, help prevent contractures in the arms and the legs, and help reduce tone in the hands. The devices also help to increase or maintain the **range of motion** of the limbs, improve stability, and reduce involuntary movements. The rehabilitation engineers and orthopedic specialists who work with the PTs and OTs must individually design all orthotic devices for the child and modify or exchange the devices as she grows older and larger and develops different needs.

PTs and OTs have another important job: consulting with parents so that they can carry through with exercises at home. Ketelaar, Vermeer, Helders, and Hart (1998) reviewed 13 research studies on the involvement of parents in intervention programs for their children with CP. They found that overall, when parents participate in intervention programs for their children, greater gains are generally made. In a related study, Lin (2000) found that, although many families had difficulty adapting to the disability of their child with CP, some were better able to cope than others. The important factors included having "positive family appraisal," "support from concerned others," "spiritual support," "personal growth and advocacy," and "positive social interaction."

Preschool programs can also serve young children with HIV/AIDS, which benefits both the child and his family. One important outcome of being in a preschool is that program personnel may play an important role in helping the child take the required medication. Children's need to take different medications is often a problem that requires careful monitoring. If a drug is missed, not only will it be less effective, but the child may develop dosage resistance (Best, 2005a).

Besides directly helping the child, preschool programs might also work with other community agencies to help facilitate stability in the home. Most young children with AIDS either have one or two parents who are infected with the disease—or have lost one or both parents—and may also have infected siblings. Life at home certainly is stressful. In the United States, most children who have HIV/AIDS are poor and live in inner cities. Their lives are complicated not only by their illness but by high rates of crime and violence, poor housing, and limited access to health care and social services. To succeed with these children, school personnel, health-care providers, social workers, and other mental health professionals and community agencies must work together closely (Spiegel & Bonwit, 2002).

## REFLECTIVE EXERCISE

#9 Do you think it is possible for personnel from different agencies to work together effectively on behalf of a student with HIV/AIDS? What do you think would facilitate or inhibit this process?

## Academic and Functional Instruction in the School Years

### Curriculum and Instruction

Determining the most appropriate individual goals for a student and placing her in the curriculum that best meets her needs are very important decisions. According to IDEA, to the extent possible, all students with disabilities are to participate in the general curriculum. Many of the students we have been discussing in this chapter should be able to do this with little difficulty. However, you should consider a few relevant issues.

Many students with physical disabilities, and especially those with health impairments, will miss an inordinate number of school days. They may not get enough sleep, they may be too weak or in too much pain, or they may be hospitalized periodically. Therefore, although these students have the cognitive ability to participate in the general curriculum, teachers and parents have to work together to help them catch up when they fall behind.

When in school, these students may miss some class time because of their disability or impairment. For example, a child may have to leave the class if an asthma attack occurs, if he is in too much pain to participate due to sickle-cell disease or HIV/AIDS, or if she has to go to the bathroom frequently or leave to check her blood sugar because she is diabetic. So again, students must have as much opportunity as possible to catch up on different learning activities.

Finally, some of these students have intellectual or learning disabilities occurring along with their physical or health challenges. When this is the case, teachers must carefully consider both their individual learning needs and the overall curriculum in which they should be placed. Stump and Bigge (2005) suggest four curricular options:

- **The general education curriculum.** Students in this curriculum work on the same learning activities as other students do. As we have said, many of the students we have been discussing perform well using the standard curriculum.
- **The general education curriculum with modifications.** Modifications might include changes in the content, desired outcomes, or levels of complexity. This curriculum may be appropriate for a student whose condition impedes success in the general curriculum without modifications—for example, a student with CP who cannot maintain the same pace as the rest of the class.
- **Life skills curriculum.** If a student needs skills necessary for succeeding in life, this is the appropriate curriculum. Participation in a life skills curriculum may either complement or supplement participation in the general curriculum with or without modifications. This curriculum is appropriate for a student who is not acquiring sufficient life skills without specific instruction or for a student who needs to learn to use adaptive devices to participate in different activities.

REFLECTIVE EXERCISE

#10 Based on what you have read about the different conditions that may affect students, how do you see some of the students fitting into the different curricula?

- **Curriculum modified in communication and task performance.** Students who need explicit instruction in communication skills in order to participate in home, school, and community life participate in learning activities in this curriculum. These students have relatively severe physical disabilities that may exist with or without concurrent intellectual disabilities.

## Classroom Considerations

With appropriate accommodations and supports, most of the students we have discussed can succeed in the general education classroom. The classroom teacher, the special education teacher, OTs and PTs, and often paraeducators must work together to ensure students' well-being and educational success. Wadsworth and Knight (1999) suggest several useful guidelines for teaching students with physical disabilities and other health impairments in the general education classroom:

### Teaching Students with Other Health Impairments in the General Education Classroom

- Know the warning signals for students with conditions such as respiratory problems, heart conditions, or other chronic health problems and how to respond to students' needs.
- Follow universal precautions to avoid contact with any communicable diseases.
- Have emergency plans in case of an equipment failure, an emergency physical problem, or problems occurring due to natural disasters.
- Be aware of routine treatments and who is responsible for carrying them out.
- Know the medication the student takes, who is to administer it, and the possible side effects.
- Know special nutritional needs such as dietary restrictions, special diets, or special eating procedures.
- Know how much the student is expected to participate in self-managing his special physical or health needs. It is essential that the student practice as much independence as possible.

### Teaching Students with Physical Disabilities in the General Education Classroom

- The school and classroom should be assessed by a physical or occupational therapist to determine its accessibility.
- School arrangements such as ramps, handrails, widening of sidewalks and doorways, and adjustment of the heights of equipment might be necessary.
- In the classroom, the teachers should make sure that there is ready access to all parts of the room, including centers and materials.
- Sometimes classroom temperatures may have to be adjusted to accommodate a student's health needs.

In addition to these considerations, teachers must be attuned to factors that are specific to the individual children in their classroom and be responsive to their needs. For example, if the cause of a student's asthma attacks can be identified, teachers can sometimes prevent them from occurring. Teachers can try to reduce any sources of antigens in their classrooms by working with the school custodial staff to ensure that a room is as clean and dust-free as possible. Further, they can help the student avoid irritants by making sure the room is adequately ventilated and having the student keep her distance from chalk dust, classroom pets, felt-tip pen fumes, cleaning products, glue, and other possible triggers. Such strategies can be applied for different students based on their needs and should be included in their individual health-care plans.

PEARSON
**myeducationlab**

Go to the Assignements and Activities section of Topic 14: Physical Disabilities & Health Impairments in the MyEducationLab for your course and complete the activities entitled *Accommodations for Students with Physical Disabilities* and *Accommodations for Students with Health Impairments*.

## Assistive Technology Devices and Services

Many students with physical disabilities and other health impairments may achieve more success if they are properly supported by an assistive technology (AT) device and AT support services. According to the Assistive Technology Act of 1998, AT devices should be provided to students in special education if one is necessary for the student to receive a free and appropriate education. AT devices include "any item, piece of equipment, or product system, whether acquired commercially off the shelf, modified, or customized, that is used to increase, maintain, or improve functional capabilities of a child with a disability" (Sec. 3[a][3]). Additionally, the law defines AT services as "any service that directly assists a child with a disability in the selection, acquisition, or use of an assistive technology device" (Sec. 3[a][4]).

A wide range of AT devices, from relatively simple to very complex, may benefit students with various types of disabilities. Many AT devices been developed specifically to help individuals with physical disabilities overcome their challenges and function more adequately in different environments (Hasselbring & Glaser, 2000), for example, by providing different ways to input information. A list of alternative input devices is included in "Technology for Access."

# TECHNOLOGY for ACCESS

## ALTERNATIVE INPUT DEVICES FOR STUDENTS WITH PHYSICAL DISABILITIES

### Switches

Switches control the flow of electrical power to a device that the user wants to turn on or off. Switches can be activated by almost any part of the body a person can voluntarily and reliably control. For example, switches are available that can be activated by the use of an arm, hand, finger, leg, foot, head, or chin. They also may be controlled by less obvious movements of the eyebrow or the rib cage, with access through controlled breathing. While the movement does not have to be big, it must be controllable and reliable. Considerable training often is required before the use of the switch is reliable.

### Basic Adaptive Keyboards

Basic keyboard adaptations that assist physically disabled students to use computers include replacing standard keys with larger keys that are easier to see and touch, reducing the number of keys on the keyboard, placing letter keys in alphabetical order, and providing keys that are brightly colored and easy to read. Other keyboards are much smaller than their traditional counterparts and have surfaces that are much more sensitive to touch. These keyboards are excellent for individuals with a limited range of motion or for those who have a difficult time applying pressure to keys.

### Touch-Sensitive Screens

Touch-sensitive screens are very popular with young computer users and with individuals who have severe developmental or physical disabilities. This technology allows the user to simply touch the computer screen to perform a function. Many touch-sensitive screens come complete with multiple screen overlays that students can use to perform a variety of tasks. Similarly, many companies provide additional software that enables the users to create their own overlays.

### Infrared Sensors with Pneumatic Switches

Use of an infrared sensor worn on the head, along with use of a pneumatic switch, can enable physically disabled students to interact with the computer. As the user looks at the computer screen, the cursor follows the user's head movement. Moving the head to the left moves the cursor in the same direction on the screen. Thus, users can position the cursor anywhere on the screen by moving their head left, right, up, or down. The pneumatic switch, which is activated by inhaling or exhaling through a plastic tube, enables the user to use the mouse. When the user sips or puffs on the switch, the computer responds as if the mouse button had been clicked. In this manner, the user can move a cursor and click on items displayed on the computer screen. Special software is used in conjunction with these movements to allow the user to type out information on a facsimile of a keyboard that is displayed on the computer monitor.

### Voice Recognition

Using voice-recognition software, the user can bypass the keyboard and speak to the computer. By programming the computer with a set of predefined instructions, the user can control the computer by verbally issuing commands into a microphone. In most cases, the reliability of the system can be enhanced by having the user train the computer to recognize his speech patterns. Voice-recognition systems allow students to operate a variety of application programs, to dictate to a word processor, and to enter data into spreadsheets.

Source: Adapted from Hasselbring, T. S., & Glaser, C. H. W. (2000). Use of computer technology to help students with special needs. *Future of Children, 10*(2), 102–122.

## Conductive Education

In the United States, the most common educational model for students with physical disabilities is to participate in the general curriculum, as much as possible, in the general education classroom. Physical and occupational therapy, and sometimes speech/language services, are provided as related services, supplementing general education or special educational services. Additionally, AT devices and services are often provided. Beyond these services, no well-recognized curriculum or instructional model is specifically designed for students with physical disabilities. In contrast is a therapeutic educational approach called "conductive education."

Conductive education, developed in Hungary by András Pető after World War II, uses a holistic approach designed to address individual goals to improve motor, language, functional living, and academic skills. It is offered through a "conductor," who is trained to provide routines to students with CP while they are supported by a parent or a caregiver. The routines are based on group participation that incorporate singing and movement during a variety of activities. Students are encouraged to use language to learn to direct their own movements as they complete functional activities.

Conductive education appeals to many parents because it focuses simultaneously and intensely on all of a student's needs. However, it requires a high level of commitment from parents or caregivers because they must provide one-to-one support for their child during the sessions. It also requires that parents pay privately for the service, because it is typically not offered in public schools. In fact, research has not found conductive education to be any more beneficial than special education and related therapies provided in most public schools, and so the schools usually do not feel that the extra cost is justifiable (Ratliffe & Sanekane, 2009).

## Transition, Adolescence, and Adult Needs and Services

Like all students, students with physical disabilities or other health impairments are interested in different aspects of school. They may think about the possibility of post-secondary education, possible jobs or careers, and they are undoubtedly consumed with social issues, dates, and hormonal changes. But in some cases these students have to cross hurdles due to their disabilities. They may approach typical areas of interest with extra concerns related to their disability or chronic illness. For example, some students with some physical disabilities have to deal with limitations due to motor-skill impairments, mobility problems, or personal care needs; and students with chronic health impairments may have issues to confront, ranging from their day-to-day lack of stamina to episodes of pain and, for some, their own mortality. As parents and teachers work together, they need to think about what the student will do beyond the high school years and how they can best prepare a student.

The students we have described in this chapter are likely to have one or more of four major conditions that will affect job options and career choices (Clark & Bigge, 2005):

- **Independence difficulties.** High levels of dependency can be a potential barrier to a job or a career. Needs such as transportation, accessibility modifications, the use of AT devices, or communication supports can be problematic.
- **Strength and stamina.** The person's ability to complete the job, side effects due to medications, or the regular need for emergency medical care can pose challenges.
- **Lack of experience in self-care and personal health management.** Generally, people in the workforce are expected to be able to take care of their personal needs. The person who has not learned to do these tasks, or cannot do them, may have difficulties.

## REFLECTIVE EXERCISE

#11 Programs like conductive education are often appealing to parents because of their intense therapeutic nature. However, by their nature, they segregate students with disabilities. Do you think the value of most separate programs outweighs the separation they require?

- **Limited social experiences.** Most important, people expect demonstration of an acceptable level of social ability in a working environment. Persons who have not learned these important skills are at a disadvantage.

If persons with physical disabilities or chronic health impairments are to have successful futures, they must be able to overcome these barriers or find situations in which their limitations are not a factor. Preparing for life career opportunities through a career education program is helpful.

The career education model has been used effectively for many years in preparing persons with different types of disabilities for the future (Clark & Bigge, 2005). It has four stages:

1. Career awareness begins during early childhood education. At this level children learn that there are many important roles that they might fill as adults and that they can be an important part of society.
2. Career exploration occurs during the elementary school years and continues into the middle school. During this stage, students explore jobs and career areas and the requirements of workers in these positions.
3. Career preparation is emphasized at the high school level, particularly for students who will not be going into postsecondary education. Students may enroll in regular or special vocational preparation classes or attend vocational or technical training schools. For some students, training at this level includes community-based instruction to help them attain a competitive or a supported employment position.
4. Career placement involves follow-up and continuing education. After training, students are placed on a job, and support is provided as long as necessary to ensure they can be succeed. Some students may also be able to continue training through postsecondary education.

Many individuals with physical disabilities will pursue successful professional careers.

## PREVAILING ISSUES, CONTROVERSIES, AND IMPLICATIONS FOR THE TEACHER

Although most of us clearly accept the right of school attendance for students with disabilities, some of the students we have discussed in this chapter (and others we have not discussed) require rather extensive supports in order to attend school. Given this context, we consider two issues that are sometimes controversial.

### To What Extent Should Schools Be Responsible for "Related Services"?

Over the years, the lines have been blurred between related educational services (i.e., a service that supports students so they can participate meaningfully in school) and medical services (DePaepe et al., 2002). For example, in an early court case (*Irving Independent School District v. Tatro,* 1984), the Supreme Court ruled that a process called clean intermittent catheterization (used to provide bladder relief to some individuals with physical disabilities) was a school-related health service that schools had to provide. The court noted that this was necessary for the child to attend school and that the school nurse or another qualified person could do it. (In fact, this procedure is now performed by many special education teachers.)

To enhance your understanding of how a classroom teacher can effectively collaborate with a school nurse, go to the IRIS Center Resources section of Topic 14: Physical Disabilities & Health Impairments in the MyEducationLab for your course and complete the Module entitled *School Nurses: Roles and Responsibilities in the School Setting.*

## THE REAL WORLD Challenges and Solutions

### When parents want more than you can offer

*Judy Ruggles really did like Mrs. Billon, and she certainly liked Cameron, Mrs. Billon's 6-year-old son. But since Cameron had enrolled in Judy's kindergarten class, she was beginning to get a real feel for how demanding some parents could be, and this feeling emanated from Jenn Billon's nearly constant, overbearing presence and from her recent request.*

*From the time the Billons learned that Cameron had CP, they committed themselves to providing the best possible treatment they could find. They wanted him to progress to the maximum extent possible in all ways: physically, intellectually, personally, socially, and academically. He was their first and only child, and their world pretty much revolved around him.*

*When Cameron was only 18 months old, Kris Billon had been transferred to Chicago, and before they even made the move, their investigations led the Billons to an affluent neighborhood known for the quality of its public education and its services for students with disabilities. The housing market being what it was, they purchased a nice home at a good price and worked diligently to provide Cameron with a life that would defy any impediments that might result from his disability. Right away they enrolled him in an early intervention program that was set in an inclusive preschool. In this setting, a pediatric PT provided frequent services, as did an OT and a speech–language pathologist. The early childhood special education teacher and the preschool teacher worked well together, and all of the children in the preschool program, including Cameron, developed excellent bonds with both teachers, their assistants, and other school personnel.*

*When Cameron was old enough to begin kindergarten, the Billons, as could be expected, became very familiar with the faculty and administration at their neighborhood elementary school. They talked to the principal, who strongly recommended Mrs. Ruggles's classroom, and then they got to know Mrs. Ruggles herself. They also met and became very close with Amanda Johnson, the special education teacher who would be supporting Cameron as he participated fully in his new classroom and school. The first IEP meeting for Cameron occurred in late May, and they felt they were ready for the coming new year.*

*But now, after only a week in Mrs. Ruggles's class, Jenn Billon was feeling like maybe Cameron needed more, and she called or visited Mrs. Ruggles nearly every day to press her about her opinion and her support. Cameron seemed happy enough with his new classmates, and the services were more than adequate, but Mrs. Billon had been learning about other services, and she wanted to know the school's position on providing them. She was interested in various types of therapies for Cameron but seemed especially interested in hippotherapy and conductive education.*

*Yesterday, Jenn came to pick up Cameron, plopped a stack of printouts about conductive education on Judy Ruggles's desk, and asked her to share them with Ms. Johnson. She told Judy that she had decided to request a new IEP meeting and she was going to request financial support from the school district to provide transportation and tuition for Cameron to be enrolled in a conductive education program that she found about 20 miles from the school. She had been reading parent comments about the program online and was convinced that it would be more beneficial for Cameron than the services he was currently receiving. She asked Judy to read about the program and be supportive of it at the IEP meeting. Judy was almost speechless.*

It is natural for parents to want the best possible services for their child. In some cases, they will spend an inordinate amount of time trying find new and different therapies or programs that they believe will be beneficial and then will look for ways to get the services provided and paid for if they themselves cannot pay for them. The teacher sometimes gets caught in the middle, as did Judy Ruggles, and can find this position a bit uncomfortable if not stressful. If you ever find yourself in this position, here is what we suggest:

- **Maintain your cool.** The parent usually believes that what she is doing or wants to do is the best thing for her child. You may become very frustrated about the conflict and the amount of time it is taking, but this all comes with the territory. Don't take the issue personally. Try to maintain an attitude of balance and fairness, and maintain your professional demeanor.

- **Do not commit or agree about what is best unless you are sure.** You can be supportive of the parents' desire to have the best for their child, but you don't have to agree with them about what is best. Your opinion is valuable, and before you give it, make sure that it is valid. An off-handed comment like "Yeah, that would be great for Cameron" may come back to you at an IEP meeting or in another legal forum.

- **Do your homework about the proposed program.** Parents may want many different services and therapies. Often they will know more about these than you do because they have spent time studying them. You should do the same. But your focus should be not only on the program itself but on any available research or evidence that supports the effectiveness of the program. You should look to see if clear evidence indicates that a student like the one in question will make more progress in the proposed program than in the one he is currently in.

- **Focus on the student's achievements.** It might be helpful for you and for the parents if you ensure they are aware of their child's progress in the current program. If they are seeking something different, they should do so in a framework of understanding the current benefit their child is receiving. Showing them documentation of how well their child is doing might help them realize that there is a lot of value in what is already available.

- **Do not let the conflict affect your relationship with the student.** Whatever happens, keep the student out of the fray, and the quality of your services, and that of other professionals, should continue. It would be inappropriate and very unprofessional to have adult discussions affect your relationship with the student.

- **Keep your relationship with the parents strong.** You should also try to maintain a generally positive attitude with the parents. Keep in mind that you will always have the potential to be more effective when you can communicate than if your relationship is severed. Also keep in mind that you may have a relationship with the parent that continues beyond the current situation. You never want to say or do something that could have a long-term aversive effect.

### Valuable Resources for the Teacher

Porter, L. (2008). *Teacher–parent collaboration: Early childhood to adolescence.* Camberwell, Australia ACER Press.

TeacherVision. (2009). *Parent–teacher collaboration.* Retrieved July 26, 2009, from http://www.teachervision.fen.com/education-and-parents/resource/3730.html

Turnbull, A. P., Taylor, R. L., Erwin, E. J., & Soodak, L. C. (2005). *Families, professionals and exceptionality: Positive outcomes through partnership and trust* (5th ed.). Upper Saddle River, NJ: Pearson Education.

### Final Thoughts

Parents will often talk to teachers about what they wish for their child, and sometimes they will wish for things that seem uncalled for. It is always important to listen and to support them in their quest to find what is best. You can do this without committing yourself, and then you can learn more about what it is they want. When you have attained a level of knowledge about what they are asking for, then you can have an honest conversation with them about its merits and limitations.

But in other cases, courts have ruled that the cost of procedures and safety issues need to be considered when deciding whether or not a specific service should be provided. The issue, then, is what should schools be required to do for students with physical or health-related disabilities, and how much should they be required to spend on an individual student? Some say that, with our limited educational budgets, we should invest in programs that will benefit the most students, especially those who are likely to gain the most from the intervention. On the other hand, isn't our treatment of those with great needs an important indicator of our quality as a nation?

## Who Should Provide AT Devices, and Who Should Pay for Them?

Cost is one of the most common reasons why a student with a disability would not have an appropriate AT device. It is important to note that IDEA 2004 specifically requires the IEP team evaluate a student's need for AT devices and services when developing the IEP. If the committee determines that a student with a disability needs an AT device in order to achieve individual goals and objectives, IDEA 2004 requires that the school system provide such a device without cost to the parents. Some AT devices can be very costly, though, and schools may balk at the idea of buying the device for the student because of limited budgets. Schools will often insist that they will only fund items that are limited to school use (a serious limitation for devices that would be useful in multiple settings), unless use of the item in the home is specified in the IEP as being necessary for the student as part of a "free and appropriate public education" (Kemp, Hourcade, & Parette, 2000; Parette, 1997; Parette & Peterson-Karlan, 2007). Even when IEP team members recognize the tremendous potential of AT to benefit students with disabilities, they may not pursue the issue further because they may not know how to access or pay for AT devices and services. Securing the funding necessary for these often expensive resources is a common frustration. In fact, funding is often the biggest barrier to acquiring AT devices and services (Kemp et al., 2000).

In these two areas, the availability of related services and the provision of AT devices, school administrators often have to deal with controversial matters or conflicting interests. However, sometimes teachers directly experience dilemmas that require some deft thinking. In "The Real World: Challenges and Solutions," we present a situation that you may find yourself in a teacher.

# 14 SUMMARY

In this chapter, we discussed two special education disability categories identified by the U.S. Department of Education: orthopedic handicaps (which we refer to as physical disabilities) and other health impairments. These categories include some specific conditions that we described in the chapter. Because of the nature of the conditions, we focused on the physical and medical aspects of the conditions.

## Definitions of Physical Disabilities and Other Health Impairments as Used in Special Education

- Physical disabilities are referred to in special education law as "orthopedic impairments," which "includes impairments caused by congenital anomaly (e.g., clubfoot, absence of some member, etc.), impairments caused by disease (e.g., poliomyelitis, bone tuberculosis, etc.), and impairments from other causes (e.g., cerebral palsy, amputations, and fractures or burns that cause contractures)."

- Health impairment means having "limited strength, vitality or alertness, including a heightened alertness to environmental stimuli, that results in limited alertness with respect to the educational environment, that is due to chronic or acute health problems such as asthma, attention deficit disorder or attention deficit hyperactivity disorder, diabetes, epilepsy, a heart condition, hemophilia, lead poisoning, leukemia, nephritis, rheumatic fever, and sickle cell anemia; and . . . adversely affects a child's educational performance."

- Not only is it necessary to exhibit physical or health limitations in order to be served in special education, but these conditions must interfere with the student's ability to receive an appropriate education.

## Major Characteristics of Students with Physical Disabilities and Other Health Impairments

- The physical characteristics of students with physical disabilities vary according to their specific disabilities. However, as we noted, persons with physical disabilities often have different reactions to life events. To help fit in, they may do things such as try to avoid calling attention to their disability, make fun of their own condition, or find a special niche among their peers. They may also try to educate their peers about their conditions.

- Students with health impairments can be affected by their lack of learning and socialization opportunities caused by missed time in school, limited play and recreational opportunities, isolation by peers, and family challenges that might result from their ongoing medical conditions.

## Prevalence of Physical Disabilities and Other Health Impairments

- Students with physical disabilities and other health impairments, as categories in special education, make up less than 1% of the total school population. About 0.10% have physical disabilities, and about 0.77% have other health impairments.

## Areas of Assessment and Planning for Students with Physical Disabilities and Health Impairments

- Assessment first occurs in the medical arena in which the condition of the student is initially diagnosed and medical interventions developed.

- Second, within schools, eligibility for special education must be determined based on the extent to which the condition affects the student's learning ability. If the child meets criteria, an individualized family service plan may be developed if he or she is served in an early intervention program, or an IEP if served in a public school.

- Third, as a part of these plans, related services such as PT or OT may be offered. In this case, additional assessments will be conducted, and plans will be developed to meet a student's needs.

- If a student is not eligible for special education services, it is still possible that a Section 504 plan may be developed in order that the student can participate in school.

## Special Considerations for Students with Physical Disabilities and Health Impairments with Regard to Instruction and Related Services

- Students with physical disabilities and health impairments may receive special education and related services at the preschool level, during school years, and as they transition into the adult years.

- Variations of the general curriculum may be provided to students based on their unique needs, but most participate in the general curriculum.

- Most students with physical disabilities and health impairments are in the general education classroom. Special considerations for their physical and health-care needs are necessary for them to participate, and some modifications in the physical structure of the classroom may be necessary. It may be particularly helpful for an OT or PT to evaluate the classroom in order to better accommodate students.

- Conductive education is a special holistic form of education that is sometimes sought by parents. Research indicates, however, that it is no more effective than current special education and related services offered in most public schools in the United States.

- Teachers should especially be attuned to classroom situations that might endanger the health of some students. For example, chalk dust may trigger an asthma attack.
- Assistive technology devices can help students participate in the general education classroom and the general curriculum.
- Students will need supports as they transition into adolescence and adulthood. Their unique physical and health-care needs will need to be considered when further educational and career possibilities are discussed.

## Major Issues Related to Teaching and Providing Services to Students with Physical Disabilities or Other Health Impairments

- Two major issues related to serving students with physical disabilities and health impairments are (1) determining the divide between the responsibilities of the educational system and educators and the medical field and health-care professionals and (2) providing appropriate assistive technology devices.

 Council for Exceptional Children

## ADDRESSING THE PROFESSIONAL STANDARDS

Council for Exceptional Children (CEC) Knowledge Standards addressed in the chapter:

ICC1K: 1, 2, 4, 5, 7; PH1K: 1, 3; ICC2K: 1–7; PH2K: 1–4; ICC3K: 1, 2; PH3K: 1; PH4K: 1, 2; ICC5K: 1–4; PH5K: 1–3; ICC6K: 3; ICC7K: 1; ICC8K: 1; PH8K: 1, 2; PH9K: 1; PH10K: 1–3

Appendix B: CEC Knowledge and Skill Standards Common Core has a full listing of the standards referenced here.

### PEARSON myeducationlab

Now go to Topic 14: Physical Disabilities & Health Impairments and Topic 16: Multiple Disabilities & TBI in the MyEducationLab for your course, where you can:

- Find learning outcomes for the broad concepts covered in this chapter along with the national standards that connect to these outcomes.
- Complete Assignments and Activities that can help you more deeply understand the chapter content.
- Examine challenging situations presented in the IRIS Center Resources.

- Apply and practice your understanding of the core concepts and skills identified in the chapter with the Building Teaching Skills and Dispositions learning units.
- Check your comprehension on the content covered in the chapter by going to the Study Plan in the Book-Specific Resources section for your text. Here you will be able to take a chapter quiz, receive feedback on your answers, and then access Review, Practice, and Enrichment activities to enhance your understanding of chapter content.

# chapter
# 15

# Academically Gifted and Talented

**by Eric Jones,**
*Bowling Green State University,*

**and W. Thomas Southern,**
*Miami University of Ohio*

## REFLECT UPON

- How is giftedness defined and classified?
- What are the primary behavioral characteristics of students with gifts and talents?
- How prevalent are students with gifts and talents, and what causal factors are associated with these characteristics?
- How are students with gifts and talents identified and assessed?
- What educational practices are used for early intervention, academic enhancements, and transitions to adult life for students with gifts and talents?
- What are the major issues confronting the education of students with gifts and talents?

## MY PROFESSION, MY STORY: JULIE LENNER

Julie Lenner is a teacher of students identified as gifted in the Sandusky city schools in northwestern Ohio. She has been on the job for 5 years. She has completed a master's degree in gifted education and has recently become a part-time instructor in gifted education at a local university.

Julie became interested in these children almost by chance. As an undergraduate elementary education major, she frequently sought out opportunities to volunteer in a wide variety of educational settings, including summer camps and community programs. During the summer following her junior year, Julie was hired to serve as a counselor in a summer program for students with gifts and talents. Her curiosity was piqued by the enthusiasm of the students and the range of the challenges they pursued. During the following summer, she not only participated in the same program (this time as a residential director) but also took graduate classes in the field of gifted education. At the same time she was looking for a job. Jobs in elementary education turned out to be highly competitive. However, she noticed a posted opening in Sandusky. While she had not completed her licensure in gifted education (required under state of Ohio law), she applied. Julie had student-taught in this district, and staff members had already expressed interest in her.

Julie's initial appointment was wide-ranging and intense. She met with students identified as gifted. In addition, she was expected to develop curricula for the program in language arts and mathematics, provide counseling for students and consultation with students' general classroom teachers, meet with and counsel parents, develop individual written plans for each student, and assist in identifying students for the following year. Julie describes her first group of students as "great." She was concerned about some identified students who were experiencing difficulty and worried about whether or not she was providing appropriate experiences. Because her district has a culturally diverse student body, she struggled with the issues of identifying students with inappropriate instruments and dealing with students who might be missed by the district's policy. And there were other challenges. Some students seemed unconnected to the curriculum, even when their abilities and precocities were evident in nonacademic exchanges. Some were confrontational; others were too quietly compliant or behaviorally difficult (challenging her initial assumptions that gifted students would accept and rise to challenges). She also noted that classroom teachers were often unaware of the kinds of difficulties gifted students experienced in educational settings. They seemed to feel that these kids could make it on their own with little problem and that the services they received were not as essential as those provided in the general classroom.

Julie's typical day starts with meetings with general education classroom teachers at 7:30 A.M., planning the logistics of the day. From 8:00 to 11:10, she meets with students in math and language arts in the upper grades. She also meets with grade-level groups of five or six students each for 40 minutes. During the lunch hour, she eats with the building staff to keep up with what's going on in the school and chat about students, hash out ideas, and so on. Julie has a 35-minute planning period, but it is frequently taken up with administrative and parent concerns. She also has supervisory duty (recess, lunch, etc.) or a demonstration lesson for whole-grade groups of students. From 1:00 to 2:15, she repeats the morning schedule with other grades and students. Then until 3:30 she has dismissal duty and meeting and planning responsibilities with peers, administrators, and parents.

Julie Lenner is an excellent example of a teacher who realizes that it is important to take care of herself in order to take care of her students. To do this, she participates in professional organizations and accesses professional development opportunities often. From time to time the pressures of external mandates and difficult performance expectations intrude on a teacher's ability to provide conscionable instruction. In gifted education, this is amplified by the attitudes of some of the general education staff and administrators, who are unaware of the difficulties and needs experienced by students who are gifted. She deals with these pressures by finding peers at building, district, state, and national levels to support her.

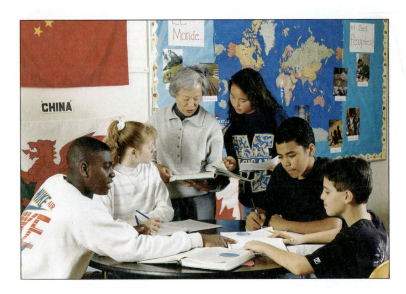

It is a myth that students with gifts and talents will thrive without special attention; the population is very diverse, and their needs are complex and varied.

One basic reason students come to school is to learn things that they do not already know. Of course, time is needed to refine and improve certain skills. Certainly, it is also important for students to become socialized in their schools, make friends, and learn to deal with authority. Academic achievement is, however, the primary reason that students are expected to attend school. While some students have difficulty profiting from our best efforts to teach them, others demonstrate exceptional abilities to gain impressive levels of competence rapidly and appear more insightful and creative than their peers. These precocious students appear to learn with very little effort; however, their exceptional aptitudes often challenge the talents, skills, and patience of their teachers.

Certainly children and youth with high intelligence or impressive talents are likely to have advantages coping with the challenges of learning and socialization. However, it is a mistake to assume that they can be left to their own devices. It is a bit of popular mythology that students with gifts and talents will thrive without special attention from their teachers, counselors, and parents. Overlooked and unfulfilled geniuses are such common themes that we have proverbs, novels, and feature-length films about them. Nonetheless, students whose capacities to learn and achieve are significantly greater than those of their peers (and sometimes greater than their teachers and other adults in their lives) require special interventions. Despite the many stereotypes of giftedness, the population of students with gifts and talents is very diverse, and their needs are complex and varied (see the "FAQ Sheet"). Although it may seem that persons with exceptional potential to learn do not need special education, there is broad agreement among parents and educators that such services are needed.

## DEFINITIONS AND CLASSIFICATION CRITERIA FOR GIFTEDNESS

### Defining Giftedness

Attempts to identify the concept of giftedness have resulted in an assortment of definitions (Coleman, 2004). A central theme in all the conceptualizations of giftedness is the concept of high ability. Beyond that, however, concepts of giftedness vary widely. Some definitions consider a wide spectrum of different abilities, such as intellectual abilities, creative thinking, artistic talents, or social leadership. Others are concerned primarily with intellectual abilities, motivations, attitudes, and personal dispositions. Still other definitions focus on demonstrated achievement, while others are concerned with potential abilities. Ironically, the educational needs of students with gifts are not directly addressed in most efforts.

Definitions have changed as views of intelligence, talent, and motivation have changed. Often these changes have been influenced by changes in the technologies for measuring those traits. Cultural, societal, and historical factors have also influenced assumptions about the appropriate goals for both general education and gifted education. We focus on three commonly accepted definitions of giftedness.

## FAQ Sheet

### STUDENTS WITH GIFTS AND TALENTS

| | |
|---|---|
| Who are they? | • Children and youth in some states who meet a threshold in IQ or achievement<br>• Children in some states who far exceed peers in learning pace or attainment<br>• Children who have demonstrated performance abilities at high levels in visual or performing arts, creativity, or leadership |
| What are typical characteristics? | • Academic or creative performance that vastly exceeds that of their age mates<br>• Ability to understand complex and abstract ideas at ages earlier than expected<br>• Socially well adjusted at early ages but with concerns about later socialization<br>• High levels of task commitment<br>• Advanced language skills and development<br>• Advanced sense of humor<br>• Advanced vocabulary and sophisticated use of language |
| What are the demographics? | • Between 5% and 20% of the population<br>• Roughly equivalent numbers of males and females<br>• Nonproportional lower representation of African American, Hispanic, and Native American students<br>• Lower-than-proportional representation of economically disadvantaged students |
| Where are students educated? | • Most are educated in inclusive settings with smaller numbers educated in resource room pullouts, self-contained classrooms, and special schools for the gifted. |
| What are the outcomes? | • Most are successful in school, though evidence indicates that many underachieve.<br>• Identified gifted students graduate from college and achieve advanced degrees in greater percentages than do nongifted peers. |

## The Marland Federal Definition

The most widely cited definition of giftedness was originally developed by Marland (1972) as a guide for federal funding of education programs presented to the U.S. Congress:

> Gifted and talented children are those identified by professionally qualified persons who by virtue of outstanding abilities are capable of high performance. These are children who require differentiated educational programs and/or services beyond those normally provided by the regular school program in order to realize their contribution to self and society. Children capable of high performance include those with demonstrated achievement and/or potential ability in any of the following areas:

- General intellectual ability
- Specific academic ability
- Creative or productive thinking
- Leadership ability
- Visual and performing arts
- Psychomotor ability (p. 5)

The Marland (1972) definition (and its subsequent modification in 1979) is significant for several reasons. First, it stressed the complexity of the concept of giftedness. Second, it stated clearly that giftedness may be identified by either demonstrated performance or demonstration of potential for ability. Third, and perhaps most important, the definition called for special education services for students with gifts and talents beyond those provided to students in general education programs.

During the past 20 years, several important alternative definitions for giftedness have been proposed. Generally, they reflect varied perceptions of the importance and nature of intelligence and their relationship to talent and nonintellectual traits such as persistence and self-esteem.

### REFLECTIVE EXERCISE

#1 Although students with gifts and talents can learn very rapidly, they often share emotional maturities and interests similar to those of their age-level peers. They often challenge our abilities to provide services that meet their educational needs and their social/emotional development. Do you have the temperament to work with children and youth who are precocious learners?

Many students with gifts and talent engage in creative acts that require divergent thinking.

## REFLECTIVE EXERCISE

#2 Compare Renzulli's model for giftedness with the Marland definition. Which model has greater importance for educators?

## Renzulli's Three-Ring Conception of Giftedness

Renzulli (2002) defines giftedness as behavior that is the result of the combination of three ingredients: well-above-average ability, task commitment, and creativity. In developing this definition of giftedness, Renzulli (1977) addressed two major problems with the Marland (1972) definition. First, the Marland definition did not include motivational factors. Renzulli considered task commitment, or the motivation to persevere with a task, as an important attribute of giftedness. Second, the Marland effort included several traits that seemed to overlap in their effects on performance. Renzulli contended that some traits such as creativity or leadership do not exist apart from the performance areas in which they are applied. For example, a creative jazz musician is not necessarily expected to demonstrate creativity in areas such as writing, debate, or science.

According to Renzulli's model, well-above-average ability can be defined by performances that indicate either general intellectual abilities or specific talents. General abilities include abstract thinking, spatial relations, and logical reasoning. These abilities are considered important and are frequently measured by intelligence tests. Specific abilities may be shown in areas such as academics, art, or social behavior. Renzulli (1986) observed that task commitment is a trait that has been consistently associated with giftedness. He found consensus among studies of accomplished and talented people that motivation to work hard and to persevere through difficulties to meet high personal expectations for quality are dependably associated with giftedness. Thus, motivation to learn and produce is an essential ingredient in his conceptualization of giftedness. Renzulli's studies of productive and talented persons supported the inclusion of a third ingredient—creativity. Genius has usually been recognized because of creative productivity. Originality, constructively ingenious problem solving, and divergent thinking are considered to be traits of creativity. Unfortunately, these traits are difficult to assess in everyday situations.

## Gardner's Definition Using Multiple Intelligences

Gardner and colleagues (e.g., Gardner, 1983; Gardner & Hatch, 1989; Walters & Gardner, 1986; Ramos-Ford & Gardner, 1991) believe that intelligence and giftedness are not general traits and therefore should not be viewed as the general factors that IQ tests purport to measure. Consequently, they developed a theory of multiple types of intelligences in which intelligence is defined as "the capacity to solve problems or to fashion products that are valued in one or more cultural settings" (Gardner & Hatch, 1989, p. 5). Gardner and co-workers describe eight areas of intelligence: logical-mathematical, linguistic, musical, spatial, bodily-kinesthetic, interpersonal, intrapersonal, and naturalistic. Figure 15.1 lists the eight intelligences with examples of roles and abilities generally associated with each. Gardner (1983) allowed

Some students with gifts and talents excel in the visual and performing arts.

## FIGURE 15.1 • GARDNER'S MULTIPLE INTELLIGENCES

1. Linguistic (sensitivity to the meaning and order of words)
2. Logical-mathematical (ability in numbering/reasoning and other logical systems)
3. Musical (ability to understand and create music)
4. Spatial (ability to perceive the visual world accurately and re-create or alter it)
5. Bodily-kinesthetic (ability to use one's body in a skilled way—e.g., a dancer)
6. Interpersonal (ability to perceive and understand other individuals)
7. Intrapersonal (ability to understand one's own emotions; self-knowledge)
8. Naturalistic (ability to discriminate among elements of natural world; knowledge of nature)

that the list may not be exhaustive and that other intelligences could be identified. However, it does include a set of competencies that, although they may usually operate in combination, are capable of functioning individually. Thus, each talent may be studied, identified, and developed apart from the others (Henshon, 2006).

## Classification Criteria for Identifying Giftedness

The two most frequently used classification systems in the education of the students with gifts and talents are (1) types of gifts and (2) levels of giftedness.

### Types of Gifts and Talents

When students are classified by type of gift or talent, criteria from the Marland (1972) federal definition are used. For example, *general intellectual ability* refers to scores on IQ tests, and *specific academic aptitude* refers to high abilities in content-specific areas (most frequently mathematics, science, social studies, reading, and writing). Creativity describes students who have numerous, useful, and original ideas. Leadership describes students who are natural or developing leaders. Students with talents in visual and performing arts excel in instrumental or local performance, two- or three-dimensional arts, dance, or theater.

Another distinction among the types is what some researchers characterize as gifts versus talents. Intellectual and academic performances are often referred to as gifts, while the others are labeled talents. Many theorists view this distinction as invalid (all observed behaviors are manifestations of gifts) and portray the talent areas as less important or remarkable. For example, Gagné (1999) suggests that initial gifts in the individual become recognized talents after opportunity, instruction, environment, and chance factors contribute to their development and exposure. This more ecological view appears to be winning approval in the field.

### Levels of Giftedness

The notion that giftedness should be sorted into levels arose with the study of individuals with high IQ scores. Hollingsworth (1940) suggested that individuals with IQs higher than 180 are very different from those with lower IQs still in the gifted range. Other researchers attempted to determine if bands of intelligence might have different characteristics and needs. This led to a designation of levels of giftedness:

IQ 130–145: Gifted
IQ 145–160: Highly gifted
Above IQ 160: Profoundly gifted

Still, many are not pleased with this classification system. They feel that IQ alone is an inadequate measure to accurately classify types of giftedness and that the performance of students at each level is not that dissimilar. Nonetheless, some researchers still advocate for and refer to such a system in texts on students who are gifted, and research into individuals who are profoundly gifted is still being conducted (e.g., Delisle, 2003; Gross, 2004; Silverman, 1990).

**REFLECTIVE EXERCISE**

#3 What is your opinion of the theory of multiple intelligences? Do you believe these specific areas exist? Do you believe that intelligence can be reduced to eight specific areas? Explain.

PEARSON
**myeducationlab**

Go to the Assignments and Activities section of Topic 17: Gifted & Talented in the MyEducationLab for your course and complete the activities entitled *Definitions of Giftedness* and *Multiple Intelligences in the Classroom*.

**REFLECTIVE EXERCISE**

#4 How much influence should IQ test scores have in the determination of giftedness? What other factors should be part of the classification system?

# PRIMARY BEHAVIORAL CHARACTERISTICS OF STUDENTS WITH GIFTS AND TALENTS

As we have discussed, the term *giftedness* suggests a range of different patterns of behavior. Next we consider some of the early stereotypes of students with gifts and then identify empirically derived characteristics.

## Early Conceptualizations

Early written accounts of students with gifts and talents presented a variety of physical, cognitive, and affective characteristics. Lombroso (1891), a 19th-century writer, described them as being near-sighted, physically weak, and oversensitive. He claimed that genius was a force that burned the body's substance and put sanity at risk. The cliché that "genius is separated from madness by a fine line" was originally one of Lombroso's assertions.

Terman (1925) conducted a study of the characteristics of more than 1,500 students with IQs above 140 in order to investigate Lombroso's characterizations. He concluded that students identified as gifted were physically larger and healthier, more likely to mature into adults who were also highly productive, and had superior mental health compared to their average peers. Terman's and Lombroso's characterizations are contradictory, but they are both represented in current stereotypes of giftedness. Neither characterization is adequately supported. Terman's more scientific study was flawed because it was based primarily on white middle-class students from advantaged backgrounds. The characteristics he found might not be typical of students who demonstrate exceptional abilities in today's diverse multicultural communities.

## Current Views

Students with gifts and talents vary greatly in physical, cognitive, and affective characteristics. Some students exhibit traits that can be viewed quite positively. For example, some students show high degrees of empathy for others, task commitment, motivation to excel, or desire to fulfill teacher expectations. On the other hand, high-ability students may exhibit behaviors that are viewed negatively. They may display impatience with peers' inability to rapidly learn information, question authority and become rebellious, or express distaste for tasks that require drill and repetition.

Some students with gifts and talents are disorganized and appear flighty and unfocused. Ironically, some traits associated with creative students may actually interfere with their being selected to participate in gifted education programs (Richert, Alvino, & McDonnel, 1982). Unusual responses may be considered flaky and off-the-wall. Questioning rules and authority may be viewed as rudeness or sarcasm. A high degree of risk-taking behavior may result in the adoption of attitudes and behaviors that ostracize the student from peers and teachers.

### Developmental Factors

The characteristics of students who are gifted also vary according to developmental age. As these children go through school, more specific sorts of talent develop. Young children may be well developed in all the school tasks. They may be able to accomplish most of the learning in early grades with apparent ease. However, by the time a student reaches middle grades, preferences, strengths, and comparative weaknesses become more apparent. Some students excel in mathematics or science, while others express high achievement in writing or history (Winner, 2000). Some of these differences arise because, in later grades, content becomes more specific and directed.

Cognitive, affective, and physical development are not uniform. For example, young children may display very large vocabularies or advanced problem-solving skills. They may also engage in temper tantrums and emotional displays common to other children their age. When students with gifts and talents enter school, their school-related fine-motor skills may not match their cognitive development. Faced with tasks such as handwriting and coloring, they may experience frustration. Young boys often express impatience with the cumbersome process of handwriting, even developing a strong dislike for the entire writing process. Students who enter school early or skip grades are not as apt to participate in varsity athletics as their chronological-age peers. While they may continue to participate in sports, lower levels of physical maturation may disadvantage young students if they have to compete with grade-level peers. Many students will pursue other interests and choose not to compete or participate in interscholastic sports (Olenchak & Hebert, 2002).

## Adolescence

Adolescence is perhaps the most challenging period of development for high-ability students. Buescher (1991) describes adolescence as a time of personal redefinition for all youth. The role of "good student" and "high achiever" may be questioned in the light of the intense physical and emotional changes occurring during this period (Foust, Rudasill, & Callahan, 2006). Some students begin to distrust their ability and question whether they really have gifts and talents. Others may change priorities and acquire greater preferences for relations with peers that conflict with goals for advanced achievement. For females, this can sometimes include rejection of mathematics and science as a course of study (Reis & Graham, 2005). For males, it may result in adopting more rebellious and noncompliant roles. It is important that teachers remember that these changes are more a function of adolescence than of giftedness (Buescher, 1991; Foust et al., 2006).

As students with gifts and talents progress further in school, a major task facing them is the selection of training and career options. For many students, interests and abilities have been channeled for some time. They have identified career choices (or an area of knowledge to pursue) early and clearly. For others, these choices are more difficult. Some students with gifts, particularly those with multiple talents, experience difficulties making decisions about which options to pursue (Berger, 1994).

Postsecondary education is the time when students redefine themselves, this time as young adults with different responsibilities. At this point they may, and frequently do, change career aspirations and goals. For instance, students who might have identified a long graduate educational course may change their minds and choose a more direct career path.

## Adulthood

Studies of adults with gifts and talents tend to take the form of biographical surveys, usually of the famous and the eminent (e.g., Goertzel & Goertzel, 1962; Roe, 1952). While these life histories provide insight into some of the later development of individuals with gifts and talents, the sample is biased. Studies that have identified and followed groups of "typical" individuals with gifts and talents through adulthood are scarce. Terman (1925) completed the most noteworthy longitudinal study. Although that study relied on the IQ data of a very narrow sample, it provides a glimpse of how highly capable students progress into adulthood. The group, as a whole, was stable, in both personal and professional relationships. The males in Terman's group were generally satisfied with their life achievements. Some members of the group were near the top of their professions. Females told a different story. Few of the women identified in the group had engaged in careers. When they were interviewed as adults, the women expressed disappointment that they had not fulfilled their academic potential. Given the societal roles and expectations for women at the time of the study, that result is not surprising. More recent studies (e.g., Arnold, 1993; Tomlinson-Keasey & Keasey, 1993) have also indicated that high-achieving women do not find it easy to resolve professional and family options.

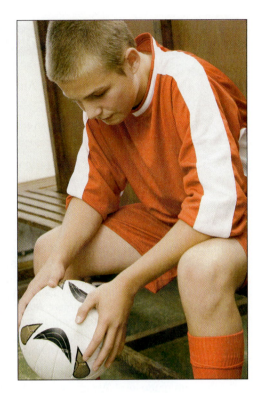

Due to lower levels of maturation, accelerated students may have difficulty participating fully in school-based sports and recreation activities.

## REFLECTIVE EXERCISE

#5 What were your initial thoughts regarding the characteristics of students with gifts and talents? How do the empirically derived characteristics compare with your initial thoughts?

# CAN YOU HELP ME WITH THIS STUDENT?

| To... | Sonia Telsky, Area Superintendent |
| --- | --- |
| From... | Megan Lee, Assistant Principal |
| Subject: | Addressing the placement needs of a gifted child |

Hi Sonia,

I hope you are having a great school year. I also hope that you can help us with a situation with one of our students. I believe you are familiar with Wes Andrews, one of our young gifted students who is performing far above grade level. I recall you were quoted in a newspaper story a couple years ago in which Mrs. Andrews feigned annoyance that the 3-year-old Wes was repeatedly pulling volumes of the *World Book Encyclopedia* from the shelf and paging through them. He never seemed to harm them, but it was an "irritation" for her to have to continually replace them. In that story she recounted how Wes would point at a picture caption and ask, "What's this word, Mommy?" She told him and then asked why he wanted to know. He replied, "Because I can read all the other words." Without instruction, Wes had taught himself to read at the age of 3.

Wes is now 5 and has been in kindergarten for a month. Achievement tests indicate that he is reading above the sixth-grade level. Along with Mrs. Andrews, several of our administrators and related service personnel want him to skip kindergarten, but the kindergarten teacher is adamant that he will miss valuable skills and that gaps in instruction would later limit his progress. She opposes acceleration to an advanced grade, citing immaturity and poor foundations in certain reading and math skills (e.g., making inferences, problem solving).

Do you have any guidance on how we should proceed? You are the district's recognized expert in gifted education. Any resources to share with the parties would also be helpful. Thanks for your prompt attention to this escalating situation.

Meg

---

To: Megan Lee
From: Sonia Telsky
Subject: RE: Addressing the placement needs of a gifted child

This is a tough one, Meg, and a circumstance that requires attention to Wes's unique characteristics. A program for a gifted student like Wes cannot be based just on standardized tests and follow a boilerplate set of steps. Areas such as psychological readiness and how Wes learns best must be considered in program development. I would suggest a 6-week trial in kindergarten with a review of placement at the end of that time. At the review the team should consider various aspects of Wes's development, noting things beyond just standardized test scores. I would also suggest use of independent observers who target specific aspects of social and academic development. I suggest these resources to guide the development and evaluation of the trial period:

Coleman, L. J., & Cross, T. L. (2005). *Being gifted in school: An introduction to development, guidance, and teaching.* Waco, TX: Prufrock Press.

Winner, E. (2000). The origins and ends of giftedness. *American Psychologist, 55*(1), 159–169.

Roedell, W. (2000). Nurturing giftedness in young children. Retrieved July 10, 2009, from http://www.kidsource.com/kidsource/content/nurturing_giftedness.html

Let me know how things progress. Wes is a special kid and deserves a program that matches his needs.

ST

# PREVALENCE AND CAUSAL FACTORS

## Prevalence

Estimates of the numbers of students who are gifted and talented vary so widely that it is difficult to find consensus among them (Belanger & Gagne, 2006). The estimates differ as a function of three variables: (1) the prevailing conceptualizations of giftedness, (2) services offered for gifted students, and (3) the quality of the general education program. Gagné (1991) reported that most prevalence estimates are based on IQs of 130 or on academic achievement at the 95th percentile. Accordingly, we would expect to find that about 5% of the school-age population is gifted, but actual numbers vary considerably from that estimate. Renzulli (1986) argued that performances on standardized, norm-referenced tests do not provide adequate bases for the identification of giftedness and talent. More liberal criteria would allow for the identification of 15% to 20% of the school's population as potentially gifted. It seems that the general public shares the liberal criteria. Gagné, Bélanger, and Motard (1993) surveyed noneducators regarding their estimates of the prevalence of school-age children with gifts and talents. They found that estimates varied widely for both labels. An average of 19% of school-age children were estimated to be gifted, while the average estimate of talented students was 36%.

From these data we can draw three conclusions. First, estimates of prevalence vary widely depending on how closely you adhere to the IQ model of giftedness. Second, professionals offer lower estimates than nonprofessionals do. Third, estimates vary if the notion of high ability is broadened from cognitive or academic abilities to include artistic, creative, social, and psychomotor talents. Also keep in mind that the demand for special education for students with gifts and talents increases if the general curriculum is inadequate to meet their instructional needs. Schools with high academic demands, well-designed curricula, and good instruction experience less pressure for special services. Thus, variations in local education programs are accompanied by variations in demands for educational services.

## Causal Factors

Where does giftedness come from? Answers to that question rarely seem adequate. To many, the term *gifted* suggests something mystical. However, most of the professional discussion on causality centers on inheritance and environment. While the debate has waxed and waned, most theorists believe that both genetic and environmental factors are important in the development of intellectual gifts. Gagné (1993) and Feldhusen (1992) offer models of talent development that describe a genetic and environmental interaction. In Gagné's model, for example, giftedness is a predisposed set of inborn abilities that allows a range of development in the child. These abilities, however, interact with environmental factors such as guidance from other significant people, appropriate early instruction, and even chance. The environment also impacts motivational and personality traits important for the development of talent.

While innate abilities may provide the bases for giftedness, the preponderance of relatively advantaged students in programs for gifted students clearly suggests that the socioeconomics of communities, schools, and families also play critical causal roles. Specifically, where you live and the school you attend can influence the development of giftedness. More affluent communities, schools, and families tend to have more opportunities for intellectual and creative efforts. Gifted education programs are only sporadically available in rural and low-income school districts (Southern & Jones, 1992).

# IDENTIFICATION AND ASSESSMENT

Educators use a wide assortment of evaluation procedures to identify students for gifted education programs. These varied procedures contribute to the diverse characteristics and different numbers of students who are identified as gifted. Test-driven identification systems tend to be based on rather simple conceptualizations that identify only 2% to 5% of the school population as gifted. The major problem is that tests alone do not identify many students who consistently demonstrate significant talent and capabilities. Standardized tests offer only general predictions and are not very useful in identifying students for programs that provide for diverse opportunities for individual enrichment. Currently, the most useful identification processes are based on the use of multiple criteria (Davis & Rimm, 2003), including intelligence tests, achievement tests, creativity tests, teacher nominations, peer nominations, parent nominations, product sampling, and self-nominations.

## Intelligence Tests

Intelligence tests provide information that is often useful for predicting future school performance. Scores are highly reliable and relatively stable. Critics, however, argue that IQ tests have several limitations. First, they are based on limited conceptualizations of intelligence because they only test convergent and analytical reasoning. Second, IQ tests do not adequately identify students from special populations. Third, IQ tests become less useful in determining specific abilities and talents as students grow older.

## Achievement Tests

Achievement tests offer more specific information about student learning and also provide norm-referenced comparative data. Achievement tests are generally organized into subtests that provide information on academic strengths and weaknesses. For this reason achievement test batteries are often used to identify specific academic abilities. However, these tests have potential drawbacks.

The content of standardized achievement tests is made up of samples of items that test what is taught, or what should be taught, in schools. However, great variations in the contents of local curricula exist among school districts. Frequently, what is tested is not what is taught, so norm-referenced comparisons may not be valid. Moreover, achievement tests may lack sufficient numbers of difficult questions to reliably measure the achievement of very capable students. The tests are fairly easy; and although the students earn high scores, their achievement is not thoroughly tested.

## Creativity Tests

During the 1950s, researchers developed instruments to assess divergent thinking and creativity. Many tests of creativity measure traits such as creative fluency, or the ability to produce large numbers of responses; flexibility, or the ability to produce responses in a large number of categories; elaboration, or the ability to link words or symbols together to make new ideas; and originality, or the ability to generate responses that are unusual or unique. Research with creativity tests has shown some lower correlation with IQ testing. Proponents therefore claim that the instruments are measuring a construct different from intelligence. Nonetheless, links among creativity-test performance and adult productivity have not been clearly established, and some research claiming that creativity is linked to school achievement has been called into question (Piirto, 1992).

## Teacher Nominations

Teachers often participate in the process of identifying students who may benefit from specialized programs. Usually they are asked either to supply ratings of students' strengths and weaknesses or to nominate students they think would benefit from special services. Teachers do not rate and nominate only students who appear to be academically precocious. They are frequently asked to provide ratings on different abilities or aptitudes, such as creativity, content ability, artistic aptitude, and motivation. The importance of teachers' participation should not be ignored. Teachers directly observe students' academic performance. They also observe the performances of their students in comparison to one another in academic and relevant nonacademic settings. Teacher ratings/nominations are also inexpensive and easily collected.

Still, teachers' judgments should be used cautiously. Some researchers have found that teachers are relatively poor at identifying both students with high IQs and students with specific academic aptitudes (Pegnato & Birch, 1959; Terman & Oden, 1947). Some teachers orient to indicators that are not highly related to gifted behaviors. For example, they might view neatness, grammatical speech, or exact compliance with assignments as highly related to student ability when, in fact, such traits may be irrelevant. The literature on the use of teacher evaluations suggests several guidelines. First, teacher ratings are perhaps most useful if they are used to indicate talents and abilities that may be missed in formal testing. Second, because some teachers may have dramatically high rates of nominations while others nominate relatively few students, teachers should be trained in rating and nominating students. Third, even if training is provided, teachers' evaluations should be used cautiously because differences do not disappear with training. Fourth, teachers should provide capable students with instruction that requires the students to use abstract reasoning, creativity, or problem solving. If students do not have opportunities to show their cognitive abilities, teachers will not be able to observe them.

## Peer Nominations

When observing their fellow students, peers see a wider variety of behaviors than do teachers. Consequently, peers can be asked questions that help identify giftedness. Difficulties, however, can be associated with peer nomination. First, young students may be overly influenced by teacher praise of student peers. Peer judgment may reflect the teacher's judgments. Second, older peers tend to be less informative because they are reluctant or they take the process less seriously than younger students do. Third, peer judgments are frequently influenced by behaviors that have little to do with aptitudes or abilities of their peers. For example, students who irritate others or belittle their peers will probably not be selected as frequently as other students will. Fourth, the number of nominations needed to identify a student is open to question. Given some of the factors that cause students to undernominate certain students, peer nominations should be used cautiously.

## Parent Nominations

Arguably, parents are the greatest source of nominations of students (Jones & Southern, 1991). Parents know a great deal about their child's behavior. Thus, they are often asked to participate in assessments by filling out forms or rating scales or are simply asked if their son or daughter should be a part of a program for the gifted and talented. Parents can provide extensive information about current habits, skills, leisure activities, and preferred learning tasks. Determining the value of some types of parental information can be difficult, however. Unless they have kept accurate records, questions about milestone events in a child's life (e.g., the age at which speech began or the age at which an interest in books emerged) are difficult to interpret and recall. Unlike teachers, parents are apt to lack a comparative frame of reference. For example, questions about the size of their child's vocabulary or the relative sophistication of the child's sense of humor are difficult for many parents to answer accurately.

## Product Sampling

Products provide information about how students perform in terms of critical and creative thinking in various content areas or provide information about prior achievements or awards. Products collected over time have the advantage of showing a profile of student growth and learning, but they also have limitations. First, it can be difficult to assess the relative performance of students with product samples because evaluation criteria frequently are not clear and well defined. Second, using multiple judges and holistic scoring can increase the cost of the assessment process. Third, teachers and program administrators do not often have access to products and achievements of students outside school (or outside the teacher's classroom), and important information may be missing.

## Self-Nomination

Perhaps the most direct method of assessment involves self-nomination by the student for various programs. Though many would guess that such a procedure would result in massive amounts of overreferral, evidence indicates that self-nomination is as effective as other nomination methods. Shore and Tsiamis (1986) conducted a study in which they selected students for a university-based summer program in two ways. One group was required to submit standardized achievement test data and teacher checklists. The other group was asked only to submit a letter from a teacher saying the student might benefit from the program. In fact, the letters were never examined and were used only to ensure a minimal amount of student interest. When the two groups of students were compared, the researchers discovered that they were equivalent in aptitude and achievement. Students who had selected themselves actually had the same characteristics as those who underwent external review.

The value of self-referrals has several limitations. First, young children may not be aware of their abilities to perform in novel settings. Descriptions that emphasize the fun and exciting elements of programs and underplay the difficulty of the academic demands may be so appealing that they attract students who are more hopeful than accurate about their abilities to perform adequately. Self-nomination does, however, provide the benefit of opening involvement in programs and can help students identify interests that school personnel may not have witnessed.

## Interpreting Data Collected During Assessment

Educators use three basic approaches to analyzing assessment data and determining which students are eligible for services in gifted education. The first approach is to gather several measures on relevant traits and set acceptable minimum criteria or thresholds for each measure. Students who do not meet the minimum criteria on any individual measures are then eliminated from the selection process. The second approach is to organize the data into matrices. This involves assigning values to various levels of performance for each of the instruments. Results are then summed, and students are selected for participation based on their overall scores.

A third approach is to create profiles of students' abilities. Profiles are visual representations of the information collected in the assessment. They can illustrate the relative ability levels within individual students as well characterize the patterns of talent of the group of students that is participating in or seeking service from an existing program. Profile analysis has three advantages over the other two methods. First, it allows for consideration of data that are not drawn from test scores (e.g., student awards and achievements, whether the student has participated in gifted programs in the past). Second, it allows for comparisons of the patterns of talents and interests that may go beyond the specific focus of the program, thus letting educators, students, and parents make judgments about the appropriateness of a special program or academic option (Southern, Spicker, Kierouz, & Kelly, 1990).

None of the selection processes are without potential problems, and errors in selection will occasionally occur. Students may be erroneously excluded from or placed in programs. It is therefore good practice to develop and expect to use an appeals process. Appeals may be made by teachers, parents, or students. The process should allow new information to be introduced that might be relevant to reconsiderations of initial selection decisions.

**REFLECTIVE EXERCISE**

#6 Describe an evaluation system that you believe would result in more equitable identifications among economically disadvantaged and ethnically diverse students.

# EDUCATIONAL PRACTICES

We recommend using evidence-based educational practices to address the instructional and social needs of students with gifts and talents. We first address the thorny issue of early intervention and then focus on strategies for providing academic and social support.

## Early Intervention

Early intervention for students with gifts and talents is not mandated by law as it is for students with disabilities. Early identifications are usually made when a young child demonstrates very atypical performances that alert or even alarm their parents. Parents often seek interventions when children learn to read without instruction at 3 or 4 years of age, when they solve problems adults do not expect them to perform, or when they have rapidly expanding and astonishing supplies of knowledge. Keep in mind that the absence of these kinds of behaviors doesn't mean a child is not gifted. However, when such evidence is observed, it is a signal to parents and educators that some unusual and rather immediate efforts may be needed. Early intervention for students with gifts and talents, however, is rare. Schools in most states are not required to provide services, and parents are generally unaware of potential need and benefit. Hence, most instances of these services revolve around prodigious achievement. Many districts actively discourage parents from pursuing any service. When suggestions are made, they generally revolve around some form of acceleration (e.g., early admission or grade skipping).

As students progress though school, the pressure for services generally increases for those who have mastered the curriculum or for those who are not adapting to school-related provisions. These students are mismatched with the curriculum. Various other issues may come into consideration, but choices of whether to offer accelerative options or enrichment options generally revolve around the following five factors:

1. **Adequacy of general education curriculum.** For some students, educators may have serious questions about whether or not the curriculum is too "dumbed down" (Renzulli, 2002) to be of significant value even if the student could proceed through it rapidly.

2. **Ability of student to handle the demands of more rapid presentation of content or placement in higher-level classes.** Determine if the student can adapt to the rapid pace of instruction and the increasing complexity of the material being presented.

3. **Separation from age-level peers.** If parents or educators think that there is too much risk to social/emotional adjustment, accelerative options such as grade skipping and early entrance are rejected in favor of options that allow the student to remain with age-level peers.

4. **Skepticism about accelerating the curriculum.** If school personnel are opposed to acceleration, they may consciously or unconsciously place road blocks in the way of the intervention.

5. **Missing important instruction.** Not having certain instruction could disadvantage the student during future learning activities. (Shore, Cornell, Robinson, & Ward, 1991).

**my education lab**

Go to the Assignments and Activities section of Topic 17: Gifted & Talented in the MyEducationLab for your course and complete the activities entitled *Challenging Gifted Students* and *Differentiated Instruction*.

## Academic Interventions

For students with gifts and talents, academic interventions center on six dimensions: *content; complexity; abstraction; pacing; documenting achievement;* and *choice and independence* (Maker & Nielson, 1996).

### Content

Students who are identified as gifted require advanced content instruction either because they have generally mastered content at earlier ages or because they can master content at a faster pace. Perhaps the most easily identifiable characteristic of such students is their vast store of information. It is critical that a teacher offer greater and more varied academic content to such learners.

### Complexity

The content for students with gifts and talents should be more complex. It should include multiple perspectives, multiple implications, and advanced demands on the learner to see interactions with other areas of study. Compared to students with more typical academic capacities, students with gifts and talents are capable of considering more variables as they contemplate problems. They are also capable of understanding abstractions to a greater degree than other children of the same chronological age. In fact, most gifted children relish this capacity. Unlike children with cognitive deficits, they are capable of intuitive leaps. However, without providing gifted students with access to opportunities to demonstrate their capacities, their teachers will not be able to observe the facility with which they can learn. Limits to opportunities result in limits in achievement.

### Abstraction

For many children with exceptionalities, a major challenge for educators is to provide concrete instruction that avoids ambiguities and abstractions. With children who have gifts, differentiation of instruction requires efforts to allow increased abstraction of principles, ideas, and examples. These students ask a great many more questions, such as

> What if the events in history did not happen?
> Why were the outcomes of the War of 1812 so beneficial to the status quo?
> What would have occurred if steam had become the predominant motorcar fuel in the 1920s?

### Pacing

If the most apparent trait of children identified as gifted is their ability to learn quickly and easily, then the most important implication is that they should be provided a rapid or accelerated pace of instruction. Teachers must be aware of the need to quickly and efficiently assess the current state of learning for their students. They also need to adequately assess this learning and to document it for the next levels of instruction.

### Documenting Achievement

The teacher must prove that the student has met achievement criteria. In our age of accountability, this is difficult. For a third-grade teacher to assure a fourth-grade teacher (or a fifth- or sixth-grade teacher) that a student is truly competent, he must provide very thorough documentation of curriculum compacting and must participate in consultations during the process. It can sometimes be a challenge to collaborate and to document achievement across grade levels.

### Choice and Independence

Nearly every theorist in gifted education suggests that student choice is extremely important. Four variables are key in exercising choice (Treffinger & Barton, 1988):

- Content, or the area of interest to be studied
- Process, or the way one should pursue the investigation
- Product, or the way one will show the results of the investigation
- Evaluation, or the way one will view the success of the investigation

Treffinger and Barton (1988) note that students are not generally encouraged to make choices. Teachers typically provide the content to be studied, the media for learning, and the product to be delivered. Students with gifts and talents, however, should be given these choices.

## Transition to Adult Life

Very little research has been done on the transition to adulthood among those with gifts and talents. The available data are from longitudinal studies of very specific populations of students (e.g., Noble, Subotnik, & Arnold, 1999). Individuals identified as gifted often choose career paths and academic interests early and concentrate on achieving career goals. Others, however, seem paralyzed by the multiplicity of options available, even to the point where they cannot choose. As adults, these individuals often express regret for choices made and options not selected (Berger, 1994).

If we are to assist these students, we need to make them aware of the implications of choices they are making along the way in school and of the fact that as adults they may pursue multiple careers and pathways. A major goal of counseling students with gifts and talents about adulthood is to prepare them for careers and career change.

Providing choices in content as well as how it is studied, represented, and evaluated are critical variables in instruction for students with gifts and talents.

Educators can facilitate transitions to higher levels of academic demand and social expectation through counseling that focuses on (1) early academic guidance and (2) dealing with transition stages.

### Early Academic Guidance

Students with gifts and talents, especially those who are exceptionally capable, benefit from early guidance that points out ways to access the academic pathways open to them. Casey and Shore (2000) noted that these students are often unaware of potential careers and may have choices pressed on them by family or caregivers that are not consistent with their temperament and/or their abilities. Any discussions of accelerative options should also be accompanied by counseling on curricular and adjustment issues. Such guidance and counseling are appropriate considerations for students in upper elementary programs on through early entrants to college and university. Students intending to access more advanced studies will need advice on what preliminary or related coursework to take. They will also benefit from considerations of the potential repercussions of their decisions. Early on, advisors can help easily. As the student becomes more advanced, however, helping becomes more difficult. For example, if a child is doing fourth-grade work in the second grade, the curricular issues and personal challenges are fairly easy to predict. If the student is doing 11th-grade work in middle school, it is more difficult to readily anticipate issues or concerns. A freshman taking graduate courses may baffle the most informed counselor.

As students with gifts and talents advance through the school curriculum and the established grades, it is very important to have a well-written plan that both documents progress and provides a mentor to help navigate each level of schooling. The more these students diverge from "normal" development, the greater the need for explicit planning statements.

### Dealing with Transition Stages

Gifted individuals experience several predictable transition stages. As mentioned, the students may choose dysfunctional ways to redefine themselves. To assist in the transitions, it is important for teachers to help students know that changes are coming, to arm them with awareness of pitfalls, and to help them select constructive ways of dealing with new academic and societal expectations. Counseling for successful transitions for gifted children involves life skills, just as it does for other exceptionalities.

## REFLECTIVE EXERCISE

#7 How can teachers provide choices to students without giving up control over the curriculum?

Like students with other exceptionalities, students with gifts and talents who are transitioning to adulthood often require instruction and counseling in essential life skills.

## PREVAILING ISSUES, CONTROVERSIES, AND IMPLICATIONS FOR THE TEACHER

The most important issues affecting gifted education are related to the difficulties of defining intelligence, creativity, and giftedness. These concepts are critical to defining the nature of giftedness, but researchers show little substantive agreement on what the terms mean. On the other hand, debates about the nature and varieties of intelligence have been constructive. We now have a broader appreciation for the nature of intelligence and a broader view of student needs. More discussion is needed about the concepts of talent and creativity; those issues are even more ill defined than intelligence and giftedness. Unfortunately, the imprecision makes advocacy and programming difficult.

Other factors linked directly to policies concerning gifted students include (1) - declining quality of education and reform; (2) underrepresented groups of students; and (3) accountability.

### Declining Quality of Education and Reform

Demands on schools to be accessible to and successful for all students are increasing. These demands often lead to simplification of curriculum materials for general education (Renzulli & Reis, 1991). The issue is important because high-quality educational programs are at the core of the best gifted education.

The most recent round of educational reform efforts began more than a decade ago in response to general and growing dissatisfaction with public education. While the reforms raise possibilities for improving education for students with gifts and talents, reforms also pose threats. Gallagher (1993) argues that school failure is not only rooted in educational problems. It is also likely to be the result of societal problems. Renzulli and Reis (1991) observe that reform proposals consistently address goals of excellence in achievement for the most promising students and/or goals of equal opportunity and access for disadvantaged and at-risk students. These may be viewed as competing goals. For the teacher, this may cause anxiety or a rejection of one of the other general goals. It does not need to be so. Schools can pursue excellence and rigor for all students.

Teachers are bombarded by reformist calls for the elimination of ability grouping, implementation of cooperative learning, adoption of middle school student–teacher teaming, establishment of master or mentor teachers, institution of site-based

# THE REAL WORLD Challenges and Solutions
## Increasing cultural diversity in gifted programs

*Susan Victor noticed it immediately. Hired to coordinate the gifted education programs for the Central Valley School District, she observed that almost all of the students identified and educated in academically oriented accelerated and enrichment programs were White. Most were from fairly affluent homes where English is the primary if not the only language. Still, Central Valley, like most of our nation, is increasingly multicultural, and Susan knew from her studies that the inclusion of students from diverse cultures in academic programs for gifted students remains an important goal. Clearly, a comprehensive plan of action for the district was necessary and overdue. But, where should she begin?*

In pursuit of greater inclusiveness, three issues are of particular importance: identification, retention, and curriculum. The most important components of these efforts include the following:

- Train teachers to be thoughtful, fair, and watchful in looking for behaviors that indicate precocious learning or potential for achievement or talent in all populations.
- Consider which characteristics tend to hide students in various populations from identification for gifted programs.
- Identify instruments that are the most representative for local populations and curricular offerings.
- Frequently analyze local outcomes of evaluations that include gender, ethnicity, and race, as well as socioeconomic status representations in the identified gifted population.
- Examine the degree to which transportation and other financial demands disenfranchise various culturally and economically diverse groups.
- Consider inequities of opportunities for culturally diverse students to access the logistics and resources of gifted programs.

Susan recognizes that once identification practices are improved, greater efforts must also be made to retain students in programs. Culturally diverse students leave programs at higher rates than do middle-class White students. Many students from culturally diverse backgrounds perceive gifted programs as culturally alien places. When they are included in gifted programs, culturally diverse students often see fewer (if any) students like themselves. It is difficult for them to not have feelings of alienation from more typically identified gifted students. They also may feel pressured to avoid acculturation into White, middle-class expectations and values (Ford & Harris, 2000).

As a consequence, ethnically diverse students leave these programs at rates that accelerate with age. Clearly, if culturally diverse students don't feel welcome, they will not stay.

Susan has found that one way to make culturally diverse students feel welcome is to make the program's curriculum responsive to changing demographics of our nation and to represent varied interests and strengths in programming (Ford & Whiting, 2008). The following contribute to a better fit between student and curriculum:

1. Be inclusive of the groups targeted for differential identification and retention.
2. Ensure that the curriculum samples from experiences of culturally diverse groups.
3. Avoid materials, texts, and activities that are culturally biased.
4. Program appropriate opportunities to express and explore cultural differences among names, experiences, holidays, and literature.
5. Be aware of how cultural differences are related to performance expectations. For example, some groups of children do not feel comfortable in competitive situations, and others may shy away from face-to-face confrontation.
6. Recognize accomplishment but remember that, within some cultures, individual praise may not be perceived as rewarding.

### Valuable Resources for the Teacher

Ford, D. Y., & Grantham, T. C. (2003). Providing access for culturally diverse gifted students: From deficit to dynamic thinking. *Theory into Practice, 42*(3), 217–225.

Ford, D. Y., & Whiting, G. W. (2008). Cultural competence: Preparing gifted students for a diverse society. *Roeper Review, 30,* 104–110.

Harris, B., Rapp, K. E., Martinez, R. S., & Plucker, J. A. (2007). Identifying English language learners for gifted and talented programs: Current practices and recommendations for improvement. *Roeper Review, 29,* 26–29.

### Final Thoughts

Experience with and sensitivity to diverse cultural perspectives yields many benefits and is essential to providing adequate services for students who show evidence of high aptitude. For gifted students from culturally diverse backgrounds, careful and open-minded planning and the selection of relevant curriculum are especially important issues.

management, accountability, and adoption of inclusion policies. Each of these elements of reform has important merits; but unfortunately, as policy initiatives, many are based on misinterpretations and misapplications of the research.

## Underrepresented Groups of Students

As with students from culturally and linguistically diverse backgrounds (see "The Real World"), students who are challenged by economic disadvantage are also hard to identify as having gifts and talents and are difficult to retain in specialized programs. Economically disadvantaged students face disruptions, pressures, and distractions that threaten their educational careers (Maker, 1989). They face greater demands to work in order to support their own financial needs and perhaps the needs of their families. It is important for teachers to be aware of these problems and to encourage and assist in retention.

Students with gifts and talents who also have disabilities represent another group that is seriously underserved. These students can be difficult to identify, and their unique programming needs can be difficult to meet in gifted programs. The disability need not result in a decrease in ability or aptitude, but it may necessitate alternate approaches to assessment and instruction. All teachers need to separate the disability from the underlying gifts. Some children actually use their gifts and talents to mask their disabilities in other areas.

## Accountability

Providing for the special educational needs of students with gifts and talents requires expenditures of time and resources. It is important to base gifted education programs on defensible service models. Educators should also evaluate local implementations of gifted education programs to determine their effectiveness. It is important to evaluate instructional arrangements that involve high-ability students but are not specifically designed for their benefit—particularly if the application is potentially controversial. For example, cooperative learning is a widely recommended practice in general education classrooms (Slavin, Hurley, & Chamberlain, 2003), but discussions in the literature suggest that it is a controversial arrangement for gifted students (Patrick, Bangel, Jeon, & Townsend, 2005; Robinson, 1990). The fact is that cooperative learning arrangements are applied in general education programs, and high-achieving students are included. The challenge for teachers is to make data-based decisions about implementing any educational option.

# 15 SUMMARY

Students with gifts and talents have demonstrated or show potential for achieving knowledge and skills at significantly higher levels and at faster rates than their age-level peers. The tasks for teachers are the same as the tasks of educators of students with other special learning needs. Gifted children must be identified; decisions must be made about what and how they should be taught. Their progress needs to be evaluated and planned for.

## Definitions and Classification Criteria

- Three common definitions of giftedness are the Marland federal definition, Renzulli's three-ring conceptualization, and Gardner's multiple intelligences approach.
- Giftedness is usually classified by (1) types of gifts and talents and (2) level of giftedness.

## Primary Behavioral Characteristics

- Early conceptualizations of giftedness were flawed and perpetuated mistaken stereotypes of individuals with superior mental health or of people who were physically weak, oversensitive, and highly productive.
- Current studies have found that students with gifts and talents vary greatly and have a range of positive and negative traits and patterns of behavior.
- As students with gifts progress in school, a major challenge is redefining their life roles, clarifying aspirations, and selecting careers.

## Prevalence and Causal Factors

- Prevalence rates of students with gifts and talents vary widely and typically range from 5% to 20% of the school-age population.

- Although speculations as to where giftedness comes from remain controversial, most believe that it is rooted in a genetic/environmental interaction.

### Identification and Assessment

- Standardized intelligence tests alone are not useful for identifying students who could benefit from gifted programming.
- The most useful identification processes use multiple criteria that supplement intelligence tests with achievement tests, creativity tests, teacher nominations, peer nominations, parent nominations, student self-nominations, and product samples.

### Educational Practices

- Early intervention for students with gifts and talents is rare and usually provided to those with prodigious achievement.
- The decision to offer accelerative or enrichment options for students in school revolves around five factors: adequacy of the general education curriculum, ability of students to handle demands, risk of separation from age-related peers, skepticism about acceleration, and the risk of missing instruction.
- Successful academic interventions for students with gifts and talents focus on content, complexity, abstraction, pacing, documenting achievement, and choice and independence.
- Transitions to higher levels of academic demand are facilitated by counseling that focuses on early academic guidance, awareness of self-perception, and strategies for dealing with change.

### Prevailing Issues

- The most important issues affecting the education of students with gifts and talents relate to the difficulties inherent in defining intelligence and creativity.
- Factors influencing policies toward the education of students with gifts and talents include the declining quality of general education and school reform efforts, underrepresentation of certain groups among those identified as having gifts and talents, and accountability.

## ADDRESSING THE PROFESSIONAL STANDARDS

Council for Exceptional Children (CEC) Knowledge Standards addressed in the chapter:

ICC1K5, GC1K1, GC4K5, ICC4S3, ICC5K4, GC7S2, ICC10S2

Appendix B: CEC Knowledge and Skill Standards Common Core has a full listing of the standards referenced here.

**myeducationlab** PEARSON

Now go to Topic 17: Gifted & Talented in the MyEducationLab for your course, where you can:

- Find learning outcomes for the broad concepts covered in this chapter along with the national standards that connect to these outcomes.
- Complete Assignments and Activities that can help you more deeply understand the chapter content.
- Apply and practice your understanding of the core concepts and skills identified in the chapter with the Building Teaching Skills and Dispositions learning units.

- Check your comprehension on the content covered in the chapter by going to the Study Plan in the Book-Specific Resources section for your text. Here you will be able to take a chapter quiz, receive feedback on your answers, and then access Review, Practice, and Enrichment activities to enhance your understanding of chapter content.
- Access video clips of CCSSO National Teachers of the Year award winners responding to the questions, "Why Do I Teach?" in the Teacher Talk section.

# A Successful Career

## Growing in Your Profession

part four

chapter

# 16

# Continuing a Successful Career

## Professionalism, Effective Instruction, and Reflection

**REFLECT UPON**

- What activities and actions help beginning teachers develop into special education professionals?
- What key elements of support help new special education teachers navigate early career development?
- What actions can new teachers of students with disabilities take to contribute, maintain, and represent ongoing personal and professional growth?
- What strategies help keep special educators invigorated and committed to their students and profession?

"Highly effective special education teachers recognize that their initial preparation is just the start of their professional development. Reading the current literature, attending conferences sponsored by professional organizations, listening to students' family members, and interacting with other experienced educators are all opportunities for beginning teachers to hone their craft and better serve their students."

Michael S. Rosenberg

"The most effective special education teachers are those who can effectively manage the educational system so that the needs of students with disabilities are met using effective practices. This is often a very difficult task that is unique for each student and requires teachers to continually learn and grow as professionals. Professional educators engage in this work for one reason—they care so deeply for each child they serve."

James McLeskey

"Being an effective professional is a life style, not a life outcome. To become an effective professional, a teacher needs to view learning as an ongoing process. One of the most interesting things about teaching students with special needs is that one student's needs can be very different from those of another. This requires you to seek out new opportunities to learn so that you can be an effective educator for all of the students you teach. Undoubtedly, your experience will give you an invaluable set of tools to succeed in the classroom, but you also need to take advantage of more formal opportunities to learn."

David L. Westling

As we begin this final chapter of the text, we would like you to reflect back to several of the more personal topics presented in Chapter 1. Recall that we introduced the themes of professionalism, effective instruction, and reflection; presented what is special about special education; and highlighted the roles, responsibilities, and work settings typical of special education teachers. Most important, we highlighted the keys to being a good teacher of all students—attributes, dispositions, attitudes, and characteristics—that are prerequisites for a successful teaching career. For example, we emphasized that effective teachers value diversity and recognize that it is their responsibility to teach all students regardless of needs or challenging conditions. We concluded the chapter by asking you to reflect on whether providing service to others, helping influence the lives of young people, and improving society could provide you with the personal satisfaction you might want in a career.

In the other chapters of the text, we introduced you to exceptional special educators. We illustrated how individuals with the appropriate personal qualities find their roles and experience the rewards of teaching students with various

Many beginning teachers experience difficulties due to feelings of isolation, confusion about role expectations, and excessive paperwork.

REFLECTIVE EXERCISE

# 1 Put yourself in the role of a committee member seeking to fill several special education teaching positions in your school district. What essential qualities, characteristics, and dispositions are you looking for in applicants?

PEARSON
**myeducationlab**

To check your comprehension on the content covered in Chapter 16, go to the Book-Specific Resources section in the MyEducationLab for your course, select your text, and complete the Study Plan. Here you will be able to take a chapter quiz, receive feedback on your answers, and then access Review, Practice, and Enrichment activities to enhance your understanding of chapter content.

"My colleagues tell me that my students tend to take on certain parts of my personality. If true, this is quite satisfying. I present a very strong work ethic, and my students reflect this in their work and when they advocate for themselves."

Monique Green, Prince Georges County, Maryland

disabilities. Our goal was to encourage those of you with the appropriate dispositions to consider a career in special education. Our hope was that you may continue pursuing this career path, taking more content-specific courses, participating in a variety of field experiences, engaging in relevant professional development, and eventually entering the classroom as a teacher. For those already teaching, perhaps we have provided you with some information on how to better serve your students and navigate through the demanding situations typical of a quick start in the classroom.

Whatever your situation, you know or will soon realize that the first years of teaching students with special education needs is challenging. Many preservice and beginning teachers have difficulties because of (1) feelings of isolation; (2) confusion regarding roles and responsibilities; and (3) work-related issues such as excessive paperwork and limited planning time (see Billingsley, 2005; Gersten, Keating, Yovanoff, & Harniss, 2001; Griffin, Kilgore, Winn, Otis-Wilborn, Hou, & Garvan, 2009; Kozleski, Mainzer, & Deshler, 2000). Some people—in fact, far too many—leave the profession completely, but you do not have to be part of this group. Those considering or beginning a career in special education help themselves by participating actively in their own professional growth and well-being. Those who thrive in the classroom understand what it means to be a professional, are aware of the supports available to help them succeed, take charge of their ongoing growth and development, and use proactive strategies to remain invigorated and enthusiastic.

## BECOMING A SPECIAL EDUCATION PROFESSIONAL

Broadly defined, **professionalism** is an inclusive pattern of behavior that includes respect, responsibility, communication, leadership, risk taking, ongoing development, and a positive attitude (see Connelly & Rosenberg, 2009; Grouse, 2003; Kramer, 2003; Phelps, 2006). Professional behavior involves persevering in the face of intermittent successes and remaining poised when encountering frustrating situations. Let's consider the variety of ways in which one develops as a professional.

### Developing Proficiency

Professions are knowledge-based occupations requiring specialized expertise. Professionals recognize that initial preparation alone is not sufficient for professional success. Teachers develop professionally by consistently enhancing their content expertise and instructional delivery skills. Areas in which teachers regularly seek to improve their proficiency include the following:

- Assess for diversity of learning styles and levels of competence among students.
- Expand their knowledge of evidence-based practices.
- Develop meaningful learning activities that bring curricular objectives, concepts, and learning principles to life.
- Provide adaptations, supports, and **assistive technology** to learners who require specialized accommodations.
- Manage the learning environment in a positive manner, ensuring that all students have an opportunity to access instruction.
- Deliver instruction in a culturally responsive fashion.

### Caring for Students and Families

Professional special educators demonstrate explicitly that they care for their students. Caring—responding regularly to the physical and emotional needs of children—facilitates and complements instruction. Caring teachers remain vigilant about in-school and out-of-school factors that impede student success. This awareness is as simple as recognizing the best time to provide a mid-morning break from reading activities to more complicated and diplomatic matters such as alerting families to free breakfast and lunch programs. On rare occasions, caring teachers have the troubling task of reporting instances of child abuse and neglect. Caring also involves advocacy for the legal rights of students with disabilities, ensuring that due process protections are honored and mandated services delivered.

When it comes to caring interactions with families, teachers communicate "more in attitude than hours" (Rosenberg, O'Shea, & O'Shea, 2006, p. 311). Connecting successfully with parents requires a host of interpersonal communication skills such as effective listening, nonjudgmental questioning, flexibility, and compromise. Through open, honest, and positive discussions designed to promote school–home coordination, professional teachers dispel the often-held perception that only appreciative, flattering, uncritical, and noninterfering interactions are welcome at school.

## Being a Public Figure

Inherent in developing professionally is recognizing that teachers are always in the public eye. What you do and how you act, both inside and outside the classroom, are topics of discussion around countless family dinner tables and community social events. Teachers are positive ambassadors to the public, highlighting the accomplishments of the school-based learning team, being responsive to parent and community concerns, and serving as sources of information (Feiman-Nemser & Floden, 1986; Kauchak & Eggen, 2005). Never underestimate the value and trust that the public places on teacher communication. Most American parents consider their child's teacher a most credible source of information on educational issues, well ahead of clergy and members of the media (Richardson, 1999). Moreover, parents in crisis over the care and safety of their children depend on the responsiveness of well-informed educators.

## Addressing Paperwork and Legal Responsibilities

Most educators agree that the paperwork requirements associated with teaching students with disabilities are excessive and burdensome. In fact, many report that they spend more time on legal and compliance paperwork than on directly teaching students with disabilities (President's Commission on Excellence in Special Education, 2002). Teachers are typically responsible for (1) screening and prereferral documentation; (2) documentation of student progress; (3) formal and informal assessments; (4) eligibility and placement information; (5) individuallzed education programs (IEPs); and (6) functional behavior assessments (FBAs). These are useful documents that contribute to the creation of effective learning environments for students and an organized workplace for adults (Rosenberg et al., 2006). Because the completion of important documentation requires attention, patience, and effort, a

## REFLECTIVE EXERCISE

#2 How can you distinguish a teacher who cares for students from one who does not? Can caring be taught in a teacher preparation program, or do you believe it is a disposition or character trait that one must have before entering teaching?

"Students need to know that their teachers care for them and respect them as individuals. I try to speak informally with each of my students throughout the day, seeking to build positive relationships. I have found that these brief interactions are an important precondition for motivation, achievement, and appropriate behavior."

Bobby Biddle, science teacher, Herndon Middle School, Fairfax County, Virginia

A professional approach to paperwork management requires patience, attention, and the use of organizational supports such as electronic case management software programs.

Special education teachers often cite the considerable paperwork as one reason for leaving the profession. What aspects of documentation can be reduced without endangering legal compliance? What specific time-management strategies can teachers use to minimize the impact of paperwork and documentation on instructional time?

professional approach to paperwork management is warranted (Billingsley, 2005; Kozleski et al., 2000; Rosenberg et al., 2006):

- Remain aware of required paperwork and frequently updated forms.
- Develop a plan for handling paperwork. Organize and review due dates and multiple requests to ensure necessity, clarify requirements, and eliminate redundancy.
- Delegate, whenever possible, routine clerical tasks to support personnel.
- Use technology and data-based software to organize relevant student data and facilitate report preparation. Electronic case-management tools can assist with record keeping, data analysis, and the monitoring of instructional accommodations.
- Develop and use standardized tools and universal design to record and document student performance.

Teachers are legally responsible for their students. **In loco parentis**—the same judgment and care exercised by parents in protecting their children—is the legal principle used to assess the extent of a teacher's professional responsibility for students' well-being. If teachers fail to protect students from injury, they are considered negligent and, with their school districts, subject to legal actions (Kauchak & Eggen, 2005). Accidents happen whenever groups of active children share a common space. However, because of their behavioral profiles, students with disabilities have an increased probability of mishaps. In addition to purchasing liability insurance (which is recommended and often offered by professional teaching associations; see Figure 16.1),

FIGURE 16.1 • **IS THERE A NEED FOR LIABILITY INSURANCE?**

Accidents and mistakes will happen, and working with challenging students can increase the probability that things may go wrong. For better or worse, there is little doubt that we live in an increasingly litigious society. From formal courtrooms to reality-based television shows, large numbers of citizens are seeking legal restitution for actions perceived as offensive, wrongful, and injurious. Regardless of how we feel about the role of malpractice lawsuits in public schools, teachers are liable for the care of their students and may be subject to legal action if students are injured. Recent data suggest that the number of lawsuits against educators has increased more than 270% in the past decade; in fact, more than 1/3 of all high school principals report having been involved in a lawsuit. Parents, students, and even colleagues may use the legal system if they feel they have been injured because of another educator's actions.

Although most school districts have liability insurance, many professional organizations, education law experts, and, not surprisingly, insurance vendors recommend that all educators consider obtaining additional liability insurance (Henderson, Gullatt, Hardin, Jannik, & Tollett, 1999). Without individual coverage, a  teacher would have no choice but to rely on the district's policies and procedures for dealing with liability and could be personally liable if the district's policy is not comprehensive. Determine your need for liability insurance:

- Review the extent of coverage provided by your districts and teacher's association.
- Determine the extent of the school's policy to provide legal representation.
- Assess your exposure to risk. For example, consider the extent of your responsibilities for supervision of challenging students who are prone to injury due to reckless behavior.
- Review the nature of your supervisory responsibilities.
- Determine how much your clinical judgment and decision making may be challenged by others.
- Assess your own emotional reactions to risk and possible legal exposure.

Keep in mind that most liability insurance plans provide up to 2 million dollars in coverage for relatively small premiums. However, most plans do not include criminal actions and corporal punishment where forbidden by law.

teacher can take several precautions to minimize risk (Kauchak & Eggen, 2005; Westling & Koorland, 1988). First and foremost, try to anticipate troubling and dangerous circumstances, and make every effort to protect students from such situations. One way is to establish and reinforce concrete rules and procedures that prompt students about potentially dangerous situations. Second, professionalism involves delivering a standard of care that corresponds to the environment, situation, and characteristics of your students. For example, taking students with severe developmental disabilities on a field trip to the mall food court requires structures, support, and supervision of much greater intensity than would be provided to typical high school students eating in their school's cafeteria.

To minimize accidents, teachers should anticipate troubling and dangerous circumstances and make every effort to protect students from such situations.

## Seeing Schools as Integrated Systems of Care

We have emphasized throughout this text that educating students with disabilities (and many without disabilities) requires more than effective academic instruction. To benefit from their education, many students require related services. Consequently, some schools have established school-based, cross-agency systems designed to deliver a comprehensive spectrum of health, mental health, and other necessary services in a coordinated fashion. These activities require teachers to collaborate professionally with other stakeholders who deliver services to students with disabilities, including school-based mental health clinicians, social workers, juvenile justice personnel, and medical professionals. The ancillary activities provided by these specialists are essential for students, and schools are a logical location for coordinating service delivery (Weist, Goldstein, Morris, & Bryant, 2003; Woodruff et al., 1998). These additional responsibilities increase already heavy teacher workloads and reduce time for planning, instruction, and recharging one's batteries. Professional teachers recognize the necessity of these additional demands and account for them within their time-management activities.

"In addition to unique talents, most of my students present unique challenges, particularly in the areas of parent and emotional support. I have found it extremely useful to use community, state, and national resources to meet the needs of these diverse learners."

Julie Lenner, teacher of students with gifts and talents, Sandusky, Ohio

### REFLECTIVE EXERCISE

#4 In earlier chapters we highlighted why wraparound programming is an essential feature of school programs for students with emotional and behavioral disabilities. How can viewing the neighborhood school as an integrated system of care promote the delivery of wraparound services to all students? How can teachers ensure that involvement in the coordination of services does not cut into instructional time?

## Being an Educated Consumer of Evidence-Based Practices

As you have read this text, you have noticed that the knowledge base for addressing learning and behavioral difficulties is substantial and useful. Unfortunately, far too few teachers apply this knowledge with consistency and regularity. Educational research is not viewed as trustworthy, readily accessible, or relevant to many

teachers' daily experiences (Kauffman, 1996; Kennedy, 1997). Consequently, empirical evidence is often ignored, and anecdote and appearance influence the selection of instructional practices. When research-based practices are employed, they are too often adapted rather than adopted. Steps in instructional protocols are modified to fit an individual teacher's values, beliefs, and situations rather than applied as intended. Unfortunately, these changes often alter components of the intervention that make it successful.

Putting research into practice can be challenging. However, increased knowledge and use of validated practices are signs of increased professionalism and occur when teachers do the following (Abbott et al., 1999; Fuchs & Fuchs, 1998; Rolewski, 2008):

One important indicator of professionalism is the pursuit of increased knowledge of evidence-based practices.

- Keep up with the relevant literature and participate in educational research activities.
- Remain educated and skeptical consumers of proposed curricular materials and content-area programs.
- Advocate for data-based decision making when making curricular decisions.
- Recognize that teaching is both an art and a science, requiring a balance between creativity and fidelity to evidence-based practices.
- Develop action research activities that allow for the data-based evaluation of classroom techniques and interventions.
- Employ strategies to overcome the obstacles that can preclude implementing evidence-based practices.

## COLLABORATIVE SUPPORT FOR BEGINNING TEACHERS

PEARSON
**myeducationlab**

Go to the IRIS Center Resources section of Topic 2: Collaboration & Co-Teaching in the MyEducationLab for your course and Complete the Case Study entitled *Beginning Teacher Support*.

Even the most enthusiastic, idealistic, and well-prepared teachers of students with disabilities experience pressure, frustration, and periods of disillusionment. These feelings are natural. Students present a wide range of complex academic and behavioral challenges, the roles and responsibilities of addressing student needs are not always well defined, and teachers seldom have enough time for adequate planning or coordination. You will undoubtedly hear from many veteran teachers that early career challenges shaped their future attitudes, practices, and path to professionalism. How can you survive the mental bumps, bruises, peaks, and valleys typical of early career development? What support systems are available to assist beginning teachers? How can you access this support?

### Support Through Learning Communities

In past years, teaching was a career characterized by rugged individualism: one knowledgeable adult responsible for the development of students in her charge. Isolated teachers were expected to handle their own classrooms and address learning and behavior problems with little assistance from others. Recent research on effective schools has found that individual teacher effectiveness is dependent on a collaborative, supportive, and encouraging professional learning community

(Hord, 2009; Louis, Marks, & Kruse, 1996). Not surprisingly, education is now placing greater emphasis on educators working together in purposeful groupings or communities.

Professional learning communities share five characteristics: supportive and shared leadership; collective learning; shared values and vision; supportive conditions in human and physical resources; and shared practice (Hord, 1997). Rather than feeling isolated, misunderstood, or not valued—reasons why many teachers leave the field—teachers in professional learning communities have a shared sense of empowerment and purpose. Members of the community believe they are useful and valued contributors to efforts that lead to student achievement.

Keep in mind, however, that learning communities have their costs. Participation requires time, commitment, diplomacy, and patience. As members of a learning community, teachers are expected to serve on committees, observe their colleagues, be observed by others, as well as participate in FBAs and behavior intervention plans (BIPs). Nonetheless, the benefits of having a professional learning community are usually worth the effort and energy. Schools that are challenging, satisfying, empowering, creative, and growth-oriented for adults achieve good outcomes for students (Saphier, 1995).

## Support Through Induction and Mentoring

Knowing that beginning teachers are both a valuable and fragile resource, many school district administrators have enhanced their induction activities and programs, which are support mechanisms geared to the needs of those new to the field. Characteristics of high-quality **induction** activities include (1) a supportive school culture in which veteran educators are committed to socializing new teachers; (2) frequent opportunities for interactions, including mentoring, between new and experienced teachers; (3) targeted professional development opportunities aimed at improving new teacher performance; and (4) graduated adjustments in the complexity and difficulty of tasks assigned to the beginning teacher (Billingsley, 2005; Griffin, Winn, Otis-Wilborn, & Kilgore, 2003; White & Mason, 2006).

> "Early in my career I came to the realization that I didn't have all of the answers and that I needed a lot more help. Thankfully, I worked with a mentor and co-teacher who was knowledgeable and patient. I learned so much from her."
>
> Carol Sprague, Thomas County, Georgia

The most powerful component in an induction program is the direct contact new teachers have with colleagues. New teachers crave purposeful contact with both experienced teachers and other beginners in similar situations. These opportunities can be a formal, comprehensive, one-to-one mentorship arrangement or part of an overall school- or peer-support team. Effective mentorship and peer-support programs share certain elements. First, ample opportunities exist to take part in problem solving and conflict-resolution team activities. Integrated into these activities is an ethic of care, characterized by frequent opportunities for dialogue, reflection, cooperation, questioning, and validation—ingredients essential in effective teams.

Second, successful induction programs give adequate attention to the emotional needs of the new teacher. Novice teachers require trusted guides and confidants, successful mentors who are supportive and empathetic rather than evaluative. Effective mentors and peers create a welcoming school environment, make frequent use of informal meetings, and provide a safe zone for beginning teachers to deal with stress, vent frustrations, and secure emotional first aid. Finally, effective mentorship activities allow novice teachers to acquire system information, the nuts and bolts of responding to school and district responsibilities and securing resources and materials (Whitaker, 2000).

**PEARSON**
**myeducationlab**

To learn more about how collaboration can effectively meet the academic needs of sudents school-wide, go to the IRIS Center Resources section of Topic 2: Collaboration & Co-Teaching in the MyEducationLab for your course and complete the Module entitled *Effective School Practices*.

You can make the most of available induction and mentoring activities by doing the following (Billingsley, 2005; Lee et al., 2006; Rosenberg, Griffin, Kilgore, & Carpenter, 1997; Rosenberg et al., 2006):

- **Get ready for mentor–mentee activities.** Consider what is expected of your role in the mentoring relationship. Reflect on how you can best build and sustain an effective, productive working relationship.
- **Attend all district, school, and department orientation meetings.** These meetings focus on general and special education policies and procedures and provide a forum for understanding the roles and responsibilities of key personnel in the school.
- **Recognize the competence of colleagues.** New teachers discover quickly that many of their colleagues—teachers, administrators, and related-service personnel—have their own ways of doing things. In some cases they contradict what you believe or how you were taught. Remain diplomatic. Rather than shutting these individuals out, recognize that much can be learned by understanding why certain professionals act in the manner that they do.
- **Communicate willingness for consultative services.** Consider all forms of assistance as a benefit provided by your school. Be aware that input from colleagues and related-service professionals will help you and your students. For example, veteran teachers and behavior specialists provide useful suggestions about discipline plans, and speech–language pathologists suggest ways to integrate communication strategies into instruction.
- **Reflect on feedback constructively.** It is difficult to avoid being defensive when presented with alternative ways of approaching your job. Nonetheless, when presented with constructive criticism, open your mind to new ideas by listening carefully and reflecting on the information being conveyed. No one expects perfection during the beginning years of a teaching career, and improvements in practice require feedback, reflection, and change.
- **Understand and respect school culture.** Schools are microcosms of society; and appropriately or not, people socialized to the school's existing culture make value judgments about newcomers, sometimes superficially. Remain patient with those who seek to overwhelm you with advice about how to reach your challenging students, and avoid flaunting your own knowledge of innovative practices, especially when no one asks your advice. Focus on the positive aspects of school culture, and avoid being soured by cynics who appear disillusioned, apathetic, and worn out.

## Support Through Collaborative Consultation and Teaming

Collaborative consultation is another structured opportunity to learn from other professionals engaged in work similar to your own. Collaborative practices may take many forms but most often occur through teacher-to-teacher consultation or in collaborative groups.

### Teacher-to-Teacher Consultation

Support through teacher-to-teacher consultation typically focuses on everyday classroom concerns (e.g., managing the behavior of disruptive students, developing alternative methods of teaching a child long division, best practices for assessing academic content of resistant students). Collaborative consultation is more than casually talking with another teacher in the hallway or teachers' lounge. It is a formal process that includes (1) specific problem identification and goal setting; (2) analysis of factors contributing to the problem and brainstorming possible problem-solving interventions; (3) planning an intervention; and (4) evaluating the outcomes (Griffin & Pugach, 2007; Salend, 2005).

**REFLECTIVE EXERCISE**

**#5** Why has teaching evolved from an isolated endeavor to a collaborative enterprise? How are the steps involved in collaborative consultation similar to other group problem-solving tasks, such as the development of functional behavior analyses?

Teacher-to-teacher consultation appears direct and straightforward. However, for the process to work, those involved must employ effective interpersonal communication skills. By interpersonal communication skills, we are referring to the processes of active listening, picking up nonverbal signals, effective and appropriate questioning, talking in nonthreatening ways, and expressing ideas clearly (Friend & Cook, 2010). Keep in mind that attitudinal factors contribute greatly to interpersonal communication (Rogers, 1965). For example, participants should convey positive regard for others—typically demonstrated through the delivery of honest feedback and specific, descriptive encouragement—during all facets of the process. Second, empathy (understanding and concern about what the other person is going through) is an essential part of the process. Finally, effective interpersonal communication requires frequent efforts to monitor congruence—the degree to which a collaborator's perceptions actually correspond to the situation being experienced by the other person. When stakeholders agree on the patterns of troublesome situations, a greater opportunity exists for honest, sincere, and productive discussions (Rosenberg et al., 2006).

### Collaborative Teaming

Collaboration also occurs as part of teacher-assistance problem-solving teams (Chalfant & Pysh, 1989; Papalia-Berardi & Hall, 2007). These teams follow steps similar to those used in teacher-to-teacher collaboration but involve groups of professionals with different types of expertise. This process provides the teacher with possible interventions for a given student situation, allowing increased opportunities for supportive activities such as classroom observations and group brainstorming.

Collaborative teams, which are often used to address schoolwide issues such as discipline and inclusion, ensure that the shared expertise of multiple professionals is integrated into the important everyday activities of the school and classroom (McLeskey & Waldron, 2000, 2002; Rosenberg & Jackman, 2003). Friend and Bursuck (2006) characterize effective collaborative teams as formal work groups that "have clear goals, active and committed members, and leaders; they practice to achieve their results; and they do not let personal issues interfere with the accomplishment of their goals" (p. 90). Successful teams share the same goal: ensuring that teachers (and other professionals) share their expertise to develop the best possible educational system that effectively meets the needs of all students.

### Support from Paraprofessionals

Many teachers of students with disabilities have the benefit of paraprofessional assistance. Paraprofessionals (1) assist teachers in delivering effective educational programs; (2) provide opportunities for flexible grouping by increasing the adult–student ratio in the classroom; (3) provide additional pairs of eyes to monitor behavior and academic performance; (4) contribute to completion of data-collection and accountability requirements; and (5) perform numerous important and time-consuming noninstructional tasks. In the teacher–paraprofessional relationship, the teacher is responsible for supervising and managing the paraprofessional, a role that few teachers are formally prepared to undertake (French, 2001).

Effective teachers treat paraprofessionals as valued members of the educational team and assign tasks in a fair and respectful manner.

How can you maximize the effectiveness of paraprofessional support? Most experts (Doyle, 2002; French & Pickett, 1997; Hague & Babkie, 2006; Wallace, Bernhardt, & Utermarck, 1999; Warger, 2002; Westling & Koorland, 1988) agree that a productive teacher–paraprofessional relationship involves the following:

- Understand and respect the roles and responsibilities of paraprofessionals.
- Clearly articulate expectations and provide guidance, mentoring, and support.
- Be diplomatic; model and maintain effective communication, and provide positive feedback for tasks completed appropriately.
- Assign tasks in a fair and reasonable manner; model how the task is to be completed.
- Share relevant information about students with the paraprofessional.
- Treat the individual as a valued member of the educational team by encouraging the sharing of observations, suggestions, and concerns.
- Schedule private opportunities to provide formal feedback of paraprofessional performance, and never criticize the paraprofessional in front of students or colleagues.

# PROFESSIONAL GROWTH AND PERSONAL DEVELOPMENT

The pursuit of success and satisfaction in teaching is a marathon rather than sprint, and those pursuing long-term careers take an active role in their own progress. How can you support yourself and facilitate your own personal and professional growth? Four areas typically require ongoing attention: being resilient, recognizing and managing stress, maintaining highly qualified status, and monitoring and documenting professional growth.

## Being Resilient: Managing the Ups and Downs of Teaching

When you work with students with special needs, you will have days when you feel ineffectual and question your decision to become a teacher. During these down times, you may doubt that you have any positive influence on your students and focus on the negative aspects of your career choice. Fortunately, on other days you will feel on top of the world, confident in your abilities to meet the social and academic needs of your students. At these times, you will experience **self-efficacy**, the belief that your professional decisions, actions, and choices result in positive outcomes in your students' lives.

Early in your career, the down days may seem to outnumber the high self-efficacy days. Consequently, it is important to remember two factors. First, events unrelated to job performance often influence a teacher's attitudes and feelings. Second, days of doubt and unease are part of the human condition. Elements such as health, family circumstances, current world events, and even the weather affect our moods and dispositions (Knowles, Cole, & Presswood, 1994). Although these pressures are always present in one form or another, the extreme emotional ups and downs will diminish over time. As teachers gain experience and learn from missteps, the frequency and intensity of hardships fade, and instances of success take their place.

Resiliency is the process of adjusting to varied situations and increasing competence in the face of adverse conditions (Gordon & Coscarelli, 1996). Strategies that contribute to the development of resiliency in teachers include the following (Billingsley, 2005; Bobek, 2002; Harvey, 2007):

- Develop and maintain significant relationships with others who value teaching, and who communicate honestly and openly, understand the challenges associated with teaching, and offer tangible suggestions for dealing with problem situations.

- Refer back, reflect upon, and make use of content and pedagogical skills acquired during professional training.
- Acknowledge your distinct contributions to your students' success, recognize that external recognitions of effort are infrequent, and remind yourself that your actions are instrumental in promoting positive student outcomes.
- Establish realistic expectations for yourself and your students; be aware that the rewards of teaching students with disabilities are often small and incremental.
- Work at a reasonable pace, employ time-management strategies, and celebrate all of the little victories associated with your work.
- Maintain a sense of humor; recognize that humor diffuses tense situations in the classroom and serves as a method for venting frustrations during and after challenging situations.

**REFLECTIVE EXERCISE**

**#6** Knowing the importance of navigating through the ups and downs of teaching students with disabilities, how would you advise a colleague who wants to improve his level of resiliency?

## Recognizing and Managing Stress

As resiliency promotes performance during adverse circumstances, excessive stress produces a series of psychological and physiological responses that inhibits effective actions. All classrooms, regardless of the number of special, at-risk, or typically achieving students, produce organizational pressures that heighten the stress level of teachers. Doyle (1986) has characterized the classroom as a public forum where the teacher is always on stage, responding with limited resources to multiple, immediate, simultaneous, and sometimes unpredictable demands. Although early recognition of the organizational pressures of the classroom can minimize stress, many teachers who work in special education have reported additional pressures—work assignment problems, role definition, feelings of isolation, minimal support—as persistent sources of stress.

Stress has specific signs and signals, some obvious and others so subtle they may be unrecognizable (see Figure 16.2). Still, teachers can minimize the stress associated with working with students with disabilities: The keys are maintaining flexibility and taking care of your physical and mental health. First and foremost, expect the unexpected. Westling and Koorland (1988) note that, in busy classrooms, events requiring immediate action and attention will

> "I make every effort not to bring the stress of teaching home with me. I navigate the tough days by reminding myself that Steve Kennedy and I provide hope and success in an environment of fairness and respect. I reflect on how what we do is important, and it gets me fired up to come back and try new methods to reach the kids."
>
> Steve Williams, Leesburg, Virginia

FIGURE 16.2 • **OBVIOUS AND SUBTLE SIGNS OF STRESS**

Obvious Indicators
- Avoidance of work
- Apathy toward students and responsibilities
- Withdrawal from colleagues
- High rate of negative self-statements regarding work and self-efficacy
- Lack of effort and perfunctory performance
- Frequent physical ailments (headaches, stomachaches, etc.)

Subtle Indicators
- Irritability with family and colleagues
- Inability to concentrate for sustained periods of time
- Decreased productivity
- Increased eating, smoking, and drinking
- Feeling bored and exhausted
- Appearing rigid and angry

happen; and unfortunately, they occur when you least think they will. Second, prepare in advance for stressful events by employing time-management strategies: Plan time for specific assignments, do not overcommit, monitor how you spend your time, and make sure to build periods of rest and reflection into your day. Finally, maintain a balanced and healthy lifestyle. Physically, stress can be managed through exercise, adequate amounts of sleep, a healthy diet, and self-verbalizations that emphasize the positive side of situations and events.

## Becoming and Remaining Highly Qualified

The requirements of the No Child Left Behind Act have many special education teachers asking a clear and direct question: What does it take to become and remain a highly qualified teacher? Unfortunately, the answer is not nearly as straightforward as the question. In past years, teachers completed an approved course of study, obtained state certification and licensure in their area of expertise, and maintained their skills and knowledge through various forms of ongoing professional development. For the most part, professional development activities were based on standards, guidelines, and requirements set by professional organizations, state education agencies, and local boards of education. Teachers' self-reflection also influenced the selection of activities. Today, the legal definition of what it means to be a highly qualified teacher drives many teachers' thoughts of professional development. Becoming and remaining highly qualified requires an understanding of teaching standards, tests, the high objective uniform state standard of evaluation (HOUSSE), and professional development alternatives (see Figure 16.3).

### Professional Teaching Standards

When we speak of professional teaching standards, we are referring to what a teacher should know and what she should be able to do (Galluzzo, 1999). Few in the educational establishment disagree with the need for professional teaching standards; they represent tangible benchmarks for initial and continual professional

FIGURE 16.3 • **BECOMING A HIGHLY QUALIFIED SPECIAL EDUCATION TEACHER**

Concurrent with the passage of NCLB and the most recent reauthorization of IDEA, there has been an increase in confusion as to what constitutes a highly qualified special education teacher. Although some professional organizations (e.g., National Education Association, National Association of State Directors of Special Education) have advocated that a special educator should be considered highly qualified if licensed or certified, special education is not recognized as a core academic subject area. Consequently, additional requirements must be met for a special educator to be considered highly qualified. How can a teacher determine his highly qualified status? Consider the following guidelines developed by NEA and NASDSE (2004):

- The highly qualified requirements apply only to those teachers who provide instruction in core academic subjects; those who provide consultative services (e.g., adapt materials, develop academic and behavioral supports and accommodations) to other highly qualified subject-area teachers do not need subject-matter competency.
- Elementary special education teachers who provide content-area instruction must either pass a state test of subject knowledge and teaching skills in reading, writing, math, and other areas of the basic elementary school curriculum or demonstrate competence in core subject areas by completing a state's HOUSSE.
- Secondary special education teachers who teach subject-area content such as math, science, history, etc., must have had an academic major of coursework equivalent to a major in each of the subjects taught, pass a test determined by their state in each of the areas, or complete HOUSSE requirements within a state-approved time period.

development. Four sets of performance standards are most relevant for those who teach students with disabilities (Dudzinski, Roszmann-Millican, & Shank, 2000):

1. **Interstate New Teacher Assessment and Support Consortium (INTASC).** INTASC standards specify the knowledge, dispositions, and performance indicators for all beginning teachers regardless of content area or grade level. Adopted in 33 states, the core elements of the 10 principles of the standards include subject-matter knowledge, child development, varied instructional strategies, assessment, reflective teaching, and lifelong development.

2. **National Board for Professional Teaching Standards (NBPTS).** NBPTS seeks to advance the quality of teaching by maintaining standards for what accomplished teachers should know and do as well as having a voluntary system for certifying teachers who meet these standards. Five core propositions serve as the foundation for the standards: (a) being committed to students and their learning; (b) knowing the subject matter one teaches and how to teach that subject to students; (c) managing and monitoring student learning; (d) thinking systematically about practice; and (e) being a member of a learning community. Certification involves a series of performance-based assessments, including portfolios, student work samples, and videotapes of teaching.

3. **Council for Exceptional Children (CEC).** Through its work as the national leader in special education advocacy, CEC has developed a series of performance-based standards that address both categorical and noncategorical licensure and preparation frameworks. In its most recent iteration of *What Every Special Educator Must Know*, CEC (2009) details (a) a code of ethics, principles to be applied when meeting day-to-day responsibilities (see Appendix C); (b) a common core of knowledge and skills in 10 areas, including foundations, characteristics, learning differences, instructional strategies, social interactions, language, planning, assessment, professional practice, and collaboration; (c) specialized knowledge and skills to meet the needs of students with specific disabilities (see Appendix B); and (d) tools and strategies for using the standards in the development of professional development plans. (Note that we have keyed the content of this text to these standards at the end of every chapter.)

4. **State standards.** Because certification and licensure are state functions, states have unique standards for initial and ongoing licensure and professional development. In many cases states augment nationally recognized professional standards with additional requirements.

## Teacher Tests

To ensure that each of its teachers is highly qualified, many states require a passing score on standardized pencil-and-paper tests of basic academic skills, principles of learning and teaching, and specific subject areas. Among states that require tests, most utilize The Praxis Series™ (www.ets.org/praxis), a product of the Educational Testing Service (ETS), to assess various facets of teacher competence. Teaching students with disabilities often requires would-be teachers to pass several Praxis tests. First, it is necessary to pass the Praxis I: Pre-Professional Skills Tests, three separate assessments that tap basic skills in reading, math, and writing. These tests are typically taken early in a student's college career and are often used as a component of admission to the teacher education program.

Second, teachers must take the Praxis II: Subject Assessments, which tests general and specific subject teaching skills and knowledge (see Appendix A). For special educators, the required tests vary as a function of the ages of the students one intends to teach, the intensity of service delivery in which these students are educated, the types of disabilities they possess, and the nature (i.e., categorical or noncategorical) of certification structure in your state. For example, a resource teacher of elementary students integrated in general education for most of her school

## REFLECTIVE EXERCISE

# 7
Although common in most states, the use of tests to determine teacher licensure remains controversial. Do you believe that a passing score on a test is predictive of success as a teacher of students with disabilities? Would you suggest consideration of any other measures to ensure that teachers are highly qualified?

day who resides in a noncategorical licensure state is likely to be required to pass (1) Education of Exceptional Students: Core Content Knowledge; (2) Special Education: Application of Core Principles Categories of Disability; and (3) Principles of Learning and Teaching: Grades K–6. However, a science teacher assigned to a self-contained classroom for secondary students who resides in a categorical licensure state is required to pass (1) Education of Exceptional Students: Core Content Knowledge, (2) Special Education: Teaching Students with Behavioral Disorders/Emotional Disturbances, and (3) a subject assessment in the specific area of science expertise.

Finally, some teachers may be assessed for licensure using the Praxis III, an on-site classroom performance measure that includes direct observation of classroom practice, reviews of documentation prepared by the teacher, and interviews with teacher and relevant colleagues. The emphases of these multiple data sources are on four interrelated domains: planning to teach, the classroom environment, instruction, and professional responsibilities.

### HOUSSE Procedures

Veteran teachers demonstrate that they are highly qualified in a variety of ways. HOUSSE is a procedure used by states to assess an existing teacher's subject-matter competency in place of a test, coursework, degree, or certification. Although HOUSSE systems vary across states, several general categories of documentation are used to document highly qualified status (Azordegan, 2004):

- **Professional development.** Participation in set amounts of professional development related to the subject taught
- **Performance evaluation.** Observations of teaching by peers or supervisors focusing on content knowledge and instructional skills
- **Portfolio.** A collection of evidence reflecting teacher practice in the subject area (we outline methods for portfolio development later in this chapter)
- **Student achievement data.** An assessment of a teacher's effect on student achievement through test scores
- **Point systems.** Teacher-accumulated points for various professional activities associated with the subject taught, including coursework, professional development activities, awards, recognitions, and student performance data

### Ongoing Professional Development

No matter how lengthy or comprehensive an initial preparation program, teachers of students with disabilities recognize quickly that they need more strategies if they are to remain successful. Professional development activities allow teachers to improve their skills by keeping pace with the many innovative changes that impact the field. Effective professional development is not a passive or time-limited undertaking. A common misconception is that professional development activities are contractually mandated presentations, usually directed by school administrators and delivered during one or two inservice days throughout the school year. However, professional development is most useful and effective when individual teachers take an active role in the process. Teachers take this responsibility by (1) recognizing that careers require a lifelong commitment to self-improvement; (2) reflecting on and articulating strengths and needs; (3) developing a development plan; (4) selecting activities that best meet their objectives; and (5) evaluating the effectiveness of selected activities.

## REFLECTIVE EXERCISE

# 8
What types of professional development do you find most appealing and beneficial? What activities are particularly rewarding? Identify activities that you find aversive. Given the opportunity, how would you plan and deliver professional development for yourself and your peers?

As you plan your own activities, keep in mind that professional development is most effective when activities are school-based, embedded in daily routines, balanced between the priorities of the school and teachers, linked directly to student outcomes, delivered in a supportive working environment, and structured in ways that allow teachers to share their expertise with each other (Dudzinski et al., 2000; Guskey & Yoon, 2009; Public Education Network, 2004). You can also contribute to your own professional development by becoming active in professional organizations, reading the professional literature, pursuing advanced degrees, and assuming leadership positions.

**Professional Organizations.** Professional organizations provide a wealth of formal and informal mechanisms for teachers to develop professionally. Most organizations set up conferences with nationally recognized speakers, sponsor staff development activities, and publish periodicals that focus on current issues and innovations in research and development. In addition to providing a wealth of instructional strategies, attendance at professional meetings serves as a source of rejuvenation—a jolt of motivation and a tangible reminder of the challenges and rewards of special education. Those who assume an active role in the governance and activities of an organization—assisting with the planning of conferences or editing newsletters—find that informal networking activities provide a sense of purpose, a source of new ideas, and a new avenue for giving and receiving emotional support.

> "It is incredibly satisfying, helping kids transition from being dependent on staff to becoming the most independent person they can become. No one knows everything, so I attend all professional development activities to learn better ways to help my kids."
>
> Kim Thomas, Heartspring School, Wichita, Kansas

**Reading the Professional Literature.** The professional literature—journals, monographs, texts—is the lifeblood of any profession. The most current validated information on issues associated with the teaching of students with disabilities is found in special education journals. Typically, journals present a variety of formats including (1) how-to articles that focus on the application of specific methods and techniques; (2) commentary and opinion pieces on controversial issues in the field; (3) program descriptions and evaluations; and (4) reports of quantitative and qualitative research efforts. While print copies of most of these journals may still be housed in district professional development centers, regional resource centers, and university libraries, most articles are now available online in electronic form through ERIC, Wilson Web, and other databases.

Although the Internet has made physical access to professional journals instantaneous, finding time and energy to read the relevant information remains a challenge. Clearly, the most desirable method for putting research into practice would be for teachers to have assigned professional development time at school for reading, applying, and discussing journal content (Westling & Koorland, 1988). Unfortunately, most time on the job is committed to instructional activities, and teachers must find other sources of time for professional reading. Here are some suggestions. First, set aside a fixed, reasonable amount of time for journal reading. Second, be selective in your reading; read the abstract to assess the applicability of the article to your needs. Finally, infuse a social component into your reading. Try to interest peers in forming a weekly lunchtime journal discussion group.

**Pursuing Advanced Degrees and Certificates.**
Most institutions of higher education offer degree and certificate programs that focus on specific aspects of the subject matter and skills associated with teaching students with disabilities. In addition to traditional full-time options, most graduate programs offer advanced degree programs that address the needs of working teachers, offering courses at convenient times and locations. For those who do not wish to pursue an

One enjoyable way of keeping up with recent advances in the field is to have friendly group discussions of current articles and books.

advanced degree, focused certificate programs are often available. In many cases these programs allow for in-depth analyses of topical issues (e.g., inclusion, comprehensive behavior management) or specialized techniques that can be used with particular populations of students with disabilities (e.g., autism spectrum disorder). Partnership programs between school districts and universities are becoming quite common, and it may be possible to secure academic credits for courses sponsored by and completed in your local school district. Sources are available that describe advanced degree programs in special education. Links to these sources are easily accessed through centers such as the National Center for Special Education Personnel and Related Service Providers (http://www.personnelcenter.org/).

**Assuming Leadership Positions.** Perhaps the most natural form of professional development is assuming leadership positions within your department, school, or district. Teacher-leadership activities include serving as a mentor, participating in curriculum review and development, facilitating parent groups, and chairing committees that govern activities and events in the school or district. Be aware that some leadership development programs combine staff development activities with internships and often lead to positions of increased responsibility, status, and compensation.

## Monitoring Your Growth: The Professional Portfolio

Professionals in many disciplines rely on portfolios as a way of displaying their best work. For example, artists and architects collect samples of their many creations, and even lawyers and physicians (particularly plastic surgeons) maintain attractive displays to showcase their efforts. For teachers, portfolios are mechanisms to record evidence of development as well as to showcase creative efforts and achievements. This documentation is quite useful when interviewing for teaching and leadership positions or for advanced graduate study. A well-presented portfolio demonstrates that you have what it takes—the knowledge, skills, creativity, and dispositions—to advance to the next level (Rosenberg et al., 2006).

Still, for teachers, portfolios serve an even greater personal and professional development purpose: Portfolios are a vehicle for allowing teachers to reflect on their own growth and development, both as educators and learners. In some cases professional boards use portfolios to measure progress in meeting advanced professional standards (e.g., National Board for Professional Teaching Standards Certification). For those experiencing a particularly frustrating day, portfolios provide comfort in that they are a tangible way to reflect upon previous successes and experience feelings of self-efficacy. Be aware that each professional teaching portfolio is unique to the individual who creates it. Consequently, portfolios vary in content, form, and emphasis, reflecting an individual's philosophy, values, and viewpoints (Hurst, Wilson, & Cramer, 1998).

Although no hard and fast rules govern portfolio content, several generic considerations are helpful when using the portfolio as a tool for both reflection and demonstration (Hurst et al., 1998; Reese, 2004; Rosenberg et al., 2006; Van Wagenen & Hibbard, 1998):

- Include evidence and artifacts that reflect who you are, what you are about, and your goals and aspirations.
- Present evidence of your achievements, and indicate how they are tied to your goals and aspirations.
- Provide actual samples of assessment, instructional, and behavioral materials that you have developed, implemented, and evaluated.
- Show evidence of student work, family involvement, and community-outreach activities.
- Align your accomplishments with professional standards that are meaningful to you and your school district.

- Maintain representations of your degrees, teaching credentials, letters of reference, and awards.
- Integrate what you have learned from your experiences, and articulate these insights into professional goals.
- Ensure that the material in the portfolio is presented in an organized and attractive manner.
- Consider the use of an electronic or digital portfolio, a vehicle that integrates paper-based and video-based evidence in a format that is easy to access, expand upon, and transport.

A final note on completing a professional portfolio: Try not to consider this activity as an additional dull paperwork responsibility. The portfolio is your personal statement, a tangible representation of who you are, why you selected a career in special education, and what you hope to accomplish as a professional. It is your running narrative of growth and, with minimal nurturance, serves as a reliable resource to reflect on your teaching career.

## FINAL THOUGHTS: STAYING INVIGORATED AND COMMITTED

In this chapter we highlighted how supports and professional development can facilitate the development of a successful and professional special education career. In concluding this chapter, we offer a few final suggestions for remaining invigorated and committed to teaching students with disabilities.

First, remember why you chose a career involving the education of students with disabilities. As you discovered in Chapter 1, a number of factors entered into your decision to pursue this challenging and rewarding career. It is likely you were committed to helping others succeed or had a desire to give back to the community. Perhaps you believed that you had a special gift or disposition for reaching children and youth from troubling backgrounds. Difficult and frustrating days may result in serious questioning of your assumptions. This is natural and healthy. As you consider your chosen career, recognize that teaching is a tough job, requiring not only specific knowledge but also a commitment of physical and mental energy and breadth of character demanded of precious few other careers. Along with having high expectations, remain patient with your students. As Banner and Cannon (1997) have observed, "patience enables teachers to suspend disappointment and frustration out of an understanding of the difficulties students have in catching on [to] what their teachers already know" (p. 96).

Second, build upon your professional and creative disposition. As we discussed at the start of this chapter, professionalism is a pattern of behaviors (e.g., Connelly & Rosenberg, 2009; Grouse, 2003; Kramer, 2003; Phelps, 2006) that includes respect, ethics, responsibility, communication, leadership, risk taking, and a positive attitude. Persevere in the face of intermittent successes, and remain poised when encountering frustrating situations. Do not let the important technical and methodical aspects of teaching overshadow artistic and inventive activities. Although scientific and research-based practices inform the selection of specific instructional methods, materials, and processes, teaching is in large part a creative act in which you share elements of your own personality, spirit, experience, and humanity. By revealing aspects of your personality and value system, you become a central figure in the lives of students. Meaningful learning occurs not only through the effective presentation of subject matter but by the thoughtful modeling of care, honor, and integrity. Regardless of the subject matter being taught, the creative force of a trusted and principled teacher facilitates life-changing learning.

"I think you can know every research-based reading program out there; but if you don't respect your students as individuals, they won't grow as individuals."

Meridith Taylor-Strout, Gainesville, Florida

Third, don't take the politics of education personally. Educational decisions, like other social policy issues requiring taxpayer contributions, are often based on practical matters such as the limited availability of resources rather than merit. Politics is the process of trying to influence the direction of decisions being made as well as urging how much and where resources should be allocated (Goor, 1995). Rather than ignoring or fearing them, recognize the energizing role of politics in teaching and special education. Be aware of changes in educational policies and trends at the national, state, and local levels, and know how such changes affect the delivery of educational programs. Whenever possible and appropriate, participate in community discussions on how best to educate students with disabilities. Participation in political-action activities of professional groups, disability-advocacy organizations, teacher associations, and local parent groups are among the most effective methods of advocating for policies and funding to enhance educational services.

Finally, take pleasure in teaching. Most of us have chosen to teach because we enjoy it. Trust your instincts. We get satisfaction in seeing our students acquire skills, master complex concepts, and grow emotionally. How can teachers maximize their pleasure in teaching? Banner and Cannon (1997) recommend (1) creating an atmosphere where students enjoy learning; (2) letting others' wit shine; (3) modeling an enduring love of learning; (4) acknowledging the challenges as well as the joys of learning; and (5) recognizing and celebrating when students learn as a result of your efforts.

Plan well, work hard, have compassion, take care, and enjoy the many pleasures in teaching students with disabilities!

# 16 SUMMARY

Those who seek a successful, long-term career in special education recognize the importance of developing as a professional, are aware of the supports available to help them grow, and take charge of their ongoing personal and professional growth.

## Developing into a Special Education Professional

- Teachers are typically expected to deliver instructional content in an effective manner, differentiate instruction for individual students in a culturally responsive manner, provide supports and adaptations, manage the learning environment, evaluate student performance, care for students, and communicate effectively with colleagues and parents.
- Expectations have expanded and include knowledge of testing accommodations, awareness and management of paperwork and legal responsibilities, and participation in schools that are both integrated systems of care and professional learning communities.

## Key Elements of Collaborative Professional Support

- Early in their career, teachers receive support through induction, mentoring, and peer coaching, activities that allow novice teachers to acquire important school-system information as well as receive critical emotional support.

- Throughout their career, teachers give and receive assistance through professional learning communities, collaborative consultation, collaborative teaming, and assistance from paraprofessionals.

## Successful Teachers Take an Active Role in Their Own Personal Growth and Professional Development

- Successful teachers are resilient, adjusting to situations and developing competence in the face of adverse conditions.
- Professional growth is predicated on recognizing and managing stress.
- Professional growth requires highly qualified status, a process that is facilitated by knowledge of standards, tests, and professional development alternatives.
- Professional growth is documented by a well-organized portfolio.

## Special Educators Remain Invigorated and Committed to Their Students and Profession

- Motivated teachers remember why they have chosen this challenging and rewarding career.
- Creative teachers do not allow the technical and political aspects of the job to overshadow the inventive aspects of teaching.
- Professionals take time to enjoy the pleasure of teaching.

**Council for Exceptional Children**

## ADDRESSING THE PROFESSIONAL STANDARDS

Council for Exceptional Children (CEC) Knowledge Standards addressed in the chapter:

ICC1K3, ICC1S1, ICC9K2, ICC9K3, ICC9K4, ICC9S1, ICC9S2, ICC9S3, ICC9S4, ICC9S8, ICC9S10, ICC9S11, ICC9S12, ICC10S3, ICC10S11

Appendix B: CEC Knowledge and Skill Standards Common Core has a full listing of the standards referenced here.

## PEARSON myeducationlab

Now go to Topic 2: Collaboration & Co-Teaching in the MyEducationLab for your course, where you can:

- Find learning outcomes for the broad concepts covered in this chapter along with the national standards that connect to these outcomes.
- Complete Assignments and Activities that can help you more deeply understand the chapter content.
- Examine challenging situations and cases presented in the IRIS Center Resources.
- Apply and practice your understanding of the core concepts and skills identified in the chapter with the Building Teaching Skills and Dispositions learning units.

- Check your comprehension on the content covered in the chapter by going to the Study Plan in the Book-Specific Resources section for your text. Here you will be able to take a chapter quiz, receive feedback on your answers, and then access Review, Practice, and Enrichment activities to enhance your understanding of chapter content.
- Access video clips of CCSSO National Teachers of the Year award winners responding to the questions, "Why Do I Teach?" in the Teacher Talk section.

# Appendix A

## Coverage of Content Areas for PRAXIS II® Test
### Special Education Core Principles: Content Knowledge (0353)

As we noted in Chapter 16, most states that require tests for certification and licensure utilize THE PRAXIS SERIES™ developed by the Educational Testing Service (ETS). For special educators, a central element in the test series is the Special Education Core Principles: Content Knowledge Assessment. This "core knowledge" centers on three areas: Understanding Exceptionalities, Legal and Societal Issues, and Delivery of Services to Students with Disabilities.

In the following grid we reference where the relevant material associated with the Praxis content areas are located in each chapter (chapter number is followed by chapter sections). We anticipate that this content will be helpful as you prepare for the test. However, keep in mind that success on PRAXIS™ exams (as well as success teaching students with and without disabilities) requires greater in-depth study and application than any broad-based introductory textbook can provide. We urge you to utilize the foundational material found in the chapters to anchor and organize future coursework and field experiences.

## I. UNDERSTANDING EXCEPTIONALITIES

| PRAXIS™ Content Area | Relevant Chapter Content |
| --- | --- |
| *Human development and behavior as related to students with disabilities* | • **Chapter 4:** Indicators of Disabilities from Infancy Through School Ages<br>• **Chapter 6:** Defining Learning Disabilities; Course and Causal Factors of LD<br>• **Chapter 7:** Defining Emotional and Behavioral Disabilities; Course and Causal Factors EBD<br>• **Chapter 8:** Defining Mild Intellectual Disabilities; Course and Causal Factors of Mild Intellectual Disabilities<br>• **Chapter 9:** Defining ADHD; Course and Causal Factors of ADHD<br>• **Chapter 10:** Defining Autism Spectrum Disabilities; Course and Causal Factors ASD<br>• **Chapter 11:** Defining Communication Disorders; Causes of Communication Disorders; Types of Language Disorders and Speech Disorders<br>• **Chapter 12:** Definitions and Classification Criteria for Students with Severe Intellectual Disabilities and Multiple Disabilities<br>• **Chapter 13:** Definitions and Classification Criteria for Sensory Disabilities<br>• **Chapter 14:** Definitions and Classification Criteria of Traumatic Brain Injury, Physical Disabilities, and Health Impairments<br>• **Chapter 15:** Defining Giftedness |

*(continues)*

| PRAXIS™ Content Area | Relevant Chapter Content |
|---|---|
| *Characteristics of students with disabilities* | • **Chapter 3:** Influence of Cultural and Linguistic Factors on Disabilities<br>• **Chapter 4:** Characteristics of Infants, Toddlers, and Preschoolers<br>• **Chapter 6:** Primary Behavioral Characteristics of Students with LD<br>• **Chapter 7:** Primary Behavioral Characteristics of EBD<br>• **Chapter 8:** Primary Behavioral Characteristics of Students with Mild Intellectual Disabilities<br>• **Chapter 9:** Primary Behavioral Characteristics of Students with ADHD<br>• **Chapter 10:** Primary Behavioral Characteristics of ASD<br>• **Chapter 11:** Types of Language Disorders and Speech Disorders; Relationship Between Communication Disorders and Other Disabilities; Prevalence of Communication Disorders<br>• **Chapter 12:** Learning Characteristics and Challenging Behavior Associated with Severe and Multiple Disabilities; Physical and Medical Problems Associated with Severe and Multiple Disabilities<br>• **Chapter 13:** Learning, Academic, and Social Characteristics of Students with Vision or Hearing Losses<br>• **Chapter 14:** Characteristics of Students with Traumatic Brain Injury, Physical Disabilities, and Health Impairments |
| *Basic concepts in special education* | • **Chapter 1:** Meaning of Special Education; Roles of Special Education Teachers and Other Professionals and Paraeducators; Importance of Evidence-Based Instruction; Rewards and Challenges of Being a Special Education Teacher; Reasons for Choosing Special Education as a Career; Dispositions and Attitudes Appropriate for Special Education Teachers<br>• **Chapter 2:** Social History of Special Education<br>• **Chapter 4:** Ways Students with Disabilities Are Recognized, Referred, and Evaluated; Types of Plans That Schools Develop; Parents' Rights; Prereferrals; Early Intervening Services; Response to Intervention (RTI)<br>• **Chapter 5:** Communicating Instruction and Behavior Management<br>• **Chapter 12:** School Programs and Related Services<br>• **Chapter 13:** Special Education Eligibility Requirements for Students with Visual or Hearing Loss; Legal Definition of Blindness; Criteria for Deaf-Blindness<br>• **Chapter 14:** Special Education Eligibility Requirements for Students with Traumatic Brain Injury, Physical Disabilities, and Health Impairments<br>• **Chapter 16:** Professionalism; Collaboration, Consultation, and Teaming; Professional Growth and Development |

## II. LEGAL AND SOCIETAL ISSUES

| PRAXIS™ Content Area | Relevant Chapter Content |
| --- | --- |
| *Federal laws and legal issues related to special education* | • **Chapter 2:** IDEA: Legal Basis for IDEA; Major Components of IDEA; IDEA Outcomes and Improvements; NCLB: Major Components of NCLB; NCLB Outcomes; Section 504; Americans with Disabilities Act<br>• **Chapter 3:** Cultural and Community Influences on Attitudes Toward Disabilities<br>• **Chapter 4:** Eligibility Requirements for Special Education; Prereferral and Referral Procedures; IEP and Section 504 Requirements; IFSP Requirements; IEP Team Members; Transition Plans<br>• **Chapter 8:** Developing Student Self-Advocacy<br>• **Chapter 9:** Section 504<br>• **Chapter 12:** Prevailing Issues, Controversies, and Implications for the Teacher<br>• **Chapter 14:** Eligibility Requirements for Students with Traumatic Brain Injury, Physical Disabilities, and Health Impairments |
| *The school's connections with the families, prospective and actual employers, and communities of students with disabilities* | • **Chapter 6:** Early Intervention for Students with LD; Transition to Adult Life Considerations for Students with LD<br>• **Chapter 7:** Early Intervention EBD; Transition to Adult Life Considerations EBD<br>• **Chapter 8:** Early Intervention for Students with Mild Intellectual Disabilities; Transition to Adult Life Considerations for Students with Mild Intellectual Disabilities<br>• **Chapter 9:** Early Intervention for Students with ADHD; Transition to Adult Life Considerations for Students with ADHD<br>• **Chapter 10:** Early Intervention ASD; Transition to Adult Life Considerations ASD<br>• **Chapter 11:** Roles of Families in Supporting Students with Communication Disorders<br>• **Chapter 12:** Prevailing Issues, Controversies, and Implications for the Teacher<br>• **Chapter 13:** Deaf People as a Culture |

## III. DELIVERY OF SERVICES TO STUDENTS WITH DISABILITIES

| PRAXIS™ Content Area | Relevant Chapter Content |
| --- | --- |
| *Background knowledge* | • **Chapter 3:** Cultural and Linguistic Considerations Regarding Curriculum and Instruction<br>• **Chapter 6:** Service Delivery for Students with LD<br>• **Chapter 7:** Service Delivery EBD<br>• **Chapter 8:** Service Delivery for Students with Mild Intellectual Disabilities<br>• **Chapter 9:** Service Delivery for Students with ADHD<br>• **Chapter 10:** Service Delivery ASD<br>• **Chapter 11:** Service Delivery for Students with Communication Disorders<br>• **Chapter 12:** School Programs and Related Services<br>• **Chapter 14:** Academic and Functional Instruction |

*(continues)*

| PRAXIS™ Content Area | Relevant Chapter Content |
|---|---|
| *Curriculum and instruction and their implementation across the continuum of educational placements* | • **Chapter 5:** Curriculum and Students with Special Needs; Approaches to Teaching; Systematic Teaching; Managing Student Behavior; Proactive Behavior Management<br>• **Chapter 6:** Academic Interventions for Students with LD<br>• **Chapter 7:** Academic and Social/Behavioral Interventions EBD<br>• **Chapter 8:** Academic Interventions for Students with Mild Intellectual Disabilities<br>• **Chapter 9:** Academic and Social/Behavioral Interventions for Students with ADHD<br>• **Chapter 10:** Academic and Social/Behavioral Interventions ASD<br>• **Chapter 11:** Intervention Procedures; Supporting Students Using AAC Devices; Service Delivery Models<br>• **Chapter 12:** School Programs and Related Services<br>• **Chapter 13:** Academic Interventions for Students with Visual or Hearing Impairments<br>• **Chapter 14:** Academic and Functional Instruction |
| *Assessment* | • **Chapter 4:** Identification Procedures for Infants and Toddlers; Preschoolers and School-Age Students; Overview of Assessment Instruments for Identification and Planning<br>• **Chapter 6:** Identification and Assessment of Students with LD<br>• **Chapter 8:** Identification and Assessment of Students with Mild Intellectual Disabilities<br>• **Chapter 9:** Identification and Assessment of Students with ADHD<br>• **Chapter 7:** Identification and Assessment of Students with EBD<br>• **Chapter 10:** Identification and Assessment of Students with ASD<br>• **Chapter 11:** Identification and Assessment of Students with Communication Disorders<br>• **Chapter 12:** Identification and Assessment of Students with Severe and Multiple Disabilities<br>• **Chapter 13:** Identification and Assessment for Students with Visual or Hearing Impairments<br>• **Chapter 14:** Identification and Assessment of Students with Traumatic Brain Injury, Physical Disabilities, and Health Impairments |

# Appendix B

## CEC Knowledge and Skill Standards Common Core

**Standard I: Foundations**

ICC1K1: Models, theories, and philosophies, and research methods that provide the basis for special education practice.

ICC1K2: Laws, policies, and ethical principles regarding behavior management planning and implementation.

ICC1K3: Relationship of special education to the organization and function of educational agencies.

ICC1K4: Rights and responsibilities of students, parents, teachers, and other professionals, and schools related to exceptional learning needs.

ICC1K5: Issues in definition and identification of individuals with exceptional learning needs, including those from culturally and linguistically diverse backgrounds.

ICC1K6: Issues, assurances, and due process rights related to assessment, eligibility, and placement within a continuum of services.

ICC1K7: Family systems and the role of families in the educational process.

ICC1K8: Historical points of view and contributions of culturally diverse groups.

ICC1K9: Impact of the dominant culture on shaping schools and the individuals who study and work in them.

ICC1K10: Potential impact of differences in values, languages, and customs that can exist between the home and school.

ICC1S1: Articulate personal philosophy of special education.

**Standard II: Development and Characteristics of Learners**

ICC2K1: Typical and atypical human growth and development.

ICC2K2: Educational implications of characteristics of various exceptionalities.

ICC2K3: Characteristics and effects of the cultural and environmental milieu of the individual with exceptional learning needs and the family.

ICC2K4: Family systems and the role of families in supporting development.

ICC2K5: Similarities and differences of individuals with and without exceptional learning needs.

ICC2K6: Similarities and differences among individuals with exceptional learning needs.

ICC2K7: Effects of various medications on individuals with exceptional learning needs.

**Standard III: Individual Learning Differences**

ICC3K1: Effects an exceptional condition(s) can have on an individual's life.

ICC3K2: Impact of learner's academic and social abilities, attitudes, interests, and values on instruction and career development.

ICC3K3: Variations in beliefs, traditions, and values across and within cultures and their effects on relationships among individuals with exceptional learning needs, family, and schooling.

ICC3K4:    Cultural perspectives influencing the relationships among families, schools, and communities as related to instruction.
ICC3K5:    Differing ways of learning of individuals with exceptional learning needs including those from culturally diverse backgrounds and strategies for addressing these differences.

## Standard IV: Instructional Strategies

ICC4K1:    Evidence-based practices validated for specific characteristics of learners and settings.
ICC4S1:    Use strategies to facilitate integration into various settings.
ICC4S2:    Teach individuals to use self-assessment, problem-solving, and other cognitive strategies to meet their needs.
ICC4S3:    Select, adapt, and use instructional strategies and materials according to characteristics of the individual with exceptional learning needs.
ICC4S4:    Use strategies to facilitate maintenance and generalization of skills across learning environments.
ICC4S5:    Use procedures to increase the individual's self-awareness, self-management, self-control, self-reliance, and self-esteem.
ICC4S6:    Use strategies that promote successful transitions for individuals with exceptional learning needs.

## Standard V: Learning Environments and Social Interactions

ICC5K1:    Demands of learning environments.
ICC5K2:    Basic classroom management theories and strategies for individuals with exceptional learning needs.
ICC5K3:    Effective management of teaching and learning.
ICC5K4:    Teacher attitudes and behaviors that influence behavior of individuals with exceptional learning needs.
ICC5K5:    Social skills needed for educational and other environments.
ICC5K6:    Strategies for crisis prevention and intervention.
ICC5K7:    Strategies for preparing individuals to live harmoniously and productively in a culturally diverse world.
ICC5K8:    Ways to create learning environments that allow individuals to retain and appreciate their own and each other's respective language and cultural heritage.
ICC5K9:    Ways specific cultures are negatively stereotyped.
ICC5K10:   Strategies used by diverse populations to cope with a legacy of former and continuing racism.
ICC5S1:    Create a safe, equitable, positive, and supporting learning environment in which diversities are valued.
ICC5S2:    Identify realistic expectations for personal and social behavior in various settings.
ICC5S3:    Identify supports needed for integration into various program placements.
ICC5S4:    Design learning environments that encourage active participation in individual and group settings.
ICC5S5:    Modify the learning environment to manage behaviors.
ICC5S6:    Use performance data and information from all stakeholders to make or suggest modifications in learning environments.
ICC5S7:    Establish and maintain rapport with individuals with and without exceptional learning needs.
ICC5S8:    Teach self-advocacy.

ICC5S9:     Create an environment that encourages self-advocacy and increased independence.

ICC5S10:    Use effective and varied behavior management strategies.

ICC5S11:    Use the least intensive behavior management strategy consistent with the needs of the individual with exceptional learning needs.

ICC5S12:    Design and manage daily routines.

ICC5S13:    Organize, develop, and sustain learning environments that support positive intracultural and intercultural experiences.

ICC5S14:    Mediate controversial intercultural issues among students within the learning environment in ways that enhance any culture, group, or person.

ICC5S15:    Structure, direct, and support the activities of paraeducators, volunteers, and tutors.

ICC5S16:    Use universal precautions.

## Standard VI: Communication

ICC6K1:     Effects of cultural and linguistic differences on growth and development.

ICC6K2:     Characteristics of one's own culture and use of language and the ways in which these can differ from other cultures and uses of languages.

ICC6K3:     Ways of behaving and communicating among cultures that can lead to misinterpretation and misunderstanding.

ICC6K4:     Augmentative and assistive communication strategies.

ICC6S1:     Use strategies to support and enhance communication skills of individuals with exceptional learning needs.

ICC6S2:     Use communication strategies and resources to facilitate understanding of subject matter for students whose primary language is not the dominant language.

## Standard VII: Instructional Planning

ICC7K1:     Theories and research that form the basis of curriculum development and instructional practice.

ICC7K2:     Scope and sequences of general and special curricula.

ICC7K3:     National, state or provincial, and local curricula standards.

ICC7K4:     Technology for planning and managing the teaching and learning environment.

ICC7K5:     Roles and responsibilities of the paraeducator related to instruction, intervention, and direct service.

ICC7S1:     Identify and prioritize areas of the general curriculum and accommodations for individuals with exceptional learning needs.

ICC7S2:     Develop and implement comprehensive, longitudinal individualized programs in collaboration with team members.

ICC7S3:     Involve the individual and family in setting instructional goals and monitoring progress.

ICC7S4:     Use functional assessments to develop intervention plans.

ICC7S5:     Use task analysis.

ICC7S6:     Sequence, implement, and evaluate individualized learning objectives.

ICC7S7:     Integrate affective, social, and life skills with academic curricula.

ICC7S8:     Develop and select instructional content, resources, and strategies that respond to cultural, linguistic, and gender differences.

ICC7S9:     Incorporate and implement instructional and assistive technology into the educational program.

ICC7S10:   Prepare lesson plans.
ICC7S11:   Prepare and organize materials to implement daily lesson plans.
ICC7S12:   Use instructional time effectively.
ICC7S13:   Make responsive adjustments to instruction based on continued observations.
ICC7S14:   Prepare individuals to exhibit self-enhancing behavior in response to societal attitudes and actions.
ICC7S15:   Evaluate and modify instructional practices in response to ongoing assessment data.

**Standard VIII: Assessment**

ICC8K1:   Basic terminology used in assessment.
ICC8K2:   Legal provisions and ethical principles regarding assessment of individuals.
ICC8K3:   Screening, prereferral, referral, and classification procedures.
ICC8K4:   Use and limitations of assessment instruments.
ICC8K5:   National, state or provincial, and local accommodations and modifications.
ICC8S1:   Gather relevant background information.
ICC8S2:   Administer nonbiased formal and informal assessments.
ICC8S3:   Use technology to conduct assessments.
ICC8S4:   Develop or modify individualized assessment strategies.
ICC8S5:   Interpret information from formal and informal assessments.
ICC8S6:   Use assessment information in making eligibility, program, and placement decisions for individuals with exceptional learning needs, including those from culturally and/or linguistically diverse backgrounds.
ICC8S7:   Report assessment results to all stakeholders using effective communication skills.
ICC8S8:   Evaluate instruction and monitor progress of individuals with exceptional learning needs.
ICC8S9:   Develop or modify individualized assessment strategies.
ICC8S10:  Create and maintain records.

**Standard IX: Professional and Ethical Practice**

ICC9K1:   Personal cultural biases and differences that affect one's teaching.
ICC9K2:   Importance of the teacher serving as a model for individuals with exceptional learning needs.
ICC9K3:   Continuum of lifelong professional development.
ICC9K4:   Methods to remain current regarding research-validated practice.
ICC9S1:   Practice within the CEC Code of Ethics and other standards of the profession.
ICC9S2:   Uphold high standards of competence and integrity and exercise sound judgment in the practice of the professional.
ICC9S3:   Act ethically in advocating for appropriate services.
ICC9S4:   Conduct professional activities in compliance with applicable laws and policies.
ICC9S5:   Demonstrate commitment to developing the highest education and quality-of-life potential of individuals with exceptional learning needs.
ICC9S6:   Demonstrate sensitivity for the culture, language, religion, gender, disability, socioeconomic status, and sexual orientation of individuals.
ICC9S7:   Practice within one's skill limit and obtain assistance as needed.
ICC9S8:   Use verbal, nonverbal, and written language effectively.

ICC9S9:     Conduct self-evaluation of instruction.

ICC9S10:    Access information on exceptionalities.

ICC9S11:    Reflect on one's practice to improve instruction and guide professional growth.

ICC9S12:    Engage in professional activities that benefit individuals with exceptional learning needs, their families, and one's colleagues.

ICC9S13:    Demonstrate Commitment to engage evidence-based practice.

## Standard X: Collaboration

ICC10K1:    Models and strategies of consultation and collaboration.

ICC10K2:    Roles of individuals with exceptional learning needs, families, and school and community personnel in planning of an individualized program.

ICC10K3:    Concerns of families of individuals with exceptional learning needs and strategies to help address these concerns.

ICC10K4:    Culturally responsive factors that promote effective communication and collaboration with individuals with exceptional learning needs, families, school personnel, and community members.

ICC10S1:    Maintain confidential communication about individuals with exceptional learning needs.

ICC10S2:    Collaborate with families and others in assessment of individuals with exceptional learning needs.

ICC10S3:    Foster respectful and beneficial relationships between families and professionals.

ICC10S4:    Assist individuals with exceptional learning needs and their families in becoming active participants in the educational team.

ICC10S5:    Plan and conduct collaborative conferences with individuals with exceptional learning needs and their families.

ICC10S6:    Collaborate with school personnel and community members in integrating individuals with exceptional learning needs into various settings.

ICC10S7:    Use group problem-solving skills to develop, implement, and evaluate collaborative activities.

ICC10S8:    Model techniques and coach others in the use of instructional methods and accommodations.

ICC10S9:    Communicate with school personnel about the characteristics and needs of individuals with exceptional learning needs.

ICC10S10:   Communicate effectively with families of individuals with exceptional learning needs from diverse backgrounds.

ICC10S11:   Observe, evaluate, and provide feedback to paraeducators.

# Appendix C

## CEC Code of Ethics and Standards for Professional Practice for Special Educators

### CEC CODE OF ETHICS FOR EDUCATORS OF PERSONS WITH EXCEPTIONALITIES

We declare the following principles to be the Code of Ethics for educators of persons with exceptionalities. Members for the special education profession are responsible for upholding and advancing these principles. Members of the Council for Exceptional Children agree to judge and be judged by them in accordance with the spirit and provisions of this Code.

- A. Special education professionals are committed to developing the highest educational and quality of life potential of individuals with exceptionalities.
- B. Special education professionals promote and maintain a high level of competence and integrity in practicing their profession.
- C. Special education professionals engage in professional activities which benefit individuals with exceptionalities, their families, other colleagues, students, or research subjects.
- D. Special education professionals exercise objective professional judgment in the practice of their profession.
- E. Special education professionals strive to advance their knowledge and skills regarding the education of individuals with exceptionalities.
- F. Special education professionals work within the standards and policies of their profession.
- G. Special education professionals seek to uphold and improve where necessary the laws, regulations, and policies governing the delivery of special education and related services and the practice of their profession.
- H. Special education professionals do not condone or participate in unethical or illegal acts, nor violate professional standards adopted by the Delegate Assembly of CEC.

### CEC STANDARDS FOR PROFESSIONAL PRACTICE

#### Professionals in Relation to Persons with Exceptionalities and Their Families

##### Instructional Responsibilities

Special education personnel are committed to the application of professional expertise to ensure the provision of quality education for all individuals with exceptionalities. Professionals strive to

1. Identify and use instructional methods and curricula that are appropriate to their area of professional practice and effective in meeting the individual needs of persons with exceptionalities.
2. Participate in the selection and use of appropriate instructional materials, equipment, supplies, and other resources needed in the effective practice of their profession.

3. Create safe and effective learning environments, which contribute to fulfillment of needs, stimulation of learning, and self concept.
4. Maintain class size and caseloads that are conducive to meeting the individual instructional needs of individuals with exceptionalities.
5. Use assessment instruments and procedures that do not discriminate against persons with exceptionalities on the basis of race, color, creed, sex, national origin, age, political practices, family or social background, sexual orientation, or exceptionality.
6. Base grading, promotion, graduation, and/or movement out of the program on the individual goals and objectives for individuals with exceptionalities.
7. Provide accurate program data to administrators, colleagues, and parents, based on efficient and objective record keeping practices, for the purpose of decision making.
8. Maintain confidentiality of information except when information is released under specific conditions of written consent and statutory confidentiality requirements.

## Management of Behavior

Special education professionals participate with other professionals and with parents in an interdisciplinary effort in the management of behavior. Professionals

1. Apply only those disciplinary methods and behavioral procedures, which they have been instructed to use and which do not undermine the dignity of the individual or the basic human rights of persons with exceptionalities, such as corporal punishment.
2. Clearly specify the goals and objectives for behavior management practices in the persons with exceptionalities individualized education program.
3. Conform to policies, statutes, and rules established by state/provincial and local agencies relating to judicious application of disciplinary methods and behavioral procedures.
4. Take adequate measures to discourage, prevent, and intervene when a colleague's behavior is perceived as being detrimental to exceptional students.
5. Refrain from aversive techniques unless repeated trials of other methods have failed and only after consultation with parents and appropriate agency officials.

## Support Procedures

Professionals

1. Seek adequate instruction and supervision before they are required to perform support services for which they have not been prepared previously.
2. May administer medication, where state/provincial policies do not preclude such action, if qualified to do so or if written instructions are on file which state the purpose of the medication, the conditions under which it may be administered, possible side effects, the physician's name and phone number, and the professional liability if a mistake is made. The professional will not be required to administer medication.
3. Note and report to those concerned whenever changes in behavior occur in conjunction with the administration of medication or at any other time.

## Parent Relationships

Professionals seek to develop relationships with parents based on mutual respect for their roles in achieving benefits for the exceptional persons. Special education professionals

1. Develop effective communication with parents, avoiding technical terminology, using the primary language of the home, and other modes of communication when appropriate.

2. Seek and use parents' knowledge and expertise in planning, conducting, and evaluating special education and related services for persons with exceptionalities.
3. Maintain communications between parents and professionals with appropriate respect for privacy and confidentiality.
4. Extend opportunities for parent education utilizing accurate information and professional methods.
5. Inform parents of the educational rights of their children and of any proposed or actual practices, which violate those rights.
6. Recognize and respect cultural diversities which exist in some families with persons with exceptionalities.
7. Recognize that the relationship of home and community environmental conditions affects the behavior and outlook of the exceptional person.

## Advocacy

Special education professionals serve as advocates for exceptional students by speaking, writing, and acting in a variety of situations on their behalf. They

1. Continually seek to improve government provisions for the education of persons with exceptionalities while ensuring that public statements by professionals as individuals are not construed to represent official policy statements of the agency that employs them.
2. Work cooperatively with and encourage other professionals to improve the provision of special education and related services to persons with exceptionalities.
3. Document and objectively report to one's supervisors or administrators inadequacies in resources and promote appropriate corrective action.
4. Monitor for inappropriate placements in special education and intervene at appropriate levels to correct the condition when such inappropriate placements exist.
5. Follow local, state/provincial, and federal laws and regulations which mandate a free appropriate public education to exceptional students and the protection of the rights of persons with exceptionalities to equal opportunities in our society.

# Professionals in Relation to Employment

## Certification and Qualification

Professionals ensure that only persons deemed qualified by having met state/provincial minimum standards are employed as teachers, administrators, and related service providers for individuals with exceptionalities.

## Employment

1. Professionals do not discriminate in hiring on the basis of race, color, creed, sex, national origin, age, political practices, family or social background, sexual orientation, or exceptionality.
2. Professionals represent themselves in an ethical and legal manner in regard to their training and experience when seeking new employment.
3. Professionals give notice consistent with local education agency policies when intending to leave employment.
4. Professionals adhere to the conditions of a contract or terms of an appointment in the setting where they practice.
5. Professionals released from employment are entitled to a written explanation of reasons for termination and to fair and impartial due process procedures.
6. Special education professionals share equitably in the opportunities and benefits (salary, working conditions, facilities, and other resources) of other professionals in the school system.

7. Professionals seek assistance, including the services of other professionals in instances where personal problems threaten to interfere with their job performance.
8. Professionals respond objectively when requested to evaluate applicants seeking employment.
9. Professionals have the right and responsibility to resolve professional problems by utilizing established procedures, including grievance procedures, when appropriate.

### Assignment and Role

1. Professionals should receive clear written communication of all duties and responsibilities, including those which are prescribed as conditions of their employment.
2. Professionals promote educational quality and intra- and interprofessional cooperation through active participation in the planning, policy development, management, and evaluation of the special education program and the education program at large so that programs remain responsive to the changing needs of persons with exceptionalities.
3. Professionals practice only in areas of exceptionality, at age levels, and in program models for which they are prepared by their training and/or experience.
4. Adequate supervision of and support for special education professionals is provided by other professionals qualified by their training and experience in the area of concern.
5. The administration and supervision of special education professionals provides for clear lines of accountability.
6. The unavailability of substitute teachers or support personnel, including aides, does not result in the denial of special education services to a greater degree than to that of other educational programs.

### Professional Development

1. Special education professionals systematically advance their knowledge and skills in order to maintain a high level of competence and response to the changing needs of persons with exceptionalities by pursuing a program of continuing education including but not limited to participation in such activities as inservice training, professional conferences/workshops, professional meetings, continuing education courses, and the reading of professional literature.
2. Professionals participate in the objective and systematic evaluation of themselves, colleagues, services, and programs for the purpose of continuous improvement of professional performance.
3. Professionals in administrative positions support and facilitate professional development.

## Professionals in Relation to the Profession and to Other Professionals

The Profession

1. Special education professionals assume responsibility for participating in professional organizations and adherence to the standards and codes of ethics of those organizations.
2. Special education professionals have a responsibility to provide varied and exemplary supervised field experiences for persons in undergraduate and graduate preparation programs.
3. Special education professionals refrain from using professional relationships with students and parents for personal advantage.

4. Special education professionals take an active position in the regulation of the profession through use of appropriate procedures for bringing about changes.

5. Special education professionals initiate, support, and/or participate in research related to the education of persons with exceptionalities with the aim of improving the quality of educational services, increasing the accountability of programs, and generally benefiting persons with exceptionalities. They
   - Adopt procedures that protect the rights and welfare of subjects participating in the research.
   - Interpret and publish research results with accuracy and a high quality of scholarship.
   - Support a cessation of the use of any research procedure that may result in undesirable consequences for the participant.
   - Exercise all possible precautions to prevent misapplication or misutilization of a research effort, by self or others.

## Other Professionals

Special education professionals function as members of interdisciplinary teams, and the reputation of the profession rides with them. They

1. Recognize and acknowledge the competencies and expertise of members representing other disciplines as well as those of members in their own disciplines.

2. Strive to develop positive attitudes among other professionals toward persons with exceptionalities, representing them with an objective regard for their possibilities and their limitations as persons in a democratic society.

3. Cooperate with other agencies involved in serving persons with exceptionalities through such activities as the planning and coordination of information exchanges, service delivery, evaluation, and training, so that duplication or loss in quality of services may not occur.

4. Provide consultation and assistance, where appropriate, to both general and special educators as well as other school personnel serving persons with exceptionalities.

5. Provide consultation and assistance, where appropriate, to professionals in nonschool settings serving persons with exceptionalities.

6. Maintain effective interpersonal relations with colleagues and other professionals, helping them to develop and maintain positive and accurate perceptions about the special education profession.

# Glossary

**5p or cri-du-chat (cry of the cat) syndrome** A rare condition in which a portion of the fifth chromosome is missing. The condition usually results in severe intellectual disabilities. The children with this condition are characterized by a high-pitched, cat-like cry.

**Ability grouping** An instructional arrangement that allows students with common learning characteristics to benefit from targeted teaching.

**Absence seizures** Seizures in which a loss of consciousness occurs for about 30 seconds.

**Adaptive behavior** Part of most definitions of intellectual disability. Includes the practical and social skills that students use to function effectively in their everyday lives.

**ADD** An acronym that was formerly used to identify students with ADHD who exhibit primarily inattentive behaviors.

**Adequate yearly progress (AYP)** The No Child Left Behind Act mandates that all students make adequate yearly progress. AYP is defined by each state and is intended to measure student progress and ensure that all students experience continuous and substantial growth in academic achievement.

**ADHD** *See* Attention-deficit hyperactivity disorder.

**ADHD-C** *See* Combined type.

**ADHD-PHI** *See* Predominantly hyperactive-impulsive type.

**ADHD-PI** *See* Predominantly inattentive type.

**Advance organizer** An explicit introduction to a lesson that shows students how current activities fit contextually with past and future activities, heightening motivation/anticipation.

**Alternative or augmentative communication (AAC) devices** A variety of techniques and devices used to supplement a person's oral speech.

**American Association on Intellectual and Developmental Disabilities (AAIDD)** The leading professional organization that addresses intellectual disabilities. The name of this group was formerly the American Association of Mental Retardation (AAMR) but was changed in January 2007.

**Americans with Disabilities Act (ADA)** An act that requires nondiscriminatory protection of civil rights and accessibility to physical facilities and applies to all segments of society with the exception of private schools and religious organizations.

**Amphetamine** A type of stimulant medication used to treat the symptoms of ADHD. Amphetamines include Adderall and Dexedrine.

**Anemia** A blood disorder characterized by a low level of healthy red blood cells.

**Applied behavior analysis (ABA)** The application of the scientific method and behavioral principles to the observation, study, and modification of behavior.

**Asperger's syndrome** This syndrome is part of the autism spectrum. It is a disorder characterized by qualitative impairments in nonverbal behaviors, social relationships, interests, and social and emotional reciprocity but, unlike autism, involves no delays in language or cognitive development.

**Assistive technology (AT)** Any item or piece of equipment, whether available commercially, modified, or customized, that is used to increase, maintain, or improve the functional capabilities of a student with a disability.

**Asymmetric tonic neck reflex** A postural reaction that occurs while a baby is lying on his back. The head turns to one side causing the arm and leg on the side that he is looking toward to extend or straighten, while his other arm and leg will flex.

**Ataxia** A form of cerebral palsy characterized by a lack of balance and uncoordinated movement.

**Athetosis** (referred to as **dyskinesia**) A form of cerebral palsy characterized by either slow, writing movements or abrupt, jerky movements.

**Attention-deficit hyperactivity disorder (ADHD)** A persistent pattern of inattention and/or hyperactivity/impulsivity that is more frequently displayed and more severe than is typically observed in individuals at a comparable level of development.

**Augmentative/alternative communication (AAC)** Simple or technologically advanced methods that support or enhance oral and mechanical modes of communication.

**Autism** A neurological disorder that appears during the first 3 years of life. It adversely affects development in the areas of social interaction and communication skills. Individuals with autism typically show difficulties in verbal and nonverbal communication, social interactions, and leisure or play activities.

**Autism rating scales** Instruments that measure specific characteristics, abilities, and behaviors associated with autism.

**Autism spectrum disorders (ASD)** ASD, also referred to as pervasive developmental disorders (PDD), are a group of developmental disorders that share common social, communicative, and stereotyped and ritualistic behavioral similarities, varying in age of onset and severity of symptoms. The group includes autism, Asperger's syndrome, pervasive developmental disorder—not otherwise specified (PDD-NOS), Rett syndrome, and childhood disintegrative disorder (CDD).

**Autistic disorder** Sometimes referred to as early infantile autism, childhood autism, or Kanner's autism, it is characterized by marked impairments in social interactions and communication, and restrictions in activities or interests.

**Behavior intervention plan (BIP)** A formal plan for students who exhibit challenging behavior. A BIP is required for students whose behavior is so challenging that is may lead to a more restrictive placement.

**Bilingualism** The ability to speak two languages. *Multilingualism* refers to the ability to speak more than two languages.

**Blindness** A visual impairment that includes a loss of useful vision that can affect educational performance even with correction.

**Bloom's taxonomy**  A useful planning tool developed by Benjamin Bloom based on the assumptions that most content can be learned at different conceptual levels and that all students can benefit from well-planned lessons.

**Braille**  A code used to present text in a tactile format, represented in a rectangular cell with six dots.

**Brown v. Board of Education, 1954**  The landmark case that struck down racial segregation in public schools based upon the equal protection provisions guaranteed by the 14th Amendment of the Constitution.

**Cerebral palsy (CP)**  A neuromuscular disorder that results in the brain's inability to control some or all of the body's muscles.

**Child-find system**  An IDEA requirement that says states must identify, locate, and evaluate all children with disabilities, aged birth to 21, who are in need of early intervention or special education services.

**Childhood disintegrative disorder**  Following 2 years of relatively normal development, the individual develops a severe loss of functioning.

**Chromosomal anomalies**  This condition is one in which strands of chromosomal material within cells are not arranged in their normal pattern. Anomalies often result in syndromes such as Down syndrome.

**Civil rights movement**  A particularly active period from the late 1950s to the early 1990s that advocated for the application of the Bill of Rights to all disenfranchised persons, whether by race, gender, or disability.

**Clinically derived classification system**  A classification system in which emotional and behavioral disability is viewed as a distinct pattern of behavior that occurs regularly among individuals with challenging behaviors.

**Collectivist culture**  A culture in which working for the common good is more highly valued than individual achievement.

**Coma**  A profound state of unconsciousness.

**Combined type (ADHD-C)**  A subtype of students with ADHD who exhibit inattentive, hyperactive, and impulsive behaviors.

**Comorbidity**  The co-occurrence of two or more disorders or diseases that are not caused by each other.

**Conceptual framework**  An organizational structure that guides beliefs and understandings about a subject of inquiry.

**Configuration of hearing loss**  Describes qualitative aspects of hearing, such as whether both ears are affected or whether different frequencies are affected differently.

**Contractures**  A physical development in which normally elastic connective tissue is replaced by inelastic fibrous tissue, making the affected area resistant to stretching and preventing normal movement.

**Core deficit scales**  Assessments that allow for the precise measurement of specific symptoms and functioning.

**Cornelia de Lange Syndrome**  Characterized by several distinctive facial features such as arched, well-defined eyebrows and curly eyelashes, small (microcephalic) heads, and other features. These children may have intellectual disabilities ranging from mild to profound.

**Criterion-referenced test**  A student's performance on a criterion-referenced test is evaluated in terms of how well he or she performs on specific standards or criteria.

**Cultural definition of deafness**  Individuals who are deaf may consider themselves members of a group because of their deafness, because they use sign language as a primary means of communication, and because they share a set of beliefs about themselves.

**Culturally or linguistically diverse (CLD)**  Students from backgrounds that are non-European American and, in some instances, non-English speaking, including African American, Hispanic, American Indian/Alaskan Native, and Asian/Pacific Islander.

**Culturally responsive teaching and management**  Classroom instruction and management that are based upon a consideration of students' cultural backgrounds.

**Culture**  The values, beliefs, traditions, and behaviors associated with a particular group of people who share a common history.

**Curriculum-based measure (CBM)**  An efficient method of monitoring student performance through the collection and monitoring of academic progress over time.

**Cytomegalovirus (CMV)**  A common virus that infects many people. The infection is usually harmless and rarely causes illness unless a person's immune system is seriously weakened. The virus remains alive but dormant in the body for life.

**Deaf**  With a capital *D,* used to describe a particular group of people who share a language (American Sign Language) and a culture (Deaf culture).

**Deaf-blindness**  Concomitant hearing and visual impairments, the combination of which causes such severe communication and other developmental and educational needs that they cannot be accommodated in special education programs solely for children with deafness or children with blindness.

**Deafness**  A hearing impairment that is so severe that the child is impaired in processing linguistic information through hearing with or without amplification which adversely affects the child's educational performance.

**Decibel (dB)**  A unit of measurement of the intensity or loudness of sound.

**Degree of hearing loss**  A measure of the degree of severity of hearing loss expressed in decibels (dB).

**Deinstitutionalization**  The policy of releasing people, particularly those with disabilities of the mind, from institutions and into community settings.

**Depression**  A pervasive and insidious group of symptoms that affect a person's mood, thoughts, and carriage.

**Developmental aphasia**  A language impairment that is assumed to be the result of some type of neurological dysfunction.

**Developmental assessments**  These assessments are intended to judge a child's development in relation to other children. They are based on the children's achievement of developmental milestones.

**Developmentally appropriate practices**  Instructional activities that are individually and age-appropriate and reflect a child's social and cultural milieu

**Diagnostic and Statistical Manual of Mental Disorders (4th ed.—Text Revision) (DSM-IV-TR)**  A manual produced by the American Psychiatric Association that includes definitions and identification criteria used to identify persons with psychiatric and other related disorders.

**Diagnostic interviews**  Semistructured narrative methods of gathering information on patterns of development and behavior.

**Direct instruction (DI)**  Systematic, explicit instruction, often based on scripted instructional materials.

**Direct observation scales**  A structured method for observing characteristics and abilities.

**Disabilities**  Defined in IDEA 2004, and includes any child determined to have "mental retardation, a hearing impairment (including deafness), a speech or language impairment, a visual impairment (including blindness), a serious emotional disturbance (referred to in this part as 'emotional disturbance'), an orthopedic impairment, autism, traumatic brain injury, an other health impairment, a specific learning disability, deaf-blindness, or multiple disabilities, and who, by reason thereof, needs special education and related services" (IDEA 2004, 300.8(a)(1)).

**Dominant genetic condition**  A condition that may be inherited if only one parent has the condition.

**Down syndrome**  A condition due to chromosomal anomaly in which there are three chromosome strands (instead of two) at pair 21 (trisomy 21). Children with Down syndrome are usually smaller than average and have slower physical, motor, language, and mental development.

**Due process**  Found in the 14th Amendment of the Constitution of the United States, it is the assurance of open and fair legal and procedural processes in which certain rights are inviolable.

**Dyscalculia**  A disability in the area of mathematics that is assumed to be the result of some type of neurological dysfunction. This disability may be manifested by difficulty in learning basic math facts, mathematical operations, and/or abstract mathematical concepts.

**Dysgraphia**  A disability in the area of writing that is assumed to be the result of some type of neurological dysfunction. This disability may be manifested by difficulty with handwriting, spelling, and/or written expression.

**Dyskinesia**  *See,* Athetosis.

**Dyslexia**  A reading disability that is assumed to be the result of some type of neurological dysfunction.

**Early intervening services**  Early intervening services are intensive interventions provided to students who are having difficulties in general education but who have not yet been referred to special education. The purpose of these services is to try to keep children from being placed in special education unless absolutely necessary.

**Echolalia**  Repeating words and parts of or whole sentences spoken by other people, with little understanding.

**Emotional and behavioral disabilities (EBD)**  Behavioral and emotional responses so different from appropriate levels that the behaviors adversely affect educational performance.

**Emotional lability**  A condition of excessive emotional reactions and frequent mood changes.

**English-language learners (ELL)**  Includes students who are learning English as a second language or those who have been previously called students with limited English proficiency.

**Entrepreneurial supports**  Supportive, self-sustaining, for-profit corporations built upon the skills and interests of those with disabilities.

**Epilepsy**  A neurological condition that makes people prone to having seizures.

**Equal protection**  A clause of the 14th Amendment to the Constitution of the United States that prohibits the denial of equal protection of the laws. As such, discrimination by race, gender, or disability is prohibited.

**Ethnic background**  A group in which individual members identify with one another, usually based on ancestry. Ethnic groups often share common practices related to factors such as culture, religion, and language.

**Eugenics**  The study and policy of "improving" the human race through selective reproductive practices.

**Evidence-based educational practices**  Scientifically based practices founded on well-conducted research, which therefore have proven in some manner their efficacy.

**Evidence-based instruction**  Strategies and tactics used for teaching that have demonstrated effectiveness based on empirical research.

**Exclusion clause**  Included in the definition of LD to ensure that the primary reason for a student's academic difficulty is a learning disability, and not another disability (e.g., intellectual disability or emotional/behavior disorder) or environmental conditions (e.g., poor teaching).

**Family-centered approach**  An approach to treatment or intervention that considers and addresses the strengths and needs of an individual's family as well as those of the individual.

**Figurative language**  A variety of figures of speech such as idioms, metaphors, analogies, similes, hyperbole, understatement, jokes, allusions, and slang.

**Fluency**  The rate and smoothness of speech.

**Fragile-X syndrome**  A genetically transmitted condition that is the most common cause of genetically transmitted intellectual disabilities. It is transmitted mostly from mothers to their sons. When inherited by boys, about 80% will have intellectual disabilities ranging from mild to severe.

**Frequency (or pitch)**  How high or low a voice is.

**Functional behavior assessment (FBA)**  A systematic, highly structured method of gathering information to determine the purpose or function of observed behaviors.

**Functional language**  Communicating with a purpose, such as being able to communicate basic wants and needs.

**Gastroesophageal reflux**  This condition occurs when the lower esophageal sphincter does not close properly and stomach contents leak back, or reflux, into the esophagus.

**Generalized anxiety**  A state of fear, worry, and tension that is continuous and often accompanied by a variety of physical symptoms such as headaches, irritability, sweating, and nausea.

**Genetic condition**  A condition inherited by a child from one or more of the parents.

**Giftedness**  With no single definition, giftedness is usually defined by one of three conceptualizations (the Marland federal definition, Renzulli's three ring conceptualization, and Gardner's multiple intelligences), each of which refers generally to enhanced talents and cognitive ability.

**Glasgow coma scale**  A neurological scale used to measure the consciousness of a person.

**Guided practice**  Closely supervised practice activities designed to reinforce appropriate practices and correct errors.

**Hearing impairment**  An impairment in hearing, whether permanent or fluctuating, that adversely affects a child's educational performance but that is not included under the IDEA definition of deafness.

**Herpes**  A common viral infection that causes oral herpes (cold sores or fever blisters) and genital herpes (genital sores or sores below the waist).

**Highly qualified teachers**  NCLB requirement that teachers be appropriately licensed and have the requisite qualifications in core academic subject areas. Special education teachers must be highly qualified in special education as well as in each of the core subject areas they teach.

**Hyperactivity**  A characteristic used to identify students with ADHD. Students who are hyperactive exhibit a high level of activity that is not appropriate in a particular setting and is not age appropriate.

**Impulsivity**   A characteristic used to identify students with ADHD. Students who are impulsive respond without thinking at a level that is not age appropriate.

**Inattention**   A characteristic used to identify students with ADHD. Students who are inattentive cannot sustain attention for age-appropriate periods of time.

**Independent practice**   Practice activities designed to build fluency such as seatwork and homework typically completed independently.

**Individualist culture**   A culture in which individual achievement and initiative are valued and self-realization is promoted.

**Individualized education program (IEP)**   A detailed, structured plan of action required by IDEA that informs and guides the delivery of instruction and related services.

**Individualized family service plan (IFSP)**   A detailed, structured plan of action required by IDEA that informs and guides the delivery of instruction and related services.

**Individuals with Disabilities Education Improvement Act of 2004 (IDEA 2004)**   Landmark legislation, originally enacted in 1975 as the Education for All Handicapped Children Act, that guides how states and school districts must educate children with disabilities.

**Induction**   Introductory experiences novice teachers have that expose them to experienced teachers and mentors, professional activities that improve performance, more and more complex tasks, and the overall culture surrounding teaching.

**In loco parentis**   Teachers are entrusted by parents to exercise responsibility toward their children in the parents' place, and with that responsibility come associated privileges and liabilities.

**Instructional technology (IT)**   A general term that refers to the hardware and software used to enhance teaching and learning.

**Intellectual disability**   A widely used term in many European countries, which is emerging in the United States as the preferred term for students who have been currently labeled *mentally retarded*. Defined as subaverage general intellectual functioning, existing concurrently with deficits in adaptive behavior and manifested during the developmental period, that adversely affects a child's educational performance.

**Intensity (of sound)**   The loudness of sound, which is measured in decibels.

**Intraindividual differences**   Varying strengths and weaknesses that exist within individual profiles of performance and functioning.

**Laryngeal tension**   A chronic voice condition due to vocal abuse and misuse.

**Larynx**   A valve structure between the trachea (windpipe) and the pharynx (the upper throat) that is the primary organ of voice production.

**Learning disabilities**   A classification used in special education for students who exhibit significant problems in academic areas (such as reading) that cannot be explained by other disabilities. Under IDEA, the term "specific learning disabilities" is used for this condition.

**Least restrictive environment (LRE)**   Services and the setting in which a free and appropriate education meets a child's individual needs while being educated with children without disabilities to the greatest extent possible.

**Legal blindness**   Central acuity of 20/200 or less in the better eye with the best possible corrections as measured on a Snellen vision chart, or a visual field of 20 degrees or less.

**Legislation**   Proposed or enacted law or set of laws.

**Lesch-Nyhan syndrome**   An X-linked recessive disease. The gene is carried by the mother and passed on to her son. A characteristic of this syndrome is self-injurious behavior, primarily lip and finger biting.

**Life-space interview (LSI)**   An intervention that occurs after an extreme behavioral event. Assumes that verbal mediation following this problematic event can result in lasting behavioral changes.

**Litigation**   A lawsuit or other action in the courts that seeks to settle a legal disagreement or issue.

**Maternal infections**   A prenatal infection of the mother that may affect the developing fetus.

**Mental retardation**   A term that is used in federal law and in many states that is being supplanted by the term *intellectual disability*.

**Metacognition**   An awareness of thinking processes and how these processes are monitored.

**Mild intellectual disability**   A developmental disability characterized by a low intelligence quotient (IQ) that is between about 55 to 70 points and by poor adaptive behavior.

**Moderate intellectual disability**   A developmental disability characterized by a low intelligence quotient (IQ) that is between about 40 to 55 points and by poor adaptive behavior.

**Morpheme**   The smallest unit of language that has meaning.

**Morphology**   How sounds and words are put together to form meaning.

**Multiple disabilities**   Concomitant impairments (such as mental retardation and blindness, or mental retardation and an orthopedic impairment) that are usually very severe and require educational provisions that are different than if the student had only one of the conditions.

**Musculoskeletal disorders**   These are disorders of the bones, connective tissue, and muscles. Examples include polio, arthritis, bone fractures or tumors, malformed bones, and joint disorders.

**Nasal cavity**   A large, air-filled space above and behind the nose in the middle of the face.

**Naturalistic study**   Research conducted in real-life situations, such as in the classroom or the school.

**No Child Left Behind Act (NCLB)**   Federal legislation that requires states to (1) assess student performance in reading, math, and science; (2) ensure that all students have highly qualified teachers; and (3) provide public school choice and supplemental services to students unable to meet adequate yearly progress (AYP) for 2 years.

**Nondiscriminatory assessment**   Assessments that are not biased against or harmful toward students who are being tested.

**Norm-referenced test**   A student's performance on a norm-referenced test is evaluated in terms of how well he or she performs in comparison to other students of the same age or grade who were included in the standardization process or test development.

**Obsessive-compulsive disorder (OCD)**   An anxiety disorder characterized by an inordinate fear or worry in the form of frequent problematic thoughts and the belief that these thoughts can be managed by the performance of repetitive actions and rituals.

**Occupational therapists**   Professionals who use treatments to develop, recover, or maintain the daily living and work skills of individuals with disabilities.

**Oral**   Related to the mouth.

**Orthotic devices** Braces and similar devices used to support feet and ankles.

**Overrepresentation** For certain demographic groups, the proportion of students identified for special education services is higher than the proportion of that group in the general population.

**Paraeducator** Also called a *paraprofessional, teacher assistant*, or *teacher's aide*, this is a person who assists a teacher in a special education or general education classroom.

**Part C services** Provided for students under the age of 3 and their families. The services are named after the part of the law (IDEA 2004) that describes them.

**Partial seizures** Seizures that originate in a specific part of the brain.

**Peer tutoring** A series of grouping alternatives that allow same-age or cross-age peers to assist classmates who are struggling with specific academic content.

**Pervasive developmental disorder—not otherwise specified (PDD-NOS)** Individuals who do not meet the criteria or the degree of severity that characterizes the four other disorders in the PDD group but who still show a pattern of impairments in social interaction, verbal and nonverbal communication skills, and stereotypical or restricted interests.

**Phonatory quality (of sound)** The quality of sound in a person's voice.

**Phoneme** A meaningful unit in the sound system of a language.

**Phonological processing** The ability to use sound-symbol correspondences to sound out words. Many students with reading disabilities have problems with phonological processing.

**Phonology** The sound system of language, including speech sounds, speech patterns, and rules that apply to those sounds.

**Physical therapists** Professionals who provide services that help restore function, improve mobility, relieve pain, and prevent or limit permanent physical disabilities of patients who have various injuries, diseased, or disabilities.

**Picture Exchange Communication System (PECS)** An augmentative/alternative communication system that uses pictures to systematically teach people to initiate communication.

**Positive behavior supports (PBSs)** A school-wide system of support that includes a continuum of proactive strategies for defining, teaching, and supporting appropriate student behaviors. PBS is used to create positive school environments in classroom and nonclassroom (hallway, restroom) settings.

**Positive support reflex** A reaction that occurs when holding a baby under his arms and allowing his feet to bounce on a flat surface, he will extend (straighten) his legs for about 20–30 seconds to support himself, before he flexes his legs again and goes to a sitting position.

**Pragmatics** The rules that govern and describe how language is used in different contexts and environments.

**Predominantly hyperactive-impulsive type (ADHD-PHI)** A subtype of students with ADHD who are primarily hyperactive and impulsive.

**Predominantly inattentive type (ADHD-PI)** A subtype of students with ADHD who are primarily inattentive.

**Prelinguistic communication** These are communication efforts that occur before the development of formal language. They include eye gaze, affective expressions, gestures, and vocalizations.

**Prenatal causes** Conditions that originate before birth.

**Prereferral intervention** Before a child is formally referred and evaluated for eligibility for special education services, prereferral intervention will be tried in the regular classroom in an attempt to improve the child's academic or behavioral functioning.

**Primitive reflexes** Reflexes that occur in infants but disappear as they grow older.

**Professionalism** The conduct, qualities, and purposes one has that reflect one's profession. It is an inclusive pattern of behavior that includes respect, responsibility, communication, leadership, risk taking, ongoing development, and a positive attitude.

**Profound intellectual disabilities** The most severe form of a developmental disability characterized by a low intelligence quotient (IQ) that is below 25 and by extremely poor adaptive behavior.

**Prophylactic antibiotics** Antibiotics used to prevent infections.

**Prosocial behaviors** A series of behaviors, such as helping, sharing, or showing empathy, intended to benefit others or to evoke a meaningful interactive response from others.

**Range of motion** Joint flexibility usually measured by the number of degrees from the starting position of a segment to its position at the end of its full range of the movement.

**Recessive genetic condition** A condition that can be inherited only if both parents have the condition or if both parents are carriers.

**Resilience** Successful adaptation in school or other settings, despite challenging or threatening life circumstances; a capacity that is available to all students and is bolstered by supportive factors.

**Respiration** Breathing.

**Respiratory infections** Multiple conditions including the common cold, viral respiratory infections, and bacterial respiratory infections.

**Response to intervention (RTI)** An approach to the identification of special education needs that is based on the assumption that students who struggle academically should only be identified with a disability if they do not respond to effective and intensive levels of instruction.

**Rett's disorder** A neurodevelopmental disorder characterized by seizures and mental retardation as well as a loss of functional or purposeful use of hands.

**Routines and procedures** Activities or structures that help teachers organize and orchestrate everyday events with effectiveness and efficiency.

**Rubella** A condition (commonly known as German measles) caused by the rubella virus that primarily affects the skin and lymph nodes.

**Scaffolding** Temporary support that teachers give students as they learn academic content.

**Screening** Determining whether a child has a broad set of behavioral characteristics that suggest the possibility of a disability and the need for further assessments.

**Section 504 of the Rehabilitation Act** Civil rights legislation that provides protections for persons with disabilities who are not eligible for services as part of IDEA. This includes students whose disability does not adversely affect educational performance, and those with disabilities that do not match the definitions under IDEA, including communicable diseases; temporary disabilities; and allergies, asthma, or illnesses due to the environment. Section 504 considers the child as having a disability if that child functions as though disabled and extends protections against discrimination beyond schools to employment and social and health services.

**Self-advocacy**  A principle and set of practices that allow people with disabilities to assume responsibility and advocate for their own lives and interests.

**Self-determination**  When persons act as the primary decision makers in their lives and make choices free from undue influence.

**Self-efficacy**  The belief that one's professional decisions, actions, and choices result in positive outcomes in students' lives.

**Self-fulfilling prophecy**  When someone behaves in ways that meet or go further below one's communicated low expectations, or when someone is unable to meet unreasonably high expectations and then becomes frustrated or depressed.

**Self-injurious behaviors (SIBs)**  These are behaviors such as hitting your own head or biting your own hand that can be potentially dangerous. They are sometimes exhibited by students with severe and profound intellectual disabilities.

**Self-management**  A range of behaviors, such as self-instructing, monitoring, evaluation, reinforcement, graphing, and advocacy, by which a student can increase independence by increasing positive behaviors and skills.

**Self-regulation strategies**  Strategies that may be used by students with disabilities to decrease inappropriate behaviors, increase appropriate behaviors, and increase academic accuracy and productivity.

**Semantics**  The study of the meaning of language, including meaning at the word, sentence, and conversational level.

**Separate class placement**  A class placement setting in which a student with a disability is educated with other students with disabilities for 60% or more of the school day.

**Separation anxiety**  Inordinate fear, worry, and distress of being away from persons to whom a child is attached.

**Severe discrepancy**  A criterion that has often been used to identify students with LD. Results when there is a severe discrepancy between expected achievement (typically based on an IQ score) and actual achievement.

**Severe intellectual disabilities**  A developmental disability characterized by a low intelligence quotient (IQ) that is between about 25 to 40 points and by poor adaptive behavior.

**Sheltered workshops**  Segregated facilities that provide noncompetitive training and employment opportunities for individuals with disabilities.

**Six-hour retarded child**  A phrase that was initially used by the President's Committee on Mental Retardation in 1969. Refers to the perspective that mild intellectual disabilities are more obvious during the school day than when students are at home or in the community.

**Smith-Magenis syndrome**  A chromosomal disorder with a recognizable pattern of physical, behavioral, and developmental features. It is characterized by infant feeding problems, low muscle tone, developmental delay, variable levels of intellectual disability, speech/language delay, middle-ear problems, skeletal anomalies, and decreased sensitivity to pain.

**Social reciprocity**  An exchange of meaningful communication that begins in infancy and continues throughout life.

**Social skills instruction**  The teaching of social interactive skills, including attending, affective, and pragmatic interaction.

**Social workers**  Professionals who assist individuals and families in different ways in their schools or communities to help solve problems related to daily living.

**Spasticity**  A form of cerebral palsy characterized by stiff muscles, labored movement, and a limited range of motion due to muscle contractures.

**Special schools**  These are separate schools that only serve students with disabilities, usually students with more severe disabilities.

**Specific language impairment (SLI)**  Difficulty with language in the absence of problems such as intellectual disabilities, hearing loss, or emotional disorders.

**Speech–language pathologists (SLPs)**  Sometimes called *speech therapists,* these professionals assess, diagnose, treat, and help to prevent disorders related to speech, language, cognitive-communication, voice, swallowing, and fluency.

**Standard American English (SAE)**  The dialect of English most common in the United States; most authorities believe it is best represented by a Midwestern accent.

**Standard course of study (SCOS)**  Learning outcomes specified by local or state education agencies for specific grades and subject areas.

**Standard English**  A controversial term that is most often used to refer to the dialect of English that is spoken by educated people.

**Statistically derived classification system**  A classification system in which emotional and behavioral disability is viewed as a cluster of extreme forms of typical behaviors and emotions.

**Stimulant medication**  Medications that are frequently used to treat students with ADHD. These medications have been found to be highly effective for many students with ADHD, because they increase attention and reduce restlessness. Stimulant medications include Ritalin and Concerta.

**Strategies intervention model (SIM)**  A combined cognitive and behavioral method of instruction that explicitly teaches a series of learning strategies that guide students in the acquisition, integration, and generalization of content.

**Stuttering**  An interruption in the smooth, easy flow of speech that includes repetitions, prolongations, interjections, and silent pauses.

**Supported employment**  A range of supports that enable people with disabilities to work in natural environments.

**Surface management techniques**  A series of teacher-based actions that address minor instances of misbehavior with little disruption to the instructional environment.

**Syntax**  The order of language, especially the way in which words are put together in phrases or sentences to produce meaning.

**Syphilis**  A sexually transmitted infection. The infection can also be passed from mother to infant during pregnancy, causing congenital syphilis.

**Talent**  An ability that is not intellectual or academic.

**Targeted interventions**  Powerful school-based actions directed toward the chronic and persistent problem behaviors of those students who do not respond to school-wide methods of discipline and behavior management.

**Thalidomide**  A drug chiefly sold and prescribed during the late 1950s and 1960s to pregnant women to combat morning sickness and as a sleeping aid. The drug resulted in children born with limb deficiencies.

**Token economy**  A common behavioral technique in which criteria are set for the exchanges of tokens for the display of positive behaviors. The tokens can be exchanged for items or activities a child finds meaningful.

**Tonic-clonic seizures** A seizure characterized by a loss of consciousness for several minutes, falling, and stiff (tonic) and then jerking (clonic) movements.

**Tonic labyrinthine reflex** A primitive reflex found in newborns in which tilting the head back while lying on the back causes the back to stiffen and even arch backwards, causes the legs to straighten, stiffen, and push together, causes the toes to point, causes the arms to bend at the elbows and wrists, and causes the hands to become fisted or the fingers to curl.

**Toxoplasmosis** An infection caused by a microscopic parasite that lives inside the cells of humans and animals, which is passed from animals, especially cats, to humans.

**Transition services** Required by IDEA 2004, must begin by age 16, and include a coordinated set of services that is results oriented, focuses on improving the academic and functional achievement of a student, and facilitates movement from school to post-school activities.

**Type of hearing loss** The point in the auditory system where the hearing loss is occurring.

**Universal design for learning (UDL)** A method of making curriculum and instructional activities accessible to all students by including supports and accommodations into the original design rather than making alterations after the fact.

**Visual acuity** How clearly a person sees at a specific distance. Expressed as a fraction. The numerator refers to the distance from the object; the denominator indicates the distance at which a person with normal eyesight could see the same object.

**Visual field** The area in space around the head that can be seen without moving the head. Frequently this is also called *peripheral vision*.

**Visual impairment** An impairment in vision that adversely affects a child's educational performance.

**Vocal chords (or vocal folds)** Muscular folds of mucous membrane that extend from the larynx wall.

**Vocal folds** *See* Vocal chords.

**Vocal nodules** Benign growths on both vocal folds that are caused by vocal abuse.

**Voice** Sound produced by air passing out through the larynx and upper respiratory tract.

**Voice output communication aids (VOCA)** Devices that are portable and allow people with difficulty in speech to communicate through the use of graphic symbols and words on computerized displays.

**Working memory** Used to temporarily store and use information. Allows an individual to see something, think about it, and then act on this information.

**Wraparound interventions** Intensive interventions that are grounded in values of family empowerment and cultural competence, which typically require the coordinated and integrated efforts of teams of professional service providers.

**Zero reject** The policy that prevents the exclusion of any child with a disability from receiving an education in the least restrictive environment.

# References

Abbott, M., Walton, C., Tapia, Y., & Greenwood, C. (1999). Research to practice: A blueprint for closing the gap in local schools. *Exceptional Children, 65,* 339–354.

Abeson, A., Bolick, N., & Hass, J. (1976). Due process of law: Background and intent. In F. J. Weintraub, A. Abeson, J. Ballard, & M. L. LaVor (Eds.), *Public policy and the education of exceptional children.* (pp. 22–32). Reston, VA: The Council for Exceptional Children.

Abrams, B. J. (2005). Becoming a therapeutic teacher of students with emotional and behavioral disorders. *Teaching Exceptional Children, 38*(2), 40–45.

Achenbach, T. M., & Rescorla, L. (2001). *Manual for the ASEBA school-age forms and profiles.* Burlington: University of Vermont, Research Center for Children, Youth, and Families.

Ahearn, E. (2003). *Specific learning disability: Current approaches to identification and proposals for change.* Alexandria, VA: National Association of State Directors of Special Education.

Ahearn, E. (2006). *Standards-based IEPs: Implementation in selected states.* Alexandria, VA: National Association of State Directors of Special Education.

Akshoomoff, N., Pierce, K., & Courchesne, E. (2002). The neurobiological basis of autism from a developmental perspective. *Development and Psychopathology, 14,* 613–634.

Albert, L. (2003). *Cooperative discipline: A teacher's handbook.* Circle Pines, MN: AGS.

Algozzine, B., Ysseldyke, J., & Elliot, J. (1998). *Strategies and tactics for effective instruction.* Longmont, CO: Sopris West.

Allbritten, D., Mainzer, R., & Ziegler, D. (2004, Winter). Will students with disabilities be scapegoats for school failures? *Educational Horizons, 82*(2).

Amenkhienan, C. (2003). *Attention deficit disorder: Student handbook.* Blacksburg: Virginia Tech, Cook Counseling Center.

American Academy of Asthma Allergy & Immunology. (2009). *Childhood asthma.* Retrieved July 27, 2009, from http://www.aaaai.org/patients/gallery/childhoodasthma.asp

American Academy of Pediatrics. (2000). Clinical practice guideline: Diagnosis and evaluation of the child with attention-deficit/hyperactivity disorder. *Pediatrics, 105*(5), 1158–1170.

American Academy of Pediatrics. (2001). Clinical practice guideline: Treatment of school-age children with attention-deficit/hyperactivity disorder. *Pediatrics, 108*(4), 1033–1044.

American Association of Colleges for Teacher Education. (2002). *Educators' preparation for cultural and linguistic diversity: A call to action. Committee on Multicultural Education.* Retrieved May 18, 2009, from http://www.aacte.org/index.php?/Programs/Multi-cultural-/-Diversity/aacte-statements-on-multicultural-education.html

American Federation of Teachers. (2008). *Sizing up state standards, 2008.* Retrieved May 11, 2009, from http://www.aft.org/pubs-reports/downloads/teachers/standards2008.pdf

American Lung Association. (2009). *Asthma & children fact sheet.* Retrieved July 20, 2009, from http://www.lungusa.org/

American Psychiatric Association. (2000). *Diagnostic and statistical manual of mental disorders* (4th ed.). Washington, DC: Author.

American Psychological Association (APA). (2003). *Guidelines for non-handicapping language in APA journals.* Retrieved August 5, 2006, from www.apastyle.org/disabilities.html

American Speech-Language-Hearing Association (ASHA). (1999). *Guidelines for the roles and responsibilities of the school-based speech-language pathologist.* Retrieved January 11, 2006, from http://search.asha.org/query.html?col=asha&qt=scope+of+practice

American Speech-Language-Hearing Association (ASHA). (2009). *Hearing assessment.* Retrieved August 3, 2009, from http://www.asha.org/public/hearing/testing/assess.htm

Anderson, G. M., & Hoshino, Y. (2005). Neurochemical studies of autism. In F. R. Volkmar, R. Paul, A. Klin, & D. Cohen (Eds.), *Handbook of autism and pervasive developmental disorders: Vol. 2. Assessment, interventions, and policy* (4th ed., pp. 453–472). Hoboken, NJ: Wiley.

Anderson, L., & Krathwohl, D. (Eds.). (2001). *A taxonomy for learning, teaching, and assessing.* New York: Longman.

Angelman Syndrome Foundation. (2009). *Facts about Angelman syndrome—7th edition.* Retrieved August 4, 2009, from http://www.angelman.org/stay-informed/facts-about-angelman-syndrome—7th-edition/

ARC. (2005). *Causes and prevention of mental retardation.* Retrieved June 1, 2009, from www.thearc.org/NetCommunity/Document.Doc?&id=147

Arick, J. R., Krug, D. A., Fullerton, A., Loos, L., & Falco, R. (2005). School-based programs. In F. R. Volkmar, R. Paul, A. Klin, & D. Cohen (Eds.), *Handbook of autism and pervasive developmental disorders: Vol. 2. Assessment, interventions, and policy* (4th ed., pp. 1003–1028). Hoboken, NJ: Wiley.

Arnold, K. D. (1993). Academically talented women in the 1930s: The Illinois valedictorian project. In K. D. Hulbert & D. T. Schuster (Eds.), *Women's lives through time* (pp. 393–414). San Francisco: Jossey-Bass.

Arroyo, C. (2008). *The funding gap. Education Trust.* Retrieved May 15, 2009, from http://www.nvasb.org/Publications/Research_Data/the_funding_gap.pdf

Ashford, R., Queen, J. A., Algozzine, B., & Mitchell, G. (2008). Perceptions and record of violence in middle and high school. *Behavioral Disorders, 33*(4), 222–232.

Autism Information Center. (2009). *Frequently asked questions: Prevalence.* Retrieved July 2, 2009, from http://www.cdc.gov/ncbddd/autism/htm

Azordegan, J. (2004, January). *Initial findings and major questions about HOUSSE.* Retrieved November 3, 2005, from http://www.ecs.org/topnav_NEW.htm

Bélanger, J., & Gagné, F. (2006). Estimating the size of the gifted/talented population from multiple identification criteria. *Journal for the Education of the Gifted, 30*(2), 131–163.

Babbidge Committee Report. (1965). *Education of the deaf in the United States: Report of the advisory committee on the education of the deaf.* Washington, DC: U.S. Government Printing Office.

Baca, L. M., & Cervantes, H. T. (2004). *The bilingual special education interface*. Upper Saddle River, NJ: Merrill/Pearson.

Baglieri, S., & Knopf, J. H. (2004). Normalizing difference in inclusive teaching. *Journal of Learning Disabilities, 37*(6), 525–529.

Bailey, D. B., McWilliam, R. A., Darkes, L. A., Hebbeler, K., Simeonsson, R. J., Spiker, D., et al. (1998). Family outcomes in early intervention: A framework for program evaluation and efficacy research. *Exceptional Children, 64,* 313–328.

Baines, L, Baines, C., & Masterson, C. (1994). Mainstreaming: One school's reality. *Phi Delta Kappan, 76*(1), 39–40, 57–64.

Baird, G., et al. (2000). A screening instrument for autism at 18 months of age: A 6-year follow-up. *Journal of the American Academy of Child and Adolescent Psychiatry, 29,* 694–702.

Bandura, A. (1977). Self-efficacy: Toward a unifying theory of behavioral change. *Psychological Review, 84,* 191–215.

Bangert, A. W., & Cooch, C. G. (2001). Facilitating teacher assistance teams: Key questions. *Bulletin, 85*(626). Retrieved December 2, 2004, from http://www.principals.org/news/bltn_tchr_asst901.cfm

Banks, J., Cochran-Smith, M., Moll, L., Richert, A., Zeichner, K., LePage, P., et al. with McDonald, M. (2005). Teaching diverse learners. In L. Darling-Hammond & J. Bransford (Eds.), *Preparing teachers for a changing world: What teachers should learn and be able to do* (pp. 232–273). San Francisco: Jossey-Bass.

Banks, J., & McGee Banks, C. (2006). *Multicultural education: Issues and perspectives* (6th ed.). Hoboken, NJ: Wiley.

Banner, J. M., & Cannon, H. C. (1997). *The elements of teaching*. New Haven, CT: Yale University Press.

Barbaresi, W., Katusic, S., Colligan, R., et al. (2002). How common is attention-deficit/hyperactivity disorder? *Archives of Pediatric Adolescent Medicine, 156,* 217–224.

Barkley, R. (2000). *Taking charge of ADHD*. New York: Guilford.

Barkley, R. (2003). Attention-deficit/hyperactivity disorder. In E. J. Mash & R. Barkley (Eds.), *Child psychopathology* (2nd ed., pp. 75–143). New York: Guilford.

Barkley, R. (2006a). Comorbid disorders, social and family adjustment. In R. Barkley (Ed.). *Attention-deficit hyperactivity disorder: A handbook for diagnosis and treatment* (3rd ed., pp. 184–218). New York: Guilford Press.

Barkley, R. (2006b). Primary symptoms, diagnostic criteria, prevalence, and gender differences. In R. Barkley (Ed.), *Attention-deficit hyperactivity disorder: A handbook for diagnosis and treatment* (3rd ed., pp. 76–121). New York: Guilford Press.

Barkley, R., Fischer, M., Smallish, L., & Fletcher, K. (2002). The persistance of attention-deficit/hyperactivity disorder into young adulthood as a function of reporting source and definition of disorder. *Journal of Abnormal Psychology, 111*(2), 279–289.

Barkley, R., Fischer, M., Smallish, L., & Fletcher, K. (2003). Does the treatment of attention-deficit/hyperactivity disorder with stimulants contribute to drug use/abuse? A 13-year prospective study. *Pediatrics, 111,* 97–109.

Barkley, R. A. (1981). *Hyperactive children: A handbook for diagnosis and treatment*. New York: Guilford.

Baron-Cohen, S., Wheelwright, S., Lawson, J., Griffen, R., Ashwin, C., Billington, J., & Chakrabarti, B. (2005). Empathizing and systematizing in autism spectrum conditions. In F. R. Volkmar, R. Paul, A. Klin, & D. Cohen (Eds.), *Diagnosis, development, neurobiology, and behavior* (4th ed., pp. 628–639). Hoboken, NJ: Wiley.

Batshaw, M. L., Pellegrino, L., & Roizen, N. J. (2007). *Children with disabilities* (6th ed.). Baltimore: Brookes.

Beirne-Smith, M., Patton, J., & Kim, S. (2006). *Mental retardation: An introduction to intellectual disabilities* (7th ed.). Upper Saddle River, NJ: Merrill/Pearson.

Bell, L. I. (2003). Strategies that close the gap. *Educational Leadership, 60*(4), 32–34.

Bempechat, J. (1998). *Against the odds*. San Francisco: Jossey-Bass.

Benard, B. (2004). *Resiliency: What we have learned*. San Francisco: WestEd.

Benner, G. J., Nelson, J. R., & Epstein, M. H. (2002). Language skills of children with EBD: A literature review. *Journal of Emotional and Behavioral Disorders, 10,* 43–59.

Bennett, A. (1932). *A comparative study of subnormal children in the elementary grades*. New York: Columbia University, Teachers College, Bureau of Publication.

Berger, S. L. (1994). *College planning for gifted students* (2nd ed.). Reston, VA: Council for Exceptional Children.

Bernas-Pierce, J., & Miller, T. (2005). *Natural environments: Service and advocacy for children who are visually impaired or deafblind* [Monograph 1]. Watertown, MA: Perkins School for the Blind.

Best, S. (2005a). Health impairments and infectious diseases. In S. J. Best, K. W. Heller, & J. L. Bigge (Eds.), *Teaching individuals with physical or multiple disabilities* (5th ed., pp. 59–85). Upper Saddle River, NJ: Merrill/Pearson.

Best, S. (2005b). Physical disabilities. In S. J. Best, K. W. Heller, & J. L. Bigge (Eds.), *Teaching individuals with physical or multiple disabilities* (5th ed., pp. 31–58). Upper Saddle River, NJ: Merrill/Pearson.

Best, S. J., & Bigge, J. L. (2005). Cerebral palsy. In S. J. Best, K. W. Heller, & J. L. Bigge (Eds.), *Teaching individuals with physical or multiple disabilities* (5th ed., pp. 87–109). Upper Saddle River, NJ: Merrill/Pearson.

Best, S. J., Heller, K. W., & Bigge, J. L. (Eds.). (2005). *Teaching individuals with physical or multiple disabilities* (5th ed.). Upper Saddle River, NJ: Merrill/Pearson Education.

Best, S. J., Reed, P., & Bigge, J. L. (2005). Assistive technology. In S. J. Best, K. Wolff Heller, & J. L. Bigge (Eds.), *Teaching Individuals with Physical or Multiple Disabilities* (5th ed., pp. 179–226). Upper Saddle River, NJ: Merrill/Pearson Education.

Bettelheim, B. (1967). *The empty fortress: Infantile autism and the birth of the self*. New York: Free Press.

Bhanpuri, H., & Sexton, S. (2006). *A look at the hidden costs of high school exit exams: CEP policy brief*. Washington, DC: Center on Education Policy. Retrieved October 20, 2006, from http://www.cep-dc.org/pubs/hseepolicybriefSep2006/

Biederman, J., Faraone, S., Keenan, K., & Tsuang, M. (1991). Evidence of a familial association between attention deficit disorder and major affective disorders. *Archives of General Psychiatry, 48,* 633–642.

Biklen, D. (1990). Communication unbound: Autism and praxis. *Harvard Educational Review, 60,* 291–314.

Billingsley, B. (2005). *Cultivating and keeping committed special educators: What principals and district administrators can do*. Thousand Oaks, CA: Corwin.

Billingsley, B. S., & Tomchin, E. M. (1992). Four beginning LD teachers: What their experiences suggest for trainers and employers. *Learning Disabilities Research and Practice, 7,* 104–112.

Billingsley, B., Fall, A., & Williams, T. O. (2006). Who is teaching students with emotional disorders? A profile and comparison to other special educators. *Behavioral Disorders, 31*(1), 252–264.

Billingsley, F. F., & Albertson, L. R. (1999). Finding a future for functional skills. *Journal of the Association for Students with Severe Disabilities, 24,* 298–302.

Billingsley, F. F., & Romer, L. T. (1983). Response prompting and the transfer of stimulus control: Methods, research, and a conceptual framework. *Journal of the Association for the Severely Handicapped, 8,* 3–12.

Blatt, B. (1970). *Exodus from pandemonium: Human abuse and a reformation of public policy.* Boston: Allyn & Bacon.

Blatt, B. (1976). *Revolt of the idiots: A story.* Glen Ridge, NJ: Exceptional Press.

Blatt, B., & Kaplan, F. (1966). *Christmas in Purgatory: A photographic essay on mental retardation* (2nd ed.). Boston: Allyn & Bacon.

Bloch, D. (1978). *"So the witch won't eat me": Fantasy and the child's fear of infanticide.* Boston: Houghton Mifflin.

Bobeck, B. L. (2002, March/April). Teacher resiliency: A key to career longevity. *Clearing House, 75*(4), 202–205.

Boe, E., & Cook, L. H. (2006). The chronic and increasing shortage of fully certified teachers in special and general education. *Exceptional Children, 72*(4) 443–460.

Bogdan, R., & Biklen, D., (1977). Handicapism. *Social Policy, 7*(5), 59–63.

Bondy, E., Ross, D. D., Gallingane, C., & Hambacher, E. (2007). Creating environments of success and resilience: Culturally responsive classroom management and more. *Urban Education, 42,* 326–348.

Books, S. (2007). Devastation and disregard: Reflections on Katrina, child poverty, and educational opportunity. In S. Books (Ed.). *Poverty and schooling in the U.S* (pp. 1–22). Mahwah, NJ: Erlbaum.

Bos, C., Nahmias, M., & Urban, M. (1999). Targeting home school collaboration for students with ADHD. *Teaching Exceptional Children, 31*(6), 4–11.

Botwinik, R. (2007). Dealing with teacher stress. *Clearing House: A Journal of Educational Strategies, Issues, and Ideas. 80,* 271–272.

Bradley, R., Danielson, L., & Doolittle, J. (2007). Responsiveness to intervention: 1997 to 2007. *Teaching Exceptional Children, 39*(5), 8–13.

Bricker, D., & Squires, J. (1999). *Ages & stages questionnaries: A parent completed child-monitoring system.* Baltimore: Brookes.

Brigance, A. (1991). *The Brigance screens.* North Billerica, MA: Curriculum Associates.

Brigham, F. J., Scruggs, T. E., & Mastropieri, M. A. (1992). Teacher enthusiasm in learning disabilities classrooms: Effects on learning and behavior. *Learning Disabilities Research and Practice, 7,* 68–73.

Brilliant, R. L., & Graboyes, M. (1999). Historical overview of low vision: Classifications and perceptions. In R. L. Brilliant (Ed.), *Essentials of low vision practice* (pp. 2–9). Boston: Butterworth Heinemann.

Brooke, V., Revell, G., & Wehman, P. (2009). Quality indicators for competitive employment outcomes: What special education teachers need to know in transition planning. *Teaching Exceptional Children, 41*(4), 58–66.

Brophy, J. E. (1998). *Motivating students to learn.* Boston: McGraw-Hill.

Browder, D. M., Spooner, F., Wakeman, S., Trela, K., & Baker, J. N. (2006). Aligning instruction with academic content standards: Finding the link. *Research and Practice for Persons with Severe Disabilities, 31,* 309–321.

Browder, D., & Spooner, F. (Eds.) (2006). *Teaching language arts, math, and science to students with significant cognitive disabilities.* Baltimore: Brookes.

Browder, D., Ahlgrim-Delzell, L., Courtade, G., Gibbs, S., & Flowers, C. (2008). Evaluation of the effectiveness of an early literacy program for students with significant developmental disabilities. *Exceptional Children, 75*(1), 33–52.

Browder, D., Spooner, F., Ahlgrim-Delzell, L., Harris, A., & Wakeman, S. (2008). A meta-analysis on teaching mathematics to students with significant cognitive disabilities. *Exceptional Children, 74*(4), 407–432.

*Brown v. Board of Education.* (1954). 348 U.S. 886, 72 S. Ct. 120.

Brown, D. F. (2004). Urban teachers' professed classroom management strategies: Reflections of culturally responsive teaching. *Urban Education, 39,* 266–289.

Brown, F., Gothelf, C. R., Guess, D., & Lehr, D. H. (1998). Self-determination for individuals with the most severe disabilities: Moving beyond chimera. *Journal of the Association for Persons with Severe Handicaps, 23,* 17–26.

Brown, L., Branston-McLean, M. B., Baumgart, D., Vincent, L., Falvey, M., & Schroeder, J. (1979). Using the characteristics of current and subsequent least restrictive environments as factors in the development of curricular content for severely handicapped students. *AAESPH Review, 4,* 407–424.

Brown, L., Nietupski, J., & Hamre-Nietupski, S. (1976). Criterion of ultimate functioning. In A. Thomas (Ed.), *Hey, don't forget about me!* Reston, VA: CEC Information Center.

Bryant, D., & Dix, J. (1999). Mathematics interventions for students with learning disabilities. In W. Bender (Ed.), *Professional issues in learning disabilities* (pp. 219–259). Austin, TX: PRO-ED.

Buck, G. H., Polloway, E. A., Smith-Thomas, A., & Cook, K. W. (2003). Prereferral intervention processes: A survey of state practices. *Exceptional Children, 69,* 349–360.

Buescher, T. M. (1991). Gifted adolescents. In N. Colangelo & G. A. Davis (Eds.), *Handbook of gifted education* (pp. 382–401). Needham Heights, MA: Allyn & Bacon.

Bullis, M. (2001). Job placement and support considerations in transition programs for adolescents with emotional disabilities. In L. M. Bullock & R. A. Gable (Eds.), *Addressing the social, academic, and behavioral needs of students with challenging behavior in inclusive and alternative settings* (pp. 31–41). Arlington, VA: Council for Exceptional Children.

Burns, B. J., & Goldman, S. K. (1998). *Promising practices in wraparound for children with serious emotional disturbance and their families:* Vol. 4. *Systems of care: promising practices in children's mental health 1998 series.* Washington, DC: Georgetown University, Child Development Center, National Technical Assistance Center for Children's Mental Health.

Burns, M. K. (2008). Response to intervention at the secondary level. *Principal Leadership, 8*(7), 12–15.

Busch, T. W., Pederson, K., Espin, C. A., & Weissenburger, J. W. (2001). Teaching students with learning disabilities: Perceptions of a first year teacher. *Journal of Special Education, 35,* 92–99.

Bussing, R., Gary, F., Mills, T., & Garvan, C. (2007). Cultural variations in parental health beliefs, knowledge, and information sources related to attention-deficit/hyperactivity disorder. *Journal of Family Issues, 28*(3), 291–318.

Byrd, C. T., & Gillam, R. B. (2010). Fluency disorders. In R. B. Gillam, T. P. Marquardt, and F. N. Martin (Eds.), *Communication sciences and disorders: From science to clinical practice* (2nd ed.). Sudbury MA: Jones & Bartlett.

Cafiero, J. M. (1998). Communication power for individuals with autism. *Focus on Autism and Other Developmental Disabilities, 13*(2), 113–122.

Carey, W. (2004). ADHD: An epidemic. Developmental Behavioral Pediatrics Online. Retrieved June 11, 2009, from http://www.dbpeds.org/articles/detail.cfm?TextID=128

Carlberg, C., & Kavale, K. (1980). The efficacy of special versus regular class placement for exceptional children: A meta-analysis. *Journal of Special Education 14*(3), 295–309.

Carlson, E., Lee, H., & Schroll, K. (2004). Identifying attributes of high quality special education teachers. *Teacher Education and Special Education, 27,* 350–359.

Carnine, D., Engelmann, S., & Steely, D. (2003). *Corrective math.* Columbus, OH: SRA.

Carnine, D., Silbert, J., Kame'enui, E., & Tarver, S. (2003). *Direct instruction reading* (4th ed.). Upper Saddle River, NJ: Merrill/Pearson.

Carter, E. W., Cushing, L. S., Clark, N. M., & Kennedy, C. H. (2005). Effects of peer support interventions on students' access to the general curriculum and social interactions. *Research and Practice for Persons with Severe Disabilities, 30,* 15–25.

Carter, E. W., & Kennedy, C. H. (2006). Promoting access to the general curriculum using peer support strategies. *Research and Practice for Persons with Severe Disabilities, 31,* 284–292.

Carter, J., & Sugai, G. (1989). Survey on prereferral practices: Response from state departments of education. *Exceptional Children, 55,* 298–302.

Casey, K. M. A., & Shore, B. M. (2000). Mentors' contributions to gifted adolescents' affective, social, and vocational development. *Roeper Review, 22,* 227–230.

Center for Applied Special Technology (CAST). (2009). *What is universal design for learning.* Retrieved May 12, 2009, from http://www.cast.org/research/udl/index.html

Center for Data Driven Reform in Education (CDDRE). (2009). Standards for research driven programs. Retrieved May 20, 2009, from http://www.bestevidence.org/resources/general/standards.pdf

Center for Effective Collaboration and Practice. (1998). *Functional behavioral assessment.* Retrieved October 14, 2009, from http://cecp.air.org/fba/problembehavior/main.htm

Center on Education Policy. (2004). *State high school exit exams: A maturing reform.* Washington, DC. Retrieved October 20, 2006, from http://www.cep-dc.org/highschoolexit/statematuringAug2004.cfm

Center on Education Policy. (2006). *State high school exit exams: A challenging year: Summary and methods.* Washington, DC. Retrieved October 20, 2006, from http://www.cep-dc.org/pubs/hseeAugust2006/

Centers for Disease Control and Prevention. (1999). *Universal precautions for prevention of transmission of HIV and other bloodborne infections.* Retrieved July 27, 2009, from http://www.cdc.gov/ncidod/dhqp/bp_universal_precautions.html

Centers for Disease Control and Prevention. (2008). *HIV/AIDS in the United States.* Retrieved July 21, 2009, from http://www.cdc.gov/hiv/resources/factsheets/us.htm

Centers for Disease Control and Prevention, National Center for Injury Prevention and Control. (2009). How many people have TBI? Retrieved June 20, 2009, from http://www.cdc.gov/ncipc/tbi/TBI.htm

Chalfant, J. C. (1998). Why Kirk stands alone. *Learning Disabilities Research and Practice, 13*(1), 2–7.

Chalfant, J. C., & Pysh, M. (1989). Teacher assistance teams: Five descriptive studies on 96 teams. *Remedial and Special Education, 10,* 49–58.

Chalfant, J. C., Pysh, M. V., & Moultrie, R. (1979). Teacher assistance teams: A model for within—Building problem solving. *Learning Disability Quarterly, 2,* 85–96.

Chandler, L. K., & Dahlquist, C. M. (2002). *Functional assessment: Strategies to prevent and remediate challenging behaviors in school settings.* Upper Saddle River, NJ: Merrill/Pearson.

Chawarska, K., & Volkmar, F. R. (2005). Autism in infancy and early childhood. In F. R. Volkmar, R. Paul, A. Klin, & D. Cohen (Eds.), *Handbook of autism and pervasive developmental disorders: Vol. 1. Diagnosis, development, neurobiology, and behavior.* (4th ed., pp. 223–246). Hoboken, NJ: Wiley.

Chen, D., Alsop, L., & Minor, L. (2000). Lessons from Project PLAI in California and Utah: Implications for early intervention services to infants who are deaf-blind and their families. *Deaf-Blind Perspectives, 7*(3), 1–5.

Cheney, D., & Bullis, M. (2004). The school-to-community transition of adolescents with emotional and behavioral disorders. In R. B. Rutherford, Jr., M. M. Quinn, & A. R. Mathur (Eds.), *Handbook of research in emotional and behavioral disorders* (pp. 369–384). New York: Guilford.

Child Welfare Information Gateway. (2008). *Longterm consequences of child abuse and neglect.* Retrieved May 15, 2009 from http://www.childwelfare.gov/pubs/factsheets/long_term_consequences.cfm

Cimera, R. E. (2003). *The truth about special education: A guide for parents and teachers.* Lanham, MD: Scarecrow Press.

Clarizo, H. F. (1994). *Assessment and treatment of depression in children and adolescents* (2nd ed.). Brandon, VT: Clinical Psychology.

Clark, G. M., & Bigge, J. L. (2005). Transition and self-determination. In S. J. Best, K. W. Heller, & J. L. Bigge (Eds.), *Teaching individuals with physical or multiple disabilities* (5th ed., pp. 367–398). Upper Saddle River, NJ: Merrill/Pearson.

Clark, R. (2004). *The essential eleven.* New York: Hyperion.

Clunies-Ross, P., Little, E., & Keinhuis, M. (2008). Self-reported and actual use of proactive and reactive classroom strategies and their relationship to teacher stress and student behaviour. *Educational Psychology, 28,* 693–710.

Cole, C., Horvath, B., Chapman, C., Deschenes, C., Ebeling, D., & Sprague, J. (2000). *Adapting curriculum & instruction in inclusive classrooms: A teachers' desk reference* (2nd ed.). Bloomington: Indiana Institute on Disability and Community.

Coleman, L. J. (2004). Is consensus on a definition in the field possible, desirable, necessary? *Roeper Review, 27*(1), 10–11.

Coleman, M., & Vaughn, S. (2000). Reading interventions for students with emotional/behavioral disorders. *Behavioral Disorders, 25*(2), 93–104.

Conchas, G. Q. (2006). *The color of success: Race and high achieving urban youth.* New York: Teachers College Press.

Connelly, V. J., Rosenberg, M. S. (2009). Special education teaching as a profession: Lessons learned from occupations that have achieved full professional standing. *Teacher Education and Special Education, 32*(3), 1–14.

Conners, C. K. (2008a). *Conners Parent Rating Scale* (3rd ed.). Los Angeles: Western Psychological Services.

Conners, C. K. (2008b). *Conners Teacher Rating Scale* (3rd ed.). Los Angeles: Western Psychological Services.

Connor, D. (2006a). Stimulants. In R. Barkley (Ed.). *Attention-deficit hyperactivity disorder: A handbook for diagnosis and treatment* (3rd ed., pp. 608–647). New York: Guilford Press.

Connor, D. (2006b). Other medications. In R. Barkley (Ed.). *Attention-deficit hyperactivity disorder: A handbook for diagnosis and treatment* (3rd ed., pp. 658–677). New York: Guilford Press.

Connor, M. H., & Boskin, J. (2001). Overrepresentation of bilingual and poor children in special education classes: A continuing problem. *Journal of Children and Poverty, 7*(1), 23–32.

Conroy, M. A., Hendrickson, J. M., & Hester, P. P. (2004). Early identification and prevention of emotional and behavioral disorders. In R. B. Rutherford, Jr., M. M. Quinn, & A. R. Mathur (Eds.), *Handbook of research in emotional and behavioral disorders* (pp. 199–215). New York: Guilford.

Cook, B. G., Cameron, D. L., & Tankersley, M. (2007). Inclusive teachers' attitudinal ratings of their students with disabilities. *Journal of Special Education, 40,* 230–238.

Cook, B. G., Tankersley, M., & Landrum, T. J. (2009). Determining evidence-based practices in special education. *Exceptional Children, 75*(3), 365–383.

Coonrod, E. E., & Stone, W. L. (2005). Screening for autism in young children. In F. R. Volkmar, R. Paul, A. Klin, & D. Cohen (Eds.), *Handbook of autism and pervasive developmental disorders: Vol. 2. Assessment, interventions, and policy* (4th ed., pp. 707–729). Hoboken, NJ: Wiley.

Cooper, H. (2001). *The battle over homework* (2nd ed.). Thousand Oaks, CA: Corwin.

Cooper H., & Nye, B. (1994). Homework for students with learning disabilities: The implications for policy and practice. *Journal of Learning Disabilities, 27*(8), 470–479.

Coping.org. (2006). *Tools for coping with life's stressors.* Retrieved July 14, 2006, from http://www.coping.org/specialneeds/assistech/aacdev.htm

Coplan, J. (1987). Deafness: Ever heard of it? *Pediatrics, 79*(2), 202–213.

Corbett, D., Wilson, B., & Williams, B. (2002). *Effort and excellence in urban classrooms.* New York: Teachers College Press.

Corbett, W. P., Clark, H. B., & Blank, W. (2002). Employment and social outcomes associated with vocational programming for youths with emotional or behavioral disorders. *Behavioral Disorders, 27,* 358–370.

Correa, V., & Tulbert, B. (1993). Collaboration between school personnel in special education and Hispanic families. *Journal of Educational and Psychological Consultation, 4*(3), 253–265.

Council for Exceptional Children. (2003). *What every special educator must know: Ethics, standards, and guidelines for special educators* (5th ed.). Arlington, VA: Author. Retrieved September 27, 2005, from http://www.cec.sped.org/bk/catalog2/Red_book_5th_edition.pdf

Council for Exceptional Children. (2007). *Position on response to intervention (RTI): The unique role of special education and special educators.* Arlington, VA: Council for Exceptional Children (CEC).

Council for Exceptional Children. (2009). *What every special educator must know: Ethics, standards, and guidelines* (6th ed.). Arlington, VA.

Coutinho, M. J., & Oswald, D. P. (2000). Disproportionate representation in special education: A synthesis and recommendations. *Journal of Child and Family Studies, 9*(2), 135–156.

Coutinho, M. J., Oswald, D. P., & Forness, S. R. (2002). Gender and sociodemographic factors and the disproportionate identification of culturally and linguistically diverse students with emotional disturbance. *Behavioral Disorders, 27*(2), 109–125.

Coyne, M., Kame'enui, E., & Carnine, D. (2007). *Effective teaching strategies that accommodate diverse learners* (3rd ed.). Upper Saddle River, NJ: Merrill/Pearson.

Crews, S. D., Bender, H., Cook, C. R., Gresham, F. M., Kern, L., & Vanderwood, M. (2007). Risk and protective factors of emotional and/or behavioral disorders in children and adolescents: A mega-analytic synthesis. *Behavioral Disorders, 23*(2), 64–77.

Cullinan, D. (2002). *Students with emotional and behavior disorders: An introduction for teachers and other helping professionals.* Upper Saddle River, NJ: Pearson Education.

Cullinan, D. (2004). Classification and definition of emotional and behavioral disorders. In R. B. Rutherford, Jr., M. M. Quinn, & A. R. Mathur (Eds.), *Handbook of research in emotional and behavioral disorders* (pp. 32–53). New York: Guilford.

Cullinan, D., & Sabornie, E. J. (2004). Characteristics of emotional disturbance in middle and high school students. *Journal of Emotional and Behavioral Disorders, 12,* 157–167.

Curwin, R. L., & Mendler, A. N. (1988). Packaged discipline programs: Let the buyer beware. *Educational Leadership, 46,* 68–71.

Curwin, R. L., & Mendler, A. N. (1999). *Discipline with dignity* (2nd ed.). Alexandria, VA: ASCD.

Cushman, K. (2003). *Fires in the bathroom: Advice for teachers from high school students.* New York: The New Press.

Cushman, K., & Rogers, L. (2008). *Fires in the middle school bathroom: Advice for teachers from middle schoolers.* New York: The New Press.

D'Agostino, J., & Murphy, J. (2004). A meta-analysis of Reading Recovery in United States schools. *Educational Evaluation and Policy Analysis, 26*(1), 23–38.

Dalston, R., & Marquardt, T. P. (2010). Laryngeal and orofacial disorders. In R. B. Gillam, T. P. Marquardt, & F. N. Martin (Eds.), *Communication sciences and disorders: From science to clinical practice* (2nd ed.). Sudbury MA: Jones & Bartlett.

*Daniel R. R. v. State Board of Education.* (1989). 874 F.2d 1036 (5th Cir.).

Darling-Hammond, L. (1998). Equal opportunity race and education: The nature of educational inequality. *Brookings Review, 16*(2), 28–32.

Darling-Hammond, L. (2001). *The research and rhetoric on teacher certification: A response to "Teacher certification reconsidered."* New York: National Commission on Teaching and America's Future (NCTAF). Retrieved April 8, 2009, from http://www.nctaf.org/resources/research_and_reports/nctaf_research_reports/index.htm

Davenport, C. (1910). *Eugenics: The science of human improvement by better breeding.* Retrieved February 5, 2005, from http://www.eugenicsarchive.org/html/eugenics/static/themes/28.html

Davis, B. L., & Bedore, L. M. (2010). Developmental speech disorders. In R. B. Gillam, T. P. Marquardt, & F. N. Martin (Eds.), *Communication sciences and disorders: From science to clinical practice* (2nd ed.). Sudbury MA: Jones & Bartlett.

Davis, G. A., & Rimm, S. B. (2003). *Education of the gifted and talented* (5th ed.). Upper Saddle River, NJ: Pearson.

Day-Vines, N. L., & Day-Hairston, B. O. (2005). Culturally congruent strategies for addressing the behavioral needs of urban, African American male adolescents. *Professional School Counseling, 8*(3), 236–243.

Deaf Culture Information. (2005). *Deaf history.* Retrieved February 5, 2005, from http://members.aol.com/deafcultureinfo/deaf_history.htm

deBettencourt, L. (2002). Understanding the differences between IDEA and Section 504. *Teaching Exceptional Children, 34*(3), 16–23.

Delisle, J. R. (2003). To be or to do: Is a gifted child born or developed? *Roeper Review, 26*(1), 12–13.

Deno, S. (1985). Curriculum-based measurement: The emerging alternative. *Exceptional Children, 52,* 219–232.

Deno, S. (2003). Developments in curriculum-based measurement. *Journal of Special Education, 37*(3), 184–192.

DePaepe, P., Garrison-Kane, L., & Doelling J. (2002). Supporting students with health needs in schools: An overview of selected health conditions. *Focus on Exceptional Children, 35*(1), 1–24.

Deshler, D. (2005). Adolescents with learning disabilities: Unique challenges and reasons for hope. *Learning Disability Quarterly, 28,* 122–124.

Deshler, D., & Schumaker, J. (Eds.). (2006). *Teaching adolescents with disabilities: Accessing the general education curriculum.* Thousand Oaks, CA: Corwin.

Deshler, D., Schumaker, J., Lenz, K., Bulgren, J., Hock, M., Knight, J., et al. (2001). Ensuring content-area learning by secondary students with learning disabilities. *Learning Disabilities Research and Practice, 16*(2), 96–108.

Dettmer, P., Thurston, L., Knackendoffel, A., & Dyck, N. (2009). *Collaboration, consultation, and teamwork for students with special needs.* Upper Saddle River, NJ: Merrill/Pearson Education.

Diaz-Rico, L. T. (2008). *A course for teaching English learners.* Boston: Allyn & Bacon.

Dickens, C. (1842). *American notes.* Retrieved February 9, 2005, from http://xroads.virginia.edu/~hyper/detoc/fem/dickens.htm

Diller, L. H. (2000). The Ritalin wars continue. *Western Journal of Medicine, 173,* 366–367.

Donnay, D., Morris, M., Schaubhut, N., & Thompson, R. (2004). *Strong Interest Inventory user's guide: Practitioner's tool for understanding, interpretation, and use of the Strong Profile and Interpretive Report.* Mountain View, CA: Consulting Psychology Press.

Doubt, L., & McColl, M. A. (2003). A secondary guy: Physically disabled teenagers in secondary schools. *Canadian Journal of Occupational Therapy, 70*(3), 139–151.

Downey, J. A. (2008). Recommendations for fostering educational resilience in the classroom. *Preventing School Failure, 53*(1), 56–64.

Downing, J. E., & Eichenger, J. (2003). Creating learning opportunities for students with severe disabilities in inclusive classrooms. *Teaching Exceptional Children, 36*(1), 26–32.

Doyle, M. B. (2002). *The paraprofessional's guide to the inclusive classroom* (2nd ed.). Baltimore: Brookes.

Doyle, W. (1986). Classroom organization and management. In Merlin C. Wittrock (Ed.), *Handbook of research on teaching* (3rd ed.). New York: Macmillan.

Drake, R. E., Skinner, J. S., Bond, G. R., & Goldman, H. H. (2009). Social Security and mental illness: Reducing disability with supported employment. *Health Affairs, 28*(3), 761–770.

Drotar, D. (2002). Behavioral and emotional problems in infants and young children: Challenges of clinical assessment and intervention. *Infants and Young Children, 14*(4), 1–5.

Dudzinski, M., Roszmann-Millican, M., & Shank, K. (2000). Continuing professional development for special educators: Reforms and implications for university programs. *Teacher Education and Special Education, 23*(2), 109–124.

Duhaney, L. (2003). A practical approach to managing the behaviors of students with ADHD. *Intervention in School and Clinic, 38*(5), 267–279.

Dunn, L. M. (1968). Special education for the mildly retarded—Is much of it justifiable? *Exceptional Children, 35,* 5–22.

DuPaul, G. (2004). *ADHD identification and assessment: Basic guidelines for educators.* Bethesda, MD: National Association for School Psychologists.

DuPaul, G. (2007). School-based interventions for students with attention deficit hyperactivity disorder: Current status and future directions. *School Psychology Review, 36*(2), 183–194.

DuPaul, G., Barkley, R., & Connor, D. (1998). Stimulants. In R. Barkley (Ed.), *Attention deficit hyperactivity disorder: A handbook for diagnosis and treatment* (2nd ed., pp. 510–551). New York: Guilford Press.

DuPaul, G., & Stoner, G. (2003). *ADHD in the schools: Assessment and intervention strategies* (2nd ed.). New York: Guilford Press.

Dwyer, K., & Osher, D. (2000). *Safeguarding our children: An action guide.* Washington, DC: U.S. Department of Education and Justice, American Institutes for Research.

Dwyer, K., Osher, D., & Warger, C. (1998). *Early warning, timely response: A guide to safe schools.* Washington, DC: U.S. Department of Education.

Eber, L., Sugai, G., Smith, C. R., & Scott, T. M. (2002). Wraparound and positive behavioral interventions and supports in the schools. *Journal of Emotional and Behavioral Disorders, 10*(3), 171–180.

Education Alliance. (2002). *The diversity kit.* Providence, RI: Author. Retrieved May 10, 2009, from http://www.alliance.brown.edu/tdl/diversitykitpdfs/dk_culture.pdf

Education Trust. (2004). *The ABCs of AYP.* Retrieved April 5, 2005, from www2.edtrust.org/nr/rdonlyres/37b8652d-84f4-4fa1-aa8d-319ead5a6d89/0/abcayp.pdf

Education Trust. (2009). *Education watch state report: California.* Retrieved May 15, 2009, from http://www2.edtrust.org/edtrust/summaries2009/California.pdf

Edyburn, D. (2000). Assistive technology and students with mild disabilities. *Focus on Exceptional Children, 32*(9), 1–23.

Edyburn, D. (2002). *What every teacher should know about assistive technology.* Boston: Allyn & Bacon.

Ehri, L., Dreyer, L., Flugman, B., & Gross, A. (2007). Reading rescue: An effective tutoring intervention model for language-minority students who are struggling readers in first grade. *American Educational Research Journal, 44*(2), 414–448.

Elbaum, B., Vaughn, S., Hughes, M., & Moody, S. (1999). Grouping practices and reading outcomes for students with disabilities. *Exceptional Children, 65*(3), 399–415.

Elliott, S. N., & Busse, R. T. (2004). Assessment and evaluation of students' behavior and intervention outcomes: The utility of rating scale methods. In R. B. Rutherford, Jr., M. M. Quinn, & A. R. Mathur (Eds.), *Handbook of research in emotional and behavioral disorders* (pp. 54–77). New York: Guilford.

Emmer, E. T., & Evertson, C. M. (2008). *Classroom management for the middle and high school teacher.* Reading MA: Addison-Wesley.

Engelmann, S., & Bruner, E. (2003). *Reading mastery classic.* Chicago: Science Research Associates.

Engelmann, S., Carnine, D., Bernadette, K., & Engelmann, O. (2003). *Connecting math concepts.* Columbus, OH: SRA.

Engelmann, S., Hanner, S., & Johnson, G. (2008). *Corrective reading.* Chicago: Science Research Associates.

Englert, C. S., Wu, X., & Zhao, Y. (2005). Cognitive tools for writing: Scaffolding the performance of students through technology. *Learning Disabilities Research and Practice, 20*(3), 184–198.

Epilepsy Foundation. (2009). *What is epilepsy?* Retrieved July 27, 2009, from http://www.epilepsyfoundation.org/

Epstein, M. H., & Sharma, J. M. (1998). *Behavioral and emotional rating scale.* Austin, TX: PRO-ED.

Escamilla, K., & Coady, M. (2001). Assessing the writing of Spanish speaking students: Issues and suggestions. In S. Hurley & J. Tinajero (Eds.), *Literacy assessment of bilingual learners* (pp. 43–63). Boston: Allyn & Bacon.

Escolar, D. M., Tosi, L. L., Rocha, A. C. T., & Kennedy, A. (2007). Muscles, bones, and nerves. In M. L. Batshaw, L. Pellegrino, & N. J. Roizen (Eds.), *Children with disabilities* (6th ed., pp. 203–215). Baltimore: Brookes.

Esquith, R. (2007). *Teach like your hair's on fire.* NY: Penguin Books.

Evertson, C., Emmer, E., & Worsham, M. (2005). *Classroom management for elementary teachers* (7th ed.). Boston: Allyn & Bacon.

Fairbanks, S., Sugai, G., Guarding, D., & Lathrop, M. (2007). Response to intervention: Examining classroom behavior support in second grade. *Exceptional Children, 73*(3), 288–310.

Farel, A. M., Meyer, R. E., Hicken, M., & Edmonds, L. (2003). Registry to referral: A promising means for identifying and referring infants and toddlers for early intervention services. *Infants and Young Children, 16,* 99–105.

FASlink. (2009). *Introduction to fetal alcohol spectrum disorders.* Retrieved August 4, 2009, from http://www.faslink.org/katoc.htm

Fass, S., & Cauthen, N. (2008). *Who are America's poor children: The official story.* Retrieved May 15, 2009, from http://www.nccp.org/publications/pub_843.html

*Federal Register.* (1993, February 10). Washington, DC: U.S. Government Printing Office.

Feiman-Nemser, S., & Floden, R. E. (1986). The cultures of teaching. In Merlin C. Wittrock (Ed.), *Handbook of research on teaching* (3rd ed.). New York: Macmillan.

Feldhusen, J. F. (1992). *Talent identification and development in education (TIDE).* Sarasota, FL: Center for Creative Learning.

Feldman, R. S. (2000). *Development across the life span* (2nd ed.). Upper Saddle River, NJ: Pearson.

Ferguson, D. L., & Baumgart, D. (1991). Partial participation revisited. *Journal of the Association for Persons with Severe Handicaps, 16,* 218–227.

Ferrell, K. (2007). *Issues in the field of blindness and low vision.* Retrieved August 5, 2009, from http://www.unco.edu/ncssd/resources/issues_bvi.pdf

Ferrell, K. A. (1997). *Reach out and teach.* New York: American Foundation for the Blind.

Ferrell, K. A. (1998). *Project PRISM: A longitudinal study of developmental patterns of children who are visually impaired* [Final report]. Greeley: University of Northern Colorado.

Ferster, C. B. (1961). Positive reinforcement and behavioral deficits of autistic children. *Child Development, 61,* 437–456.

Filipek, P. (2005). Medical aspects of autism. In F. R. Volkmar, R. Paul, A. Klin, & D. Cohen (Eds.), *Handbook of autism and pervasive developmental disorders: Vol. 1. Diagnosis, development, neurobiology, and behavior.* (4th ed., pp. 534–578). Hoboken, NJ: Wiley.

Fischer, M., Barkley, R., Smallish, L., & Fletcher, K. (2002). Young adult follow-up of hyperactive children. *Journal of Abnormal Child Psychology, 30*(5), 463–475.

Fletcher, J., Lyon, G., Fuchs, L., & Barnes, M. (2007). *Learning disabilities: From identification to intervention.* New York: Guilford Press.

Fletcher, J., Lyon, R., Barnes, M., Stuebing, K., Francis, D., Olson, R., et al. (2002). Classification of learning disabilities: An evidence-based evaluation. In R. Bradley, L. Danielson, & D. Hallahan (Eds.), *Identification of learning disabilities: Research to practice* (pp. 185–250). Mahwah, NJ: Erlbaum.

Fletcher, J., Morris, R., & Lyon, R. (2003). Classification and definition of learning disabilities: An integrative perspective. In L. Swanson, K. Harris, & S. Graham (Eds.). *Handbook of learning disabilities* (pp. 30–56). New York: Guilford.

Fletcher, T. V., & Navarrete, L. A. (2003). Learning disabilities or difference: A critical look at issues associated with misidentification and placement of Hispanic students in special education. *Rural Special Education Quarterly, 22*(4), 37–45.

Florida Department of Education. (2009). *Access points for students with significant cognitive disabilities.* Retrieved May 28, 2009, from www.floridastandards.org/page24.aspx

Fombonne, E. (2003, January). The prevalence of autism. *Journal of the American Medical Association, 289*(1), 87–89.

Foorman, B., & Torgesen, J. (2001). Critical elements of classroom and small-group instruction promote reading success in all children. *Learning Disabilities Research and Practice, 16*(4), 203–212.

Ford, A., Schnorr, R., Meyer, L., Davern, L., Black, J., & Dempsey, P. (Eds.). (1989). *The Syracuse community-referenced curriculum guide for students with moderate and severe disabilities.* Baltimore: Brookes.

Ford, D. Y., & Grantham, T. C. (2003). Providing access for culturally diverse gifted students: From deficit to dynamic thinking. *Theory into Practice, 42*(3), 217–225.

Ford, D. Y., & Harris, J. J. (2000). A framework for infusing multicultural curriculum into gifted education. *Roeper Review, 23,* 4–10.

Ford, D. Y., & Whiting, G. W. (2008). Cultural competence: Preparing gifted students for a diverse society. *Roeper Review, 30,* 104–110.

Fore, C., Martin, C., & Bender, W. N. (2002). Teacher burn-out in special education. *High School Journal, 86*(1), 36–45.

Foreman, P., Arthur-Kelly, M., Pascoe, S., & King, B. S. (2004). Evaluating the educational experiences of students with profound and multiple disabilities in inclusive and segregated classroom settings: An Australian perspective. *Research and Practice for Persons with Severe Disabilities, 29,* 183–193.

Forest, M., & Lusthaus, E. (1987). The kaleidoscope. Challenge to the cascade. In M. Forest (Ed.), *More education/integration* (pp. 1–16). Downsview, Ontario: Roeher Institute.

Forness, S. R., & Kavale, K. A. (2000). Emotional or behavioral disorders: Background and current status of the E/BD terminology and definition. *Behavioral Disorders, 25*(3), 264–269.

Forni, P. M. (2002). *Choosing civility: Twenty-five rules of considerate conduct.* New York: St. Martin's/Griffin.

Foshay, J., & Ludlow, B. (2005). Implementing computer-mediated supports and assistive technology. In M. Wehmeyer & M. Agran (Eds.), *Mental retardation and intellectual disabilities: Teaching students using innovative and research-based strategies* (pp. 101–124). Upper Saddle River, NJ: Pearson.

Foust, R. C., Rudasill, K. M., & Callahan, C. M. (2006). An investigation into the gender and age differences in the social coping of academically advanced students. *Journal of Advanced Academics, 18*(1), 60–80.

Fox, N., & Ysseldyke, J. (1997). Implementing inclusion at the middle school level: Lessons from a negative example. *Exceptional Children, 64*(1), 81–98.

Fragile X Research Foundation. (2009). *About Fragile X.* Retrieved August 4, 2009, from http://www.fraxa.org/aboutFX.aspx

Freeman, S. F. N., & Alkin, M. C. (2000). Academic and social attainments of children with mental retardation in general and special education settings. *Remedial and Special Education, 21,* 2–18.

French, N. (2001). Supervising paraprofessionals: A survey of teacher practices. *Journal of Special Education, 35*(1), 41–53.

French, N., & Pickett, A. L. (1997). Paraprofessionals in special education: Issues for teacher educators. *Teacher Education and Special Education, 20*(1), 61–73.

Frey, L. M. (2003). Abundant beautification: An effective service-learning project for students with emotional or behavioral disorders. *Teaching Exceptional Children, 35*(5), 66–75.

Friend, M., & Bursuck, W. (2006). *Including students with special needs: A practical guide for classroom teachers* (4th ed.). Boston: Allyn & Bacon.

Friend, M., & Cook, L. (2010). *Interactions: Collaboration skills for school professionals* (6th ed.). Boston: Allyn & Bacon.

Frith, U. (2003). *Autism: Explaining the enigma* (2nd ed.). Malden, MA: Blackwell.

Frost, L., & Bondy, A. (2000). *The picture exchange communication system (PECS).* Newark, DE: Pyramid Products.

Fuchs, D., & Fuchs, L. (1998). Researchers and teachers working together to adopt instruction for diverse learners. *Learning Disabilities Research and Practice, 13*(3), 126–137.

Fuchs, D., & Fuchs, L. S. (1994). Inclusive school movement and the radicalization of special education reform. *Exceptional Children, 60*(4), 294–309.

Fuchs, D., Fuchs, L., & Burish, P. (2000). Peer-assisted learning strategies: An evidence-based practice to promote reading achievement. *Learning Disabilities Research and Practice, 15*(2), 85–91.

Fuchs, D., Fuchs, L., & Compton, D. (2004). Identifying reading disabilities by responsiveness-to-instruction: Specifying measures and criteria. *Learning Disability Quarterly, 27*(4), 216–227.

Fuchs, D., Fuchs, L., Compton, D., Bryant, J., Hamlett, C., & Seethaler, P. (2007). Mathematics screening and progress monitoring at first grade: Implications for responsiveness to intervention. *Exceptional Children, 73*(3), 311–330.

Fuchs, D., Fuchs, L., Mathes, P., Lipsey, M., & Roberts, H. (2002). Is "learning disabilities" just a fancy term for low achievement? A meta-analysis of reading differences between low achievers with and without the label. In R. Bradley, L. Danielson, & D. Hallahan (Eds.). *Identification of learning disabilities: Research to practice* (pp. 737–762). Mahwah, NJ: Erlbaum.

Fuchs, L. (2003). Assessing intervention responsiveness: Conceptual and technical issues. *Learning Disabilities Research and Practice, 18*(3), 172–186.

Fuchs, L. (2004). The past, present, and future of curriculum-based measurement research. *School Psychology Review, 33*(2), 188–192.

Fuchs, L., & Fuchs, D. (2007). A model for implementing responsiveness to intervention. *Teaching Exceptional Children, 39*(5), 14–20.

Fuchs, L., Compton, D., Fuchs, D., Paulsen, K., Bryant, J., & Hamlett, C. (2005). Responsiveness to intervention: Preventing and identifying mathematics disability. *Teaching Exceptional Children, 37*(4), 60–63.

Fuchs, L., Fuchs, D., Hosp, M., & Hamlett, C. (2003). The potential for diagnostic analysis within curriculum-based measurement. *Assessment for Effective Instruction, 28*(2-3), 13–22.

Fuchs, L., Fuchs, D., & Speece, D. (2002). Treatment validity as a unifying construct for identifying learning disabilities. *Learning Disability Quarterly, 25*(1), 33–45.

Gaffney, J. S. (1987). *Seatwork: Current practices and research implications.* Paper presented at the 64th meeting of the Council for Exceptional Children, Chicago.

Gagné, F. (1991). Toward a differentiated model of giftedness and talent. In N. Colangelo & G. A. Davis (Eds.), *Handbook of gifted education* (pp. 65–80). Needham Heights, MA: Allyn & Bacon.

Gagné, F. (1993). Constructs and models pertaining to exceptional human abilities. In K. A. Heller, F. J. Monks, & A. H. Passow (Eds.), *International handbook of research and development of giftedness and talent* (pp. 69–87). Oxford, England: Pergamon.

Gagné, F. (1999). My convictions about the nature of abilities, gifts, and talents. *Journal for the Education of the Gifted, 22,* 109–136.

Gagné, F., Bélanger, J. & Motard, D. (1993). Popular estimates of the prevalence of giftedness and talent. *Roeper Review, 16,* 96–98.

Gallagher, J. J. (1993). Current status of gifted education in the United States. In K. A. Heller, F. J. Monks, & A. H. Passow (Eds.), *International handbook of research and development of giftedness and talent* (pp. 755–770). Oxford, England: Pergamon.

Gallagher, J. J. (1998). The public policy legacy of Samuel A. Kirk. *Learning Disabilities Research and Practice, 13*(1), 11–14.

Gallaudet Research Institute. (2005). *Regional and national summary report of data from the 2003–2004 annual survey of deaf and hard of hearing children and youth.* Washington, DC: Author.

Galluzzo, G. (1999). *Aligning standards to improve teacher preparation and practice.* Washington, DC: National Council for Accreditation of Teacher Education.

Gardner, H. (1983). *Frames of mind: A theory of multiple intelligences.* New York: Basic Books.

Gardner, H., & Hatch, T. (1989). Multiple intelligences go to school: Educational implications of the theory of multiple intelligences. *Educational Researcher, 18*(8), 4–9.

Gay, G. (2000). *Culturally responsive teaching.* New York: Teachers College Press.

Gay, G. (2002). Preparing for culturally responsive teaching. *Journal of Teacher Education, 53*(2), 106–116.

Geertz, C. (1973). *The interpretation of culture.* New York: Basic.

Gerber, M. (2005). Teachers are still the test: Limitations to response to intervention strategies for identifying children with learning disabilities. *Journal of Learning Disabilities, 38*(6), 516–524.

Gerhardt, P. F., & Holmes, D. L. (2005). Employment: Options and issues for adolescents and adults with autism spectrum disorders. In F. R. Volkmar, R. Paul, A. Klin, & D. Cohen (Eds.), *Handbook of autism and pervasive development disorders: Vol. 2. Assessment, interventions, and policy* (4th ed., pp. 1087–1101). Hoboken, NJ: Wiley.

Gersten, R., Compton, D., Connor, C., Dimino, J., Santoro, L., & Linan-Thompson, S., et al. (2009). *Assisting students struggling with reading: Response to Intervention and multi-tiered intervention in the primary grades*. Washington, DC: Institute for Education Sciences.

Gersten, R., Keating, T., Yovanoff, P., & Harniss, M. K. (2001). Working in special education: Factors that enhance special educators' intent to stay. *Exceptional Children, 67*(4), 549–567.

Giangreco, M. F., Broer, S. M., & Edelman, S. W. (1999). The tip of the iceberg: Determining whether paraprofessional support is needed for students with disabilities in general education settings. *Journal of the Association for Persons with Severe Handicaps, 24,* 281–291.

Giangreco, M. F., & Doyle, M. B. (2002). Students with disabilities and paraeducator supports: Benefits, balance, and Band-Aids. *Focus on Exceptional Children, 34*(7), 1–12.

Giangreco, M. F., Edelman, S. W., & Broer, S. M. (2003). Schoolwide planning to improve paraeducator supports. *Exceptional Children, 70,* 63–79.

Giangreco, M. F., Edelman, S. W., Broer, S. M., & Doyle, M. B. (2001). Paraeducator support of students with disabilities: Literature from the past decade. *Exceptional Children, 68,* 45–63.

Gil, L. (2007). Bridging the transition gap from high school to college. *Teaching Exceptional Children, 40*(2), 12–15.

Gillam, R. B., & Petersen, D. B. (2010). Language disorders in school-age children. In R. B. Gillam, T. P. Marquardt, & F. N. Martin (Eds.), *Communication sciences and disorders: From science to clinical practice* (2nd ed.). Sudbury MA: Jones & Bartlett.

Gillberg, C., & Cederlund, M. (2005). Asperger syndrome: Familial and pre- and perinatal factors. *Journal of Autism and Developmental Disorders, 35*(2), 159–166.

Goe, L. (2007). *The link between teacher quality and student outcomes: A research synthesis*. Washington, DC: National Comprehensive Center on Teacher Quality.

Goertzel, V., & Goertzel, M. G. (1962). *Cradles of eminence*. London: Constable.

Goldstein, A. P., & McGinnis, E. (1997). *Skillstreaming the adolescent: New strategies and perspectives for teaching prosocial skills*. Champaign, IL: Research Press.

Goldstein, D., Murray, C., & Edgar, E. (1998). Employment earnings and hours of high-school graduates with learning disabilities through the first decade after graduation. *Learning Disabilities Research and Practice, 13*(1), 53–64.

Gonzalez, L., Brown, M. S., & Slate, J. R. (2008). Teachers who left the teaching profession: A qualitative understanding. *The Qualitative Report, 13*(1), 1–11.

Gonzalez, N., Moll, L., & Amanti, C. (2005). *Funds of knowledge: Theorizing practices in households and classrooms*. Mahwah, NJ: Erlbaum.

Good, T., & Brophy, J. (2008). *Looking in classrooms* (10th ed.). Boston: Allyn & Bacon.

Goode, D. (1998). *The history of the Association for the Help of Retarded Children*. Retrieved March 2, 2005, from http://www.ahrcnyc.org/index.htm

Goor, M. B. (1995). *Leadership for special education administration: A case-based approach*. Fort Worth, TX: Harcourt Brace.

Gordon, K. A., & Coscarelli, W. C. (1996). Recognizing and fostering resilience. *Performance Improvement, 35*(9), 14–17.

Graham, L., Tognazzini, D., & Lyons-Holden, M. (1996). Labeling and entrance into special education. In A. Goldberg (Ed.), *Acquired Brain Injury in Childhood and Adolescence* (pp. 93–94). Springfield, IL: Charles C. Thomas.

Graham, S., & Harris, K. R. (2003). Students with learning disabilities and the process of writing: A meta-analysis of SRSD studies. In H. L. Swanson, K. R. Harris, & S. Graham (Eds.), *Handbook of learning disabilities* (pp. 323–344). New York: Guilford.

Grandin, T. (1992). An inside view of autism. In E. Schopler & G. B. Mesibov (Eds.), *High functioning individuals with autism* (pp. 105–126). New York: Plenum.

Gray, C. A. (2000). *The new social story book*. Arlington, TX: Future Horizons.

Gray, C. A., & Garand, J. D. (1993). Social stories: Improving responses of students with autism with accurate social information. *Focus on Autistic Behavior, 8*(1), 1–10.

Grayson, J. L., & Alvarez, H. K. (2008). School climate factors related to teacher burnout: A mediator model. *Teaching and Teacher Education: An International Journal of Research and Studies, 24,* 1349–1363.

Greenfield, P. M., Raeff, C., & Quiroz, B. (1996). Cultural values in learning and education. In B. Williams (Ed.), *Closing the achievement gap: A vision for changing beliefs and practices* (pp. 37–55). Alexandria. VA: Association for Supervision and Curriculum Development.

Greenman, N. P., & Kimmel, E. B. (1995). The road to multicultural education: Potholes of resistance. *Journal of Teacher Education, 46*(5), 360–368.

Gregory, A. (2007). *African-American students and the discipline gap in high schools*. UCAccord Public Policy Series. PB-014-0507. Retrieved June 11, 2009, from http://ucaccord.gseis.ucla.edu/publications/index.html.

Gregory, A., & Weinstein, R. S. (2008). The discipline gap and African Americans: Defiance or cooperation in the high school classroom. *Journal of School Psychology, 46*(4), 455–475.

Gresham, F. (2002). Responsiveness to intervention: An alternative approach to the identification of learning disabilities. In R. Bradley, L. Danielson, & D. Hallahan (Eds.), *Identification of learning disabilities: Research to practice* (pp. 467–519). Mahwah, NJ: Erlbaum.

Gresham, F. M. (1988). Social competence and motivational characteristics of learning disabled students. In M. C. Wang, M. C. Reynolds, & H. J. Walberg (Eds.), *Handbook of special education: Research and practice: Vol. 2. Mildly handicapped conditions*. Oxford, UK: Pergamon.

Gresham, F. M. (2005). Response to intervention: An alternative means of identifying students as emotionally disturbed. *Education and Treatment of Children, 28,* 328–344.

Gresham, F. M., Beebe-Frankenberger, M. E., & MacMillan, D. L. (1999). A selective review of treatments for children with autism: Description and methodological considerations. *School Psychology Review, 28*(4), 559–575.

Gresham, F. M., & Elliott, S. N. (1990). *The social skills rating system (SSRS)*. Circle Pines, MN: American Guidance Service.

Gresham, F. M., & Gansle, K. (1992). Misguided assumptions in *DSM-III-R:* Implications for school psychological practice. *School Psychology Quarterly, 7,* 79–95.

Gresham, F. M., & Kern, L. (2004). Internalizing behavior problems in children and adolescents. In R. B. Rutherford, Jr., M. M. Quinn, & A. R. Mathur (Eds.), *Handbook of research in emotional and behavioral disorders* (pp. 54–77). New York: Guilford.

Gresham, F. M., Lane, K. L., MacMillan, D. L., & Bocian, K. M. (1999). Social and academic profiles of externalizing and internalizing groups: Risk factors for emotional and behavioral disorders. *Behavioral Disorders, 24,* 231–245.

Gresham, F. M., Sugai, G., & Horner, R. H. (2001). Interpreting outcomes of social skills training for students with high-incidence disabilities. *Exceptional Children, 67,* 331–344.

Griffin, C. C., Kilgore, K. L., Winn, J. A., Otis-Wilborn, A., Hou, W., & Garvan, C. W. (2009). First-year special educators: The influence of school and classroom context factors on their accomplishments and problems. *Teacher Education and Special Education, 32*(1), 45–63.

Griffin, C. C., & Pugach, M. C. (2007). Framing the progress of collaborative teacher education. *Focus on Exceptional Children, 39*(6), 1–16.

Griffin, C. C., Winn, J. A., Otis-Wilborn, A., & Kilgore, K. L. (2003, September). *New teacher induction in special education* (COPSSE Document No. RS-5). Gainesville: University of Florida, Center on Personnel Studies in Special Education.

Griffin, H. C., Fitch, C. L., & Griffin, L. W. (2002). Causes and interventions in the area of cerebral palsy. *Infants and Young Children, 14*(3), 18–23.

Gross, M. U. M. (2004). *The use of radical acceleration in cases of extreme intellectual precocity.* Thousand Oaks, CA: Corwin.

Grossman, H. (Ed.). (1973). *Manual on terminology and classification in mental retardation* (rev. ed.). Washington, DC: AAMR.

Grouse, W. F. (2003). Reflecting on teacher professionalism: A student perspective. *Kappa Delta Pi Record, 40,* 17–37.

Gruwell, E. (2007). *Teach with your heart.* New York: Random House.

Guetzloe, E. (1999). Inclusion: The broken promise. *Preventing School Failure, 43*(3), 92–98.

Gureasko-Moore, D., DuPaul, G., & Power, T. (2005). Stimulant treatment for attention-deficit/hyperactivity disorder: Medication monitoring practices of school psychologists. *School Psychology Review, 34*(2), 232–245.

Gureasko-Moore, S., DuPaul, G., & White, G. (2006). The effects of self-management in general education classrooms on the organizational skills of adolescents with ADHD. *Behavior Modification, 30*(2), 159–183.

Guskey, T. R., & Yoon, K. S. (2009). What works in professional development? *Phi Delta Kappan, 90*(7), 495–500.

Hague, J. M., & Babkie, A. M. (2006). Develop collaborative special educator–paraprofessional teams: One para's view. *Intervention in School and Clinic, 42*(1), 51–53.

Hahn, H. (1985). Toward a politics of disability: Definitions, disciplines and policies. *Social Science Journal, 22*(4), 87–105.

Hall, D., Wiener, R., & Carey, K. (2003). What new "AYP" information tells us about schools, states, and public education. *Education Trust, 2003,* pp. 1–10.

Hammer, M. (2004). Using the self-advocacy strategy to increase student participation in IEP conferences. *Intervention in School and Clinic, 39,* 295–300.

Hampton, E. O., Whitney, D. W., & Schwartz, I. S. (2002). Weaving assessment information into intervention ideas: Planning communication interventions for young children with disabilities. *Assessment for Effective Intervention, 27,* 49–59.

Handleman, J. S., Harris, S. L., & Martins, M. P. (2005). Helping children with autism enter the mainstream. In F. R. Volkmar, R. Paul, A. Klin, & D. Cohen (Eds.), *Handbook of autism and pervasive developmental disorders: Vol. 2. Assessment, interventions, and policy* (4th ed., pp. 1029–1042). Hoboken, NJ: Wiley.

Hardman, M. L., & Mulder, M. (2004). Federal education reform: Critical issues in public education and their impact on students with disabilities. In L. M. Bullock & R. A. Gable (Eds.), *Quality personnel preparation in emotional/behavioral disorders: Current perspectives and future directions.* Denton, TX: Institute for Behavioral and Learning Differences at the University of North Texas.

Hardman, M. L., & Nagle, K. (2004). Public policy: From access to accountability in special education. In A. McCray Sorrells,

H. J. Rieth, & P. T. Sindelar (Eds.), *Critical issues in special education: Access, diversity, and accountability.* Boston: Pearson Education.

Hardman, M., & Dawson, S. (2008). The impact of federal public policy on curriculum and instruction for students with disabilities in the general classroom. *Preventing School Failure, 52*(2), 5–11.

Harlacher, J., Roberts, N., & Merrell, K. (2006). Classwide interventions with ADHD: A summary of teacher options beneficial for the whole class. *Teaching Exceptional Children, 39*(2), 6–12.

Harris, B., Rapp, K. E., Martinez, R. S., & Plucker, J. A. (2007). Identifying English language learners for gifted and talented programs: Current practices and recommendations for improvement. *Roeper Review, 29*(5), 26–29.

Harris, S. L., & Delmolino, L. (2002, January). Applied behavior analysis: Its application in the treatment of autism and related disorders in young children. *Infants and Young Children, 14*(3), 11–17.

Harris, S. L., Handleman, J. S., Gordon, R., Kristoff, B., & Fuentes, F. (1991). Changes in cognitive and language functioning of preschool children with autism. *Journal of Autism and Developmental Disabilities, 21,* 281–290.

Harris, S. L., Handleman, J. S., & Jennett, H. K. (2005). Models of educational intervention for students with autism: Home, center, and school-based programming. In F. R. Volkmar, R. Paul, A. Klin, & D. Cohen (Eds.), *Handbook of autism and pervasive developmental disorders: Vol. 2. Assessment, interventions, and policy* (4th ed., pp. 1043–1054). Hoboken, NJ: Wiley.

Harrison, P., & Oakland, T. (2003). *Adaptive behavior assessment system* (2nd ed.). San Antonio, TX: Psychological Corporation.

Hart, D., Mele-McCarthy, J., Pasternack, R., Zimbrich, K., & Parker, D. (2004). Community college: A pathway to success for youth with learning, cognitive, and intellectual disabilities in secondary settings. *Education and Training in Developmental Disabilities, 39*(1), 54–66.

Hart, J. E., & Whalon, K. J. (2008). Promote academic engagement and communication of students with autism spectrum disorder in inclusive settings. *Intervention in School and Clinic, 44*(2), 116–120.

Harvey, V. S. (2007). Raising resiliency schoolwide. *Principal Leadership, 7,* 10–14.

Hasselbring, T. S., & Glaser, C. H. W. (2000). Use of computer technology to help students with special needs. *Future of Children, 10*(2), 102–122.

Hatton, D. D. (2001). Model registry of early childhood visual impairment: First-year results. *Journal of Visual Impairment and Blindness, 95,* 418–433.

Hawbaker, B. (2006). Student-led IEP meetings: Planning and implementation strategies. *Teaching Exceptional Children Plus, 3*(5) Article 4. Retrieved April 8, 2009, from http://escholarship.bc.edu/education/tecplus/vol3/iss5/art4/

Heal, L. W., & Rusch, F. R. (1995). Predicting employment for students who leave special education high school programs. *Exceptional Children, 61*(5), 472–487.

Heber, R. (1961). A manual on terminology and classification in mental retardation (rev. ed.). *American Journal of Mental Deficiency, 64* [Monograph Supplement].

Heflin, L. J., & Alaimo, D. F. (2007). *Students with autism spectrum disorders: Effective instructional practices.* Upper Saddle River, NJ: Pearson.

Heflin, J., & Simpson, R. (1998). Interventions for children and youth with autism: Prudent choices in a world of exaggerated claims and empty promises: Part 1: Intervention and treatment option review. *Focus on Autism and Other Developmental Disabilities, 13,* 212–220.

Heller, K. W. (2004). Integrating health care and educational programs. In F. P. Orelove, D. Sobsey, & R. K. Silberman (Eds.), *Educating children with multiple disabilities: A collaborative approach* (2nd ed., pp. 379–424). Baltimore: Brookes.

Heller, K. W., & Kennedy, C. (1994). *Etiologies and characteristics of deaf-blindness*. Monmouth, OR: Teaching Research Publications.

Henderson, K., & Bradley, R. (2004). A national perspective on mental health and children with disabilities: Emotional disturbances in children. *Emotional and Behavioral Disorders in Youth, 4*(3), 67–74.

Henderson, M. V., Gullatt, D. E., Hardin, D. T., Jannik, C., & Tollett, J. R. (1999). *Preventative law curriculum guide* (ED437366). Baton Rouge: Louisiana State Board of Regents.

Hendley, S. L. (2007). Use positive behavior support for inclusion in the general education classroom. *Intervention in School and Clinic, 42*(4), 225–228.

Hendrick, I. G., & MacMillan, D. L. (1989). Selecting children for special education in New York City: William Maxwell, Elizabeth Farrell, and the development of ungraded classes, 1900–1920. *Journal of Special Education, 22*(4), 395–417.

Hendricks, D. R. (2009). Transition from school to adulthood for youth with autism spectrum disorders. *Focus on Autism and Other Developmental Disorders, 24*(2), 77–88.

Hendricks, D., & Wehman, P. (2009). Transition from school to adulthood for youth with autism: Review and recommendations. *Focus on Autism and Developmental Disabilities, 24*(2), 77–89.

Henley, M., Ramsey, R., & Algozzine, R. (2006). *Teaching students with mild disabilities* (5th ed). Boston: Pearson Education.

Henshon, S. (2006). An evolving field. *Roeper Review, 28*(4), 191–194.

Herr, S. (1995). A humanist's legacy: Burton Blatt and the origins of the disability rights movement. *Mental Retardation, 33*(5), 328–331.

Higgins, K., Boone, R., & Williams, D. (2000). Evaluating educational software for special education. *Intervention in School and Clinic, 36*(2), 109–115.

Hitchcock, C., Meyer, A., Rose, D., & Jackson, R. (2002). Providing new access to the general curriculum: Universal design for learning. *Teaching Exceptional Children, 35*(2), 8–17.

Hobbs, T., & Westling, D. L. (2000). Together and alone: A comparison of collaborative and individual inclusion planning. *Issues in Teacher Education, 9*(1), 9–38.

Hollenbeck, A. F. (2007). From IDEA to implementation: A discussion of foundational and future responsiveness-to intervention research. *Learning Disabilities Research & Practice, 22*(2), 137–146.

Hollingsworth, L.S (1940). Intelligence as an element of personality. *Yearbook of the National Society of Education, 39*, 271–275.

Hollins, E. R. (1996). *Culture in school learning: Revealing the deep meaning*. Mahwah, NJ: Erlbaum.

Holt, J. (1993). Stanford achievement test—8th edition: Reading comprehension subgroup results. *American Annals of the Deaf, 138*, 172–175.

Hoover, J. J., & Patton, J. R. (2008). The role of special educators in a multitiered instructional system. *Intervention in School and Clinic, 43*(4), 195–202.

Hord, S. M. (1997). *Professional learning communities: Communities of continuing improvement*. Austin, TX: Southwest Educational Development Laboratory.

Hord, S. M. (2009). Professional learning communities. *Journal of Staff Development, 30*(1). Retrieved on July 12, 2009, from http://vnweb.hwwilsonweb.com/

Hosp, J., & Reschly, D. (2004). Disproportionate representation of minority students in special education: Academic, demographic, and economic predictors. *Exceptional Children, 70*(2), 185–199.

Howlin, P. (1997). *Autism: Preparing for adulthood*. London: Routledge.

Howlin, P., & Asgharian, A. (1999). The diagnosis of autism and Asperger syndrome: Findings from a survey of 770 families. *Developmental Medicine and Child Neurology, 41*, 834–839.

Howlin, P., Magiati, I., & Charman, T. (2009). Systematic review of early intensive behavioral interventions for children with autism. *American Association on Intellectual and Developmental Disabilities, 114*(1), 23–41.

Howlin, P., Mawhood, L., & Rutter, M. (2000). Autism and developmental receptive language disorder—A follow-up comparison in early adult life. II: Social, behavioural, and psychiatric outcomes. *Journal of Child Psychology and Psychiatry, 41*, 561–578.

Hu-Lince, D., Craig, D. W., Huentelman, M. J., & Stephan, D. A. (2005). The autism genome project: Goals and strategies. *American Journal of Pharmacogenomics, 5*(4), 233–246.

Huebner, K. M., Merk-Adam, B., Stryker, D., & Wolffe, K. E. (2004). *The national agenda for the education of children and youths with visual impairments, including those with multiple disabilities—Revised*. New York: AFB Press.

Humphrey, G. (1962). Introduction. In J. M. G. Itard, *The wild boy of Aveyron*. New York: Appleton-Century-Crofts.

Humphries, T., & Padden, C. (1988). *Deaf in America: Voices from a culture*. Cambridge, MA: Harvard University Press.

Hunt, P., & Goetz, L. (1997). Research on inclusive educational programs, practices, and outcomes for students with severe disabilities. *Journal of Special Education, 31*, 3–29.

Hurst, B., Wilson, C., & Cramer, G. (1998). Professional teaching portfolios. *Phi Delta Kappan, 79*(8), 578–582.

Hussar, W. J. (2005). *Projections of education statistics to 2014*. Washington, DC: National Center for Education Statistics.

IDEA Law and Resources. (1999). *Law & Regulations: IDEA '97 Law and Regs*. U.S. Department of Education. Retrieved June 11, 2009, from http://www.ed.gov/offices/OSERS/Policy/IDEA/index.html

Indiana Department of Education. (2005). *2004–2005 special education statistical report*. Indianapolis: Division of Exceptional Learners. Retrieved on December 2, 2005, from http://ideanet.doe.state.in.us/exceptional/speced/welcome.html

Individuals with Disabilities Education Act (IDEA), Public Law 105-17. (1997). Retrieved November 21, 2006, from http://www.ed.gov/offices/OSERS/Policy/IDEA/index.html

Individuals with Disabilities Education Improvement Act (IDEA), Public Law 108-446 (2004). Retrieved June 11, 2009, from http://idea.ed.gov/download/statute.html

Inge, K. J., & Tilson, G. (1994). Supported employment: Issues and applications for individuals with learning disabilities. In P. J. Gerber & H. B. Reiff (Eds.), *Learning disabilities in adulthood: Persisting problems and evolving issues* (pp. 179–193). Boston: Andover Medical Publishers.

Interstate New Teacher Assessment and Support Consortium. (1992). *Model standards for beginning teacher licensing, assessment and development: A resource for state dialogue*. Retrieved June 7, 2004, from http://www.ccsso.org/content/pdfs/corestrd.pdf

Irvine, J. J. (2002). *In search of wholeness: African American teachers and their culturally specific practices*. New York: Palgrave/St. Martin's Press.

Irvine, J. J. (2003) *Educating teachers for diversity: Seeing with a cultural eye*. New York: Teachers College Press.

Itard, I. M. G. (1962). *The wild boy of Aveyron*. New York: Appleton-Century-Crafts.

Jenkins, J. R., Graff, J., & Miglioretti, D. L. (2009). Estimating reading growth using intermittent CBM progress monitoring. *Exceptional Children, 75*(2), 151–164.

Jensen, P., Kettle, L., Roper, M., et al. (1999). Are stimulants over-prescribed? Treatment of ADHD in four U.S. communities. *Journal of the American Academy of Child and Adolescent Psychiatry, 38*(7), 797–804.

Jewell, E. J., & Abate, F. (Eds.). (2001). *The new Oxford American dictionary*. New York: Oxford University Press.

Johns, B. H., & Carr, V. G. (1995). *Techniques of managing: Verbally and physically aggressive students*. Denver: Love.

Johnson, D., Johnson, R., & Holubec, E. (1993). *Circles of learning: Cooperation in the classroom*. Edina, MN: Interaction Book Company.

Johnson, D., Mellard, D., & Lancaster, P. (2007). Road to success: Helping young adults with learning disabilities plan and prepare for employment. *Teaching Exceptional Children, 39*(6), 26–32.

Johnson, D., & Thurlow, M. (2003). *A national study on graduation requirements and diploma options for youth with disabilities* (Technical Report 36). Minneapolis: University of Minnesota, National Center on Educational Outcomes.

Johnson, G. O. (1962). Special education for the mentally handicapped: A paradox. *Exceptional Children, 29*, 62–69.

Jolivette, K., McCormick, K. M., & Lingo, A. S. (2004). Embedding choices into the daily routines of young children with behavior problems: Eight reasons to build social competence. *Beyond Behavior, 13*(3), 21–26.

Jones, E. D., & Southern, W. T. (1991). Objections to early entrance and grade skipping. In W. T. Southern & E. D. Jones (Eds.), *The academic acceleration of gifted children* (pp. 51–74). New York: Teachers College Press.

Jones, V., & Jones, L. (2004). *Comprehensive classroom management: Creating communities of support and solving problems* (7th ed.). Boston: Pearson.

Justice, L. M. (2006). *Communication sciences and disorders: An introduction*. Upper Saddle River, NJ: Merrill/Pearson.

Kabat-Zinn, J. (1991). *Full catastrophe living: Using the wisdom of your body and mind to face stress, pain, and illness*. New York: Delta.

Kame'enui, E., & Carnine, D. (1998). *Effective teaching strategies that accommodate diverse learners*. Upper Saddle River, NJ: Merrill/Pearson.

Kame'enui, E., & Simmons, D. (1999). *Toward successful inclusion of students with disabilities: The architecture of instruction*. Reston, VA: Council for Exceptional Children.

Kanner, L. (1943). Autistic disturbances of affective contact. *Nervous Child, 2*, 217–250.

Kaplan, S. G., & Cornell, D. G. (2005). Threats of violence by students in special education. *Behavioral Disorders, 31*, 107–119.

Kasari, C., & Wong, C. (2002). Five early signs of autism. *Exceptional Parent, 32*(11), 60–62.

Katims, D. S. (2000). Literacy instruction for people with mental retardation: Historical highlights and contemporary analysis. *Education and Training in Mental Retardation and Developmental Disabilities, 35*, 3–15.

Kauchak, D., & Eggen, P. (2005). *Introduction to teaching: Becoming a professional* (2nd ed.). Upper Saddle River, NJ: Merrill/Prentice Hall.

Kauchak, D., Eggen, P., & Carter, C. (2002). *Introduction to teaching: Becoming a professional*. Upper Saddle River, NJ: Merrill/Pearson.

Kauffman, J. M. (1981). Introduction: Historical trends and contemporary issues in special education in the United States. In J. M. Kauffman & D. P. Hallahan (Eds.), *Handbook of special education* (pp. 3–23). Upper Saddle River, NJ: Pearson.

Kauffman, J. M. (1996). Research to practice issues. *Behavioral Disorders, 22*, 55–60.

Kauffman, J. M. (2001). *Characteristics of emotional and behavioral disorders of children and youth* (7th ed.). Upper Saddle River, NJ: Merrill/Pearson.

Kauffman J. M., Bantz, J., & McCullough, J. (2002). Separate and better: A special public school class for students with emotional and behavioral disorders. *Exceptionality, 10*(3), 149–170.

Kauffman, J. M., & Hallahan, D. P. (2005). *Special education: What it is and why we need it*. Boston: Pearson Education.

Kauffman, J. M., Mock, D. R., & Simpson, R. L. (2007). Problems related to the underservice of students with emotional or behavioral disorders. *Behavioral Disorders, 33*(1), 43–57.

Kauffman, J. M., Mostert, M. P., Trent, S. C., & Hallahan, D. P. (2002). *Managing classroom behavior: A reflective case-based approach* (3rd ed.). Boston: Allyn & Bacon.

Kavale, K., & Forness, S. (1995). *The nature of learning disabilities: Critical elements of diagnosis and classification*. Mahwah, NJ: Erlbaum.

Kavale, K., Holdnack, J., & Mostert, M. (2005). Responsiveness to intervention and the identification of specific learning disability: A critique and alternative proposal. *Learning Disability Quarterly, 28*(1), 2–16.

Kavale, K. A., Mathur, S. R., & Mostert, M. P. (2004). Social skills training and teaching social behavior to students with emotional and behavioral disorders. In R. B. Rutherford, Jr., M. M. Quinn, & A. R. Mathur (Eds.), *Handbook of research in emotional and behavioral disorders* (pp. 446–461). New York: Guilford.

Kearns, J., Burdge, M., & Kleinert, H. (2005). Alternative assessment and standards-based instruction: Practical strategies for teachers. In M. Wehmeyer, & M. Agran (Eds.). *Mental retardation and intellectual disabilities: Teaching students using innovative and research-based strategies* (pp. 3–28). Upper Saddle River, NJ: Pearson.

Kemp, C. E., Hourcade, J. J., & Parette, H. P. (2000). Building an initial information base: Assistive technology funding resources for school-aged students with disabilities. *Journal of Special Education Technology, 15*(4), 15–24.

Kendziora, K. T. (2004). Early intervention for emotional and behavioral disorders. In R. B. Rutherford, Jr., M. M. Quinn, & A. R. Mathur (Eds.), *Handbook of research in emotional and behavioral disorders* (pp. 327–351). New York: Guilford.

Kennedy, C. H., & Shukla, S. (1995). Social interaction research for people with autism as a set of past, current, and emerging propositions. *Behavioral Disorders, 21*, 21–35.

Kennedy, C. H., Meyer, K. A., Knowles, T., & Shukla, S. (2000). Analyzing the multiple functions of stereotypical behavior for students with autism: Implications for assessment and treatment. *Journal of Applied Behavioral Analysis, 33*, 559–571.

Kennedy, M. M. (1997). The connection between research and practice. *Educational Researcher, 26*(7), 4–12.

Kern, L. & State, T. M. (2009). Incorporating choice and preferred activities into classwide instruction. *Beyond Behavior, 18*(2), 3–11.

Ketelaar, M., Vermeer, A., Helders, P. J. M., & Hart, H. (1998). Parental participation in intervention programs for children with cerebral palsy: A review of research. *Topics in Early Childhood Special Education, 18*(2), 108–117.

Kewal-Ramani, A., Gilbertson, L., Fox, M., & Provasnik, S. (2007). *Status and trends in the education of racial and ethnic minorities* (NCES 2007-039). Washington, DC: National Center for Education Statistics, Institute of Education Sciences, U.S. Department of Education.

Keyser-Marcus, L., Briel, L., Sherron-Targett, P., Yasuda, S., Johnson, S., & Wehman, P. (2002). Enhancing the schooling of students with traumatic brain injury. *Teaching Exceptional Children, 34*(4), 62–67.

Kidsource. (2000). *What do parents need to know about children's television viewing?* Retrieved January 20, 2005, from http://www.kidsource.com/kidsource/content/TV.viewing.html

Kilgore, K., & Griffin, C. C. (1998). Beginning special education teachers: Problems of practice and the influence of school context. *Teacher Education and Special Education, 21,* 155–173.

Kilgore, K., Griffin, C., Otis-Wilborn, A., & Winn, J. (2003). The problems of beginning special education teachers: Exploring the contextual factors influencing their work. *Action in Teacher Education, 25,* 38–47.

Kim, K., & Turnbull, A. (2004). Transition to adulthood for students with severe intellectual disabilities: Shifting toward person-family interdependent training. *Research and Practice for Persons with Severe Disabilities, 29,* 53–57.

King, K. A., Harris-Murri, N. J., & Artiles, A. J. (2006). *Proactive culturally responsive discipline.* Tempe AZ: National Center for Culturally Responsive Educational Systems.

Kirsch, N. L., Shenton, M., Spirl, E., Rowan, J., Simpson, R., Schreckenghost, D., & LoPresti, E. F. (2004). Web-based assistive technology interventions for cognitive impairments after traumatic brain injury: A selective review and two case studies. *Rehabilitation Psychology, 49,* 200–212.

Kliewer, C., & Landis, D. (1999). Individualizing literacy instruction for young children with moderate to severe disabilities. *Exceptional Children, 66,* 85–100.

Klin, A., McPartland, J., & Volkmar, F. R. (2005). Asperger syndrome. In F. R. Volkmar, R. Paul, A. Klin, & D. Cohen (Eds.), *Handbook of autism and pervasive developmental disorders: Vol. 1. Diagnosis, development, neurobiology, and behavior* (4th ed., pp. 88–125). Hoboken, NJ: Wiley.

Klingner, J. K., Hoover, J. J., & Baca, L. M. (2008). *Why do English language learners struggle with reading? Distinguishing language acquisition from learning disabilities.* Thousand Oaks, CA: Corwin Press.

Knowles, J. G., Cole, A. L., & Presswood, C. S. (1994). *Through preservice teachers' eyes: Exploring field experience through narrative and inquiry.* New York: Macmillan.

Kochhar-Bryant, C. (2008). *Collaboration and system coordination for students with special needs.* Upper Saddle River, NJ: Merrill/Pearson Education.

Kochhar-Bryant, C., & Greene, G. (2008). *Pathways to successful transition for youth with disabilities: A developmental process* (2nd ed.). Upper Saddle River, NJ: Prentice Hall.

Koenig, L. (2000). *Smart discipline for the classroom: Respect and cooperation restored* (3rd ed.). Thousand Oaks, CA: Corwin.

Kollins, S., Barkley, R., & DuPaul, G. (2001). Use and management of medications for children diagnosed with attention deficit hyperactivity disorder (ADHD). *Focus on Exceptional Children, 33*(5), 1–24.

Konopasek, D., & Forness, S. (2004). Psychopharmacology in the treatment of emotional and behavioral disorders. In

R. B. Rutherford, Jr., M. M. Quinn, & A. R. Mathur (Eds.), *Handbook of research in emotional and behavioral disorders* (pp. 352–368). New York: Guilford Press.

Kortering, L., Braziel, P. M., & Tompkins, J. R. (2002). The challenge of school completion among youth with behavioral disorders: Another side of the story. *Behavioral Disorders, 27*(2), 142–154.

Kostewicz, D. E., & Kubina, R. M. (2008). The national reading panel guidepost: A review of reading outcome measures for students with emotional and behavioral disorders. *Behavioral Disorders, 33*(2), 62–74.

Kottler, J. A. (2002). *Students who drive you crazy: Succeeding with resistant, unmotivated, and otherwise difficult young people.* Thousand Oaks, CA: Corwin.

Kozleski, E., Mainzer, R., & Deshler, D. (2000). *Bright futures for exceptional learners: An agenda to achieve quality conditions for teaching & learning.* Arlington, VA: Council for Exceptional Children.

Kramer, C. (2004). *The effects of a self-management device on the acquisition of social skills in adolescent males with SED.* Unpublished doctoral dissertation, Johns Hopkins University, Baltimore.

Kramer, P. A. (2003). The ABC's of professionalism. *Kappa Delta Pi Record, 40,* 22–25.

Krashen, S. (1985). *The input hypothesis: Issues and implications.* London: Longman.

Krashen, S. D. (2006). *Bilingual education accelerates English language development.* Retrieved May 10, 2009, from http://www.sdkrashen.com/articles/krashen_intro.pdf

Kurtts, S., Matthews, C., & Smallwood, T. (2009). (Dis)solving the differences: A physical science lesson using universal design. *Intervention in School & Clinic, 44*(3), 151–159.

Kyle, D., McIntyre, E., Miller, K., & Moore, G. (2006). *Bridging school & home through family nights.* Thousand Oaks, CA: Corwin Press.

La Paro, K. M., Olsen, K., & Pianta, R. C. (2002). Special education eligibility: Developmental precursors over the first three years of life. *Exceptional Children, 69,* 55–66.

Ladson-Billings, G. (2009). *The dreamkeepers: Successful teachers of African American children* (2nd ed.). San Francisco: Jossey-Bass.

Laing, R. D. (1967). *The politics of experience.* New York: Ballantine.

Lambert, N., Nihira, K., & Leland, H. (1993). *AAMR adaptive behavior scale—School* (2nd ed.). Austin, TX: PRO-ED.

Lambros, K. M., Ward, S. L., Bocian, K. M., MacMillan, D. L., & Gresham, F. M. (1998). Behavioral profiles of children at-risk for emotional and behavioral disorders: Implications for assessment and classification. *Focus on Exceptional Children, 30*(5), 1–16.

Lane, K. L. (2004). Academic instruction and tutoring interventions for students with emotional and behavioral disorders: 1990 to the present. In R. B. Rutherford, Jr., M. M. Quinn, & A. R. Mathur (Eds.), *Handbook of research in emotional and behavioral disorders* (pp. 462–486). New York: Guilford.

Lane, K. L., Carter, E. W., Pierson, M. R., & Glaeser, B. C. (2006). Academic, social, and behavioral characteristics of high school students with emotional disturbances or learning disabilities. *Journal of Emotional and Behavioral Disorders, 14*(2), 108–112.

Lane, K. L., Weisenbach, J. L., Phillips, A., & Wehby, J. H. (2007). Designing, implementing, and evaluating function-based interventions using a systematic feasible approach. *Behavioral Disorders, 32*(2), 122–139.

Lane, K., Pierson, M., Robertson, E., & Little, A. (2004). Teachers' views of prereferral interventions: Perceptions of and recommendations for implementation support. *Education and Treatment of Children, 27*(4), 420–439.

Langdon, C. (1999). The fifth Phi Delta Kappa poll of teachers' attitudes toward public schools. *Phi Delta Kappan, 80*(8), 611–618.

Langer, J. A. (2000). Excellence in English in Middle and high school. How teachers' professional lives support student achievement. *American Educational Research Journal, 37*(2), 397–439.

Lapp, J., & Attridge, M. (2000). Worksite interventions reduce stress among high school teachers and staff. *International Journal of Stress Management, 7*(3), 229–232.

Larson, E. J. (2002). The meaning of human gene testing for disability rights. *University of Cincinnati Law Review, 70*, 1–26.

Larson, S., Doljanac, R., & Lakin, K. (2005). United States living arrangements of persons with intellectual and/or developmental disabilities in 1995. *Journal of Intellectual and Developmental Disability, 30*, 248–251.

Larson, S., Scott, N., & Lakin, C. (2008). Changes in the number of people with intellectual or developmental disabilities living in homes they own or rent between 1998 and 2007. *Intellectual and Developmental Disabilities, 46*(6), 487–491.

Lee, S-H., Theoharis, R., Fitzpatrick, M., Kim, K-H., Liss, J. M., Nix-Williams, T., Griswold, D. E., & Walther-Thomas, C. (2006) Create effective mentoring relationships: Strategies for mentor and mentee success. *Intervention in School and Clinic, 41*(4), 233–240.

Lehman, C. (1992, July). Job designs: A community based program for students with emotional and behavioral disorders. *Teaching Research Newsletter,* pp. 1–7.

LeNard, J. M. (2001). *How public input shapes the Clerc Center's priorities: Identifying critical needs in transition from school to postsecondary education and employment.* Washington, DC: Laurent Clerc National Center on Deaf Education.

Lenz, K., Deshler, D., & Kissam, B. (Eds.). (2004). *Teaching content to all: Evidence-based inclusive practices in middle and secondary schools.* Boston: Allyn & Bacon.

Lerner, J., & Johns, B. (2009). *Learning disabilities and related mild disabilities* (11th ed.). Boston: Houghton Mifflin.

Leslie, L. (2004). ADHD: An epidemic. Developmental Behavioral Pediatrics Online. Retrieved June 10, 2009, from http://www.dbpeds.org/articles/detail.cfm?TextID=129

Lewis, T. J., & Sugai, G. (1999). Effective behavior support: A systems approach to proactive school-wide management. *Focus on Exceptional Children, 31*(6), 1–24.

Lin, S. L. (2000). Coping and adaptation in families of children with cerebral palsy. *Exceptional Children, 66*, 201–218.

Linn, A., & Smith-Myles, B. (2004). Asperger syndrome and six strategies for success. *Beyond Behavior, 14*(1), 3–9.

Little, M. E. (2009). *Response to intervention for teachers. Classroom instructional problem solving.* Denver: Love.

Loewen, J. W. (2007). *Lies my teacher told me* (2nd ed.). New York: Simon & Schuster.

Lombroso, C. (1891). *The men of genius.* London: Scott.

Lotter, V. (1978). Follow-up studies. In M. Rutter & E. Schopler (Eds.), *Autism: A reappraisal of concepts and treatment* (pp. 475–596). New York: Plenum.

Louis, K. S., Marks, H. M., & Kruse, S. D. (1996). Teachers' professional community in restructuring schools. *American Educational Research Journal, 33*, 757–798.

Loveland, K. A., & Tunali-Kotoski, B. (2005). The school-age child with an autistic spectrum disorder. In F. R. Volkmar, R. Paul, A. Klin, & D. Cohen (Eds.), *Handbook of autism and pervasive developmental disorders: Vol. 1. Diagnosis, development, neurobiology, and behavior* (4th ed., pp. 247–287). Hoboken, NJ: Wiley.

Luckasson R., Coulter, D., Polloway, E., Reiss, S., Schalock, R., Snell, N., et al. (1992). *Mental retardation: Definition, classification, and systems of support* (9th ed.). Washington, DC: AAMR.

Luckasson, R., Borthwick-Duffy, S., Buntinx, W. H. E., Coulter, D. L., Craig, E. M., Reeve, A., et al. (2002). *Mental retardation: Definition, classification, and systems of supports* (10th ed.). Washington, DC: AAMR.

Luckner, J. L. (2002). *Facilitating the transition of students who are deaf or hard of hearing.* Austin, TX: PRO ED.

Luckner, J. L., & Howell, J. J. (2002). Suggestions for preparing itinerant teachers: A qualitative analysis. *American Annals of the Deaf, 147*(3), 54–61.

Lyon, R., Fletcher, J., Shaywitz, S., Shaywitz, B., Torgesen, J., Wood, F., et al. (2001). Rethinking learning disabilities. In C. Finn, A. Rotherham, & C. Hokanson (Eds.), *Rethinking special education for a new century* (pp. 259–287). Retrieved on December 28, 2005, from http://www.edexcellence.net/foundation/publication/index.cfm

Maag, J. (2002). A contextually based approach for treating depression in school-age children. *Intervention in School and Clinic, 37*(3), 149–155.

Maag, J. W., & Reid, R. (2006). Depression among students with learning disabilities: Assessing the risk. *Journal of Learning Disabilities, 39*(1), 3–10.

Maas, E., & Robin, D. A. (2006). Motor speech disorders: Apraxia and dysarthria. In L. M. Justice, *Communication sciences and disorders: An introduction* (pp. 180–211). Upper Saddle River, NJ: Merrill/Pearson.

Mace, A. L., Wallace, K. L., Whan, M. Q., & Steimachowicz, P. G. (1991). Relevant factors in the identification of hearing loss. *Ear and Hearing, 12*(4), 287–293.

MacLean, W. E., & Symons, F. (2002). Self-injurious behavior in infancy and young childhood. *Infants and Young Children, 14*(4), 31–41.

MacMillan, D., & Siperstein, G. (2002). Learning disabilities as operationalized by schools. In R. Bradley, L. Danielson, & D. Hallahan (Eds.), *Identification of learning disabilities: Research to practice* (pp. 287–333). Mahwah, NJ: Erlbaum.

Macmillan, D., Siperstein, G., & Leffert, J. (2006). Children with mild mental retardation: A challenge for classification practices—revised. In H. Switzky & S. Greenspan (Eds.). *What is mental retardation? Ideas for an evolving disability in the 21st century* (rev. ed., pp. 197–220). Washington, DC: American Association on Intellectual and Developmental Disabilties.

Madaus, J., & Shaw, S. (2008). The role of school professionals in implementing Section 504 for students with disabilities. *Educational Policy, (22)*3, 363–378.

Maker, C. J. (1989). *Critical issues in gifted education: Defensible programs for cultural and ethnic minorities.* Austin, TX: PRO-ED.

Maker, C. J., & Nielson, A. B. (1996). *Curriculum development and teaching strategies for gifted learners* (2nd ed.). Austin, TX: PRO-ED.

Mann, V. (2003). Language processes: Keys to reading disability. In H. L. Swanson, K. R. Harris, & S. Graham (Eds.), *Handbook of learning disabilities* (pp. 213–228). New York: Guilford.

Marcus, L. M., Kunce, L. J., & Schopler, E. (2005). Working with families. In F. R. Volkmar, R. Paul, A. Klin, & D. Cohen (Eds.), *Handbook of autism and pervasive developmental disorders: Vol. 2. Assessment, interventions, and policy* (4th ed., pp. 1055–1086). Hoboken, NJ: Wiley.

Marks, D. (2005). *Culture and classroom management: Grounded theory from a high poverty predominately African American elementary school*. Unpublished doctoral dissertation. Gainesville: University of Florida.

Marland, S. P. (1972). *Education of the gifted and talented: Report to the Congress of the United States by the U.S. Commissioner of Education*. Washington, DC: U.S. Government Printing Office.

Martin, J., Marshall, L., Maxon, L., & Jerman, P. (1997). *The self-directed IEP*. Longmont, CO: Sopris West.

Martin, J., Van Dycke, J., Christensen, W., Greene, B., Gardner, J., & Lovett, D. (2006). Increasing student participation in IEP meetings: Establishing the self-directed IEP as an evidence-based practice. *Exceptional Children, 72(3)*, 299–316.

Martinez, R. S., Nellis, L. M., & Prendergast, K. A. (2006). Closing the achievement gap series: Part II Response to Intervention (RTI)—Basic elements, practical applications, and policy recommendations. *Center for Evaluation & Education Policy, 4*(8).

Marzano, R., Pickering, D., & Pollock, J. (2001). *Classroom instruction that works*. Alexandria, VA: ASCD.

Mason, C., Field, S., & Sawilowsky, S. (2004). Implementation of self-determination activities and student participation in IEPs. *Exceptional Children, 70(4)*, 441–451.

Mason, C., McGahee-Kovac, M., Johnson, L., & Stillerman, S. (2002). Implementing student-led IEPs: Student participation and student and teacher reactions. *Career Development for Exceptional Individuals, 25*(2), 171–192.

Masten, A. S., Best, K. M., & Garmezy, N. (1990). Resilience and development: Contributions from the study of children who overcome adversity. *Development and Psychopathology, 2*, 425–444.

Mastropieri, M. A. (2001). Introduction to the special issue: Is the glass half full or half empty? Challenges encountered by first year special education teachers. *Journal of Special Education, 35*, 66–74.

Mastropieri, M., & Scruggs, T. (2005). Feasibility and consequences of response to intervention: Examination of the issues and scientific evidence as a model for the identification of individuals with learning disabilities. *Journal of Learning Disabilities, 38*(6), 525–531.

Mastropieri, M., & Scruggs, T. (2007). *The inclusive classroom: Strategies for effective instruction* (3rd ed.). Upper Saddle River, NJ: Merrill/Pearson.

Mastropieri, M., & Scruggs, T. (2010). *The inclusive classroom: Strategies for effective instruction* (4th ed.). Upper Saddle River, NJ: Prentice Hall.

Mathes, P., Howard, J., Babyak, A., & Allen, S. (2000). Peer-assisted learning strategies for first-grade readers: A tool for preventing early reading failure. *Learning Disabilities Research and Practice, 14*(1), 50–60.

Mattison, R. E. (2004). Psychiatric and psychological assessment of emotional and behavioral disorders during school mental health consultation. In R. B. Rutherford, Jr., M. M. Quinn, & A. R. Mathur (Eds.), *Handbook of research in emotional and behavioral disorders* (pp. 54–77). New York: Guilford.

Maurice, C. (1993). *Let me hear your voice*. New York: Knopf.

Mayer, G. R. (2001). Antisocial behavior: Its causes and prevention within our schools. *Education and Treatment of Children, 24*(4), 414–429.

Mayes, S., & Calhoun, S. (2006). Frequency of reading, math, and writing disabilities in children with clinical disorders. *Learning and Individual Differences, 16*, 145–157.

McCaleb, K. N. (2006). The relationship between brain injury and the provision of school services. *Physical Disabilities: Education and Related Services, 25*, 61–76.

McConnell, M. E., Hilvitz, P. B., & Cox, C. J. (1998). Functional assessment: A systematic approach for assessment and intervention in general and special education classrooms. *Intervention in School and Clinic, 34*, 10–20.

McGahee, M., Mason, C., Wallace, T., & Jones, B. (2001). *Student-led IEPs: A guide for student involvement*. Arlington, VA: CEC.

McGinnis, E., & Goldstein, A. P. (1997). *Skillstreaming in early childhood: New strategies and perspectives for teaching prosocial skills*. Champaign, IL: Research Press.

McKenzie, A. R., & Lewis, S. (2008). The role and training of paraprofessionals who work with students who are visually impaired. *Journal of Visual Impairment & Blindness, 102*, 459–471.

McLean, L. K., Brady, N. C., & McLean, J. E. (1996). Reported communication abilities of individuals with severe mental retardation. *American Journal on Mental Retardation, 100*, 580–591.

McLean, M. (2004). Assessment and its importance in early intervention/early childhood special education. In M. McLean, M. Wolery, & D. B. Bailey, Jr. (Eds.), *Assessing infants and preschoolers with special needs* (3rd ed., pp. 1–21). Upper Saddle River, NJ: Merrill/Pearson.

McLeskey, J. (Ed.). (2007). *Reflections on inclusion: Classic articles that shaped our thinking*. Arlington, VA: Council for Exceptional Children.

McLeskey, J., & Billingsley, B. (2008). How does the quality and stability of the teaching force influence the research-to-practice gap? A perspective on the teacher shortage in special education. *Remedial and Special Education, 29*(5), 293–305.

McLeskey, J., Henry, D., & Axelrod, M. (1999). Inclusion of students with LD: An examination of data from *Reports to Congress*. *Exceptional Children, 65*, 55–66.

McLeskey, J., Henry, D., & Hodges, D. (1999). Inclusion: What progress is being made across disability categories? *Teaching Exceptional Children, 31*(3), 60–64.

McLeskey, J., Hoppey, D., Williamson, P., & Rentz, T. (2004). Is inclusion an illusion? An examination of national and state trends toward the education of students with learning disabilities in general education classrooms. *Learning Disabilities Research and Practice, 19*(2), 109–115.

McLeskey, J., & Pacchiano, D. (1994). Mainstreaming students with LD: Are we making progress? *Exceptional Children, 60*, 508–517.

McLeskey, J., Rosenberg, M., & Westling, D. (2010). *Inclusion: Highly effective practices for all students*. Upper Saddle River, NJ: Merrill/Pearson Education.

McLeskey, J., & Ross, D. D. (2004). The politics of teacher education in the new millennium: Implications for special education teacher educators. *Teacher Education and Special Education, 27*(6), 342–349.

McLeskey, J., Tyler, N., & Flippin, S. S. (2004). The supply of and demand for special education teachers: A review of research regarding the nature of the chronic shortage of special education teachers. *The Journal of Special Education, 38*(1), 5–21.

McLeskey, J., & Waldron, N. (2000). *Inclusive education in action: Making differences ordinary*. Alexandria, VA: ASCD.

McLeskey, J., & Waldron, N. (2002, September). School change and inclusive schools: Lessons learned from practice. *Phi Delta Kappan, 84*(1), 65–72.

McLeskey, J., & Waldron, N. (2006). Comprehensive school reform and inclusive schools: Improving schools for all students. *Theory into Practice, 45*(3), 269–278.

McMaster, K., Kung, S., Han, I., & Cao, M. (2008). Peer-assisted learning strategies: A "Tier 1" approach to promoting English learners' response to intervention. *Exceptional Children, 74*(2), 194–214.

Meadows, N. B., & Stevens, K. B. (2004). Teaching alternative behaviors to students with emotional and behavioral disorders. In R. B. Rutherford, Jr., M. M. Quinn, & A. R. Mathur (Eds.), *Handbook of research in emotional and behavioral disorders* (pp. 385–398). New York: Guilford.

Mellard, D., & Lancaster, P. (2003). Incorporating adult community services in students' transition planning. *Remedial and Special Education, 24*(6), 359–368.

Mercer, C., & Pullen, P. (2009). *Students with learning disabilities* (7th ed.). Upper Saddle River, NJ: Merrill/Pearson Education.

Merrell, K. W., & Walker, H. M. (2004). Deconstructing a definition: Social maladjustment versus emotional disturbance and moving the ebd field forward. *Psychology in the Schools, 41*(8), 899–910.

Merrill, E. (2005). Preattentive orienting in adolescents with mental retardation. *American Journal on Mental Retardation, 110*(1), 28–35.

Meyer, G. A., & Batshaw, M. L. (2001). Fragile X syndrome. In M. L. Batshaw (Ed.), *Children with disabilities* (5th ed., pp. 321–331). Baltimore: Brookes.

Michaud, L. J., Duhaime, A., Wade, S. L., Rabin, J. P., Jones, D. O., & Lazar, M. F. (2007). Traumatic brain injury. In M. L. Batshaw, L. Pellegrino, & N. J. Roizen (Eds.), *Children with disabilities* (6th ed., pp. 461–476). Baltimore: Paul H. Brookes.

Miller, A. (1999). Appropriateness of psychostimulant prescriptions to children: Theoretical and empirical perspectives. *Canadian Journal of Psychiatry, 44,* 1017–1024.

Miller, C. J., Sanchez, J., & Hynd, G. W. (2003). Neurological correlates of reading disabilities. In H. L. Swanson, K. R. Harris, & S. Graham (Eds.), *Handbook of learning disabilities* (pp. 242–255). New York: Guilford.

Minskoff, E. H. (1998). Sam Kirk: The man who made special education special. *Learning Disabilities Research and Practice, 13*(1), 15–21.

Mitchell, R. (2005). *A brief summary of estimates for the size of the deaf population in the USA based on available federal data and published research.* Retrieved August 2, 2005, from http://gri.gallaudet.edu/Demographics/deaf-US.php

Moll, L. C., Armanti, C., Neff, D., & Gonzalez, N. (1992). Funds of knowledge for teaching: Using a qualitative approach to connect homes and classrooms. *Theory into Practice, 31*(1), 132–141.

Monroe, C. R. (2006). Misbehavior or misinterpretation? *Kappa Delta Pi Record. 42,* 161–165.

Montague, M., Enders, C., Dietz, S., Dixon, J., & Cavendish, W. M. (2008). A longitudinal study of depressive symptomology and self-concept in adolescents. *The Journal of Special Education, 42*(2), 67–78.

Mooney, J., & Cole, D. (2000). *Learning outside the lines.* New York: Simon & Shuster.

Mostert, M. (2001). Facilitated communication since 1995: A review of published studies. *Journal of Autism and Developmental Disorders, 31,* 287–313.

Mostert, M. P., & Crockett, J. B. (2000). Reclaiming the history of special education for more effective practice. *Exceptionality, 8*(2), 133–143.

Mount, B., & Zwernik, K. (1988). *It's never too early, it's never too late.* St. Paul, MN: Metropolitan Council.

Mrug, S., & Wallander, J. L. (2002). Young people with physical disabilities: Does integration play a role? *International Journal of Disabilities, 49*(3), 267–280.

MTA Cooperative Group. (1999). A 14-month randomized clinical trial of treatment strategies for attention-deficit/hyperactivity disorder. *Archives of General Psychiatry, 56,* 1073–1086.

Murdick, N., Gartin, B., & Crabtree, T. (2002). *Special education law.* Upper Saddle River, NJ: Merrill/Pearson.

Murphy, C., Yeargin-Allsopp, M., Decoufle, P., & Drews, C. (1995). The administrative prevalence of mental retardation in 10-year-old children in metropolitan Atlanta. *American Journal of Public Health, 85*(3), 319–323.

Muscott, H. S. (2000). A review and analysis of service learning programs involving students with emotional/behavioral disorders. *Education and Treatment of Children, 23*(3), 346–368.

National Alliance for Autism Research (NAAR). (2005). *What is autism: An overview.* Retrieved November 5, 2005, from http://www.autismspeaks.org/whatisit/index.php

National Association for Down Syndrome. (2009). *Down syndrome facts.* Retrieved August 4, 2009, from http://www.nads.org/pages_new/facts.html

National Association of the Deaf. (2000). *Cochlear implants: Position statement.* Retrieved August 4, 2009, from http://www.nad.org/issues/technology/assistive-listening/cochlear-implants

National Association of the Deaf. (2009a). *About us.* Retrieved August 6, 2009, from http://www.nad.org/about-us

National Association of the Deaf. (2009b). *American Sign Language.* Retrieved August 6, 2009, at http://www.nad.org/issues/american-sign-language

National Association of the Deaf. (2009c). *Educational Placments.* Retrieved August 3, 2009 at: http://www.nad.org/issues/education/educational-placements

National Association of the Deaf. (2009d). *Position statement on inclusion.* Retrieved August 6, 2009, from http://www.nad.org/issues/education/k-12/inclusion

National Center for Education Statistics (NCES). (2002). *The condition of education.* Retrieved March 23, 2005, from http://nces.ed.gov/pubsearch/pubsinfo.asp?pubid=2002025

National Center for Education Statistics (NCES). (2005). *NAEP 2004 trends in academic progress: Three decades of student performance in reading and mathematics: Findings in brief.* Retrieved May 10, 2009, from http://nces.ed.gov/pubsearch/pubsinfo.asp?pubid=2005463

National Center for Education Statistics. (2006). *How many English language learner (ELL) students are receiving services in U.S. public schools?* Retrieved May 10, 2009, from http://nces.ed.gov/fastfacts/display.asp?id=96

National Center for Education Statistics. (2007). *Condition of education.* Retrieved May 15, 2009, from http://nces.ed.gov/programs/coe/2007/section2/indicator16.asp

National Center for Education Statistics. (2008). *Digest of educational statistics 2007.* Retrieved May 15, 2009, from http://nces.ed.gov/programs/digest/d07/tables/dt07_049.asp?referrer=list

National Center for Hearing Assessment and Management. (2008). *Universal Newborn Hearing Screening Fact Sheet*. Retrieved August 4, 2009, from http://www.infanthearing.org/index.html

National Center on Birth Defects and Developmental Disabilities. (2009). *Cerebral palsy*. Retrieved July 27, 2009, from http://www.cdc.gov/ncbddd/dd/ddcp.htm

National Commission on Teaching and America's Future. (2003). *No dream denied: A pledge to America's children*. Retrieved May 18, 2009, from www.nctaf.org/documents/no-dream-denied_summary_report.pdf

National Consortium on Deaf-Blindness (NCDB). (2008). *The 2007 National Child Count of Children and Youth who are Deaf-Blind*. Retrieved August 4, 2009, from http://www.nationaldb.org/documents/products/2007-Census-Tables.pdf

National Council of Teacher Education. (2008). *Professional standards for the accreditation of teacher preparation institutions*. Washington, D.C.: Author. Retrieved April 17, 2009, from http://www.ncate.org/documents/standards/NCATE%20Standards%202008.pdf

National Dissemination Center for Children with Disabilities. (2009). *Spina bifida*. Retrieved July 27, 2009, from http://www.nichcy.org/Disabilities/Specific/Pages/SpinaBifida.aspx

National Down Syndrome Society. (2009). *About Down syndrome*. Retrieved August 4, 2009, from http://www.ndss.org/index.php?option=com_content&view=category&id=35&Itemid=57

National Education Association (NEA). (2003). *The status of the American public school teacher 2000–2001*. Retrieved December 13, 2005, from http://www.nea.org/newsreleases/2003/nr030827.html

National Fragile-X Foundation. (2009). *Summary of Fragile X syndrome*. Retrieved August 4, 2009, from http://www.fragilex.org/html/summary.htm

National Institute of Allergy and Infectious Diseases (NIAID). (2004). *HIV infection in infants and children*. Retrieved July 27, 2009, from http://www.niaid.nih.gov/factsheets/hivchildren.htm

National Institute on Deafness and Other Communication Disorders (NIDCD). (2007). *Cochlear implants*. Retrieved August 4, 2009, from http://www.nidcd.nih.gov/health/hearing/coch.asp

National Institute on Deafness and Other Communication Disorders. (2008). *Statistics on voice, speech, and language*. Retrieved May 25, 2009, from http://www.nidcd.nih.gov/health/statistics/vsl.asp#2

National Longitudinal Transition Study 2 (NLTS2). (2009). Data Tables. Retrieved August 5, 2009, from http://www.nlts2.org/data_tables/index.html

National Research Council (NRC). (2001). *Educating children with autism*. Washington, DC: National Academy Press.

National Resource Center on AD/HD. (2005). *College issues for students with ADHD*. Retrieved October 13, 2005, from http://www.help4adhd.org/en/education/college/collegeissues

National Technical Assistance Consortium for Children and Young Adults Who Are Deaf-Blind (NTAC). (2004). *National deaf-blind child count*. Retrieved August 16, 2006, from http://www.tr.wou.edu/ntac/documents/census/2004-Census-Tables.pdf

National Vaccine Information Center. (2005). *Autism and vaccines: A new look at an old story*. Retrieved December 7, 2005, from http://www.909shot.com/Diseases/autismsp.htm

NEA and NASDSE. (2004). The path to "highly qualified" special education teacher under the Individuals with Disabilities Education Improvement Act of 2004. Retrieved May 8, 2005 from http://www.nea.org/specialed/hqspecial.html

Neece, C., Kraemer, R., & Blacher, J. (2009). Transition satisfaction and family well being among parents of young adults with severe intellectual disabilities. *Intellectual and Developmental Disabilities, 47*(1), 31–43.

Neel, R. S., & Cessna, K. K. (1990). Behavioral intent: Instructional content for students with behavior disorders. In K. K. Cessna (Ed.), *Instructionally differentiated programming* (pp. 31–40). Denver: Colorado Department of Education.

Nelson, J. R. (1996). Designing schools to meet the needs of students who exhibit disruptive behavior. *Journal of Emotional and Behavioral Disorders, 4*(3), 147–161.

Newcomer, P. L., Barenbaum, E., & Pearson, N. (1995). Depression and anxiety in children and adolescents with learning disabilities, conduct disorders, and no disability. *Journal of Emotional and Behavioral Disorders, 3*(1), 27–39.

Newman, L., Wagner, M., Cameto, R., Knokey, A. M. (2009). *The post-high school outcomes of youth with disabilities up to 4 years after high school. A report from the National Longitudinal Transition Study-2 (NLTS2)* (NCSER 2009-3017). Menlo Park, CA: SRI International.

Nieto, S., & Bode, P. (2007). *Affirming diversity: The sociopolitical context of multicultural education* (5th ed.). Boston: Allyn & Bacon.

No Child Left Behind Act. (2001). 20 U.S.C. § 6301 et seq.

Noble, K. D., Subotnik, R. F. & Arnold, K. D. (1999). To thine own self be true: A new model of female talent development. *Gifted Child Quarterly, 43*, 140–149.

Noddings, N. (1988, December 7). Schools face crisis in caring. *Education Week*, p. 32.

Nybo, T., & Koskiniemi, M. (1999). Cognitive indicators of vocational outcomes after severe traumatic brain injury (TBI) in childhood. *Brain Injury, 13*, 759–766.

Nybo, T., Sainio, M., & Müller, K. (2004). Stability of vocational outcome in adulthood after moderate to severe preschool brain injury. *Journal of the International Neuropsychological Society, 10*, 719–723.

O'Leary, K., & Becker, W. (1967). Behavior modification of an adjustment class: A token reinforcement program. *Exceptional Children, 9*, 637–642.

O'Neil, P. (2001). Special education and high stakes testing for high school graduation: An analysis of current law and policy. *Journal of Law and Education, 30*(2), 185–222.

Ochs, E., Kremer-Sadlik, T., Solomon, O., & Sirota, K. G. (2001). Inclusion as social practice: Views of children with autism. *Social Development, 10*(3), 399–419.

Odom, S. L., Brantlinger, E., Gersten, R., Horner, R. H., Thompson, B., & Harris, K. R. (2005). Research in special education: Scientific methods and evidenced-based practices. *Exceptional Children, 71*, 137–148.

Odom, S. L., & DeKlyen, M. (1986). *Social withdrawal in childhood*. Unpublished manuscript.

Office of Special Education Programs (OSEP). (2003). *Identifying and treating attention deficit hyperactivity disorder: A resource for school and home*. Washington, DC: Author.

Olenchak, F. R., & Hebert, T. P. (2002). Endangered academic talent: Lessons learned from gifted first generation college males. *Journal of College Student Development, 28*, 195–212.

Olley, G. J. (2005). Curriculum and classroom structure. In F. R. Volkmar, R. Paul, A. Klin, & D. Cohen (Eds.), *Handbook of autism and pervasive developmental disorders: Vol. 2*.

*Assessment, interventions, and policy* (4th ed., pp. 863–881). Hoboken, NJ: Wiley.

Orelove, F. P., Sobsey, D., & Silberman, R. K. (Eds.). (2004). *Educating children with multiple disabilities: A collaborative approach* (4th ed.). Baltimore: Paul H. Brookes.

Orkwis, R., & McLane, K. (1998). *A curriculum every student can use: Design principles for student access*. Reston, VA: Council for Exceptional Children, ERIC Clearinghouse on Disabilities and Gifted Education.

Osher, D., Morrison, G., & Bailey, W. (2003). Exploring the relationship between student mobility and dropout among students with emotional and behavioral disorder. *Journal of Negro Education, 72,* 79–96.

Overton, T. (2009). *Assessing learners with special needs: An applied approach* (6th ed.). Upper Saddle River, NJ: Merrill/Pearson Education.

Owen-DeSchryver, J. S., Carr, E. G., Cale, S. I., & Blakeley-Smith, A. (2008). Promoting social interactions between students with autism spectrum disorders and their peers in inclusive settings. *Focus on Autism and Other Developmental Disorders, 23*(1), 15–28.

Owens, R. E., Metz, D. E., & Haas, A. (2003). *Introduction to communication disorders: A life span perspective* (2nd ed.). Boston: Allyn & Bacon.

Paine, S. C., Radicci, J., Rosellini, L. C., Deutchman, L., & Darch, C. B. (1983). *Structuring your classroom for academic success*. Champaign, IL: Research Press Company.

Papalia-Berardi, A., & Hall, T. E. (2007). Teacher assistance team social validity: A perspective from general education teachers. *Education and Treatment of Children, 30*(2), 89–110.

Parette, H. P. (1997). Assistive technology devices and services. *Education and Training in Mental Retardation and Developmental Disabilities, 32,* 267–280.

Parette, H. P., & Peterson-Karlan, G. R. (2007). Facilitating student achievement with assistive technology. *Education and Training in Developmental Disabilities, 42,* 387–397.

Parrish, T. B. (2003). *Financing (or the Cost of) Special Education*. Presented to the Education Writers Association, Nashville. Retrieved July 2, 2009 at: http://csef.air.org/publications/related/edwriters.pdf

Patrick, H., Bangel, N. J., Jeon, K., & Townsend, M. A. R. (2005). Reconsidering the issue of cooperative learning with gifted students. *Journal for the Education of the Gifted, 29*(1), 90–108.

Patrick, H., Turner, J., Meyer, D. K., & Midgley, C. (2003). How teachers establish psychological environments during the first days of school: Associations with avoidance in mathematics. *Teachers College Record, 105,* 1521–1558.

Patterson, G. R., Reid, J. B., Jones, R. R., & Conger, R. E. (1975). *A social learning approach to family intervention: Vol. 1. Families with aggressive children*. Eugene, OR: Castalia.

Patton, J., Polloway, E., Smith, T., Edgar, E., Clark, G., & Lee, S. (1996). Individuals with mild mental retardation: Postsecondary outcomes and implications for educational policy. *Education and Training in Mental Retardation and Developmental Disabilities, 31,* 77–85.

Paul, R. (2005). Assessing communication in autism spectrum disorders. In F. R. Volkmar, R. Paul, A. Klin, & D. Cohen (Eds.), *Handbook of autism and pervasive developmental disorders: Vol. 2. Assessment, interventions, and policy* (4th ed., pp. 799–816). Hoboken, NJ: Wiley.

Paul, R. (2009). Parents ask: Am I risking autism if I vaccinate my children? *Journal of Autism and Developmental Disorders, 39,* 962–963.

Paul, R., Orlovski, S. M., Marcinko, H.C., Volkmar, F. (2009). Conversational behaviors in youth with high-functioning ASD and asperger syndrome. *Journal of Autism and Developmental Disorders, 39,* 115–125.

Peña, E. D., & Davis, B. L. (2010). Language disorders in infants, toddlers, and preschoolers. In R. B. Gillam, T. P. Marquardt, & F. N. Martin (Eds.), *Communication sciences and disorders: From science to clinical Practice* (2nd ed.). Sudbury MA: Jones & Bartlett.

Pearman, E., Elliott, T., & Aborn, L. (2004). Transition services model: Partnership for student success. *Education and Training in Developmental Disabilities, 39,* 26–34.

Pegnato, C. W., & Birch, J. W. (1959). Locating gifted children in junior high schools—A comparison of methods. *Exceptional Children, 25,* 300–304.

Pellegrino, L. (2007). Cerebral palsy. In M. L. Batshaw, L. Pellegrino, & N. J. Roizen (Eds.), *Children with disabilities* (6th ed., pp. 387–408). Baltimore: Brookes.

Pelo, A., & Davidson, F. (2000). *That's not fair! A teacher's guide to activism with young children*. St. Paul, MN: Redleaf.

Penno, D. A., Frank, A. R., & Wacker, D. P. (2000). Instructional accommodations for adolescent students with severe emotional or behavioral disorders. *Behavioral Disorders, 25,* 325–343.

Peske, H., & Haycock, K. (2006). *How poor and minority students are shortchanged on teacher quality. Education Trust.* Retrieved May 15, 2009, from http://www2.edtrust.org/NR/rdonlyres/010DBD9F-CED8-4D2B-9E0D-91B446746ED3/0/TQReportJune2006.pdf

Peterson's Guide. (2003). *Colleges with programs for students with learning disabilities or attention deficit disorders* (7th ed.). Lawrenceville, NJ: Thomson Learning.

Phelps, L., & Grabowski, J. (1991). Autism: Etiology, differential diagnosis, and behavioral assessment update. *Journal of Psychopathology and Behavioral Assessment, 13*(2), 107–125.

Phelps, P. (2006). The three Rs of professionalism. *Kappa Delta Pi Record, 42,* 69–71.

Pierce, C. D., Reid, R., & Epstein, M. H. (2004). Teacher mediated interventions for children with EBD and their academic outcomes. *Remedial and Special Education, 25*(3), 175–188.

Piers, E., & Harris, D. (1984). *The Piers-Harris children's self-concept scale*. Nashville, TN: Counselor Recordings and Tests.

Pierson, M., Carter, E., Lane, K., & Glaeser, B. (2008). Factors influencing the self-determination of transition-age youth with high-incidence disabilities. *Career Development for Exceptional Individuals, 31*(2), 115–125.

Piirto, J. N. (1992). *Understanding those who create*. Dayton: Ohio Psychology Press.

Platt, J. M. (1987). Substitute teachers can do more than just keep the lid on. *Teaching Exceptional Children, 19*(2), 28–31.

Polloway, E. (1984). The integration of mildly retarded students in the schools: A historical review. *Remedial and Special Education, 5*(4), 18–28.

Polloway, E., Chamberlain, J., Denning, C., Smith, J., & Smith, T. (1999). Levels of deficits or supports in the classification of mental retardation: Implementation practices. *Education and Training in Mental Retardation and Developmental Disabilities, 34,* 200–206.

Polsgrove, L., & Smith, A. W. (2004). Informed practice in teaching self-control to children with emotional and behavioral disorders. In R. B. Rutherford, Jr., M. M. Quinn, & A. R. Mathur (Eds.), *Handbook of research in emotional and behavioral disorders* (pp. 399–425). New York: Guilford Press.

Postman, N., & Weingartner, C. (1969). *Teaching as a subversive activity*. New York: Delta.

Prader-Willi Syndrome Association. (2009). *What is Prader-Willi syndrome?* Retrieved August 4, 2009, from http://www.pwsausa.org/syndrome/index.htm

President's Commission on Excellence in Special Education. (2002). *A new era: Revitalizing special education for children and their families*. Jessup, MD: Education Publications Center, U.S. Department of Education.

President's Committee on Mental Retardation. (1969). *The six-hour retarded child*. Washington, DC: U.S. Government Printing Office.

Psychological Corporation. (2001). *Wechsler individual achievement test* (2nd ed.). San Antonio, TX: Author.

Psychological Corporation. (2009). *Wechsler individual achievement test* (3rd ed.). San Antonio, TX: Author.

Public Education Network. (2004). *Teacher professional development: A primer for parents & community members*. Washington, DC: Author.

Putnam, J. (1998). *Cooperative learning and strategies for inclusion* (2nd ed.). Baltimore: Brookes.

Quinn, M. M., Osher, D., Warger, C., Hanley, T., Bader, B. D., Tate, R., et al. (2000). *Educational strategies for children with emotional and behavioral problems*. Washington, DC: Center for Effective Collaboration and Practice, American Institutes for Research.

Racino, J. A. (1995). Community living for adults with developmental disabilities: A housing and support approach. *Journal of the Association for Persons with Severe Handicaps, 20,* 300–310.

Ramey, S. L., & Ramey, C. T. (1998). The transition to school: Opportunities and challenges for children, families, educators, and communities. *Elementary School Journal, 98*(4), 293–295.

Ramos-Ford, V., & Gardner, H. (1991). Giftedness from a multiple intelligences perspective. In N. Colangelo & G. A. Davis (Eds.), *Handbook of gifted education* (pp. 55–64). Needham Heights, MA: Allyn & Bacon.

Rapport, M., Scanlan, S., & Denney, C. (1999). Attention deficit/hyperactivity disorder and scholastic achievement: A model of dual developmental pathways. *Journal of Child Psychology and Psychiatry and Applied Disciplines, 40*(8), 1169–1183.

Ratliffe, K. T., & Sanekane, C. (2009). Conductive education: Benefits and challenges. *Teaching Exceptional Children, 41*(5), 66–72.

Raver, C. C., & Knitze, J. (2002). *Ready to enter: What research tells policymakers about strategies to promote social and emotional school readiness among three- and four-year-olds* (Policy Paper No. 3). Columbia University: National Center for Children in Poverty.

Redcav, E., & Courchesne, E. (2005). When is the brain enlarged in autism? A meta-analysis of all brain size reports. *Biological Psychiatry, 58*(1), 1–9.

Redl, F., & Wineman, D. (1957). *The aggressive child*. New York: Free Press.

Reed, V. A., & Spicer, L. (2003). The relative importance of selected communication skills for adolescents' interactions with their teachers: High school teachers' opinions. *Language, Speech, and Hearing Services in Schools, 34,* 343–357.

Reese, S. (2004, May). Teacher portfolios: Displaying the art of teaching. *Techniques, 79*(5), 18–21.

Regenbogen, L., & Coscas, G. (1985). *Oculo-auditory syndromes*. New York: Masson.

Rehabilitation Research and Training Center on Independent Living Management. (2002). *Disability history timeline*. Retrieved July 7, 2005, from http://courses.temple.edu/neighbor/ds/disabilityrightstimeline.htm

Reid, D. H., Parsons, M. B., Green, C. W., & Browning, L. B. (2001). Increasing one aspect of self-determination among adults with severe multiple disabilities in supported work. *Journal of Applied Behavior Analysis, 34,* 341–344.

Reid, R., & Lienemann, T. (2006). *Strategy instruction for students with learning disabilities*. New York: Guilford Press.

Reid, R., Trout, A., & Schartz, M. (2005). Self-regulation interventions for children with attention deficit/hyperactivity disorder. *Exceptional Children, 71*(4), 361–377.

Reiff, M. (2004). *ADHD: A complete and authoritative guide*. Elk Grove Village, IL: American Academy of Pediatrics.

Reis, S. M., & Graham, C. (2005). Needed: Teachers to encourage girls in math, science, and technology. *Gifted Child Today, 28,* 14–21.

Renzulli, J. S. (1977). *The enrichment triad model: A guide for developing defensible programs for the gifted and talented*. Mansfield, CT: Creative Learning Press.

Renzulli, J. S. (1986). The three ring conception of giftedness: A developmental model for creative productivity. In R. Sternberg & J. E. Davidson (Eds.), *Conceptions of giftedness* (pp. 53–92). New York: Cambridge University Press.

Renzulli, J. S. (2002). Emerging conceptions of giftedness: Building a bridge to the new century. *Exceptionality, 10,* 67–75.

Renzulli, J. S., & Reis, S. M. (1991). The reform movement and the quiet crisis in gifted education. *Gifted Child Quarterly, 35*(1), 26–35.

Reschly, D. (2005). Learning disabilities identification: Primary intervention, secondary intervention, and then what? *Journal of Learning Disabilities, 38*(6), 510–515.

Reynolds, C., & Kamphaus, R. (2004). *Behavior Assessment System for Children (2nd ed.). (BASC-2)*. Circle Pines, MN: American Guidance Service.

Rhode, G., Jenson, W., & Reavis, K. (1998). *The tough kid book: Practical classroom management strategies*. Longmont, CO: Sopris West.

Rhodes, W. C. (1967). The disturbing child: A problem in ecological management. *Exceptional Children, 33,* 449–455.

Richards, D. (2003). *The top Section 504 errors: Expert guidance to avoid 25 common compliance mistakes*. Horsham, PA: LRP.

Richards, H. V., Brown, A. F., & Forde, T. B. (2006). *Addressing diversity in schools: Culturally responsive pedagogy*. Tempe AZ: National Center for Culturally Responsive Educational Systems.

Richardson, J. (1999, February/March). Engaging the public builds support for schools. *Tools for Schools*. Retrieved October 5, 2005, from http://www.nsdc.org/library/publications/tools/tools2-99rich.cfm

Richert, E. S., Alvino, J., & McDonnel, R. (1982). *The national report on identification of gifted and talented youth: Assessment and recommendations for comprehensive identification of gifted and talented youth*. Sewell, NJ: Educational Improvement Center South.

Ritzman, M. J., Sanger, D., & Coufal, K. L. (2006), A case study of a collaborative speech-language pathologist. *Communication Disorders Quarterly, 27*(4), 221–231.

Rivera, G. (2004). *Early biography*. Retrieved June 27, 2005, from http://www.geraldo.com/index.php?/archives/14_EARLY_BIO.html

Rivkin, S., Hanushek, E., & Kain, J. (2001). *Teachers, schools, and academic achievement*. Political Economy Working Paper 09/01. Richardson: University of Texas at Dallas.

Rivkin, S., Hanushek, E., & Kain, J. (2002). *Teachers, schools, and academic achievement*. Dallas, TX: University of Texas—Dallas Texas Schools Project.

Robertson, E. J., & Lane, K. L. (2007). Supporting middle school students with academic and behavioral concerns: A methodological illustration for conducting secondary interventions within three-tiered models of support. *Behavioral Disorders, 33*(1), 5–22.

Robins D., Fein, D., Barton, M., & Green, J. (2001). The modified checklist for autism in toddlers. *Journal of Autism and Developmental Disorders, 31*(2), 131–144.

Robinson, A. (1990). Cooperation or exploitation? The argument against cooperative learning for talented students. *Journal for the Education of the Gifted, 14,* 9–27.

Rock, E. E., Fessler, M. A., & Church, R. P. (1997). The concomitance of learning disabilities and emotional/behavioral disorders: A conceptual model. *Journal of Learning Disabilities, 30*(3), 245–263.

Roe, A. (1952). A psychologist examines 64 eminent scientists. *Scientific American, 187,* 21–25.

Roedell, W. C. (1990) *Nurturing giftedness in young children. ERIC Digest E487.* Reston, VA: ERIC Clearinghouse on Disabilities and Gifted Education. (ERIC Document Reproduction Service No. ED321492). Retrieved July 28, 2009, from http://www.kidsource.com/kidsource/content/nuturing_giftedness.html

Rogan, J. (2000). Learning strategies: Recipes for success. *Beyond Behavior, 10*(1), 18–22.

Rogers, C. (1965). *Client centered therapy.* Boston: Houghton Mifflin.

Roid, G. (2003). *Stanford-Binet intelligence test* (5th ed.). Itasca, IL: Riverside.

Roizen, N. J. (2001). Down syndrome. In M. L. Batshaw (Ed.), *Children with disabilities* (5th ed., pp. 307–320). Baltimore: Brookes.

Rolewski, M. (2008). Overcoming obstacles to adopting and implementing evidence-based practices. In *Best Evidence Encyclopedia (BEE).* Retrieved July 14, 2009, from http://www.bestevidence.org/resources/general/obstacles.htm

Rorschach, H. (1932). *Psychodiagnostic: Methodik und Ergebnisse eines Wahrnehmungs-diagnostischen Experiments* (2nd ed.). Bern, Switzerland: Huber.

Rosenberg, M. S., Griffin, C., Kilgore, K., & Carpenter, S. L. (1997). Beginning teachers in special education: A model for providing individualized support. *Teacher Education and Special Education, 20*(4), 301–321.

Rosenberg, M. S., & Jackman, L. A. (1997). Addressing student and staff behavior: The PAR model. *Fourth R, 79,* 1–12.

Rosenberg, M. S., & Jackman, L. A. (2003). Development, implementation, and sustainability of comprehensive school-wide behavior management systems. *Intervention in School and Clinic, 39*(1), 10–21.

Rosenberg, M. S., O'Shea, L., & O'Shea, D. J. (2006). *Student teacher to master teacher: A practical guide for educating students with special needs* (4th ed.). Upper Saddle River, NJ: Merrill/Pearson.

Rosenberg, M. S., & Sindelar, P. (2007). Alternative route programs to certification in special education: Program infrastructure, instructional delivery, and participant characteristics. *Exceptional Children, 73*(X), 224–241.

Rosenberg, M. S., Wilson, R. J., Maheady, L., & Sindelar, P. T. (2004). *Educating students with behavior disorders* (3rd ed.). Boston: Pearson Education.

Rosenfeld, J. S. (2005). Section 504 and IDEA: Basic similarities and differences. *Learning Disabilities OnLine.* Retrieved November 29, 2005, from http://www.ldonline.org/ld_indepth/legal_legislative/edlaw504.html

Rosenshine, B., & Stevens, R. (1986). Teaching functions. In M. C. Wittrock (Ed.), *Handbook of research on teaching* (3rd ed., pp. 376–391). New York: Macmillan.

Ross, J. A. (1994). The impact of an inservice to promote cooperative learning on the stability of teacher efficacy. *Canadian Journal of Education, 17,* 51–65.

Ross, K. S., Neeley, R. A., & Baggs, T. W. (2007). The relationship between discipline infractions and communication disorders in public school students. *Education, 128*(2), 202–210.

Roth, F. P., & Worthington, C. K. (1996). *Treatment resource manual for speech-language pathology.* San Diego: Singular.

Rothstein, R. (2004). *Class and schools.* Washington, DC: Economic Policy Institute.

Rothstein, R. (2008). Whose problem is poverty? *Educational Leadership, 56*(7), 8–13.

Rotter, J. B. (1966). Generalized expectancies for internalized versus externalized control of reinforcement. *Psychological Monographs, 80,* 1–28.

Rowland, A., Umback, D., Stallone, L., et al. (2002). Prevalence of medication treatment for attention deficit-hyperactivity disorder among elementary school children in Johnston County, North Carolina. *American Journal of Public Health, 92,* 231–234.

Rubin, K. H., Coplan, R. J., & Bowker, J. C. (2009). Social withdrawal in childhood. *Annual Review of Psychology, 60,* 141–71.

Rusch, F. R. & Braddock, D. (2004). Adult day programs versus supported employment (1988–2002): Spending and service practices of mental retardation and developmental disabilities' state agencies. *Research and Practice for Persons with Severe Disabilities, 29,* 237–242.

Rutter, M. (1978). Diagnosis and definition. In M. Rutter & E. Schopler (Eds.), *Autism: A reappraisal of concepts and treatment* (pp. 1–26). New York: Plenum.

Ryan, A., Halsey H., & Matthews, W. (2003). Using functional assessment to promote desirable student behavior in schools. *Teaching Exceptional Children, 35,* 8–15.

Ryan, J. B., & Peterson, R. L. (2004). Physical restraint in school. *Behavioral Disorders, 29*(2), 154–168.

Safford, P. J., & Safford, E. J. (1996). *A history of childhood and disability.* New York: Teachers College Press.

Safran, J. S. (2002). Supporting students with Asperger's syndrome in general education. *TEACHING Exceptional Children, 34*(5), 60–66.

Salend, S. (2008). *Creating inclusive classrooms: Effective and reflective practices for all students* (6th ed.). Upper Saddle River, NJ: Merrill/Prentice Hall.

Salend, S., & Duhaney, L. (1999). The impact of inclusion on students with and without disabilities and their educators. *Remedial and Special Education, 20,* 114–126.

Salend, S., & Garrick Duhaney, L. (2007). Research related to inclusion and program effectiveness: Yesterday, today, and tomorrow. In J. McLeskey (Ed.), *Reflections on inclusion: Classic articles that shaped our thinking* (pp. 125–129, 147–159). Arlington, VA: Council for Exceptional Children.

Salend, S., & Rohena, E. (2003). Students with attention deficit disorders: An overview. *Intervention in School and Clinic, 38*(5), 259–266.

Salisbury, C. L., & Smith, B. J. (1993). *Effective practices for preparing young children with special needs for school.* ERIC Digest #E519. Reston VA: ERIC Clearinghouse on Special Needs and Gifted Education. (ED358675).

Salvia, J., Ysseldyke, J., & Bolt, S. (2010). *Assessment in special and inclusive education* (11th ed.). Belmont, CA: Wadsworth.

Sameroff, A. (1990). Neo-environmental perspectives on developmental theory. In R. Hodapp, J. Burack, & E. Zigler (Eds.), *Issues in the developmental approach to mental retardation* (pp. 93–113). New York: Cambridge University Press.

Sample, P. (1998). Postschool outcomes for students with significant emotional disturbance following best-practice transition services. *Behavioral Disorders, 23*(4), 231–242.

Sanders, W., & Horn, S. (1998). Research findings from the Tennessee Value-Added Assessment System (TVAAS) database: Implications for educational evaluation and research. *Journal of Personnel Evaluation in Education, 12*(3), 247–256.

Sands, D., & Wehmeyer, M. (2005). Teaching goal setting and decision making to students with developmental disabilities. In M. Wehmeyer & M. Agran (Eds.), *Mental retardation and intellectual disabilities: Teaching students using innovation and research-based strategies* (pp. 273–296). Upper Saddle River, NJ: Pearson.

Sansosti, F. J., Powell-Smith, K. A., & Kincaid, D. (2004). A research synthesis of social story interventions for children with autism spectrum disorders. *Focus on Autism and Other Developmental Disabilities, 19*(4), 194–204.

Santos, M. (2002). From mystery to mainstream: Today's school-based speech-language pathologist. *Educational Horizons, 80*, 93–96.

Saphier, J. D. (1995). *Bonfires and magic bullets. Making teaching a true profession: The step without which other reforms will neither take nor endure.* Carlisle, MA: Research for Better Teaching.

Scheff, T. (1966). *Being mentally ill: A sociological theory.* Chicago: Aldine.

Scheffler, R., Hinshaw, S., Modrek, S., & Levine, P. (2007). The global market for ADHD medications. *Health Affairs, 26*(2), 450–457.

Schirmer, B. R. (2000). *Language and literacy development in children who are deaf* (2nd ed.). Needham Heights, MA: Allyn & Bacon.

Schirmer, B. R. (2001a). *Psychological, social, and educational dimensions of deafness.* Boston: Allyn & Bacon.

Schirmer, B. R. (2001b). Using research to improve literacy practice and practice to improve literacy research. *Journal of Deaf Studies and Deaf Education, 6*(2), 83–91.

Schnoes, C., Reid, R., Wagner, M., & Marder, C. (2006). ADHD among students receiving special education services: A national survey. *Exceptional Children, 72*(4), 483–496.

Schoenbrodt, L., Kumin, L., & Sloan, J. M. (1997). Learning disabilities existing concomitantly with language disorder. *Journal of Learning Disabilities, 30*, 264–281.

Schopler, E. (2005). Cross-cultural program priorities and reclassification of outcome research methods. In F. R. Volkmar, R. Paul, A. Klin, & D. Cohen (Eds.), *Handbook of autism and pervasive developmental disorders: Vol. 2. Assessment, interventions, and policy* (4th ed., pp. 1174–1192). Hoboken, NJ: Wiley.

Schreibman, L., & Ingersoll, B. (2005). Behavioral interventions to promote learning in individuals with autism. In F. R. Volkmar, R. Paul, A. Klin, & D. Cohen (Eds.), *Handbook of autism and pervasive developmental disorders: Vol. 2. Assessment, interventions, and policy* (4th ed., pp. 882–896). Hoboken, NJ: Wiley.

Schumaker, J., & Deshler, D. (2006). Teaching adolescents to be strategic learners. In D. Deshler & J. Schumaker (Eds.), *Teaching adolescents with disabilities* (pp. 121–156). Thousand Oaks, CA: Corwin.

Schumm, J. (1999) *Adapting reading and math materials for the inclusive classroom.* Reston, VA: Council for Exceptional Children.

Schwab Foundation for Learning. (1999). *Learning special needs: Common warning signs.* Retrieved November 1, 2004, from http://www.schwablearning.org/index.asp

Schworm, R., & Birnbaum, R. (1989). Symptom expression in hyperactive children: An analysis of observation. *Journal of Learning Disabilities, 22*, 35–40.

Scott, E. M., Smith, T. E. C., Hendricks, M. D., & Polloway, E. A. (1999). Prader-Willi syndrome: A review and implications for educational intervention. *Education and Training in Mental Retardation and Developmental Disabilities, 34*, 110–116.

Scott, K. (1999). Cognitive instructional strategies. In W. Bender (Ed.), *Professional issues in learning disabilities* (pp. 55–82). Austin, TX: PRO-ED.

Scott, T. M., Alter, P. J., Rosenberg, M. S., & Borgmeier, C. (2009). *A continuum of secondary and tertiary interventions within school-wide systems of positive behavioral support.* Manuscript submitted for publication.

Scott, T. M., & Kamps, D. M. (2007). The future of functional behavioral assessment in school settings. *Behavioral Disorders, 32*(3), 146–157.

Scruggs, T., & Mastropieri, M. (2002). On babies and bathwater: Addressing the problems of identification of learning disabilities. *Learning Disability Quarterly, 25*(3), 155–168.

Segal, N. L. (2005). Twin study summaries. *Twin Research and Human Genetics, 8*(4), 411-2, 413-4.

Selig, R. A. (2005). *The Revolution's black soldiers.* Retrieved May 18, 2009, from http://americanrevolution.org/blk.html.

Seltzer, M., Floyd, F., Greenberg, J., Lounds, J., Lindstron, M., & Hong, J. (2005). Life course impacts of mild intellectual deficits. *American Journal of Mental Retardation, 110*, 451–468.

Shackelford, J. (2006). *State and jurisdictional eligibility definitions for infants and toddlers with special needs under IDEA* (NECTAC Notes No. 20). Chapel Hill: University of North Carolina, FPG Child Development Institute, National Early Childhood Technical Assistance Center. Retrieved June 22, 2006, from http://www.nectac.org/%7Epdfs/pubs/nnotes20.pdf

Shalock, R., Luckasson, R., & Shogren, K. (2007). The renaming of *mental retardation:* Understanding the change to the term *intellectual disability. Intellectual and Developmental Disabilities, 45*(2), 116–124.

Shapiro, D. A. (1999). *Stuttering intervention: A collaborative journey to fluency freedom.* Austin, TX: PRO-ED.

Shapiro, E. S., Miller, D. N., Sawka, K., Gardill, M. C., & Handler, M. W. (1999). Facilitating the inclusion of students with EBD into general education classrooms. *Journal of Emotional and Behavioral Disorders, 7*(2), 83–93.

Shaw, S. F., & Madaus, J. W. (2008). Preparing school personnel to implement Section 504. *Intervention in School and Clinic, 43*(4), 226–230.

Shaywitz, B., Shaywitz, S., Blachman, B., Pugh, K., Fulbright, R., Skudlarski, P., et al. (2004). Development of left occipito-temporal systems for skilled reading in children after a phonologically-based intervention. *Biological Psychiatry, 55*, 926–933.

Shea, V., & Mesibov, G. B. (2005). Adolescents and adults with autism. In F. R. Volkmar, R. Paul, A. Klin, & D. Cohen (Eds.), *Handbook of autism and pervasive developmental disorders: Vol. 1. Diagnosis, development, neurobiology, and behavior* (4th ed., pp. 288–311). Hoboken, NJ: Wiley.

Shippen, M. E., Simpson, R. G., & Crites, S. A. (2003). A practical guide to functional behavioral assessment. *Teaching Exceptional Children, 35*, 36–44.

Shore, B. M., Cornell, D. G., Robinson, A., & Ward, V. S. (1991). *Recommended practices in gifted education.* New York: Teachers College Press.

Shore, B. M., & Tsiamis, A. (1986). Identification by provision: Limited field test of a radical alternative for identifying gifted students. In K. A. Heller & J. F. Feldhusen (Eds.), *Identifying and nurturing the gifted: An international perspective* (pp. 93–109). Toronto: Huber.

Shuell, T. (1996). Teaching and learning in a classroom context. In D. Berliner & R. Calfee (Eds.), *Handbook of educational psychology* (pp. 726–764). New York: Macmillan.

Siegel, L. S. (2003). Basic cognitive processes and reading disabilities. In H. L. Swanson, K. R. Harris, & S. Graham (Eds.), *Handbook of learning disabilities* (pp. 158–181). New York: Guilford.

Sigman, M., & Capps, L. (1997). *Children with autism: A developmental perspective*. Cambridge, MA: Harvard University Press.

Silverman, L. K. (1990). Social and emotional education of the gifted: The discoveries of Leta Hollingworth. *Roper Review, 12,* 171–178.

Simonsen, C. E., & Vito, G. F. (2003). *Juvenile justice today* (4th ed). Upper Saddle River, NJ: Prentice Hall.

Simpson, R. L., de Boer-Ott, S. R., & Smith-Myles, B. (2003). Inclusion of learners with autism spectrum disorders in general education settings. *Topics in Language Disorders, 23*(2), 116–133.

Simpson, R. L., McKee, M., Teeter, D., & Beytien, A. (2007). Evidence-based methods for children and youth with autism spectrum disorders: Stakeholder issues and perspectives. *Exceptionality, 15*(4), 203–218.

Sindelar, P. T., Griffin, C. C., Smith, S. W., & Watanabe, A. K. (1992). Pre-referral intervention: Encouraging notes on preliminary findings. *Elementary School Journal, 92,* 245–259.

Sitlington, P. L., & Nuebert, D. A. (2004). Preparing youths with emotional or behavioral disorders for transition to adult life: Can it be done within the standards-based reform movement? *Behavioral Disorders, 29*(3), 279–288.

Skiba, R., Poloni-Staudinger, L., Gallini, S., Simmons, A., & Feggins-Azziz, R. (2006). Disparage access: The disproportionality of African American students with disabilities across educational environments. *Exceptional Children, 72*(4), 411–424.

Skiba, R., Simmons, A., Ritter, S., Gibb, A., Rausch, M., Cuadrado, J., & Chung, C. (2008). Achieving equity in special education: History, status, and current challenges. *Exceptional Children, 74*(3), 264–288.

Skinner, R., & Staresina, L. (2004). State of the states. In *Education Week* [special issue]: *Special education in an era of standards: Count me in,* pp. 97–123.

Slavin, R. (2008). Perspectives on evidence-based research in education—What works? Issues in synthesizing educational program evaluations. *Educational Researcher, 37*(1), 51–14.

Slavin, R., Hurley, E., & Chamberlain, A. (2003). Cooperative learning and achievement theory and research. In I. Weiner, W. Reynolds, & G. Miller (Eds.); *Handbook of psychology, Volume 7: Educational psychology* (pp. 177–197). Hoboken, NJ: John Wiley.

Slavin, R., & Madden, N. (2006). *Success for all: Summary of research on achievement out comes.* Baltimore: Johns Hopkins University, Center for Data-Driven Reform in Education.

Slavin, R. E. (1990a). Ability grouping, cooperative learning and the gifted. *Journal for the Education of the Gifted, 14,* 3–8.

Slavin, R. E. (1990b). *Cooperative learning: Theory, research, and practice.* Upper Saddle River, NJ: Pearson.

Sleeter, C. (1995). Radical structuralist perspectives on the creation and use of learning disabilities. In T. Skrtic (Ed.), *Disability & democracy: Reconstructing (special) education for postmodernity* (pp. 153–165). New York: Teachers College Press.

Smith, B., Barkley, R., & Shapiro, C. (2006). Attention deficit/hyperactivity disorder. In E. Mash & R. Barkley (Eds.). *Treatment of childhood disorders* (3rd ed., pp. 65–136). New York: Guilford.

Smith, D. D., & Rivera, D. P. (1995). Discipline in special education and general education settings. *Focus on Exceptional Children, 27*(5), 1–14.

Smith, D. J. (1998). Histories of special education: Stories from our past, insights for our future. *Remedial and Special Education, 19*(4), 196–200.

Smith, P. (2007). Have we made any progress? Including students with intellectual disabilities in regular education classrooms. *Intellectual and Developmental Disabilities, 45*(5), 297–309.

Smith, S. W., & Gilles, D. L. (2003). Using key instructional elements to systematically promote social skill generalization for students with challenging behavior. *Intervention in School and Clinic, 39*(1), 30–37.

Smith, T. E. C. (2001). Section 504, the ADA, and public schools. *Remedial and Special Education, 22*(6), 335–343.

Smith-Myles, B., & Simpson, R. L. (2001). Effective practices for students with Asperger's syndrome. *Focus on Exceptional Children, 34,* 1–16.

Snell, M. E., & Brown, F. (Eds.). (2005). *Instruction of students with severe disabilities* (6th ed.). Upper Saddle River, NJ: Merrill/Pearson.

Snow, K. (2006). *People first language.* Retrieved August 1, 2006, from http://www.disabilityisnatural.com/peoplefirstlanguage.htm

Soto, G., & Goetz, L. (1998). Self-efficacy beliefs and the education of students with severe disabilities. *Journal of the Association for Persons with Severe Handicaps, 23,* 134–143.

Southern, W. T., & Jones, E. D. (1992). Programming, grouping, and acceleration in rural school districts: A survey of attitudes and practices. *Gifted Child Quarterly, 36,* 172–117.

Southern, W. T., Spicker H. H., Kierouz, K., & Kelly, K. (1990). *The Indiana guide for the identification of the gifted and talented* (K. Kierouz, Ed.). Indianapolis: Indiana Department of Education.

Sparrow, S. S., Cicchetti, D. V., & Balla, D. A. (2005). *Vineland adaptive behavior scales* (2nd ed.). Circle Pines, MN: American Guidance Service.

Spectrum K12. (2009). *Response to intervention (RTI) adoption survey.* Retrieved April 8, 2009, from http://www.spectrumk12.com/

Spiegel, H. M. L., & Bonwit, A. M. (2002). HIV infection in children. In M. L. Batshaw (Ed.), *Children with disabilities* (5th ed., pp. 123–139). Baltimore: Brookes.

Spooner, F., Dymond, S. K., Smith, A., & Kennedy, C. H. (2006). What we know and need to know about accessing the general curriculum for students with significant cognitive disabilities. *Research and Practice for Persons with Severe Disabilities, 31,* 277–283.

Sprague, J. R., & Walker, H. M. (2005). *Safe and healthy schools: Practical prevention strategies.* New York: Guilford.

Stehr-Green P., et al. (2003). Autism and Thimerosal-containing vaccines: Lack of consistent evidence for an association. *American Journal of Preventive Medicine, 25*(2), 101–106.

Stein, M., Silbert, J., & Carnine, D. (1997). *Designing effective mathematics instruction: A Direct Instruction approach* (3rd ed.). Upper Saddle River, NJ: Merrill/Pearson.

Strauss A., & Lehtinen, L. (1947). *Psychopathology and education of the brain-injured child* (vol. I). New York: Grune & Stratton.

Stronge, J. H. (2002). *Qualities of effective teachers.* Alexandria, VA: Association for Supervision and Curriculum Development.

Stump, C. S., & Bigge, J. (2005). Curricular options for individuals with physical, health, or multiple disabilities. In S. J. Best, K. W. Heller, & J. L. Bigge (Eds.), *Teaching individuals with physical or multiple disabilities* (5th ed., pp. 278–318). Upper Saddle River, NJ: Merrill/Pearson.

Sugai, G., & Lewis, T. J. (1996). Preferred and promising practices for social skills instruction. *Focus on Exceptional Children, 29*(4), 1–16.

Sulzer-Azaroff, B., Hoffman, A. O., Horton, C. B., Bondy, A., & Frost, L. (2009). The picture exchange communication system (PECS): What do the data say? *Focus on Autism and Other Developmental Disabilities, 24*(2), 89–103.

Sunderland, L. C. (2004). Speech, language, and audiology services in public schools. *Intervention in School and Clinic, 39,* 209–217.

Swanson, L., & Saez, L. (2003). Memory difficulties in children and adults with learning disabilities. In H. L. Swanson, K. R. Harris, & S. Graham (Eds.), *Handbook of learning disabilities* (pp. 182–198). New York: Guilford.

Symons, F. J. (1995). Self-injurious behavior: A brief review of theories and current treatment perspectives. *Developmental Disabilities Bulletin, 23,* 91–104.

Tager-Flusberg, H., Paul, R., & Lord, C. (2005). Language and communication in autism. In F. R. Volkmar, R. Paul, A. Klin, & D. Cohen (Eds.), *Handbook of autism and pervasive developmental disorders: Vol. 1. Diagnosis, development, neurobiology, and behavior.* (4th ed., pp. 335–364). Hoboken, NJ: Wiley.

Taylor, R., Richards, S. B., & Brady, M. (2005). *Mental retardation: Historical perspectives, current practices, and future directions.* Boston: Pearson/Allyn & Bacon.

Terman, L. M. (1925). *Mental and physical traits of a thousand gifted children.* Vol. 1 of L. M. Terman (Ed.), *Genetic studies of genius.* Stanford, CA: Stanford University Press.

Terman, L. M., & Oden, M. H. (1947). *The gifted child grows up: Twenty-five years' follow-up of a superior group.* Stanford, CA: Stanford University Press.

Test, D., Mason, C., Hughes, C., Konrad, M., Neale, M., & Wood, W. (2004). Student involvement in individualized education program meetings. *Exceptional Children, 70*(4), 391–412.

Thatcher, K. L., Fletcher, K., & Decker, B. (2008). Communication disorders in the school: Perspectives on academic and social success an introduction. *Psychology in the Schools, 45,* 579–581.

Thoma, C., & Getzel, E. (2005). "Self-determination is what it's all about": What post-secondary students with disabilities tell us are important considerations for success. *Education and Training in Developmental Disabilities, 40,* 234–242.

Thomson, J., & Raskind, W. (2003). Genetic influences on reading and writing disabilities. In H. L. Swanson, K. R. Harris, & S. Graham (Eds.), *Handbook of learning disabilities* (pp. 256–270). New York: Guilford.

Thuppal, M., & Sobsey, D. (2004). Children with special health care needs. In F. P. Orelove, D. Sobsey, & R. K. Silberman (Eds.), *Educating children with multiple disabilities: A collaborative approach* (2nd ed., pp. 311–377). Baltimore: Brookes.

Thurlow, M. L., Elliott, J. L., & Ysseldyke, J. E. (2003). *Testing students with disabilities: Practical strategies for complying with district and state requirements* (2nd ed.). Thousand Oaks, CA: Corwin.

Tileson, D.W., & Darling, S. K. (2008). *Why culture counts: Teaching children of poverty.* Bloomington, IN: The Solution Tree.

Tobin, T., Sugai, G., & Colvin, G. (1996). Patterns in middle school discipline records. *Journal of Emotional and Behavioral Disorders, 4*(2), 82–94.

Tomlinson-Keasey, C., & Keasey, C. B. (1993). Graduating from college in the 1930's: The Terman genetic studies of genius. In K. D. Hulbert & D. T. Schuster (Eds.), *Women's lives through time* (pp. 63–92). San Francisco: Jossey-Bass.

Torgesen, J. (2000). Individual differences in response to early interventions in reading: The lingering problem of treatment resisters. *Learning Disabilities Research and Practice, 15*(1), 55–64.

Torgesen, J. (2002). Empirical and theoretical support for direct diagnosis of learning disabilities by assessment of intrinsic processing weakness. In R. Bradley, L. Danielson, & D. Hallahan (Eds.), *Identification of learning disabilities: Research to practice* (pp. 565–613). Mahwah, NJ: Erlbaum.

Torgesen, J., Alexander, A., Wagner, R., Rashotte, C., Voeller, K., & Conway, T. (2001). Intensive remedial instruction for children with severe reading disabilities: Immediate and long-term outcomes from two instructional approaches. *Journal of Learning Disabilities, 34*(1), 33–58, 78.

Towbin, K. E., Mauk, J. E., & Batshaw, M. L. (2002). Pervasive developmental disorders. In M. L. Batshaw (Ed.), *Children with disabilities* (5th ed.). Baltimore: Brooks.

Traxler, C. B. (2000). The Stanford achievement test, 9th edition: National norming and performance for deaf and hard-of-hearing students. *Journal of Deaf Studies and Deaf Education, 5*(4), 337–348.

Treffinger, D. J., & Barton, B. L. (1988). Fostering independent learning. *Gifted Child Today, 11,* 28–30.

Trumbull, E., Rothstein-Fisch, C., & Greenfield, P. M. (2000). *Bridging cultures in our schools: New approaches that work.* San Francisco: WestEd.

Tsal, Y., Shalev, L., & Mevorach, C. (2005). The diversity of attention deficits in ADHD. *Journal of Learning Disabilities, 38*(2), 142–157.

Tschannen-Moran, M., Woolfolk Hoy, A., & Hoy, W. K. (1998). Teacher efficacy: Its meaning and measure. *Review of Educational Research, 68,* 202–248.

Turnbull, H. R., Stowe, M., & Huerta, N. E. (2007). *Free appropriate public education: The law and children with disabilities.* Denver: Love.

Tyler, N., Yzquierdo, Z., Lopez-Reyna, N., & Flippin, S. (2004). Cultural and linguistic diversity and the special education workforce: A critical overview. *Journal of Special Education, 38*(1), 22–38.

United States Census Bureau. (2007). Retrieved May 15, 2009, from http://factfinder.census.gov/servlet/STTable?_bm=y&-geo_id=01000US&-qr_name=ACS_2007_3YR_G00_S1601&-ds_name=ACS_2007_3YR_G00

United States Census Bureau. (2008). *National population projections: Released 2008.* Retrieved May 11, 2009, from http://www.census.gov/population/www/projections/summarytables.html

U.S. Department of Education. (2003). *Identifying and implementing educational practices supported by rigorous evidence: A user friendly guide.* Washington, DC: Author.

U.S. Department of Education. (2003). *25th annual report to Congress on the implementation of the Individuals with Disabilities Education Act: To assure the free appropriate public education of all children with disabilities.* Washington, DC: Author.

U.S. Department of Education. (2005a). Assistance to states for the education of children with disabilities. *Federal Register, 70*(118), 34 CFR, parts 300, 301, amend. 304, sec. 300.8.

U.S. Department of Education. (2005b). *IDEA 2004 resources.* Retrieved June 11, 2006, from http://www.ed.gov/policy/speced/guid/idea/idea2004.html

U.S. Department of Education. (2005c). *Individuals with Disabilities Education Act (IDEA) data.* Retrieved October 13, 2005, from http://www.ideadata.org/

U.S. Department of Education. (2005d). *26th annual report to Congress on the implementation of the Individuals with Disabilities Education Act* (Vol. 1). Washington, DC: Author.

U.S. Department of Education. (2006a). *Assistance to states for the education of children with disabilities and preschool grants for children with disabilities*. [34 CFR Parts 300 and 301]. Washington, DC: Author.

U.S. Department of Education. (2006b). *Individuals with Disabilities Education Act data*. Retrieved June 11, 2006, from https://www.ideadata.org/index.html

U.S. Department of Education. (2006c). *IDEA regulations: Identification of specific learning disabilities*. Retrieved November 15, 2006, from http://idea.ed.gov/explore/home

U.S. Department of Education. (2008). Individuals with Disabilities Education Act (IDEA) data. Retrieved July 31, 2009, from http://www.ideadata.org

U.S. Department of Education. (2009). *28th Annual Report to Congress on the Implementation of the Individuals with Disabilities Education Act, 2006*, vol. 2, Washington, D.C. Retrieved April 7, 2009, from http://www.ed.gov/about/reports/annual/osep/2006/parts-b-c/28th-vol-2.pdf

U.S. Department of Education. (2009). Individuals with Disabilities Education Act (IDEA) Data. Retrieved June 11, 2009, from http://www.ideadata.org/

U.S. Department of Education. (n.d.). *History: 25 years of progress in educating children with disabilities through IDEA*. Retrieved March, 10, 2005, http://www.ed.gov/policy/speced/leg/idea/history.html

U.S. Food and Drug Administration. (2009). *Cochlear implants*. Retrieved August 4, 2009, from http://www.fda.gov/MedicalDevices/ProductsandMedicalProcedures/ImplantsandProsthetics/CochlearImplants/default.htm

U.S. Department of Health and Human Services. (2006). *Child neglect: A guide for prevention, assessment and intervention*. Retrieved May 15, 2009, from http://www.childwelfare.gov/pubs/umnew.cfm

U.S. Department of Health and Human Services. (2009). *Child maltreatment 2007*. Retrieved May 15, 2009, from http://www.acf.hhs.gov/programs/cb/pubs/cm07/insidecover.htm

Uzgiris, I. C. (1970). Sociocultural factors in cognitive development. In H. C. Haywood (Ed.), *Social-cultural aspects of mental retardation* (pp. 7–58). New York: Appleton-Century-Crofts.

Van Acker, R., Loncola, J. A., & Van Acker E. Y. (2005). Rett syndrome: A pervasive developmental disorder. In F. R. Volkmar, R. Paul, A. Klin, & D. Cohen (Eds.), *Handbook of autism and pervasive developmental disorders: Vol. 1. Diagnosis, development, neurobiology, and behavior* (4th ed., pp. 126–164). Hoboken, NJ: Wiley.

Van Hulle, A., & Hux, K. (2006). Improvement patterns among survivors of brain injury: Three case examples documenting the effectiveness of memory compensation strategies. *Brain Injury, 20*, 101–109.

Van Wagenen, L., & Hibbard, K. M. (1998, February). Building teacher portfolios. *Educational Leadership, 55*(5), 26–29.

Vandercook, T., York, J., & Forest, M. (1989). The McGill Action Planning System (MAPS): A strategy for building the vision. *Journal of the Association for Persons with Severe Handicaps, 14*, 205–215.

Vaughn, S., Bos, C., & Schumm, J. (2007). *Teaching students who are exceptional, diverse, and at-risk in the general education classroom* (4th ed.). Boston: Allyn & Bacon.

Vaughn, S., & Fuchs, L. (2003). Redefining learning disabilities as inadequate response to instruction: The promise and potential problems. *Learning Disabilities Research and Practice, 18*(3), 137–146.

Vaughn, S., Gersten, R., & Chard, D. (2000). The underlying message in LD intervention research: Findings from research syntheses. *Exceptional Children, 67*(1), 99–114.

Vaughn, S., LaGreca, A., & Kuttler, A., (1999). The why, who, and how of social skills. In W. Bender (Ed.), *Professional issues in learning disabilities* (pp. 187–217). Austin, TX: PRO-ED.

Vaughn, S., & Roberts, G. (2007). Secondary interventions in reading: Providing additional instruction for students at risk. *Teaching Exceptional Children, 39*(5), 40–46.

Vavrus, M. (2001). Deconstructing the multicultural animus held by monoculturalists. *Journal of Teacher Education, 52*(1), 70–77.

Vellutino, F., Scanlon, D., Small, S., & Fanuele, D. (2006). Response to intervention as a vehicle for distinguishing between children with and without reading disabilities. *Journal of Learning Disabilities, 39*(2), 157–169.

Venn, J. J. (2006). *Assessing students with special needs* (4th ed.). Upper Saddle River, NJ: Merrill/Pearson Education.

Verplaetse, S., & Migliacci, N. (Eds.) (2007). *Inclusive pedagogy for English language learners: A handbook of research-informed practices*. New York: Erlbaum.

Vocke, K. S. (2007). *Where do we go from here?: Meeting the unique educational needs of migrant students*. Thousand Oaks, CA: Corwin Press.

Volkmar, F. R., & Klin, A. (2005). Issues in the classification of autism and related conditions. In F. R. Volkmar, R. Paul, A. Klin, & D. Cohen (Eds.), *Handbook of autism and pervasive developmental disorders: Vol. 1. Diagnosis, development, neurobiology, and behavior* (4th ed., pp. 5–41). Hoboken, NJ: Wiley.

Volkmar, F. R., Szatmari, P., & Sparrow, S. S. (1993). Sex differences in pervasive developmental disorders. *Journal of Autism and Developmental Disorders, 23*, 579–591.

Wadsworth, D. E. D., & Knight, D. (1999). Preparing the inclusion classroom for students with special physical and health needs. *Intervention in School and Clinic, 34*, 170–175.

Wagner, M., Blackorby, J., Cameto, R., Hebbeler, K., & Newman, L. (1993). *The transition experiences of young people with disabilities: A summary of findings from the national longitudinal transition study of special education students*. Menlo Park, CA: SRI International.

Wagner, M., D'Amico, R., Marder, C., Newman, L., & Blackorby, J. (1992). *What happens next? Trends in postschool outcomes of youth with disabilities. The second comprehensive report from the National Longitudinal Transition Study of Special Education Students*. Menlo Park, CA: SRI International.

Wagner, M., Newman, L., Camero, R., Garza, N., & Levine, P. (2005). *After high school: A first look at the postschool experience of youth with disabilities. A report from the National Longitudinal Transition Study-2 (NLTS2)*. Menlo Park, CA: SRI International.

Wagner, M. M., & Blackorby, J. (1996). Transition from high school to work or college: How special education students fare. *Special Education for Students with Disabilities, 6*(1), 103–120.

Wagner, M. M., Kutash, K., Duchnowski. A. J., Epstein, M. H., & Sumi, W. C. (2005). The children and youth we serve: A national picture of the characteristics of students with emotional disturbances receiving special education. *Journal of Emotional and Behavioral Disorders, 13*(2), 79–96.

Wald, J., & Losen, D. J. (2007). Out of sight: The journey through the school-to-prison pipeline. In S. Books (Ed.), *Invisible children in the society and its schools* (pp. 23–37). Mahwah, NJ: Erlbaum.

Waldron, N., & McLeskey, J. (1998). The impact of a full-time inclusive school program (ISP) on the academic achievement of students with mild and severe learning disabilities. *Exceptional Children, 64*(2), 395–405.

Waldron, N., & McLeskey, J. (2009). Establishing a collaborative culture through comprehensive school reform. *Journal of Educational and Psychological Consultation,* in press.

Walker, H., Colvin, G., & Ramsey, E. (1995). *Antisocial behavior in school: Strategies and best practices.* Pacific Grove, CA: Brooks/Cole.

Walker, H. M. (1983). *Walker problem behavior identification checklist.* Los Angeles: Western Psychological Services.

Walker, H. M., Horner, R. H., Sugai, G., Bullis, M., Sprague, J. R., Bricker, M., et al. (1996). Integrated approaches to preventing antisocial behavior patterns among school-age children and youth. *Journal of Emotional and Behavioral Disorders, 4*(4), 194–209.

Walker, H. M., McConnell, S. R., Holmes, D., Todis, B., Walker, J., & Golden, N. (1983). *ACCEPTS: A children's curriculum for effective peer and teacher skills.* Austin, TX: PRO-ED.

Walker, H. M., Ramsey, E., & Gresham, F. M. (2004). *Antisocial behavior in school: Strategies and best practices* (2nd ed.). Pacific Grove, CA: Brooks/Cole.

Walker, H. M., & Severson, H. H. (1992). *Systematic screening for behavior disorder (SSBD): User's guide and technical manual* (2nd ed.). Longmont, CO: Sopris West.

Walker, H. M., Severson, H. H., & Feil, E. G. (1995). *The early screening project: A proven child-find process.* Longmont, CO: Sopris West.

Walker, H. M., & Walker, J. E. (1991). *Coping with noncompliance in the classroom: A positive approach for teachers.* Austin, TX: PRO-ED.

Wallace, T., Bernhardt, J., & Utermarck, J. (1999). *Minnesota paraprofessional guide.* Minneapolis: University of Minnesota, Institute on Community Integration, Minnesota Paraprofessional Project.

Walsh, K. (2001). *Teacher certification reconsidered: Stumbling for quality.* Baltimore: Abell Foundation. Retrieved April 2009 from http://www.abell.org/pubsitems/ed_cert_1101.pdf

Walters, J. M., & Gardner, H. M. (1986). The theory of multiple intelligences: Some issues and answers. In R. J. Sternberg & R. K. Wagner (Eds.), *Practical intelligence: Origins and nature of competence in the everyday world* (pp. 161–182). New York: Cambridge University Press.

Warger, C. (2002). *Supporting paraeducators: A summary of current practices* (ED475383). Arlington, VA: ERIC Clearinghouse on Disabilities and Gifted Education.

Wasserman, R., Kelleher, K., Bocian, A., et al. (1999). Identification of attentional and hyperactivity problems in primary care: A report from pediatric research in office settings and the ambulatory sentinel practice network. *Pediatrics, 103*(3), 661.

Waters, G., & Doehring, D. (1990). Reading acquisition in congenitally deaf children who communicate orally: Insights from an analysis of competent reading, language, and memory skills. In T. Carr & B. A. Levy (Eds.), *Reading and its development* (pp. 323–368). San Diego: Academic.

Watkins, S. (1987). Long term effects of home intervention with hearing-impaired children. *American Annals of the Deaf, 132,* 267–271.

Wechsler, D. (2003). *Wechsler intelligence scale for children* (4th ed.). San Antonio, TX: Psychological Corporation.

Wehby, J. H., Lane, K. L., & Falk, K. B. (2003). Academic instruction for students with emotional and behavioral disorders. *Journal of Emotional and Behavioral Disorders, 11*(4), 194–197.

Wehman, P., & Kregel, J. (Eds.). (2004). *Functional curriculum for elementary, middle and secondary students with special needs.* Austin, TX: Pro-Ed.

Wehmeyer, M. (1996). Self-determination as an educational outcome: Why is it important to children, youth, and adults with disabilities? In D. Sands & M. Wehmeyer (Eds.), *Self-determination across the life span: Independence and choice for people with disabilities* (pp. 17–36). Baltimore: Brookes.

Wehmeyer, M. (2003). Defining mental retardation and ensuring access to the general curriculum. *Education and Training of Developmental Disabilities, 38,* 271–277.

Wehmeyer, M. (2006). Self-determination and individuals with severe disabilities: Reexamining meanings and misinterpretations. *Research and Practice in Severe Disabilities, 30,* 113–120.

Wehmeyer, M., & Fields, S. (2007). *Self-determination: Instructional and assessment strategies.* Thousand Oaks, CA: Corwin Press.

Wehmeyer, M. L. & Agran, M. (2006). Promoting access to the general curriculum for students with significant cognitive disabilities. In D. M. Browder & F. Spooner (Eds.), *Teaching Language Arts, Math, & Science to Students with Significant Cognitive Disabilities* (pp. 15–37). Baltimore: Paul H. Brookes.

Wehmeyer, M. L., Lance, G. D., & Bashinski, S. (2002). Promoting access to the general curriculum for students with mental retardation: A multi-level model. *Education and Training in Mental Retardation and Developmental Disabilities, 37*(3), 223–234.

Weinstein, C. S., Tomlinson-Clarke, S. T., & Curran, M. (2004). Toward a conception of culturally responsive classroom management. *Journal of Teacher Education, 55*(1), 25–38.

Weinstein, S. (2002). Epilepsy. In M. L. Batshaw (Ed.), *Children with disabilities* (5th ed., pp. 493–523). Baltimore: Brookes.

Weinstein, S., & Gaillard, W. D. (2007). Epilepsy. In M. L. Batshaw, L. Pellegrino, & N. J. Roizen (Eds.), *Children with disabilities* (6th ed., pp. 439–460). Baltimore: Brookes.

Weintraub, F. J., & Abeson, A. (1976). New education policies for the handicapped: The quiet revolution. In F. J. Weintraub, A. Abeson, J. Ballard, & M. L. LaVor (Eds.), *Public policy and the education of exceptional children* (pp. 7–13). Reston, VA: Council for Exceptional Children.

Weist, M. D., Goldstein, A., Morris, L., Bryant, T. (2003). Integrating expanded school mental health programs and school-based health centers. *Psychology in the Schools, 40*(3), 297–308.

Wenar, C., & Kerig, P. (2006). *Developmental psychopathology: From infancy through adolescence.* Boston: McGraw-Hill.

Westat Corp. (2002). *A high-quality teacher for every classroom (SPeNSE Summary Sheet).* Retrieved April 8, 2009, from http://ferdig.coe.ufl.edu/spense/SummaryReportserviceproviders.pdf.

Westling, D. L., & Fox, L. (2009). *Teaching students with severe disabilities* (4th ed.). Upper Saddle River, NJ: Merrill/Pearson Education.

Westling, D. L., & Koorland, M. A. (1988). *The special educator's handbook.* Boston: Allyn & Bacon.

Wetherby, A. M., Goldstein, H., Cleary, J., Allen, L., & Kublin, K. (2003). Early identification of children with communication disorders: Concurrent and predictive validity of the CSBS developmental profile. *Infants and Young Children, 16,* 161–174.

Whitaker, S. D. (2000). Mentoring beginning special education teachers and the relationship to attrition. *Exceptional Children, 66,* 546–566.

White, M., & Mason, C. Y. (2006) Components of a successful mentoring program for beginning special education teachers: Perspectives from new teachers and mentors. *Teacher Education and Special Education, 29*(3), 191–201.

White, R. (1996). Unified discipline. In B. Algozzine (Ed.), *Problem behavior management: An educator's resource service* (pp. 11:28–11:36). Gaithersburg, MD: Aspen.

White, R., Algozzine, B., Audette, R., Marr, M. B., & Ellis, E. D. (2001). Unified discipline: A schoolwide approach for managing problem behavior. *Intervention in School and Clinic, 37*(1), 3–8.

White, S. W., Keonig, K., & Scahill, L. (2007). Social skills development in children with autism spectrum disorders: A review of the intervention research. *Journal of Autism and Developmental Disorders, 37,* 1858–1868.

Wilder, L. K., Taylor Dyches, T., Obiakor, F. E., & Algozzine, B. (2004). Multicultural perspectives on teaching students with autism. *Focus on Autism and Other Developmental Disabilities, 19*(2), 105–113.

Wilens, T., Faraone, S., Biederman, J., & Gunawardene, S. (2003). Does stimulant therapy of attention deficit hyperactivity disorder beget later substance abuse? Meta-analytic review of the literature. *Pediatrics, 111,* 179–185.

Wilkinson, L. A. (2005). Supporting the inclusion of students with emotional and behavioural disorders: Examples using conjoint behavioural consultation and self-management. *International Journal of Special Education, 20*(2), 73–84.

Willard-Holt, C. (1998). Academic and personality characteristics of gifted students with cerebral palsy: A multiple case study. *Exceptional Children, 65,* 37–50.

Williamson, P., McLeskey, J., Hoppey, D., & Rentz, T. (2006). Educating students with mental retardation in general education classrooms. *Exceptional Children, 72,* 347–361.

Willis, S. M. (1996). *Childhood depression in school age children* (ERIC Document Reproduction Service No. ED415973).

Wilson, B. L., & Corbett, H. D. (2001). *Listening to urban kids.* Albany: SUNY Press.

Wing, L. (1981). Asperger's syndrome: A clinical account. *Psychological Medicine, 11,* 115–129.

Winner, E. (2000). The origins and ends of giftedness. *American Psychologist, 55*(1), 159–169.

Winzer, M. A. (1998). A tale often told: The early progression of special education. *Remedial and Special Education, 19*(4), 212–218.

Witt, J., VanDerHeyden, A., & Gilbertson, D. (2004). Troubleshooting behavioral interventions: A systematic process for finding and eliminating problems. *School Psychology Review, 33,* 363–383.

Wolery, M., & Bailey, D. B. (2002). Early childhood special education research. *Journal of Early Intervention, 25,* 88–99.

Wolery, M., Ault, M. J., & Doyle, P. M. (1992). *Teaching students with moderate to severe disabilities: Use of response prompting strategies.* New York: Longman.

Wolfensberger, W. (1985). An overview of social role valorization and some reflections on elderly mentally retarded persons. In M. Janicki & H. Wisniewski (Eds.), *Expanding systems of service delivery for persons with developmental disabilities* (pp. 127–148). Baltimore: Brookes.

Wolffe, K. (1996). Career education for students with visual impairments. *RE:view, 28*(2), 89–93.

Wolk, S., & Allen, T. E. (1984). A 5-year follow-up of reading comprehension achievement of hearing-impaired students in special education programs. *Journal of Special Education, 18,* 161–176.

Wong, S. W., & Hughes, J. N. (2006). Ethnicity and language contributions to dimensions of parent involvement. *School Psychology Review, (35)*4, 645–662.

Wood, T., & McCarthy, C. (2004). *Understanding and preventing teacher burnout.* (ERIC Document Reproduction Service No. ED477726)

Woodcock, R. W., McGrew, K. S., & Mather, N. (2001). *Woodcock-Johnson III tests of cognitive abilities.* Itasca, IL: Riverside.

Woodruff, D. W., Osher, D., Hoffman, C. C., Gruner, A., King, M. A., et al. (1998). *Systems of care: Promising practices in children's mental health. 1998 series: Vol. 3. The role of education in a system of care: Effectively serving children with emotional or behavioral disorders.* Washington, DC: Center for Effective Collaboration and Practice, American Institute for Research.

Woods, J. J., & Wetherby, A. M. (2003, July). Early identification of and early intervention for infants and toddlers who are at risk for autism spectrum disorder. *Language, Speech, and Hearing Services in Schools, 34,* 180–193.

Wright-Strawderman, C., & Lindsay, P. (1996). Depression in students with disabilities: Recognition and intervention strategies. *Intervention in School and Clinic, 31*(5), 261–265.

Wunsch, M. J., Conlon, C. J., & Scheidt, P. C. (2001). Substance abuse: A preventable threat to development. In M. L. Batshaw (Ed.), *Children with disabilities* (5th ed., pp. 107–122). Baltimore: Brookes.

Xu, C., Reid, R., & Steckelberg, A. (2002). Technology applications for children with ADHD: Assessing the empirical support. *Education and Treatment of Children, 25*(2), 224–248.

Yeargin-Allsopp, M., Rice, C., Karapurkar, T., Doernberg, N., Boyle, C., & Murphy, C. (2003). Prevalence of autism in a U.S. metropolitan area. *Journal of the American Medical Association, 289*(1), 49–55.

Yell, M. L., & Drasgow, E. (2005). *No child left behind: A guide for Professional.* Upper Saddle River, NJ: Pearson.

Yirmiya, N., Sigman, M. D., Kasari, C., & Mundy P. (1992). Empathy and cognition in high-functioning children with autism. *Child Development, 63*(1), 150–160.

Yoshinaga-Itano, C. (1987). Aural habilitation: A key to the acquisition of knowledge, language, and speech. *Seminars in Hearing, 8*(2), 169–174.

Yoshinaga-Itano, C., Coulter, D., & Thomson, V. (2000). Infant hearing impairment and universal hearing screening. The Colorado Newborn Hearing Screening Project: Effects on speech and language development for children with hearing loss. *Journal of Perinatology, 20,* S131–S136.

Ysseldyke, J., Dennison, A., & Nelson, R. (2004). *Large-scale assessment and accountability systems: Positive consequences for students with disabilities* (Technical Report 51). Minneapolis: University of Minnesota, National Center on Educational Outcomes.

Zafft, C., Hart, D., & Zimbrich, K. (2004). College career connection: A study of youth with intellectual disabilities and the impact of postsecondary education. *Education and Training in Developmental Disabilities, 39,* 45–53.

Zentall, S. (2006). *ADHD and education: Foundations, characteristics, methods, and collaboration.* Upper Saddle River, NJ: Prentice Hall.

Zhang, D., & Katsiyannis, A. (2002). Minority representation in special education: A persistent challenge. *Remedial and Special Education, 23*(3), 180–187.

Zirkel, P. A. (2009). What does the law say? New Section 504 student eligibility standards. *Teaching Exceptional Children, 41*(4), 68–71.

Zirkel, P. A., & Krohn, N. (2008). RTI after IDEA: A survey of state laws. *Teaching Exceptional Children, 40*(3), 71–73.

Zito, J., Safer, D., dosReis, S., et al. (1999). Psychotherapeutic medication patterns for youth with attention deficit hyperactivity disorder. *Archives of Pediatric and Adolescent Medicine, 153*(12), 1257–1263.

Zito, J., Safer, D., dosReis, S., et al. (2000). Trends in the prescribing of psychotropic medications in preschoolers. *Journal of the American Medical Association, 283*(8), 1025–1030.

# Author Index

# Subject Index

Certifications
  professional development and, 435–436
  special education teachers and, 101–103
  state governments and, 433
CF (Cystic fibrosis), 378
Challenging behavior
  behavior management and, 131–132
  preschoolers with special needs and, 91
CHAT (Checklist for Autism in Toddlers), 272
Checklist for Autism in Toddlers (CHAT), 272
Child abuse, rate of, 53
Child Behavior Checklist (CBCL), 184–185
Child find systems, 35, 88, 356
Childhood disintegrative disorder, 260, 261
Child neglect, 53
A Children's Curriculum for Effective Peer and
  Teacher Skills (ACCEPTS), 192
Children's literature, culturally relevant
  curriculum, 72
The Child Who Stutters at School: Notes to the
  Teacher (Scott), 299
Chromosomal anomalies, 88, 327
Chromosomes, 327
Chronic health conditions, 376–378, 378–381
Civility, in communication, 109, 110
Civil rights movement, and special education
  history, 29–30
Classification criteria
  for emotional and behavioral disorders,
    172–173
  for English language learners, 53
  for giftedness, 403
  for intellectual disabilities, 204–207
  for learning disabilities, 142–144, 151
  for profound intellectual disabilities, 204, 205
  for students with attention deficit hyperactivity
    disorder, 236–238
  for students with autism spectrum disorders,
    260, 262–263
  for students with gifts and talents, 403
  for students with multiple disabilities, 322
  for students with sensory impairments, 346,
    347–350
  for students with traumatic brain injuries,
    321–322
Classroom environment
  physical environment design, 124, 125
  sense of community in, 68
Classroom interventions
  evidence-based teaching approaches and,
    133–134
  speech/language pathologists and, 308–309, 312
  students with attention deficit hyperactivity
    disorder and, 246–248
  students with intellectual disabilities and,
    216–222
  students with learning disabilities and, 154–161
CLD. See Culturally or linguistically diverse (CLD)
Clinical Exploitation of Life Events (CELE), 193
Clinically derived system, 172–173
Clinton, Hillary, 73
CMV (cytomegalovirus), 327, 354, 383–384
Cochlear implants, 357, 367
Code of ethics, 451
Cognitive approaches, instructional delivery, 117
Cognitive characteristics
  of students with communication disorders,
    302–305
  of students with emotional and behavioral
    disorders, 179
  of students with intellectual disabilities, 209–210
  of students with sensory impairments, 350
Cognitive skill deficits, students with learning
  disabilities, 146–147

Collaboration
  general education teachers and special
    education teachers, 9–10, 13–14, 165
  speech/language pathologists and, 312,
    313–314
  support for beginning teachers and, 426–430
  teaming and, 428, 429
Collectivist cultures, 60, 61, 72, 74
College Career Connection (CCC), 227
Colleges with Programs for Students with Learning
  Disabilities or Attention Deficit Disorders
  (Peterson's Guide), 162
Coma, 321
Combined type (ADHD-C), 236, 245
Communication
  authentic relationships and, 108–109
  behavior management and, 108–111
  of caring, 67–71, 108–109
  civility and respect and, 109, 110
  credibility, dependability, and assertiveness
    and, 109, 110
  facilitated communication, 283
Communication delays, indicators of, 89, 90, 91
Communication disorders. See also Students with
  communication disorders
  causal factors and, 306
  cerebral palsy and, 305
  communication differences versus, 301–302
  definition of, 292
  language disorders, 292–294, 302, 305–306
  speech disorders, 295–301
Communication skills
  disorders affecting, 292–301
  students with autism spectrum disorders and,
    264, 267
Community, sense of, in classroom, 68
Comorbidity, 177
Complex phonological naming tasks, 308
Comprehensive program models, students with
  autism spectrum disorders, 278, 280
Computer-assisted instruction (CAI), 249
Conceptual framework, of special education, 24
Concussions, 321
Conductive education, 392, 394
Confidentiality, IDEA 2004, 39
Configuration of the hearing loss, 347
Connecting Math Concepts, 220
Conners' Parent Rating Scale, 243
Conners' Teaching Rating Scale, 243
Consequences
  students with attention deficit hyperactivity
    disorder and, 246
  tangible management plan and, 127–129, 131
Conspicuous strategies, curriculum design,
  158–161
Consultation, 10, 359, 362, 428–429
Content area instruction, 132, 134
Content disorders, 292, 294
Content expertise, 101–103
Continuum of services, 9, 35, 37, 46
Contractures, 210, 323
Controversies
  of content area instruction for students with
    severe disabilities, 132, 134
  of disproportionate behavior management
    referrals, 134–135
  of meeting accountability standards, 103
  of providing highly qualified teachers, 101–103
  of students with attention deficit hyperactivity
    disorder, 248–250, 254–256
  of students with autism spectrum disorders,
    282–283, 285
  of students with communication disorders,
    312, 314

  of students with emotional and behavioral
    disorders, 195–196
  of students with gifts and talents, 414, 416
  of students with intellectual disabilities,
    227–229
  of students with learning disabilities, 141,
    162–164, 164
  of students with multiple disabilities, 341
  of students with physical disabilities or other
    health impairments, 393, 394, 395
  of students with sensory impairments, 366–367
  of students with traumatic brain injuries, 339
Cooperative learning
  students with emotional and behavioral
    disorders and, 188
  systematic teaching and, 118
Cooperative Research Act (1954), 33
Core deficit scales, 272
Cornelia de Lange syndrome, 91
Corrective Math, 220
Corrective Reading, 220
Co-teaching, 5, 9–10, 102–103
Council for Exceptional Children (CEC), 30, 433,
  451–455
Counselors, 15
Course
  of attention deficit hyperactivity disorder, 241
  of autism spectrum disorders, 269–270
  of emotional and behavioral disorders, 180–181
  of intellectual disabilities, 211–212
  of learning disabilities, 148–149
  of multiple disabilities, 325, 327
  of traumatic brain injuries, 324–325
CP. See Cerebral palsy (CP)
Craine, Andrea, 201–202, 210, 215, 229
Creativity tests, 408–409
Credibility, in communication, 109, 110
Cri-du-chat syndrome, 91
Crisis management, tangible management plan,
  130–131
Criterion-referenced tests, 102
Cultural definitions, of deafness, 347–348
Culturally or linguistically diverse (CLD)
  graduation rates and, 57
  lack of as teachers, 58
  student population and, 53
  students with gifts and talents and, 414, 416
Culturally relevant curriculum
  connecting pedagogy to students, 72–73
  students' needs and, 71–73
Culturally relevant instructional methods, 40
Culturally responsive classroom management,
  defined, 65
Culturally responsive teaching
  academic achievement and, 65
  behavior management and, 109
  belief all children can be reached and, 71
  communicating caring, 67–71, 108–109
  culturally relevant curriculum and, 71–73
  defined, 65
  disproportionate behavior management
    referrals and, 134
  perceptions and, 58–59, 65–67
  student backgrounds and experiences
    and, 68
  students with gifts and talents and, 415
Cultural norms, 60, 64
Cultural sensitivity, communication, 109
Culture
  cultural norms, 60, 64
  ethnicity and class and, 61–62
  impact on behavior management referrals,
    134–135
  impact on education, 60–61

students with gifts and talents, 413
students with intellectual disabilities, 222–227
students with learning disabilities, 161–162
students with multiple disabilities, 337–338
students with other health impairments,
    392–393
students with physical disabilities or other
    health impairments, 392–393
students with sensory impairments, 364–366
students with TBI and multiple disabilities,
    337–338
Traumatic brain injuries (TBI). *See also* Students
    with traumatic brain injuries
    causal factors, 325
    course of, 324–325
    defined, 8
    intellectual disabilities distinguished
        from, 204
    prevalence of, 324
Treatment and Education of Autistic and Related
    Communication Handicapped Children
    (TEACCH), 278, 280
Tutoring programs, 118–119
Type 1 diabetes, 378
Type of hearing loss, 347

UDL (Universal design for learning), 114–115, 220,
    222, 223
Underrepresentation, students with gifts and
    talents, 416
University of Kansas Center for Learning, 117
U.S. Census Bureau, 52
U.S. Constitution, 40–41
U.S. Department of Education, 41, 140, 152,
    237, 244
Use disorders, 292, 294
U.S. Supreme Court, 40–41, 393

Vaccines, students with autism spectrum disorders,
    282–283
Vanguard, 311
Variable intellectual functioning, students with
    autism spectrum disorders, 268
Vineland Adaptive Behavior Scales, 214
Violence prevention, 123
Visual acuity, 349
Visual disabilities, identifying preschoolers with
    special needs, 89
Visual field, 349
Visual impairment including blindness. *See also*
    Blindness; Students with sensory impairments
    causal factors, 354
    defined, 8, 349
    educational practices, 356, 358, 361–364,
        365–366
    learning characteristics of, 350–352
    transition to adult life, 365–366
Vocal chords, 297
Vocal folds, 297
Vocal nodules, 299–300
Vocational education, students with emotional and
    behavioral disorders, 194–195
Vocational support
    students with attention deficit hyperactivity
        disorder and, 251
    students with autism spectrum disorders
        and, 281
    students with intellectual disabilities and, 222,
        224, 226
    students with learning disabilities and, 161–162
    students with TBI and multiple disabilities
        and, 337–338
VOCA (voice output communication aids), 277
Voice, 295
Voice Craft, 333

Voice disorders, 297–300
Voice output communication aids (VOCA), 277
Voice recognition, 391

Wait-to-fail approach, 141, 163
Walker Problem Behavior Identification
    Checklist, 184
WatchMinder, 333
Wechsler Individual Achievement Test-II
    (WIAT-II), 150, 214
Wechsler Intelligence Scale for Children (4th ed.),
    150, 214
*What Every Special Educator Must Know,* 433
The What Works Clearinghouse, 133
WIAT-II (Wechsler Individual Achievement Test-
    II), 150, 214
Wild Boy of Aveyon, 25, 27
Williams, Steve, 169, 170
Willowbrook State School, 30
Women, as teachers, 58
Woodcock-Johnson Tests of Achievement-III,
    150, 214
Working memory, 146
Wraparound interventions
    behavior management and, 131–132
    students with autism spectrum disorders and, 275
    students with emotional and behavioral
        disorders and, 194
Wright, Jeremiah, 73
Writing skills
    big ideas and, 155
    students with gifts and talents and, 405
    students with learning disabilities and, 146, 158
Written referral form, for evaluation, 85
*Wyatt v. Stickney* (1972), 34

Zero reject, defined, 34